THE
KURMA PURANA
A SYSTEM OF HINDU MYTHOLOGY AND TRADITION

BIBLIOTHECA INDICA;

A

COLLECTION OF ORIENTAL WORKS

PUBLISHED BY THE

ASIATIC SOCIETY OF BENGAL

NEW SERIES, NOS. 559, 589, 602, 618, 642, 655, 687, 699, 743.

THE
KURMA PURANA

A SYSTEM OF HINDU MYTHOLOGY AND TRADITION

EDITED BY

NILMANI MUKHOPADHYAYA

NYAYALANKARA M.A., B.L.

PROFESSOR OF SANSKRIT, PRESIDENCY COLLEGE,
CALCUTTA;
FELLOW OF THE CALCUTTA UNIVERSITY, AND
MEMBER OF THE ASIATIC SOCIETY OF BENGAL.

Published by

GYAN

Gyan Publishing House
5, Ansari Road
Daryaganj, New Delhi-110002
Phone: 011-47034999, 9811692060
E-mail: books@gyanbooks.com

Distribution Network
gyanbooks.com
India, USA, Canada, UK, Australia, France

ISBN : 978-81-212-2506-9 (HB)
First Published, 1890

2nd Impression 2021

Printed at: Gyan Press, Delhi.

The
Kurma Purana
Edited by: Nilmani Mukhopadhyaya

BIBLIOTHECA INDICA;

A

COLLECTION OF ORIENTAL WORKS

PUBLISHED BY THE

ASIATIC SOCIETY OF BENGAL.

NEW SERIES, NOS. 559, 589, 602, 618, 642, 655, 687, 699, 743.

THE KÚRMA PURÁNA

A SYSTEM OF HINDU MYTHOLOGY AND TRADITION

EDITED BY

NÍLMAṆI MUKHOPÁDHYÁYA

NYÁYÁLANKÁRA M. A., B. L.

PROFESSOR OF SANSKRIT, PRESIDENCY COLLEGE, CALCUTTA;
FELLOW OF THE CALCUTTA UNIVERSITY, AND
MEMBER OF THE ASIATIC SOCIETY
OF BENGAL.

CALCUTTA:

PRINTED BY ŚASIBHÚSHAṆA BHAṬṬÁCHÁRYYA, AT THE GIRIŚA-VIDYÁRATNA PRESS,
24, GIRIŚA-VIDYÁRATNA'S LANE, UPPER CIRCULAR ROAD.
AND PUBLISHED BY THE
ASIATIC SOCIETY, 57, PARK STREET.

1890.

कूर्म्मपुराणम्

श्रीलश्री

वङ्गदेशीयासियाटिकसमितेरनुज्ञया

कलिकाता-प्रेसिडेन्सीकलेज-संस्कृताध्यापकेन

श्रीनीलमणिमुखोपाध्याय-

न्यायालङ्कारेण

संशोधितम्

कलिकाताराजधान्याम्

२४संख्यके गिरिश-विद्यारत्न-वर्त्मस्थे

गिरिश-विद्यारत्न-यन्त्रे

श्रीशशिभूषणभट्टाचार्य्येण

मुद्रितम्

१८९०

NOTICE OF MSS.

The Kúrmapuráṇa is edited from a collection of MSS. such as is not often available for the publication of old Sanskrit works. Considering that it contains very little that is new and that whatever it contains can be found elsewhere in a more attractive and elaborate form, and considering also that the book is seldom read and cited as an authority for any religious practices that obtain now-a-days, it is a wonder that so many well-written MSS. in a well-preserved state should have been received from different quarters for the purpose of collection.

I have received eight MSS. for my use ; they are named respectively A, B, C, D, E, F, G and H.

I have been indebted to M. M. Maheśachandra Nyáyaratna for the loan of MS. A, from the library of the Sobhábázár Ráj Family. It is the best MS. in my collection. It is written in the Devanágri character with a neat hand. The copy was made at Benares in A. D. 1777.

The scribe adds the following colophon—

काश्यां विन्दुमाधवसन्निधौ संवत् १८३४, शके १६९९। कीलकसंवत्सरे उत्तरायणे शशिकृतौ। फाल्गुन शुदि ६ बुधे समाप्तिमगमत्।

For B also I am under obligations to the above-named gentleman who has procured it from the library of the late Śivanáráyaṇa Ghosha of Páthuriághāta. It is written in the Bengali character, and abounds in accuracies, omissions, variations of readings, transpositions of stanzas, and, now and then, interpolations. As this is the only MS. prepared in Bengal, for MS. A, though belonging to a native of that province, was transcribed at Benares, I suspected in the first instance that B must represent a different rescension of the Kúrmapuráṇa. But on a close examination I had to change that opinion. B contains no colophon, but its age cannot be longer than 50 years. C, D and F follow B now and then, and serve as checks on it. The remaining six MSS. are all written in the Devanágri character and have been received from the Asiatic Society of Bengal.

C is complete but here and there rubbed up and illegible. It contains the following at the end—संवत् १८६८ * * * * भाद्रमासे कृष्णपत्ते ।

D is only a fragment. It breaks off in the midst of the fiftieth chapter of Part I (पूर्व्वविभाग) ।

E is received from the Deccan College. It forms No. 342 of the Viśrámabág collection. It is complete and generally agrees with A, but is too often incorrect and full of *lacunae*.

F is incomplete and breaks off in the midst of the forty-fourth chapter of Part I. It has been received from the same place as E, and forms No. 1151 of the above-mentioned collection.

G is the oldest MS. in my possession. It bears date संवत् १६१५, corresponding to 1559 A.D. It is generally well preserved and compares well with A in correctness and neatness of writing. The colophon runs thus : संवत् १६१५ दशम्यां तिथौ रविदिनेऽद्येह श्रीवृद्धनगरे * * * वास्तव्या: * * * दामोदरेण लिखितमिदम् ।

It belongs to the Govt. Collection 1881-82, and is numbered 41 in the Deccan College Library.

H was purchased from Jasalmere and deposited in the Deccan College constituting, No. 16 of the Government Collection 1873-74. At the end is written,—संवत् १६२२ वर्षे माघे शनौ लिखितमिति । This MS. ranks next to G in point of seniority, being junior to it by seven years only.

Of the above eight MSS., only A, G and H contain a table of contents, which is called अनुक्रमणिका ।

PREFACE.

The word Puráṇa means 'what has occurred before,' hence something that is simply ancient. The vast body of Sanskṛit literature which is known under the general appellation of Puráṇa, is so named, not because it was composed and compiled in remote ages, but because it records ancient traditions and customs which have governed the Hindus from times immemorial, both in their worldly and spiritual concerns.

The definition of a Puráṇa given by Amara Siṃha is found in the body of the Puráṇas with little or no variation. Wilson says that the great lexicographer, being one of the gems at the court of Vikramáditya, must have flourished 56 years B. C.* But, according to the calculation made by Colebrooke, which seems to be better founded, the age of Amara Siṃha falls in the tenth century of the Christian era,† so that the oldest Puráṇas such as the Vishṇu, the Brahma, the Padma &c., must have been in existence before that time. That a change was subsequently introduced into the composition of the Puráṇas is, however, evidenced by what is narrated on the subject at the end of the Brahma-vaivarta. Wilson considers that Puráṇa to be of a recent origin and with very good reason. According to it, the five characteristics of a Puráṇa described by Amara Siṃha are to be attributed to what are called Upa-puráṇas or minor Puráṇas; but to a Mahá-puráṇa, such as the Vishṇu, the Brahma, &c, belong ten characteristics; viz, 1 Primary creation, 2 Secondary creation, 3 Growth of the world, 4 Its preservation (by incarnations of Hari), 5 Transmigration of deeds through their consequences,

---

* In the preface to his dictionary, Wilson abandons this hypothesis and places Amara in the 5th. century, as a contemporary of Varáha-mihira.

† See preface to his edition of the Amarakośa.

6 Narration of Manu's reigns, 7 Description of dissolutions, 8 Determination of final liberation, 9 Eulogistic description of Hári, 10 That of the gods. *

The first, the second, and the sixth, in the above list, are the same as the Sarga, Pratisarga and Manvantara of Amara, and consequently should have been omitted. The ninth is given in conformity with the sectarian character of the Purána. Under the fifth and sixth heads are to be included all those later additions, the Máhátmyas (eulogistic descriptions of holy places &c.), the Vratas (periodical fastings and offerings), Práyaśchittas (expiations) &c., &c.

That new matter, under various names, has been incorporated into the Puráṇas from time to time admits of very little doubt; and one can separate the new from the old material by applying the two standards supplied by Amara and the Brahma-vaivarta, respectively.

All the Puráṇas give a list of the eighteen Puráṇas, and some, such as the Matsya, the Bhágavata, the Brahma-vaivarta &c., even specify the number of stanzas contained in each. This circumstance has given rise to the belief that the Puráṇas are the production of one author, viz., Kṛishṇa-Dvaipáyana, *alias* Vyása. There are abundant proofs, however, in the varying style, scope and contents of these Puráṇas themselves to

---

* सृष्टिश्चापि विसृष्टिश्चोत्थितिस्तेषाञ्च पालनम्। कर्म्मणां वासना वार्त्ता मनूनाञ्च क्रमेण च। वर्णनं प्रलयानाञ्च मोक्षस्य च निरूपणम्। उत्कीर्त्तनं हरेरेव देवानाञ्च पृथक् पृथक्। दशाधिकं लक्षणञ्च महतां परिकीर्त्तितम्॥ In the Bhágavata there is a different specification of the ten characteristics of a Mahá-Puráṇa, thus—1 Sarga or cosmogony, 2 Visarga or secondary creation, 3 Vṛitti or growth of the world, 4 Rakshá or incarnations of God Hari, 5 Reigns of Manus, 6 Vaṃśa or descent of Brahmá's sons, 7 Vaṃśánucharita or narration of their deeds, 8 Dissolution, 9 Hetu or souls existing before creation, 10 Upáśraya, the Supreme Spirit.

discredit such a belief. True it is that the internal evidence supplied by language is not always satisfactory. But it is only credulous ignorance and superstitious bigotry that would discard all evidence, internal and external, and cling to the belief that the Vishṇu, the Bhágavata, and the Brahma-vaivarta are creations of the same brain. The Puráṇas generally affirm that, that sage has communicated this or that Puráṇa to his disciples, and that it was revealed to him by some higher authority. But in a passage in the Matsya Puráṇa it is asserted that Vyása Deva was the author of the eighteen Puráṇas which had a priority over the Mahábhárata.* Similar passages are not wanting in the Puráṇas, but, such as they are, they might be considered interpolations inserted to support the popular belief. The disciple of Vyása who was made by him the depositary of the Puráṇas was Súta, who acquired the title of Lomaharshaṇa by virtue of his having so regaled his preceptor with the recital that his hair stood on end. The son of Súta was Ugraśravas, *alias* Sauti, *alias* Lomaharshaṇi, who figures as a reciter of the Puráṇas at the holy place of the Naimisháraṇya in Oude, where the great sage Śaunaka, entitled Kulapati, lived in his hermitage with a host of many thousand disciples.

But Súta is a generic name. Those who were born of a Kshatriya father and Bráhmaṇí mother formed a separate caste†,

---

* अष्टादश पुराणानि कृत्वा सत्यवतीसुतः। भारताख्यानमखिलं चक्रे तदुपबृंहितम् ॥ See p. 223, Chap. 53, Jívánanda's edition.

† ब्राह्मण्यां क्षत्रियात् सूतः। Another version of the story is given in the Puráṇas:—त्वं हि स्वायम्भुवे यज्ञे सुत्याहे वितते सति। सम्भूतः संहितां वक्तुं स्वांशेन पुरुषोत्तमः ॥ See Kúrma Puráṇa, Chap. I., p. 2. Again—वैण्यपुत्रस्य वितते पुरा पैतामहे मखे। सूतः पौराणिको यज्ञे मायारूपः स्वयं हरिः ॥ प्रवक्ता सर्व्वशास्त्राणां धर्म्मज्ञो गुरुवत्सलः। तं मां वित्त मुनिश्रेष्ठाः पूर्व्वोद्भूतं सनातनम् ॥ अस्मिन्मन्वन्तरे व्यासः कृष्णद्वैपायनः स्वयम्। श्रावयामास मां प्रीत्या पुराणपुरुषो हरिः ॥ मदन्वये तु ये सूताः सम्भूता वेदवर्ज्जिताः। तेषां पुराणवक्तृत्वं वृत्तिरासीदजाज्ञया ॥ See Chap. 14, p. 151.

and their vocation was either that of charioteers or reciters of sacred stories. Though the Súta-caste, by reason of their superior mothers and inferior fathers, was considered a Pratiloma játi, or a mixed caste of perverted parentage, still on account of their sacred calling, they were invested with superior sanctity. Indeed Baladeva, after having killed Sauti in a fit of anger, considered himself guilty of Bráhmaṇicide and imposed upon himself a severe mode of expiation.* As these Sútas had the privilege of being the depositaries and reciters of the Puráṇas, they did not scruple to enhance the dignity of their profession by engrafting on them additions from time to time and from generation to generation. In the course of time such additions became crystallised and came to form part and parcel of the original text. It is no wonder, therefore, that interpolations should abound in all the Puráṇas to a more or less extent. Now-a-days, it is the Bráhmaṇas who, under the different appellations of Páṭhakas and Kathakas, have the exclusive right to recite the Mahábhárata, the Harivaṃśa, the Káśíkhaṇḍa from the Skandapuráṇa, the Rámáyaṇa of Válmíki and the Adhyátma Rámáyaṇa. The Súta caste has long been extinct, but the time when they began to be replaced by the Bráhmaṇas in their peculiar vocation, and die out, it is very difficult to trace. It must have taken place at some period before the Mahomedans conquered India, and after the successive accretions had been fossilized in the body of the different Puráṇas.

---

* ब्राह्मं स्थानं गतो ह्येष यत्सूतो विनिपातित:। तथा ह्येते द्विजा: सर्व्वे मामवेच्य विनिर्गता:। शरीरस्य च मे गन्धो लोहस्येवासुखावह:। आत्मानञ्चावगच्छामि ब्रह्मघ्नमिव कुत्सितम्। धिगमर्षं तथा मद्यमतिमानमभीरुताम्। यैराविष्टेन सुमहत् मया पापमिदङ्कृतम्। तत्क्षयार्थं चरिष्यामि व्रतं द्वादशवार्षिकम्। स्वकर्म्मख्यापनं कुर्व्वन् प्रायश्चित्तमनुत्तमम्॥ See Márkaṇḍeya Puráṇa, Chap. 6, p. 58.

Every Puráṇa begins with a salutation to a particular deity in its own peculiar style and fashion, and contains some mention or other of the great Vyása; but very few of them claim him as their author directly. The successive authors of the Puráṇas studiously kept themselves in the back-ground, and in their anonymous character perpetrated a sort of pious fraud by encouraging the popular belief in the universal authorship of Vyása, and thereby enhancing the sanctity of their own works. The Puráṇas were composed and compiled to serve more or less sectarian purposes; it is no wonder, therefore, that their authors should have vied with each other in strictly keeping their incognitos and merging themselves into the gigantic personality of the author of the Mahábhárata, the son of the great sage Parásara, the father of the self-enlightened Śuka, the progenitor of the Páṇḍavas, the arranger of the Vedas, and the propounder of the Brahma-sútras. Such an instance of combined and absolute anonymity is unique and unparalleled; but the facts stated above are inexorable, and they all militate against the hypothesis of Vyása's universal authorship and tend to demolish it.

Some of the Puráṇas not only contain a list of the eighteen Puráṇas but also a list of the Upa-puráṇas; there is, however, some uncertainty as to the number of these last. The Matsya Puráṇa enumerates only 4 Upa-puráṇas;* the Brahma-vaivarta says that, there are 18 Upa-puráṇas, but does not mention any by name; while the Kúrma-puráṇa recounts 18 Upa-puráṇas. †

* Nárasiṃha, Nandipuráṇa, Sámba and Áditya. See Chap. 53.

† 1 Sanatkumárokta, 2 Nárasiṃha, 3 Skanda, 4 Sivadharmákhya, 5 Durvásasokta, 6 Náradíya, 7 Kapila, 8 Vámana, 9 Uśanasokta, 10 Brahmáṇḍa, 11 Varuṇa, 12 Kálikákhya, 13 Maheśvara, 14 Sámba, 15 Saura, 16 Paráśarokta, 17 Márícha, 18 Bhárgava.

On looking through the shelves of the Sanskrit College Library, in

But nowhere is given either the number of stanzas that each Upa-puráṇa consists of, or the grand total which they all together aggregate. Both the Matsya and the Kúrma content themselves with stating that the minor Puráṇas are mere abridgments, compiled from the principal ones, which contain no less than four hundred thousand stanzas.

The insertion of the names of the minor Puráṇas furnishes an additional proof of the extent to which interpolations have been interspersed in the body of the principal Puráṇas. Yet there are paṇḍits who go to the length of ascribing the authorship of these Upa-puráṇas also to Kṛishṇa-Dvaipáyaṇa!

The Puráṇas are the store-houses in which are collected the traditions of many by-gone ages. Stories and legends touching the sages that are interspersed throughout the Upánishadas and Áraṇyakas are also therein amplified and embellished.

They are replete with repetitions, and abound in exaggerations; but the language is always easy and smooth though diffuse, and everything is couched in a form which is popular, and as free from vedic archaism on the one hand, as from the terseness of the Saṃhitás and the sententious gravity of the Sútras on the other. From the Saṃhitás or Dharma-śástras,

---

addition to these I find several others not included in the above list—Ádi-puráṇa, Átma-puráṇa, Kalki-puráṇa and Gaṇeśa-puráṇa. Compare with the lists given by Wilson.

Raghunandana, called the Smárta, professes to give in his Malamásatattva a list of Upa-puráṇas from the Kúrma, but his list does not tally with the above. He says—1 Sanatkumárokta, 2 Nárasiṃha, 3 Váyavíya, 4 Śivadharmákhya, 5 Durvásokta, 6 Náradíya, 7 Nandikeśvara-puráṇa, 8 Vṛihat-Nandikeśvara-puráṇa, 9 Uśanasokta, 10 Varuṇa, 11 Kapila, 12 Śámba, 13 Kálliká-puráṇa, 14 Maheśvara, 15 Padma, 16 Deví-puráṇa, 17 Márícha, 18 Bháskara.

the Puráṇas have gathered materials bearing on the usages of the fourfold stages or A'śramas and of the fourfold castes or Varṇas; also on various forms of expiations (Práyaśchittas) recommended for the cleansing of sins.

Among the different schools of philosophy or Darśanas, the Sáṅkhya supplies the cardinal doctrine which pervades the Puráṇas. The duality of Prakṛiti and Purusha, by which the followers of Kapila understand nature and soul, or matter and mind, has been eagerly seized upon by the Puráṇas which have interpreted them into the creative principle (Śakti) and the Supreme spirit (Paramátman). Kálidása, in conformity with this modified interpretation of the Sáṅkhya doctrine, puts the following stanza into the mouth of Vṛihaspati, the spiritual guide of the gods, when, oppressed by the demon Tárakásura, they sought the protection of Brahman :—"They declare that thou art the Prakṛiti engaged in bringing about fruition and liberation, as desired by the Purusha; and thou also art the Purusha who witnesses her doings unconcerned."* With this modified form of the Sáṅkhya doctrine, the Puráṇas have intermixed the pantheistic theory of illusion (Máyá) taken from the system of Vedántism. They affirm that, the Supreme Spirit exists in everything, and everything exists in Him; that the universe has emanated from Him, and into Him it will be absorbed at the time of dissolution or Pralaya. In some of the Puráṇas, such as the Kúrma, the Brahma, &c., the mysticism of the Yoga school has found favour, and prominence has been given to the practice of mental abstraction, and such postures and bodily exercises as come under what is called the Haṭha-yoga.

It will thus be seen that, the material, which the Puráṇas

---

* त्वामामनन्ति प्रकृतिं पुरुषार्थप्रवर्त्तिनीम्। तद्दर्शिनमुदासीनं त्वामेव पुरुषं विदुः॥
See Canto 2, Kumára Sambhava.

have borrowed and collected from the Upanishads, the Dharma-śástras and the Darsanas, is varied and abundant. But what has been engrafted upon the old material is out of all proportion to the old material itself. The Puráṇas, as has already been stated, have been composed more or less to serve sectarian purposes. To enforce their particular dogmas they have multiplied the *Vratas* which are religious observances attended with fasting, feasting the Bráhmaṇas, and the worship of particular deities.

These Vratas are repeated from year to year till they are concluded with a grand ceremony. Sometimes, as in the case of the Sávitrí and Ananta vratas, these religious observances are carried on for 14 years. There are vratas even, that are enjoined to be observed through life; such as the Janmáshṭamí or Kṛishṇa's birth-day festival, the Maháshṭamí or the second day of the Durgá-pújá festival, the Śiva-chaturdaśí or the 14th. day of the dark fortnight sacred to Śiva, the Rámanavamí or Ráma's birth-day festival, &c. Vratas occupy a considerable portion of the majority of the Puráṇas, but by far the greater space is alloted to what are called the Máhátmyas, which are the eulogistic descriptions of sacred places or Tírthas, religious observances, religious books, &c. These Máhátmyas sometimes assume vast proportions and constitute altogether separate works. The Káśíkhaṇḍa, the Utkalakhaṇḍa of the Liṅgapuráṇa, and the Adhyátma Rámáyaṇa of the Brahmáṇḍa* are remarkable instances under this head.

Like Vratas and Máhátmyas, there also abound in the Puráṇas, legends bearing witness to the efficacy of particular

---

* It is said that, the Adhyátma Rámáyaṇa was composed by Śaṅkaráchárya and included in the Brahmáṇḍa Puráṇa to impart to it additional sanctity.

forms of faith inculcated by them. These legends are peculiar to the Puráṇas; they are never found in earlier works, the Upanishads and Áraṇyakas. They are either inventions or embodiments of loose traditions floating in the atmosphere of Hindu mythology.

The really interesting and historical element in the Puráṇas consists in the description and enumeration of kings of the solar and lunar races who flourished after Ráma and Paríkshit, respectively. To preserve the sanctity and ancient character of the Puráṇas, these descriptions are given as predictions, but they are necessarily meagre and loose, and do not warrant any convincing conclusions touching ancient history and chronology.

Be that as it may, the Puráṇas form an important portion of the religious literature of the Hindus, and, together with the Dharma-śástras and Tantras, govern their conduct and regulate their religious observances at the present day. The Vedas are studied by the antiquarian, the Upanishads by the philosopher; but every orthodox Hindu must have some knowledge of the Puráṇas, directly or vicariously, to shape his conduct and to perform the duties essential to his worldly and spiritual welfare. The form of faith enjoined by the Vedas, is, element-worship; and that sanctioned by the Saṃhitás is, ancestor-worship; while the Puráṇas advocate hero-worship and image-worship, and the Tantras inculcate devotion to the creative principle called Sakti, and enjoin oblations to her various forms after the example and in imitation of the Puráṇas. These different forms of worship are blended into one harmonious whole, and constitute the cardinal doctrines which regulate the religious observances of the orthodox Hindu at the present day: bigotry and sectarianism are now-a days at a discount; especially amongst the higher classes.

The Kúrma Puráṇa.

This Puráṇa is named Kúrma, because it was communicated by the divine Kúrma or the tortoise incarnation of Hari to those Rishis who sang his praise at the churning of the Ocean.

The Kúrma Puráṇa, says Súta, has existed in four distinct forms or Saṃhitás (collections) which are called Bráhmí, Bhágavatí, Saurí, and Vaishṇaví. It is the Bráhmí Saṃhitá that was recited by Súta to the ascetics of the Naimisha-forest. It consists of six thousand stanzas. But the Bhágavata Puráṇa says that, the Kúrma has 17000 ślokas, while the Matsya and Brahma-vaivarta concur in holding that it contains 18000. The eight MSS. that I have received from different quarters represent only the Bráhmí-Saṃhitá. It is, therefore, probable that this collection, together with the other three collections which have perhaps become extinct, must have altogether comprised 17 or 18 thousand stanzas, as stated by the above authorities.

There are three channels referred to at the end, through which the descent of this Puráṇa is to be traced.

1. Nárada, the son of Brahmá, received the Kúrma-puráṇa from Náráyaṇa, and communicated it to Gautama, who again imparted it to Paráśara. The last in his turn narrated the Puráṇa to a number of Rishis at a place called Gaṅgádvára. The second channel consists in Brahman imparting it to Sanaka, Sanaka to Devala, and Devala to Pañchaśikha. Brahman also communicated the Puráṇa to Sanatkumára, another of his mind-begotten sons, Sanatkumára to Vyása, and he to Lomaharshaṇa. This is the third medium of descent.

The Kúrma Puráṇa, as it is now edited, forms a consistent whole and does not seem incomplete in any of the essential parts of a Mahá-puráṇa. Not only does it conform to the simple definition of Amara-Siṃha, but it also tallies with the ten characteristics laid down by the Bhágavata and the Brahma-vaivarta. It is, therefore, reasonable to conclude that, this Puráṇa must have been composed after the time of Amara in the 10th. century and before the age of the Bhágavata, which, according to one theory, was, written by Vopadeva, the grammarian, who flourished towards the end of the 12th. century of the Christian era.

The comparatively modern origin of the Kúrma-puráṇa might be inferred from its having mentioned one of the Tantras by name (Yámala), and alluded to a class of devotees who are called the left-handed (Vámáchárí).* But one cannot help demurring to the way in which the above conclusion is sought to be corroborated on the ground of its having referred to the practices of the Yoga system of philosophy. There is no reason to question the antiquity of that school, whose founder is reckoned one of the Rishis, and must have flourished before the Christian era. Similarly, exception might be taken to another argument advanced in favour of the belief in the recent origin of the Kúrma-puráṇa, which is based on the circumstance that this Puráṇa adverts to that sect of heretics who are known as Jains. Now the Jains, though heretics from the orthodox religion of the Hindus, are, as a sect, older than the Christian era. I have seen lists of Jaina Tírthaṅkaras, called Jaina-paṭṭávalís, in which the birth of the first Tírthaṅkara is dated Samvat 4, *i. e.*, 52 B. C.

The Kúrma is a Śaiva Puráṇa; it is not, as might be inferred to its title, one of that class of Puráṇas, which are consecrated to the advocacy of a faith in Hari. Though Śaiva in its character, it is not intolerant in its spirit. It glorifies Śiva above all others, but manifests no prejudice against the votaries of Vishṇu.

---

* See Chap. 12, p. 137.

The Kúrma-puráṇa consists of two sections, Púrva-vibhága and Uttara-vibhága. The former comprises 53, and the latter 45 chapters.

SECTION I.

At the outset there is a point of some interest which requires explanation. The list of Puráṇas given at page 3 names 19, instead of 18 Puráṇas, though immediately after, it is mentioned that the Brahmáṇḍa, the last named, is the 18th, and that the sages having 'heard the 18 Puráṇas, succinctly recounted the Upa-puráṇas.' This difficulty might be obviated by reading अथा-त्रेयं in the place of अथाग्नेयं. But the adoption of the former reading would lead to absurdities. In the first place, it is incorrect and occurs only in three out of the eight MSS. I have in my possession, viz., C, E and F. Dr. Hall in his edition of Wilson's Vishṇu-puráṇa says that, it occurs in Wilson's MS.,* but is wanting in the four MSS. that he consulted. In the second place, even if अथात्रेयं were corrected into अथो त्रेयं or अथ त्रेयं; there would still occur another difficulty not easy to get over. At p. 4, the Kúrma-puráṇa is styled as the 15th.; and it is so ranked in every other list that I have seen. But, if the reading अथो त्रेयं be adopted and the Agni-puráṇa left out, the Kúrma will take the fourteenth and not the fifteenth place in the above list.

The above considerations have induced the present editor to prefer the other reading अथाग्नेयं। But the question, though extricated from one horn of the dilemma, is yet entangled in the other. For the list, as it stands in the present edition, apparently contains nineteen instead of eighteen Puráṇas, viz.,

* On the strength of this single MS. Wilson says that, there is no mention of the Ágneya in the list given by the Kúrma. But it should be noted, that, that Puráṇa is mentioned in every other list which I have seen, and is nowhere omitted.

1 Bráhma, 2 Pádma, 3 Vaishṇava, 4 S'aiva, 5 Bhágavata, 6 Bhavishya, 7 Náradíyaka, 8 Márkaṇḍeya, 9 A'gneya, 10 Brahma-vaivarta, 11 Laiṅga, 12 Váráha, 13 Skánda, 14 Vámana, 15 Kaurma, 16 Mátsya, 17 Gáruḍa, 18 Váyavíya, 19 Brahmáṇḍa. Wilson attempts to identify the S'aiva with the Váyavíya on the ground that, as on the one hand the list given by the Bhágavata, the Vishṇu and the Márkaṇḍeya, mentions the S'aiva but leaves out the Váyavíya, so on the other in the list supplied by the A'gneya and the Mátsya, the Váyavíya occurs while the S'aiva does not; and that to both of the Puráṇas, S'aiva and Váyavíya, are assigned 24,000 stanzas. This seems to be a mere beating about the bush. The Váyavíya has been edited by Rájá Rájendralála Mitra C. I. E. under the auspices of the Asiatic Society of Bengal, and the S'aiva by Gaṇapat Kṛishṇa of Bombay. I have compared the one with the other, and found them to be two entirely different works, as has all along been held to be the case.

Wilson, however, supplies the data * to solve the difficulty

* See his preface to the Vishṇu-puráṇa, p. 86.

The copy of the Brahmáṇḍa I have procured turns out on comparison to be an entirely different work from the Váyavíya. I have a strong suspicion, that the book I have in my possession is not a Mahá-puráṇa, but an Upa-puráṇa. Both the Kúrma-puráṇa and the Revá-khaṇḍa make mention of an Upa-puráṇa of that name. The MS. of Part II. of the Brahmáṇḍa-puráṇa which I have seen in the shelves of Calcutta Sanskrit College Library corroborates the remarks of Wilson on the Brahmáṇḍa as a Mahá-puráṇa. The omission of the Váyavíya in the Bhágavata, the Vishṇu and the Márkaṇḍeya-puráṇas stands to reason, as it is included in the Brahmáṇḍa. But the Ágneya and the Mátsya are doubly inconsistent, firstly in rejecting the S'aiva, and secondly in including both the Váyavíya and the Brahmáṇḍa as two separate works. In the first place, it will not do to say that, the S'aiva is an Upa-puráṇa and, therefore, should not be included in a list of Mahá-puráṇas. For under that name there are two

above adverted to. He says that, god Váyu is the teacher or narrator of the first section of Brahmáṇḍa-puráṇa, which is identical with what is known by the name of the Váyavíya-puráṇa. It is, therefore, clear that the word Váyavíya in the text does not stand for a new work, but qualifies the expression Brahmáṇḍa and means "narrated by Váyu" ; so it seems that, in avoiding Scylla, the editor runs no risk of falling into Charybdis, and that in rejecting the reading अष्टौ शैवं, he is not in danger of overstating the number of the Mahá-puráṇas.

The Kúrma Puráṇa opens with the great sages singing the praises of the divine Tortoise, the incarnation of Vishṇu who bore the weight of Mount Mandara at the churning of the ocean. When the goddess Śrí or Lakshmí issued forth from the ocean, Vishṇu took her as his consort and imparted to the Rishis a knowledge of her who was the all creating, all-sustaining, and all-destroying energy of the Supreme spirit. It was that lotus-dwelling goddess, continued the divine narrator, who appeared to the Bráhmaṇa Indradyumna as he was engaged in propitiating Mahádeva, the lord of all beings, by penances, fastings and oblations into the fire. Indradyumna had been a king* in his previous birth. Having built a city and governed the earth, he was born a Bráhmaṇa in his next birth through his devotion to Hari. When the goddess appeared to him, he sang praises to her and sought from her the way to a knowledge of that omnipotent lord of the universe,—Mahádeva. Having revealed to the supplicant Bráhmaṇa the secret that such a

---

works, one a Mahá-puráṇa, and the other an Upa-puráṇa. In the second place, there is no authority in support of the contention that what goes by the name of the Brahmáṇḍa-puráṇa is a conglomeration of two works, the first constituting the Váyavíya, and the second the Brahmáṇḍa proper.

* Indradyumna was a king of Avantí in Málava and built the temple of Jagannátha at Níláchala, as Purí was then called.

knowledge must be communicated by none other than Vishṇu, she disappeared. He then propitiated Vishṇu, who exhorted him to worship Mahádeva with his whole heart, so as to secure the blessings of salvation. The Bráhmaṇa then renounced the world, and took to contemplative devotion. Having at last attained the powers which are sought by those who strive after final liberation, he, once upon a time, at the advice of the Sun, journeyed through the air to the mountain to the north of Lake Mánasarovara in order to see god Brahman. He now beheld the god and attained that imperishable state, which is called Moksha or beatitude.

In order to impart, to the sages assembled in the nether world, that true knowledge based on righteousness which he had revealed to the ascetic Indradyumna, the divine Kúrma commenced to narrate the Kúrma-puráṇa.

This episode of Indradyumna is apparently introduced to exalt a faith in Mahádeva and to enhance the value of contemplative devotion which is the essence of the Yoga-school of philosophy. The Kúrma-puráṇa does not breathe a spirit of intolerance ;* it sings praises to Vishṇu and Brahman alike, and advocates only a preferential, and not an exclusive, devotion to Mahádeva.

The second chapter contains a succinct description of the four castes, Bráhmaṇas, Kshatriyas, Vaiśyas and Śúdras, and their several occupations, as also of the four stages, or Áśramas, with the duties incumbent on each. These things as stated are in complete accord with the spirit and language of the Mánava Dharma-śástra. The fourfold objects of life,—virtue, riches, enjoyments, and beatitude,—are also briefly adverted to. Then in Chap. III, the efficacy of knowledge when combined

* See Chap. 2, p. 32.

with acts, (penances, oblations &c.) and the desirability of making over the fruits of such acts to the Supreme spirit are touched upon, much in the style of the Bhagavadgítá.

In Chapter IV the creation of the Universe is described, generally in conformity with the evolution-theory of the Sáṅkhyas. Here and there are mixed up with it scraps of the doctrine of the primordial mundane egg from the Manu-saṃhitá, and of the Vedantic theory of air evolving from ether, light from air, water from light, and earth from water.

Chapter V gives the subdivisions of time from the minutest to the grandest cycles of Manvantaras and Kalpas.*

Chapter VI adverts to the Earth being raised from the Ocean by the Boar incarnation of Vishṇu, who is here described as indentical with Brahman, and also to the levelling of the earth and planting it with mountains.

Chapter VII continues the first characteristic of a Puráṇa, Sarga or cosmogony. From the Supreme spirit, wrapped in a state of unconsciousness, first emanates darkness, then come mountains, then animals and the rest, then gods, and lastly man.

The above order is not however maintained when Brahman,

---

* 15 Twinklings are equal to a Káshṭhá, 30 Káshṭhás = a Kalá, 30 Kalás = a Muhúrta, 30 Muhúrtas = a day, 30 days = a Mása or month, 6 months = an Ayana, 2 Ayanas = a Year or a day of the gods, 12000 celestial years = 4 Yugas (Satya, Tretá, Dvápara and Kali), 71 cycles of 4 Yugas = a Manvantara, 14 Manvantaras or 1000 Cycles of 4 Yugas = a Kalpa or a day of Brahman, 360 Kalpas = 1 year of Brahman, 100 years of Brahman = 1 Parárddha.

A minor dissolution, or Khaṇḍa-pralaya, of the world takes place during each night of Brahman's life, as a creation during the day. But at the end of Brahman's life, which endures 100 years, the grand dissolution, or Mahá-pralaya, takes place, when the whole universe, with the gods, Brahman, Vishṇu and Mahádeva, is dissolved into nature (Prakṛiti).

being in a state of consciousness, creates,—first matter, secondly the elements, thirdly the organs of sense, fourthly immovables (mountains, trees &c.), fifthly animals and birds, sixthly the gods, seventhly man, eighthly spirits, and lastly his will-begotten sons.

Creation is then considered in another aspect, inasmuch as the birth of the Asuras is assigned to the first day, of the gods to the second day, of the manes to the third, of man to the fourth, and lastly of the lower animals, plants &c. to the fifth day.

Chap. VIII deals with creation in further details much in the strains of Manu, describing how Brahman, dividing his body into twain, made a male from one and a female from the other half; and how from this couple the race of man multiplied.

In Chap. IX, it is described how Brahman was born in the lotus of Vishṇu's navel, and how he insisted on the duality of godhead and denied its trinity, when the three-eyed Mahádeva, the lord of beings, appeared on the scene in his full glory; whereupon Brahman, disabused of his illusion, sought Mahádeva's protection; and Mahádeva, granting him a boon, declared that there existed a perfect identity between Vishṇu and himself, and that no ascetic should find grace with him unless he had previously sought the protection* of the former.

The greater portion of Chapter X is taken up in Brahman chanting hymns in praise of Mahádeva, and in his receiving encouragement and promises of help from the latter in furtherance of his work of creation.

Chap. XI touches upon Mahádeva's dividing his body into two parts, male and female; from the former of which eleven

---

* See p. 85.

Rudras were born, whilst from the latter numerous Śaktis or Vibhútis sprang. It is then mentioned that there is no difference between Śakti and Śaktimat ; as one is the goddess that is enjoyed and the other is the god (Mahádeva)who is the enjoyer. This is followed in Chapter XII,by the description,how Himavat and his wife Mená obtained, through penances, the privilege of begetting goddess Śakti as their daughter,how a long protracted dialogue followed between the father and the daughter, how the former sang her praises and the latter imparted to him a knowledge of her identity with Mahádeva, and, lastly, how Himavat, at the request of Brahman, married her to Mahádeva.

The above is apparently a digression, and might have a fitting place in a book intended for inculcating a faith in Śákta worship.

Chap. XIII touches upon the progeny of Bhṛigu and several other patriarchs.

Chap. XIV gives a genealogy of Manu, the son of Svayambhú. From this royal line was born Suśíla, who was initiated into the mysteries of Śiva's worship by the sage Śvetáśvatara. Daksha, one of the will-born sons of Brahman, was for his arrogance cursed by Rudra and became in his second birth a great-grandson of Suśíla.

In Chapter XV is mentioned, how Daksha commenced a sacrifice under the protection of Vishṇu, inviting all the gods except his daughter Satí and her husband Mahádeva. Whereupon Maháleva in a rage created Vírabhadra, who struck the gods with paralysis, put out the eyes of their king Indra, pulled out the teeth of the Sun, hurled down the Moon with his toes, cut off the hands and tongue of Fire, kicked the sages on the head, pierced Vishṇu with sharp arrows, stopped his weapon Sudarśana, and drove Garuḍa away. At last Maháleva with his consort appears on the scene, when the gods with Daksha chant praises to him and are pardoned. Several incidents, as mentioned here in connection with the sacrifice of Daksha, appear to be new, and fit in with the sectarian character of the Puráṇa.

Chap. XVI makes mention of the sixty daughters of Daksha and their progeny; of the two sons of Diti, the demons Hiraṇyáksha and Hiraṇyakaśipu; of Vishṇu's assuming the incarnation of Nṛisiṃha, half man and half lion, to slay the latter; of the installation of Prahláda, the son of Hiraṇyakaśipu, through his devotion to Hari; and lastly of Prahláda's subsequent renunciation of the world. Then Andhakásura ascends the throne and attempts to carry off Párvatí, the consort of Mahádeva, and is slain by him.

In this chapter it is stated that Rudra and Vishṇu conjointly invented certain sciences for deception, such as Kápála, Nakula, Váma, oriental and occidental, Pañcharátras, Páśupata and many thousands of a like nature. Mention is made of certain Bráhmaṇas who had lost the privilege of studying the Vedas through the curse of the sage Gautama, and who were directed by the above gods to write on and teach other sciences of a perverted character, showing their utility for the confounding of the wicked,* and thereby find a way to the expiation of their sins. It is not easy to describe what those sciences were, but one thing is clear, that all this means a covert attack aimed at the schisms consequent on that nascent spirit of innovation exhibited in the various forms of Śákta, Vaishṇava and Śaiva worship, which sprung up in medieval India, after Buddhism had been stamped out.

Chap. XVII and Chap. XVIII continue the genealogy of Prahláda and advert to the Dwarf incarnation of Vishṇu, by

---

* See Chap. 16, p. 184—85.

whom his grandson Bali was punished, and Indra was reinstated in his celestial realm.

Chap. XIX begins with the marriage of Pulastya, one of the patriarchs, from whom the Rákshasas, Rávaṇa, Kumbhakarṇa &c., were descended; and concludes with a description of Vasishṭha, who married Arundhatí. Vasishṭha begot Śakti, Śakti begot Paráśara the omniscient ascetic, and Paráśara begot the incomparable Kṛishṇadvaipáyana, whose son was no less a personage than Śuka, an incarnation of god Śaṅkara himself.

Chapters XX and XXI give a list of the kings of the solar race down to the fourteenth descent from Ráma, Śrutáyu being the last king of that line.

The lunar race with its several branches is described at a greater length in Chapters XXII—XXVII, the last three Chapters being devoted to Śríkṛishṇa, the incarnation of Vishṇu, who belonged to the Yádava branch of that line.

A point of considerable interest to devotees is dwelt upon in pp. 239—42.

Amongst the five sons of Kártavíryya, a famous king of the Haihaya branch of the lunar dynasty, a quarrel broke out as to the preferential claim for worship of a particular deity. The dispute was referred to the Seven Rishis (Pleiades), who then laid down the following canons of worship for the guidance of the princes.

1. That every one is to follow the bent of his inclination in worshipping a deity.

2. That particular deities are to be worshipped for the attainment of particular objects.

3. That princes shall worship specially gods Vishṇu, Mahádeva and Purandara.

4. That Bráhmaṇas shall worship specially gods Fire, Sun, Mahádeva and Brahman.

5. That to the gods are assigned for worship Vishṇu and Mahádeva.

6. That to the Gandharvas and Yakshas is allotted the god Moon; to the Vidyádharas, Sarasvatí, the goddess of speech; to the Siddhas, the all-powerful Vishṇu; to the Rákshasas, Rudra; to the Kinnaras, Párvatí; to the Rishis, Brahman and Mahádeva; to women, the goddess Umá, Vishṇu, Mahádeva and the Sun; to house-holders, all gods without distinction; to Brahmachárís (students of the vedas), Brahma (vedas)*; to ascetics, the Sun; to anchorites, Mahádeva; and, lastly, to Bhútas (spirits), Brahman.

But the tolerant and liberal exposition of devotional worship adverted to above is somewhat neutralised † by the statement that Kṛishṇa, the incarnation of Vishṇu, had himself to practise austerities to propitiate Mahádeva, in order to have a son for his favourite wife Jámbavatí. Mahádeva was propitiated, and himself took birth in the womb of Kṛishṇa's wife. He was known by the name of Śámba.‡ While Kṛishṇa was practising penances, the sage Márkaṇḍeya came to him and asked the reason for his doing so. In reply to him, Kṛishṇa expatiated on the efficacy of worshiping Mahádeva in his symbolic representation, the great Liṅga, and incidentally touched upon the origin of phallic worship.

With Kṛishṇa ended the line of the Yádava branch of the lunar race. No mention is made of the Kauravas and Páṇḍavas, the most famous branch of the above line, except that Arjuna, while wending his way back after performing the last rites to

* वेदस्तत्त्वं तपोब्रह्म इत्यमरः ।

† See p. 262—94.

‡ There is an Upa-puráṇa of that name in which Śámba figures as the chief interlocutor.

Kṛishṇa, his relative and friend, met the renowned Kṛishṇa-dvaipáyana. This is the purport of the short chapter that follows.

In Chapters XXIX and XXX, the sage relates to Arjuna the characteristics of the Kali-yuga or iron age which, as he foretells, is coming on apace. The Puráṇas, as a rule, take a pessimist view of the fourth Yuga and expatiate on its evil propensities and evil doings. Every thing is said in the tone of prophecy; as it is supposed that, the Puráṇas, or rather the chief interlocutors who figure in them, flourished before the advent of Kali. After shortly depicting the characteristics of the Satya, or the golden age, the Tretá or the silver age, and the Dvápara or the copper age, Kṛishṇa-dvaipáyana draws a picture of the Kali-yuga in glowing colours. He says,——— "In the Satya yuga righteousness exists in its perfect state; in the Tretá it progresses; but being mixed up with evil in the Dvápara, it dies in the Kali-yuga."*

"In the iron age, there shall occur epidemics, famines, droughts, and revolutions." "Men shall be devoid of virtue, possessed of slender powers, irascible, covetous, and untruthful." "The Bráhmaṇas shall not study the Vedas, perform ablutions, offer oblations, repeat hymns, give alms, and worship the gods." "They shall associate with the Śúdras, and join with them in the performance of religious rites." "Princes, surrounded with the Śúdras, shall persecute the Bráhmaṇas." "People shall speak disparagingly of Mahádeva, the Bráhmaṇas, the Vedas, the Śástras, and the Puráṇas."

"The Bráhmaṇas shall not cling to their religion; the Śúdras shall occupy higher seats than the Bráhmaṇas, and princes shall insult them."

---

* See p. 302—11.

"There shall be a large number of beggars amongst the people ; short life, lassitude, disease, and misery shall prevail as consequences of sin and ignorance."

"Both the Bráhmaṇas and the Kshatriyas shall take to the practices of the Vámas, the Pásupatas, and the Pañcharátrikas."

"In the iron age, even Mahádeva, the lord of all beings, the god of gods, shall be no divinity to man." "But that bestower of blessings shall have his many incarnations * for the good of his devotees, and the re-establishment of rites, sanctioned by revelation and tradition, Śruti and Smṛiti."

"Though the Kali-yuga is tainted with many vices, there is one merit in it, for one can attain to a state of blessedness with no great trouble."

"In this age, the worship of Mahádeva makes amends for all demerits ; hence, leaving other deities, who are powerless, one should devote oneself to the great lord Mahádeva, if one should aspire to the highest place." "Alms-giving, penances, and sacrifices shall be of no avail to those who do not in this Yuga worship Rudra, who is worshipped by the gods."

After having thus dwelt on the characteristics of the different Yugas and of the Kali-yuga in particular, the sage launches fourth into a description of the sacred place, Váráṇasí,† to which the next five chapters are devoted. Váráṇasí is peculiarly sacred to Mahádeva and stands pre-emiment among the holy places of India. This city bestows beatitude on those that die in its precincts, for Mahádeva himself whispers to their dying ears that immortality-giving name, called Táraka-

---

* See Chap. 53.

† Benares. अयोध्या मथुरा माया काशी काञ्ची अवन्तिका। पुरी द्वारावती चैव सप्तैता मोक्षदायिकाः॥

Brahma. The god never leaves the place, whence it goes by the name of Avimukta or undeserted.

Several secret emblematic representations or Lingas of Váráṇasí are described with the traditional accounts associated with them, but they cannot now be identified. Pilgrims cannot now trace where Oṅkáreśvara on the bank of the Matsyodarí was; or ascertain if such places as Kṛittiváseśvara, Kaparthíśvara, and Madhyameśvara are still in existence.

In the four subsequent Chapters, the máhátmya of Prayága or modern Allahabad is related. In connection with Prayága a few places of peculiar sanctity are mentioned, such as Kambaláśvatara on the southern bank of the Yamuná, Abaṭa, Sarva-samudra, Pratishṭháua on the east side of the Ganges, Haṃsa-prapatana to the north of Prátishṭhána, Urvasí-pulina, Sandhyávaṭa, and, lastly, Tripathá that abounds in many ghats and hermitages. But no trace of all these places, which were considered peculiarly holy by the writer of the Kúrma-Puráṇa, can be found now. It is also worthy of note that, in describing places of interest both in Váráṇasi and in Prayága, no mention is made of those spots which are now-a-days considered holy and resorted to by pilgrims.*

The next eleven chapters (from Chapter XL to Chapter L) are devoted to, what may be called, transcendental geography and transcendental astronomy. Here and there, however, the chaff may be separated from the corn, and the truth disentangled from imaginary descriptions and false assumptions.

Some peculiar sanctity is attached to number seven.† For

---

* See p. 320.

† It would be interesting to quote here an extract from Mr. Gladstone's address at Oxford delivered to the Union Debating Society on Wednesday morning, the 5th of February, 1890. "Then as to the use of number seven, the only prominent one in Homer was the description

the earth is divided into seven continents surrounded by seven oceans. The heaven is divided into seven spheres, and the nether world into seven regions.

Fanciful diameters and distances are given to the different planets. The distance of the sun from the earth is given as eight hundred thousand miles; that of the moon from the sun is also asserted to be the same. The distance of Mercury from the sphere of the asterisks, that of Venus from Mercury, of Mars from Venus, of Jupiter from Mars, and of Saturn from Jupiter are all given as 1,60,000 miles. At the distance of 8,00,000 miles from Saturn is the great Bear, and at a similar distance from the latter is the polar star, where the almighty Vishṇu, the embodiment of righteousness has his abode.

The diameter of the sun is only 72,000 miles, and its circumference is three times its diameter; the diameter of the moon is twice that of the sun; Venus's circumference is one-sixteenth of that of the moon, Jupiter's three-fourths of Venus's, those of Mars and Saturn are both three-fourths of that of Jupiter, and Mercury's three-fourths of that of either of them.

The above is, I presume, a fair specimen of what I mean by transcendental geography and transcendental astronomy.

Chapter LI adverts to the seven Manvantaras, of which six are past and the seventh, called Vaivasvata, is the current one; and concludes with a eulogium on Vishṇu.

The next chapter speaks of Vyása and his 25 incarnations in the different Dvápara-yugas of the Vaivasvata Manvantara.

---

of Thebes, and its seven gates; then there were the seven winds. Again as to the flood legend, its duration was of seven days, as is the description or cosmogony in Genesis. Then the war in heaven was carried on by seven spirits; also the under-world was shut in by seven gates."

Then are mentioned his five disciples, of whom Paila was appointed as teacher of the Rigveda, Vaiśampáyana, of the Yajurveda, Jaimini, of the Sáma-veda, Sumantu, of the Atharva-veda, and Súta of Itihásas and Puráṇas.

In imitation of the foregoing description but in perfect keeping with the sectarian character of the Puráṇa, the concluding chapter of Section I mentions by name twenty-six incarnations of Mahádeva and of his one hundred and six disciples. In every incarnation the god had four disciples who were all initiated into the practice of Yoga or mental abstraction, had a contented mind, and were distinguished by self-restraint and reverential attachment to their respective lords. They were remarkable for purity, devotion, knowledge and meditation. To do good to the Bráhmaṇas and to re-establish the authority of the Vedas, these disciples can have incarnations of their own, at the command of their respective masters, the different incarnations of Mahádeva. It is enjoined that those Bráhmaṇas who always meditate upon, bow to, gratify and worship these disciples of Mahádeva, shall obtain the knowledge of the Supreme spirit.

Section II.

The second Section is also called the Vyása-gítá, as at this stage of Súta's narration Vyása appears on the scene, and relates, at the request of his disciple, in *propria persona*, the occult knowledge of contemplative devotion and other transcendental themes to the assembled sages of Naimisháraṇya. This very secret knowledge was originally revealed by Mahádeva, at the desire of Vishṇu, to a number of Rishis who were practising austerities at the celebrated shrine of Vadariká-śrama. The first eleven Chapters of Section II are taken up with Vyása's propounding these themes of high import in the words and style of Mahádeva himself; and, hence, they constitute what is called I′śvara-gítá.

The next eight chapters (from XII to XIX) deal with various directions as to the way in which a Bráhmaṇa should conduct himself. The directions descend to the minutest details of his daily life, such as, his ablutions, meals, sleeping, reading, repeating prayers &c. &c.

Chapters XX—XXIII describe the several ways of offering oblations to the manes under different circumstances. In chapter XXIII, the directions for the observance of mourning are specified.

Chapter XXIV deals with the worship and cherishing of the fire, Chapter XXV with the means of livelihood allowable to a Bráhmaṇa, and Chapter XXVI with various kinds of gifts and merits attached to them.

The foregoing fifteen Chapters all refer to the duties of a house-holder or Gṛihastha.

Chapter XXVII touches upon the mode of embracing and practising asceticism and the duties connected with it. This is the third stage, called Vánaprastha A′śrama.

The following two Chapters are taken up in describing what is called Yatidharma or the duties of an anchorite at the last stage of life.

The next five chapters, XXX—XXXIV, treat of various kinds of expiations for the cleansing of sins. This subject is concluded with a dissertation on chastity, enlivened with the story of Sítá, who was saved from the hands of the evil-minded Rávaṇa by the god of fire.

The above twenty-three chapters supply a code of morals with penalties attached to violations thereof, and extend to the minutest and most trivial details. As, for instance, when bitten by a dog one is subjected to an expiation; even the touching of liquor or the body of a Chaṇḍála is attended with penalties. The materials of these chapters are drawn from the Saṃhitás, chiefly from the Manusaṃhitá, though there are additions here and there.

Chapters XXXV—XLIII are devoted to the description of holy places throughout India. This subject, it will be remembered, has already occupied a considerable space; for the description of the two greatest Tírthas, Váráṇasí and Prayága, extends over nine chapters in the first section of the work.

Chapter XLIV adverts to the dissolution of the Universe. The next chapter begins with a dissertation on the greatness of Mahádeva and the mode of worshiping him, either directly or indirectly, through Brahman, or Váyu, or Agni, or Indra. Having thus brought his theme to a conclusion, the divine Kúrma stopped, and the sages chanted praises to him. After this Súta makes a brief recapitulation of the whole Puráṇa, describing the merit attached to its recital, and concludes with an invocation to Vyása, his preceptor, and to the divine Kúrma "from whom everything emanates and into whom everything merges."

ERRATA.

Page	*Line*	*For*	*Read*
vi	9	Collection	Collation
vi	23	accuracies	inaccuracies
vii	23	ten	ten additional
viii	8	sixth	tenth
xiv	20	alloted	allotted
xvii	27	to	from
xxxi	26	a eulogium	an eulogium
xxxiii	21	Vánaprastha áśrama	the Vánaprastha áśrama

अनुक्रमणिका।

कूर्म्मपुराणम् ।

प्रथमोऽध्यायः ।

ओँ नमो गणेशाय ।

नमस्कृत्याप्रमेयाय विष्णवे कूर्म्मरूपिणे ।
पुराणं संप्रवक्ष्यामि यदुक्तं विश्वयोनिना ॥
सत्रान्ते* सूतमनघं† नैमिषेया महर्षयः ।
पुराणसंहितां पुण्यां पप्रच्छू रोमहर्षणम् ॥
त्वया सूत महाबुद्धे भगवान् ब्रह्मवित्तमः‡ ।
इतिहासपुराणार्थं व्यासः सम्यगुपासितः ॥
तस्य ते सर्व्वरोमाणि वचसा हृषितानि यत् ।
द्वैपायनस्य तु भवांस्ततो वै रोमहर्षणः ॥

---

* सवान्ते इति B.

† सूतमनघा इति D.

‡ ब्रह्मसंयुतः इति A and E.

भवन्तमेव भगवान् व्याजहार स्वयं प्रभुः ।
मुनीनां संहितां* वक्तुं व्यासः पौराणिकीं पुरा ॥
त्वं हि स्वायम्भुवे यज्ञे सुत्याहे† वितते सति‡ ।
संभूतः संहितां वक्तुं स्वांशेन पुरुषोत्तमः ॥
तस्माद्भवन्तं पृच्छामः पुराणं कौर्म्ममुत्तमम् ।
वक्तुमर्हसि चास्माकं पुराणार्थविशारद ॥
मुनीनां वचनं श्रुत्वा सूतः पौराणिकोत्तमः ।
प्रणम्य मनसा प्राह गुरुं सत्यवतीसुतम् ॥

रोमहर्षण उवाच ।

नमस्कृत्य जगद्योनिं कूर्म्मरूपधरं हरिम् ।
वक्ष्ये पौराणिकीं दिव्यां कथां पापप्रणाशिनीम् ॥
यां श्रुत्वा पापकर्म्मापि गच्छेत§ परमाङ्गतिम् ।
न नास्तिके कथां पुण्यामिमां ब्रूयात्कदाचन ॥
श्रद्दधानाय शान्ताय धार्म्मिकाय द्विजातये ।
इमां कथामनुब्रूयात्साक्षान्नारायणेरिताम् ॥

---

* संहिता वक्तुं व्यासः पौराणिकीः पुरा इति E.

† सत्यादौ इति B. सत्राहे इति C. सुत्याहे सुत्या यज्ञार्थं स्नानं तस्याः अहः तस्मिन् ।

‡ हरिः इति E.

§ गच्छेत इति आर्षमात्मनेपदम् ।

सर्गश्च प्रतिसर्गश्च वंशो मन्वन्तराणि च।
वंशानुचरितञ्चैव पुराणं पञ्चलक्षणम्॥
ब्राह्मं पुराणं प्रथमं पाद्मं वैष्णवमेव च*।
शैवं भागवतञ्चैव भविष्यं नारदीयकम्॥
मार्कण्डेयमथाग्नेयं ब्रह्मवैवर्त्तमेव च।
लैङ्गं तथा च वाराहं† स्कान्दं वामनमेव च॥
कौर्म्मं मात्स्यं गारुडञ्च‡ वायवीयमनन्तरम्§।
अष्टादशं समुद्दिष्टं ब्रह्माण्डमिति संज्ञितम्॥
अन्यान्युपपुराणानि मुनिभिः कथितानि तु।
अष्टादश पुराणानि श्रुत्वा संक्षेपतो द्विजाः॥
आद्यं सनत्कुमारोक्तं नारसिंहमतःपरम्।
तृतीयं स्कान्दमुद्दिष्टं कुमारेण तु भाषितम्॥
चतुर्थं शिवधर्म्माख्यं साक्षान्नन्दीशभाषितम्।
दुर्व्वाससोक्तमाश्चर्य्यं नारदीयमतःपरम्॥
कापिलं वामनञ्चैव तथैवोशनसेरितम्।
ब्रह्माण्डं वारुणञ्चैव कालिकाह्वयमेव च॥

---

* वैष्णवमुच्यते इति D.

† वराहञ्च इति C.

‡ मात्स्यञ्च गरुडम् इति C.

§ मनुत्तमम् इति D.

माहेश्वरं तथा शाम्बं सौरं सर्व्वार्थसञ्चयम्।
पराशरोक्तं मारीचं तथैव* भार्गवाह्वयम्॥
इदन्तु पञ्चदशमं पुराणं कौर्म्ममुत्तमम्।
चतुर्द्धा संस्थितं पुण्यं संहितानां प्रभेदतः॥
ब्राह्मी भागवती सौरी वैष्णवी च प्रकीर्त्तिताः।
चतस्रः संहिताः पुण्या धर्म्मकामार्थमोक्षदाः† ॥
इयन्तु संहिता ब्राह्मी चतुर्व्वेदैस्तु सम्मिता।
भवन्ति षट् सहस्राणि श्लोकानामत्र संख्यया॥
यत्र धर्म्मार्थकामानां मोक्षस्य च मुनीश्वराः।
माहात्म्यमखिलं ब्रह्म ज्ञायते परमेश्वरः‡ ॥
सर्गश्च प्रतिसर्गश्च वंशो मन्वन्तराणि च।
वंशानुचरितं पुण्या दिव्या प्रासङ्गिकी कथा॥
ब्राह्मणाद्यैरियं धार्य्या धार्म्मिकैर्वेदपारगैः§ ।
तामहं वर्णयिष्यामि व्यासेन कथितां पुरा॥
पुरामृतार्थं दैतेयदानवैः सह देवताः।
मन्थानं मन्दरं कृत्वा ममन्थुः क्षीरसागरम्॥

---

* पराशरीक्तमपरं मारीचम् इति A, C and D.

† सर्व्वपापप्रणाशनाः इति A and E.

‡ ब्रह्मन् ज्ञायते पारमेश्वरम् इति E, F and H.

§ शान्तमानसैरिति A, D, E and H.

मथ्यमाने तदा तस्मिन् कूर्म्मरूपी जनार्द्दनः ।
बभार* मन्दरं† देवो देवानां‡ हितकाम्यया ॥
देवाश्च तुष्टुवुर्देवं नारदाद्या महर्षयः ।
कूर्म्मरूपधरं दृष्ट्वा साक्षिणं विष्णुमव्ययम् ॥
तदन्तरे§ऽभवद्देवी श्रीर्नारायणवल्लभा ।
जग्राह भगवान् विष्णुस्तामेव पुरुषोत्तमः ॥
तेजसा विष्णुमव्यक्तं¶ नारदाद्या महर्षयः ।
मोहिताः सह शक्रेण श्रेयोवचन‖मब्रुवन् ॥
भगवन् देवदेवेश नारायण जगन्मय ।
कैषा देवी विशालाक्षी यथावद्ब्रूहि पृच्छताम्** ॥
श्रुत्वा तेषां तदा वाक्यं विष्णुर्दानवमर्द्दनः ।
प्रोवाच देवीं संप्रेक्ष्य नारदादीनकल्मषान् ॥
इयं सा परमा शक्तिर्मन्मयी ब्रह्मरूपिणी ।
माया मम प्रियानन्ता ययेदं धार्य्यते†† जगत् ॥

---

* दधार मन्दरं देवो लोकानाम् इति D.

† It is supposed to be the mountain so named in Bhágalpur, which is held sacred.

‡ लोकानामिति F and H.

§ तदन्तरे तत्र अवकाशे तदा इत्यर्थः ।

¶ तेजसा अव्यक्तं दुर्दर्शेन ज्योतिषा अस्पष्टदृष्टमित्यर्थः ।

‖ श्रेयोवचनं श्रेयःप्रधानं वचनं प्रशस्ततमं वचनमित्यर्थः ।

** यथावद्वक्तुमर्हसि इति D. पृच्छतां नः, सम्बन्धविवक्षायां षष्ठी ।

†† मोहितमिति A, C, D, F and H.

अनयैव जगत्सर्व्वं सदेवासुरमानुषम् ।
मोहयामि द्विजश्रेष्ठा ग्रसामि विसृजामि च ॥
उत्पत्तिं प्रलयञ्चैव भूतानामागतिङ्गतिम् ।
विद्यया वीक्ष्य चात्मानं तरन्ति विपुलामिमाम्* ॥
अस्यास्त्वंशानधिष्ठाय शक्तिमन्तोऽभवन् सुराः† ।
ब्रह्मेशानादयः सर्व्वे सर्व्वशक्तिरियं मम ॥
सैषा सर्व्वजगत्सूतिः प्रकृतिस्त्रिगुणात्मिका ।
प्रागेव मत्तः संजाता श्रीः कल्पे पद्मवासिनी‡ ॥
चतुर्भुजा शङ्खचक्रपद्महस्ता स्रगन्विता§ ।
कोटिसूर्य्यप्रतीकाशा मोहिनी सर्व्वदेहिनाम् ॥
नालं देवा न पितरो मानवा वासवोऽपि च ।
मायामेतां समुत्तर्त्तुं ये चान्ये भुवि देहिनः ॥
इत्युक्ता वासुदेवेन मुनयो विष्णुमब्रुवन् ।
ब्रूहि त्वं पुण्डरीकाक्ष यद्वि कालत्रयेऽपि च¶ ॥

---

* विज्ञायान्वीक्ष्य चात्मानं भवन्ति इति B. विज्ञायोद्वीक्ष्य इति C. विज्ञाय वीक्ष्य इति D.

† द्विजाः इति B, D, F and H.

‡ पद्मे कल्पवासिनी इति A, F and H.

§ शुभान्विता इति B and D. सुकान्तिका इति C.

¶ यदि कालत्रयेऽपि सः इति B. येन सा तारिता पुरा इति C. यथा कालत्रयेऽपि च इति D.

अथोवाच हृषीकेशो मुनीन्मुनिगणार्च्चितः* ।
अस्ति द्विजातिप्रवर इन्द्रद्युम्न इति श्रुतः ॥
पूर्व्वजन्मनि राजासावधृष्यः शङ्करादिभिः ।
दृष्ट्वा मां कूर्म्मसंस्थानं श्रुत्वा पौराणिकीं† स्वयम् ॥
संहितां मन्मुखाद्दिव्यां पुरस्कृत्य मुनीश्वरान् ।
ब्रह्माणञ्च महादेवं देवांश्चान्यान् स्वशक्तिभिः ॥
मच्छक्तौ संस्थितान् बुद्ध्वा मामेव शरणङ्गतः ।
सम्भाषितो मया चाथ‡ विप्रयोनिङ्गमिष्यसि ॥
इन्द्रद्युम्न इति ख्यातो जातिं स्मरसि पौर्व्विकीम् ।
सर्व्वेषामेव भूतानां देवानामप्यगोचरम् ॥
वक्तव्यं यद्गुह्यतमं दास्ये ज्ञानं तवानघ ।
लब्ध्वा तन्मामकं ज्ञानं मामेवान्ते प्रवेक्ष्यसि ॥
अंशान्तरेण§ भूम्यान्त्वं तत्र तिष्ठ सुनिर्वृतः ।
वैवस्वतेऽन्तरेऽतीते कार्य्यार्थं मां प्रवेक्ष्यसि ॥
मां प्रणम्य पुरीं कृत्वा¶ पालयामास मेदिनीम् ।
कालधर्म्मङ्गतः कालाच्छ्वेतद्वीपे मया सह ॥

---

* मुनीनां पुरतः प्रभुः इति C.

† पौराणिकान्वयमिति G and H.

‡ स चोदितो मया चैव इति D.

§ अंशावतारे इति F, G and H.

¶ गत्वा इति F and H.

भुक्त्वा तान् वैष्णवान्* भोगान् योगिनामप्यगोचरान्।
मदाज्ञया मुनिश्रेष्ठा जज्ञे विप्रकुले पुनः॥
ज्ञात्वा मां वासुदेवाख्यं यत्र द्वे निहितेऽक्षरे।
विद्याविद्ये गूढ़रूपं† यद्ब्रह्म परमं विदुः॥
सोऽर्च्चयामास भूतानामाश्रयं परमेश्वरम।
व्रतोपवासनियमैर्होमैर्ब्राह्मणतर्पणैः॥
तदाशीस्तन्नमस्कारस्तन्निष्ठस्तत्परायणः।
आराधयन्महादेवं योगिनां हृदि संस्थितम्॥
तस्यैवं वर्त्तमानस्य कदाचित्परमा कला।
स्वरूपं दर्शयामास दिव्यं विष्णुसमुद्भवम्॥‡
दृष्ट्वा प्रणम्य शिरसा विष्णोर्भगवतः प्रियाम्§।
संस्तूय विविधैः स्तोत्रैः कृताञ्जलिरभाषत॥

इन्द्रद्युम्न उवाच।

का त्वं देवि विशालाक्षि विष्णुचिह्नाङ्किते शुभे।
याथातथ्येन वै भावं तवेदानीं ब्रवीहि¶ मे॥

---

* विपुलान् इति F and H.

† गूढ़रूपे इति C and D.

‡ श्लोकोऽयं B पुस्तके नास्ति।

§ प्रभामिति F, G and H.

¶ आर्षः प्रयोगः, ब्रूहि।

तस्य तद्वाक्यमाकर्ण्य सुप्रसन्ना सुमङ्गला।
हसन्ती संस्मरन्* विष्णुं प्रियं ब्राह्मणमब्रवीत्॥

श्रीरुवाच।

न मां पश्यन्ति मुनयो देवाः शक्रपुरोगमाः।
नारायणात्मिकामेकां मायाहं तन्मयी परा॥
न मे नारायणाद्भेदो विद्यते हि विचारतः।
तन्मय्यहं परं ब्रह्म स विष्णुः परमेश्वरः॥
येऽर्च्चयन्तीह भूतानामाश्रयं† पुरुषोत्तमम्।
ज्ञानेन कर्म्मयोगेन न तेषां प्रभवाम्यहम्॥
तस्मादनादिनिधनं कर्म्मयोगपरायणः।
ज्ञानेनाराधयानन्तं‡ ततोमोक्षमवाप्स्यसि॥
इत्युक्तः स मुनिश्रेष्ठ इन्द्रद्युम्नो महामतिः।
प्रणम्य शिरसा देवीं प्राञ्जलिः पुनरब्रवीत्॥
कथं स भगवानीशः शाश्वतो निष्कलोऽच्युतः।
ज्ञातुं हि शक्यते देवि ब्रूहि मे परमेश्वरि॥
एवमुक्ताथ विप्रेण§ देवी कमलवासिनी।
साक्षान्नारायणो ज्ञानं दास्यतीत्याह तं मुनिम्॥

---

* आर्षः प्रयोगः। संस्मरन्ती।

† भूतानामालयम् इति C and D.

‡ ज्ञानेनाराधयेशानम् इति A, F and H.

§ एवमुक्ता तु देवेन इति B.

उभाभ्यामथ हस्ताभ्यां संस्पृश्य प्रणतं मुनिम् ।*
स्मृत्वा परात्परं विष्णुं तत्रैवान्तरधीयत ॥
सोऽपि नारायणं द्रष्टुं परमेण समाधिना ।
आराधयद्धृषीकेशं प्रणतार्त्तिप्रभञ्जनम्† ॥
ततो बहुतिथे काले गते नारायणः स्वयम् ।
प्रादुरासीत्‡ महायोगी पीतवासा जगन्मयः ॥
दृष्ट्वा देवं समायान्तं विष्णुमात्मानमव्ययम् ।
जानुभ्यामवनीं गत्वा तुष्टाव गरुड़ध्वजम् ॥

इन्द्रद्युम्न उवाच ।

यज्ञेशाच्युत गोविन्द माधवानन्त केशव ।
कृष्ण विष्णो हृषीकेश तुभ्यं विश्वात्मने नमः ॥
नमोऽस्तु ते पुराणाय हरये विश्वमूर्त्तये§ ।
सर्गस्थितिविनाशानां हेतवेऽनन्तशक्तये ॥
निर्गुणाय नमस्तुभ्यं निष्कलाय नमोनमः¶ ।
पुरुषाय नमस्तेऽस्तु विश्वरूपाय ते नमः ॥
नमस्ते वासुदेवाय विष्णवे विश्वयोनये ।

---

* एष श्लोकार्द्धः D पुस्तके नास्ति ।

† आद्यं परं हृषीकेशम् इति C. प्रणतार्त्तिप्रणाशनम् इति B, E, F and H.

‡ आविरासीत् इति E, F and H.

§ विष्णवे विश्वयोनये इति B.

¶ निष्कलायामलात्मने इति C, D, E, F and H.

आदिमध्यान्तहीनाय ज्ञानगम्याय ते नमः ॥
नमस्ते निर्विकाराय निष्प्रपञ्चाय ते नमः ।
भेदाभेदविहीनाय नमोऽस्त्वानन्दरूपिणे* ॥
नमस्ताराय शान्ताय नमोऽप्रतिहतात्मने ।
अनन्तमूर्त्तये तुभ्यममूर्त्ताय नमोनमः ॥
नमस्ते परमार्थाय मायातीताय ते नमः ।†
नमस्ते परमेशाय ब्रह्मणे परमात्मने ॥
नमोऽस्तु ते सुसूक्ष्माय महादेवाय ते नमः‡ ।
नमः शिवाय शुद्धाय§ नमस्ते परमेष्ठिने ॥
त्वयैतत्सृष्टमखिलं¶ त्वमेव परमा गतिः ।
त्वं पिता सर्व्वभूतानां त्वं माता पुरुषोत्तम ॥
त्वमक्षरं परं धाम चिन्मात्रं व्योम निष्कलम्‖ ।
सर्व्वस्याधारमव्यक्तमनन्तं तमसः परम् ॥

---

* नमस्त्वानन्दमूर्त्तये इति C and D.

† ‘नमस्ते निर्विकाराय’ इत्यारभ्य ‘मायातीताय ते नमः’ इत्यन्तं E, F, G and H पुस्तकेषु न दृश्यते ।

‡ मायातीताय ते नमः इति D and G.

§ नमस्ते शिवरूपाय इति D.

¶ त्वयैव सृष्टमखिलम् इति B, D, E, F and H.

‖ व्योमसंस्थितम् इति C.

प्रपश्यन्ति परात्मानं* ज्ञानदीपेन केवलम् ।
प्रपद्ये भवतो रूपं† तद्विष्णोः परमं पदम् ॥
एवं स्तुवन्तं भगवान् भूतात्मा भूतभावनः ।
उभाभ्यामथ हस्ताभ्यां पस्पर्श प्रहसन्निव ॥
स्पृष्टमात्रो भगवता विष्णुना मुनिपुङ्गवः ।
यथावत्परमं तत्त्वं ज्ञातवांस्त्वत्प्रसादतः ॥
ततः प्रहृष्टमनसा प्रणिपत्य जनार्द्दनम् ।
प्रोवाचोन्निद्रपद्माक्षं‡ पीतवाससमच्युतम् ॥
त्वत्प्रसादादसन्दिग्धमुत्पन्नं पुरुषोत्तम ।
ज्ञानं ब्रह्मैकविषयं परमानन्दसिद्धिदम् ॥
नमो भगवते तुभ्यं वासुदेवाय वेधसे§ ।
किं करिष्यामि योगेश¶ तन्मे वद जगन्मय ॥
श्रुत्वा नारायणो वाक्यमिन्द्रद्युम्नस्य माधवः‖ ।
उवाच सस्मितं वाक्यमशेषं जगतो हितम्** ॥

---

* प्रविशन्ति महात्मान इति A, प्रपश्यन्ति महात्मान इति E, F and H.

† प्रपद्यन्ते ततो रूपम् इति C and D.

‡ प्रोवाच तं स पद्माक्षम् इति C and D.

§ हेतवे इति A, D, E, F and H.

¶ योगेन इति E, F and H.

‖ धीमतः इति H, धीमते: इति E and F.

** मशेषजगतो हितमिति E, F and H.

श्रीभगवानुवाच।

वर्णाश्रमाचारवतां पुंसां देवो महेश्वरः।
ज्ञानेन भक्तियोगेन पूजनीयो न चान्यथा॥
विज्ञाय तत्परं तत्त्वं विभूतिं कार्य्यकारणम्।
प्रवृत्तिञ्चापि मे ज्ञात्वा मोक्षार्थीश्वरमर्च्चयेत्॥
सर्व्वसङ्गान्परित्यज्य ज्ञात्वा मायामयं जगत्।
अद्वैतं भावयात्मानं द्रक्ष्यसे* परमेश्वरम्॥
त्रिविधां भावनां ब्रह्मन् प्रोच्यमानां निबोध मे†।
एका मद्विषया तत्र द्वितीया व्यक्तसंश्रया‡॥
अन्या च भावना ब्राह्मी विज्ञेया सा गुणातिगा।
आसामन्यतमाञ्चाथ भावनां भावयेद्बुधः॥
अशक्तः संश्रयेदाद्यामित्येषा वैदिकी श्रुतिः॥
तस्मात्सर्व्वप्रयत्नेन तन्निष्ठस्तत्परायणः।
समाराधय विश्वेशं ततो मोक्षमवाप्स्यसि॥

इन्द्रद्युम्न उवाच।

किन्तत्परतरं तत्त्वं का विभूतिर्जनार्द्दन।
किङ्कार्य्यं कारणं कस्त्वं प्रवृत्तिश्चापि का तव॥

---

* आत्मनेपदमार्षम्।

† निशामय इति A, E, F and H. मया शृणु इति D.

‡ चाचसंश्रया इति E, F, G and H.

श्रीभगवानुवाच ।

परात्परतरं तत्त्वं परं ब्रह्मैकमव्ययम् ।
नित्यानन्दमयं* ज्योतिरक्षरं तमसः परम् ॥
ऐश्वर्य्यं तस्य यन्नित्यं विभूतिरिति गीयते ।
कार्य्यं जगदथाव्यक्तं कारणं शुद्धमक्षरम् ॥
अहं हि सर्व्वभूतानामन्तर्य्यामीश्वरः परः ।†
सर्गस्थित्यन्तकर्तृत्वं प्रवृत्तिर्मम गीयते ॥
एतद्विज्ञाय भावेन यथावदखिलं द्विज ।
ततस्त्वं कर्म्मयोगेन शाश्वतं सम्यगर्च्चय ॥

इन्द्रद्युम्न उवाच ।

के ते वर्णाश्रमाचारा यैः समाराध्यते परः ।
ज्ञानञ्च कीदृशं दिव्यं‡ भावनात्रयसंस्थितम्§ ॥
कथं सृष्टमिदं पूर्व्वं कथं संह्रियते पुनः ।
कियत्यः सृष्टयो लोके वंशा मन्वन्तराणि च ॥
कानि तेषां प्रमाणानि पावनानि व्रतानि च ।
तीर्थान्यर्कादिसंस्थानं पृथिव्यायामविस्तरम्¶ ॥

---

* नित्यानन्दं परम् इति A, D, E, F and H.

† अहं हि सर्व्वभावानामीश्वरः प्रभुरव्ययः इति D. अन्तर्यामीति G.

‡ पुण्यम् इति C.

§ मिश्रितम् इति D.

¶ पृथिव्या आयामो दैर्घं विस्तरो विस्तारश्च तयोः समाहारः तत् । The whole length and breadth of the earth. विस्तारे इति A.

कति द्वीपाः समुद्राश्च पर्व्वताश्च नदीनदाः ।
ब्रूहि मे पुण्डरीकाक्ष यथावदधुना पुनः* ॥
श्रीकूर्म्म उवाच ।
एवमुक्तोऽथ तेनाहं भक्तानुग्रहकाम्यया ।
यथावदखिलं सम्यगवोचं† मुनिपुंगवाः ॥
व्याख्यायाशेषमेवेदं यत्पृष्टोऽहं द्विजेन तु ।
अनुगृह्य च तं विप्रं तत्रैवान्तर्हितोऽभवम् ॥
सोऽपि तेन विधानेन मदुक्तेन द्विजोत्तमाः ।
आराधयामास परं भावपूतः‡ समाहितः ॥
त्यक्त्वा पुत्रादिषु स्नेहं निर्द्वन्द्वो निष्परिग्रहः ।
स न्यस्य§ सर्व्वकर्म्माणि परं वैराग्यमाश्रितः ॥
आत्मन्यात्मानमन्वीक्ष्य स्वात्मन्येवाखिलं जगत् ।
संप्राप्य भावनामन्त्यां ब्राह्मीमक्षरपूर्व्विकाम् ॥
अवाप परमं योगं येनैकं¶ परिपश्यति ।
यं विनिद्राजितश्वासाः‖ कांक्षन्ते मोक्षकांक्षिणः ॥

---

* यथावदखिलं मम इति B.

† सर्व्वमवोचम् इति A, C, D, E, F and H.

‡ भावैः सदभिप्रायैः पूत इत्यर्थः । भावयुक्तः इति B and D.

§ संन्यस्य इति B and D.

¶ येनैव इति A and E.

‖ विनिद्रया अनालस्येन जितो वशीकृतः श्वासो यैस्तथोक्ताः ।

ततः कदाचिद्योगीन्द्रो ब्रह्माणं द्रष्टुमव्ययम्* ।
जगामादित्यनिर्द्देशान्मानसोत्तरपर्व्वतम्† ॥
आकाशेनैव विप्रेन्द्रो योगैश्वर्य्यप्रभावतः ।
विमानं सूर्य्यसङ्काशं प्रादुर्भूतमनुत्तमम् ॥
अन्वगच्छन्देवगणा गन्धर्वाप्सरसां गणाः ।
दृष्ट्वान्ये‡ पथि योगीन्द्रं सिद्धा ब्रह्मर्षयो ययुः ॥
ततः स गत्वानुगिरिं विवेश सुरवन्दितम् ।
स्थानं तद्योगिभिर्जुष्टं यत्रास्ते परमः पुमान् ॥
संप्राप्य परमं स्थानं सूर्य्यायुतसमप्रभम् ।
विवेश चान्तर्भवनं देवानाञ्च दुरासदम् ॥
विचिन्तयामास परं शरण्यं सर्व्वदेहिनाम् ।
अनादिनिधनं चैव§ देवदेवं पितामहम् ॥
ततः प्रादुरभूत्तस्मिन् प्रकाशः¶ परमाद्भुतः‖ ।
तन्मध्ये पुरुषं पूर्व्व** मपश्यत्परमं पदम् ॥

---

* द्रष्टुमुद्यतः इति D.

† मानसोत्तरपर्व्वतम् मानससरसः उत्तरस्यां दिशि स्थितं पर्व्वतं मेरुमित्यर्थः ।

‡ दृष्टीयैः पथि योगीन्द्र इति E, F and H.

§ देवमिति B, C, D, E, F and H.

¶ प्रकाशः ज्योतिरित्यर्थः ।

‖ परमात्मनः इति B and C.

** सर्व्व इति A, E, F and H.

महान्तं तेजसो राशिमगम्यं ब्रह्मविद्विषाम् ।
चतुर्मुख* मुदाराङ्गमर्चिर्भिरुपशोभितम् ॥
सोऽपि योगिनमन्वीक्ष्य प्रणमन्तमुपस्थितम् ।
प्रत्युद्गम्य स्वयं देवो विश्वात्मा परिषस्वजे ॥
परिष्वक्तस्य देवेन द्विजेन्द्रस्याथ देहतः ।
निर्गत्य महती ज्योत्स्ना विवेशादित्यमण्डलम् ॥
ऋग्यजुःसामसंज्ञं तत्सवित्रममलं पदम् ।
हिरण्यगर्भो भगवान् यत्रास्ते हव्यकव्यभुक् ॥
द्वारं तद्योगिनामाद्यं वेदान्तेषु प्रतिष्ठितम् ।
ब्रह्मतेजोमयं श्रीमद्द्रष्टा† चैव मनीषिणाम् ॥
दृष्टमात्रो भगवता ब्रह्मणार्चिर्म्मयो मुनिः ।
अपश्यदैश्वरं तेजः शान्तं सर्वत्रगं शिवम् ॥
स्वात्मानमक्षरं व्योम यत्र विष्णोः परं पदम् ।
आनन्दमचलं‡ ब्रह्मस्थानं तत्पारमेश्वरम् ॥
सर्वभूतात्मभूतस्थः§ परमैश्वर्य्यमास्थितः ।
प्राप्तवानात्मनो धाम यत्तन्मोक्षाख्यमव्ययम् ॥

---

* चतुर्भुज इति D.

† श्रीमन्निष्ठा इति B and C. यन्ता देवमनीषिणामिति D.

‡ आनन्दनपरमिति C and D.

§ भूतः सः इति B.

तस्मात्सर्वप्रयत्नेन वर्णाश्रमविधौ स्थितः ।
समाश्रित्यान्तिमं भावं मायां लक्ष्मीं तरेद्बुधः ॥

सूत उवाच ।

व्याहृता हरिणा त्वेवं नारदाद्या महर्षयः ।
शक्रेण सहिताः सर्वे पप्रच्छुर्गरुड़ध्वजम् ॥

ऋषय ऊचुः ।

देवदेव हृषीकेश नाथ नारायणाव्यय* ।
तद्वदाशेषमस्माकं यदुक्तं भवता पुरा ॥
इन्द्रद्युम्नाय विप्राय ज्ञानं धर्म्मादिगोचरम्† ।
शुश्रूषुश्चाप्ययं शक्रः सखा तव जगन्मय ॥
ततः स भगवान् विष्णुः कूर्म्मरूपी जनार्द्दनः ।
रसातलगतो देवो नारदाद्यैर्महर्षिभिः ॥
पृष्टः प्रोवाच सकलं‡ पुराणं कौर्म्ममुत्तमम् ।
सन्निधौ देवराजस्य तद्वक्ष्ये भवतामहम् ॥
धन्यं यशस्यमायुष्यं पुण्यं मोक्षप्रदं नृणाम् ।
पुराणश्रवणं विप्राः कथनञ्च विशेषतः ॥

---

* नारायणामल इति B and C.

† धर्म्मार्थगोचरम् इति C and D.

‡ भगवान् इति E, F and H.

श्रुत्वा चाध्यायमेवैकं सर्वपापैः प्रमुच्यते।
उपाख्यानमथैकं* वा ब्रह्मलोके महीयते॥
इदं पुराणं परमं कौर्म्मं कूर्म्मस्वरूपिणा।
उक्तं वै देवदेवेन† श्रद्धातव्यं द्विजातिभिः॥

इति श्रीकूर्म्मपुराणे इन्द्रद्युम्नमोचे प्रथमोऽध्यायः।

---

* मथाश्रम इति A, E, F and H.

† देवाधिदेवेन इति B.

द्वितीयोऽध्यायः ।

कूर्म्म उवाच ।

शृणुध्वमृषयः* सर्व्वे यत्पृष्टोऽहं जगद्धितम् ।
वक्ष्यमाणं मया सर्व्वमिन्द्रद्युम्नाय भाषितम् ॥
भूतैर्भव्यैर्भवद्भिश्च† चरितैरुपवृंहितम् ।
पुराणं पुण्यदं नृणां मोक्षधर्म्मानुकीर्त्तनम् ‡ ॥
अहं नारायणो देवः पूर्व्वमासन्न मे परम्§ ।
उपास्य विपुलां निद्रां भोगिशय्यां समाश्रितः ।
चिन्तयामि पुनः सृष्टिं निशान्ते प्रतिबुध्य तु ॥
ततो मे सहसोत्पन्नः प्रसादो मुनिपुंगवाः ।
चतुर्मुखस्ततो जातो ब्रह्मा लोकपितामहः ॥
तदन्तरेऽभवत्क्रोधः कस्माच्चित्कारणात्तदा ।
आत्मनो¶ मुनिशार्दूलास्तत्र देवो महेश्वरः ॥

---

* शृणुध्वं मुनयः इति B.

† भूतैर्भव्यैर्भविष्यद्भिः इति A, E, F and H. भवन्ति इति भवाः भवा एव भव्याः वर्त्तमानाः । यद्यपि भव्यशब्दः भविष्यदर्थे रूढ़स्तथाप्यत्र तद्धित-य-प्रत्ययसिद्धतया न तदर्थबोधकः ।

‡ मोक्षधर्म्मानुवर्त्तिनाम् इति D.

§ अहं पूर्व्वमासं, मे परं मत्तः अन्यत् किञ्चित् न आसीदिति शेषः ।

¶ आत्मना इति B and C.

रुद्रः क्रोधात्मको जज्ञे शूलपाणिस्त्रिलोचनः।
तेजसा सूर्य्यसङ्काशस्त्रैलोक्यं संदहन्निव* ॥
तदा श्रीरभवद्देवी कमलायतलोचना।
सुरूपा सौम्यवदना मोहिनी सर्व्वदेहिनाम् ॥
शुचिस्मिता सुप्रसन्ना† मङ्गला महिमास्पदा।
दिव्यकान्तिसमायुक्ता दिव्यमाल्योपशोभिता ॥
नारायणी महामाया मूलप्रकृतिरव्यया।
स्वधाम्ना पूरयन्तीदं मत्पार्श्वं समुपाविशत् ॥
तां दृष्ट्वा भगवान् ब्रह्मा मामुवाच जगत्पतिम्।
मोहायाशेषभूतानां नियोजय‡ सुरूपिणीम् ॥
येनेयं विपुला सृष्टिर्वर्द्धते§ मम माधव।
तथोक्तोऽहं श्रियं देवीमब्रवं¶ प्रहसन्निव ॥
देवीदमखिलं विश्वं सदेवासुरमानुषम्।
मोहयित्वा ममादेशात्संसारे विनिपातय ॥

---

* निर्द्दहन्निव इति B, संहरन्निव इति C.

† सुसम्पन्ना इति E, F, G and H.

‡ मन्नियोगान्नियोजय इति A, E, F and H.

§ वर्त्तते इति A and H.

¶ तथोक्तः स श्रियं देवीमब्रवीत् इति C, F and H.

ज्ञानयोगरतान्दान्तान् ब्रह्मिष्ठान् ब्रह्मवादिनः* ।
अक्रोधनान् सत्यपरान्दूरतः परिवर्ज्जय ॥
ध्यायिनो निर्म्ममान् शान्तान्धार्म्मिकान्वेदपारगान् ।
याजिनस्तापसान्विप्रान्दूरतः परिवर्ज्जय ॥†
वेदवेदान्तविज्ञानसंछिन्नाशेषसंशयान् ।
महायज्ञपरान्विप्रान्दूरतः परिवर्ज्जय ॥
ये यजन्ति जपैर्होमैर्द्देवदेवं महेश्वरम् ।
स्वाध्यायेनेज्यया दूरात्तान् प्रयत्नेन वर्ज्जय‡ ॥
भक्तियोगसमायुक्तानीश्वरार्पितमानसान् ।
प्राणायामादिषु रतान्दूरात्परिहरामलान् ॥
प्रणवासक्तमनसोरुद्रजप्यपरायणान् ।
अथर्वशिरसो§ वेत्तॄन्¶ धर्म्मज्ञान् परिवर्ज्जय ॥
बहुनात्र किमुक्तेन स्वधर्म्मपरिपालकान् ।
ईश्वराराधनरतान्मन्नियोगान्न मोहय ॥

---

* शान्तान्धार्म्मिकान् वेदपारगान् इति A, E, F and H.

† अक्रोधनानित्यारभ्य सार्द्धैकश्लोकः A, E, F and H पुस्तकेषु नास्ति ।

‡ दूरात्प्रयत्नेन विवर्ज्जय इति C and D.

§ An epithet of महापुरुष when masculine. Williams. अथर्वणः शिरइव ब्रह्मविद्याप्रतिपादकतया श्रेष्ठत्वात् स्वनामख्याते अथर्वोपनिषद्भेदे । वाचस्पत्यम् ।

¶ अथर्वशिरसोऽध्येतॄन् इति B, शास्त्रेष्वभिरतान्धीरान् इति C, शास्त्रवृत्तिरतान्धीरान् इति D.

एवं मया महामाया प्रेरिता हरिवल्लभा ।
यथादेशं चकारासौ तस्माल्लक्ष्मीं समर्च्चयेत् ॥
श्रियं ददाति विपुलां पुष्टिं मेधां यशो बलम् ।
अर्च्चिता भगवत्पत्नी तस्माल्लक्ष्मीं समर्च्चयेत् ॥
ततोऽसृजत्स भगवान् ब्रह्मा लोकपितामहः ।
चराचराणि भूतानि यथापूर्व्वं ममाज्ञया ॥
मरीचिभृग्वङ्गिरसं पुलस्त्यं पुलहं क्रतुम् ।
दक्षमत्रिं वसिष्ठञ्च सोऽसृजद्योगविद्यया ॥
नवैते ब्रह्मणः पुत्रा ब्राह्मणा* ब्राह्मणोत्तमाः ।
ब्रह्मवादिन एवैते मरीच्याद्यास्तु साधकाः ॥
ससर्ज्ज ब्राह्मणान्वक्त्रात् क्षत्रियांश्च भुजाद्विभुः ।
वैश्यानूरुद्वयाद्देवः पद्भ्यां शूद्रान् पितामहः ॥
यज्ञनिष्पत्तये ब्रह्मा शूद्रवर्ज्जं ससर्ज्ज ह ।
गुप्तये सर्व्वदेवानां तेभ्यो यज्ञो हि निर्बभौ ॥
ऋचो यजूंषि सामानि तथैवाथर्व्वणानि च ।
ब्रह्मणः सहजं रूपं नित्यैषा शक्तिरव्यया ॥
अनादिनिधना दिव्या वागुत्सृष्टा स्वयम्भुवा ।
आदौ वेदमयी भूता यतः सर्व्वाः प्रवृत्तयः† ॥

---

* ब्रह्मणा इति E, F and H. ब्रह्मणा तपसा ब्राह्मणोत्तमा इत्यर्थः। "वेदस्तत्त्वं तपोब्रह्म" इत्यमरः ।

† माला एताः पूर्व्वाः प्रवृत्तयः इति D.

अतोऽन्यानि हि* शास्त्राणि पृथिव्यां यानि कानिचित्।
न तेषु रमते धीरः पाषण्डी रमते बुधः† ॥
वेदार्थवित्तमैः कार्य्यं यत्स्मृतं मुनिभिः पुरा।
स ज्ञेयः परमो धर्म्मो नान्यशास्त्रेषु संस्थितः ॥
या वेदबाह्याः स्मृतयो याश्च काश्च कुदृष्टयः।
सर्व्वास्ता निष्फलाः प्रेत्य तमोनिष्ठा हि ताः स्मृताः ॥
पूर्वकल्पे प्रजा जाताः सर्व्वबाधाविवर्ज्जिताः।
शुद्धान्तःकरणाः सर्व्वाः स्वधर्म्मपरिपालकाः‡ ॥
ततः कालवशात्तासां रागद्वेषादिकोऽभवत्।
अधर्म्मो मुनिशार्दूलाः स्वधर्म्मप्रतिबन्धकः ॥
ततः सा सहजा सिद्धिस्तासां नातीव जायते।
रजोमात्रात्मिकास्तासां सिद्धयोऽन्यास्तदाभवन् ॥
तासु क्षीणास्वशेषासु कालयोगेन ताः पुनः।
वार्त्तोपायं पुनश्चक्रुर्हस्तसिद्धिञ्च कर्म्मजाम् ॥
ततस्तासां विभुः§ ब्रह्मा कर्म्माजीवमकल्पयत्।
स्वायम्भुवो मनुः पूर्व्वं धर्म्मान्प्रोवाच सर्व्वदृक् ॥

---

* अथान्यानि तु शास्त्राणि इति D. अन्यान्यानि हि शास्त्रानि इति G. अन्यान्यपि हि शास्त्राणि इति E, F and H.

† पाषण्डी तेन जायते इति B, C and H, पाषण्डी जायते पुनः इति D, E and F, पाषण्डी रमते पुनः इति G.

‡ स्वधर्म्मनिरताः सदा इति B.

§ पिता इति D.

साक्षात्प्रजापतेर्मूर्त्तिर्निसृष्टा ब्रह्मणो द्विजाः* ।
भृग्वादयस्तद्वदनाच्छ्रुत्वा धर्म्मानथोचिरे ॥
यजनं याजनं दानं ब्राह्मणस्य प्रतिग्रहः ।
अध्यापनं चाध्ययनं षट् कर्म्माणि द्विजोत्तमाः ॥
दानमध्ययनं यज्ञो धर्म्मः क्षत्त्रियवैश्ययोः ।
दण्डोयुद्धं क्षत्त्रियस्य कृषिर्वैश्यस्य शस्यते ॥
शुश्रूषैव† द्विजातीनां शूद्राणां धर्म्मसाधनम् ।
कारुकर्म्म तथाजीवः पाकयज्ञादि धर्म्मतः‡ ॥
ततः स्थितेषु वर्णेषु स्थापयामास चाश्रमान् ।
गृहस्थञ्च वनस्थञ्च भिक्षुकं ब्रह्मचारिणम् ॥
अग्नयोऽतिथिशुश्रूषा यज्ञो दानं सुरार्च्चनम् ।
गृहस्थस्य समासेन धर्म्मोऽयं मुनिपुंगवाः ॥
होमोमूलफलाशित्वं स्वाध्यायस्तप एव च ।
संविभागो यथान्यायं धर्म्मोऽयं वनवासिनाम् ॥
भैक्षाशनञ्च मौनित्वं तपो ध्यानं विशेषतः ।
सम्यग्ज्ञानञ्च वैराग्यं धर्म्मोऽयं भिक्षुके मतः ॥

---

* ब्रह्मणा द्विजाः इति A, E and F.　ब्रह्मणः पुरा इति C.

† शुश्रूषा वै इति A, E and F.

‡ वणिज्यादि क्रयविक्रयणं तथा इति A, E and F.

भिक्षाचर्य्या* च शुश्रूषा गुरोः स्वाध्याय एव च ।
सन्ध्याकर्म्माग्निकार्य्यञ्च धर्म्मोऽयं ब्रह्मचारिणाम् ॥
ब्रह्मचारिवनस्थानां भिक्षुकाणां द्विजोत्तमाः ।
साधारणं ब्रह्मचर्य्यं प्रोवाच कमलोद्भवः ॥
ऋतुकालाभिगामित्वं स्वदारेषु न चान्यतः ।
पर्व्ववर्ज्जं गृहस्थस्य ब्रह्मचर्य्यमुदाहृतम् ॥
आगर्भधारणादाज्ञा कार्य्या तेनाप्रमादतः ।
अकुर्वाणस्तु विप्रेन्द्रा भ्रूणहा तूपजायते† ॥
वेदाभ्यासोऽन्वहं शक्त्या श्राद्धञ्चातिथिपूजनम् ।
गृहस्थस्य परो धर्म्मो देवताभ्यर्च्चनं तथा ॥
वैवाह्यमग्निमिन्धीत‡ सायं प्रातर्यथाविधि ।
देशान्तरगतो वाथ मृतपत्नीक एव च ॥
त्रयाणामाश्रमाणान्तु गृहस्थो योनिरुच्यते ।
अन्ये तमुपजीवन्ति तस्माच्छ्रेयान् गृहाश्रमी ॥
ऐकाश्रम्यं गृहस्थस्य चतुर्णां श्रुतिदर्शनात् ।
तस्माद्गार्हस्थ्यमेवैकं विज्ञेयं धर्मसाधनम् ॥

---

* भिक्षाशनम् इति D.

† भ्रूणहा तु प्रजायते इति B. भ्रूणहा चोपजायते इति D.

‡ मन्वीत इति C, मासीत इति D.

परित्यजेदर्थकामौ यौ स्यातां धर्मवर्जितौ ।
सर्वलोकविरुद्धञ्च धर्म्ममप्याचरेन्न तु ॥
धर्मात्संजायते ह्यर्थो धर्मात्कामोऽभिजायते ।
धर्म्म एवापवर्गाय तस्माद्धर्म्मं समाश्रयेत् ॥
धर्मश्चार्थश्च कामश्च त्रिवर्गस्त्रिगुणो मतः ।
सत्वं रजस्तमश्चेति तस्माद्धर्मं समाश्रयेत् ॥
ऊर्द्धं गच्छन्ति सत्वस्था मध्ये तिष्ठन्ति राजसाः ।
जघन्यगुणवृत्तिस्था अधो गच्छन्ति तामसाः ॥*
यस्मिन्धर्म्मसमायुक्तौ ह्यर्थकामौ व्यवस्थितौ ।
इहलोके सुखी भूत्वा प्रेत्यानन्त्याय कल्पते ॥
धर्मात्संजायते मोक्षो ह्यर्थात्कामोऽभिजायते ।
एवं साधनसाध्यत्वं चातुर्विध्ये† प्रदर्शितम् ॥
य एवं वेद धर्म्मार्थकाममोक्षस्य‡ मानवः ।
माहात्म्यं चानुतिष्ठेत§ सचानन्त्याय कल्पते ॥

---

* 'ऊर्द्धं गच्छन्ति सत्त्वस्था अधो गच्छन्ति तामसाः' इति श्लोकार्द्धं F पुस्तके न दृश्यते । 'मध्ये तिष्ठन्ति राजसाः जघन्यगुणवृत्तिस्थाः' इति अंशश्च A, E, F and H पुस्तकेषु नास्ति ।

† चातुर्विद्ये इति A, B, E, F and H. चतस्रः विद्याः—आन्वीक्षिकी-त्रयी-वार्त्ता-दण्डनीत्यः एव चातुर्विद्यं तस्मिन् इत्यर्थः ।

‡ धर्म्मस्य अर्थस्य कामस्य तैः सहितो मोक्षस्तस्य इति विग्रहः ।

§ आत्मनेपदमार्षम् ।

तस्मादर्थञ्च कामञ्च त्यक्त्वा धर्म्मं समाश्रयेत्।
धर्म्मात्संजायते सर्वमित्याहुर्ब्रह्मवादिनः॥
धर्म्मेण धार्यते सर्वं जगत्स्थावरजङ्गमम्।
अनादिनिधना शक्तिः सैषा ब्राह्मी द्विजोत्तमाः॥
कर्म्मणा प्राप्यते धर्म्मो ज्ञानेन च न संशयः।
तस्माज्ज्ञानेन सहितं कर्मयोगं समाश्रयेत्*॥
प्रवृत्तञ्च निवृत्तञ्च द्विविधं कर्म्म वैदिकम्।
ज्ञानपूर्वं निवृत्तं स्यात्प्रवृत्तं यदतोऽन्यथा॥
निवृत्तं सेवमानस्तु याति तत्परमं पदम्।
तस्मान्निवृत्तं संसेव्यमन्यथा संसरेत्पुनः†॥
क्षमा दमो दया दानमलोभस्त्याग एव च।
आर्जवं चानसूया च तीर्थानुसरणं तथा॥
सत्यं सन्तोष‡मास्तिक्यं श्रद्धा चेन्द्रियनिग्रहः।
देवताभ्यर्चनं पूजा ब्राह्मणानां विशेषतः॥
अहिंसा प्रियवादित्वमपैशून्यमकल्कता§।
सामासिकमिमं धर्म्मं चातुर्वर्ण्येऽब्रवीन्मनुः॥

---

* समाचरेत् इति B and D.

† सञ्चरेत्पुन इति F.

‡ सन्तोषमिति क्लीवत्वमार्षम्।

§ मकल्पता इति B, मवक्रता इति C, मजल्पना इति D.

प्राजापत्यं ब्राह्मणानां स्मृतं स्थानं क्रियावताम्।
स्थानमैन्द्रं क्षत्रियाणां संग्रामेष्वपलायिनाम्॥
वैश्यानां मारुतं स्थानं स्वधर्म्ममनुवर्त्तताम्*।
गान्धर्वं शूद्रजातीनां परिचारेण वर्त्तताम्*॥
अष्टाशीतिसहस्राणामृषीणामूर्द्ध्वरेतसाम्।
स्मृतं तेषान्तु यत्स्थानं तदेव गुरुवासिनाम्†॥
सप्तर्षीणान्तु यत्स्थानं स्मृतं तद्वै वनौकसाम्।
प्राजापत्यं गृहस्थानां स्थानमुक्तं स्वयंभुवा॥
यतीनां जितचित्तानां न्यासिनां‡मूर्द्ध्वरेतसाम्।
हैरण्यगर्भं तत्स्थानं यस्मान्नावर्त्तते पुनः॥
योगिनाममृतं स्थानं व्योमाख्यं परमक्षरम्§।
आनन्दमैश्वरं धाम सा काष्ठा सा परा गतिः॥

ऋषय ऊचुः।

भगवन्देवतारिघ्न हिरण्याक्षनिषूदन।
चत्वारो ह्याश्रमाः प्रोक्ता योगिनामेक उच्यते॥

---

* अत्र आत्मनेपदित्वेऽपि शत्रर्थः।

† गुरुदासिनाम् इति A. गुरवे दासन्ते आत्मानमर्पयन्ति ये तेषाम्। अस्य श्लोकस्य शेषार्द्धं परश्लोकस्य च प्रथमार्द्धं E, F and H पुस्तकेषु नास्ति।

‡ न्यासिनां सन्न्यासवतामित्यर्थः।

§ परमाक्षरमिति B, E, F and H. यत् स्थानं परमक्षरमिति C. यत् स्थानं पारमेश्वरमिति D.

कूर्म्म उवाच ।

सर्व्वकर्म्माणि संन्यस्य समाधिमचलं श्रितः ।
य आस्ते निश्चलो योगी स सन्न्यासी च* पञ्चमः ॥
सर्व्वेषामाश्रमाणान्तु द्वैविध्यं श्रुतिदर्शितम्† ।
ब्रह्मचार्य्युपकुर्व्वाणो नैष्ठिको ब्रह्मतत्परः ॥
योऽधीत्य विधिवद्वेदान् गृहस्थाश्रममाव्रजेत् ।
उपकुर्व्वाणको ज्ञेयो नैष्ठिको मरणान्तिकः ॥
उदासीनः साधकश्च गृहस्थो द्विविधो भवेत् ।
कुटुम्बभरणायत्तः साधकोऽसौ गृही भवेत् ॥
ऋणानि त्रीण्यपाकृत्य‡ त्यक्त्वा भार्य्याधनादिकम् ।
एकाकी यस्तु विचरेदुदासीनः स मौक्षिकः ॥
तपस्तप्यति योऽरण्ये यजेद्देवान् जुहोति च ।
स्वाध्याये चैव निरतो वनस्थस्तापसोमतः ॥
तपसा कर्षितोऽत्यर्थं यस्तु ध्यानपरो भवेत् ।
सान्न्यासिकः स विज्ञेयो वानप्रस्थाश्रमे स्थितः ॥
योगाभ्यासरतो§ नित्यमारुरुक्षुर्जितेन्द्रियः ।
ज्ञानाय वर्त्तते भिक्षुः प्रोच्यते पारमेष्ठिकः ॥

---

* न इति B, D, E and H.

† द्वैविध्यं श्रुतिदर्शनमिति B and G.

‡ त्रीण्युपाहृत्य इति B, त्रीण्युपाकृत्य इति C.

§ योगमभ्यस्यते इति D.

यस्त्वात्मरतिरेव स्यान्नित्यतृप्तो महामुनिः ।
सम्यग्दर्शनसम्पन्नः स योगी भिक्षुरुच्यते ॥
ज्ञानसन्न्यासिनः केचिद्वेदसन्न्यासिनोऽपरे ।
कर्म्मसन्न्यासिनः केचित्त्रिविधाः पारमेष्ठिकाः ॥
योगी च त्रिविधो ज्ञेयो भौतिकः* सांख्य एव च ।
तृतीयो ह्याश्रमी प्रोक्तो योगमुत्तममाश्रितः ॥
प्रथमा भावना पूर्व्वे सांख्ये त्वक्षरभावना ।
तृतीये चान्तिमा प्रोक्ता भावना पारमेश्वरी ॥
तस्मादेतद्विजानीध्वम्† आश्रमाणां चतुष्टयम् ।
सर्व्वेषु वेदशास्त्रेषु पञ्चमो नोपपद्यते ॥
एवं वर्णाश्रमान् सृष्ट्वा देवदेवो निरञ्जनः ।
दक्षादीन्प्राह विश्वात्मा सृजध्वं‡ विविधाः प्रजाः ॥
ब्रह्मणो वचनात्पुत्रा दक्षाद्या मुनिसत्तमाः ।
असृजन्त प्रजाः सर्व्वे देवमानुषपूर्व्वकाः ॥
इत्येवं भगवान् ब्रह्मा स्रष्टृत्वे§ संव्यवस्थितः ।
अहं वै पालयामीदं संहरिष्यति शूलभृत् ॥

---

* वैदिक इति D.

† विजानीयादिति C.

‡ आत्मनेपदमार्षम् ।

§ स्रष्टेदमिति C and D.

तिस्रस्तु मूर्त्तयः प्रोक्ता ब्रह्मविष्णुमहेश्वराः ।
रजःसत्वतमोयोगात्परस्य परमात्मनः ॥
अन्योन्यमनुरक्तास्ते ह्यन्योन्यमुपजीविनः ।
अन्योन्यप्रणताश्चैव लीलया परमेश्वराः ॥
ब्राह्मी माहेश्वरी चैव तथैवाक्षरभावना ।
तिस्रस्तु भावना रुद्रे वर्त्तन्ते सततं द्विजाः ॥
प्रवर्त्तते मय्यजस्रमाद्या त्वक्षरभावना* ।
द्वितीया ब्रह्मणः प्रोक्ता देवस्याक्षरभावना ॥
अहं चैव महादेवो न भिन्नः परमार्थतः ।
विभज्य स्वेच्छयात्मानं सोऽन्तर्यामीश्वरः स्थितः ॥
त्रैलोक्यमखिलं स्रष्टुं सदेवासुरमानुषम् ।
पुरुषः परतोऽव्यक्तो ब्रह्मत्वं समुपागमत् ॥
तस्माद्ब्रह्मा महादेवो विष्णुर्विश्वेश्वरः परः ।
एकस्यैव स्मृतास्तिस्रस्तद्वत्कार्यवशात्प्रभोः ॥
तस्मात्सर्व्वंप्रयत्नेन वन्द्याः पूज्याः विशेषतः ।
यदीच्छेदचिरात्स्थानं यत्तन्मोक्षाख्यमव्ययम् ॥
वर्णाश्रमप्रयुक्तेन धर्म्मेण प्रीतिसंयुतः ।
पूजयेद्भावयुक्तेन यावज्जीवं प्रतिज्ञया ॥

---

* चाक्षरभावना इति A, E, F and H. प्रवर्त्तन्ते मय्यजस्रमन्याश्चाक्षरभावनाः इति B.

चतुर्णामाश्रमाणान्तु प्रोक्तोऽयं विधिवद्द्विजाः ।
आश्रमो वैष्णवो ब्राह्मो हराश्रम इति त्रयः ॥
तल्लिङ्गधारी नियतं* तद्भक्तजनवत्सलः ।
ध्यायेदथार्च्चयेदेतान् ब्रह्मविद्यापरायणः ॥
सर्वेषामेव भक्तानां शम्भोर्लिङ्गमनुत्तमम् ।
सितेन भस्मना कार्य्यं ललाटे तु त्रिपुण्ड्रकम् ॥
यस्तु नारायणं देवं प्रपन्नः परमं पदम् ।
धारयेत्सर्व्वदा शूलं ललाटे गन्धवारिभिः ॥
प्रपन्ना ये जगद्वीजं ब्रह्माणं परमेष्ठिनम् ।
तेषां ललाटे तिलकं धारणीयन्तु सर्वदा ॥
योऽसावनादिर्भूतादिः† कालात्मासौ धृतो भवेत् ।
उपर्य्यधोभावयोगात्त्रिपुण्ड्रस्य तु धारणात् ॥
यत्तत्प्रधानं त्रिगुणं ब्रह्मविष्णुशिवात्मकम् ।
धृतन्तु शूल‡धरणाद्भवत्येव न संशयः ॥
ब्रह्मतेजोमयं शुक्लं यदेतन्मण्डलं रवेः ।
भवत्येव धृतं स्थानमैश्वरं तिलके कृते ॥

---

* सततमिति B.

† भगवान् इति D.

‡ धृतं त्रिशूल इति C.

तस्मात्कार्यं त्रिशूलाङ्कं* तथा च तिलकं शुभम्।
आयुष्यञ्चापि भक्तानां त्रयाणां विधिपूर्वकम्॥
यजेत जुहुयादग्नौ जपेद्दद्याज्जितेन्द्रियः।
शान्तो दान्तो जितक्रोधो वर्णाश्रमविधानवित्॥
एवं परिचरेद्देवान् यावज्जीवं समाहितः।
तेषां स्वस्थानमचलं† सोऽचिरादधिगच्छति॥

इति श्रीकूर्म्मपुराणे वर्णाश्रमवर्णनं नाम द्वितीयोऽध्यायः।

---

* क्लीवलमार्षम्।

† ततस्तत्स्थानमचलमिति D.

तृतीयोऽध्यायः ।

ऋषय ऊचुः ।

वर्णा भगवतोद्दिष्टाश्चत्वारोऽप्याश्रमास्तथा ।
इदानीं क्रममस्माकमाश्रमाणां वद प्रभो ॥

कूर्म्म उवाच ।

ब्रह्मचारी गृहस्थश्च वानप्रस्थो यतिस्तथा ।
क्रमेणैवाश्रमाः प्रोक्ताः कारणादन्यथा भवेत्* ॥
उत्पन्नज्ञानविज्ञानो वैराग्यं परमं गतः ।
प्रव्रजेद्ब्रह्मचर्यात्तु† यदीच्छेत्परमां गतिम् ॥
दारानाहृत्य विधिवदन्यथा विविधैर्मखैः ।
यजेदुत्पादयेत्पुत्रान् विरक्तो यदि संन्यसेत् ॥
अनिष्ट्वा विधिवद्यज्ञैरनुत्पाद्य तथात्मजान् ।
न गार्हस्थं गृही त्यक्त्वा‡ संन्यसेद्बुद्धिमान् द्विजः ॥
अथ वैराग्यवेगेन स्थातुं नोत्सहते गृहे ।
तत्रैव संन्यसेद्विद्वाननिष्ट्वापि द्विजोत्तमः ॥

---

* कारणादन्यथाभवन् इति D, E and F.

† ब्रह्मचर्य्याद्वा इति D.

‡ गृहीत्वा तु इति B. गृहीत्वैव इति E, F, G and H.

तथापि* विविधैर्यज्ञैरिष्ट्वा वनमथाश्रयन्† ।
तपस्तप्त्वा तपोयोगाद्विरक्तः संन्यसेद्यदि:‡ ॥
वानप्रस्थाश्रमं गत्वा न गृहं प्रविशेत्पुनः ।
न सन्न्यासी वनञ्चाथ ब्रह्मचर्यञ्च साधकः§ ॥
प्राजापत्यान्निरूप्येष्टिमाग्नेयीमथवा द्विजः ।
प्रव्रजेत्तु¶ गृही विद्वान् वनाद्वा श्रुतिचोदनात् ॥
प्रकर्त्तुमसमर्थोऽपि जुहोति यजति‖ क्रियाः ।
अन्धः पङ्गुर्दरिद्रो वा विरक्तः संन्यसेद्द्विजः ॥
सर्वेषामेव वैराग्यं संन्यासे तु** विधीयते ।
पतत्येवाविरक्तो यः†† संन्यासं कर्त्तुमिच्छति ॥

---

* अन्यथा इति B. अथापि इति E, F and H.

† वनमथाश्रयेत् इति B. वनमथाव्रजेत् इति D.

‡ संन्यसेद्यदि इति B, C, E, F, G and H. संन्यसेद्यतिः इति D.

§ असन्न्यासी वनञ्चाथ ब्रह्मचर्य्यानुसाधकः इति B. न संन्यासी वनं चाथ ब्रह्मचर्यंन्न साधकः इति C. न संन्यासी वने वासं ब्रह्मचर्यं न साधकः इति D. ब्रह्मचर्य्यं न साधकमिति E, F and H.

¶ प्रव्रजेत इति E, F and H.

‖ जपति इति E, F and H.

** संन्यासाय इति B. संन्यासे तु विभाव्यते इति D.

†† एतत्सेवी विरक्तो वा इति E, F, G and H.

एकस्मिन्नथवा सम्यग्वर्त्तेतामरणान्तिकम्* ।
श्रद्धावानाश्रमे युक्तः सोऽमृतत्वाय कल्पते ॥
न्यायागतधनः† शान्तो ब्रह्मविद्यापरायणः ।
स्वधर्मपालको नित्यं ब्रह्मभूयाय कल्पते ॥
ब्रह्मण्याधाय कर्म्माणि निःसङ्गः कामवर्ज्जितः ।
प्रसन्नेनैव मनसा कुर्वाणो याति तत्पदम् ॥
ब्रह्मणा दीयते देयं ब्रह्मणे संप्रदीयते ।
ब्रह्मैव दीयते चेति ब्रह्मार्पणमिदं परम् ॥
नाहं कर्त्ता सर्वमेतद्ब्रह्मैव कुरुते तथा ।
एतद्ब्रह्मार्पणं प्रोक्तमृषिभिस्तत्त्वदर्शिभिः ॥
प्रीणातु भगवानीशः कर्म्मणानेन शाश्वतः ।
करोति सततं बुद्ध्या ब्रह्मार्पणमिदं परम् ॥
यद्वा फलानां‡ संन्यासं प्रकुर्यात्परमेश्वरे ।
कर्म्मणामेतदप्याहुर्ब्रह्मार्पणमनुत्तमम् ॥
कार्यमित्येव यत्कर्म्म नियतं सङ्गवर्ज्जितम् ।
क्रियते विदुषा कर्म्म तद्भवेदपि मोक्षदम् ॥

---

* मरणाद्विजाः इति B.

† न्यायाधनगतः इति G. न्यायेन अधनं धनाभावं गतः प्राप्तः, न्यायेन दत्तसर्व्वस्व इत्यर्थः ।

‡ फलार्थं इति B.

अथवा* यदि कर्म्माणि कुर्य्यान्नित्यान्यपि द्विजः।
अकृत्वा फलसंन्यासं बध्यते तत्फलेन तु॥
तस्मात्सर्व्वप्रयत्नेन त्यक्त्वा कर्म्माश्रितं फलम्।
अविद्वानपि कुर्व्वीत कर्म्माप्नोति चिरात्पदम्॥
कर्म्मणा क्षीयते पापमैहिकं पौर्व्विकं तथा।
मनःप्रसादमन्वेति ब्रह्मविज्ज्ञायते नरः॥†
कर्म्मणा सहिताज्ज्ञानात् सम्यग्योगोऽभिजायते।
ज्ञानं च कर्म्मसहितं जायते दोषवर्जितम्॥
तस्मात्सर्व्वप्रयत्नेन यत्र तत्राश्रमे रतः।‡
कर्म्माणीश्वरतुष्ट्यर्थं कुर्य्यान्नैष्कर्म्म्यमाप्नुयात्॥
संप्राप्य परमं ज्ञानं नैष्कर्म्म्यं तत्प्रसादतः।
एकाकी निर्म्ममः शान्तो जीवन्नेव§ विमुच्यते॥
वीक्षते परमात्मानं परं ब्रह्म महेश्वरम्।
नित्यानन्दी निराभासः¶ तस्मिन्नेव लयं व्रजेत्॥

---

* अन्यथा इति B, C and D.

† मनः प्रसादमन्वेति ब्रह्म विज्ञायते ततः इति B, C and D.

‡ कर्म्मणा सहितादित्यादि सार्द्धश्लोकः C पुस्तके न दृश्यते।

§ जीवन्नपि इति C and D.

¶ नित्यानन्दं निराभासं इति C and D.

तस्मात्सेवेत सततं कर्म्मयोगं प्रसन्नधीः* ।
तृप्तये परमेशस्य तत्पदं याति शाश्वतम् ॥
एतद्वः कथितं सर्वं चातुराश्रम्यमुत्तमम्† ।
न ह्येतत्समतिक्रम्य सिद्धिं विन्दति मानवः‡ ॥

इति श्रीकूर्म्मपुराणे चातुराश्रम्यकथनं नाम तृतीयोऽध्यायः ।

---

* प्रशस्तधीः इति C and D.

† सम्यग्वर्णाश्रममनुत्तमम् इति B.

‡ विन्दन्ति मानवाः इति B and C.

चतुर्थोऽध्यायः ।

सूत उवाच ।

श्रुत्वाश्रमविधिं कृत्स्नमृषयो हृष्टचेतसः* ।
नमस्कृत्य हृषीकेशं पुनर्वचनमब्रुवन् ॥

मुनय ऊचुः ।

भाषितं भवता सर्वं चातुराश्रम्यमुत्तमम् ।
इदानीं श्रोतुमिच्छामो यथा सम्भवते† जगत् ॥
कुतः सर्वमिदं जातं कस्मिंश्च लयमेष्यति ।
नियन्ता कश्च सर्वेषां वदस्व‡ पुरुषोत्तम ॥
श्रुत्वा नारायणो वाक्यमृषीणां कूर्मरूपधृक् ।
प्राह गम्भीरया वाचा भूतानां प्रभवोऽव्ययः ॥

कूर्म्म उवाच ।

महेश्वरः परोऽव्यक्तः§ चतुर्व्यूहः¶ सनातनः ।
अनन्तश्चाप्रमेयश्च नियन्ता सर्व्वतोमुखः ॥

---

* हृष्टमानसाः इति B, C and D.

† आर्षमात्मनेपदम् । प्राप्त्यर्थकत्वे तु वैकल्पिकमात्मनेपदं भवति ।

‡ वदस्व इति आत्मनेपदमार्षम् ।

§ परोऽव्यक्तात् इति A, E, F and H.

¶ चत्वारः व्यूहा अवस्थानभेदा यस्य तथोक्तः । चातुर्विध्यञ्च दण्डभोगमण्डला-संहतभेदात् । तथाच—"तिर्य्यग्वृत्तिश्च दण्डः स्यात्, भोगोऽन्वावृत्तिरेव च । मण्डलं सर्व्वतोवृत्तिः, पृथग्वृत्तिरसंहतः" । यद्यपि व्यूहपदं सैन्यरचनायां रूढं तथाप्यत्र महेश्वरस्य सर्वव्यापित्वात् सर्वावस्थामयत्वेन स चतुर्व्यूह इत्युच्यते ।

अव्यक्तं कारणं यत्तन्नित्यं सदसदात्मकम् ।
प्रधानं प्रकृतिश्चेति यमाहुस्तत्त्वचिन्तकाः ॥
गन्धवर्ण*रसैर्हीनं शब्दस्पर्शविवर्ज्जितम् ।
अजरं† ध्रुवमक्षय्यं नित्यं स्वात्मन्यवस्थितम् ॥
जगद्योनिर्महाभूतं परब्रह्म‡ सनातनम् ।
विग्रहः सर्वभूतानामात्मनाधिष्ठितं महत् ॥
अनाद्यन्तमजं सूक्ष्मं त्रिगुणं प्रभवाव्ययम् ।
असाम्प्रत§मविज्ञेयं ब्रह्माग्रे समवर्त्तत ॥
गुणसाम्ये तदा तस्मिन् पुरुषे वात्मनि¶ स्थिते ।
प्राकृतः प्रलयो ज्ञेयो यावद्विश्वसमुद्भवः ॥
ब्राह्मी रात्रिरियं प्रोक्ता ह्यहःसृष्टि‖रुदाहृता ।
अहर्न विद्यते तस्य न रात्रिर्ह्युपचारतः** ॥
निशान्ते प्रतिबुद्धोऽसौ जगदादिरनादिमान्†† ।
सर्वभूतमयोऽव्यक्तादन्तर्यामीश्वरः परः ॥

---

* वर्णः रूपमित्यर्थः ।

† अध्रुवम् इति B. चाक्षरम् इति D.

‡ परमिति E, F and H.

§ असाम्प्रतं सम्प्रति न भवम्, त्रिकालव्यापि शाश्वतमित्यर्थः ।

¶ चात्मनि इति B, E, F and H.

‖ अहःसृष्टिरिति E, F and H.

** रात्रिरुपचारतः इति C and D.

†† जगदादिरनामयः इति B.

प्रकृतिं पुरुषं चैव प्रविश्याशु महेश्वरः।
चोभयामास योगेन परेण परमेश्वरः॥
यथा मदो नरस्त्रीणां यथा वा माधवोऽनिलः।
अनुप्रविष्टः चोभाय तथासौ योगमूर्त्तिमान्*॥
स एव चोभको विप्राः चोभ्यश्च परमेश्वरः।
स संकोचविकाशाभ्यां प्रधानत्वे व्यवस्थितः॥
प्रधानात्चोभ्यमानाच्च तथा पुंसः पुरातनात्।
प्रादुरासीन्महद्वीजं प्रधानपुरुषात्मकम्॥
महानात्मा मतिर्ब्रह्मा† प्रबुद्धिः ख्यातिरीश्वरः।
प्रज्ञा धृतिः स्मृतिः संविदेतस्मादिति‡ तत्स्मृतम्॥
वैकारिकस्तैजसश्च भूतादिश्चैव तामसः।
त्रिविधोऽयमहंकारो महतः संबभूव ह॥
अहंकारोऽभिमानश्च कर्त्ता मन्ता§ च स स्मृतः¶।
आत्मा च मत्परो‖ जीवो यतः सर्वाः प्रवृत्तयः॥

---

* पुरुषोत्तमः इति C.

† गतिर्ब्रह्मा इति B and C.

‡ संविदैश्वरश्चेति C and D.

§ हर्त्ता इति C and D.

¶ संस्कृत इति G. संस्मृत इति H.

‖ पुष्कल इति B. प्रबल इति C. पुद्गल इति F and H. पुद्गलः परमाणुरूपः। पुरुष इति G.

पञ्चभूतान्यहंकारात्तन्मात्राणि च जज्ञिरे ।
इन्द्रियाणि च सर्वाणि* सर्वं तस्मात्मजं† जगत् ॥
मनस्त्वव्यक्तजं प्रोक्तं विकारः प्रथमः स्मृतः ।
येनासौ‡ जायते कर्त्ता भूतादींश्चानुपश्यति ॥
वैकारिकादहंकारात्सर्गो वैकारिकोऽभवत्§ ।
तैजसानीन्द्रियाणि स्युर्देवा वैकारिका दश ॥
एकादशं मनस्तत्र स्वगुणेनोभयात्मकम् ।
भूततन्मात्रसर्गोऽयं भूतादेरभवद्द्विजाः ॥
भूतादिस्तु विकुर्वाणः शब्दमात्रं ससर्ज्ज ह ।
आकाशो¶ जायते तस्मात्तस्य शब्दो गुणो मतः ॥
आकाशस्तु विकुर्वाणः स्पर्शमात्रं ससर्ज्ज ह‖ ।
वायुरुत्पद्यते तस्मात्तस्य स्पर्शं गुणं विदुः ॥
वायुश्चापि विकुर्वाणो रूपमात्रं ससर्ज्ज ह ।
ज्योतिरुत्पद्यते वायोस्तद्रूपगुणमुच्यते ॥

---

* इन्द्रियाणि तथा देवाः इति B and C.

† तस्मात्मकम् इति B, D, E, F, G and H.

‡ एतस्मादिति A, E, F and H.

§ सर्गो वैकारिकोऽभवदित्यारभ्य भूततन्मात्रेत्यन्तं C पुस्तके न दृश्यते ।

¶ आकाशं शुषिरं तस्मादुत्पन्नं शब्दलक्षणम् इति B.

‖ आकाश इत्यारभ्य ससर्ज्ज हेत्यन्तः श्लोकः C पुस्तके न दृश्यते ।

ज्योतिश्चापि विकुर्वाणं रसमात्रं ससर्ज्ज ह।
सम्भवन्ति ततोऽम्भांसि रसाधाराणि तानि च॥
आपश्चापि विकुर्वाणा* गन्धमात्रं ससर्ज्जिरे।†
सङ्घातो जायते तस्मात्तस्य गन्धो गुणो मतः‡॥
आकाशं शब्दमात्रं तु स्पर्शमात्रं समावृणोत्।
द्विगुणस्तु ततो वायुः शब्दस्पर्शात्मकोऽभवत्॥
रूपं तथैवाविशतः शब्दस्पर्शौ गुणावुभौ।
त्रिगुणः स्यात्ततो वह्निः स शब्दस्पर्शरूपवान्॥
शब्दः स्पर्शश्च रूपञ्च रसमात्रं समाविशत्।
तस्माच्चतुर्गुणा आपो§ विज्ञेयास्तु रसात्मकाः॥
शब्दः स्पर्शश्च रूपञ्च रसो गन्धं समाविशत्।
तस्मात्पञ्चगुणा भूमिः स्थूला भूतेषु शब्द्यते¶॥
शान्ता घोराश्च मूढ़ाश्च विशेषास्तेन ते स्मृताः।
परस्परानुप्रवेशाद्धारयन्ति परस्परम्॥
एते सप्त महात्मानो ह्यन्योन्यस्य समाश्रयात्।
नाशक्नुवन् प्रजाः स्रष्टुमसमागम्य कृत्स्नशः॥

---

* विकुर्वंत्य इति A, C, E, F and H.

† आत्मनेपदमार्षम्।

‡ गन्धो गुणो मत इत्यारभ्य रूपं तथैवाविशत इत्यन्तं C पुस्तके न दृश्यते।

§ गुणास्त्वाप इति C. गुणाश्चाप इति D.

¶ शस्यते इति C, E and F. पठ्यते इति D.

पुरुषाधिष्ठितत्वाच्च अव्यक्तानुग्रहेण च।
महदादयो विशेषान्ता ह्यण्डमुत्पादयन्ति ते॥
एककालसमुत्पन्नं जलबुद्बुदवच्च तत्।
विशेषेभ्योऽण्डमभवद्बृहत्तदुदकेशयम्॥
तस्मिन् कार्यस्य करणं* संसिद्धं परमेष्ठिनः।
प्राकृतेऽण्डे विवृद्धे तु क्षेत्रज्ञो ब्रह्मसंज्ञितः॥
स वै शरीरी प्रथमः स वै पुरुष उच्यते।
आदिकर्त्ता स भूतानां ब्रह्माग्रे समवर्त्तत॥
यमाहुः पुरुषं हंसं प्रधानात्परतः स्थितम्।
हिरण्यगर्भं कपिलं छन्दोमूर्त्तिं सनातनम्॥
मेरुरुल्वं†मभूत्तस्य जरायुश्चापि पर्वताः‡।
गर्भोदकं समुद्राश्च तस्यासन्परमात्मनः॥
तस्मिन्नण्डेऽभवद्विश्वं सदेवासुरमानुषम्।
चन्द्रादित्यौ सनक्षत्रौ सग्रहौ सह वायुना॥
अद्भिर्दशगुणाभिश्च बाह्यतोऽण्डं समावृतम्।
आपो दशगुणेनैव तेजसा बाह्यतो वृताः॥

---

* कार्य्यस्य कारणं तस्मिन् इति A, E, F and H.

† उल्वं गर्भवेष्टनचर्म्म।

‡ जरायुश्च महीधराः इति D.

तेजोदशगुणेनैव वाह्यतो वायुना वृतम्।
आकाशेनावृतो वायुः खं तु भूतादिना वृतम्* ॥
भूतादिर्महता तद्वदव्यक्तेनावृतो महान्।
एते लोका महात्मानः सर्वे† तत्त्वाभिमानिनः ॥
वसन्ति तत्र पुरुषास्तदात्मानो व्यवस्थिताः‡।
ईश्वरायोगधर्म्माणो ये चान्ये तत्त्वचिन्तकाः§ ॥
सर्वज्ञाः शान्तरजसो नित्यं मुदितमानसाः।
एतैरावरणैरण्डं प्राकृतैः सप्तभिर्वृतम् ॥
एतावच्छक्यते वक्तुं मायैषा गहना द्विजाः।
एतत्प्राधानिकं कार्य्यं यन्मया वीजमीरितम्¶ ॥
प्रजापतेः परा‖ मूर्त्तिरितीयं वैदिकी श्रुतिः।
ब्रह्माण्डमेतत्सकलं सप्तलोकबलान्वितम्** ॥

---

* आकाशेनावृतो वायुरित्यादि श्लोकार्द्धं D पुस्तके न दृश्यते, परन्तु "वायुर्दशगुणेनैव आकाशेनावृतो वह्निः। भूतादिना दशगुणेनाकाशो वहिरावृतः ॥" इति श्लोको दृश्यते।

† सर्वतत्त्वाभिमानिनः इति A, E, F and H.

‡ नभःस्थिताः इति A, E, F and H.

§ योगचिन्तकाः इति B.

¶ पूर्व्वमीरितम् इति B.

‖ पुरा इति D.

** सप्तलोकतलान्वितम् इति B and C. सप्तलोककुलान्वितम् इति D.

द्वितीयं तस्य देवस्य शरीरं परमेष्ठिनः ।
हिरण्यगर्भो भगवान् ब्रह्मा वै कनकाण्डजः ॥
तृतीयं भगवद्रूपं प्राहुर्वेदार्थवेदिनः ।
रजोगुणमयं चान्यद्रूपं तस्यैव धीमतः ॥
चतुर्मुखस्तु* भगवान् जगत्सृष्टौ प्रवर्त्तते ।
सृष्टं च† पाति सकलं विश्वात्मा विश्वतोमुखः ॥
सत्वं गुणमुपाश्रित्य विष्णुर्विश्वेश्वरः स्वयम् ।
अन्तकाले स्वयं देवः सर्वात्मा परमेश्वरः ॥
तमोगुणं समाश्रित्य रुद्रः संहरते जगत् ।
एकोऽपि सन्महादेवस्त्रिधासौ समवस्थितः ॥
सर्गरक्षालयगुणैर्निर्गुणोऽपि निरञ्जनः ।
एकधा स द्विधा चैव त्रिधा च बहुधा गुणैः‡ ॥
योगेश्वरः शरीराणि करोति विकरोति च ।
नानाकृतिक्रियारूपनामवन्ति स्वलीलया ॥
हिताय चैव भक्तानां स एव ग्रसते पुनः ।
त्रिधा विभज्य चात्मानं त्रैलोक्ये संप्रवर्त्तते ॥
सृजते ग्रसते चैव वीक्षते च विशेषतः ।
यस्मात्सृष्ट्वानुगृह्णाति ग्रसते च पुनः प्रजाः ॥

---

* चतुर्मुखः स इति B and C. चतुर्मुखश्च इति D.

† संसृज्य इति C.

‡ गुण इति E, F and H.

गुणात्मकत्वात्त्रैकाल्ये* तस्मादेकः स उच्यते ।
अग्रे हिरण्यगर्भः स प्रादुर्भूतः सनातनः ॥
आदित्वादादिदेवोऽसावजातत्वादजः† स्मृतः ।
पाति यस्मात्प्रजाः सर्वाः प्रजापतिरिति स्मृतः ॥
देवेषु च महादेवो महादेव इति स्मृतः‡ ।
बृहत्त्वाच्च स्मृतो ब्रह्मा परत्वात्परमेश्वरः ॥
वशित्वादप्यवश्यत्वादीश्वरः परिभाषितः ।
ऋषिः सर्व्वत्रगत्वेन हरिः सर्व्वहरो यतः§ ॥
अनुत्पादाच्च¶ पूर्वत्वात्स्वयंभूरिति स स्मृतः ।
नराणामयनं यस्मात्तेन नारायणः स्मृतः ॥
हरः संसारहरणाद्विभुत्वाद्विष्णुरुच्यते ।
भगवान्सर्वविज्ञानादवनादोमिति स्मृतः‖ ॥
सर्वज्ञः सर्वविज्ञानात्सर्वः सर्वमयो यतः ।
शिवः स्यान्निर्म्मलो यस्माद्विभुः सर्वगतो यतः ॥

---

* गुणात्मकत्वात्त्रैलोक्ये इति B and D.

† ज्ञातत्वादज इति E, F and H.

‡ देवेषु चेति श्लोकार्द्धं D पुस्तके नास्ति ।

§ सर्व्वगुरुरिति A, E, F and H.

¶ अनुत्पादाच्च पूर्व्वत्वादित्यारभ्य सर्व्वः सर्व्वमयो यतः इत्यन्तं E, F, G and H पुस्तकेषु नास्ति ।

‖ देवनाद्देवता स्मृतः इति D.

तारणात्सर्वदुःखानां तारकः परिगीयते।
बहुनाऽत्र किमुक्तेन सर्वं ब्रह्ममयं* जगत्॥
अनेकभेदभिन्नस्तु क्रीड़ते† परमेश्वरः।
इत्येष प्राकृतः सर्गः संक्षेपात्कथितो मया।
अबुद्धिपूर्वकां‡ विप्रा ब्राह्मीं सृष्टिं निबोधत॥

इति श्रीकूर्म्मपुराणे प्राकृतसर्गो नाम चतुर्थोऽध्यायः।

---

* विष्णुमयं इति B.

† आत्मनेपदमार्षम्।

‡ अबुद्धिपूर्व्वकां नास्ति बुद्धिः महत्तत्त्वं पूर्व्वा प्रथमा यत्र तथोक्ताम्। प्राकृतसर्गे तु प्रथमं प्रकृतेर्म्महान्, ततो महतोऽहङ्कारः, इत्येवम्प्रकारेण क्रमेण सर्गो भवति। ब्राह्मे तु सर्गे न तथा इति विशेषः।

पञ्चमोऽध्यायः ।

कूर्म्म उवाच ।

स्वयम्भुवो निवृत्तस्य* कालसंख्या द्विजोत्तमाः । †
न शक्यते समाख्यातुं‡ बहुवर्षैरपि स्वयम् ॥
कालसंख्या समासेन परार्द्धद्वयकल्पिता ।
स एव स्यात्परः कालस्तदन्ते सृज्यते पुनः§ ॥
निजेन तस्य मानेन चायुर्वर्षशतं स्मृतम् ।
तत्परार्द्धं तदर्द्धं वा¶ परार्द्धमभिधीयते ॥

---

* स्वयम्भुवोऽपि वृत्तस्य इति B.

† इतः परम्

अनुत्पादाच्च पूर्व्वस्मात् स्वयम्भुरिति स स्मृतः ।
नराणामयनो यस्मात्तेन नारायणः स्मृतः ॥
हरः संसारहरणाद्विभुत्वाद्विष्णुरुच्यते ।
भगवान् सर्व्ववित् ज्ञानादवनादोमिति स्मृतः ॥
सर्व्वज्ञः सर्व्वविज्ञानात्सर्व्वः सर्व्वमयो यतः । इति E, F and H पुस्तकेषु दृश्यते ।

‡ मयाख्यातुं इति C.

§ तदन्ते प्रतिगृह्यते इति B. तदन्ते परिगृह्यते इति C. तदन्ते प्रतिसृज्यते इति D.

¶ तत्पराख्यं तदूर्द्धञ्च इति B. तत्पराख्यं तदर्द्धञ्च इति C and D. तदर्द्धञ्च इति E and F. तदर्द्धञ्चा इति H.

काष्ठा पञ्चदश ख्याता* निमेषा द्विजसत्तमाः ।
काष्ठात्रिंशत् कला त्रिंशत्कला मौहूर्त्तिकी गतिः ॥
तावत्सङ्ख्यैरहोरात्रं मुहूर्त्तैर्मानुषं स्मृतम् ।
अहोरात्राणि तावन्ति मासः पक्षद्वयात्मकः ॥
तैः षड्भिरयनं वर्षं द्वेऽयने दक्षिणोत्तरे ।
अयनं दक्षिणं रात्रिर्देवानामुत्तरं दिनम् ॥
दिव्यैर्वर्षसहस्रैस्तु कृतत्रेतादिसंज्ञितम् ।
चतुर्युगं द्वादशभिस्तद्विभागं निबोधत ॥
चत्वार्याहुः सहस्राणि वर्षाणां तत्कृतं युगम् ।
तस्य तावच्छती सन्ध्या सन्ध्यांशश्च कृतस्य तु ॥
त्रिशती द्विशती सन्ध्या तथा चैकशती क्रमात् ।
अंशकं षट्शतं तस्मात्कृतसन्ध्यांशकैर्विना ॥
त्रिद्व्येकधा च साहस्रं† विना सन्ध्यांशकेन तु ।
त्रेता द्वापरतिष्याणां‡ कालज्ञाने§ प्रकीर्त्तितम् ॥
एतद्द्वादशसाहस्रं साधिकं परिकल्पितम्¶ ।
तदेकसप्ततिगुणं‖ मनोरन्तरमुच्यते ॥

---

* पञ्चदशाख्यास्तु इति D.

† त्रिद्व्येकसाहस्रमिती इति B and C. त्रिभिर्द्व्येकसहस्राणामिति D.

‡ तिष्याद्यामिति G. तिष्यापमिति E and F.

§ लोकज्ञाने इति H.

¶ परिकीर्त्तितमिति A, E, F and H.

‖ तदेकसप्ततियुगमिति D.

ब्रह्मणो दिवसे विप्रा मनवश्च* चतुर्द्दश।
स्वायम्भुवादयः सर्व्वे ततः सावर्णिकादयः॥
तैरियं पृथिवी सर्व्वा सप्तद्वीपा सपर्व्वता।
पूर्णं युगसहस्रं वै परिपाल्या नरेश्वरैः॥
मन्वन्तरेण चैकेन सर्व्वाण्येवान्तराणि वै।
व्याख्यातानि न सन्देहः कल्पे कल्पे न चैव हि॥
ब्राह्ममेकमहः कल्पस्तावती रात्रिरिष्यते।
चतुर्युगसहस्रं तु कल्पमाहुर्मनीषिणः॥
त्रीणि कल्पशतानि स्युस्तथा षष्टिर्द्दिजोत्तमाः।
ब्रह्मणो वत्सरस्तज्ज्ञैः कथितो वै द्विजोत्तमाः॥
स च कालः शतगुणः परार्द्धं चैव तद्विदुः।†
तस्यान्ते सर्व्वसत्त्वानां स्वहेतौ प्रकृतौ लयः॥
तेनायं प्रोच्यते सद्भिः प्राकृतः प्रतिसंचरः।
ब्रह्मनारायणेशानां त्रयाणां प्रकृतौ लयः॥
प्रोच्यते कालयोगेन पुनरेव च सम्भवः।
एवं ब्रह्मा च भूतानि वासुदेवोऽपि शङ्करः॥
कालेनैव तु सृज्यन्ते सएव ग्रसते पुनः।
अनादिरेष भगवान् कालोऽनन्तोऽजरोऽमरः॥

---

* मनवः स्युरिति B. मनवस्तु इति C.

† ब्रह्मणः कथितं वर्षं पराख्यं तच्च तत्परम् इति B. ब्रह्मणः कथितं सर्व्वं परार्द्धं तच्छतं विदुः इति C and D.

सर्वगत्वात्स्वतन्त्रत्वात्सर्वात्मत्वान्महेश्वरः ।
ब्रह्माणो बहवो रुद्रा ह्यन्ये* नारायणादयः ॥
एको हि भगवानीशः कालः कविरिति श्रुतिः ।
एकमत्र व्यतीतं तु† परार्द्धं ब्रह्मणो द्विजाः ॥
साम्प्रतं वर्त्तते त्वर्द्धं तस्य कल्पोऽयमग्रजः‡ ।
योऽतीतः सोऽन्तिमः कल्पः पाद्म§ इत्युच्यते बुधैः ।
वाराहो वर्त्तते कल्पस्तस्य वक्ष्यामि विस्तरम् ॥

इति श्रीकूर्म्मपुराणे कालसंख्याकथनं नाम पञ्चमोऽध्यायः ।

---

* तत इति B. येन्ये इति C.

† एवमत्र व्यतीतं तत् इति B.

‡ कल्पोऽयमग्रतः इति C and D.

§ पद्म इति E, F and H.

अथ षष्ठोऽध्यायः ।

कूर्म्म उवाच ।

आसीदेकार्णवं घोरमविभागं तमोमयम् ।
शान्तवातादिकं सर्वं न प्राज्ञायत किञ्चन ॥
एकार्णवे तदा तस्मिन्नष्टे स्थावरजङ्गमे ।
तदा समभवद्ब्रह्मा सहस्राक्षः सहस्रपात् ॥
सहस्रशीर्षा पुरुषो रुक्मवर्णो ह्यतीन्द्रियः ।
ब्रह्मा नारायणाख्यस्तु सुष्वाप सलिले तदा ॥
इमं चोदाहरन्त्यत्र श्लोकं नारायणं प्रति ।
ब्रह्मस्वरूपिणं देवं जगतः प्रभवाव्ययम् ॥
आपो नारा इति प्रोक्ता आपो वै नरसूनवः* ।
अयनं तस्य ता यस्मात्तेन नारायणः स्मृतः ॥
तुल्यं युगसहस्रस्य नैशं कालमुपास्य† सः ।
शर्वर्यन्ते प्रकुरुते‡ ब्रह्मत्वं सर्गकारणात् ॥
ततस्तु सलिले तस्मिन् विज्ञायान्तर्गतां महीम् ।
अनुमानात्तदुद्धारं कर्त्तुकामः प्रजापतिः ॥

---

* नाम्ना पूर्व्वं इति श्रुतः इति B.   नाम्ना पूर्व्वमिति श्रुतिः इति D, E, F, G and H.

† अपास्य इति H.

‡ सर्व्वयत्नेन कुरुते इति D.

जलक्रीड़ासु रुचिरं वाराहं रूपमास्थितः ।
अधृष्यं मनसाप्यन्यैर्वाङ्मयं* ब्रह्मसंज्ञितम् ॥
पृथिव्युद्धरणार्थाय प्रविश्य च रसातलम् ।
दंष्ट्रयाभ्युज्जहारैनामात्माधारो धराधरः ॥
दृष्ट्वा दंष्ट्राग्रविन्यस्तां पृथ्वीं प्रथितपौरुषम् ।
अस्तुवञ्जनलोकस्थाः† सिद्धा ब्रह्मर्षयो हरिम् ॥

ऋषय ऊचुः ।

नमस्ते देवदेवाय ब्रह्मणे परमेष्ठिने‡ ।
पुरुषाय पुराणाय शाश्वताय जयाय च ॥
नमः स्वयम्भुवे तुभ्यं स्रष्ट्रे सर्वार्थवेदिने ।
नमो हिरण्यगर्भाय वेधसे परमात्मने ॥
नमस्ते वासुदेवाय विष्णवे विश्वयोनये§ ।
नारायणाय देवाय देवानां हितकारिणे ॥
नमोऽस्तु ते चतुर्वक्त्रशार्ङ्गचक्रासिधारिणे ।
सर्वभूतात्मभूताय कूटस्थाय¶ नमो नमः ॥
नमो वेदरहस्याय नमस्ते वेदयोनये ।
नमो बुद्धाय शुद्धाय नमस्ते ज्ञानरूपिणे ॥

---

* ब्रह्माद्यैः इति D.

† जनलोकस्थाः जननामकभुवनवर्त्तिनः इत्यर्थः ।

‡ ब्रह्मणे परमेष्ठिने इत्यारभ्य नमस्ते वासुदेवाय इत्यन्तं B पुस्तके न दृश्यते ।

§ विष्णवे विश्वयोनये नारायणाय देवाय—एष भागः C पुस्तके न दृश्यते ।

¶ कूटस्थाय—"एकरूपतया तु यः कालव्यापी स कूटस्थः" तस्मै इत्यर्थः ।

नमोऽस्त्वानन्दरूपाय साक्षिणे जगतां नमः* ।
अनन्तायाप्रमेयाय कार्य्याय कारणाय च ॥
नमस्ते पञ्चभूताय पञ्चभूतात्मने नमः ।
नमो मूलप्रकृतये मायारूपाय ते नमः ॥
नमोऽस्तु ते वराहाय नमस्ते मत्स्यरूपिणे ।
नमो योगाधिगम्याय नमः संकर्षणाय ते ॥
नमस्त्रिमूर्त्तये तुभ्यं त्रिधाम्ने दिव्यतेजसे ।
नमः सिद्धाय पूज्याय गुणत्रयविभागिने ॥
नमोऽस्त्वादित्यरूपाय† नमस्ते पद्मयोनये‡ ।
नमोऽमूर्त्ताय मूर्त्ताय§ माधवाय नमो नमः ॥
त्वयैव सृष्टमखिलं त्वय्येव सकलं स्थितम्¶ ।
पालयैतज्जगत्सर्वं त्राता त्वं शरणं गतिः‖ ॥
इत्थं स भगवान् विष्णुः सनकाद्यैरभिष्टुतः ।
प्रसादमकरोत्तेषां वराहवपुरीश्वरः ॥

---

* नमोऽस्त्वनन्तरूपाय साक्षिणे जगतो नमः इति B.

† आदित्यवर्णाय इति E, F and H.

‡ विश्वयोनये इति G.

§ शान्ताय इति E, F and H.

¶ लयमेष्यति इति B and C.

‖ शरणं गतः इति B. शरणङ्गतान् इति D.

ततः स्वस्थान*मानीय पृथिवीं पृथिवीधरः।
मुमोच रूपं मनसा धारयित्वा धराधरः† ॥
तस्योपरि जलौघस्य महती नौरिव स्थिता।
विततत्वाच्च‡ देहस्य न मही याति संप्लवम् ॥
पृथिवीं स§ समीकृत्य पृथिव्यां सोऽचिनोद्गिरीन्।
प्राक् सर्गदग्धानखिलान्ततः सर्गेऽदधन्मनः ॥

इति श्रीकूर्म्मपुराणे पृथिव्युद्धारे षष्ठोऽध्यायः।

---

* संस्थानमिति E, F and H.

† प्रजापतिः इति B.

‡ पीनत्वाच्चैव इति B and C.

§ तु इति B and C.

सप्तमोऽध्यायः ।

कूर्म्म उवाच ।

सृष्टिं चिन्तयतस्तस्य कल्पादिषु यथा पुरा ।
अबुद्धिपूर्वकः सर्गः प्रादुर्भूतस्तमोमयः ॥
तमो मोहो महामोहस्तामिस्रश्चान्धसंज्ञितः* ।
अविद्या पञ्चमी तेषां† प्रादुर्भूता महात्मनः ॥
पञ्चधावस्थितः सर्गो ध्यायतः सोऽभिमानिनः ।
संवृतस्तमसा चैव वीजकुम्भवदावृतः ॥
वहिरन्तश्चाप्रकाशस्तब्धो निःसङ्ग एव च ।
मुख्या नगा इति प्रोक्ता मुख्यसर्गस्तु स स्मृतः ॥
तं दृष्ट्वाऽसाधकं‡ सर्गममन्यदपरं§ प्रभुः ।
तस्याभिध्यायतः सर्गं तिर्य्यक्स्रोतोऽभ्यवर्त्तत ॥
यस्मात्तिर्य्यक् प्रवृत्तः स तिर्य्यक्स्रोतः ततः स्मृतः ।
पश्वादयस्ते विख्याता उत्पथग्राहिणो¶ द्विजाः ॥
तमप्यसाधकं ज्ञात्वा सर्गमन्यं ससर्ज्ज ह ।
ऊर्द्ध्वस्रोत इति प्रोक्तो देवसर्गस्तु सात्विकः ॥

---

* तामिस्त्री ह्यन्धसंज्ञितः इति B and C.

† पञ्चपर्व्वैषा इति A, C, E, F and H. पञ्च सर्व्वेषां इति B.

‡ असाधकं न सर्व्वार्थप्रतिपादकम् असम्पूर्णमित्यर्थः ।

§ ममन्यत परं इति B. अमन्यदित्यार्षम् ।

¶ तत्पथग्राहिणः इति B.

ते सुखप्रीतिबहुला बहिरन्तस्त्वनावृताः ।
प्रकाशा बहिरन्तश्च स्वभावाद्देवसंज्ञिताः ॥
ततोऽभिध्यायतस्तस्य सत्याभिध्यायिनस्तदा* ।
प्रादुरासीत्तदा व्यक्तादर्वाक्स्रोतस्तु साधकः† ॥
तत्र प्रकाशबहुलास्तमोद्रिक्ता‡ रजोऽधिकाः ।
दुःखोत्कटाः सत्वयुता§ मनुष्याः परिकीर्त्तिताः ॥
तं दृष्ट्वा चापरं सर्गममन्यद्भगवानजः ।
तस्याभिध्यायतः सर्गं सर्गो भूतादिकोऽभवत् ॥
ते परिग्रहिणः सर्वे संविभागरताः पुनः ।
खादिनश्चाप्यशालाश्च¶ भूताद्याः परिकीर्त्तिताः ॥
इत्येते पञ्च कथिताः सर्गा वै द्विजपुंगवाः ।
प्रथमो महतः सर्गो विज्ञेयो ब्रह्मणस्तु सः ॥
तन्मात्राणां द्वितीयस्तु भूतसर्गो हि संस्मृतः‖ ।
वैकारिकस्तृतीयस्तु सर्ग ऐन्द्रियकः स्मृतः ॥

---

* सर्व्वाभिध्यायिनस्तथा इति D.

† स्रोतः स साधक इति E, F and H. स सर्गः साधकः सर्व्वार्थप्रतिपादक-इत्यर्थः ।

‡ तमःप्रक्ता इति B.

§ दुःखोत्कायः सत्वयुता इति E and F.

¶ शीलाश्च इति E, F and H.

‖ स स्मृतः इति B, C, E, F and H. तथा स्मृतः इति D.

इत्येष प्राकृतः सर्गः संभूतो बुद्धिपूर्व्वकः ।
मुख्यसर्गश्चतुर्थस्तु मुख्या वै स्थावराः स्मृताः ॥
तिर्य्यक्स्रोतस्तु यः प्रोक्तस्तिर्यग्योन्यः स पञ्चमः ।
तथोर्द्ध्वस्रोतसां षष्ठो देवसर्गस्तु स स्मृतः ॥
ततोऽर्वाक्स्रोतसां सर्गः सप्तमः स तु मानुषः ।
अष्टमो भौतिकः सर्गो भूतादीनां प्रकीर्त्तितः ॥
नवमश्चैव कौमारः प्राकृता वैकृतास्त्विमे ।
प्राकृतास्तु त्रयः पूर्व्वे सर्गास्ते बुद्धिपूर्व्वकाः ॥
बुद्धिपूर्वं प्रवर्त्तन्ते मुख्याद्या मुनिपुंगवाः ।
अग्रे ससर्ज्ज वै ब्रह्मा मानसानात्मनः समान् ॥
सनकं सनातनं चैव* तथैव च सनन्दनम् ।
क्रतुं† सनत्कुमारं च पूर्वमेव प्रजापतिः ॥
पञ्चैते योगिनो विप्राः परं वैराग्यमाश्रिताः‡ ।
ईश्वरासक्तमनसो न सृष्टौ दधिरे मतिम् ॥
तेष्वेवं निरपेक्षेषु लोकसृष्टौ प्रजापतिः ।
मुमोह मायया सद्यो मायिनः परमेष्ठिनः ॥
संबोधयामास च तं§ जगन्मायो महामुनिः ।

---

* 'सनकं सनातनञ्चैव' इति नवभिरक्षरैरपि क्वचिदनुष्टुप् भवति ।

† विभुं इति B. ऋभुं इति C and D.

‡ आस्थिता इति B.

§ तं बोधयामास सुतं इति C and D.

नारायणो महायोगी योगिचित्तानुरञ्जनः ॥
बोधितस्तेन विश्वात्मा तताप परमं तपः।
स तप्यमानो* भगवान्न किञ्चित्प्रत्यपद्यत ॥
ततो दीर्घेण कालेन दुःखात्क्रोधोऽभ्यजायत।
क्रोधाविष्टस्य नेत्राभ्यां प्रापतन्नश्रुबिन्दवः ॥
भ्रुकुटीकुटिलात्तस्य ललाटात्परमेष्ठिनः।
समुत्पन्नो महादेवः शरण्यो नीललोहितः ॥
स एव भगवानीशस्तेजोराशिः सनातनः।
यं प्रपश्यन्ति विद्वांसः स्वात्मस्थं परमेश्वरम्† ॥
ओंकारं समनुस्मृत्य प्रणम्य च कृताञ्जलिः।
तमाह भगवान् ब्रह्मा सृजेमा विविधाः प्रजाः ॥
निशम्य भगवद्वाक्यं‡ शंकरो धर्मवाहनः।
आत्मना§ सदृशान् रुद्रान्¶ ससर्ज मनसा शिवः।
कपर्दिनो निरातङ्कांस्त्रिनेत्रान्नीललोहितान् ॥

---

* संतप्यमान इति A.

† परमेष्ठिनम् इति B.

‡ भगवान् वाक्यम् इति E, F and H.

§ स्वात्मना इति E, F and H.

¶ पुत्रान् इति B and C.

तं प्राह भगवान् ब्रह्मा जन्ममृत्युयुताः प्रजाः ।
सृजेति सोऽब्रवीदीशो नाहं मृत्युजरान्विताः ।
प्रजाः स्रक्ष्ये जगन्नाथ सृज त्वमशुभाः प्रजाः ॥
निवार्य्य स तदा रुद्रं ससर्ज कमलोद्भवः ।
स्थानाभिमानिनः* सर्वान्† गदतस्तान्निबोधत‡ ॥
आपोऽग्निरन्तरिक्षं च द्यौर्वायुः पृथिवी तथा ।
नद्यः समुद्राः शैलाश्च वृक्षा वीरुध एव च ।
लवाः काष्ठाः कलाश्चैव मुहूर्त्ता दिवसाः क्षपाः ।
अर्द्धमासाश्च मासाश्च अयनाब्दयुगादयः§ ।
स्थानाभिमानिनः सृष्ट्वा साधकानसृजत्पुनः¶ ॥
मरीचिभृग्वङ्गिरसः पुलस्त्यं पुलहं क्रतुम् ।
दक्षमत्रिं वसिष्ठं च धर्म्मं संकल्पमेव च ॥
प्राणाद्ब्रह्मासृजद्दक्षं चक्षुर्भ्यां च मरीचिनम् ।
शिरसोऽङ्गिरसं देवो‖ हृदयाद्भृगुमेव च ।
नेत्राभ्यामत्रिनामानं धर्म्मं च व्यवसायतः ।

---

* ज्ञानाभिमानिनः इति B.

† तेषामिति E, F and H.

‡ निबोध मे इति C.

§ अयनञ्च युगादयः इति B.

¶ प्रभुः इति B.

‖ चैव इति D.

संकल्पं चैव संकल्पात्सर्वलोकपितामहः।
पुलस्त्यं च तथोदानाद्व्यानाच्च* पुलहं मुनिम्।†
अपानात्‡ क्रतुमव्यग्रं समानाच्च वसिष्ठकम्।
इत्येते ब्रह्मणा सृष्टाः साधका गृहमेधिनः॥
आस्थाय मानवं रूपं धर्म्मस्तैः संप्रवर्त्तितः।
ततो देवासुरपितॄन्§ मनुष्यांश्च चतुष्टयम्।
सिसृक्षुर्भगवानीशः स्वमात्मानमयोजयत्¶॥
युक्तात्मनस्तमोमात्रा ह्युद्रिक्ताभूत्प्रजापतेः।
ततोऽस्य जघनात्पूर्वमसुरा जज्ञिरे सुताः॥
उत्ससर्जासुरान् सृष्ट्वा तां तनुं पुरुषोत्तमः।
सा चोत्सृष्टा तनुस्तेन सद्यो रात्रिरजायत॥
सा तमोबहुला यस्मात्प्रजास्तस्यां स्वपन्त्यतः॥
सत्त्वमात्रात्मिकां देवस्तनुमन्यां गृहीतवान्‖।
ततोऽस्य मुखतो देवा दीव्यतः संप्रजज्ञिरे**॥

---

* तथापानाद्व्यानाच्च इति D.

† प्रभुं इति C and D.

‡ उदानात् इति D.

§ देवान् ततोऽसुरपितॄन् इति C.

¶ सिसृक्षुर्भगवानेतान् स्वमात्मानमयूयुजत् इति C and D.

‖ अगृह्णत इति B, C and D.

** दीप्तिमन्तः प्रजज्ञिरे इति D.

त्यक्ता सापि तनुस्तेन सत्त्वप्रायमभूद्दिनम्।
तस्माद्‌हो धर्म्मयुक्ता* देवताः समुपासते॥
सत्त्वमात्रात्मिकामेव ततोऽन्यां जगृहे तनुम्।
पितृवन्मन्यमानस्य पितरः संप्रजज्ञिरे† ॥
उत्ससर्ज पितॄन् सृष्ट्वा ततस्तामपि विश्वसृक्‡।
सापविद्धा तनुस्तेन सद्यः सन्ध्या व्यजायत§॥
तस्मादहर्द्देवतानां रात्रिः स्याद्देवविद्विषाम्।
तयोर्मध्ये पितॄणां तु मूर्त्तिः सन्ध्या गरीयसी¶॥
तस्माद्देवासुराः सर्वे मुनयो मानवास्तदा‖।
उपासते सदा** युक्ता†† रात्र्यह्नोर्मध्यमां तनुम्॥
रजोमात्रात्मिकां ब्रह्मा तनुमन्यां ततोऽसृजत्‡‡।
ततोऽस्य जज्ञिरे पुत्रा मनुष्याः रजसावृताः॥

---

* धर्म्मयुक्ता धार्म्मिका देवताः सूर्य्यादीन् समुपासते इत्यर्थः।

† पितरस्तस्य जज्ञिरे इति D.

‡ विश्वधृक् इति B and C.

§ सन्ध्याप्यजायत इति D.

¶ महीयसी इति D.

‖ मनवो मानवास्तथा इति B. मनवो मानवाः सदा इति C.

** तदा इति C.

†† युक्ता अवहिता इत्यर्थः।

‡‡ तनुमन्यामगृह्णत इति B and C. रजोमात्रात्मिकामन्यां ब्रह्मा तनुमगृह्णत इति D.

तामथाशु* स तत्याज तनुं सद्यः प्रजापतिः ।
ज्योत्स्ना सा चाभवद्विप्राः प्राक्सन्ध्या याभिधीयते ॥
ततः स भगवान्ब्रह्मा संप्राप्य द्विजपुंगवाः ।
मूर्त्तिं तमोरजःप्रायां† पुनरेवाभ्यपूजयत्‡ ॥
अन्धकारे क्षुधाविष्टा राक्षसास्तस्य जज्ञिरे ।
पुत्रास्तमोरजःप्राया बलिनस्ते निशाचराः ॥
सर्पा यक्षास्तथा§ भूताः¶ गन्धर्वाः संप्रजज्ञिरे ।
रजस्तमोभ्यामाविष्टांस्ततोऽन्यानसृजत्प्रभुः‖ ॥
वयांसि वयसः सृष्ट्वा अवीन्वै वक्षसोऽसृजत् ।
मुखतोऽजान् ससर्जान्यान्** उदराद्गाश्च निर्ममे ॥
पद्भ्यां चाश्वान्समातङ्गान्रासभान्†† गवयान्मृगान् ।
उष्ट्रानश्वतरांश्चैव न्यङ्कूनन्याश्च जातयः‡‡ ॥

---

* तामप्याशु इति C and D.

† इतः परं चरणचतुष्टयं D पुस्तके न दृश्यते ।

‡ न्यपूजयत् इति B. पुनरेव ह्ययूयुजत् इति H.

§ तत इति C.

¶ सर्पा भूतास्तथा यक्षाः इति B.

‖ पुनः इति A, E, F and H.

** ससर्जाथ इति A, E, F and H.

†† रक्षसः इति C. पद्भ्याश्चैवाश्वमातङ्गान् रक्षसः इति D.

‡‡ न्यङ्कूनन्यांश्च जातय इति E, F and H.

ओषध्यः फलमूलानि* रोमभ्यस्तस्य जज्ञिरे।
गायत्रं च ऋचश्चैव† त्रिवृत्स्तोमं रथन्तरम्‡॥
अग्निष्टोमं च यज्ञानां निर्म्ममे प्रथमान्मुखात्।
यजूंषि त्रैष्टुभं छन्दस्तोमं पञ्चदशं तथा॥
बृहत्साम तथोक्थञ्च दक्षिणादसृजन्मुखात्।
सामानि जागतं छन्दस्तोमं§ सप्तदशं तथा।
वैरूपमतिरात्रं च पश्चिमादसृजन्मुखात्॥
एकविंशमथर्वाणमाप्तोर्यामाणमेव च¶।
अनुष्टुभं सवैराजमुत्तरादसृजन्मुखात्॥
उच्चावचानि भूतानि गात्रेभ्यस्तस्य जज्ञिरे।
ब्रह्मणो हि प्रजासर्गं सृजतस्तु प्रजापतेः‖।
यक्षान् पिशाचान् गन्धर्वांस्तथैवाप्सरसः शुभाः॥

---

* मूलिन्य इति E, F and H.

† ऋतश्चैव इति D.

‡ औद्गात्रञ्च ऋचश्चैव त्रिष्टुप्साम रथन्तरम् इति C.

§ जगतीच्छन्दस्तोमं इति B.

¶ माप्तोर्यामानमेव च इति B, D, E, F and H.

‖ अनुष्टुभमित्यारभ्य प्रजापतेरित्यन्तं C पुस्तके नास्ति।

सृष्ट्वा चतुष्टयं सर्गं देवर्षिपितृमानुषम्* ।
ततोऽसृजच्च† भूतानि स्थावराणि चराणि च ।
नरकिन्नररक्षांसि वयःपशुमृगोरगान् ।
अव्ययं च व्ययं चैव द्वयं स्थावरजङ्गमम् ॥
तेषां ये यानि कर्म्माणि प्राक् सृष्टेः प्रतिपेदिरे ।
तान्येव ते प्रपद्यन्ते सृज्यमानाः पुनः पुनः ॥
हिंस्राहिंस्रे मृदुक्रूरे धर्म्माधर्म्मावृतानृते ।
तद्भाविताः‡ प्रपद्यन्ते तस्मात्तत्तस्य रोचते ॥
महाभूतेषु नानात्वमिन्द्रियार्थेषु मूर्त्तिषु ।
विनियोगं च भूतानां धातैव§ व्यदधात्स्वयम् ।
नामरूपं च भूतानां प्राकृतानां प्रपञ्चनम्¶ ।
वेदशब्देभ्य एवादौ‖ निर्म्ममे स महेश्वरः ॥

---

* देवर्षिपितृमानवम् इति B. सदेवासुरमानवम् इति C. देवर्षिपितृमानवान् इति D.

† ततोऽसृजत इति A. ततोऽसृजत्स इति D.

‡ उद्भाविता इति C.

§ तथैव इति C and D.

¶ दृष्टानाञ्च प्रपञ्चनम् इति B. कृतानाञ्च प्रपञ्चनम् इति C. नृणां ये पञ्चभूतानां प्राकृतानां प्रपञ्चनम् इति D.

‖ वेदशब्दापशब्दौ च इति A, E, F and H.

आर्षाणि चैव नामानि याश्च वेदेषु दृष्टय:* ।
शर्व्वर्य्यन्ते प्रसूतानां† तान्येवैभ्यो ददात्यज: ॥
यावन्ति प्रतिलिङ्गानि‡ नानारूपाणि पर्य्यये ।
दृश्यन्ते तानि तान्येव तथा भावा युगादिषु ॥

इति श्रीकूर्म्मपुराणे सप्तमोऽध्याय: ।

* दृष्टय इति A, C, E, F and H.

† शर्व्वर्य्यन्ते च भूतानाम् इति B.

‡ यथार्त्तावृतुलिङ्गानि इति E, F and H. यथा ऋतौ नानारूपाणि ऋतु-लिङ्गानि सन्ति तानि तानि पर्य्यये पुनर्व्वत्सरान्तरे दृश्यन्ते च इत्यर्थ: ।

अष्टमोऽध्यायः ।

कूर्म उवाच ।

एवं भूतानि सृष्टानि स्थावराणि चराणि च ॥

यदास्य ताः* प्रजाः सृष्टा न व्यवर्द्धन्त धीमतः ।

तमोमात्रावृतो† ब्रह्मा तदाशोचत दुःखितः ॥

ततः स विदधे‡ बुद्धिमर्थनिश्चयगामिनीम् ॥

अथात्मनि§ समद्राक्षीत्तमोमात्रां नियामिकाम् ।

रजः सत्वं च संवृत्तं वर्त्तमानं स्वधर्म्मतः ॥

तमस्तु व्यनुदत्पश्चाद्रजः सत्वेन संयुतः¶ ।

तत्तमः प्रतिनुन्नं‖ वै मिथुनं समजायत ॥

अधर्माचरणो** विप्रा हिंसा चाशुभलक्षणा ।

---

* यदा तस्य इति B. यदा चास्य इति C.

† तमोमयोवृतः इति B.

‡ संविदधे इति B.

§ तथात्मनि इति A, E, F and H.

¶ संवृतः इति B.

‖ प्रतिलभं इति B प्रतिभानुस्रमिति D.

** अधर्म्माचरणमेव इति अधर्म्माचरणः । स्वार्थे षण् । "क्वचित् स्वार्थिकाः प्रकृतितो लिङ्गवचनान्यतिवर्त्तन्ते" राक्षसवत् इति मृग्यम् ।

स्वां तनुं स ततो* ब्रह्मा तामपोहत भास्वराम्† ॥
द्विधाकरोत्पुनर्द्देहमर्द्धेन पुरुषोऽभवत् ।
अर्द्धेन नारी पुरुषो‡ विराजमसृजत्प्रभुः ॥
नारीं च§ शतरूपाख्यां योगिनीं ससृजे शुभाम् ।
सा दिवं पृथिवीं चैव महिम्ना व्याप्य संस्थिता¶ ।
योगैश्वर्य्यबलोपेता ज्ञानविज्ञानसंयुता ॥
योऽभवत्पुरुषात्पुत्रो विराड़्व्यक्तजन्मनः ।
स्वायंभुवो मनुर्द्देवः सोऽभवत्पुरुषो मुनिः ॥
सा देवी शतरूपाख्या तपः कृत्वा सुदुश्चरम्‖ ।
भर्त्तारं दीप्तयशसं** मनुमेवान्वपद्यत ॥
तस्माच्च शतरूपा सा पुत्रद्वयमसूयत ।
प्रियव्रतोत्तानपादौ कन्याद्वयमनुत्तमम् ॥
तयोः प्रसूतिं दक्षाय मनुः कन्यां ददे†† पुनः ॥

---

* सततं इति B.

† भासुरामिति C and D.

‡ पुरुषात् इति B.

§ तां नारीमिति C and D.

¶ तिष्ठति इति B.

‖ सुदुस्तरम् इति B.

** ब्रह्मणः पुत्रं इति B.

†† ददौ इति B.

प्रजापतिरथाकूतिं मानसो* जगृहे रुचिः ।
आकूत्या मिथुनं जज्ञे मानसस्य रुचेः शुभम्† ।
यज्ञश्च दक्षिणा चैव याभ्यां संवर्द्धितं जगत्‡ ॥
यज्ञस्य दक्षिणायां च पुत्रा द्वादश जज्ञिरे ।
यामा इति समाख्याता देवाः स्वायंभुवेऽन्तरे ॥
प्रसूत्यां च तथा दक्षश्चतस्रो विंशतिं तथा ।
ससर्ज्ज कन्या नामानि तासां सम्यक् निबोधत ।
श्रद्धा लक्ष्मीर्धृतिस्तुष्टिः पुष्टिर्मेधा क्रिया तथा§ ॥
बुद्धिर्लज्जा वपुः शान्तिः¶ सिद्धिः कीर्त्तिस्त्रयोदशी ।
पत्न्यर्थं प्रतिजग्राह धर्म्मो दाक्षायणीः शुभाः‖ ॥
ताभ्यः शिष्टा यवीयस्य एकादश सुलोचनाः ।
ख्यातिः सत्यथ संभूतिः स्मृतिः प्रीतिः क्षमा तथा ।
सन्ततिश्चानसूया** च ऊर्ज्जा स्वाहा स्वधा तथा ॥

---

* मनसा इति C and D.

† सुतः इति C and D.

‡ इदं श्लोकार्द्धं D पुस्तके नास्ति ।

§ तथा क्रिया इति B, C and D.

¶ कान्तिः इति B.

‖ प्रभुरिति D.

** सन्नतिश्चानसूया इति B.

भृगुर्भवो* मरीचिश्च तथा चैवाङ्गिरा मुनिः।
पुलस्त्यः पुलहश्चैव क्रतुः परमधर्म्मवित्।
अत्रिर्वसिष्ठो वह्निश्च पितरश्च† यथाक्रमम्।
ख्यात्याद्या जगृहुः कन्या मुनयो ज्ञानसत्तमाः॥
श्रद्धाया आत्मजः कामो दर्पो लक्ष्मीसुतः स्मृतः।
धृत्यास्तु नियमः पुत्रस्तुष्ट्याः सन्तोष उच्यते॥
पुष्ट्या लाभः‡ सुतश्चापि मेधापुत्रः शमस्तथा।
क्रियायाश्चाभवत्पुत्रो दण्डश्च नय एव च§॥
बुद्ध्या बोधः सुतस्तद्वदप्रमादोऽप्यजायत¶।
लज्जाया विनयः पुत्रो वपुषो व्यवसायकः॥
क्षेमः शान्तिसुतश्चापि सिद्धः‖ सिद्धेरजायत।
यशः कीर्त्तिसुतस्तद्वदित्येते धर्म्मसूनवः॥
कामस्य हर्षः पुत्रोऽभूद्देवानन्दोऽप्यजायत**।
इत्येष वै सुखोदर्कः सर्गो धर्म्मस्य कीर्त्तितः॥

---

* भग इति B.

† पतयश्च इति G.

‡ लोभ इति C and D.

§ क्रियायामभवत् पुत्रो दण्डः समय उच्यते इति C and D.

¶ व्यजायत इति B.

‖ सुखमिति C and D.

** पुत्रो वै वेदानन्दो व्यजायत इति B.

जज्ञे हिंसा त्वधर्म्माद्वै निकृतिं चानृतं सुतम्।
निकृते*स्तनयो† जज्ञे भयं नरकमेव च॥
माया च वेदना चैव मिथुनं त्विदमेतयोः।
भयाज्जज्ञेऽथ‡ वै माया मृत्युं भूतापहारिणम्॥
वेदना च सुतं चापि दुःखं जज्ञेऽथ रौरवात्।
मृत्योर्व्याधिर्जराशोकौ तृष्णा क्रोधश्च§ जज्ञिरे॥
दुःखोत्तराः स्मृता ह्येते सर्वे चाधर्म्मलक्षणाः।
नैषां भार्य्यास्ति पुत्रो वा सर्वे ते ह्यूर्द्ध्वरेतसः॥
इत्येष तामसः सर्गो जज्ञे धर्म्मनियामकः।
संक्षेपेण मया प्रोक्ता विसृष्टिर्मुनिपुङ्गवाः॥

इति श्रीकूर्म्मपुराणे मुख्यादिसर्गकथने अष्टमोऽध्यायः।

---

* निकृत्यास्तु सुत इति C and D.

† निकृत्यनृतयोः इति B.

‡ जज्ञे जनयामास इत्यर्थः, अन्तर्भूतः प्रेरणार्थः, यथा कुमारसम्भवे "अनुग्रहं संस्मरणप्रवृत्तं, इच्छामि संवर्द्धितुमाज्ञया ते" इति।

§ व्याधिजराशोकतृष्णाक्रोधाश्च इति B.

नवमोऽध्यायः।

सूत उवाच।

एतच्छ्रुत्वा तु वचनं नारदाद्या महर्षयः।
प्रणम्य वरदं विष्णुं पप्रच्छुः संशयान्विताः॥

मुनय ऊचुः।

कथितो भवता सर्गो मुख्यादीनां जनार्द्दन।
इदानीं संशयं चेममस्माकं छेत्तुमर्हसि॥
कथं स भगवानीशः पूर्व्वजोऽपि पिनाकधृक्।
पुत्रत्वमगमच्छंभुर्ब्रह्मणोऽव्यक्तजन्मनः॥
कथं च भगवाञ्जज्ञे ब्रह्मा लोकपितामहः*।
अण्डतो† जगतामीशस्तन्नो वक्तुमिहार्हसि॥

कूर्म्म उवाच।

शृणुध्वमृषयः सर्वे शङ्करस्यामितौजसः।
पुत्रत्वं ब्रह्मणस्तस्य पद्मयोनित्वमेव च॥
अतीतकल्पावसाने‡ तमोभूतं जगत्त्रयम्।
आसीदेकार्णवं घोरं§ न देवाद्या न चर्षयः¶॥

---

* कमलसम्भवः इति B.

† अण्डजः इति E, F and H.

‡ कल्पापसरे इति C and D.

§ सर्व्वं इति B, C and D.

¶ नारदाद्या महर्षयः इति D.

तत्र नारायणो देवो निर्ज्जने निरुपप्लवे* ।
आश्रित्य शेषशयनं सुष्वाप पुरुषोत्तमः ॥
सहस्रशीर्षा भूत्वा स सहस्राक्षः सहस्रपात् ।
सहस्रबाहुः सर्वज्ञश्चिन्त्यमानो मनीषिभिः ।
पीतवासा विशालाक्षो नीलजीमूतसन्निभः ।
ततो† विभूतियोगात्मा योगिनां तु दयापरः‡ ॥
कदाचित्तस्य सुप्तस्य लीलार्थं दिव्यमद्भुतम्§ ।
त्रैलोक्यसारं विमलं नाभ्यां पङ्कजमुद्बभौ ।
शतयोजनविस्तीर्णं तरुणादित्यसन्निभम् ।
दिव्यगन्धमयं पुण्यं कर्णिकाकेसरान्वितम् ॥
तस्यैवं सुचिरं कालं वर्त्तमानस्य शार्ङ्गिणः ।
हिरण्यगर्भो भगवांस्तं देशमुपचक्रमे ॥
स तं करेण विश्वात्मा समुत्थाप्य सनातनम् ।
प्रोवाच मधुरं वाक्यं मायया तस्य मोहितः ॥
अस्मिन्नेकार्णवे घोरे निर्जने तमसावृते ।
एकाकी को भवांश्छेते ब्रूहि मे पुरुषर्षभ ॥

---

* निर्ज्जनो निरुपप्लवः इति B.

† महा इति B, C and D.

‡ योगिनां हृदयालयः इति B, C and D

§ दिव्यमुत्तमम् इति B and D.

तस्य तद्वचनं श्रुत्वा विहस्य गरुड़ध्वजः।
उवाच देवं ब्रह्माणं मेघगम्भीरनिःस्वनः॥
भो भो नारायणं देवलोकानां* प्रभवाव्ययम्।
महायोगीश्वरं मां वै† जानीहि पुरुषोत्तमम्॥
मयि पश्य जगत्कृत्स्नं त्वं च लोकपितामहः‡।
सपर्व्वतमहाद्वीपं समुद्रैः सप्तभिर्वृतम्॥
एवमाभाष्य विश्वात्मा प्रोवाच पुरुषं हरिः।
जानन्नपि महायोगी को भवानिति वेधसम्॥
ततः प्रहस्य भगवान् ब्रह्मा वेदनिधिः प्रभुः।
प्रत्युवाचाम्बुजाभाक्षं सस्मितं श्लक्ष्णया गिरा॥
अहं धाता विधाता च स्वयम्भूः प्रपितामहः।
मय्येव संस्थितं विश्वं ब्रह्माहं विश्वतोमुखः॥
श्रुत्वा वाचं स भगवान्विष्णुः§ सत्यपराक्रमः।
अनुज्ञाप्याथ¶ योगेन प्रविष्टो ब्रह्मणस्तनुम्॥

---

* देवं लोकानां इति B, E, F and H.

† त्वं इति B.

‡ त्वां च लोकपितामहम् इति B and D.

§ श्रुत्वेत्थं भगवान् विष्णुः सत्यः सत्यपराक्रमः इति D.

¶ अनुज्ञयाथ इति E, F and H.

त्रैलोक्यमेतत्सकलं सदेवासुरमानुषम्।
उदरे तस्य देवस्य दृष्ट्वा विस्मयमागतः* ॥
तदास्य वक्त्रान्निष्क्रम्य पन्नगेन्द्रनिकेतनः।
अथापि भगवान्विष्णुः† पितामहमथाब्रवीत् ॥
भवानप्येवमेवाद्य शाश्वतं हि ममोदरम्।
प्रविश्य लोकान्पश्यैतान्विचित्रान्पुरुषर्षभ ॥
ततः प्रह्लादिनीं वाणीं श्रुत्वा तस्याभिनन्द्य च।
श्रीपतेरुदरम्भूयः प्रविवेश कुशध्वजः ॥
तानेव लोकान्गर्भस्थानपश्यत्सत्यविक्रमः।
पर्यटित्वाथ‡ देवस्य ददृशेऽन्तं न वै हरेः§ ॥
ततो द्वाराणि सर्वाणि पिहितानि महात्मना।
जनार्द्दनेन ब्रह्मासौ नाभ्यां द्वारमविन्दत ॥
तत्र योगबलेनासौ प्रविश्य कनकाण्डजः।
उज्जहारात्मनो रूपं पुष्कराच्चतुराननः ॥
विरराजारविन्दस्थः¶ पद्मगर्भसमद्युतिः।
ब्रह्मा स्वयंभूर्भगवाञ्जगद्योनिः पितामहः ॥

---

* विस्मयमागमत् इति B.

† अजातश्मश्रुर्भगवान् इति B.

‡ पर्य्यटित्वा पर्य्यट्य इति साधु। आर्षः यप्प्रत्ययाभावः।

§ ददृशे तत्र वै हरेः इति B.

¶ विरराजारविन्देऽस्मिन् इति D.

स मन्यमानो विश्वेशमात्मानं परमं पदम् ।
प्रोवाच विष्णुं पुरुषं मेघगम्भीरया गिरा ॥
कृतं किं भवतेदानीमात्मनो जयकांक्षया* ।
एकोऽहं प्रबलो नान्यो मा वै कोऽभिभविष्यति† ॥
श्रुत्वा नारायणो वाक्यं ब्रह्मणोक्तमतन्द्रितः‡ ।
सान्त्वपूर्वमिदं वाक्यं बभाषे मधुरं हरिः ॥
भवान्धाता विधाता च स्वयंभूः प्रपितामहः ।
न मात्सर्याभियोगेन§ द्वाराणि पिहितानि मे ॥
किन्तु लीलार्थमेवैतन्न त्वां बाधितुमिच्छया ।
को हि बाधितुमन्विच्छेद्देवदेवं पितामहम्¶ ॥
न हि त्वं बाध्यसे ब्रह्मन्‖ मान्यो हि सर्वथा भवान् ।
मम क्षमस्व कल्याण** यन्मयापकृतं तव ॥

---

* भवतैवाद्य नन्मनोजयकाङ्क्षया इति D.

† मां हि कोऽभिभविष्यति इति B. समानोऽपि च विद्यते इति D.

‡ ब्रह्मणो लोकमन्त्रिणः इति D. ब्रह्मणः परमेष्ठिनः इति G. मन्त्रिणः परमेष्ठिन- इति E, F and H.

§ त्वन्मात्सर्य्याभियोगेन इति D.

¶ श्लोकोऽयं D पुस्तके नास्ति ।

‖ न तेऽन्यथावमन्तव्यमिति B, C and D.

** मम मर्षय कल्याणं यन्मयापहृतं तव इति B and G. सर्व्वमन्वयकल्याण- मिति C. सर्व्वधर्म्मैककल्याण इति D.

अस्माच्च कारणाद्ब्रह्मन्पुत्रो भवतु मे भवान्।
पद्मयोनिरिति ख्यातो मत्प्रियार्थं जगन्मय॥
ततः स भगवान्देवो वरं दत्त्वा किरीटिने।
प्रहर्षमतुलं गत्वा पुनर्विष्णुमभाषत॥
भवान्सर्व्वात्मकोऽनन्तः सर्वेषां परमेश्वरः।
सर्वभूतान्तरात्मा वै परं ब्रह्म सनातनम्॥
अहं वै सर्वलोकानामात्मालोको महेश्वरः* ।
मन्मयं सर्व्वमेवेदं ब्रह्मणः पुरुषः परः† ॥
नावाभ्यां विद्यते ह्यन्यो लोकानां परमेश्वरः।
एका मूर्तिर्द्विधा भिन्ना नारायणपितामहौ‡ ॥
तेनैवमुक्तो ब्रह्माणं वासुदेवोऽब्रवीदिदम्।
इयं प्रतिज्ञा भवतो विनाशाय भविष्यति॥
किं न पश्यसि योगेन§ ब्रह्माधिपतिमव्ययम्।
प्रधानपुरुषेशानं वेदाहं परमेश्वरम्॥
यं न पश्यन्ति योगीन्द्राः सांख्या अपि महेश्वरम्।
अनादिनिधनं ब्रह्म तमेव शरणं व्रज॥

---

* मात्मा लोकपितामहः इति B.

† ब्रह्माहं पुरुषः परः इति B. ब्रह्माख्यं पुरुषर्षभ इति C and D.

‡ एकोऽस्मीति द्विधा भिन्नौ इति E, F, G and H.

§ योगेशमिति B.　देवेशमिति D.

ततः क्रुद्धोऽम्बुजाभाक्षं ब्रह्मा प्रोवाच केशवम्।
भगवन्नूनमात्मानं* वेद्मि तत्परमाक्षरम्॥
ब्रह्माणं जगतामेकमात्मानं परमं पदम्।
नावाभ्यां विद्यते त्वन्यो लोकानां परमेश्वरः॥
संत्यज्य निद्रां विपुलां स्वमात्मानं विलोकय।
तस्य तत्क्रोधजं वाक्यं श्रुत्वापि† स तदा प्रभुः॥
मा मैवं वद कल्याण परिवादं महात्मनः।
न मे ह्यविदितं ब्रह्मन् नान्यथाहं वदामि ते॥
किन्तु मोहयति ब्रह्मन्ननन्ता‡ पारमेश्वरी।
मायाशेषविशेषाणां हेतुरात्मसमुद्भवा॥
एतावदुक्त्वा भगवान्विष्णुस्तूष्णीं बभूव ह।
ज्ञात्वा तत्परमं तत्त्वं स्वमात्मानं सुरेश्वरः§॥
कुतो ह्यपरिमेयात्मा भूतानां परमेश्वरः।
प्रसादं ब्रह्मणे कर्त्तुं प्रादुरासीत्ततो हरः॥
ललाटनयनो देवो¶ जटामण्डलमण्डितः।
त्रिशूलपाणिर्भगवान्तेजसां परमो निधिः॥

---

* भवान्न नूनमात्मानं विन्देत परमेश्वर इति B and D.

† श्रुत्वा विष्णुरभाषत इति B, C and D.

‡ भवन्तमिति B, C and D.

§ महेश्वरमिति B, C and D.

¶ ऽनन्त इति B, C and D.

विद्याविलास*ग्रथितां ग्रहैः सार्केन्दुतारकैः ।
मालामत्यद्भुताकारां धारयन्पादलम्बिनीम् ॥
तं दृष्ट्वा देवमीशानं ब्रह्मा लोकपितामहः ।
मोहितो माययात्यर्थं पीतवाससमब्रवीत् ॥
क एष पुरुषो नीलः† शूलपाणिस्त्रिलोचनः ।
तेजोराशिरमेयात्मा समायाति‡ जनार्दन ॥
तस्य तद्वचनं श्रुत्वा विष्णुर्दानवमर्दनः ।
अपश्यदीश्वरं देवं ज्वलन्तं विमलेऽम्भसि§ ॥
ज्ञात्वा तं परमं भावमैश्वरं ब्रह्मभावनः¶ ।
प्रोवाचोत्थाय भगवान्देवदेवं पितामहम् ॥
अयं देवो महादेवः स्वयं ज्योतिः सनातनः ।
अनादिनिधनोऽचिन्त्यो लोकानामीश्वरो महान् ॥
शङ्करः शम्भुरीशानः सर्वात्मा परमेश्वरः ।
भूतानामधिपो योगी महेशो विमलः शिवः ॥

---

* दिव्यां विशालां ग्रथितामिति C and D.

† पुरुषोऽनन्त इति B and D.

‡ समायातः इति D.

§ जटिलं तमथाम्भसि इति D.

¶ ब्रह्मभावितः इति B.

एष धाता विधाता च प्रधानप्रभुरव्ययः* ।
यं प्रपश्यन्ति यतयो ब्रह्मभावेन भाविताः† ॥
सृजत्येष जगत्कृत्स्नं पाति संहरते तथा ।
कालो भूत्वा महादेवः केवलो निष्कलः शिवः ॥
ब्रह्माणं विदधे पूर्वं भवन्तं यः सनातनः ।
वेदांश्च प्रददौ तुभ्यं सोऽयमायाति शङ्करः ॥
अस्यैव चापरां मूर्त्तिं विश्वयोनिं सनातनीम् ।
वासुदेवाभिधानं मामवेहि प्रपितामह ॥
किं न पश्यसि योगेशं ब्रह्माधिपतिमव्ययम् ।
दिव्यं भवतु ते चक्षुर्येन द्रक्ष्यसि तत्परम्‡ ॥
लब्ध्वा चैवं तदा चक्षुर्विष्णोर्लोकपितामहः ।
बुबुधे परमं§ ज्ञानं पुरतः समवस्थितम् ॥
स लब्ध्वा परमं ज्ञानमैश्वरं प्रपितामहः ।
प्रपेदे शरणं देवं तमेव पितरं शिवम् ॥
ओङ्कारं समनुस्मृत्य संस्तभ्यात्मानमात्मना ।
अथर्वशिरसा देवं तुष्टाव च कृताञ्जलिः ॥

---

* पुरुषेश्वरः इति B, C and D.

† भवितुमिति C and D.

‡ तत्पदम् इति B.

§ परमीशानमिति B, परमेशानमिति C and D.

संस्तुतस्तेन भगवान्* ब्रह्मणा परमेश्वरः।
अवाप परमां प्रीतिं व्याजहार स्मयन्निव† ॥
मत्समस्त्वं न सन्देहो वत्स भक्तश्च मे भवान्‡।
मयैवोत्पादितः पूर्वं लोकसृष्ट्यर्थमव्ययः॥
त्वमात्मा ह्यादिपुरुषो मम देहसमुद्भवः।
वरं वरय विश्वात्मन्वरदोऽहं तवानघ॥
स देवदेववचनं निशम्य कमलोद्भवः।
निरीक्ष्य विष्णुं पुरुषं प्रणम्योवाच शङ्करम्§॥
भगवन्भूतभव्येश महादेवाम्बिकापते।
त्वामेव पुत्रमिच्छामि त्वया वा सदृशं सुतम्॥
मोहितोऽस्मि महादेव मायया सूक्ष्मया त्वया।
न जाने परमं भावं याथातथ्येन ते शिव¶॥
त्वमेव देव भक्तानां माता भ्राता पिता सुहृत्।
प्रसीद तव पादाब्जं नमामि शरणागतः॥
स तस्य वचनं श्रुत्वा जगन्नाथो वृषध्वजः।
व्याजहार तदा पुत्रं समालोक्य जनार्दनम्॥

---

* देवेन इति B.

† स्मयन्निव स्मितं कुर्वन्निव इत्यर्थः। स्मयन्नित्यार्षं स्मयमानः।

‡ मद्भक्तश्च यतो भवान् इति B.

§ प्रणम्याह वृषध्वजमिति B.

¶ तेऽनघ इति B.

यदर्थितं भगवता तत्करिष्यामि पुत्रक ।
विज्ञानमैश्वरं दिव्यमुत्पत्स्यति तवानघम्* ॥
त्वमेव सर्व्वभूतानामादिकर्त्ता नियोजितः ।
कुरुष्व तेषु देवेश† मायां लोकपितामह ॥
एष नारायणो मत्तो‡ ममैव परमा तनुः ।
भविष्यति तवेशान योगक्षेमवहो§ हरिः ॥
एवं व्याहृत्य हस्ताभ्यां प्रीतः स¶ परमेश्वरः ।
संस्पृश्य देवं ब्रह्माणं‖ हरिं वचनमब्रवीत् ॥
तुष्टोऽस्मि सर्व्वथाहं ते भक्तस्त्वं च** जगन्मय ।
वरं वृणीष्व नावाभ्यामन्योऽस्ति परमार्थतः†† ॥

---

* उत्पत्स्यतीत्यत्र आत्मनेपदमार्षम् । तवानघ इति B.

† तथा कुरुष्व देवेश इति B, C and D.

‡ नारायणोऽनन्त इति B.

§ योगक्षेमवहः—अलब्धस्य लाभो योगः, लब्धस्य परिरक्षणं क्षेमं तयोर्निर्व्वाहक इत्यर्थः ।

¶ प्रीतात्मा इति B.

‖ ततो नारायणः साक्षादिति D. अतः पूर्व्वं श्लोकार्द्धत्रयं D पुस्तके नास्ति ।

** भक्त्या तव इति B.

†† न ह्यावां विभिन्नौ परमार्थतः इति B.

श्रुत्वाथ देववचनं विष्णुर्विश्वमयं जगत्* ।
प्राह प्रसन्नया वाचा समालोक्य च तन्मुखम्† ॥
एष एव वरः श्लाघ्यो यदहं परमेश्वरम् ।
पश्यामि परमात्मानं भक्तिर्भवतु मे त्वयि ॥
तथेत्युक्त्वा महादेवः पुनर्विष्णुमभाषत ।
भवान् सर्वस्य कार्यस्य कर्त्ताहमधिदैवतम्‡ ॥
त्वन्मयं मन्मयं चैव सर्वमेतन्न संशयः ।
भवान् सोमस्त्वहं सूर्यो भवान्रात्रिरहं दिनम् ॥
भवान् प्रकृतिरव्यक्तमहं पुरुषएव च ।
भवान् ज्ञानमहं ज्ञाता भवान्मायाहमीश्वरः ॥
भवान्विद्यात्मिका§ शक्तिः शक्तिमानहमीश्वरः ।
योऽहं स निष्कलो देवः सोऽसि नारायणः प्रभुः ॥
एकीभावेन पश्यन्ति योगिनो ब्रह्मवादिनः ।
त्वामनाश्रित्य¶ विश्वात्मन्न योगी मामुपैष्यति ॥
पालयैतज्जगत्कृत्स्नं सदेवासुरमानुषम् ॥

---

* विश्वजगन्मयः इति B, C and D.

† समालोक्य चतुर्म्मुखमिति C and D.

‡ कर्त्ता हर्त्ताधिदैवतमिति C and D.

§ चिदात्मिका इति D.

¶ त्वामनादृत्य इति D.

इतीदमुक्त्वा भगवाननादिः
स्वमायया मोहितभूतभेदः ।
जगाम जन्मर्द्धिविनाशहीनं*
धामैकमव्यक्तमनन्तशक्तिः ॥

इति श्रीकूर्म्मपुराणे पद्मोद्भवप्रादुर्भावे नवमोऽध्यायः ।

---

* जन्मस्थितिनाशहीनमिति C and D.

दशमोऽध्यायः ।

कूर्म्म उवाच ।

गते महेश्वरे देवे भूयएव* पितामहः ।
तदेव सुमहत्पद्मं भेजे नाभिसमुत्थितम् ॥
अथ दीर्घेण कालेन तत्राप्रतिमपौरुषौ ।
महासुरौ समायातौ भ्रातरौ मधुकैटभौ ॥
क्रोधेन महताविष्टौ महापर्वतविग्रहौ ।
कर्णान्तरसमुद्भूतौ देवदेवस्य शार्ङ्गिणः ॥
तावागतौ समीक्ष्याह नारायणमजो विभुः† ।
त्रैलोक्यकण्टकावेतावसुरौ हन्तुमर्हसि ॥
तदस्य वचनं श्रुत्वा हरिर्नारायणः प्रभुः ।
आज्ञापयामास तयोर्वधार्थं पुरुषावुभौ ॥
तदाज्ञया महद्युद्धं तयोस्ताभ्यामभूद्द्विजाः‡ ।
व्यजयत्कैटभं जिष्णुः विष्णुश्च व्यजयन्मधुम् ॥
ततः पद्मासनासीनं जगन्नाथः पितामहम् ।
बभाषे मधुरं वाक्यं स्नेहाविष्टमना हरिः ॥

---

* सोऽधिवासमिति B and C. स विशालमिति D.

† नारायणमथो विभुः इति G.

‡ तयोरासीत् समाः शतम् इति D.

अस्मान्मयोह्यमानस्त्वं पश्चादवतर प्रभो।
नाहं भवन्तं शक्नोमि वोढुं* तेजोमयं गुरुम्॥
ततोऽवतीर्य विश्वात्मा देहमाविश्य चक्रिणः।
अवाप वैष्णवीं निद्रामेकीभूतोऽथ† विष्णुना॥
सह तेन तयाविश्य‡ शङ्खचक्रगदाधरः।
ब्रह्मा नारायणाख्योऽसौ सुष्वाप सलिले तदा॥
सोऽनुभूय चिरं कालमानन्दं परमात्मनः।
अनाद्यनन्तमद्वैतं स्वात्मानं ब्रह्मसंज्ञितम्॥
ततः प्रभाते योगात्मा भूत्वा देवश्चतुर्मुखः।
ससर्ज्ज सृष्टिं तद्रूपां वैष्णवं भावमाश्रितः॥
पुरस्तादसृजद्देवः सनन्दं सनकं तथा।
ऋभुं सनत्कुमारं च पूर्वजं तं§ सनातनम्॥
ते द्वन्द्वमोहनिर्मुक्ताः परं वैराग्यमास्थिताः।
विदित्वा परमं भावं ज्ञाने विदधिरे मतिम्¶॥

---

* सोढुमिति D.

† मेकीभूयाथ इति B.

‡ सहस्रशीर्षनयन इति B and C. सहस्रशीर्षस्तनय इति D.

§ पूर्वजन्तु इति B.

¶ न सृष्टौ दधिरे मतिमिति B, C and D.

तेष्वेवं निरपेक्षेषु लोकसृष्टौ पितामहः ।
बभूव नष्टचेता वै मायया परमेष्ठिनः* ॥
ततः पुराणपुरुषो जगन्मूर्त्तिः सनातनः ।
व्याजहारात्मनः पुत्रं मोहनाशाय पद्मजम् ॥

विष्णुरुवाच ।

कच्चिन्नु† विस्मृतो देवः शूलपाणिः सनातनः ।
यदुक्तो वै पुरा शम्भुः पुत्रत्वे भव शङ्करः‡ ॥
अवाप संज्ञां§ गोविन्दात्पद्मयोनिः पितामहः ।
प्रजाः स्रष्टुं मनश्चक्रे तपः परमदुस्तरम्¶ ॥
तस्यैवं तप्यमानस्य न किञ्चित्समवर्त्तत ।
ततो दीर्घेण कालेन दुःखात्क्रोधोऽभ्यजायत ॥
क्रोधाविष्टस्य नेत्राभ्यां प्रापतन्नश्रुबिन्दवः ।
ततस्तेभ्यः समुद्भूताः‖ भूताः प्रेतास्तदाभवन् ॥
सर्वांस्तानग्रतो दृष्ट्वा ब्रह्मात्मानमविन्दत** ।
जहौ प्राणांश्च भगवान् क्रोधाविष्टः प्रजापतिः ॥

---

* परिवेष्टित इति B.

† कच्चिन्न इति B, C and D.

‡ यदुक्तवानात्मनोऽसौ पुत्रत्वे तव शङ्करः इति B.

§ प्रयुक्तवान् मनो योऽसौ पुत्रत्वेन तु शङ्करः । अवाप्तसंज्ञः इति D.

¶ प्रजाः स्रष्टुमनास्तेपे तपः परमदुश्चरम् इति B.

‖ ततस्तेभ्योऽश्रुबिन्दुभ्य इति B.

** मनिन्दत इति D.

तदा प्राणमयो रुद्रः प्रादुरासीत्प्रभोर्मुखात्।
सहस्रादित्यसङ्काशो युगान्तदहनोपमः॥
रुरोद सुस्वरङ्घोरं देवदेवः स्वयं शिवः।
रोदमानं* ततो ब्रह्मा मा रोदीरित्यभाषत॥
रोदनाद्रुद्र इत्येवं लोके ख्यातिं गमिष्यसि।
अन्यानि सप्त नामानि पत्नीः पुत्रांश्च शाश्वतान्॥
स्थानानि तेषामष्टानां ददौ लोकपितामहः।
भवः शर्वस्तथेशानः पशूनां पतिरेव च।
भीमश्चोग्रो महादेवस्तानि नामानि सप्त वै॥
सूर्यो जलं मही वह्निर्वायुराकाशमेव च।
दीक्षितो ब्राह्मणश्चन्द्र इत्येता अष्टमूर्त्तयः॥
स्थानेष्वेतेषु ये रुद्राञ्ध्यायन्ति प्रणमन्ति च।
तेषामष्टतनुर्देवो† ददाति परमं पदम्॥
सुवर्च्चला तथैवोमा‡ विकेशी च शिवा तथा।
स्वाहा दिशश्च दीक्षा च रोहिणी चेति पत्नयः§॥
शनैश्चरस्तथा शुक्रो लोहिताङ्गो मनोजवः।
स्कन्दः सर्गोऽथ सन्तानो बुधश्चैषां सुताः स्मृताः॥

---

* आर्षमात्मनेपदित्वं भौवादिकत्वञ्च।

† माद्या तनुरिति E and F.

‡ वीषा इति E and H.

§ पत्नय: इत्यार्षम्।

एवम्प्रकारो भगवान्देवदेवो महेश्वरः।
प्रजा धर्म्मञ्च कामञ्च त्यक्त्वा वैराग्यमाश्रितः॥
आत्मन्याधाय चात्मानमैश्वरं भावमास्थितः।
पीत्वा तदक्षरं ब्रह्म शाश्वतं परमामृतम्॥
प्रजाः सृजेति चादिष्टो ब्रह्मणा नीललोहितः।
स्वात्मना सदृशानुद्रान्* ससर्ज्ज मनसा शिवः॥
कपर्द्दिनो निरातङ्कान्नीलकण्ठान् पिनाकिनः।
त्रिशूलहस्तानुद्रिक्तान् सदानन्दांस्त्रिलोचनान्॥
जरामरणनिर्मुक्तान् महावृषभवाहनान्।
वीतरागांश्च सर्व्वज्ञान् कोटिकोटिशतान्प्रभुः॥
तान्दृष्ट्वा विविधानुद्रान्निर्म्मलान्नीललोहितान्।
जरामरणनिर्मुक्तान् व्याजहार हरं गुरुः॥
मा स्राक्षीरीदृशीर्देव प्रजा मृत्युविवर्ज्जिताः।
अन्याः सृजस्व† भूतेश जन्ममृत्युसमन्विताः॥
ततस्तमाह भगवान् कपर्द्दी कामशासनः।
नास्ति मे तादृशः सर्गः‡ सृज त्वं विविधाः§ प्रजाः॥

---

* सदृशान् पुत्रानिति B.

† आत्मनेपदमार्षम्। सृजस्व देवेश इति B.

‡ तादृशी शक्तिरिति D.

§ सृज त्वमशुभाः इति B.

ततः प्रभृति देवोऽसौ न प्रसूते शुभाः प्रजाः ।
स्वात्मजैरेव* तैरुद्रैर्निवृत्तात्मा ह्यतिष्ठत† ॥
स्थाणुत्वं तेन तस्यासीद्देवदेवस्य शूलिनः ॥
ज्ञानं वैराग्यमैश्वर्यं तपः सत्यं क्षमा धृतिः ।
द्रष्टृत्वमात्मसंबोधो ह्यधिष्ठातृत्वमेव च ।
अव्ययानि दशैतानि नित्यं तिष्ठन्ति शङ्करे ॥
एवं स शङ्करः साक्षात्पिनाकी परमेश्वरः ॥
ततः स भगवान् ब्रह्मा वीक्ष्य देवं त्रिलोचनम् ।
सहैव मानसै रुद्रैः प्रीतिविस्फारलोचनः ।
ज्ञात्वा परतरं भावमैश्वरं ज्ञानचक्षुषा ।
तुष्टाव जगतामीशं कृत्वा शिरसि चाञ्जलिम् ॥

ब्रह्मोवाच ।

नमस्तेऽस्तु महादेव नमस्ते परमेश्वर ।
नमः शिवाय देवाय नमस्ते ब्रह्मरूपिणे ॥
नमोऽस्तु ते महेशाय नमः शान्ताय हेतवे ।
प्रधानपुरुषेशाय योगाधिपतये‡ नमः ॥
नमः कालाय रुद्राय महाग्रासाय शूलिने ।
नमः पिनाकहस्ताय त्रिनेत्राय नमोनमः ॥

---

* आत्मजैरपि इति B.

† व्यतिष्ठत इति B.

‡ यज्ञाधिपतये इति D.

नमस्त्रिमूर्त्तये तुभ्यं ब्रह्मणे* जनकाय ते।
ब्रह्मविद्याधिपतये ब्रह्मविद्याप्रदायिने॥
नमो वेदरहस्याय कालकालाय ते नमः।
वेदान्तसारसाराय नमो वेदात्म†मूर्त्तये॥
नमो बुद्धाय रुद्राय‡ योगिनां गुरवे नमः।
प्रहीणशोकैर्विविधैर्भूतैः परिवृताय ते॥
नमो ब्रह्मण्यदेवाय ब्रह्माधिपतये नमः।
त्र्यम्बकायादिदेवाय नमस्ते परमेष्ठिने॥
नमो दिग्वाससे तुभ्यं नमो मुण्डाय दण्डिने।
अनादिमलहीनाय ज्ञानगम्याय ते नमः॥
नमस्ताराय§ तीर्थाय नमो योगर्द्धिहेतवे।
नमो धर्म्मादिगम्याय योगगम्याय ते नमः॥
नमस्ते निष्प्रपञ्चाय निराभासाय ते नमः।
ब्रह्मणे विश्वरूपाय नमस्ते परमात्मने॥
त्वयैव सृष्टमखिलं त्वय्येव सकलं स्थितम्।
त्वया संह्रियते विश्वं प्रधानाद्यं जगन्मय॥

---

* ब्रह्मणो जनकाय इति C and D.

† वेदान्तमूर्त्तये इति B, C and D.

‡ शुद्धाय इति B, C and D.

§ ताराय—तारयतीति तारः, पचाद्यच्, तस्मै। नमस्ताराय इत्यारभ्य योगगम्याय ते नमः इत्येतदन्तं G and H पुस्तकयोर्नास्ति।

त्वमीश्वरो महादेवः परं ब्रह्म महेश्वरः ।
परमेष्ठी शिवः शान्तः पुरुषो निष्कलो हरः ॥
त्वमक्षरं परं ज्योतिस्त्वं कालः परमेश्वरः ।
त्वमेव पुरुषोऽनन्तः प्रधानं प्रकृतिस्तथा ॥
भूमिरापोऽनलो वायुर्व्योमाहङ्कार एव च ।
यस्य रूपं नमस्यामि भवन्तं ब्रह्मसंज्ञितम् ॥
यस्य द्यौरभवन्मूर्द्धा पादौ पृथ्वी दिशो भुजाः ।
आकाशमुदरं तस्मै विराजे प्रणमाम्यहम् ॥
सन्तापयति यो नित्यं स्वभाभिर्भासयन् दिशः* ।
ब्रह्मतेजोमयं विश्वं तस्मै सूर्य्यात्मने नमः ॥
हव्यं वहति यो नित्यं रौद्री तेजोमयी तनुः ।
कव्यं पितृगणानां च तस्मै वह्न्यात्मने नमः ॥
आप्याययति यो नित्यं स्वधाम्ना सकलं जगत् ।
पीयते देवतासङ्घैस्तस्मै चन्द्रात्मने† नमः ॥
बिभर्त्त्यशेषभूतानि यान्तश्चरति सर्व्वदा ।
शक्तिर्म्माहेश्वरी तुभ्यं तस्मै वाय्वात्मने नमः ॥
सृजत्यशेषमेवेदं यः स्वकर्म्मानुरूपतः ।
आत्मन्यवस्थितस्तस्मै चतुर्वक्त्रात्मने नमः‡ ॥

---

* सम्भावयति यो नित्यं स्वधाम्ना सकलं जगदिति D.

† सोमात्मने इति B.

‡ चतुर्वक्त्राय ते नम इति C.

यः शेते शेषशयने विश्वमावृत्य मायया ।
स्वात्मानुभूतियोगेन तस्मै विष्णात्मने* नमः ॥
बिभर्त्ति शिरसा नित्यं द्विसप्तभुवनात्मकम् ।
ब्रह्माण्डं योऽखिलाधारस्तस्मै शेषात्मने नमः ॥
यः परान्ते† परानन्दं पीत्वा दिव्यैकसाक्षिकम्‡ ।
नृत्यत्यनन्तमहिमा तस्मै रुद्रात्मने नमः ॥
योऽन्तरा सर्वभूतानां नियन्ता तिष्ठतीश्वरः ।
तं सर्वसाक्षिणं देवं नमस्ये§ विश्वतस्तनुम्¶ ॥
यं विनिद्रा जितश्वासाः सन्तुष्टाः समदर्शिनः|| ।
ज्योतिः पश्यन्ति युञ्जानास्तस्मै** योगात्मने नमः ॥
यया सन्तरते मायां योगी संक्षीणकल्मषः ।
अपारतरपर्य्यन्तां†† तस्मै विद्यात्मने नमः ॥

---

* विश्वात्मने नम इति E, F and H.

† परान्ते जगतां चरमे प्रलये इत्यर्थः ।

‡ दिव्हैकसाक्षिक इति E and F.

§ नमस्ये नमः करोमि । आर्षमात्मनेपदम् ।

¶ विश्वतस्तनवो यस्य अष्टमूर्त्तिमित्यर्थः । यस्य केशेषु जीमूता नद्यः सर्व्वाङ्गसन्धिषु।
कुक्षौ समुद्राश्चत्वारस्तस्मै तोयात्मने नमः ॥ इत्यतिरिक्तं D पुस्तके दृश्यते ।

|| समवर्त्तिन इति C.

** युञ्जाना योगं कुर्व्वाणा इत्यर्थः ।

†† अतिशयेन अपारः अपारतरः पर्य्यन्तः यस्यास्ताम् ।

यस्य भासा विभात्यर्कौ मही यत्तमसः* परम् ।
प्रपद्ये तत्परं तत्त्वं तद्रूपं पारमेश्वरम् ॥
नित्यानन्दं निराधारं निष्कलं परमं शिवम् ।
प्रपद्ये परमात्मानं भवन्तं परमेश्वरम् ॥
एवं स्तुत्वा महादेवं ब्रह्मा तद्भावभावितः ।
प्राञ्जलिः प्रणतस्तस्थौ गृणन् ब्रह्म सनातनम् ॥
ततस्तस्य महादेवो दिव्यं योगमनुत्तमम् ।
ऐश्वरं ब्रह्मसद्भावं वैराग्यं च ददौ† हरः ॥
कराभ्यां सुशुभाभ्यां च संस्पृश्य प्रणतार्त्तिहा ।
व्याजहार स्मयन्नेव‡ सोऽनुगृह्य पितामहम् ॥
यत्त्वयाभ्यर्थितं ब्रह्मन् पुत्रत्वे भवता मम ।
कृतं मया तत्सकलं सृजस्व विविधं जगत् ॥
त्रिधा भिन्नोऽस्म्यहं ब्रह्मन् ब्रह्मविष्णुहराख्यया ।
सर्गरक्षालयगुणैर्निष्कलः परमेश्वरः ॥
स त्वं ममाग्रजः पुत्रः सृष्टिहेतोर्विनिर्म्मितः ।
ममैव दक्षिणादङ्गाद्वामाङ्गात्पुरुषोत्तमः ॥
तस्य देवाधिदेवस्य शम्भोर्हृदयदेशतः ।
सम्बभूवाथ रुद्रो वा सोऽहं तस्य परा तनुः ॥

---

* विभातीदमद्वयं तमसः परमिति B, C and D.

† वैराग्यं प्रददौ इति B.

‡ स्वयं देव इति B.

ब्रह्मविष्णुशिवा ब्रह्मन्* सर्गस्थित्यन्तहेतवः ।
विभज्यात्मानमेकोऽपि स्वेच्छया शङ्करः स्थितः ॥
तथान्यानि च रूपाणि मम मायाकृतानि च ।
अरूपः† केवलः स्वस्थो महादेवः स्वभावतः ॥
य एभ्यः परतो‡ देवस्त्रिमूर्त्तिः परमा तनुः§ ।
माहेश्वरी त्रिनयना योगिनां शान्तिदा सदा ॥
तस्या एव परां मूर्त्तिं मामवेहि¶ पितामह ।
शाश्वतैश्वर्यविज्ञानं तेजोयोगसमन्वितम्‖ ॥
सोऽहं ग्रसामि सकलमधिष्ठाय तमोगुणम् ।
कालोभूत्वा न मनसा मामन्योऽभिभविष्यति** ॥
यदा यदा हि मां नित्यं विचिन्तयसि पद्मज ।
तदा तदा मे सान्निध्यं भविष्यति तवानघ ॥
एतावदुक्त्वा ब्रह्माणं सोऽभिवन्द्य गुरुं हरः ।
सहैव मानसैः पुत्रैः†† क्षणादन्तरधीयत ॥

---

* ह्येते इति D. ब्रह्मविष्णुशिवास्तस्मिन् इति E, F and H.

† नीरूप इति C and D.

‡ एभ्यः परतरः इति B, C and D.

§ परमात्मनः इति B.

¶ एवापरा मूर्त्तिर्ममैव हि इति C.

‖ तपोयोगेति D.

** भूत्वा न तमसा सामान्योहि भविष्यतीति C, E, F and H.

†† रुद्रैरिति B.

सोऽपि योगं समास्थाय ससर्ज विविधं जगत्।
नारायणाख्यो भगवान्यथापूर्वं प्रजापतिः॥
मरीचिभृग्वङ्गिरसः पुलस्त्यं पुलहं क्रतुम्।
दक्षमत्रिं वसिष्ठञ्च सोऽसृजद्योगविद्यया* ॥
नव ब्रह्माण इत्येते पुराणे निश्चयो मतः† ।
सर्वे ते ब्रह्मणा तुल्याः साधका ब्रह्मवादिनः॥
सङ्कल्पञ्चैव धर्म्मञ्च युगधर्म्मांश्च शाश्वतान्।
स्थानाभिमानिनः सर्व्वान्यथा ते कथितं पुरा॥

इति श्रीकूर्म्मपुराणे रुद्रसृष्टिर्नाम दशमोऽध्यायः।

एकादशोऽध्यायः।

कूर्म्म उवाच।

एवं सृष्ट्वा मरीच्यादीन्देवदेवः पितामहः।
सहैव मानसैः पुत्रैस्तताप परमं तपः॥
तस्यैवं तपतो वक्त्राद्रुद्रः कालाग्निसम्भवः* ।
त्रिशूलपाणिरीशानः प्रादुरासीत्त्रिलोचनः॥

---

* मायया इति D.

† निश्चयज्ञताः इति B, C and D.

* कालाग्निसन्निभः इति B, C and D.

अर्द्धनारीनरवपुः* दुष्प्रेक्ष्योऽतिभयङ्करः।
विभजात्मानमित्युक्ता ब्रह्मा चान्तर्द्दधे भयात्॥
तथोक्तोऽसौ द्विधा स्त्रीत्वं पुरुषत्वं तथाकरोत्।
बिभेद पुरुषत्वञ्च दशधा चैकधा पुनः॥
एकादशैते कथिता रुद्रास्त्रिभुवनेश्वराः।
कपालीशादयो† विप्रा देवकार्य्ये नियोजिताः॥
सौम्यासौम्यैस्तथा शान्ताशान्तैः स्त्रीत्वञ्च स प्रभुः।
बिभेद बहुधा देवः स्वरूपैरसितैः सितैः॥
ता वै विभूतयो‡ विप्रा विश्रुताः शक्तयो भुवि।
लक्ष्म्यादयो यद्वपुषा§ विश्वं व्याप्नोति शाङ्करी॥
विभज्य पुनरीशानी स्वात्मांशमकरोद्द्विजाः¶।
महादेवनियोगेन पितामहमुपस्थिता॥
तामाह भगवान् ब्रह्मा दक्षस्य दुहिता भव।
सापि तस्य नियोगेन प्रादुरासीत्प्रजापतेः॥
नियोगाद्ब्रह्मणो देवीं ददौ रुद्राय तां सतीम्।
दाक्षीं‖ रुद्रोऽपि जग्राह स्वकीयामेव शूलभृत्॥

---

* अर्द्धनारीश्वरवपुरिति B.

† कापालिकादय इति D.

‡ ते वै चिन्तयतः इति D.

§ याभिरीशा इति B.

¶ आत्मानं शङ्कराद्विभोः इति B. स्वात्मांशमकरोद्विभोः इति E, F and H.

‖ दक्षात् इति C and D.

प्रजापतिविनिर्द्दिष्टात्कालेन* परमेश्वरी† ।
मेनायामभवत्पुत्री तदा हिमवतः सती ॥
स चापि पर्व्वतवरो ददौ रुद्राय‡ पार्व्वतीम् ।
हिताय सर्व्वदेवानां§ त्रैलोक्यस्यात्मनो द्विजाः¶ ॥
सैषा माहेश्वरी देवी शङ्करार्द्धशरीरिणी ।
शिवा सती हैमवती सुरासुरनमस्कृता ॥
तस्याः प्रभावमतुलं सर्व्वे देवाः सवासवाः ।
वदन्ति‖ मुनयो वेत्ति शङ्करो वा स्वयं हरिः** ॥
एतद्वः कथितं विप्राः पुत्रत्वं परमेष्ठिनः ।
ब्रह्मणः पद्मयोनित्वं शङ्करस्यामितौजसः ॥

इति श्रीकूर्म्मपुराणे देव्यवतारे एकादशोऽध्यायः ।

---

* कोपेन इति D.

† विभज्य पुनरीशानी आत्मानं शङ्कराद्विभोरिति श्लोकार्द्धं B पुस्तके दृश्यते ।

‡ शर्व्वाय इति B.

§ सर्व्वलोकानामिति B and D.

¶ त्रैलोक्यस्यात्मनोऽपि च इति B and D.

‖ विदन्ति मुनयोवेत्तीति E. विन्दन्ति मुनयोवेत्तीति F and H.

** हरिः स्वयमिति B.

द्वादशोऽध्यायः।

सूत उवाच।

इत्याकर्ण्याथ मुनयः कूर्म्मरूपेण भाषितम्।
विष्णुना पुनरेवेमं* पप्रच्छुः प्रणता हरिम्॥

ऋषय ऊचुः।

कैषा भगवती देवी शङ्करार्द्धशरीरिणी।
शिवा सती हैमवती यथावद्ब्रूहि पृच्छताम्॥
तेषां तद्वचनं श्रुत्वा मुनीनां पुरुषोत्तमः।
प्रत्युवाच महायोगी ध्यात्वा† स्वं परमं पदम्‡॥

कूर्म्म उवाच।

पुरा पितामहेनोक्तं मेरुपृष्ठे सुशोभने।
रहस्यमेतद्विज्ञानं गोपनीयं विशेषतः॥
साङ्ख्यानां परमं साङ्ख्यं ब्रह्मविज्ञानमुत्तमम्।
संसारार्णवमग्नानां जन्तूनामेकमोचनम्॥
या सा माहेश्वरी शक्तिर्ज्ञानरूपातिलालसा।
व्योमसंज्ञा§ परा काष्ठा सेयं हैमवती मता॥
शिवा सर्व्वगतानन्ता गुणातीतातिनिष्कला¶।

---

* पुनरेवैनं इति B. पुनरेवेत्थमिति D.

† ध्यात्वेदमिति D.

‡ स परमास्पदमिति B.

§ व्योमरूपा इति A.

¶ गुणातीता तु निष्कला इति C, D, E, F and H.

एकानेकविभागस्था* ज्ञानरूपातिलालसा ॥
अनन्या निष्कले तत्त्वे संस्थिता तस्य तेजसा।
स्वाभाविकी च तन्मूला प्रभा भानोरिवामला ॥
एका माहेश्वरी शक्तिरनेकोपाधियोगतः।
परावरेण† रूपेण क्रीड़ते तस्य सन्निधौ ॥
सेयं करोति सकलं‡ तस्याः कार्य्यमिदं जगत्।
न कार्य्यं नापि करणमीश्वरस्येति सूरयः ॥
चतस्रः शक्तयो देव्याः स्वरूपत्वेन संस्थिताः।
अधिष्ठानवशात्तस्याः शृणुध्वं मुनिपुङ्गवाः ॥
शान्तिर्विद्या प्रतिष्ठा च निवृत्तिश्चेति§ ताः स्मृताः।
चतुर्व्यूहस्ततो देवः¶ प्रोच्यते परमेश्वरः ॥
अनया परया देवः स्वात्मानन्दं समश्नुते।
चतुर्ष्वपि च वेदेषु‖ चतुर्मूर्त्तिर्महेश्वरः ॥
अस्यास्त्वनादिसंसिद्धमैश्वर्य्यमतुलं** महत्।
तत्सम्बन्धादनन्तैषा†† रुद्रेण परमात्मना ॥

---

* एवं नानाविभागस्था इति A.

† परापरेण इति B, C and D.

‡ सङ्कल्पं इति C and D.

§ निवृत्तिरितीति B.

¶ चतुर्व्यूहः शुभो देवः इति B.

‖ देवेषु इति C and D. भेदेषु इति E, F and H.

** ममलमिति D.

†† तत्सम्बन्धादनन्ता या इति B, E, F and H.

सैषा सर्व्वेश्वरी देवी सर्व्वभूतप्रवर्त्तिका।
प्रोच्यते भगवान् कालो हरिः* प्राणो महेश्वरः॥
तत्र सर्व्वमिदं प्रोतमोतञ्चैवाखिलं जगत्।
स कालाग्निर्हरो देवो† गीयते वेदवादिभिः॥
कालः सृजति भूतानि कालः संहरति‡ प्रजाः।
सर्वे कालस्य वशगा न कालः कस्यचिद्वशः§॥
प्रधानं पुरुषस्तत्त्वं¶ महानात्मा त्वहङ्कृतिः।
कालेनान्यानि तत्त्वानि‖ समाविष्टानि** योगिना॥
तस्य सर्व्वजगन्मूर्त्तिः†† शक्तिर्मायेति विश्रुता।
तयेयं भ्रामयेदीशो मायावी पुरुषोत्तमः॥
सैषा मायात्मिका शक्तिः सर्व्वाकारा सनातनी।
विश्वरूपं महेशस्य सर्व्वदा सम्प्रकाशयेत्॥
अन्याश्च शक्तयो मुख्यास्तस्य देवस्य निर्म्मिताः।
ज्ञानशक्तिः क्रियाशक्तिः प्राणशक्तिरिति त्रयम्॥

---

* हरः इति C and D.

† रुद्रो इति B, C and D.

‡ संहरते इति B, C and D.

§ वशे इति C and D.

¶ प्रधानपुरुषत्वञ्च इति B.

‖ भूतानि समधिष्ठानि इति D.

** समाविश्यानि इति B.

†† जगत्प्रतिरिति B, C, E, F, G and H.

सर्व्वासामेव शक्तीनां शक्तिमन्तो* विनिर्म्मिताः ।
माययैवाथ विप्रेन्द्राः सा चानादिरनश्वरा† ॥
सर्वशक्त्यात्मिका माया दुर्निवारा दुरत्यया ।
मायावी सर्व्वशक्तीशः कालः कालकरः प्रभुः ॥
करोति कालः सकलं संहरेत्काल एव हि ।
कालः स्थापयते विश्वं कालाधीनमिदं जगत् ॥
लब्ध्वा देवाधिदेवस्य सन्निधिं परमेष्ठिनः ।
अनन्तस्याखिलेशस्य शम्भोः कालात्मनः प्रभोः ॥
प्रधानं पुरुषो माया माया सैव प्रपद्यते‡ ।
एका सर्व्वगतानन्ता केवला निष्कला शिवा ॥
एका शक्तिः शिवैकोऽपि शक्तिमानुच्यते शिवः ।
शक्तयः शक्तिमन्तोऽन्ये सर्व्व§शक्तिसमुद्भवाः ॥
शक्तिशक्तिमतोर्भेदं वदन्ति परमार्थतः ।
अभेदञ्चानुपश्यन्ति योगिनस्तत्त्वचिन्तकाः ॥
शक्तयो गिरिजा देवी शक्तिमानथ शङ्करः¶ ।

---

* शक्तिमानीश्वरीमत इति D.

† माययैवाच विप्रेन्द्राः स्थानादिकमनन्तया इति D.

‡ माययैवं प्रभिद्यते इति B and D. माया चैवं इति C.

§ सर्व्वें इति D.

¶ शक्तिमानथशङ्कर इत्यारभ्य भोग्या विश्वेश्वरी देवी इत्यन्तं B पुस्तके नास्ति ।
विशेषः कथ्यते वायुपुराणे ब्रह्मवादिभिः ।
भोग्या विश्वेश्वरी देवी शक्तिमन्तोऽथ शङ्करः ॥
इदं श्लोकार्द्धद्वयं प्रक्षिप्तं प्रतिभाति, केवलं A पुस्तके एव दृश्यते ।

विशेषः कथ्यते चायं पुराणे ब्रह्मवादिभिः ॥
भोग्या विश्वेश्वरी देवी महेश्वरपतिव्रता।
प्रोच्यते भगवान्भोक्ता कपर्द्दी नीललोहितः ॥
मन्ता विश्वेश्वरो देवः शङ्करो मन्मथान्तकः।
प्रोच्यते मतिरीशानी मन्तव्या च विचारतः ॥
इत्येतदखिलं विप्राः शक्तिशक्तिमदुद्भवम्*।
प्रोच्यते सर्व्ववेदेषु मुनिभिस्तत्त्वदर्शिभिः ॥
एतत्प्रदर्शितं दिव्यं देव्या माहात्म्यमुत्तमम्।
सर्व्ववेदान्तवादेषु निश्चितं ब्रह्मवादिभिः ॥
एकं सर्व्वगतं सूक्ष्मं कूटस्थमचलं ध्रुवम्।
योगिनस्तत्प्रपश्यन्ति महादेव्याः परं पदम् ॥
आनन्दमक्षरं ब्रह्म केवलं निष्कलं परम्।
योगिनस्तत्प्रपश्यन्ति महादेव्याः परं पदम् ॥
परात्परतरं तत्त्वं शाश्वतं शिवमच्युतम्।
अनन्तप्रकृतौ† लीनं देव्यास्तत्परमं पदम् ॥
शुभं निरञ्जनं शुद्धं निर्गुणं द्वैतवर्ज्जितम्।
आत्मोपलब्धिविषयं देव्यास्तत्परमं पदम् ॥
सैषा धात्री विधात्री च परमानन्दमिच्छताम्।
संसारतापानखिलान्निहन्तीश्वरसंश्रयात् ॥
तस्माद्विमुक्तिमन्विच्छन् पार्व्वतीं परमेश्वरीम्।

---

* शक्तिसमुद्भवमिति E, F and H.

† अनन्तं प्रकृतौ इति B.

आश्रयेत्सर्व्वभूतानामात्मभूतां शिवात्मिकाम् ॥
लब्ध्वा च पुत्रीं सर्व्वाणीं तपस्तप्त्वा सुदुश्चरम् ।
सभार्य्यः शरणं यातः पार्व्वतीं परमेश्वरीम् ॥
तां दृष्ट्वा जायमानाञ्च स्वेच्छयैव वराननाम् ।
मेना हिमवतः पत्नी प्राहेदं पर्व्वतेश्वरम्* ॥

मेना उवाच ।

पश्य बालामिमां राजन्राजीवसदृशाननाम् ।
हिताय सर्व्वभूतानां जाता च तपसावयोः ॥
सोऽपि दृष्ट्वा ततो देवीं तरुणादित्यसन्निभाम् ।
कपर्द्दिनीं चतुर्वक्त्रां त्रिनेत्रामतिलालसाम् । †
अष्टहस्तां विशालाक्षीं चन्द्रावयवभूषणाम् ।
निर्गुणां सगुणां साक्षात्सदसद्व्यक्तिवर्ज्जिताम् ॥
प्रणम्य शिरसा भूमौ तेजसा चातिविह्वलः ।
भीतः कृताञ्जलिस्तस्याः प्रोवाच परमेश्वरीम् ॥

हिमवानुवाच ।

का त्वं देवि विशालाक्षि शशाङ्कावयवाङ्किते‡ ।
न जाने त्वामहं वत्से यथावद्ब्रूहि पृच्छते ॥
गिरीन्द्रवचनं श्रुत्वा ततः सा परमेश्वरी ।
व्याजहार महाशैलं योगिनामभयप्रदा ॥

---

* परमेश्वरमिति G. परमेश्वरं पतिमित्यर्थः ।

† श्लोकार्द्धमिदं A पुस्तके नास्ति ।

‡ शशाङ्कावयवान्विता इति B.

श्रीदेव्युवाच।

मां विद्धि परमां शक्तिं महेश्वरसमाश्रयाम्।
अनन्यामव्ययामेकां यां पश्यन्ति मुमुक्षवः॥
अहं हि सर्व्वभावानामात्मा सर्व्वात्मना* शिवा।
शाश्वतैश्वर्य्यविज्ञानमूर्त्तिः† सर्व्वप्रवर्त्तिका॥
अनन्तानन्तमहिमा संसारार्णवतारिणी।
दिव्यं ददामि ते चक्षुः पश्य मे रूपमैश्वरम्॥
एतावदुक्त्वा विज्ञानं दत्त्वा हिमवते स्वयम्।
स्वं रूपं दर्शयामास दिव्यं तत्पारमेश्वरम्॥‡
कोटिसूर्य्यप्रतीकाशं तेजोबिम्बं निराकुलम्।
ज्वालामालासहस्राढ्यं कालानलशतोपमम्॥
दंष्ट्राकरालं दुर्द्धर्षं जटामण्डलमण्डितम्।§
त्रिशूलवरहस्तञ्च घोररूपं भयानकम्॥
प्रशान्तं सौम्यवदनमनन्ताश्चर्य्यसंयुतम्¶।
चन्द्रावयवलक्ष्माणं चन्द्रकोटिसमप्रभम्॥
किरीटिनं गदाहस्तं नूपुरैरुपशोभितम्।
दिव्यमाल्याम्बरधरं दिव्यगन्धानुलेपनम्॥

---

* सर्व्वान्तरा इति C, F and H.

† शाश्वती सर्वविज्ञानमूर्त्तिरिति D.

‡ इदं श्लोकार्द्धं C, D पुस्तकयोर्नास्ति।

§ इतः परं B पुस्तके किरीटिनं गदाहस्तं शङ्खचक्रधरं तथा इत्यधिकं दृश्यते।

¶ अनन्तैश्वर्य्यसंयुतम इति C.

शङ्खचक्रधरं काम्यं* त्रिनेत्रं कृत्तिवाससम् ।
अण्डस्थं चाण्डवाह्यस्थं वाह्यमाभ्यन्तरं परम्† ॥
सर्व्वशक्तिमयं शुभ्रं सर्व्वाकारं सनातनम्‡ ।
ब्रह्मेन्द्रोपेन्द्रयोगीन्द्रैर्व्वन्द्यमानपदाम्बुजम् ॥
सर्व्वतः पाणिपादान्तं सर्व्वतोऽक्षिशिरोमुखम् ।
सर्व्वमावृत्य तिष्ठन्तीं§ ददर्श परमेश्वरीम् ॥
दृष्ट्वा तदीदृशं रूपं देव्या माहेश्वरं परम् ।
भयेन च समाविष्टः स राजा हृष्टमानसः ॥
आत्मन्याधाय चात्मानमोङ्कारं समनुस्मरन् ।
नाम्नामष्टसहस्रेण तुष्टाव परमेश्वरीम् ॥

हिमवानुवाच ।

शिवोमा परमा शक्तिरनन्ता निष्कलामला ।
शान्ता माहेश्वरी नित्या शाश्वती परमाक्षरा ॥
अचिन्त्या केवलानन्त्या शिवात्मा परमात्मिका ।
अनादिरव्यया शुद्धा देवात्मा सर्व्वगाचला ॥
एकानेकविभागस्था मायातीता सुनिर्म्मला ।
महामाहेश्वरी सत्या महादेवी निरञ्जना ॥
काष्ठा सर्व्वान्तरस्था च चिच्छक्तिरतिलालसा ।

---

* सौम्यमिति D.

† पुरमिति A. पुरं शरीरमित्यर्थः ।

‡ सर्व्वाधारमनामयमिति D.

§ तिष्ठन्तं सर्व्वतः श्रुतिमत्परमिति D.

नन्दा* सर्व्वात्मिका विद्या ज्योतीरूपामृताक्षरा ॥
शान्तिः प्रतिष्ठा सर्व्वेषां निवृत्तिरमृतप्रदा ।
व्योममूर्त्तिर्व्योमलया व्योमाधाराच्युतामरा ॥
अनादिनिधनामोघा कारणात्माकुलाकुला ।
स्वतः† प्रथमजा नाभिरमृतस्यात्मसंश्रया ॥
प्राणेश्वरप्रिया माता महामहिषवासिनी‡ ।
प्राणेश्वरी प्राणरूपा प्रधानपुरुषेश्वरी ॥ ¶
सर्व्वशक्तिकलाकारा ज्योत्स्ना द्यौर्म्महिमास्पदा ।
सर्व्वकार्य्यनियन्त्री च सर्व्वभूतेश्वरेश्वरी‖ ॥
संसारयोनिः सकला सर्व्वशक्तिसमुद्भवा ।
संसारपोता** दुर्व्वारा दुर्निरीक्ष्या दुरासदा ॥
प्राणशक्तिः प्राणविद्या योगिनी परमा कला ।
महाविभूतिर्दुर्द्धर्षा मूलप्रकृतिसम्भवा ॥
अनाद्यनन्तविभवा परमाद्यापकर्षिणी ।
सर्गस्थित्यन्तकरणी सुदुर्व्वाच्या†† दुरत्यया ॥‡‡

---

* तारा इति B and C.

† ऋतुरिति E, F and H.

‡ महामहिषघातिनी इति B. वाहिनीति C and D.

¶ इतः परं B पुस्तके महामाया सुदुष्पूरा मूलप्रकृतिरीश्वरी इत्यधिकं दृश्यते ।

‖ अतः परम् अनादिरव्यक्तगुणेति श्लोकार्द्धचयं E, F, H पुस्तकेषु दृश्यते ।

** संसारपारा इति B.

†† दुराराध्या इति B.

‡‡ इतः पूर्व्वं श्लोकार्द्धसप्तकं C, D पुस्तकयोः मूलप्रकृतिरीश्वरीत्यस्मात्परं दृश्यते ।

शब्दयोनिः शब्दमयी नादाख्या नादविग्रहा ।
अनादिरव्यक्तगुणा* महानन्दा सनातनी ॥
आकाशयोनिर्योगस्था महायोगेश्वरेश्वरी ।
महामाया सुदुष्पारा मूलप्रकृतिरीश्वरी ॥
प्रधानपुरुषातीता प्रधानपुरुषात्मिका ।
पुराणा† चिन्मयी पुंसामादिपूरुषरूपिणी ॥
भूतान्तरस्था‡ कूटस्था महापुरुषसंज्ञिता ।
जन्ममृत्युजरातीता सर्व्वशक्तिसमन्विता§ ॥
व्यापिनी चानवच्छिन्ना प्रधानानुप्रवेशिनी ।
क्षेत्रज्ञशक्तिरव्यक्तलक्षणा मलवर्जिता¶ ॥
अनादिमायासम्भिन्ना त्रितत्त्वा प्रकृतिग्रहा ।
महामायासमुत्पन्ना तामसी पौरुषी ध्रुवा ॥
व्यक्ताव्यक्तात्मिका कृष्णा रक्ता शुक्ला प्रसूतिका ।
अकार्य्या कार्य्यजननी नित्यं प्रसवधर्म्मिणी ॥
सर्गप्रलयनिर्म्मुक्ता सृष्टिस्थित्यन्तधर्म्मिणी ।
ब्रह्मगर्भा चतुर्व्विंशा‖ पद्मनाभाच्युतात्मिका ॥

---

* अनादिरव्यक्तगुणेति श्लोकार्द्धत्रयं B, E, F, G, H पुस्तकेषु सर्व्वभूतेश्वरेश्वरीत्यस्मात्परं दृश्यते ।

† पुराणी इति B, C, D, E, F and H.

‡ भूतान्तरात्मा इति B.

§ समुद्भवा इति A, C, D, E, F and H.

¶ सत्त्ववर्जिता इति E, F, G and H.

‖ चतुर्भेदा इति B. चतुर्विंशा चतुर्विंशतितत्त्वरूपा इति भावः । चतुर्वेदा इति C.

वैद्युती शाश्वती* योनिर्जगन्मातेश्वरप्रिया।
सर्व्वाधारा महारूपा सर्व्वैश्वर्य्यसमन्विता॥
विश्वरूपा महागर्भा विश्वेशेच्छानुवर्त्तिनी।
महीयसी ब्रह्मयोनिः† महालक्ष्मीसमुद्भवा॥
महाविमानमध्यस्था महानिद्रात्महेतुका‡।
सर्व्वसाधारणी सूक्ष्मा ह्यविद्या पारमार्थिकी॥
अनन्तरूपानन्तस्था देवी पुरुषमोहिनी।§
अनेकाकारसंस्थाना कालत्रयविवर्ज्जिता॥
ब्रह्मजन्मा हरेर्मूर्त्तिर्ब्रह्मविष्णुशिवात्मिका।
ब्रह्मेशविष्णुजननी ब्रह्माख्या ब्रह्मसंश्रया॥
व्यक्ता प्रथमजा ब्राह्मी महती ब्रह्मरूपिणी¶।
वैराग्यैश्वर्य्यधर्म्मात्मा ब्रह्ममूर्त्तिर्हृदि स्थिता॥
अपां योनिः स्वयम्भूतिर्मानसी तत्त्वसम्भवा‖।
ईश्वराणी च शर्व्वाणी शङ्करार्द्धशरीरिणी॥
भवानी चैव रुद्राणी महालक्ष्मीरथाम्बिका।
महेश्वरसमुत्पन्ना भुक्तिमुक्तिफलप्रदा॥

---

* भास्वती इति C and D.

† महामाया महायोनिः इति B.

‡ महानिद्रार्थहेतुका इति B.

§ इदं श्लोकार्द्धं B पुस्तके नास्ति।

¶ ज्ञानरूपिणीति B, C and D.

‖ तत्त्वसंश्रया इति B.

सर्व्वेश्वरी सर्व्ववन्द्या नित्यं मुदितमानसा ।
ब्रह्मेन्द्रोपेन्द्रनमिता शङ्करेच्छानुवर्त्तिनी ॥
ईश्वरार्द्धासनगता महेश्वरपतिव्रता ।
सकृद्विभाता सर्व्वार्त्तिसमुद्रपरिशोषिणी* ॥
पार्व्वती हिमवत्पुत्री परमानन्ददायिनी ।
गुणाढ्या योगजा† योग्या ज्ञानमूर्त्तिर्विकाशिनी ॥
सावित्री कमला लक्ष्मीः श्रीरनन्तोरसि स्थिता ।
सरोजनिलया गङ्गा‡ योगनिद्रा सुरार्द्दिनी§ ॥
सरस्वती सर्व्वविद्या जगज्ज्येष्ठा सुमङ्गला ।
वाग्देवी वरदावाच्या¶ कीर्त्तिः सर्व्वार्थसाधिका‖ ॥
योगीश्वरी** ब्रह्मविद्या महाविद्या सुशोभना ।
गुह्यविद्यात्मविद्या च धर्म्मविद्यात्मभाविता ॥
स्वाहा विश्वम्भरा सिद्धिः स्वधा मेधा धृतिः श्रुतिः ।
नीतिः सुनीतिः सुकृतिर्माधवी नरवाहिनी ॥
पूज्या विभावती†† सौम्या भोगिनी भोगशायिनी ।

---

* अजा दुस्तरसंसारसमुद्रपरिशोषिणी इति D.

† योगदा इति B.

‡ मुद्रा इति B.

§ सुगन्धिनी इति C. शुचिव्रता इति D.

¶ वरदा अवाच्या अनवद्या इत्यर्थः । वरदा वाणी इति B.

‖ सर्व्वातिशायिका इति C and D.

** वागीश्वरीति B, C and D.

†† विभावरीति B. विभाविनीति C and D.

शोभा च शङ्करी* लोला मालिनी परमेष्ठिनी ॥
त्रैलोक्यसुन्दरी नम्या† सुन्दरी कामचारिणी ।
महानुभावा सत्त्वस्था‡ महामहिषमर्द्दिनी ॥
पद्मनाभा§ पापहरा विचित्रमुकुटाङ्गदा¶ ।
कान्ता चित्राम्बरधरा दिव्याभरणभूषिता ॥
हंसाख्या व्योमनिलया जगत्सृष्टिविवर्द्धिनी ।
नियन्त्री यन्त्रमध्यस्था|| नन्दिनी भद्रकालिका ॥
आदित्यवर्णा कौवेरी** मयूरवरवाहना ।
वृषासनगता गौरी महाकाली सुरार्च्चिता†† ॥
अदितिर्नियता रौद्रा पद्मगर्भा विवाहना ।
विरूपाक्षी लेलिहाना महासुरविनाशिनी‡‡ ॥
महाफलानवद्याङ्गी कामरूपा विभावरी ।
विचित्ररत्नमुकुटा प्रणतार्त्तिप्रभञ्जनी ॥

---

* वंशकरीति B.

† रम्या इति B, C and D.

‡ मध्यस्था इति B.

§ पद्ममाला इति B, C and D.

¶ विचित्रमुकुटानना इति B.

|| यन्त्रवाह्यस्था इति B.

** कौमारीति B, C and D.

†† सुगर्व्विता इति E, F and H.

‡‡ इतः परं B पुस्तके कान्ता चित्राम्बरेत्यारभ्य जगत्सृष्टिविवर्द्धिनीत्यन्तं पुनर्दृश्यते। महापुरनिवासिनीति C, D पुस्तकयोर्दृश्यते।

कौशिकी कर्षणी रात्रिस्त्रिदशार्त्तिविनाशिनी।
बहुरूपा स्वरूपा च* विरूपा रूपवर्जिता॥
भक्तार्त्तिशमनी भव्या भवतापविनाशिनी†।
निर्गुणा नित्यविभवा निःसारा निरपत्रपा॥
तपस्विनी सामगीतिर्भवाङ्कनिलयालया‡।
दीक्षा विद्याधरी दीप्ता महेन्द्रविनिपातिनी॥
सर्व्वातिशायिनी विश्वा§ सर्व्वसिद्धिप्रदायिनी¶।
अकलङ्का निराधारा नित्यसिद्धा निरामया॥
कामधेनुर्बृहद्गर्भा धीमती मोहनाशिनी।
निःसङ्कल्पा निरातङ्का विनया विनयप्रिया॥
ज्वालामालासहस्राढ्या देवदेवी मनोमयी‖।
महाभगवती भर्गा वासुदेवसमुद्भवा॥
महेन्द्रोपेन्द्रभगिनी** भक्तिगम्या परावरा††।

---

* ब्रह्मरूपा सुरूपा चेति B and G. बहुरूपा सुरूपा च इति E, F and H.

† भवभारविनाशिनीति B. भवभावविनाशिनीति E, F and H.

‡ यशस्विनी सामगीतिर्भवाङ्कनिलयालया इति B.

§ तरङ्गिणी समाधिस्था इति B.

¶ इतः परं B, C, D, E, F, H पुस्तकेषु "सर्व्वेश्वरप्रिया भार्य्या समुद्रान्तरवासिनी" इत्यधिकं दृश्यते।

‖ मनोन्मनी इति A, C, E, F and H. मनसामुन्मादनीत्यर्थः। प्रयोगोऽयमार्षः।

** महेन्द्रभगिनी भव्या इति D.

†† परायणा इति B.

ज्ञानज्ञेया जरातीता* वेदान्तविषया गतिः ॥
दक्षिणा दहती दीर्घा† सर्व्वभूतनमस्कृता ।
योगमाया विभागज्ञा महामोहा गरीयसी‡ ॥
सन्ध्या सर्व्वसमुद्भूतिर्ब्रह्मविद्याश्रयादिभिः§ ।
वीजाङ्कुरसमुद्भूतिर्महाशक्तिर्महामतिः ॥
क्षान्तिः¶ प्रज्ञा चितिः सच्चिन्महाभोगीन्द्रशायिनी ।
विकृतिः शाङ्करी शास्तिर्गणगन्धर्व्वसेविता‖ ॥
वैश्वानरी महाशाला महासेना** गुहप्रिया ।
महारात्रिः शिवानन्दा†† शची दुःस्वप्ननाशिनी ॥
इज्या पूज्या जगद्धात्री दुर्विनेया‡‡ सुरूपिणी§§ ।
गुहाम्बिका¶¶ गुणोत्पत्तिर्महापीठा मरुत्सुता‖‖ ॥

---

* जनातीता इति D.

† दहना दक्षा इति B. दहना दार्व्वी इति E, F, G and H. दहना माया इति C. दहनाऽरूढ़ा इति D.

‡ महीयसी इति B.

§ ब्रह्मब्रह्माश्रया नतिरिति B. ब्रह्मब्रह्माश्रयादितिरिति D, E, F, G and H.

¶ ख्यातिरिति B, E, F and H. ज्योतिः प्रज्ञा धृतिः सर्पौ इति D.

‖ शान्तिर्गन्धर्व्वगणसेविता इति D.

** देवसेना इति C and D.

†† शिवामन्दा इति B.

‡‡ दुर्विज्ञेया इति E, F and H. दुर्विज्ञेयस्वरूपिणी इति C and D.

§§ तपस्विनी समाधिस्था त्रिनेत्रा दिवि संस्थिता इत्यधिकं D पुस्तके दृश्यते ।

¶¶ गुणात्मिका इति B.

‖‖ महाप्रौढ़ा निरुत्सुका इति C and D.

हव्यवाहान्तरागादिः* हव्यवाहसमुद्भवा।
जगद्योनिर्जगन्माता जन्ममृत्युजरातिगा॥
बुद्धिर्महाबुद्धिमती† पुरुषान्तरवासिनी।
तरस्विनी समाधिस्था त्रिनेत्रा दिवि संस्थिता॥
सर्व्वेन्द्रियमनोमाता‡ सर्व्वभूतहृदि स्थिता।
संसारतारणी विद्या§ ब्रह्मवादिमनोलया॥
ब्रह्माणी बृहती ब्राह्मी ब्रह्मभूता भवारणी।
हिरण्मयी महारात्रिः संसारपरिवर्त्तिका॥
सुमालिनी सुरूपा च भाविनी हारिणी¶ प्रभा।
उन्मीलनी सर्व्वसहा सर्व्वप्रत्ययसाक्षिणी॥
सुसौम्या चन्द्रवदना ताण्डवासक्तमानसा।
सत्त्वशुद्धिकरी‖ शुद्धिर्मलत्रयविनाशिनी॥
जगत्प्रिया जगन्मूर्त्तिस्त्रिमूर्त्तिरमृताश्रया।
निराश्रया निराहारा निरङ्कुशपदोद्भवा** ॥
चन्द्रहस्ता†† विचित्राङ्गी स्रग्विणी पद्मधारिणी।

---

* हव्यवाहातुरा गाङ्गीति B.

† बुद्धिमती बुद्धिमतीति A. बुद्धिमाता बुद्धिमतीति E, F and H.

‡ भावा इति D.

§ नित्या इति B.

¶ तारिणीति B.

‖ तत्त्वशुद्धिकरीति A.

** निरङ्कुशवनोद्भवा इति B. निःशङ्का पद्मजोद्भवा इति D.

†† चक्रहस्ता इति C and D.

परावरविधानज्ञा महापुरुषपूर्व्वजा ॥
विश्वेश्वरप्रिया विद्युद्विद्युज्जिह्वा* जितश्रमा।
विद्यामयी सहस्राक्षी सहस्रवदनात्मजा ॥
सहस्ररश्मिः सत्त्वस्था† महेश्वरपदाश्रया।
क्षालिनी मृण्मयी‡ व्याप्ता तैजसी पद्मबोधिका ॥
महामायाश्रया मान्या महादेवमनोरमा।
व्योमलक्ष्मीः सिंहरथा§ चेकितानामितप्रभा ॥
वीरेश्वरी¶ विमानस्था विशोका शोकनाशिनी।
अनाहता कुण्डलिनी नलिनी पद्मभासिनी‖ ॥
सदानन्दा सदाकीर्त्तिः सर्वभूताश्रयस्थिता**।
वाग्देवता ब्रह्मकला कलातीता कलारणी ॥††
व्योमशक्तिः‡‡ क्रियाशक्तिर्ज्ञानशक्तिः परा गतिः।
क्षोभिका बन्धिका भेद्या भेदाभेदविवर्ज्जिता ॥

---

* विद्या विद्युज्जिह्वा इति B.

† तत्त्वस्था इति D.

‡ ज्वालिनी सन्मना इति B. सन्मयी इति E, F and H.

§ सिंहवाहा इति D.

¶ विश्वेश्वरीति B.

‖ पद्मजा पद्मवासिनी इति D.

** शतानन्दा सतां कीर्त्तिः सर्व्वभूताशयस्थिता इति B.

†† इतः परं "ब्रह्मश्रीर्ब्रह्महृदया ब्रह्मविष्णुशिवप्रिया" इति श्लोकार्द्धं B, C, D पुस्तकेषु दृश्यते।

‡‡ कामशक्तिरिति D.

अभिन्ना भिन्नसंस्थाना वंशिनी* वंशहारिणी।
गुह्यशक्तिर्गुणातीता सर्वदा सर्वतोमुखी॥
भगिनी भगवत्पत्नी सकला कालहारिणी†।
प्रक्रिया योगमाता च गङ्गा विश्वेश्वरेश्वरी॥
कलिला कपिला‡ कान्ता कमलाभा§ कलान्तरा।
पुण्या पुष्करिणी भोक्त्री पुरन्दरपुरस्सरा॥
पोषणी परमैश्वर्य्यभूतिदा भूतिभूषणा।
पञ्चब्रह्म¶समुत्पत्तिः परमार्थार्थविग्रहा‖॥
धर्म्मोदया भानुमती** योगिज्ञेया मनोजवा।
मनोरमा†† मनोरस्का‡‡ तापसी वेदरूपिणी॥
वेदशक्तिर्वेदमाता वेदविद्याप्रकाशिनी।
योगेश्वरेश्वरी§§ माता महाशक्तिर्मनोमयी॥

---

* वंशिनीति B, C and D.

† कालवारिणीति B. इतः परं "सर्व्ववित् सर्व्वतोभद्रा गुह्यातीता गुहावलिः" इति श्लोकार्द्धं B, G पुस्तकयोर्दृश्यते। D, E, F, H पुस्तकेषु च गुह्या गूढ़ा गुणारणीति दृश्यते।

‡ कपिला कापिला इति B.

§ कनकाभा इति B, C and D.

¶ गणेशभास्करशिवविष्णुशक्तय इति पञ्चविधं ब्रह्म।

‖ परमात्मार्थविग्रहा इति B.

** धर्म्मसुखी इति D.

†† मनोहरीति B, C and D.

‡‡ महोरःस्था इति D.

§§ वागीश्वरेश्वरीति E, F and H.

विश्वावस्था वियन्मूर्त्तिर्विद्युन्माला विहायसी।
किन्नरी सुरभी विद्या* नन्दिनी नन्दिवल्लभा† ॥
भारती परमानन्दा परापरविभेदिका।
सर्वप्रहरणोपेता काम्या‡ कामेश्वरेश्वरी ॥
अचिन्त्यानन्तविभवा§ भूलेखा कनकप्रभा।
कूष्माण्डी धनरत्नाढ्या सुगन्धा गन्धदायिनी¶ ॥
त्रिविक्रमपदोद्भूता धनुष्पाणिः शिवोदया।
सुदुर्लभा धनाध्यक्षा धन्या पिङ्गललोचना ॥
शान्तिः‖ प्रभावती दीप्तिः पङ्कजायतलोचना।
आद्या भूः कमलोद्भूता** गवां माता रणप्रिया ॥
सत्क्रिया गिरिशा शुद्धिर्नित्यपुष्टा†† निरन्तरा‡‡।
दुर्गा कात्यायनी चण्डी चर्च्चिताङ्गा सुविग्रहा§§ ॥

---

* सुरभिर्वन्द्या इति B.

† नन्दवल्लभा इति C, D, E, F and H.

‡ कामा कामेश्वरेश्वरी इति E, F and H.

§ अचिन्त्याचिन्त्यविभवा इति B. अचिन्त्यानन्दविभवा हृल्लेखा इति C, D, E, F and H.

¶ गन्धवाहिनीति D.

‖ भ्रान्तिरिति B.

** हृत्कमलोद्भूता इति B. हृल्लेखा इति G.

†† शुक्ला नित्यशुद्धा इति B.

‡‡ गिरिजा शुद्धा नित्यतुष्टा निरञ्जना इति D.

§§ चर्च्चिता शान्तविग्रहा इति B.

हिरण्यवर्णा जगती* जगद्यन्त्रप्रवर्त्तिका ।
मन्दराद्रि†निवासा च शरद्धा‡ स्वर्णमालिनी ॥
रत्नमाला रत्नगर्भा पुष्टिर्विश्वप्रमाथिनी§ ।
पद्मनाभा¶ पद्मनिभा नित्यरुष्टामृतोद्भवा‖ ॥
धुन्वती दुष्प्रकम्प्या च सूर्य्यमाता दृषद्वती ।
महेन्द्रभगिनी सौम्या** वरेण्या वरदायिका ॥
कल्याणी कमलावासा पञ्चचूड़ा वरप्रदा ।
वाच्यामरेश्वरी विद्या†† दुर्ज्जया दुरतिक्रमा ॥
कालरात्रिर्महावेगा वीरभद्रप्रिया हिता ।
भद्रकाली जगन्माता भक्तानां भद्रदायिनी‡‡ ॥
कराला पिङ्गलाकारा कामभेदा महास्वना§§ ।
यशस्विनी¶¶ यशोदा च षड़ध्वपरिवर्त्तिका‖‖ ॥

---

* रजनीति B.

† महाराज्ञीति D.

‡ शारदा इति B.

§ पृथ्वी विश्वप्रमाथिनीति B. प्रसाधनीति D.

¶ पद्मानना इति B.

‖ नित्यतुष्टा इति B and G.

** मान्या इति B.

†† वाच्या वरेश्वरी वन्द्या इति B and G. वाच्या वरेश्वरीति E, F and H.

‡‡ भक्तिदायिनीति B.

§§ महामदा इति B.

¶¶ तपस्विनीति B.

‖‖ षड़र्त्तुपरिवर्त्तिनीति B. पञ्चस्थपरिवर्तिनीति D.

शङ्खिनी पद्मिनी साङ्ख्या साङ्ख्ययोगप्रवर्त्तिका* ।
चैत्रा संवत्सरारूढ़ा जगत्सम्पूरणी ध्वजा† ॥
शुम्भारिः खेचरी‡ स्वस्था कम्बुग्रीवा कलिप्रिया ।
खगध्वजा खगारूढ़ा वाराही पूगमालिनी§ ॥
ऐश्वर्य्यपद्मनिलया विरक्ता गरुड़ासना ।
जयन्ती हृद्गुहागम्या गह्वरेष्ठा गणाग्रणीः ॥
सङ्कल्पसिद्धा साम्यस्था सर्व्वविज्ञानदायिनी¶ ।
कलिः कल्कविहन्त्री च‖ गुह्योपनिषदुत्तमा ॥
निष्ठा** दृष्टिः स्मृतिर्व्याप्तिः पुष्टिस्तुष्टिः†† क्रियावती ।
विश्वामरेश्वरेशाना भुक्तिर्मुक्तिः शिवामृता ॥
लोहिता सर्पमाला‡‡ च भीषणी वनमालिनी ।
अनन्तशयनानन्ता§§ नरनारायणोद्भवा ॥

---

* सङ्ख्यासङ्ख्ययोगप्रवर्त्तिका इति E, F and H.

† चैत्रा संवत्सरी रुद्रा जगत्संपूरणीन्द्रजा इति B.

‡ शुभा विश्वचरीति D.

§ पराय्यौ परमालिनीति B. वराही इति G. वराही भगमालिनीति C, D, E, F and H.

¶ दायिका इति B.

‖ कलिकल्मषहन्त्री चेति B.

** नित्या इति B.

†† सृष्टिरिति E, F and H.

‡‡ सर्व्वमाता इति B and D.

§§ शयनानन्या इति E, F and H.

नृसिंही दैत्यमथनी शङ्खचक्रगदाधरा ।
सङ्कर्षणी* समुत्पत्तिरम्बिका पादसंश्रया ॥
महाज्वाला महाभूतिः† सुमूर्त्तिः सर्व्वकामधुक् ।
शुभ्रा च‡ सुस्तना सौरी धर्म्मकामार्थमोक्षदा ॥
भ्रूमध्यनिलया पूर्व्वा पुराणपुरुषारणिः§ ।
महाविभूतिदा मध्या सरोजनयना समा ॥
अष्टादशभुजानाद्या नीलोत्पलदलप्रभा ।
सर्व्वशक्त्यासनारूढा¶ धर्म्माधर्म्मविवर्ज्जिता‖ ॥
वैराग्यज्ञाननिरता निरालोका निरिन्द्रिया ।
विचित्रगहनाधारा** शाश्वतस्थानवासिनी ॥
स्थानेश्वरी निरानन्दा त्रिशूलवरधारिणी ।
अशेषदेवतामूर्त्तिर्द्दैवता वरदेवता ॥
गणाम्बिका गिरेः पुत्री निशुम्भविनिपातिनी ।
अवर्णा†† वर्णरहिता त्रिवर्णा जीवसम्भवा ॥

---

* सङ्कर्षण इति B.

† महामूर्त्तिरिति B and D. महासूतिरिति B, E, F and H.

‡ सुप्रभा इति B. सुश्रोणिरिति D.

§ रतिरिति D.

¶ सर्व्वशक्त्या समारूढ़ा इति B, C and D.

‖ सर्व्वधर्म्मार्थवर्जिता इति B.

** धीरा इति B.

†† स्ववर्णा इति D.

अनन्तवर्णानन्यस्था शङ्करी शान्तमानसा* ।
अगोत्रा† गोमती गोप्त्री‡ गुह्यरूपा गुणोत्तरा ॥
गौर्गीर्गव्यप्रिया गौणी§ गणेश्वरनमस्कृता ।
सत्यभामा¶ सत्यसन्धा त्रिसन्ध्या सन्धिवर्ज्जिता ॥
सर्व्ववादाश्रया‖ सङ्ख्या साङ्ख्ययोगसमुद्भवा ।
असंख्येयाप्रमेयाख्या शून्या शुद्धकुलोद्भवा ॥
विन्दुनादसमुत्पत्तिः शम्भुवामा शशिप्रभा ।
पिशङ्गा** भेदरहिता मनोज्ञा मधुसूदनी ॥
महाश्रीः श्रीसमुत्पत्तिस्तमःपारे प्रतिष्ठिता ।
त्रितत्त्वमाता†† त्रिविधा सुसूक्ष्मपदसंश्रया ॥
शान्ताभीता मलातीता‡‡ निर्विकारा शिवाश्रया§§ ।
शिवाख्या चित्तनिलया शिवज्ञानस्वरूपिणी ॥

---

* नान्यमानसा इति A, E, F and H. शङ्करीत्यारभ्य सत्यभामेत्यन्तं B पुस्तके विन्दुनादसमुत्पत्तिरित्यतः परं दृश्यते ।

† अगाधा इति D.

‡ योक्त्रीति B.

§ दुर्गा शिवप्रिया गौरीति D.

¶ सत्यमाता इति C, D, E, F and H.

‖ अर्थवाचाश्रया इति D.

** विसर्गा इति B.

†† धामा इति D.

‡‡ शान्त्यतीता मनोऽतीता इति B.

§§ नराश्रया इति B.

दैत्यदानवनिर्म्माथी* काश्यपी कालकर्णिका ।
शास्त्रयोनिः क्रियामूर्त्तिश्चतुर्वर्गप्रदर्शिका ॥
नारायणी नरोत्पत्तिः† कौमुदी लिङ्गधारिणी ।
कामुकी कलिताभावा‡ परावरविभूतिदा§ ॥
पराङ्गजातमहिमा¶ बड़वा वामलोचना ।
सुभद्रा देवकी सीता वेदवेदाङ्गपारगा ॥
मनस्विनी मन्युमाता महामन्युसमुद्भवा ।
अमन्युरमृतास्वादा पुरुहूता पुरुष्टुता‖ ॥
अशोच्या** भिन्नविषया†† हिरण्यरजतप्रिया ।
हिरण्यरजनी हैमा‡‡ हेमाभरणभूषिता ॥
विभ्राजमाना दुर्ज्ञेया ज्योतिष्टोमफलप्रदा ।
महानिद्रासमुद्भूतिरनिद्रा सत्यदेवता ॥
दीर्घा ककुद्मिनी हृद्या शान्तिदा शान्तिवर्द्धनी ।

---

* निर्मोचीति B, E, F, G and H.

† नरोद्भूतिरिति B.

‡ ललिताभावा इति C, D, E, F and H.

§ परापरेति B.

¶ परात्मज्ञानमहिमा इति D.

‖ पुरस्कृता इति B.

** अमोघा इति C.

†† भिन्नहृदया इति D.

‡‡ हिरण्यराजती हैमा इति B. हिरण्यानी हैमवती इति D.

लक्ष्म्यादिशक्तिजननी शक्तिचक्रप्रवर्त्तिका ॥*
त्रिशक्तिजननी जन्या षडूर्म्मिपरिवर्ज्जिता† ।
सुधौता‡ कर्म्मकरणी युगान्तदहनात्मिका ॥
सङ्कर्षणी जगद्धात्री कामयोनिः किरीटिनी ।
ऐन्द्री त्रैलोक्यनमिता वैष्णवी परमेश्वरी ॥
प्रद्युम्नदयिता दात्री§ युग्मदृष्टिस्त्रिलोचना ।
मदोत्कटा हंसगतिः प्रचण्डा चण्डविक्रमा ॥
वृषावेशा¶ वियन्माता विन्ध्यपर्व्वतवासिनी ।
हिमवन्मेरुनिलया कैलासगिरिवासिनी ॥
चाणूरहन्तृतनया नीतिज्ञा कामरूपिणी ।
वेदविद्या व्रतस्नाता ब्रह्मशैलनिवासिनी‖ ॥
वीरभद्रप्रजा** वीरा महाकामसमुद्भवा ।
विद्याधरप्रिया सिद्धा विद्याधरनिराकृतिः ॥
आप्यायनी हरन्ती च पावनी पोषणी कला ।

---

* इतः परं श्लोकार्द्धत्रयं B पुस्तके नास्ति ।

† षड्वर्गपरिवर्त्तिका इति D. षड्वर्गः—कामादिगणः । षडूर्म्मिपदमपि तदर्थकमिति सम्भावयामः ।

‡ सुधामा इति B सुधातेति D.

§ दान्ता इति B, C and D.

¶ वृषे धर्म्मे आवेशो यस्याः इत्यर्थः । वृषवेगा इति C and D.

‖ धर्म्मशैलानिलाशनेति C and D. ब्रह्मशैलानिवासनीति E, F and H.

** वीरभद्रा प्रजा इति E, F and H. वीरभद्रप्रिया इति C and D.

मातृका मन्मथोद्भूता वारिजा वाहनप्रिया ॥
करीषिणी सुधावाणी* वीणावादनतत्परा ।
सेविता सेविका सेव्या† सिनीवाली गरुत्मती ॥
अरुन्धती हिरण्याक्षी मृगाङ्का मानदायिनी ।
वसुप्रदा वसुमती वसोर्द्धारा वसुन्धरा ॥
धाराधरा‡ वरारोहा परावाससहस्रदा§ ।
श्रीफला श्रीमती श्रीशा श्रीनिवासा शिवप्रिया ॥
श्रीधरा श्रीकरी¶ कल्या श्रीधरार्द्धशरीरिणी ।
अनन्तदृष्टिरक्षुद्रा धात्रीशा धनदप्रिया ॥
निहन्त्री दैत्यसङ्घानां सिंहिका सिंहवाहना ।
सुवर्च्चला च सुश्रोणी‖ सुकीर्त्तिश्छिन्नसंशया ॥
रसज्ञा रसदा रामा लेलिहानामृतस्रवा** ।
नित्योदिता स्वयं ज्योतिरुत्सुका मृतजीवनी†† ॥
वज्रदण्डा‡‡ वज्रजिह्वा वैदेही वज्रविग्रहा ।

---

* सुधाधारा इति B. स्वधावाणी इति C. स्वधावीणा इति D.

† सेवा इति B, C and D.

‡ वरानना इति B and C.

§ परावरसहस्रदा इति C, E, F and H.

¶ श्रीकरा इति B.

‖ सुवेषा चन्द्रनिलया इति B.

** स्वरा इति C.

†† मृगजीवनीति E, F and H.

‡‡ वज्रचण्डा इति C.

मङ्गल्या मङ्गला माला निर्म्मला* मलहारिणी ॥
गान्धर्व्वी करुणा† चान्द्री कम्बलाश्वतरप्रिया ।
सौदामिनी जनानन्दा‡ भ्रुकुटीकुटिलानना ॥
कर्ण्णिकारकरा कच्चा§ कंसप्राणापहारिणी ।
युगन्धरा युगावर्त्ता त्रिसन्ध्या¶ हर्षवर्द्धनी ॥
प्रत्यक्षदेवता दिव्या दिव्यगन्धा दिवः परा‖ ।
शक्रासनगता शाक्री साध्या चारुशरासना** ॥
इष्टा विशिष्टा शिष्टेष्टा शिष्टाशिष्टप्रपूजिता ।
शतरूपा शतावर्त्ता विनता सुरभिः सुरा†† ॥
सुरेन्द्रमाता सुद्युम्ना सुषुम्ना सूर्य्यसंस्थिता ।
समीक्ष्या सत्प्रतिष्ठा च निवृत्तिर्ज्ञानपारगा‡‡ ॥
धर्म्मशास्त्रार्थकुशला धर्म्मज्ञा धर्म्मवाहना ।
धर्म्माधर्म्मविनिर्म्मोची धार्म्मिकाणां शिवप्रदा ॥

---

* मलिना इति B. मालिनीति C and D.

† गारुड़ीति B.

‡ निजानन्दा इति D.

§ चाचा इति D. चाची इत्यर्थः ।

¶ त्रिवर्म्मा इति C. त्रिविधा इति D.

‖ दिवा परा इति B. दिवाकरा इति C and D. दिवाकरी इत्यर्थः ।

** साध्या वीराशरासना इति D.

†† सुता इति D.

‡‡ वेदपारगा इति B.

धर्म्मशक्तिर्धर्म्ममयी विधर्म्मा विश्वधर्म्मिणी ।
धर्म्मान्तरा धर्म्ममयी* धर्म्मपूर्व्वा धनावहा ॥
धर्म्मोपदेष्ट्री धर्म्मात्मा† धर्म्मगम्या धराधरा ।
कापाली शकला‡ मूर्त्तिः कलाकलितविग्रहा ॥
सर्व्वशक्तिविनिर्मुक्ता सर्व्वशक्त्याश्रयाश्रया§ ।
सर्व्वा सर्व्वेश्वरी सूक्ष्मा सूक्ष्मज्ञानस्वरूपिणी ॥
प्रधानपुरुषेशेशा¶ महादेवैकसाक्षिणी‖ ।
सदाशिवा वियन्मूर्त्तिर्वेदमूर्त्तिरमूर्त्तिका** ॥
एवं नाम्नां सहस्रेण स्तुत्वासौ हिमवान्गिरिः ।
भूयः प्रणम्य भीतात्मा प्रोवाचेदं कृताञ्जलिः ॥
यदेतदैश्वरं रूपं घोरन्ते†† परमेश्वरि ।
भीतोऽस्मि साम्प्रतं दृष्ट्वा रूपमन्यत्प्रदर्शय ॥
एवमुक्ताथ सा देवी तेन शैलेन पार्व्वती ।
संहृत्य दर्शयामास स्वरूपमपरम्पुनः ॥

---

* धर्म्मान्तरा धर्म्मवेद्या इति D.

† धर्म्मस्था इति D.

‡ कापालीशकरा इति B.

§ सर्व्वशक्तिसमाश्रया इति B.

¶ प्रधानपुरुषेशी च इति D.

‖ महादेवतसाक्षिणीति B.

** अमूर्त्तिगा इति D.

†† घोरं तदिति D.

नीलोत्पलदलप्रख्यं नीलोत्पलसुगन्धि च* ।
द्विनेत्रं द्विभुजं† सौम्यं नीलालकविभूषितम् ॥
रक्तपादाम्बुजतलं सुरक्तकरपल्लवम् ।
श्रीमद्विलाससद्वृत्तं‡ ललाटतिलकोज्ज्वलम् ॥
भूषितं चारुसर्व्वाङ्गं भूषणैरतिकोमलम् ।
दधानमुरसा मालां विशालां हेमनिर्म्मिताम् ॥§
ईषत्स्मितं सुबिम्बोष्ठं नूपुरारावसंयुतम् ।
प्रसन्नवदनं दिव्यमनन्तमहिमास्पदम् ॥
तदीदृशं समालोक्य स्वरूपं शैलसत्तमः ।
भीतिं सन्त्यज्य हृष्टात्मा बभाषे परमेश्वरीम् ॥

हिमवानुवाच ।

अद्य मे सफलं जन्म अद्य मे सफलं तपः ।
यन्मे साक्षात्त्वमव्यक्ता प्रपन्ना दृष्टिगोचरम्¶ ॥
त्वया सृष्टं जगत्सर्व्वं प्रधानाद्यं त्वयि स्थितम् ।
त्वय्येव लीयते देवि त्वमेव परमा गतिः‖ ॥
वदन्ति केचित्त्वामेव प्रकृतिं प्रकृतेः पराम् ।

---

* नीलोत्पलसुगन्धिकमिति B.

† त्रिनेत्रं सुभुजं इति D.

‡ श्रीमद्विशालसंवृत्तमिति B. श्रीमद्विशालसंवृद्धमिति H.

§ श्लोकार्द्धमिदं E, F, H पुस्तकेषु न दृश्यते।

¶ प्रसन्ना दृष्टिगोचरा इति B.

‖ त्वमेव च परा गतिरिति B.

अपरे परमार्थज्ञाः शिवेति शिवसंश्रयात्॥
त्वयि प्रधानं* पुरुषो महान्ब्रह्मा तथेश्वरः।
अविद्या नियतिर्माया कलाद्याः शतशोऽभवन्† ॥
त्वं हि सा परमा शक्तिरनन्ता परमेष्ठिनी‡।
सर्व्वभेदविनिर्मुक्ता सर्व्वभेदाश्रयाश्रया॥
त्वामधिष्ठाय योगेशि महादेवो महेश्वरः।
प्रधानाद्यं जगत्सर्व्वं§ करोति विकरोति च॥
त्वयैव सङ्गतो देवः स्वात्मानन्दं¶ समश्नुते।
त्वमेव परमानन्दस्त्वमेवानन्ददायिनी॥
त्वमक्षरं परं व्योम महज्ज्योतिर्निरञ्जनम्।
शिवं सर्व्वगतं सूक्ष्मं परं ब्रह्म सनातनम्॥
त्वं शक्रः‖ सर्व्वदेवानां ब्रह्मा ब्रह्मविदामसि।
वायुर्बलवतां देवि योगिनां त्वं कुमारकः॥
ऋषीणाञ्च वसिष्ठस्त्वं व्यासो वेदविदामसि।**
साङ्ख्यानां कपिलो देवो रुद्राणाञ्चापि†† शङ्करः॥

---

* प्रधानपुरुषो इति C and D.

† शक्तयोऽभवन्निति B.

‡ परमेश्वरीति B.

§ जगत्कृत्स्नमिति B.

¶ स्वमानन्दमिति B, C and D.

‖ शक्तिरिति D.

** श्लोकार्द्धमिदं D, E, F पुस्तकेषु न दृश्यते।

†† रुद्राणामपि इति B.

आदित्यानामुपेन्द्रस्त्वं वसूनाञ्चैव पावकः।
वेदानां सामवेदस्त्वं गायत्री* छन्दसामसि॥
अध्यात्मविद्या विद्यानां गतीनां परमा गतिः।
माया त्वं सर्व्वशक्तीनां कालः कलयतामसि॥
ओङ्कारः सर्व्वगुह्यानां वर्णानाञ्च द्विजोत्तमः।
आश्रमाणां गृहस्थस्त्वमीश्वराणां महेश्वरः॥
पुंसां त्वमेकः पुरुषः† सर्व्वभूतहृदि स्थितः।
सर्व्वोपनिषदां देवि गुह्योपनिषदुच्यसे‡॥
ईशानश्चापि§ कल्पानां युगानां कृतमेव च।
आदित्यः सर्व्व¶मार्गाणां वाचां देवी सरस्वती॥
त्वं लक्ष्मीश्चारुरूपाणां विष्णुर्मायाविनामसि।
अरुन्धती सतीनां त्वं सुपर्णः पततामसि॥
सूक्तानां पौरुषं सूक्तं सामज्येष्ठं‖ च सामसु।
सावित्री चापि जाप्यानां** यजुषां शतरुद्रियम्॥
पर्व्वतानां महामेरुरनन्तो भोगिनामपि††।

---

* सावित्रीति C and D.

† त्वमेकपुरुष इति B.

‡ मध्ये ब्रह्मोपनिषदुच्यते इति D.

§ ईश्वरश्चापि इति B.

¶ सर्गेति B.

‖ सूक्तानां पौरुषं सूक्तं ज्येष्ठसाम इति B.

** चासि जप्यानामिति B.

†† भोगिनामसि इति B and D.

सर्व्वेषां त्वं परं ब्रह्म त्वन्मयं सर्व्वमेव हि ॥

रूपं तवाशेषविकारहीन*-
मगोचरं निर्म्मलमेकरूपम्† ।
अनादिमध्यान्तमनन्तमाद्यं
नमामि सत्यं तमसः परस्तात् ॥

यदेव पश्यन्ति जगत्प्रसूतिं
वेदान्तविज्ञानविनिश्चितार्थाः ।
आनन्दमात्रं प्रणवाभिधानं
तदेव रूपं शरणं प्रपद्ये ॥

अशेषभूतान्तरसन्निविष्टं‡
प्रधानपुंयोगवियोगहेतुम् ।
तेजोमयं जन्मविनाशहीनं
प्राणाभिधानं प्रणतोऽस्मि रूपम् ॥

आद्यन्तहीनं जगदात्मरूपं§
विभिन्नसंस्थं प्रकृतेः परस्तात् ।
कूटस्थमव्यक्तवपुस्तथैव¶
नमामि रूपं पुरुषाभिधानम् ॥

---

* तवाशेषकलाविहीन इति B, E, F, G and H.

† निर्म्मलरूपमेकमिति B.

‡ सन्निधिस्थमिति D.

§ जगदात्मभूतमिति B and D.

¶ करस्थमव्यक्तवपुस्तथैव इति B.

सर्व्वाश्रयं सर्व्वजगद्विधानं
सर्व्वत्रगं जन्मविनाशहीनम्।
सूक्ष्मं विचित्रं त्रिगुणं प्रधानं
नतोऽस्मि ते रूपमरूपभेदम्॥
आद्यं महान्तं पुरुषाभिधानं*
प्रकृत्यवस्थं त्रिगुणात्मबीजम्।
ऐश्वर्य्यविज्ञानविरोधधर्म्मैः†
समन्वितं देवि नतोऽस्मि रूपम्‡॥
द्विसप्तलोकात्मकमम्बुसंस्थं
विचित्रभेदं पुरुषैकनाथम्।
अनेक§भेदैरधिवासितं ते
नतोऽस्मि रूपं जगदण्डसंज्ञम्॥
अशेषवेदात्मकमेकमाद्यं
त्वत्तेजसा¶ पूरितलोकभेदम्।
त्रिकालहेतुं परमेष्ठिसंज्ञं
नमामि रूपं रविमण्डलस्थम्॥
सहस्रमूर्द्धानमनन्तशक्तिं

---

* पुरुषात्मरूपमिति B, E, F, G and H.

† विरागधर्म्मैरिति B.

‡ श्लोकद्वयमिदं D पुस्तके न दृश्यते।

§ अनन्तेति B. अनन्तभूतैरिति C. अनन्तरूपैरिति D.

¶ स्वतेजसा इति B, C and D.

सहस्रबाहुं पुरुषं पुराणम् ।
शयानमन्तःसलिले तवैव*
नारायणाख्यं प्रणतोऽस्मि रूपम् ॥
दंष्ट्राकरालं त्रिदशाभिवन्द्यं
युगान्तकालानलकर्त्तृरूपम्† ।
अशेषभूताण्डविनाशहेतुं
नमामि रूपं तव कालसंज्ञम् ॥
फणासहस्रेण विराजमानं
भोगीन्द्रमुख्यैरपि पूज्यमानम्‡ ।
जनार्द्दनारूढ़तनुं प्रसुप्तं
नतोऽस्मि रूपं तव शेषसंज्ञम् ॥
अव्याहतैश्वर्य्यमयुग्मनेत्रं
ब्रह्मामृतानन्दरसज्ञमेकम्§ ।
युगान्तशेषं दिवि नृत्यमानं
नतोस्मि रूपं तव रुद्रसंज्ञम् ॥
प्रहीनशोकं प्रविहीनरूपं¶
सुरासुरैरर्च्चितपादपद्मम् ।

---

* तथैव इति B and C. तदेव इति D.

† कल्परूपमिति B and D.

‡ रतिपूज्यमानमिति B. रभिपूज्यमानमिति C. रसि पूज्यमानमिति D.

§ विसंज्ञमेकमिति C. ममसंज्ञमेकमिति D.

¶ विमलं पवित्रमिति B, C and D.

सुकोमलं देवि विभासि शुभ्रं
नमामि ते रूपमिदं भवानि ॥
ओँ नमस्तेऽस्तु महादेवि नमस्ते परमेश्वरि।
नमो भगवतीशानि शिवायै ते नमो नमः॥
त्वन्मयोऽहं त्वदाधारस्त्वमेव च गतिर्मम।
त्वामेव शरणं यास्ये प्रसीद परमेश्वरि॥
मया नास्ति समो लोके देवो वा दानवोऽपि वा।
जगन्मातैव* मत्पुत्री सम्भूता तपसा यतः† ॥
एषा तवाम्बिके देवि किलाभूत्पितृकन्यका।
मेनाशेषजगन्मातुरहो मे पुण्यगौरवम्‡ ॥
पाहि माममरेशानि मेनया सह सर्व्वदा।
नमामि तव पादाब्जं व्रजामि शरणं शिवम्§ ॥
अहो मे सुमहद्भाग्यं महादेवीसमागमात्।
आज्ञापय महादेवि किं करिष्यामि शङ्करि॥
एतावदुक्त्वा वचनं तदा हिमगिरीश्वरः।
संप्रेच्चमाणोा¶ गिरिजां प्राञ्जलिः पार्श्वगोऽभवत्|| ॥

---

* भूतात्मा चैव इति E, F, G and H.

† सा स्वयं यतः इति D.

‡ अहो पुण्यस्य गौरवमिति B, C and D.

§ शिवामिति B.

¶ संप्रेक्ष्यमाणः इति H.

|| पार्श्वतोऽभवदिति B.

अथ सा तस्य वचनं निशम्य जगतोऽरणिः ।
सस्मितं प्राह पितरं स्मृत्वा पशुपतिं पतिम् ॥

श्रीदेव्युवाच ।

शृणुष्व चैतत्प्रथमं* गुह्यमीश्वरगोचरम् ।
उपदेशं गिरिश्रेष्ठ सेवितं ब्रह्मवादिभिः ॥
यन्मे साक्षात्परं रूपमैश्वरं दृष्टमद्भुतम् ।
सर्व्वशक्तिसमायुक्तमनन्तं प्रेरकं परम् ॥
शान्तः समाहितमना मानाहङ्कारवर्ज्जितः† ।
तन्निष्ठस्तत्परो भूत्वा तदेव शरणं व्रज ॥
भक्त्या त्वनन्यया तात मद्भावं परमाश्रितः ।
सर्व्वयज्ञतपोदानैस्तदेवार्च्चय सर्व्वदा ॥
तदेव मनसा पश्य तद्ध्यायस्व यजस्व तत् ।
ममोपदेशात्संसारं नाशयामि तवानघ ॥
अहं त्वां परया भक्त्या ऐश्वरं योगमास्थितम्‡ ।
संसारसागरादस्मादुद्धराम्यचिरेण तु ॥
ध्यानेन कर्म्मयोगेन भक्त्या ज्ञानेन चैव हि ।
प्राप्याहन्ते गिरिश्रेष्ठ नान्यथा कर्म्मकोटिभिः ॥
श्रुतिस्मृत्युदितं सम्यक्कर्म्म वर्णाश्रमात्मकम् ।
अध्यात्मज्ञानसहितं मुक्तये सततं कुरु ॥

---

* चैतत्परममिति B, C and D.

† दम्भाहङ्कारवर्जितः इति B, C and D.

‡ अहं वै मत्परान् भक्तानैश्वरं योगमास्थितानिति B.

धर्म्मात्संजायते भक्तिर्भक्त्या संप्राप्यते परम्।
श्रुतिस्मृतिभ्यामुदितो धर्म्मो यज्ञादिको मतः॥
नान्यतो जायते धर्म्मो वेदाद्धर्म्मो हि* निर्बभौ।
तस्मान्मुमुक्षुर्धर्म्मार्थी मद्रूपं वेदमाश्रयेत्† ॥
ममैवैषा परा शक्तिः‡ वेदसंज्ञा पुरातनी।
ऋग्यजुःसामरूपेण सर्गादौ संप्रवर्त्तते॥
तेषामेव च गुप्त्यर्थं वेदानां भगवानजः।
ब्राह्मणादीन्ससर्जाथ स्वे स्वे कर्म्मण्ययोजयत्॥
येन कुर्व्वन्ति मद्धर्म्मन्तदर्थं§ ब्रह्मनिर्म्मिताः।
तेषामधस्तान्नरकांस्तामिस्रादीनकल्पयत्॥
न च वेदादृते किञ्चिच्छास्त्रं धर्म्माभिधायकम्।
योऽन्यत्र रमते सोऽसौ न सम्भाष्यो द्विजातिभिः॥
यानि शास्त्राणि दृश्यन्ते लोकेऽस्मिन्विविधानि¶ तु।
श्रुतिस्मृतिविरुद्धानि निष्ठा तेषां हि तामसी॥
कापालं भैरवञ्चैव‖ यामलं वाममार्हतम्।
एवंविधानि चान्यानि मोहनार्थानि तानि तु॥

---

* वेदाद्धर्म्मोऽपि इति B. वेदार्थात्सहि निर्बभौ इति D.

† धर्म्मार्थं श्रद्धया वेदमाश्रयेदिति D.

‡ मूर्त्तिरिति B.

§ तद्धर्म्ममिति C, E, F, and H. तं धर्म्ममिति D.

¶ लोकेऽस्मिंस्तिविधानि इति B.

‖ पञ्चरात्रञ्च इति B.

ये कुशास्त्राभियोगेन मोहयन्तीह मानवान् ।
मया सृष्टानि शास्त्राणि मोहायैषां भवान्तरे* ॥
वेदार्थ†वित्तमैः कार्य्यं यत्स्मृतं कर्म्म वैदिकम् ।
तत्प्रयत्नेन कुर्व्वन्ति मत्प्रियास्ते हि ये नराः ॥
वर्णानामनुकम्पार्थम्मन्नियोगाद्विराट् स्वयम् ।
स्वायम्भुवो मनुर्द्धर्म्मान्मुनीनां पूर्व्वमुक्तवान् ॥
श्रुत्वा चान्येऽपि मुनयस्तन्मुखाद्धर्म्ममुत्तमम् ।
चक्रुर्द्धर्म्मप्रतिष्ठार्थं धर्म्मशास्त्राणि चैव हि ॥
तेषु चान्तर्हितेष्वेवं युगान्तेषु महर्षयः ।
ब्रह्मणो वचनात्तानि करिष्यन्ति युगे युगे ॥
अष्टादश पुराणानि व्यासाद्यैः‡ कथितानि तु ।
नियोगाद्ब्रह्मणो राजंस्तेषु धर्म्मः प्रतिष्ठितः ॥
अन्यान्युपपुराणानि तच्छिष्यैः कथितानि तु§ ।
युगे युगेऽत्र सर्व्वेषां कर्त्ता वै धर्म्मशास्त्रवित् ॥
शिक्षा कल्पो व्याकरणं निरुक्तं छन्द एव च ।
ज्योतिःशास्त्रं न्यायविद्या¶ सर्व्वेषामुपबृंहणम्‖ ॥

---

* भवार्णवे इति B.

† वेदान्तेति B.

‡ व्यासेन इति B and D.

§ नियोगादित्यारभ्य त्वित्यन्तं G, H पुस्तकयोर्नास्ति । वै कृतानि तु इति D.

¶ ज्योतिःशास्त्राध्यात्मविद्या इति H.

‖ मीमांसा चोपबृंहणमिति B.

एवं चतुर्द्दशैतानि तथा हि द्विजसत्तमाः* ।
चतुर्वेदैः सहोक्तानि धर्म्मो नान्यत्र विद्यते ॥
एवं पैतामहं धर्म्मं मनुव्यासादयः परम् ।
स्थापयन्ति ममादेशाद्यावदाभूतसंप्लवम्† ॥
ब्रह्मणा‡ सह ते सर्व्वे संप्राप्ते प्रतिसञ्चरे ।
परस्यान्ते कृतात्मानः§ प्रविशन्ति परम्पदम्¶ ॥
तस्मात्सर्व्वप्रयत्नेन धर्म्मार्थी वेदमाश्रयेत् ।
धर्म्मेण सहितं ज्ञानं परं ब्रह्म प्रकाशयेत् ॥
ये तु सङ्गान्‖ परित्यज्य मामेव शरणं गताः ।
उपासते सदा भक्त्या योगमैश्वरमास्थिताः ॥
सर्व्वभूतदयावन्तः शान्ता दान्ता विमत्सराः ।
अमानिनो बुद्धिमन्तस्तापसाः शंसितव्रताः ॥
मच्चित्ता मद्गतप्राणा मज्ज्ञानकथने** रताः ।
सन्न्यासिनो गृहस्थाश्च वनस्था ब्रह्मचारिणः ॥
तेषां नित्याभियुक्तानां मायातत्त्वं समुत्थितम्†† ।

---

* विद्यास्थानानि सत्तम इति B, C and D.

† अत्र यावत्पदं निरर्थकम्, आ इति उपसर्गेण गतार्थत्वात् ।

‡ ब्राह्मणैरिति B.

§. परस्यान्तःकृतात्मान इति E, F and H.

¶ परस्परमिति B. प्रवेक्ष्यन्ति परं पदमिति D.

‖ स्वर्गमिति B. येऽन्यसङ्गानिति D.

** मद्भावकथने इति A.

†† मायातनुसमुत्थितमिति B.

नाशयामि तमः कृत्स्नं ज्ञानदीपेन नो चिरात्* ॥
ते सुनिर्द्धूततमसो† ज्ञानेनैकेन मन्मयाः ।
सदानन्दास्तु संसारे न जायन्ते पुनः पुनः ॥
तस्मात्सर्व्वप्रकारेण मद्भक्तो मत्परायणः ।
मामेवार्च्चय सर्व्वत्र मनसा शरणं गतः ॥
अशक्तो यदि मे ध्यातुमैश्वरं रूपमव्ययम् ।
ततो मे परमं‡ रूपं कालाद्यं§ शरणं व्रज ॥
यद्यत्स्वरूपं¶ मे तात मनसो गोचरं तव ।
तन्निष्ठस्तत्परो भूत्वा तदर्च्चनपरो भव ॥
यत्तु मे निष्कलं रूपं चिन्मात्रं केवलं शिवम् ।
सर्व्वोपाधिविनिर्मुक्तमनन्तममृतं परम् ॥
ज्ञानेनैकेन तल्लभ्यं क्लेशेन परमं पदम् ।
ज्ञानमेव प्रपश्यन्तो मामेव प्रविशन्ति ते ॥
तद्बुद्धयस्तदात्मानस्तन्निष्ठास्तत्परायणाः ।
गच्छन्त्यपुनरावृत्तिं ज्ञाननिर्द्धूतकल्मषाः ॥
मामनाश्रित्य परमं निर्व्वाणममलं‖ पदम् ।

---

* मा चिरादिति B, D, E, F and H.

† ते तु निर्द्धूतमनस इति B, E, F and H.. तेषु निर्द्धूतमनस इति G.

‡ सकलमिति B. ततः सर्वकलमिति C and D.

§ कलाख्यमिति E, F and H. कलाख्यं पूर्णम् ।

¶ यद्यदिति E. F and H.

‖ सफलप्रदमिति E, F and H.

प्राप्यते न हि राजेन्द्र ततो मां शरणं व्रज ॥
एकत्वेन पृथक्त्वेन तथा चोभयथापि वा।
मामुपास्य महीपाल* ततो यास्यसि तत्पदम्† ॥
मामनाश्रित्य तत्त्वं स्वभावविमलं शिवम्।
ज्ञायते नहि राजेन्द्र ततो मां शरणं व्रज ॥
तस्मात्त्वमक्षरं रूपं नित्यं वा रूपमैश्वरम्।
आराधय प्रयत्नेन ततोऽन्यत्वं‡ प्रहास्यसि ॥
कर्म्मणा मनसा वाचा शिवं सर्व्वत्र सर्व्वदा।
समाराधय भावेन ततो यास्यसि तत्पदम्§ ॥
न वै यास्यन्ति तं देवं¶ मोहिता मम मायया।
अनाद्यनन्तं परमं महेश्वरमजं शिवम् ॥
सर्व्वभूतात्मभूतस्थं सर्व्वाधारं निरञ्जनम्।
नित्यानन्दं निराभासं निर्गुणं तमसः परम् ॥
अद्वैतमचलं ब्रह्म निष्कलं निष्प्रपञ्चकम्।
स्वसंवेद्यमवेद्यं तत्परे‖ व्योम्नि व्यवस्थितम् ॥
सूक्ष्मेण तमसा नित्यं वेष्टिता मम मायया।

---

* महाराज इति B, C and D.

† मत्पदमिति B.

‡ बन्धमिति C and D.

§ मत्पदमिति B.

¶ न वै पश्यन्ति तत्तत्त्वमिति B and G. न वै पश्यन्ति तं देवमिति E, F and H.

‖ स्वसर्गाद्यमरैर्भ्यस्तत्परमिति B.

संसारसागरे घोरे जायन्ते च पुनः पुनः॥
भक्त्या त्वनन्यया राजन् सम्यग्ज्ञानेन चैव हि।
अन्वेष्टव्यं हि तद्ब्रह्म जन्मबन्धनिवृत्तये॥
अहङ्कारञ्च मात्सर्य्यं कामं क्रोधपरिग्रहम्।
अधर्म्माभिनिवेशञ्च त्यक्त्वा वैराग्यमास्थितः॥
सर्व्वभूतेषु चात्मानं सर्व्वभूतानि चात्मनि।
अवेक्ष्य* चात्मनात्मानं ब्रह्मभूयाय कल्पते॥
ब्रह्मभूतः प्रसन्नात्मा सर्व्वभूताभयप्रदः।
ऐश्वर्य्यं† परमां भक्तिं विन्देतानन्यभाविनीम्‡॥
वीक्ष्यते तत्परं तत्त्वमैश्वरं ब्रह्म निष्कलम्।
सर्व्वसंसारनिर्मुक्तो ब्रह्मण्येवावतिष्ठते॥
ब्रह्मणोऽयं प्रतिष्ठानां§ परस्य परमः शिवः।
अनन्यश्चाव्ययश्चैकश्चात्माधारो महेश्वरः॥
ज्ञानेन कर्म्मयोगेन भक्त्या योगेन वा नृप¶।
सर्व्वसंसारमुक्त्यर्थमीश्वरं शरणं व्रज॥
एष गुह्योपदेशस्ते मया दत्तो गिरीश्वर।
अन्वीक्ष्य चैतदखिलं यथेष्टं कर्त्तुमर्हसि॥

---

* अन्वीक्ष्य इति B.

† ऐश्वरीमिति B.

‡ विन्देतानन्यगामिनीमिति B and D.

§ ब्राह्मणो हि प्रतिष्ठेयमिति B. प्रतिष्ठायामिति C, E, F and H.

¶ पुनरिति B.

अहं वै याचिता देवैः सञ्जाता परमेश्वरात् ।
विनिन्द्य दक्षं पितरं महेश्वरविनिन्दकम् ॥
धर्म्मसंस्थापनार्थाय तवाराधनकारणात् ।
मेनादेहसमुत्पन्ना त्वामेव पितरं श्रिता ॥
स त्वं नियोगाद्देवस्य ब्रह्मणः परमात्मनः ।
प्रदास्यसे मां रुद्राय स्वयंवरसमागमे ॥
तत्सम्बन्धान्तरे* राजन् सर्व्वे देवाः सवासवाः ।
त्वां नमस्यन्ति वै तात प्रसीदति च शङ्करः ॥
तस्मात्सर्व्वप्रयत्नेन मां विद्धीश्वरगोचराम् ।
संपूज्य† देवमीशानं शरण्यं शरणं व्रज ॥
स एवमुक्तो हिमवान्‡ देवदेव्या गिरीश्वरः ।
प्रणम्य शिरसा देवीं प्राञ्जलिः पुनरब्रवीत् ॥
विस्तरेण महेशानि योगं माहेश्वरं परम् ।
ज्ञानं वै चात्मनो योगं साधनानि प्रचक्ष्व मे ॥
तस्यैतत्परमं ज्ञानमात्मनो योगमुत्तमम्§ ।
यथावद्व्याजहारेशा¶ साधनानि च विस्तरात् ॥
निशम्य वदनाम्भोजाद्गिरीन्द्रो लोकपूजितः ।

---

* तत्सम्बन्धाच्च ते इति B.

† सन्तोष्य इति B.

‡ भगवानिति B, C and D.

§ मात्मयोगमनुत्तममिति D.

¶ व्याजहारेषा इति B.

लोकमातुः परं ज्ञानं योगासक्तोऽभवत्पुनः ॥
प्रददौ च महेशाय पार्व्वतीं भाग्यगौरवात् ।
नियोगाद्ब्रह्मणः साध्वीं देवानाञ्चैव सन्निधौ ॥
यइमं पठतेऽध्यायं देव्या माहात्म्यकीर्त्तनम् ।
शिवस्य सन्निधौ भक्त्या शुचिस्तद्भावभावितः ॥
सर्व्वपापविनिर्म्मुक्तो दिव्य*योगसमन्वितः ।
उल्लङ्घ्य ब्रह्मणो लोकं देव्या स्थानमवाप्नुयात् ॥
यश्चैतत्पठति स्तोत्रं ब्राह्मणानां समीपतः ।
समाहितमनाः सोऽपि† सर्व्वपापैः प्रमुच्यते ॥
नाम्नामष्टसहस्रन्तु देव्या यत्समुदीरितम् ।
ज्ञात्वार्कमण्डलगतामावाह्य‡ परमेश्वरीम् ॥
अभ्यर्च्य गन्धपुष्पाद्यैर्भक्तियोगसमन्वितः ।
संस्मरन्परमं भावं देव्या माहेश्वरं परम् ॥
अनन्यमानसो नित्यं जपेदामरणाद्द्विजः ।
सोऽन्तकाले स्मृतिं लब्ध्वा परं ब्रह्माधिगच्छति ॥
अथवा जायते विप्रो ब्राह्मणस्य शुचौ कुले§ ।
पूर्व्वसंस्कारमाहात्म्यात्¶ ब्रह्मविद्यामवाप्नुयात् ॥

---

* देव्या इति B, C and D.

† देव्याः समाहितमना इति B, C and D.

‡ सम्भाव्य इति B, C and D.

§ कुले शुचौ इति B.

¶ सर्व्वसंस्कारमाहात्म्यादिति E, F, G and H.

सम्प्राप्य योगं परमं दिव्यं तत्पारमेश्वरम्।
शान्तः सुसंयतो* भूत्वा शिवसायुज्यमाप्नुयात्॥
प्रत्येकञ्चाथ नामानि जुहुयात्सवनत्रयम्†।
महामारि‡कृतैर्दोषैर्ग्रहदोषैश्च मुच्यते॥
जपेद्वाहरहर्नित्यं संवत्सरमतन्द्रितः।
श्रीकामः पार्व्वतीं देवीं पूजयित्वा विधानतः॥
सम्पूज्य पार्श्वतः§ शम्भुन्त्रिनेत्रं भक्तिसंयुतः।
लभते महतीं लक्ष्मीं महादेव¶प्रसादतः॥
तस्मात्सर्व्वप्रयत्नेन जप्तव्यं हि द्विजातिभिः।
सर्व्वपापापनोदार्थं देव्या नामसहस्रकम्॥

सूत उवाच।

प्रसङ्गात्कथितं विप्रा देव्या माहात्म्यमुत्तमम्।
अतःपरं प्रजासर्गं भृग्वादीनां निबोधत॥

इति श्रीकूर्म्मपुराणे देव्या माहात्म्ये द्वादशोऽध्यायः।

—:—

---

* सर्व्वगत इति B, C and D.

† कुसुमत्रयमिति E, F, G and H.

‡ पूतनादीति B, C and D.

§ साद्धंत इति E, F, G and H. अर्द्धयुक्तं गौरीसहितं हरिसहितं वा इत्यर्थः।

¶ महादेवप्रभावत इति G and H.

त्रयोदशोऽध्यायः।

सूत उवाच।

भृगोः ख्यात्यां समुत्पन्ना लक्ष्मीर्नारायणप्रिया।
देवौ धाताविधातारौ मेरोर्जामातरौ शुभौ॥
आयतिर्नियतिश्चैव मेरोः कन्ये महात्मनः।
तयोर्धातृविधातृभ्यां यौ च जातौ सुतावुभौ* ॥
प्राणश्चैव मृकण्डुश्च मार्कण्डेयो मृकण्डुतः† ।
तथा वेदशिरा नाम प्राणस्य द्युतिमान्सुतः॥
मरीचेरपि सम्भूतिः पूर्णमास‡मसूयत।
कन्याचतुष्टयञ्चैव सर्व्वलक्षणसंयुतम्॥
तुष्टिर्ज्येष्ठा§ तथा वृष्टिः कृष्टि¶श्चापचितिस्तथा।
विरजाः पर्व्वतश्चैव पूर्णमासस्य|| तौ सुतौ॥
क्षमा तु सुषुवे पुत्रान्पुलहस्य प्रजापतेः।
कर्द्दमञ्च वरीयांसं सहिष्णुं मुनिसत्तमम्॥
तथैव च कनीयांसं तपोनिर्द्धूतकल्मषम्।

---

* धाताविधात्रोस्ते भार्य्ये तयोर्जातौ सुतावुभौ इति D.

† मृकण्डुज इति C and D.

‡ पौर्णमासमिति C and D.

§ कृषिरिति E, F and H.

¶ दृष्टिरिति B. पुष्टिश्चितिरिति C and D.

|| पौर्णमासस्य इति C and D.

अनसूया तथैवात्रेर्जज्ञे* पुत्रानकल्मषान् ॥
सोमं दुर्व्वाससञ्चैव दत्तात्रेयञ्च योगिनम्।
स्मृतिश्चाङ्गिरसः पुत्री जज्ञे लक्षणसंयुता ॥
सिनीवालीं कुहूञ्चैव राकामनुमतीमपि।
प्रीत्यां पुलस्त्यो भगवान्दम्भोजि†मसृजत्प्रभुः ॥
पूर्व्वजन्मनि सोऽगस्त्यः स्मृतः स्वायम्भुवेऽन्तरे।
देवबाहुस्तथा कन्या द्वितीया‡ नाम नामतः ॥
पुत्राणां षष्टिसाहस्रं सन्ततिः सुषुवे क्रतोः।
ते चोर्द्ध्वरेतसः सर्व्वे बालखिल्या इति स्मृताः ॥
वसिष्ठश्च तथोर्ज्जायां सप्त पुत्रानजीजनत्।
कन्याञ्च पुण्डरीकाक्षां सर्व्वशोभासमन्विताम् ॥
रजोमात्रोर्द्ध्वबाहुश्च§ सवनश्चानघस्तथा¶।
सुतपाः शुक्र इत्येते सप्त पुत्रा महौजसः ॥
योऽसौ रुद्रात्मको वह्निर्ब्रह्मणस्तनयो द्विजाः।
स्वाहा तस्मात्सुतान् लेभे त्रीनुदारान्महौजसः‖ ॥

---

* जनयामास इत्यर्थः, क्वचिदन्तर्भूतण्यर्थः सम्भवति।

† दत्तामिति B. दत्तोनिमिति E, F and H. दम्भोलीमिति C. दम्भोलि-निति D.

‡ सन्नतीति B.

§ राजोहश्चोर्द्ध्वबाहुश्चेति C. रजोहश्चोर्द्ध्वबाहुश्चेति D.

¶ सवनोऽनशनस्तथा इति D.

‖ त्रीनग्नीनमितौजस इति D.

पावकः पवमानश्च शुचिरग्निश्च रूपतः* ।
निर्म्मथ्यः पवमानः स्याद्वैद्युतः पावकः स्मृतः† ॥
यश्चासौ तपते सूर्य्ये शुचिरग्निस्त्वसौ स्मृतः ।
तेषान्तु सन्ततावन्ये चत्वारिंशच्च पञ्च च ॥
पवमानः पावकश्च शुचिस्तेषां पिता च यः‡ ।
एते चैकोनपञ्चाशद्वह्नयः परिकीर्त्तिताः ॥
सर्व्वे तपस्विनः प्रोक्ताः सर्व्वे यज्ञेषु भागिनः§ ।
रुद्रात्मकाः स्मृताः सर्व्वे त्रिपुण्ड्राङ्कितमस्तकाः ॥
अयज्वानश्च¶ यज्वानः पितरो‖ ब्रह्मणः सुताः ।
अग्निष्वात्ता वर्हिषदो द्विधा तेषां व्यवस्थितिः ॥
तेभ्यः स्वधा सुतां जज्ञे** मेनां वै धारिणीं†† तथा ।
ते उभे ब्रह्मवादिन्यौ योगिन्यौ मुनिसत्तमाः ॥
असूत मेना मैनाकं क्रौञ्चन्तस्यानुजन्तथा ।
गङ्गा हिमवतो यज्ञे सर्व्वलोकैकपावनी ॥

---

* ते त्रय इति C, D, E, F, G and H.

† इतः परं सपादश्लोकार्द्धद्वयं B पुस्तके न दृश्यते ।

‡ महाबल इति C. पितामह इति D.

§ भोगिन इति E, F, G and H.

¶ अयज्वानोऽपीति B.

‖ इतरे इति F and H.

** जनयामास इत्यर्थः ।

†† वैतरणीमिति B, C and D.

स्वयोगाग्निबलाद्देवीं पुत्रीं लेभे महेश्वरीम्* ।
यथावत्कथितं पूर्व्वं देव्या माहात्म्यमुत्तमम् ॥
धारिणी मेरुराजस्य पत्नी पद्मसमानना ।
देवौ धाताविधातारौ मेरोर्जामातरावुभौ† ॥
एषा दक्षस्य कन्यानां मयापत्यानुसन्ततिः ।
व्याख्याता भवतां सद्यो‡ मनोः सृष्टिं निबोधत ॥

इति श्रीकूर्म्मपुराणे त्रयोदशोऽध्यायः ।

चतुर्द्दशोऽध्यायः ।

सूत उवाच ।
प्रियव्रतोत्तानपादौ मनोः स्वायम्भुवस्य तु ।
धर्म्मज्ञौ तौ महावीर्यौ शतरूपा व्यजीजनत् ॥
ततस्तूत्तानपादस्य* ध्रुवो नाम सुतोऽभवत् ।
भक्त्या नारायणे देवे प्राप्तवान्† स्थानमुत्तमम् ॥

---

* स्वयोगात्मबलाद्देवी पतिं लेभे महेश्वरमिति A, E, F and H.

† एष श्लोकः B, C, D पुस्तकेषु नास्ति ।

‡ भवतामद्य इति B, C and D.

---

* तयोरुत्तानपादस्येति B, C and D.

† भक्तो नारायणाद्देवादिति C and D.

ध्रुवाच्छिष्टिश्च भाव्यश्च भाव्याच्छम्भुर्व्यजायत* ।
शिष्टेराधत्त सुच्छाया पञ्च पुत्रानकल्मषान् ॥
वसिष्ठवचनाद्देवी तपस्तप्त्वा सुदुश्चरम् ।
आराध्य पुरुषं विष्णुं शालग्रामे जनार्द्दनम् ॥
रिपुं रिपुञ्जयं विप्रं कपिलं† वृषतेजसम्‡ ।
नारायणपराञ्शुद्धान्स्वधर्म्मपरिपालकान् ॥
रिपोराधत्त महिषी चाक्षुषं सर्व्वतेजसम् ।
सोऽजीजनत्पुष्करिण्यां सुरूपं§ चाक्षुषं मनुम् ॥
प्रजापतेरात्मजायां वीरणस्य¶ महात्मनः ।
मनोरजायन्त दश सुतास्ते सुमहौजसः‖ ॥
कन्यायां सुमहावीर्य्यौ वैराजस्य प्रजापतेः ।
ऊरुः पूरुः शतद्युम्नस्तपस्वी सत्यवाक्** शुचिः ॥
अग्निष्टुदतिरात्रश्च सुद्युम्नश्चाभिमन्युकः ।
ऊरोरजनयत्पुत्रान्षड़ाग्नेयी महाबलान् ॥
अङ्गं सुमनसं ख्यातिं†† क्रतुमाङ्गिरसं शिवम् ।

---

* ध्रुवात्स्वष्टिश्च धान्यश्च भार्य्या शम्भुर्व्यजायत इति A, E, F and H.

† विकलमिति B, E, F and H. वृकलमिति C वृकूलमिति D.

‡ वृकतेजसमिति B, C and D.

§ वैरणमिति B. वीरिणामिति D.

¶ मरणस्य इति B, E, F, G and H. वीरणस्य इति D.

‖ नकुलायां महौजस इति B. त इलायामिति D.

** सत्यवानिति B.

†† ख्यातिमिति E, F and H.

अङ्गाद्वेणोऽभवत्पश्चाद्वेण्यो वेणादजायत ॥
योऽसौ पृथुरिति ख्यातः प्रजापालो महाबलः ।
येन दुग्धा मही पूर्व्वं प्रजानां हितकाम्यया* ।
नियोगाद्ब्रह्मणः सार्द्धं देवेन्द्रेण महौजसा ॥
वेणपुत्रस्य वितते पुरा पैतामहे मखे ।
सूतः पौराणिको जज्ञे मायारूपः स्वयं हरिः ॥
प्रवक्ता सर्व्वशास्त्राणां धर्म्मज्ञो गुरुवत्सलः† ।
तं मां वित्त मुनिश्रेष्ठाः पूर्व्वोद्भूतं सनातनम् ॥
अस्मिन्मन्वन्तरे व्यासः कृष्णद्वैपायनः स्वयम् ।
श्रावयामास मां प्रीत्या पुराणः‡ पुरुषो हरिः ॥
मदन्वये तु ये सूताः सम्भूता वेदवर्ज्जिताः ।
तेषां पुराणवक्तृत्वं वृत्तिरासीदजाज्ञया ॥
स च वैण्यः पृथुर्धीमान्सत्यसन्धो जितेन्द्रियः ।
सार्व्वभौमो महातेजाः स्वधर्म्मपरिपालकः ॥
तस्य बाल्यात्प्रभृत्येव भक्तिर्नारायणेऽभवत् ।
गोवर्द्धनगिरिं§ प्राप्तस्तपस्तेपे जितेन्द्रियः ॥
तपसा भगवान्प्रीतः शङ्खचक्रगदाधरः ।
आगत्य देवो राजानं प्राह दामोदरः स्वयम् ॥

---

* हितकारणादिति B.

† गुणवत्सलः इति B, C and D.

‡ पुराणमिति B.

§ सम्बस्थनगिरिमिति E, F, G and H.

धार्म्मिकौ रूपसम्पन्नौ सर्व्वशस्त्रभृतां वरौ ।
मत्प्रसादादसन्दिग्धौ पुत्रौ तव भविष्यतः ॥
एवमुक्त्वा हृषीकेशः स्वकीयां प्रकृतिं गतः ॥
वैण्योऽपि वेदविधिना निश्चलां भक्तिमुद्वहन् ।
सोऽपालयत्स्वकं राज्यं चिन्तयन्मधुसूदनम् ॥
अचिरादेव तन्वङ्गी भार्य्या तस्य शुचिस्मिता ।
शिखण्डिनं हविर्द्धानमन्तर्द्धानाद्व्यजायत ॥
शिखण्डिनोऽभवत्पुत्रः सुशील इति विश्रुतः ।
धार्म्मिको रूपसम्पन्नो वेदवेदाङ्गपारगः ॥
सोऽधीत्य विधिवद्वेदान्धर्म्मेण तपसि स्थितः ।
मतिञ्चक्रे भाग्ययोगात्सन्न्यासम्प्रति धर्म्मवित् ॥
स कृत्वा तीर्थसंसेवां स्वाध्याये तपसि स्थितः ।
जगाम हिमवत्पृष्ठं* कदाचित्सिद्धसेवितम् ॥
तत्र धर्म्मवनं† नाम धर्म्मसिद्धिप्रदं वनम् ।
अपश्यद्योगिनां गम्यमगम्यं ब्रह्मविद्विषाम् ॥
तत्र मन्दाकिनी नाम सुपुण्या विमला नदी ।
पद्मोत्पलवनोपेता सिद्धाश्रमविभूषिता ॥
स तस्या दक्षिणे तीरे मुनीन्द्रैर्योगिभिर्युतम्‡ ।
सुपुण्यमाश्रमं रम्यमपश्यत्प्रीतिसंयुतः ॥

---

* शृङ्गमिति B.

† धर्म्मपदमिति B.

‡ योगिभिर्युते इति B.

मन्दाकिनीजले स्नात्वा सन्तर्प्य पितृदेवताः ।
अर्च्चयित्वा महादेवं पुष्पैः पद्मोत्पलादिभिः ॥
ध्यात्वार्कसंस्थमीशानं शिरस्याधाय चाञ्जलिम् ।
सम्प्रेचमाणो भास्वन्तं तुष्टाव परमेश्वरम् ॥
रुद्राध्यायेन गिरिशं रुद्रस्य चरितेन च ।
अन्यैश्च विविधैः स्तोत्रैः शाम्भवैर्वेदसम्भवैः ॥
अथास्मिन्नन्तरेऽपश्यत्समायान्तं महामुनिम् ।
श्वेताश्वतरनामानं महापाशुपतोत्तमम् ॥
भस्मसन्दिग्धसर्व्वाङ्गं कौपीनाच्छादनान्वितम् ।
तपसा कर्षितात्मानं* शुक्लयज्ञोपवीतिनम् ॥
समाप्य संस्तवं† शम्भोरानन्दास्राविलेचणः ।
ववन्दे शिरसा पादौ प्राञ्जलिर्वाक्यमब्रवीत् ॥
धन्योऽस्म्यनुगृहीतोऽस्मि यन्मे साचान्मुनीश्वर ।
योगीश्वरोऽद्य भगवान्दृष्टो योगविदां वरः ॥
अहो मे सुमहद्भाग्यं तपांसि सफलानि मे ।
किं करिष्यामि शिष्योऽहन्तव मां पालयानघ ॥
सोऽनुगृह्याथ राजानं सुशीलं शीलसंयुतम् ।
शिष्यत्वे प्रतिजग्राह तपसा चीणकल्मषम् ॥
सान्न्यासिकं विधिङ्कृत्स्नं कारयित्वा विचचणः ।
ददौ तदैश्वरं ज्ञानं स्वशाखाविहितव्रतम् ॥

---

* हर्षितात्मानमिति E, F and H.

† संस्तवपदं परिचयार्थे रूढमपि अत्र सम्यक् स्तवरूपे वर्त्तते इति मन्तव्यम् ।

अशेषं* वेदसारन्तत्पशुपाशविमोचनम् ।
अन्त्याश्रममिति ख्यातं ब्रह्मादिभिरनुष्ठितम् ॥
उवाच शिष्यान्संप्रेक्ष्य ये तदाश्रमवासिनः ।
ब्राह्मणाः क्षत्रिया वैश्या ब्रह्मचर्य्यपरायणाः ॥
मया प्रवर्त्तितां शाखामधीत्यैवेह योगिनः ।
समासते महादेवं ध्यायन्तो विश्वमैश्वरम्† ॥
इह देवो महादेवो रममाणः सहोमया ।
अध्यास्ते भगवानीशो भक्तानामनुकम्पया ॥
इहाशेषजगद्धाता पुरा नारायणः स्वयम् ।
आराधयन्महादेवं लोकानां हितकाम्यया ॥
इहैनं देवमीशानं देवानामपि दैवतम् ।
आराध्य महतीं सिद्धिं लेभिरे देवदानवाः ॥
इहैव मुनयः सर्व्वे‡ मरीचाद्या महेश्वरम् ।
दृष्ट्वा तपोबलाज्ज्ञानं लेभिरे सार्व्वकालिकम्§ ॥
तस्मात्त्वमपि राजेन्द्र तपोयोगसमन्वितः ।
तिष्ठ¶ नित्यं मया सार्द्धं ततः सिद्धिमवाप्स्यसि ॥
एवमाभाष्य विप्रेन्द्रो देवं ध्यात्वा पिनाकिनम् ।

---

* अशेषवेदसारमिति B.

† निष्कलं शिवमिति B.

‡ पूर्व्वमिति B.

§ सार्व्वकामिकमिति B.

¶ आस्स्व इति C and D.

आचचक्षे महामन्त्रं यथावत्सर्व्वसिद्धये* ॥
सर्व्वपापोपशमनं वेदसारं विमुक्तिदम् ।
अग्निरित्यादिकं† पुण्यं ऋषिभिः सम्प्रवर्त्तितम् ॥
सोऽपि तद्वचनाद्राजा सुशीलः श्रद्धयान्वितः ।
साक्षात्पाशुपतो भूत्वा वेदाभ्यासरतोऽभवत्‡ ॥
भस्मोद्धूलितसर्व्वाङ्गः कन्दमूलफलाशनः ।
शान्तो दान्तो जितक्रोधः सन्न्यासविधिमाश्रितः ॥
हविर्धानस्तथाग्नेय्यां§ जनयामास वै सुतम्¶ ।
प्राचीनवर्हिषं नाम्ना धनुर्व्वेदस्य पारगम् ॥
प्राचीनवर्हिर्भगवान्सर्व्वशस्त्रभृतां वरः ।
समुद्रतनयायां वै दश पुत्रानजीजनत् ॥
प्रचेतसस्ते विख्याता राजानः प्रथितौजसः ।
अधीतवन्तः स्वं वेदं‖ नारायणपरायणाः ॥
दशभ्यस्तु प्रचेतोभ्यो मारिषायां प्रजापतिः ।
दक्षो जज्ञे महाभागो यः पूर्व्वं ब्रह्मणः सुतः ॥
स तु दक्षो महेशेन रुद्रेण सह धीमता ।

---

* स्वार्थसिद्धये इति B and C. तथा तत्कार्य्यसिद्धये इति D.

† अस्तिरिति E, F and H.

‡ वेदात्मा सततोऽभवदिति D.

§ हविर्धातुस्तथाग्नेय्यामिति B, E, F and H.

¶ सत्सुतमिति B, E, F and H. सुव्रतमिति C and D.

‖ स्वे वेदमिति C and D.

कृत्वा विवादं रुद्रेण शप्तः प्राचेतसोऽभवत् ॥
समायान्तं महादेवो दक्षं देव्या गृहं हरः ।
दृष्ट्वा यथोचितां पूजां दक्षाय प्रददौ स्वयम् ॥
तदा वै तमसाविष्टः सोऽधिकां ब्रह्मणः सुतः ।
पूजामनर्हामन्विच्छञ्जगाम कुपितो गृहम् ॥
कदाचित्स्वगृहं प्राप्तां सतीं दक्षः सुदुर्म्मनाः ।
भर्त्त्रा सह विनिन्द्यैनां भर्त्सयामास वै रुषा ॥
अन्ये जामातरः श्रेष्ठा भर्त्तुस्तव पिनाकिनः ।
त्वमप्यसत्सुतास्माकं गृहाद्गच्छ* यथागतम् ॥
तस्य तद्वाक्यमाकर्ण्य सा देवी शङ्करप्रिया ।
विनिन्द्य पितरं दक्षं ददाहात्मानमात्मना ॥
प्रणम्य पशुभर्त्तारं† भर्त्तारं कृत्तिवाससम् ।
हिमवद्दुहिता साभूत्तपसा तस्य तोषिता ॥
ज्ञात्वा तां‡ भगवानुद्रः प्रपन्नार्त्तिहरो हरः ।
शशाप दक्षं कुपितः समागत्याथ तद्गृहम् ॥
त्यक्त्वा देहमिमं ब्राह्मं क्षत्रियाणां कुले भव ।
स्वस्यां सुतायां मूढात्मा पुत्रमुत्पादयिष्यसि ॥
एवमुक्त्वा§ महादेवो ययौ कैलासपर्व्वतम् ।

---

* त्वमप्यस्मद्गृहाद्गच्छ सुतास्माकमिति B.

† पशुभर्त्तारं—पशूनां जीवानां भर्त्तारं पशुपतिमित्यर्थः ।

‡ तु इति B.

§ एवं शप्त्वा इति D.

स्वायम्भुवोऽपि कालेन दक्षः प्राचेतसोऽभवत् ॥
एतद्वः कथितं सर्व्वं मनोः स्वायम्भुवस्य तु ।
निसर्गं* दक्षपर्य्यन्तं शृण्वतां पापनाशनम् ॥

इति श्रीकूर्म्मपुराणे राजवंशानुकीर्त्तने चतुर्द्दशोऽध्यायः ।

पञ्चदशोऽध्यायः ।

नैमिषेया ऊचुः ।
देवानां दानवानाञ्च गन्धर्व्वोरगरक्षसाम् ।
उत्पत्तिं विस्तराद्ब्रूहि सूत* वैवस्वतेऽन्तरे ॥
स शप्तः शम्भुना पूर्व्वं दक्षः प्राचेतसो नृपः ।
किमकार्षीन्महाबुद्धिः श्रोतुमिच्छाम साम्प्रतम् ॥
सूत उवाच ।
वक्ष्ये नारायणेनोक्तं पूर्व्वकल्पानुषङ्गिकम् ।
त्रिकालबद्धं† पापघ्नं प्रजासर्गस्य विस्तरम् ॥

---

* विसर्गमिति B.

---

* विस्तरात्सूत ब्रूहीति B.

† त्रिकालवन्तमिति E, F and H.

स शप्तः शम्भुना पूर्व्वं दक्षः प्राचेतसो नृपः।
विनिन्द्य* पूर्व्ववैरेण गङ्गाद्वारे† नायजद्भवम्‡॥
देवाश्च सर्व्वे भागार्थमाहूताः§ विष्णुना सह।
सहैव मुनिभिः सर्व्वैरागता मुनिपुङ्गवाः॥
दृष्ट्वा देवकुलं कृत्स्नं शङ्करेण विनागतम्।
दधीचो¶ नाम विप्रर्षिः प्राचेतसमथाब्रवीत्॥

दधीच‖ उवाच।

ब्रह्माद्यास्तु पिशाचान्ता यस्याज्ञानुविधायिनः।
स देवः साम्प्रतं रुद्रो विधिना किन्न पूज्यते॥

दक्ष उवाच।

सर्व्वेष्वेव हि यज्ञेषु न भागः परिकल्पितः।
न मन्त्रा भार्य्यया सार्द्धं शङ्करस्येति नेज्यते**॥
विहस्य दक्षं कुपितो वचः प्राह महामुनिः।
शृण्वतां सर्व्वदेवानां सर्व्वज्ञानमयः स्वयम्††॥

---

* विचिन्त्येति B.

† Gangádwára here means Haridwára about two miles below Hurdwar. There is Kankhan (Kanakhala) where tradition places the abode of Daksha.

‡ नायजद्भवमिति C, D पुस्तकयोरेव दृश्यते, तच्च समीचीनतया प्रतिभाति।

§ भोगार्थमाहूता इति E and F.

¶ दधीचिर्नामेति C and D.

‖ दधीचिरिति C and D.

** नेष्यते इति E, F and H.

†† सर्व्वज्ञानमयो हि स इति B.

दधीच* उवाच ।

यतः प्रवृत्तिर्विश्वात्मा यश्चासौ† परमेश्वरः ।
सम्पूज्यते सर्व्वयज्ञैर्विदित्वा किन्न शङ्करः ॥

दक्ष उवाच ।

न ह्ययं शङ्करो रुद्रः संहर्त्ता तामसो हरः ।
नग्नः कपाली विदितो विश्वात्मा नोपपद्यते ॥
ईश्वरो हि जगत्स्रष्टा प्रभुर्नारायणो हरिः‡ ।
सत्वात्मकोऽसौ भगवानिज्यते सर्व्वकर्म्मसु ॥

दधीच§ उवाच ।

किं त्वया भगवानेष सहस्रांशुर्न दृश्यते ।
सर्व्वलोकैकसंहर्त्ता कालात्मा परमेश्वरः ॥
यं गृणन्तीह विद्वांसो धार्म्मिका ब्रह्मवादिनः ।
सोऽयं साक्षी¶ तीव्ररुचिः कालात्मा शाङ्करी तनुः ॥
एष रुद्रो महादेवः कपाली|| च घृणी हरः ।
आदित्यो भगवान्सूर्य्यो नीलग्रीवो विलोहितः ॥
संस्तूयते सहस्रांशुः सामगाध्वर्युहोतृभिः ।
पश्यैनं विश्वकर्म्माणं रुद्रमूर्त्तिं त्रयीमयम् ॥

---

* दधीचिरिति C and D.

† यश्चास्य इति B.

‡ स्वराडिति B, C and D.

§ दधीचिरिति C and D.

¶ सोऽर्थसाक्षीति E, F, G and H.

|| कपर्द्दीति B, C and D.

दक्ष उवाच ।

य एते द्वादशादित्या आगता यज्ञभागिनः ।
सर्व्वे सूर्य्या इति ज्ञेया न ह्यन्यो विद्यते रविः ॥
एवमुक्ते तु मुनयः समायाता दिदृक्षवः ।
बाढ़मित्यब्रुवन्दक्षं तस्य साहाय्यकारिणः ॥
तमसाविष्टमनसो न पश्यन्तो* वृषध्वजम् ।
सहस्रशोऽथ शतशो बहुशो भूय एव हि† ॥
निन्दन्तो वैदिकान्मन्त्रान् सर्व्वभूतपतिं हरम् ।
अपूजयन्दक्षवाक्यं‡ मोहिता विष्णुमायया ॥
देवाश्च सर्व्वे भागार्थमागता वासवादयः ।
नापश्यन्देवमीशानमृते नारायणं हरिम् ॥
हिरण्यगर्भो भगवान्ब्रह्मा ब्रह्मविदां वरः ।
पश्यतामेव सर्व्वेषां क्षणादन्तरधीयत ॥
अन्तर्हिते भगवति दक्षो नारायणं हरिम् ।
रक्षकं जगतां देवं जगाम शरणं स्वयम् ॥
प्रवर्त्तयामास च तं यज्ञं दक्षोऽथ निर्भयः ।
रक्षको भगवान्विष्णुः शरणागतरक्षकः ॥
पुनः प्राह च तं दक्षं दधीचो भगवानृषिः ।
संप्रेक्ष्यर्षिगणान्देवान्सर्व्वान्वै रुद्रविद्विषः ॥

---

* मन्यन्ते इति E, F and H.

† भूयएव विनिन्द्यते इति B.

‡ विष्णुवाक्यमिति E, F and H.

अपूज्यपूजने चैव पूज्यानाञ्चाप्यपूजने ।
नरः पापमवाप्नोति महद्वै नात्र संशयः ॥
असतां प्रग्रहो यत्र सताञ्चैव विमानना ।
दण्डो दैवकृतस्तत्र सद्यः पतति दारुणः ॥
एवमुक्त्वाथ* विप्रर्षिः शशापेश्वरविद्विषः ।
समागतान्ब्राह्मणांस्तान्दक्षसाहाय्यकारिणः ॥
यस्माद्बहिःकृतो वेदाद्भवद्भिः† परमेश्वरः ।
विनिन्दितो महादेवः शङ्करो लोकवन्दितः‡ ॥
भविष्यन्ति§ त्रयीबाह्याः सर्व्वेऽपीश्वरविद्विषः ।
निन्दन्तीह्यैश्वरं मार्गं कुशास्त्रासक्तचेतसः¶ ॥
मिथ्याधीतसमाचारा मिथ्याज्ञानप्रलापिनः ।
प्राप्य घोरं कलियुगं कलिजैः परिपीड़िताः‖ ॥
त्यक्त्वा तपोबलं कृत्स्नं गच्छध्वं नरकान्पुनः ।
भविष्यति हृषीकेशः स्वाश्रितोऽपि पराङ्मुखः ॥
एवमुक्त्वाथ विप्रर्षिर्विरराम तपोनिधिः ।
जगाम मनसा रुद्रमशेषाघविनाशनम् ॥

---

* एवमुक्त्वा स इति B, E, F and H.

† देवो भवद्भिरिति B.

‡ लोकपूजित इति B.

§ भविष्यध्वमिति B, C and D.

¶ निन्दन्ती ह्यैश्वरं मार्गं कुशास्त्रासक्तमानसा इति B.

‖ परिवर्ज्जिता इति B.

एतस्मिन्नन्तरे देवी महादेवं महेश्वरम् ।
पतिं पशुपतिं देवं ज्ञात्वैतत्प्राह सर्व्वदृक् ॥

श्रीदेव्युवाच ।

दक्षो यज्ञेन यजते पिता मे पूर्व्वजन्मनि ।
विनिन्द्य भवतो भावमात्मानं चापि शङ्कर ॥
देवा महर्षयश्चासन्तत्र* साहाय्यकारिणः ।
विनाशयाशु तं यज्ञं वरमेतं वृणोम्यहम् ॥
एवं विज्ञापितो देव्या देवदेवः परः† प्रभुः ।
ससर्ज्ज सहसा रुद्रं दक्षयज्ञजिघांसया ॥
सहस्रशिरसं क्रुद्धं‡ सहस्राक्षं महाभुजम् ।
सहस्रपाणिं दुर्द्धर्षं युगान्तानलसन्निभम् ॥
दंष्ट्राकरालं दुष्प्रेक्ष्यं शङ्खचक्रधरं प्रभुम्§ ।
दण्डहस्तं महानादं शार्ङ्गिणं भूतिभूषणम् ॥
वीरभद्र इति ख्यातं देवदेवसमन्वितम्¶ ।
स जातमात्रो देवेशमुपतस्थे कृताञ्जलिः ॥
तमाह दक्षस्य मखं विनाशय शिवोऽस्तु ते‖ ।

---

* देवाः सप्तर्षिभिस्तत्र येन इति B.

† देवी देववर इति B.

‡ सहस्रशीर्षपादश्चेति B.

§ शङ्खचक्रगदाधरमिति B.

¶ देवदेवसमन्विषमिति B. देवं देवसमन्वितमिति H.

‖ तमाह दक्षस्य मुखं विनाशय शिवन्त्विति इति B.

विनिन्द्य* मां स यजते गङ्गाद्वारे गणेश्वर ॥
ततो बन्धप्रमुक्तेन सिंहेनैकेन† लीलया ।
वीरभद्रेण दक्षस्य विनाशमगमत्क्रतुः ॥
मन्युना चोमया सृष्टा भद्रकाली महेश्वरी ।
तया च सार्द्धं वृषभं समारुह्य ययौ गणः ॥
अन्ये सहस्रशो रुद्रा निसृष्टास्तेन धीमता ।
रोमजा इति विख्यातास्तस्य साहाय्यकारिणः ॥
शूलशक्तिगदाहस्ता दण्डोपलकरास्तथा ।
कालाग्निरुद्रसङ्काशा नादयन्तो दिशो दश ॥
सर्वे वृषभमारूढाः‡ सभार्य्याश्चातिभीषणाः ।
समावृत्य गणश्रेष्ठं ययुर्दक्षमखम्प्रति ॥
सर्वे सम्प्राप्य तन्देशङ्गङ्गाद्वारमिति श्रुतम् ।
ददृशुर्यज्ञदेशं वै§ दक्षस्यामिततेजसः¶ ॥
देवाङ्गनासहस्राढ्यमप्सरोगीतनादितम् ।
वेणुवीणानिनादाढ्यं वेदवादाभिनादितम् ॥
दृष्ट्वा सहर्षिभिर्देवैः समासीनम्प्रजापतिम्‖ ।

---

* विनीय इति E, F and H. विनीय लघूकृत्य इत्यर्थः ।

† एकेन सिंहेन इव इति शेषः ।

‡ वृषसमारूढा इति B.

§ ददृशुर्यज्ञदेशं वै इत्यस्मात्परं दृष्ट्वा सहर्षिभिर्देवैरित्यन्तं G पुस्तके न दृश्यते ।

¶ समासीनं प्रजापतिमिति E, F and H.

‖ देवादि-पङ्क्तित्रयमिति E, F, H पुस्तकेषु नास्ति ।

उवाच स प्रियो रुद्रैर्वीरभद्रः स्मयन्निव ॥
वयं ह्यनुचराः सर्वे शर्वस्यामिततेजसः ।
भागार्थं लिप्सया भागान् प्राप्ता यच्छत्वभीप्सितान्* ॥
अथ चेत्कस्यचिदियं माया† मुनिवरोत्तमाः ।
भागो भवद्भ्यो देयस्तु नास्मभ्यमिति कथ्यताम् ॥
तम्ब्रूताज्ञापयति यो वेत्स्यामो हि वयं ततः‡ ।
एवमुक्ता गणेशेन प्रजापतिपुरःसराः ॥

देवा ऊचुः ।

प्रमाणं वो न जानीमो भागे मन्त्रा इति प्रभुम्§ ।
मन्त्रा ऊचुः सुरा यूयं तमोपहतचेतसः ।
येनाध्वरस्य राजानं पूजयेयुर्महेश्वरम् ॥
ईश्वरः सर्वभूतानां सर्वदेवतनुर्हरः¶ ।
पूज्यते सर्वयज्ञेषु सर्वाभ्युदयसिद्धिदः ॥
एवमुक्ता महेशानमायया‖ नष्टचेतनाः ।
न मेनिरे ययुर्मन्त्रा देवान्मुक्ता स्वमालयम् ॥

---

* भागाभिलिप्सया प्राप्ता भागान्यच्छध्वमीप्सितानिति B.

† कस्यचिदियमाज्ञा मुनिसुरोत्तमा इति B and H.

‡ विनंक्ष्यामो वयं तत इति B.

§ नेज्यते यज्ञभागेन न च मन्त्रा इति प्रभुरिति B.

¶ सर्व्वभूततनुर्हरिरिति B.

‖ महेशानमिति E, F and H.

ततः सभद्रो भगवान्* सभार्य्यः सगणेश्वरः ।
स्पृशन् कराभ्यां विप्रर्षिं दधीचं† प्राह देवहा ॥
मन्त्राः प्रमाणं न कृता युष्माभिर्बलदर्पितैः ।
यस्मात्प्रसह्य तस्माद्वो नाशयाम्यद्य गर्वितान् ॥
इत्युक्त्वा यज्ञशालां तां ददाह गणपुङ्गवः ।
गणेश्वराश्च संक्रुद्धा यूपानुत्पाद्य चिक्षिपुः ॥
प्रस्तोत्रा सह‡ होत्रा च अश्वञ्चैव गणेश्वराः ।
गृहीत्वा भीषणाः सर्वे गङ्गास्रोतसि चिक्षिपुः ॥
वीरभद्रोऽपि दीप्तात्मा शक्रस्यैवोद्यतं करम्§ ।
व्यष्टभयददीनात्मा तथान्येषां दिवौकसाम् ॥
भगनेत्रे तथोत्पाद्य कराग्रेणैव¶ लीलया ।
निहत्य मुष्टिना दन्तान् पूष्णश्चैवमपातयत् ॥
तथा चन्द्रमसं देवं पादाङ्गुष्ठेन लीलया ।
धर्षयामास बलवान् स्मयमानो गणेश्वरः ॥
वह्नेर्हस्तद्वयं छित्त्वा जिह्वामुत्पाद्य लीलया ।
जघान मूर्ध्नि पादेन मुनीनपि मुनीश्वराः ॥

---

* ततः स रुद्री भगवानिति E, F, G and H.

† ब्रह्मर्षिं दधीचमिति B.

‡ प्रस्तोत्रा सह इत्यस्मात्परं गङ्गास्रोतसि चिक्षिपुरित्यन्तं E, F, G, H पुस्तकेषु नास्ति ।

§ शक्रस्योद्यच्छतः करमिति B.

¶ भगस्य नेत्रे चोत्पाद्य करजाग्रेण इति B.

तथा विष्णुं सगरुड़ं समायान्तं महाबलः।
विव्याध निशितैर्वाणैः स्तम्भयित्वा सुदर्शनम्॥
समालोक्य महाबाहुरागत्य गरुड़ो गणम्।
जघान पक्षैः सहसा ननादाम्बुनिधिर्यथा॥
ततः सहस्रशो रुद्रः* ससर्ज गरुड़ान् स्वयम्।
वैनतेयादभ्यधिकान् गरुड़ं ते† प्रदुद्रुवुः॥
तान्दृष्ट्वा गरुड़ो धीमान् पलायत‡ महाजवः।
विसृज्य माधवं वेगात्तदद्भुतमिवाभवत्॥
अन्तर्हिते वैनतेये भगवान् पद्मसम्भवः।
आगत्य वारयामास वीरभद्रञ्च केशवम्॥
प्रसादयामास च तं गौरवात्परमेष्ठिनः।
संस्तूय भगवानीशं शम्भुस्तत्रागमत्स्वयम्॥
वीक्ष्य देवाधिदेवं तमुमां सर्वगुणैर्वृताम्।
तुष्टाव भगवान् ब्रह्मा दक्षः सर्वे दिवौकसः॥
विशेषात्पार्वतीं देवीमीश्वरार्द्धशरीरिणीम्।
स्तोत्रैर्नानाविधैर्दक्षः प्रणम्य च कृताञ्जलिः॥
ततो भगवती देवी प्रहसन्ती महेश्वरम्।
प्रसन्नमनसा रुद्रं वचः प्राह घृणानिधिः§॥

---

* भद्र इति B.

† गरुड़न्तमिति A.

‡ धीमानपायत इति G and H. अपायत पलायत, अप-अय-त।

§ घृणानिधिः करुणालयः। "कारुण्यं करुणा घृणा" इत्यमरः।

त्वमेव जगतः स्रष्टा शासिता चैव रक्षिता* ।
अनुग्राह्यो भगवता दक्षश्चापि दिवौकसः ॥
ततः प्रहस्य भगवान् कपर्द्दी नीललोहितः ।
उवाच प्रणतान्देवान् प्राचेतसमथो हरः ॥
गच्छध्वं† देवताः सर्वाः प्रसन्नो भवतामहम् ।
संपूज्यः सर्वयज्ञेषु न निन्द्योऽहं विशेषतः ॥
त्वञ्चापि शृणु मे दक्ष वचनं सर्वरक्षणम्‡ ।
त्यक्त्वा लोकैषणामेतां§ मद्भक्तो भव यत्नतः ॥
भविष्यसि गणेशानः कल्पान्तेऽनुग्रहान्मम ।
तावत्तिष्ठ ममादेशात्स्वाधिकारेषु निर्वृतः ॥
एवमुक्त्वा तु¶ भगवान् सपत्नीकः सहानुगः ।
अदर्शनमनुप्राप्तो दक्षस्यामिततेजसः ॥
अन्तर्हिते महादेवे शङ्करे पद्मसम्भवः ।
व्याजहार स्वयं दक्षमशेषजगतो हितम् ॥

ब्रह्मोवाच ।

किञ्चायं भवतो मोहः‖ प्रसन्ने वृषभध्वजे ।

---

* रक्षक इति B.

† गच्छध्वमित्यार्षं, गच्छत इति साधु ।

‡ सर्व्वलक्षणमिति B.

§ लोकैषणां लोकानामेषणां प्रेषणां दुष्प्रवर्त्तनामित्यर्थः ।

¶ स इति B.

‖ किं तवापगतो मोह इति B.

यदा च स स्वयं देवः पालयेत्त्वामतन्द्रितः ॥
सर्व्वेषामेव भूतानां हृद्येष परमेश्वरः* ।
पश्यन्ति यं† ब्रह्मभूता विद्वांसो वेदवादिनः ॥
स चात्मा सर्व्वभूतानां स वीजं परमा गतिः ।
स्तूयते वैदिकैर्मन्त्रैर्देवदेवो महेश्वरः ॥
तमर्च्चयन्ति ये रुद्रं स्वात्मना च‡ सनातनम् ।
चेतसा भावयुक्तेन ते यान्ति§ परमं पदम् ॥
तस्मादनादिमध्यान्तं विज्ञाय परमेश्वरम् ।
कर्म्मणा मनसा वाचा समाराधय यत्नतः ॥
यत्नात्परिहरेशस्य निन्दां स्वात्मविनाशनीम्¶ ।
भवन्ति‖ सर्व्वदोषाय निन्दकस्य क्रिया हि ताः** ॥
यस्तु चैष महायोगी रक्षको विष्णुरव्ययः ।
स देवो भगवान्रुद्रो†† महादेवो न संशयः ॥
मन्यन्ते ये जगद्योनिं विभिन्नं विष्णुमीश्वरात् ।
मोहादवेदनिष्ठत्वात्ते यान्ति नरकं नराः ॥

---

* वसतीश्वर इति B.

† पश्यन्त्येनमिति B.

‡ तमर्चयति यो रुद्रं स्वात्मन्येकमिति B.

§ स याति इति B.

¶ निन्दामात्मविनाशिनीमिति B.

‖ तरन्तीति B.

** क्रिया यत इति B.

†† स देवदेवो भगवानिति B.

वेदानुवर्त्तिनो रुद्रं देवं नारायणं तथा ।
एकीभावेन पश्यन्ति मुक्तिभाजो भवन्ति ते ॥
यो विष्णुः स स्वयं रुद्रो यो रुद्रः स जनार्द्दनः ।
इति मत्वा भजेद्देवं स याति परमां गतिम् ॥
सृजत्येष जगत्सर्वं विष्णुस्तत्पश्यतीश्वरः* ।
इत्थं जगत्सर्वमिदं रुद्रनारायणोद्भवम् ॥
तस्मात्त्यक्त्वा हरेर्निन्दां हरे चापि समाहितः ।
समाश्रय महादेवं शरण्यं ब्रह्मवादिनाम् ॥
उपश्रुत्याथ वचनं विरिञ्चस्य प्रजापतिः ।
जगाम शरणं देवं गोपतिं कृत्तिवाससम् ॥
येऽन्ये शापाग्निनिर्द्दग्धा दधीचस्य महर्षयः ।
द्विषन्तो मोहिता देवं सम्बभूवुः कलिष्वथ ॥
त्यक्त्वा तपोबलं कृत्स्नं विप्राणां कुलसम्भवाः ।
पूर्वसंस्कारमाहात्म्याद्ब्रह्मणो वचनादिह ॥
मुक्तशापास्ततः सर्वे कल्पान्ते रौरवादिषु ।
निपात्यमानाः कालेन सम्प्राप्यादित्यवर्चसम् ॥
ब्रह्माणं जगतामीशमनुज्ञाताः स्वयम्भुवा ।
समाराध्य तपोयोगादीशानं त्रिदशाधिपम् ।
भविष्यन्ति यथापूर्वं शङ्करस्य प्रसादतः ॥

---

* सृजत्येव जगत्सर्वं विष्णुस्तस्याऽर्द्धमहेश्वर इति A. विष्णुस्तस्य महेश्वर इति E, F, G and H.

एतद्वः कथितं सर्वं दक्षयज्ञनिषूदनम् ।
शृणुध्वं दक्षपुत्रीणां सर्वासां चैव सन्ततिम् ॥

इति श्रीकूर्म्मपुराणे दक्षयज्ञविध्वंसो नाम पञ्चदशोऽध्यायः ।

—:—

षोड़शोऽध्यायः ।

सूत उवाच ।

प्रजाः सृजेति सन्दिष्टः* पूर्व्वं दक्षः स्वयंभुवा ।
ससर्ज देवान् गन्धर्व्वानृषींश्चैवासुरोरगान् ॥
यदास्य सृजतः पूर्व्वं† न व्यवर्द्धन्त ताः प्रजाः ।
तदा ससर्ज भूतानि मैथुनेनैव सर्व्वतः‡ ॥
असिक्नरां§ जनयामास वीरणस्य प्रजापतेः ।
सुतायां धर्म्मयुक्तायां पुत्राणान्तु सहस्रकम् ॥
तेषु पुत्रेषु नष्टेषु मायया नारदस्य तु ।
षष्टिं दक्षोऽसृजत्कन्या वैरिण्यां¶ वै प्रजापतिः ॥

---

* व्यादिष्ट इति B.

† सृज्यमानस्येति B.

‡ धर्म्मत इति B.

§ असक्त्यामिति E, F, and H.

¶ वैरण्यामिति E, F and H.

ददौ स* दश धर्म्माय कश्यपाय त्रयोदश।
विंशत्सप्त च† सोमाय चतस्रोऽरिष्टनेमये॥
द्वे चैव बहुपुत्राय द्वे कृशाश्वाय धीमते।
द्वे चैवाङ्गिरसे तद्वत्तासां वक्ष्येऽथ विस्तरम्॥
मरुत्वती वसुर्यामी लम्बा भानुररुन्धती।
सङ्कल्पा च मुहूर्त्ता च साध्या विश्वा च भामिनी॥
धर्म्मपत्न्यो दश त्वेतास्तासां पुत्रान्निबोधत।
विश्वेदेवास्तु विश्वायां साध्या साध्यानजीजनत्॥
मरुत्वत्यां मरुत्वन्तो वस्वास्तु‡ वसवस्तथा§।
भानोस्तु भानवाश्चैव मुहूर्त्तास्तु मुहूर्त्तजाः॥
लम्बायाश्चाथ घोषोवै नागवीथी तु यामिजा¶।
पृथिवीविषयं सर्व्वमरुन्धत्यामजायत॥
सङ्कल्पायास्तु सङ्कल्पो धर्म्मपुत्रा दश स्मृताः।
ये त्वनेकवसुप्राणा देवा ज्योतिःपुरोगमाः॥
वसवोऽष्टौ समाख्यातास्तेषां वक्ष्यामि विस्तरम्‖।
आपोध्रुवश्च सोमश्च धरश्चैवानलोऽनिलः** ॥

---

* चेति B.

† सप्तविंशतिरिति B.

‡ वसोस्तु इति E, F and H.

§ मरुत्वन्तो मरुत्वत्यां वसवोऽष्टौ वसोः सुता इति B.

¶ वागवीथी तु यामिजा इति G.

‖ ये त्वनेकेत्यारभ्य विस्तरमित्यन्तं B पुस्तके नास्ति।

** धवश्चैवानिलोऽनल इति B.

प्रत्यूषश्च प्रभासश्च* वसवोऽष्टौ प्रकीर्त्तिताः।
आपस्य पुत्रो वैतण्ड्यः श्रमः श्रान्तोध्वनिस्तथा॥
ध्रुवस्य† पुत्रोभगवान् कालोलोकप्रकालनः।
सोमस्य भगवान्वर्चा धरस्य द्रविणः सुतः॥
मनोजवो‡ नलस्यासादविज्ञातगतिस्तथा।
कुमारो ह्यनिलस्यासीत्सेनापतिरिति स्मृतः॥
देवलो भगवान्योगी प्रत्यूषस्याभवत्सुतः।
विश्वकर्म्मा प्रभासस्य शिल्पकर्त्ता प्रजापतिः॥
अदितिर्द्दितिर्द्दनुस्तद्वदरिष्टा§ सुरसास्तथा।
सुरभिर्विनता चैव ताम्रा क्रोधवशा त्विरा¶॥
कद्रुर्मुनिश्च धर्मज्ञा तत्पुत्रान्वै निबोधत।
अंशो धाता भगस्त्वष्टा मित्रोऽथ वरुणोऽर्य्यमा॥
विवस्वान् सविता पूषा ह्यंशुमान्विष्णुरेव च।
तुषिता नाम ते पूर्व्वं चाक्षुषस्यान्तरे मनोः॥
वैवस्वतेऽन्तरे प्रोक्ता आदित्याश्चादितेः सुताः‖।
दितिः पुत्रद्वयं लेभे कश्यपाद्बलगर्वितम्**।

---

* प्रभावश्च इति B.

† धवस्य इति B.

‡ पुरोजव इति B.

§ क्वचित् नवाक्षरोऽपि पादो दृश्यते।

¶ क्रोधवशाङ्गिरा इति B.

‖ ह्यादित्या अदितेः सुता इति B.

** बलसंयुतमिति B.

हिरण्यकशिपुं ज्येष्ठं हिरण्याक्षं तथानुजम्* ॥
हिरण्यकशिपुर्दैत्यो महाबलपराक्रमः।
आराध्य तपसा देवं ब्रह्माणं परमेश्वरम्† ।
दृष्ट्वा लेभे वरान्दिव्यांस्तुत्वासौ विविधैस्तवैः ॥
अथ तस्य बलाद्देवाः सर्वएव महर्षयः‡ ।
बाधितास्ताड़िता जग्मुर्देवदेवं पितामहम् ॥
शरण्यं शरणं देवं शम्भुं सर्वजगन्मयम् ।
ब्रह्माणं लोककर्त्तारं त्रातारं पुरुषं परम् ।
कूटस्थं जगतामेकं पुराणं पुरुषोत्तमम् ॥
स याचितो देववरैः§ मुनिभिश्च मुनीश्वराः ।
सर्वदेवहितार्थाय जगाम कमलासनः ॥
संस्तूयमानः प्रणतैर्मुनीन्द्रैरमरैरपि ।
क्षीरोदस्योत्तरं कूलं यत्रास्ते हरिरीश्वरः ॥
दृष्ट्वा देवं जगद्योनिं विष्णुं विश्वगुरुं शिवम् ।
ववन्दे चरणौ मूर्ध्ना कृताञ्जलिरभाषत ॥

ब्रह्मोवाच ।

त्वं गतिः सर्वभूतानामनन्तोऽस्यखिलात्मकः ।
व्यापी सर्वामरवपुर्महायोगी सनातनः ॥

---

* तथापरमिति B.

† परमेष्ठिनमिति B.

‡ सुरर्षय इति B.

§ देवदेवैरिति B.

त्वमात्मा सर्वभूतानां प्रधानप्रकृतिः* परा ।
वैराग्यैश्वर्यनिरतो वागतीतो निरञ्जनः ॥
त्वङ्कर्त्ता चैव भर्त्ता च विहन्ता च सुरद्विषाम् ।
त्रातुमर्हस्यनन्तेश त्रातासि परमेश्वरः ॥
इत्थं स विष्णुर्भगवान् ब्रह्मणा सम्प्रबोधितः ।
प्रोवाचोन्निद्रपद्माक्षः पीतवासाः सुरान्द्विजाः† ॥
किमर्थं सुमहावीर्याः सप्रजापतिकाः सुराः ।
इमं देशमनुप्राप्ताः किं वा कार्यं करोमि वः ॥

देवा ऊचुः ।

हिरण्यकशिपुर्नाम ब्रह्मणोवरदर्पितः ।
बाधते भगवन्दैत्यो देवान् सर्व्वान् सहर्षिभिः ॥
अवध्यः सर्व्वभूतानां त्वामृते पुरुषोत्तमम् ।
हन्तुमर्हसि सर्व्वेषां त्रातासि‡ त्वं जगन्मय ॥
श्रुत्वा तद्दैवतैरुक्तं स विष्णुर्लोकभावनः ।
वधाय दैत्यमुख्यस्य सोऽसृजत्पुरुषं स्वयम् ॥
मेरुपर्व्वतवर्ष्माणं घोररूपं भयानकम् ।
शङ्खचक्रगदापाणिं तं प्राह गरुड़ध्वजः ॥
हत्वा तं दैत्यराजानं§ हिरण्यकशिपुं पुनः ।

---

* प्रधानं प्रकृतिरिति B.

† सुरार्च्चित इति B.

‡ त्वं त्रातासीति B.

§ दैत्यराजमिति साधु ।

इमं देशं समागन्तुं चिप्रमर्हसि पौरुषात् ॥
निशम्य वैष्णवं वाक्यं प्रणम्य पुरुषोत्तमम् ।
महापुरुषमव्यक्तं ययौ दैत्यमहापुरम् ॥
विमुञ्चन् भैरवं नादं शङ्खचक्रगदाधरः ।
आरुह्य गरुड़ं देवो महामेरुरिवापरः ॥
आकर्ण्य दैत्यप्रवरा महामेघरवोपमम् ।
समं च चक्रिरे* नादं तथा दैत्यपतेर्भयात् ॥

असुरा ऊचुः ।

कश्चिदागच्छति महान् पुरुषो देवनोदितः ।
विमुञ्चन् भैरवं नादं तं जानीमो जनार्द्दनम् ॥
ततः सहासुरवरैर्हिरण्यकशिपुः स्वयम् ।
सन्नद्धैः सायुधैः पुत्रैः सप्रह्लादैस्†तदा ययौ ॥
दृष्ट्वा तं गरुड़ारूढं‡ सूर्य्यकोटिसमप्रभम् ।
पुरुषं पर्व्वताकारं नारायणमिवापरम् ।
दुद्रुवुः केचिदन्योन्यमूचुः सम्भ्रान्तलोचनाः ॥
अयं स देवो देवानां गोप्ता नारायणोरिपुः ।
अस्माकमव्ययो नूनं तत्सुतोवा समागतः ॥
इत्युक्त्वा शस्त्रवर्षाणि ससृजुः पुरुषाय ते ।

---

* समाचचक्रिरे इति B.

† प्रह्लादाद्यैरिति B.

‡ गरुड़ासीनमिति B.

स तानि चाच्युतोदेवो* नाशयामास लीलया ॥
हिरण्यकशिपोः पुत्राः†श्चत्वारः प्रथितौजसः।
पुत्रं‡ नारायणोद्भूतं युयुधुर्म्मेघनिःस्वनाः ॥
प्रह्लादश्चानुह्लादश्च संह्लादो ह्लादएव च ॥
प्रह्लादः प्राहिणोद्ब्राह्ममनुह्लादोऽथ वैष्णवम्।
संह्लादश्चापि कौमारमाग्नेयं ह्लादएव च ॥
तानि तं पुरुषं प्राप्य चत्वार्य्यस्त्राणि वैष्णवम्।
न शेकुश्चालितुं§ विष्णुं वासुदेवं यथातथम् ॥
अथासौ चतुरः पुत्रान्महाबाहुर्म्महाबलः।
प्रगृह्य पादेषु करैश्चिक्षेप च ननाद च ॥
विमुक्तेष्वथ पुत्रेषु हिरण्यकशिपुः स्वयम्।
पादेन ताड़यामास वेगेनोरसि तं बली ॥
स तेन पीड़ितोऽत्यर्थं गरुड़ेन सहानुगः¶।
अदृश्यः प्रययौ तूर्णं यत्र नारायणः प्रभुः ॥
गत्वा विज्ञापयामास प्रवृत्तमखिलं तदा।
सञ्चिन्त्य मनसा देवः सर्व्वज्ञानमयोऽमलः।
नरस्यार्द्धतनुं कृत्वा सिंहस्यार्द्धतनुं तथा।

---

* तानि चाशेषतो देव इति B. तांस्तु स चाच्युतो देव इति E, F, G and H.

† तदा हिरण्यकशिपोरिति B.

‡ पुत्रा इति B, E, F and H.

§ बाधितुमिति B.

¶ यथाऽनुग इति B.

नृसिंहवपुरव्यक्तो हिरण्यकशिपोः पुरे ।
आविर्बभूव सहसा मोहयन्दैत्यदानवान्* ।
दंष्ट्राकरालो योगात्मा युगान्तदहनोपमः ॥
समारुह्यात्मनः शक्तिं सर्वसंहारकारिकाम् ।
भाति नारायणोऽनन्तो यथा मध्यन्दिने रविः ॥
दृष्ट्वा† नृसिंहं पुरुषं प्रह्लादं ज्येष्ठपुत्रकम् ।
वधाय प्रेरयामास नरसिंहस्य सोऽसुरः ॥
इमं नृसिंहं पुरुषं पूर्वस्मादूनशक्तिकम्‡ ।
सहैव तेऽनुजैः सर्वैर्नाशयाशु मयेरितः ॥
स तन्नियोगादसुरः प्रह्लादो विष्णुमव्ययम् ।
युयुधे सर्वयत्नेन नरसिंहेन निर्जितः ॥
ततः संमोहितो§ दैत्यो हिरण्याक्षस्तदानुजः ।
ध्यात्वा पशुपतेरस्त्रं ससर्ज च ननाद च ॥
तस्य देवाधिदेवस्य विष्णोरमिततेजसः ।
न हानिमकरोदस्त्रं यथा देवस्य शूलिनः ॥
दृष्ट्वा पराहतं त्वस्त्रं प्रह्लादो भाग्यगौरवात् ।
मेने सर्व्वात्मकं देवं वासुदेवं सनातनम् ॥
सन्त्यज्य सर्वशस्त्राणि सत्त्वयुक्तेन चेतसा ।

---

* दैत्यपुङ्गवानिति B.

† दृष्ट्वा इत्यारभ्य इमभित्यन्तं G, H पुस्तकयोर्नास्ति ।

‡ पूर्व्वस्मादरशक्तिकमिति B.

§ सञ्चोदित इति B.

ननाम शिरसा देवं योगिनां हृदयेशयम् ॥
स्तुत्वा नारायणं स्तोत्रैः ऋग्यजुःसामसम्भवैः ।
निवार्य्य पितरं भ्रातॄन् हिरण्याक्षं तदाब्रवीत् ॥
अयं नारायणोऽनन्तः शाश्वतो भगवानजः ।
पुराणः पुरुषो* देवो महायोगी जगन्मयः ॥
अयं धाता विधाता च स्वयंज्योतिर्निरञ्जनः ।
प्रधानं पुरुषं तत्त्वं मूलप्रकृतिरव्यया† ॥
ईश्वरः सर्व्वभूतानां‡मन्तर्यामी गुणातिगः ।
गच्छध्वमेनं शरणं विष्णुमव्यक्तमव्ययम् ॥
एवमुक्तो§ सुदुर्बुद्धिर्हिरण्यकशिपुः स्वयम् ।
प्रोवाच पुत्रमत्यर्थं मोहितो विष्णुमायया ॥
अयं सर्व्वात्मना वध्यो नृसिंहोऽल्पपराक्रमः ।
समागतोऽस्मद्भवनमिदानीं कालचोदितः ॥
विहस्य पितरं पुत्रो वचः प्राह महामतिः ।
मा निन्दस्वैनमीशानं¶ भूतानामेकमव्ययम् ॥
कथं देवो महादेवः शाश्वतः कालवर्जितः ।
कालेन हन्यते विष्णुः कालात्मा कालरूपधृक् ॥

---

* प्रधानपुरुष इति B.

† अव्यय इति B.

‡ भावानामिति B.

§ एवमुक्त इति B.

¶ निन्दस्व इति आर्षमात्मनेपदम् ।

ततः सुवर्णकशिपुर्दुरात्मा कालचोदितः* ।
निवारितोऽपि पुत्रेण युयुधे हरिमव्ययम् ॥
संरक्तनयनोऽनन्तो हिरण्यनयनाग्रजम् ।
नखैर्विदारयामास प्रह्लादस्यैव पश्यतः ॥
हते हिरण्यकशिपौ हिरण्याक्षो महाबलः ।
विसृज्य पुत्रं प्रह्लादं दुद्रुवे भयविह्वलः ॥†
अनुह्लादादयः पुत्रा अन्ये च शतशोऽसुराः ।
नृसिंहदेहसम्भूतैः सिंहैर्नीता यमक्षयम्‡ ॥
ततः संहृत्य तद्रूपं हरिर्नारायणः प्रभुः ।
स्वमेव परमं रूपं ययौ नारायणाह्वयम् ॥
गते नारायणे दैत्यः प्रह्लादोऽसुरसत्तमः ।
अभिषेकेण युक्तेन हिरण्याक्षमयोजयत् ॥
स बाधयामास सुरान्रणे जित्वा मुनीनपि ।
लब्ध्वान्धकं महापुत्रं तपसाराध्य शङ्करम् ॥
देवाञ्जित्वा सदेवेन्द्रान् क्षुब्ध्वा§ च धरणीमिमाम् ।
नीत्वा रसातलं चक्रे वेदान्वै निष्प्रभांस्तथा¶ ॥
ततः सब्रह्मका देवाः परिम्लानमुखश्रियः ।

---

* प्रोवाच विधिनोदित इति A, E and H.

† श्लोकोऽयं A and D पुस्तकयोर्नास्ति ।

‡ यमक्षयं यमस्य क्षयमालयम्, क्षिधातोर्वासार्थकादधिकरणे अल् ।

§ बद्ध्वा इति B and D.

¶ वन्दीमिन्दीवरप्रभामिति B.

गत्वा विज्ञापयामासुर्विष्णवे हरिमन्दिरम् ॥
स चिन्तयित्वा विश्वात्मा तद्वधोपायमव्ययः ।
सर्व्वदेवमयं शुभ्रं वाराहञ्च पुरा दधे* ॥
गत्वा हिरण्यनयनं हत्वा तं पुरुषोत्तमः ।
दंष्ट्रयोद्धारयामास† कल्पादौ धरणीमिमाम् ॥
त्यक्त्वा वाराहसंस्थानं संस्थाप्यैवं सुरद्विषः‡ ।
स्वामेव प्रकृतिं दिव्यां ययौ विष्णुः परं पदम् ॥
तस्मिन् हतेऽमररिपौ प्रह्लादो विष्णुतत्परः ।
अपालयत्स्वकं राज्यं भावं त्यक्त्वा तदासुरम् ॥
यजते§ विधिवद्देवान्विष्णोराराधने रतः ।
निःसपत्नं सदा राज्यं तस्यासीद्विष्णुवैभवात् ॥
ततः कदाचिदसुरो ब्राह्मणं गृहमागतम् ।
न च सम्भाषयामास¶ देवानाञ्चैव मायया ॥
स तेन तापसोऽत्यर्थं मोहितेनावमानितः ।
शशापासुरराजानं‖ क्रोधसंरक्तलोचनः ॥
यत्तद्बलं** समाश्रित्य ब्राह्मणानवमन्यसे ।

---

* वाराहं वपुरादधे इति B and D.

† दंष्ट्रयोर्धारयामास इति B.

‡ संस्थाप्य च सुरद्विष इति B and D.

§ इयाजेति B.

¶ तापसं नार्हयामासेति B.

‖ असुरराजमिति साधु ।

** यद्बलञ्च इति B.

सा शक्तिर्वैष्णवी* दिव्या विनाशन्ते गमिष्यति ॥
इत्युक्त्वा प्रययौ तूर्णं प्रह्लादस्य गृहाद्द्विजः।
मुमोह राज्यसंसक्तः सोऽपि शापबलात्ततः ॥
बाधयामास विप्रेन्द्रान्न विवेद जनार्द्दनम्।
पितुर्वधमनुस्मृत्य क्रोधं चक्रे हरिं प्रति ॥
तयोः समभवद्युद्धं सुघोरं रोमहर्षणम्।
नारायणस्य देवस्य प्रह्लादस्यामरद्विषः ॥
कृत्वा स सुमहद्युद्धं विष्णुना तेन निर्जितः।
पूर्व्वसंस्कारमाहात्म्यात्परस्मिन्पुरुषे हरौ।
सञ्जातं तस्य विज्ञानं शरण्यं शरणं ययौ ॥
ततःप्रभृति दैत्येन्द्रो ह्यनन्यां भक्तिमुद्वहन्।
नारायणे महायोगमवाप पुरुषोत्तमे ॥
हिरण्यकशिपोः पुत्रे योगसंसक्तचेतसि।
अवाप तन्महद्राज्यमन्धकोऽसुरपुङ्गवः ॥
हिरण्यनेत्रतनयः शम्भोर्देहसमुद्भवः।
मन्दरस्थामुमां देवीं चकमे पर्वतात्मजाम् ॥
पुरा दारुवने पुण्ये मुनयो गृहमेधिनः।
ईश्वराराधनार्थाय तपश्चेरुः सहस्रशः ॥
ततः कदाचिन्महती कालयोगेन दुस्तरा।
अनावृष्टिरतीवोग्रा ह्यासीद्भूतविनाशिनी ॥
समेत्य सर्वे मुनयो गौतमं तपसां निधिम्।

---

* भक्तिरिति D, E and H.

अयाचन्त क्षुधाविष्टा आहारं* प्राणधारणम् ॥
स तेभ्यः प्रददावन्नं मृष्टं बहुतरं बुधः ।
सर्वे बुभुजिरे विप्रा निर्विशङ्केन चेतसा ॥
गते च द्वादशे वर्षे कल्पान्त इव शङ्करी ।
बभूव वृष्टिर्महती यथापूर्वमभूज्जगत्† ॥
ततः सर्वे मुनिवराः समामन्त्र्य परस्परम् ।
महर्षिं गौतमं प्रोचुर्गच्छाम इति वेगतः ॥
निवारयामास च तान् कञ्चित्कालं यथासुखम् ।
उषित्वा मद्गृहेऽवश्यं गच्छध्वमिति पण्डिताः ॥
ततो मायामयीं सृष्ट्वा कृष्णां गां‡ सर्व एव ते ।
समीपं प्रापयामासुर्गौतमस्य महात्मनः ॥
सोऽनुवीक्ष्य कृपाविष्टस्तस्याः संरक्षणोत्सुकः ।
गोष्ठे तां बन्धयामास स्पृष्टमात्रा ममार सा ॥
स शोकेनाभिसन्तप्तः कार्याकार्यं महामुनिः ।
न पश्यति स्म सहसा तमृषिं मुनयोऽब्रुवन् ॥
गोवध्येयं§ द्विजश्रेष्ठ यावत्तव शरीरगा ।
तावत्तेऽन्नं न भोक्तव्यं गच्छामो वयमेव हि ॥

---

* ह्याहारमिति B.

† यथापूर्णमभूदिति E, G and H.

‡ कृशाङ्गीमिति B. कृशां गामिति D.

§ गोवध्येयं—गौः वध्या हत्या, क्यपि भावे हनो वधादेश आर्षः ।

तेनातोऽनुमताः सन्तो देवदारुवनं शुभम्* ।
जग्मुः पापवशन्नीत्वा† तपश्चर्त्तुं यथा पुरा ॥
स तेषां मायया जातां गोवध्यां गौतमोमुनिः ।
केनापि हेतुना ज्ञात्वा शशापातीवकोपतः‡ ॥
भविष्यन्ति त्रयीवाह्या महापातकिभिः समाः ।
बहुशस्ते तथा शापाज्जायमानाः पुनः पुनः ॥
सर्व्वै संप्राप्य देवेशं शङ्करं विष्णुमव्ययम् ।
अस्तुवन् लौकिकैः स्तोत्रैरुच्छिष्टा इव सर्व्वगौ§ ॥
देवदेवौ महादेवौ भक्तानामर्त्तिनाशनौ ।
कामवृत्त्या महायोगी पापान्नस्त्रातुमर्हतः ॥
तदा पार्श्वस्थितं विष्णुं संप्रेक्ष्य वृषभध्वजः ।
किमेतेषां भवेत्कार्य्यं प्राह पुण्यैषिणामिति ॥
ततः स भगवान्विष्णुः शरण्यो भक्तवत्सलः ।
गोपतिं प्राह विप्रेन्द्रानालोक्य प्रणतान् हरिः¶ ॥
न वेदवाह्ये पुरुषे पुण्यलेशोऽपि शङ्कर ।
सङ्गच्छते महादेव धर्मो वेदाद्विनिर्बभौ‖ ॥

---

* एवमुक्त्वा मुनिवरं गौतमं तपसां निधिमति D.

† नीता इति B and D.

‡ कोपन इति B.

§ रुच्छिष्टैरिव सर्व्वगैरिति D.

¶ प्रणतो हरिरिति A, E and H.

‖ विनिर्ययौ इति B.

तथापि भक्त*वात्सल्याद्रक्षितव्या महेश्वर ।
अस्माभिः सर्व्वं एवैते गन्तारो नरकानपि ॥
तस्माद्धि† वेदवाह्यानां रक्षणार्थाय पापिनाम् ।
विमोहनाय शास्त्राणि करिष्यामो‡ वृषध्वज ॥
एवं सम्बोधितो रुद्रो माधवेन मुरारिणा ।
चकार मोहशास्त्राणि केशवोऽपि शिवेरितः ॥
कापालं नाकुलं§ वामं भैरवं पूर्व्वपश्चिमम् ।
पञ्चरात्रं पाशुपतं तथान्यानि सहस्रशः ।
सृष्ट्वा तानाह¶ निर्व्वेदाः कुर्व्वाणाः शास्त्रचोदितम् ।
पतन्तो नरके घोरे बहून् कल्पान् पुनः पुनः ॥
जायन्तो‖ मानुषे लोके क्षीणपापचयास्ततः ।
ईश्वराराधनबलाद्गच्छध्वं सुकृताङ्गतिम् ॥
वर्त्तध्वं मत्प्रसादेन नान्यथा निष्कृतिर्हि वः ॥
एवमीश्वरविष्णुभ्यां चोदितास्ते महर्षयः ।
आदेशं प्रत्यपद्यन्त शिवस्यासुरविद्विषः ॥
चक्रुस्तेऽन्यानि शास्त्राणि तत्र तत्र रताः पुनः ।

---

* भक्ता इति H.

† तस्माद्वै इति B.

‡ करिष्याव इति B.

§ लाकुलमिति A, D, E and H.

¶ तावूचतुरिति B. तान्याह इति E, G and H.

‖ जायन्ते इति B. जायन्त इत्यत्र ग्रहरार्षः ।

शिष्यानध्यापयामासुर्दर्शयित्वा फलानि च ॥
मोहापसदनं* लोकमवतीर्य्य महीतले ।
चकार शङ्करो भिक्षां हितायैषां द्विजैः सह ।
कपालमालाभरणः प्रेतभस्मावगुण्ठितः ।
विमोहयँल्लोकमिमं जटामण्डलमण्डितः ॥
निक्षिप्य पार्व्वतीन्देवीं विष्णावमिततेजसि ।
नियोज्य भगवान्रुद्रो भैरवं दुष्टनिग्रहे ।
दत्त्वा नारायणे देव्यानन्दनं† कुलनन्दनम् ॥
संस्थाप्य तत्र च गणान्देवानिन्द्रपुरोगमान् ॥
प्रस्थिते च महादेवे विष्णुर्विश्वतनुः स्वयम् ।
स्त्रीरूपधारी नियतं सेवते स्म महेश्वरीम् ॥
ब्रह्मा हुताशनः शक्रो यमोऽन्ये सुरपुंगवाः ।
सिषेविरे महादेवीं स्त्रीरूपं शोभनङ्कृताः ॥
नन्दीश्वरश्च भगवान् शम्भोरत्यन्तवल्लभः ।
द्वारदेशे गणाध्यक्षो यथापूर्व्वमतिष्ठत ॥
एतस्मिन्नन्तरे दैत्यो ह्यन्धकोनाम दुर्मतिः ।
आहर्त्तुकामो गिरिजामाजगामाथ मन्दरम् ॥
सम्प्राप्तमन्धकं दृष्ट्वा शङ्करः कालभैरवः‡ ।
न्यषेधयदमेयात्मा कालरूपधरो हरः ॥

---

* मोहयन्त इमं लोकमिति D. मोहाय स इमं लोकमिति E and H.

† देवीं नन्दिनमिति E and H.

‡ कालचोदित इति B.

तयोः समभवद्युद्धं सुघोरं रोमहर्षणम्।
शूलेनोरसि तन्दैत्यमाजघान वृषध्वजः॥
ततः सहस्रशो दैत्याः संहस्राण्यन्धकसञ्ज्ञिताः*।
नन्दीश्वरादयो† दैत्यैरन्धकैरभिनिर्जिताः॥
घण्टाकर्णो मेघनादश्चण्डेशश्चण्डतापनः।
विनायको मेघवाहः सोमनन्दी च वैद्युतः‡।
सर्वेऽन्धकन्दैत्यवरं सम्प्राप्यातिबलान्विताः।
युयुधुः शूलशक्त्यृष्टिगिरिकूटपरश्वधैः॥
भ्रामयित्वा तु हस्ताभ्यां गृहीत्वा चरणद्वये।
दैत्येन्द्रेणातिबलिना क्षिप्तास्ते शतयोजनम्॥
ततोऽन्धकनिसृष्टा ये§ शतशोऽथ सहस्रशः।
कालसूर्य्यप्रतीकाशा भैरवञ्चाभिदुद्रुवुः¶॥
हा हेति‖ शब्दः सुमहान् बभूवातिभयङ्करः।
युयुधे भैरवो देवः** शूलमादाय भैरवम्††॥
दृष्ट्वान्धकानां सुबलं दुर्जयन्निर्जितो हरः।

---

* दैत्यः ससर्जान्धकसंज्ञितानिति B.

† नन्दिकेशादय इति B.

‡ विश्वां पतिरिति B.

§ निसृष्टास्ते इति B.

¶ भैरवन्त्वभिदुद्रुवुरिति B.

‖ जहीति इति E, G and H.

** रुद्र इति B.

†† भीषणमिति B.

जगाम शरणन्देवं वासुदेवमजं विभुम् ॥
सोऽसृजद्भगवान्विष्णुर्देवीनां शतमुत्तमम् ।
देवीपार्श्वस्थितो देवो विनाशाय सुरद्विषाम् ॥
तदान्धकसहस्रन्तु देवीभिर्यमसादनम्* ।
नीतं केशवमाहात्म्याल्लीलयैव रणाजिरे ॥
दृष्ट्वा पराहतं सैन्यमन्धकोऽपि महासुरः ।
पराङ्मुखो रणात्तस्मात्पलायत महाजवः ॥
ततः क्रीड़ां महादेवः कृत्वा द्वादशवार्षिकीम् ।
हिताय भक्तलोकानामाजगामाथ मन्दरम्† ॥
सम्प्राप्तमीश्वरं ज्ञात्वा सर्वएव गणेश्वराः ।
समागम्योपतिष्ठन्त भानुमन्तमिव द्विजाः ॥
प्रविश्य भवनं‡ पुण्यमयुक्तानां दुरासदम् ।
ददर्श नन्दिनन्देवं भैरवं केशवं शिवः ॥
प्रणामप्रवणं देवं सोऽनुगृह्याथ नन्दिनम् ।
प्रीत्यैनं पूर्वमीशानः§ केशवं परिषस्वजे ॥
दृष्ट्वा देवी महादेवीं प्रीतिविस्फारितेक्षणाम्¶ ।

---

* सदनमेव सादनं, स्वार्थे अण् ।

† जगाम सच मन्दरमिति B.

‡ भुवनमिति E and H.

§ आघ्राय मूर्द्धमीशान इति B.

¶ दृष्ट्वा देवी महादेवं प्रीतिविस्फारितेक्षणा इति B.

प्रणतः* शिरसा तस्याः† पादयोरीश्वरस्य च ॥
न्यवेदयज्जयन्तस्मै शङ्करायाथ शङ्करः ।
भैरवो विष्णुमाहात्म्यम्प्रतीतः‡ पार्श्वगोऽभवत् ॥
श्रुत्वा तं विजयं शम्भुर्विक्रमङ्केशवस्य च ।
समास्ते भगवानीशो देव्या सह वरासने ॥
ततो देवगणाः सर्वे मरीचिप्रमुखा द्विजाः ।
आजग्मुर्मन्दरन्द्रष्टुं देवदेवं त्रिलोचनम् ॥
येन तद्विजितं पूर्वन्देवीनां शतमुत्तमम् ।
समागतन्दैत्यसैन्यमीशदर्शनकाङ्क्षया§ ॥
दृष्ट्वा वरासनासीनन्देव्या चन्द्रविभूषणम् ।
प्रणेमुरादराद्देव्यो गायन्ति स्मातिलालसाः ॥
प्रणेमुर्गिरिजां देवीं वामपार्श्वे पिनाकिनः ।
देवासनगतान्देवीं नारायणमनोमयीम् ॥
दृष्ट्वा सिंहासनासीनन्देव्यो नारायणं तथा ।
प्रणम्य देवमीशानं पृष्टवत्यो वराङ्गनाः ॥

कन्या ऊचुः ।

कस्त्वं विभ्राजसे कान्त्या केयम्बाला रविप्रभा ।

---

* ननाम इति B and D.

† तस्य इति B, E and H.

‡ प्रणत इति B.

§ वाञ्छया इति B.

को न्वयम्भाति वपुषा पङ्कजायतलोचनः* ॥
निशम्य तासां वचनं वृषेन्द्रवरवाहनः।
व्याजहार महायोगी भूताधिपतिरव्ययः ॥
अयन्नारायणो गौरी जगन्माता सनातनः।
विभज्य संस्थितो देवः स्वात्मानं बहुधेश्वरः ॥
न मे विदुः परन्तत्त्वं देव्याश्च† न महर्षयः।
एकोऽयं वेदविश्वात्मा‡ भवानी विष्णुरेव च ॥
अहं हि निस्पृहः शान्तः केवलोनिष्परिग्रहः।
मामेव केशवं प्राहुर्लक्ष्मीं देवीमथाम्बिकाम् ॥
एष धाता विधाता च कारणं कार्यमेव च।
कर्त्ता कारयिता विष्णुर्भुक्तिमुक्तिफलप्रदः ॥
भोक्ता पुमानप्रमेयः संहर्त्ता कालरूपधृक्।
स्रष्टा पाता§ वासुदेवो विश्वात्मा विश्वतोमुखः ॥
कूटस्थो ह्यक्षरो व्यापी योगी नारायणोऽव्ययः¶।
तारकः पुरुषो ह्यात्मा केवलं परमं पदम् ॥
सैषा माहेश्वरी गौरी मम शक्तिर्निरञ्जना।
शान्ता सत्या सदानन्दा परम्पदमिति श्रुतिः ॥

---

* कोन्वियम्भाति वपुषा पङ्कजायतलोचना इति G. का त्वियं भाति वपुषा इति H.

† देवाद्या इति B.

‡ देवदेवात्मा इति B.

§ धाता इति B.

¶ नारायणः स्वयमिति B.

अस्याः सर्वमिदञ्जातमत्रैव लयमेष्यति।
एषैव सर्वभूतानाङ्गतीनामुत्तमा गतिः॥
तयाहं सङ्गतो देव्या केवलो निष्कलः परः।
पश्याम्यशेषमेवाहं* परमात्मानमव्ययम्॥
तस्मादनादिमद्वैतं विष्णुमात्मानमीश्वरम्।
एकमेव विजानीथ ततो यास्यथ निर्वृतिम्॥
मन्यन्ते विष्णुमव्यक्तमात्मानं श्रद्धयान्विताः।
ये भिन्नदृष्ट्या चेशानं पूजयन्तो न मे प्रियाः॥
द्विषन्ति ये जगत्सूतिं मोहिता रौरवादिषु।
पच्यमाना न मुच्यन्ते कल्पकोटिशतैरपि॥
तस्मादशेषभूतानां रक्षकोविष्णुरव्ययः।
यथावदिह विज्ञाय ध्येयः सर्वापदि प्रभुः॥
श्रुत्वा भगवतोवाक्यं देवाः सर्वे गणेश्वराः†।
नेमुर्नारायणं देवन्देवीं च हिमशैलजाम्॥
प्रार्थयामासुरीशाने भक्तिं भक्तजनप्रिये।
भवानीपादयुगले नारायणपदाम्बुजे॥
ततो नारायणन्देवङ्गणेशा मातरोऽपि च।
न पश्यन्ति जगत्सूतिन्तदद्भुतमिवाभवत्॥
तदन्तरे महादैत्यो ह्यन्धकोमन्मथान्धकः।
मोहितो गिरिजान्देवीमाहर्त्तुङ्गिरिमाययौ॥

---

* मेवेदमिति B.

† देव्यः सर्व्वगणेश्वरा इति B.

अथानन्तवपुः श्रीमान्योगी नारायणोऽमलः।
तत्रैवाविरभूद्दैत्यैर्युद्धाय पुरुषोत्तमः॥

क्वत्वाथ पार्श्वे भगवन्तमीशो
युद्धाय विष्णुङ्गणदेवमुख्यैः।
शिलादपुत्रेण च मातृकाभिः
सकालरुद्रोऽपि जगाम देवः॥
त्रिशूलमादाय कृशानुकल्पं
स देवदेवः प्रययौ पुरस्तात्।
तमन्वयुस्ते गणराजवर्या-
जगाम देवोऽपि सहस्रबाहुः॥
रराज मध्ये भगवान् सुराणां
विवाहनो वारिजपर्णवर्णः।
तदा सुमेरोः शिखराधिरूढ़-
स्त्रिलोकदृष्टिर्भगवानिवार्कः॥
जयन्ननादिर्भगवानमेयो*
हरः† सहस्राकृतिराविरासीत्।
त्रिशूलपाणिर्गगने सुघोषः
पपात देवोपरि पुष्पवृष्टिः॥
समागतं वीक्ष्य गणेशराजं
समावृतं दैत्यरिपुं गणेशैः।

* जयत्यनादिर्भगवानमेय इति B and G. जगत्यनादिरिति E and H.

† हरिरिति E and H.

युयोध शक्रेण समाहृताभि-
र्गणैरशेषैरमरप्रधानैः ॥
विजित्य सर्वानपि बाहुवीर्यात्
स संयुगे शम्भुरनन्तधामा ।
समाययौ यत्र सकालरुद्रो-
विमानमारूह्य विहीनसत्त्वः ॥
दृष्ट्वान्धकं समायान्तं भगवान् गरुड़ध्वजः ।
व्याजहार महादेवं भैरवं भूतिभूषणम् ॥
हन्तुमर्हसि दैत्येशमन्धकं लोककण्टकम् ।
त्वामृते भगवान् शक्तो हन्ता नान्योऽस्य विद्यते ॥
त्वं हर्त्ता सर्वलोकानां कालात्मा ह्यैश्वरी तनुः ।
स्तूयते विविधैर्मन्त्रैर्वेदविद्भिर्विचक्षणैः* ॥
स वासुदेवस्य वचो निशम्य भगवान् हरः ।
निरीक्ष्य विष्णुं हनने दैत्येन्द्रस्य मतिन्दधौ ॥
जगाम देवतानीकङ्गणानां हर्षवर्द्धनम्† ।
स्तुवन्ति भैरवन्देवमन्तरीक्षचरा जनाः ॥
जयानन्त महादेव कालमूर्त्ते सनातन ।
त्वमग्निः सर्वभावानामन्तस्तिष्ठसि सर्वगः‡ ॥

---

* स्तुत्वा स विविधैरिति D.

† हर्षमुद्वहन्निति A.

‡ सर्व्वभूतानामन्तश्चरसि नित्यश इति B.

त्वमन्तको* लोककर्त्ता त्वन्धाता हरिरव्ययः ।
त्वं ब्रह्मा त्वं महादेवस्त्वन्धाम परमं पदम् ॥
ओंकारमूर्त्तिर्योगात्मा† त्रयीनेत्रस्त्रिलोचनः ।
महाविभूतिर्विश्वेशो‡ जयानन्तजगत्पते§ ॥
ततः कालाग्निरुद्रोऽसौ गृहीत्वान्धकमीश्वरः ।
त्रिशूलाग्रेषु विन्यस्य प्रननर्त्त सताङ्गतिः ॥
दृष्ट्वान्धकन्देवगणाः शूलप्रोतं पितामहः ।
प्रणेमुरीश्वरं देवं भैरवम्भवमोचनम् ॥
अस्तुवन्मुनयः सिद्धा जगुर्गन्धर्वकिन्नराः ।
अन्तरीक्षेऽप्सरःसङ्घा¶ नृत्यन्ति स्म मनोहराः ॥
संस्थापितोऽथ शूलाग्रे सोऽन्धको दग्धकिल्विषः ।
उत्पन्नाखिलविज्ञानस्तुष्टाव परमेश्वरम्|| ॥

अन्धक उवाच ।

नमामि मूर्ध्ना भगवन्तमेकं
समाहितोऽयं विदुरीशतत्त्वम् ।
पुरातनं पुण्यमनन्तरूपं

---

* त्वं यज्ञस्त्वं वषट्कार इति B.

† ओंकारमूर्त्तिरीशात्मा इति B.

‡ देवेश इति B.

§ जयाशेषजगत्पते इति B.

¶ अन्तरीक्षेऽप्सरसः सर्व्वा इति B.

|| पुरुषोत्तममिति B.

कालं कविं योगवियोगहेतुम् ॥
दंष्ट्राकरालं दिवि नृत्यमानं*
हुताशवक्त्रं ज्वलनार्करूपम्।
सहस्रपादाक्षिशिरोभियुक्तं
भवन्तमेकं प्रणमामि रुद्रम् ॥
जयादिदेवामरपूजिताङ्घ्रे
विभागहीनामलतत्त्वरूप।
त्वमग्निरेको बहुधाभिपूज्यो
वाय्वादिभेदैरखिलात्मरूपः ॥
त्वामेकमाहुः पुरुषं पुराण-
मादित्यवर्णन्तमसः परस्तात्।
त्वं पश्यसीदं परिपास्यजस्रं
त्वमन्तको योगिगणानुजुष्टः† ॥
एकोऽन्तरात्मा बहुधा निविष्टो
देहेषु देहादिविशेषहीनः‡।
त्वमात्मतत्त्वं परमात्मशब्दं§
भवन्तमाहुः शिवमेव केचित् ॥
त्वमक्षरं ब्रह्म परं पवित्र-

---

* दंष्ट्राकरालञ्च विनर्त्तमानमिति A. नृत्यमानमित्यत्र आर्षमात्मनेपदम्।

† अनुसृष्ट इति E and H.

‡ इतः परं B पुस्तके त्वमिन्द्ररूप इति श्लोकः पठितः।

§ परमात्मभूतमिति B.

आनन्दरूपं प्रणवाभिधानम् ।
त्वमीश्वरो वेदविदां प्रसिद्धः*
स्वायम्भुवोऽशेषविशेषहीनः ॥
त्वमिन्द्ररूपो वरुणोऽग्निरूपो
हंसः प्राणो मृत्युरन्तोऽसि यज्ञः† ।
प्रजापतिर्भगवानेकरूपो‡
नीलग्रीवः स्तूयसे वेदविद्भिः ॥
नारायणस्त्वं जगतामनादिः§
पितामहस्त्वं प्रपितामहश्च ।
वेदान्तगुह्योपनिषत्सु गीतः
सदाशिवस्त्वं परमेश्वरोऽसि ॥
नमः परस्मै तमसः परस्ता-
त्परात्मने¶ पञ्चनवान्तराय‖ ।
त्रिशक्त्यतीताय निरञ्जनाय
सहस्रशक्त्यासनसंस्थिताय ॥

---

* वेदपदेष्वसिद्ध इति B.

† ऽधियज्ञ इति E and H. मृत्युमन्तासि यज्ञ इति D.

‡ भगवानेकरुद्र इति A, D, E and H.

§ जगतामथादिरिति B.

¶ तमसः परस्तात् परात्मने पञ्च इति G पुस्तके नास्ति ।

‖ पञ्चनवान्तराय—पञ्च नव च चतुर्द्दश इत्यर्थः अन्तराणि अवकाशाः यस्य तथोक्ताय चतुर्द्दशलोकव्यापिने इत्यर्थः । पञ्चपदान्तराय इति B. पञ्चपरान्तराय इति D. नमः परस्मै च परान्तराय इति E and H.

त्रिमूर्त्तयेऽनन्तपदात्ममूर्त्ते
जगन्निवासाय जगन्मयाय* ।
नमो जनानां हृदि संस्थिताय
फणीन्द्रहाराय नमोऽस्तु तुभ्यम् ॥
मुनीन्द्रसिद्धार्च्चितपादपद्म
ऐश्वर्य्यधर्म्मासनसंस्थिताय ।
नमः परान्ताय भवोद्भवाय
सहस्रचन्द्रार्कसहस्रमूर्त्तेः† ॥
नमोऽस्तु सोमाय सुमध्यमाय
नमोऽस्तु देवाय‡ हिरण्यबाहो ।
नमोऽग्निचन्द्रार्कविलोचनाय§
नमोऽम्बिकायाः पतये मृड़ाय¶ ॥
नमोऽस्तु गुह्याय गुहान्तराय
वेदान्तविज्ञानविनिश्चिताय ।
त्रिकालहीनामलधामधाम्ने
नमो महेशाय नमः शिवाय ॥

---

* B, D, E, G, H पुस्तकेषु "नमो ललाटार्पितलोचनाय" इत्यधिकं दृश्यते।

† सहस्रचन्द्रार्कविलोचनाय इति B.

‡ ते देव इति B.

§ नमोऽग्निचन्द्रार्कविलोचनाय इति पादः B पुस्तके नास्ति ।

¶ नमोऽम्बिकायाः इत्यारभ्य गुहान्तराय इत्यन्तं B, E, G, H पुस्तकेषु नास्ति।
गुहा मनीषा अन्तरम् अवकाशः यस्य मनीषिणाम् अन्तश्चराय इत्यर्थः।

एवं स्तुतः स* भगवान् शूलाग्रादवतार्य्य तम्।
तुष्टः प्रोवाच हस्ताभ्यां स्पृष्ट्वा च परमेश्वरः॥
प्रीतोऽहं सर्वथा दैत्य स्तवेनानेन साम्प्रतम्।
सम्प्राप्य गाणपत्यं मे सन्निधाने सदा वस†॥
अरोगश्छिन्नसन्देहो देवैरपि सुपूजितः।
नन्दीश्वरस्यानुचरः सर्व्वदुःखविवर्जितः॥
एवं व्याहृतमात्रे तु देवदेवेन देवताः।
गणेश्वरं महादैत्यमन्धकं देवसन्निधौ।
सहस्रसूर्य्यसङ्काशं त्रिनेत्रं चन्द्रचिह्नितम्।
नीलकण्ठं जटामौलिं शूलासक्तं महाकरम्।
दृष्ट्वा तन्तुष्टुवुर्दैत्यमाश्चर्य्यं परमङ्गताः।
उवाच भगवान्विष्णुर्देवदेवं स्मयन्निव॥
स्थाने तव महादेव प्रभावः पुरुषो महान्।
नेच्छति ज्ञातिजान्‡ दोषान् गृह्णाति च गुणानपि॥
इतीरितोऽथ भैरवो गणेशदेवपुङ्गवः§।
सकेशवः सहान्धको जगाम शङ्करान्तिकम्॥
निरीक्ष्य देवमागतं स शङ्करः सहान्धकम्।
समाधवं समात्मकं जगाम निर्वृतिं हरः॥

---

* एवं स्तुवन्तमिति B.

† वसामर इति B.

‡ ज्ञानजानिति B.

§ गणेशो देवपुङ्गवैरिति D. गणेशः इति E and H.

प्रगृह्य पाणिनेश्वरी हिरण्यलोचनात्मजम् ।
जगाम यत्र शैलजा विमानमीशवल्लभा ॥
विलोक्य सा समागतं पतिम्भवार्त्तिहारिणम्* ।
उवाच† सान्धकं सुखं प्रसादमन्धकम्प्रति ॥
अथान्धको महेश्वरीं ददर्श देवपार्श्वगाम् ।
पपात दण्डवत् क्षितौ ननाम पादपद्मयोः ॥
नमामि देववल्लभामनादिमद्रिजामिमाम् ।
यतः प्रधानपूरुषौ निहन्ति याखिलञ्जगत् ॥
विभाति या शिवासने शिवेन साकमव्यया ।
हिरण्मयेऽतिनिर्म्मले नमामि तां हिमाद्रिजाम्‡ ॥
यदन्तराखिलञ्जगज्जगन्ति यान्ति सङ्क्षयम् ।
नमामि यत्र तामुमामशेषदोषवर्ज्जिताम्§ ॥
न जायते न हीयते न वर्द्धते च तामुमाम् ।
नमामि तां गुणातिगाङ्गिरीशपुत्रिकामिमाम् ॥
क्षमस्व देवि शैलजे कृतं मया विमोहितम् ।
सुरासुरैर्नमस्कृतं¶ नमामि ते पदाम्बुजम् ॥
इत्थं भगवती देवी भक्तिनम्रेण पार्व्वती ।

---

* भवम्भवार्त्तिहारिणमिति B.

† अवापेति B.

‡ नमामि तामिमामजामिति B.

§ सुरासुरैर्यदर्च्चितमिति B, E and H.

¶ तत्पदमशेषदोषवर्ज्जितमिति E and H.

संस्तुता दैत्यपतिना पुत्रत्वे जगृहेऽम्बकम् ॥
ततः स मातृभिः सार्द्धं भैरवो रुद्रसम्भवः ।
जगाम त्वाज्ञया शम्भोः पातालं परमेश्वरः ॥
यत्र सा तामसी विष्णोर्मूर्त्तिः संहारकारिका ।
समास्ते हरिरव्यक्तो नृसिंहाकृतिरीश्वरः ॥
ततोऽनन्ताकृतिः शम्भुः शेषेणापि सुपूजितः ।
कालाग्निरुद्रो भगवान् युयोजात्मानमात्मनि ॥
युञ्जतस्तस्य देवस्य सर्व्वा एवाथ मातरः ।
बुभुक्षिता महादेवं प्रणम्याहुस्त्रिलोचनम् ॥

मातर ऊचुः ।

बुभुक्षिता महादेव त्वमनुज्ञातुमर्हसि* ।
त्रैलोक्यं भक्षयिष्यामो नान्यथा तृप्तिरस्ति नः ॥
एतावदुक्त्वा वचनं मातरो विष्णुसम्भवाः ।
भक्षयाञ्चक्रिरे सर्व्वं त्रैलोक्यं सचराचरम् ॥
ततः स भैरवो देवो नृसिंहवपुषं हरिम् ।
दध्यौ नारायणन्देवं† प्रणम्य च कृताञ्जलिः ॥
उमेशचिन्तितं ज्ञात्वा क्षणात्प्रादुरभूद्धरिः ।
विज्ञापयामास च तं भक्षयन्तीह मातरः ।

---

* त्वनुज्ञा दीयतां त्वया इति B.

† इतः परं "प्रणम्य च कृताञ्जलिः उमेशचिन्तितं ज्ञात्वा" इति पादद्वयं B पुस्तके नास्ति ।

निवारयाशु* त्रैलोक्यं त्वदीया भगवन्निति ॥
संस्मृता विष्णुना देव्यो नृसिंहवपुषा पुनः ।
उपतस्थुर्म्महादेवं नरसिंहाकृतिं ततः† ॥
सम्प्राप्य सन्निधिं विष्णोः सर्व्वाः संहारकारिकाः ।
प्रददुः शम्भवे शक्तिं भैरवायातितेजसे ॥
अपश्यंस्ता जगत्सूतिं नृसिंहमतिभैरवम् ।
क्षणादेकत्वमापन्नं शेषाहिश्चापि मातरः ॥
व्याजहार हृषीकेशो ये भक्ताः शूलपाणये ।
ये च मां‡ संस्मरन्तीह पालनीयाः प्रयत्नतः ॥
ममैव मूर्त्तिरतुला सर्व्वसंहारकारिका ।
महेश्वराङ्गसम्भूता§ भुक्तिमुक्तिप्रदायिनी ॥
अनन्तो भगवान् कालो द्विधावस्था ममैव तु¶ ।
तामसी राजसी मूर्त्तिर्देवदेवश्चतुर्मुखः ॥
सोऽहं‖ देवो दुराधर्षः कालो लोकप्रकालनः ।
भक्षयिष्यामि कल्पान्ते रौद्रेण** निखिलं जगत् ॥

---

* विनाशयन्तीति A, E and H.

† नरसिंहाकृतिश्च तमिति B.

‡ ये धर्म्मानिति E, G, H.

§ महेश्वरांशसम्भूतेति B.

¶ शिवस्य च इति B.

‖ सोऽयमिति B.

** भक्षयिष्यति कल्पान्ते रुद्रात्मा इति B.

या सा विमोहिनी मूर्त्तिर्मम* नारायणाह्वया।
सत्त्वोद्रिक्ता जगत्सर्व्वं† संस्थापयति नित्यदा॥
स विष्णुः परमं ब्रह्म‡ परमात्मा परा गतिः।
मूलप्रकृतिरव्यक्ता सदानन्देति कथ्यते॥
इत्येवं बोधिता देव्यो विष्णुना विष्णुमातरः।
प्रपेदिरे महादेवं तमेव शरणं परम्§॥
एतद्वः कथितं सर्व्वं मयान्धकनिषूदनम्¶।
माहात्म्यं देवदेवस्य भैरवस्यामितौजसः‖॥

इति श्रीकूर्म्मपुराणे राजवंशानुकीर्त्तने षोड़शोऽध्यायः।

---

* या सा विमोहिका मूर्त्तिरस्य इति E.

† जगत्कृत्स्नमिति B.

‡ सहि विष्णुः परं विप्राः इति B.

§ हरमिति B.

¶ निवर्हणमिति B.

‖ भैरवस्यामिततेजस इति B.

सप्तदशोऽध्यायः।

सूत उवाच।

अन्धके निगृहीते वै प्रह्लादस्य महात्मनः।
विरोचनो नाम बली* बभूव नृपतिः सुतः† ॥
देवाञ्जित्वा सदेवेन्द्रान् बह्वन्वर्षान्महासुरः।
पालयामास धर्म्मेण त्रैलोक्यं सचराचरम् ॥
तस्यैवं वर्त्तमानस्य कदाचिद्विष्णुचोदितः।
सनत्कुमारो भगवान् पुरं प्राप महामुनिः ॥
गत्वा‡ सिंहासनगतो ब्रह्मपुत्रं महासुरः।
ननामोत्थाय शिरसा प्राञ्जलिर्वाक्यमब्रवीत् ॥
धन्योऽस्म्यनुगृहीतोऽस्मि सम्प्राप्तो मे पुरोत्तमम्§।
योगीश्वरोऽद्य भगवान्यतोऽसौ¶ ब्रह्मवित्स्वयम् ॥
किमर्थमागतो ब्रह्मन् स्वयन्देवः पितामहः।
ब्रूहि मे ब्रह्मणः पुत्र किङ्कार्य्यं करवाण्यहम् ॥
सोऽब्रवीद्भगवान्देवो धर्म्मयुक्तं महासुरम्।
द्रष्टुमभ्यागतोऽहं वै भवन्तं भाग्यवानसि ॥

---

* पुत्र इति B.

† पुरा इति B.

‡ दृष्ट्वा इति B.

§ पुरातन इति B. पुरान्तरमिति D. पुरोत्तमं—पुरेषु उत्तमं सर्व्वोत्कृष्टपुरमित्यर्थः।

¶ भगवान् यतात्मा इति D.

सुदुर्लभा मीतिरेषा* दैत्यानान्दैत्यसत्तम ।
त्रिलोके धार्म्मिको नूनं त्वादृशोऽन्यो न विद्यते ॥
इत्युक्तोऽसुरराजोऽसौ† पुनः प्राह महामुनिम् ।
धर्म्माणां परमं धर्म्मं ब्रूहि मे ब्रह्मवित्तम ॥
सोऽब्रवीद्भगवान्योगी दैत्येन्द्राय महात्मने ।
सर्व्वगुह्यतमं धर्म्ममात्मज्ञानमनुत्तमम् ॥
स लब्ध्वा परमं ज्ञानं दत्त्वा च गुरुदक्षिणाम् ।
निधाय पुत्रे तद्राज्यं योगाभ्यासरतोऽभवत् ॥
स तस्य पुत्रो मतिमान्‡ बलिर्नाम महासुरः ।
ब्रह्मण्यो धार्म्मिकोऽत्यर्थं विजिग्येऽथ पुरन्दरम् ॥
कृत्वा तेन महद्युद्धं शक्रः सर्व्वामरैर्वृतः ।
जगाम निर्जितो विष्णुन्देवं शरणमच्युतम् ॥
तदन्तरेऽदितिर्देवी देवमाता सुदुःखिता ।
दैत्येन्द्राणां वधार्थाय पुत्रो मे स्यादिति स्वयम् ।
ततापं सुमहाघोरं§ तपोराशिं ततः परम् ।
प्रपन्ना विष्णुमव्यक्तं शरण्यं शरणं हरिम्¶ ॥

---

* सुदुर्लभान्यतरेषाञ्च इति D.

† राजसु इति B.

‡ भगवानिति A, E and H.

§ सुमहद्घोरमिति B.

¶ शिवमिति A, E and H.

कृत्वा हृत्पद्मकिञ्जल्के* निष्कलं परमम्पदम् ।
वासुदेवमनाद्यन्तमानन्दं व्योम केवलम् ॥
प्रसन्नो भगवान्विष्णुः शङ्खचक्रगदाधरः ।
आविर्ब्बभूव योगात्मा देवमातुः पुरो हरिः ॥
दृष्ट्वा समागतं विष्णुमदितिर्भक्तिसंयुता ।
मेने कृतार्थमात्मानं तोषयामास केशवम् ॥

अदितिरुवाच ।

जयाशेषदुःखौघनाशैकहेतो
जयानन्तमाहात्म्य योगाभियुक्त ।
जयानादिमध्यान्त विज्ञानमूर्त्ते
जयाकाशकल्पामलानन्दरूप ॥
नमो विष्णवे कालरूपाय तुभ्यं
नमो नारसिंहाय शेषाय तुभ्यम् ।
नमः कालरुद्राय संहारकर्त्रे
नमो वासुदेवाय तुभ्यं नमस्ते ॥
नमो विश्वमायाविधानाय तुभ्यं
नमो योगगम्याय सत्याय तुभ्यम् ।
नमो धर्म्मविज्ञाननिष्ठाय तुभ्यं
नमस्ते वराहाय भूयो नमस्ते ॥
नमस्ते सहस्रार्कचन्द्राभमूर्त्ते

---

* किञ्जल्कमध्ये तु इति E and H.

नमो वेदविज्ञानधर्म्माभिगम्य* ।
नमो भूधरायाप्रमेयाय तुभ्यं†
प्रभो विश्वयोनेऽथ भूयो नमस्ते ॥
नमः शम्भवे सत्यनिष्ठाय तुभ्यं
नमो हेतवे विश्वरूपाय तुभ्यम् ।
नमो योगपीठान्तरस्थाय तुभ्यं
शिवायैकरूपाय भूयो नमस्ते ॥

एवं स भगवान् विष्णुर्देवमात्रा‡ जगन्मयः ।
तोषितश्छन्दयामास वरेण प्रहसन्निव ॥
प्रणम्य शिरसा भूमौ सा वव्रे वरमुत्तमम् ।
त्वामेव पुत्रं देवानां हिताय वरये वरम् ॥
तथास्त्वित्याह भगवान् प्रपन्नजनवत्सलः ।
दत्त्वा वरानप्रमेयस्तत्रैवान्तरधीयत ॥
ततो बहुतिथे काले भगवन्तं जनार्द्दनम् ।
दधार गर्भं देवानां माता नारायणं स्वयम् ॥
समाविष्टे हृषीकेशे देवमातुरथोदरम् ।
उत्पाता जज्ञिरे घोरा बलेर्वैरोचनेः पुरे ॥
निरीक्ष्य सर्व्वानुत्पातान्दैत्येन्द्रो भयविह्वलः ।
प्रह्लादमसुरं वृद्धं प्रणम्याह पितामहम् ॥

---

* वेदविज्ञानाय धर्म्माभिगम्य इति B.

† नमो देवदेवादिदेवाय तुभ्यमिति B.

‡ कृष्णो देवमात्रा इति B.

बलिरुवाच ।

पितामह महाप्राज्ञ जायन्तेऽस्मिन्पुरान्तरे* ।
किमुत्पातो भवेत्कार्य्यमस्माकं किंनिमित्तकः ॥†
निशम्य तस्य वचनञ्चिरं ध्यात्वा महासुरः ।
नमस्कृत्य हृषीकेशमिदं वचनमब्रवीत् ॥

प्रह्लाद उवाच ।

यो यज्ञैरिज्यते विष्णुर्यस्य सर्व्वमिदं जगत् ।
दधारासुरनाशार्थं माता तं त्रिदिवौकसाम् ॥
यस्मादभिन्नं सकलं भिद्यते योऽखिलादपि ।
स वासुदेवो देवानां मातुर्द्देहं समाविशत् ॥
न यस्य देवा जानन्ति स्वरूपं परमार्थतः ।
स विष्णुरदितेर्द्देहं स्वेच्छयाद्य समाविशत् ॥
यस्माद्भवन्ति भूतानि यत्र संयान्ति संक्षयम् ।
सोऽवतीर्णो महायोगी पुराणपुरुषो हरिः ॥
न यत्र विद्यते नामजात्यादिपरिकल्पना ।
सत्तामात्रात्मरूपोऽसौ विष्णुरंशेन जायते‡ ॥
यस्य सा जगतां माता शक्तिस्तद्धर्म्मधारिणी§ ।

---

* जायन्तेऽस्मत्पुरेऽधुना इति B.

† किमुत्पातैर्भवेत्कार्य्यमस्माकं किंनिमित्तकैरिति D. किमुत्पाता भवेत्कार्य्यमस्माकं किंनिमित्तका इति E and H.

‡ विष्णुरूपेण जायते इति B, E and H.

§ धर्म्मिणीति B.

माया भगवती लक्ष्मीः सोऽवतीर्णो जनार्द्दनः ॥
यस्य सा तामसी मूर्त्तिः शङ्करी राजसी तनुः ।
ब्रह्मा सञ्जायते विष्णुरंशेनैकेन सत्वधृक्* ॥
इति सञ्चिन्त्य गोविन्दं भक्तिनम्रेण चेतसा ।
तमेव गच्छ शरणं ततो यास्यसि निर्वृतिम् ॥
ततः प्रह्लादवचनाद्बलिर्वैरोचनिर्हरिम् ।
जगाम शरणं विश्वं पालयामास धर्मवित् ॥
काले प्राप्ते महाविष्णुं देवानां हर्षवर्द्धनम् ।
असूत कश्यपाच्चैनं देवमातादितिः स्वयम् ॥
चतुर्भुजं विशालाक्षं श्रीवत्साङ्कितवक्षसम् ।
नीलमेघप्रतीकाशं भ्राजमानं श्रिया वृतम् ॥
उपतस्थुः सुराः सर्वे सिद्धाः साध्याश्च चारणाः ।
उपेन्द्र इन्द्रप्रमुखा ब्रह्मा चर्षिगणैर्वृतः ॥
कृतोपनयनो वेदानध्यैष्ट भगवान् हरिः ।
सदाचारं† भरद्वाजात्त्रिलोकाय प्रदर्शयन् ॥
एवञ्च‡ लौकिकं मार्गं प्रदर्शयति स प्रभुः ।
स यत्प्रमाणं कुरुते लोकस्तदनुवर्त्तते ॥
ततः कालेन मतिमान् बलिर्वैरोचनिः स्वयम् ।
यज्ञैर्यज्ञेश्वरं विष्णुमर्च्चयामास सर्व्वगम् ॥

---

* सत्वभृदिति B.

† समाचारमिति B, E and H.

‡ एवं हि इति B.

ब्राह्मणान्पूजयामास दत्त्वा बहुतरं धनम् ।
ब्रह्मर्षयः समाजग्मुर्यज्ञवाटं महात्मनः ॥
विज्ञाय विष्णुर्भगवान् भरद्वाजप्रचोदितः ।
आस्थाय वामनं रूपं यज्ञदेशमथागमत् ॥
कृष्णाजिनोपवीताङ्ग* आषाढेन विराजितः ।
ब्राह्मणो जटिलो वेदानुद्गिरन् सुमहाद्युतिः† ॥
सम्प्राप्यासुरराजस्य समीपं भिक्षुको हरिः ।
स्वपादैः क्रमितं देशमयाचत बलिस्त्रिभिः ॥
प्रक्षाल्य चरणौ विष्णोर्बलिर्भावसमन्वितः ।
आचामयित्वा‡ भृङ्गारमादाय स्वर्णनिर्म्मितम् ॥

दास्ये तथेदम्भवते§ पदत्रयं
प्रीणातु देवो हरिरव्ययाकृतिः ।
विचिन्त्य देवस्य कराग्रपल्लवे
निपातयामास सुशीतलञ्जलम् ॥
विचक्रमे पृथिवीमेष चैता-
मथान्तरिक्षन्दिवमादिदेवः ।
व्यपेतरागन्दितिजेश्वरन्तं
प्रकर्त्तुकामः शरणं प्रपन्नम् ॥

---

* कृष्णाजिनोत्तरीयाङ्ग इति B.

† भस्ममण्डित इति B.

‡ आचमय्य इति साधु ।

§ ददाम्यथेदम्भवते इति D.

आक्रम्य लोकत्रयमीशपादः
प्राजापत्याद्ब्रह्मलोकं जगाम।
प्रणेमुरादित्यमुखाः सुरेन्द्राः*
ये तत्र लोके निवसन्ति सिद्धाः॥
अथोपतस्थे भगवाननादिः
पितामहस्तोषयामास विष्णुम्।
भित्त्वा तदण्डस्य कपालमूर्द्धं
जगाम दिव्याभरणोऽथ† भूयः॥
अथाण्डभेदान्निपपात शीतलं
महाजलं पुण्यकृद्भिश्च जुष्टम्।
प्रवर्त्तिता‡ चापि सरिद्वरा सा§
गङ्गेत्युक्ता¶ ब्रह्मणा व्योमसंस्था॥
गत्वा महान्तं प्रकृतिं ब्रह्मयोनिं||
ब्रह्माणमेकं पुरुषं विश्वयोनिम्**।
अतिष्ठदीशस्य पदं तदव्ययं
दृष्ट्वा देवास्तत्र तत्र स्तुवन्ति॥

---

* प्रणेमुरादित्यसहस्रकल्पमिति B.

† दिव्याभरणानीति B.

‡ प्रवर्त्तते इति B.

§ सरिद्वरा तदेति B.

¶ गङ्गेति नाम्ना ननु इति E and H.

|| प्रधानमिति B.

** विश्वबीजमिति B.

आलोक्य तं पुरुषं विश्वकायं
महान् बलिर्भक्तियोगेन विष्णुम्।
ननाम नारायणमेकमव्ययं
स्वचेतसा यं प्रणमन्ति वेदाः॥
तमब्रवीद्भगवानादिकर्त्ता
भूत्वा पुनर्वामनो वासुदेवः।
ममैव दैत्याधिपतेऽधुनेदं
लोकत्रयं भवता भावदत्तम्॥
प्रणम्य मूर्द्ध्ना पुनरेव दैत्यो
निपातयामास जलं कराग्रे।
दास्ये तवात्मानमनन्तधाम्ने
त्रिविक्रमायामितविक्रमाय॥
प्रगृह्य सूनोरपि सम्प्रदत्तं
प्रह्लादसूनोरथ शङ्खपाणिः।
जगाद वश्यं* जगदन्तरात्मा
पातालमूलं प्रविशेति भूयः॥
समास्यतां भवता तत्र नित्यं
भुक्त्वा भोगान्देवतानामलभ्यान्।
ध्यायस्व† मां सततं भक्तियोगा-
त्प्रवेक्ष्यसे कल्पदाहे पुनर्माम्॥

---

* दैत्यमिति B.

† ध्यायस्वेति आर्षमात्मनेपदम्।

उक्त्वैवं दैत्यसिंहं तं विष्णुः* सत्यपराक्रमः।
पुरन्दराय त्रैलोक्यं ददौ जिष्णुरुरुक्रमः॥
संस्तुवन्ति महायोगं सिद्धा देवर्षिकिन्नराः।
ब्रह्मा शक्रोऽथ भगवान्रुद्रादित्यमरुद्गणाः॥
कृत्वैतदद्भुतं कर्म्म विष्णुर्वामनरूपधृक्।
पश्यतामेव सर्व्वेषां तत्रैवान्तरधीयत॥
सोऽपि दैत्यवरः श्रीमान्पातालं प्राप नोदितः।
प्रह्लादेनासुरवरैर्विष्णुभक्तस्तु तत्परः॥
अपृच्छद्विष्णुमाहात्म्यं भक्तियोगमनुत्तमम्।
पूजाविधानं प्रह्लादं तदाहासौ चकार सः॥

अथ रथचरणं सशङ्खपाणिं†
सरसिजलोचनमीशमप्रमेयम्।
शरणमुपययौ स भावयोगा-
त्प्रणयगतिं प्रणिधाय कर्मयोगम्॥

एष वः कथितो विप्रा वामनस्य पराक्रमः।
स देवकार्य्याणि सदा करोति पुरुषोत्तमः॥‡

इति श्रीकूर्म्मपुराणे त्रिविक्रमचरिते सप्तदशोऽध्यायः।

---

* सिंहन्तु विष्णुरिति B. सिंहं तं जिष्णुरिति E and H.

† रथचरणाब्जशङ्खपाणिमिति B.

‡ एष श्लोकः E, G, H पुस्तकेषु न दृश्यते।

अष्टादशोऽध्यायः ।

सूत उवाच ।

बलेः पुत्रशतं त्वासीन्महाबलपराक्रमम् ।
तेषां प्रधानो द्युतिमान्वाणो नाम महाबलः* ॥
सोऽतीव शङ्करे भक्तो राजा राज्यमपालयत् ।
त्रैलोक्यं वशमानीय बाधयामास वासवम् ॥
ततः शक्रादयो देवा गत्वोचुः कृत्तिवाससम् ।
त्वदीयो बाधते ह्यस्मान्वाणो नाम महासुरः ॥
व्याहृतो दैवतैः सर्वैर्देवदेवो महेश्वरः ।
ददाह वाणस्य पुरं शरेणैकेन लीलया ॥
दह्यमाने पुरे तस्मिन्वाणो रुद्रं त्रिशूलिनम् ।
ययौ शरणमीशानङ्गोपतिं नीललोहितम् ॥
मूर्द्धन्याधाय तल्लिङ्गं शाम्भवं रागवर्ज्जितः† ।
निर्गत्य तु पुरात्तस्मात्तुष्टाव परमेश्वरम् ॥
संस्तुतो भगवानीशः शङ्करो नीललोहितः ।
गाणपत्येन वाणं तं योजयामास भावतः ॥
अथैवच्च‡ दनोः पुत्रास्ताराद्याश्चातिभीषणाः§ ।

---

* महाबलपराक्रम इति A, E and H. महासुर इति D.

† भीतिवर्जित इति B.

‡ अथाभवन्निति B.

§ ताराद्यास्तु विभीषणा इति B.

तारस्तथा शम्बरश्च कपिलः शङ्करस्तथा* ।
स्वर्भानुर्वृषपर्वा च प्राधान्येन प्रकीर्त्तिताः† ॥
सुरसायाः सहस्रन्तु सर्पाणामभवद्द्विजाः ।
अनेकशिरसां तद्वत्खेचराणां महात्मनाम् ॥
अरिष्टा जनयामास गन्धर्वाणां सहस्रकम् ।
अनन्ताद्याः महानागाः काद्रवेयाः प्रकीर्त्तिताः ॥
ताम्रा च जनयामास षट् कन्या द्विजपुङ्गवाः ।
शुकीं श्येनीञ्च भासीञ्च सुग्रीवां‡ गृध्रिकां शुचिम् ॥
गास्तथा जनयामास सुरभिर्महिषीस्तथा ।
इरा§वृक्षलतावल्लीतृणजातीश्च सर्व्वशः ।
तथा वै यक्षरक्षांसि मुनिरप्सरसस्तथा ।
रक्षोगणं क्रोधवशाज्जनयामास सत्तमाः ॥
विनतायाश्च पुत्रौ द्वौ प्रख्यातौ गरुड़ारुणौ ।
तयोश्च¶ गरुड़ो धीमान्तपस्तप्त्वा सुदुश्चरम् ।
प्रसादाच्छूलिनः प्राप्तो वाहनत्वं हरेः स्वयम् ॥
आराध्य तपसा देवं‖ महादेवं तथारुणः ।

---

* सञ्चरस्तथा इति B.

† प्रतिष्ठिता इति B.

‡ सुग्रीवीमिति B.

§ तारा इति B.

¶ तयोस्तु इति B.

‖ रुद्रमिति B.

सारथ्ये कल्पितः पूर्व्वं प्रीतेनार्कस्य शम्भुना ॥
एते कश्यपदायादाः कीर्त्तिताः स्थाणुजङ्गमाः ।
वैवस्वतेऽन्तरे ह्यस्मिन् शृखतां पापनाशनम् ॥
सप्तविंशसुताः प्रोक्ताः सोमपत्न्यश्च सुव्रताः ।
अरिष्टनेमिपत्नीनामपत्यानां ह्यनेकशः* ॥
बहुपुत्रस्य विदुषश्चतस्रो विद्युतः स्मृताः† ।
तद्वदङ्गिरसः श्रेष्ठाः‡ ऋषयो ब्रषसत्कृताः§ ॥
कृशाश्वस्य तु देवर्षेर्द्देवः प्रहरणः सुतः¶ ।
एते युगसहस्रान्ते जायन्ते पुनरेव हि ।
मन्वन्तरेषु नियतन्तुल्यकार्य्यैः स्वनामभिः ॥

इति श्रीकूर्म्मपुराणे वंशानुकीर्त्तनेऽष्टादशोऽध्यायः ।

—:—

ऊनविंशोऽध्यायः ।

सूत उवाच ।

एतानुत्पाद्य पुत्रांस्तु प्रजासन्तानकारणात् ।
कश्यपः पुत्रकामस्तु चचार सुमहत्तपः ॥

---

* मपत्यानीह षोड़श इति B.

† सुता इति B.

‡ पुत्रा इति B.

§ ब्रह्मसत्कृता इति B.

¶ देवप्रहरणाः सुता इति B.

तस्यैवन्तपतोऽत्यर्थं प्रादुर्भूतौ सुताविमौ ।
वत्सरश्चासितश्चैव तावुभौ ब्रह्मवादिनौ ॥
वत्सरान्नैध्रुवो* जज्ञे रैभ्यश्च† सुमहायशाः ।
रैभ्यस्य‡ जज्ञिरे शूद्राः§ पुत्रा द्युतिमतां वराः ॥
च्यवनस्य सुता भार्या¶ नैध्रुवस्य महात्मनः ।
सुमेधा जनयामास पुत्रान्वै कुण्डपायिनः‖ ॥
असितस्यैकपर्णायां** ब्रह्मिष्ठः समपद्यत ।
नाम्ना वै देवलः पुत्रो योगाचार्यो महातपाः ॥
शाण्डिल्यः परमः†† श्रीमान् सर्व्वतत्त्वार्थविच्छुचिः‡‡ ।
प्रसादात्पार्वतीशस्य योगमुत्तमवाप्तवान्§§ ॥
शाण्डिल्यो नैध्रुवो रैभ्यः¶¶ त्रयः पुत्रास्तु काश्यपाः ।

---

* वत्सराद्दैध्रुव इति B.

† वैद्यश्च इति B.

‡ वैद्यस्य इति B.

§ वैद्या इति B.

¶ पत्नीति B.

‖ याजिन इति B.

** वर्णायामिति B.

†† शाण्डिल्यानां पर इति B.

‡‡ चित्सुधी इति B.

§§ योगमुत्तममाप्तवानिति B.

¶¶ वैद्य इति B.

नरप्रकृतयो* विप्रा पुलस्त्यस्य वदामि वः ॥
तृणविन्दोः सुता विप्रा नाम्ना ऐलविला स्मृता ।
पुलस्त्याय तु राजर्षिस्ताङ्कन्यां प्रत्यपादयत् ॥
ऋषिस्त्वैलविलस्तस्यां विश्रवाः समपद्यत ।
तस्य पत्न्यश्चतस्रस्तु पौलस्त्यकुलवर्द्धिकाः ॥
पुष्पोत्कटा च वाका† च कैकसी‡ देववर्ण्णिनी§ ।
रूपलावण्यसम्पन्नास्तासाञ्च शृणुत प्रजाः ॥
ज्येष्ठं वैश्रवणन्तस्य सुषुवे देववर्ण्णिनी¶ ।
कैकस्यजनयत्पुत्रं रावणं राक्षसाधिपम् ॥
कुम्भकर्णं शूर्पणखान्तथैव च विभीषणम् ।
पुष्पोत्कटाप्यजनयत्पुत्रान्विश्रवसः शुभान् ॥
महोदरं प्रहस्तञ्च महापार्श्वं खरन्तथा ।
कुम्भीनसीन्तथा कन्यां वाकायाः सृजत‖ प्रजाः ॥
त्रिशिरादूषणश्चैव विद्युज्जिह्वो महाबलः ।
इत्येते क्रूरकर्म्माणः पौलस्त्या राक्षसा दश ॥
सर्व्वे तपोबलोत्कृष्टा रुद्रभक्ताः सुभीषणाः ।

---

* नवप्रकृतय इति B.

† वाक्या इति B.

‡ निकषा इति रामायणेऽभिधीयते ।

§ वेदरूपिणीति B.

¶ वेदरूपिणीति B.

‖ शृणुत इति D, E and H.

पुलहस्य* मृगाः पुत्राः सर्व्वे व्यालाश्च दंष्ट्रिणः ॥
भूताः पिशाचा ऋक्षाश्च† शूकरा हस्तिनस्तथा ।
अनपत्यः क्रतुस्तस्मिन् स्मृतो वैवस्वतेऽन्तरे ।
मरीचेः कश्यपः पुत्रः स्वयमेव प्रजापतिः ॥
भृगोरथाभवच्छुक्रो‡ दैत्याचार्य्यो महातपाः ।
स्वाध्याययोगनिरतो हरभक्तो महाद्युतिः ॥
अत्रेः पुत्रोऽभवद्वह्निः सोदर्य्यस्तस्य नैध्रुवः§ ।
कृशाश्वस्य तु विप्रर्षेः¶ घृताच्यामिति नः श्रुतम् ॥
स तस्याञ्जनयामास|| स्वस्यात्रेयान्महौजसः ।
वेदवेदाङ्गनिरतांस्तपसा हतकिल्बिषान् ॥
नारदस्तु वसिष्ठाय ददौ देवीमरुन्धतीम् ।
ऊर्द्ध्वरेतास्तु तत्रैव** शापाद्दक्षस्य नारदः ॥
हर्य्यश्वेषु तु नष्टेषु मायया नारदस्य तु†† ।
शशाप नारदं दक्षः क्रोधसंरक्तलोचनः ॥

---

* पुलस्त्यस्य इति E and H.

† सर्पाश्च इति D. रक्षाश्च इति E and H.

‡ भृगोरप्यभवच्छुक्र इति B.

§ सोदर्य्यास्ताः पतिव्रताः इति B.

¶ विप्रेन्द्रा इति B.

|| सुतास्तु जनयामास इति B and D.

** ऊर्द्ध्वरेतास्तत्र मुनिरिति B.

†† च इति B.

यस्मान्मम सुताः सर्व्वे भवता* मायया द्विज।
त्वयन्नीतास्त्वशेषेण निरपत्यो भविष्यति॥
अरुन्धत्यां वसिष्ठस्तु शक्तिमुत्पादयत्सुतम्।
शक्तेः पराशरः श्रीमान् सर्व्वज्ञस्तपतां वरः॥
आराध्य देवदेवेशमीशानन्त्रिपुरान्तकम्।
लेभे त्वप्रतिमं पुत्रङ्कृष्णद्वैपायनं प्रभुम्॥
द्वैपायनाच्छुको जज्ञे भगवानेव शङ्करः।
अंशांशेनावतीर्य्योर्व्व्यां स्वं प्राप परमं पदम्॥
शुकस्यास्याभवन् पुत्राः पञ्चात्यन्ततपस्विनः।
भूरिश्रवाः प्रभुः शम्भुः कृष्णो गौरश्च पञ्चमः॥
कन्या कीर्त्तिमती चैव योगमाता धृतव्रताः।
एतेऽत्रिवंशाः कथिताः ब्रह्मणा ब्रह्मवादिनाम्॥
अत ऊर्द्ध्वं निबोधध्वङ्कश्यपाद्राजसन्ततिम्॥

इति श्रीकूर्म्मपुराणे ऋषिवंशे एकोनविंशोऽध्यायः।

——:——

* भवत इति B, E and H.

विंशोऽध्यायः ।

सूत उवाच ।

अदितिः सुषुवे पुत्रमादित्यं कश्यपात्प्रभुम् ।
तस्यादित्यस्य चैवासीद्भार्य्याणान्तु चतुष्टयम् ॥
संज्ञा राज्ञी* प्रभा छाया पुत्रांस्तासान्निबोधत ।
संज्ञा त्वाष्ट्री† तु सुषुवे सूर्य्यान्मनुमनुत्तमम् ॥
यमञ्च यमुनाञ्चैव राज्ञी‡ रेवन्तमेव च ।
प्रभा प्रभातमादित्या छाया सावर्णिमात्मजम्§ ॥
शनिञ्च तपतीञ्चैव विष्टिञ्चैव¶ यथाक्रमम् ।
मनोस्तु प्रथमस्यासन्नव पुत्रास्तु तत्समाः ॥
इक्ष्वाकुश्चैव नाभागो धृष्टः शर्य्यातिरेव च ।
नरिष्यन्तश्च नाभागो ह्यरिष्टः करूषस्तथा ॥
पृषध्रश्च महातेजा|| नवैते शक्रसन्निभाः ।
इला ज्येष्ठा वरिष्ठा च सोमवंशं व्यवर्द्धयत्** ॥

---

* रात्रिरिति D.

† त्वाष्ट्री—त्वष्टुः विश्वकर्म्मणः अपत्यं स्त्री ।

‡ रात्री इति D.

§ सावर्णिनामानं मनुमित्यर्थः ।

¶ शनिञ्चैव तपन्तीञ्च इति B.

|| महाभाग इति B.

** सोमवंशविवृद्धये इति B.

बुधस्य गत्वा भवनं सोमपुत्त्रेण सङ्गता ।
असूत सोमजाद्देवी पुरूरवसमुत्तमम् ॥
पितॄणां तृप्तिकर्त्तारं बुधादिति हि नः श्रुतम् ।
प्राप्य पुत्त्रं सुविमलं सुद्युम्न इति विश्रुतम् ॥
इला पुत्त्रत्रयं लेभे पुनः स्त्रीत्वमविन्दत ।
उत्कलश्च गयश्चैव विनतश्च तथैव च ॥
सर्व्वे तेऽप्रतिमप्रख्याः प्रपन्नाः कमलोद्भवम् ।
इक्ष्वाकोश्चाभवद्वीरो विकुक्षिर्नाम पार्थिवः ॥
ज्येष्ठपुत्त्रः स तस्यासीद्दश पञ्च च तत्सुताः ।
तेषां ज्येष्ठः ककुत्स्थोऽभूत्काकुत्स्थस्तु सुयोधनः ॥
सुयोधनात्पृथुः श्रीमान्विश्वकश्च पृथोः सुतः ।
विश्वकादार्द्रको धीमान्युवनाश्वश्च तत्सुतः ॥
स गोकर्ण*मनुप्राप्य युवनाश्वः प्रतापवान् ।
दृष्ट्वासौ गौतमं विप्रं तपन्तमनलप्रभम् ॥
प्रणम्य दण्डवद्भूमौ पुत्त्रकामो महीपतिः ।
अपृच्छत्कर्म्मणा केन धार्म्मिकं प्राप्नुयात्सुतम् ॥

गौतम उवाच ।

आराध्य पुरुषं पूर्व्वं† नारायणमनामयम् ।
अनादिनिधनं देवन्धार्म्मिकं प्राप्नुयात्सुतम् ॥

---

* A place of pilgrimage, sacred to Siva, on the west coast near Mangalore.

† पूर्व्वपुरुषमिति B.

तस्य* पुत्रः स्वयं ब्रह्मा पौत्रः स्यान्नीललोहितः ।
तमादिकृष्णमीशानमाराध्याप्नोति सत्सुतम् ॥
न यस्य भगवान् ब्रह्मा प्रभावं वेत्ति तत्त्वतः ।
तमाराध्य हृषीकेशं प्राप्नुयाद्धार्म्मिकं सुतम्† ॥
स गौतमवचः श्रुत्वा युवनाश्वो महीपतिः ।
आराधयन् हृषीकेशं वासुदेवं सनातनम् ॥
तस्य पुत्रोऽभवद्वीरः सावस्तिरिति‡ विश्रुतः ।
निर्म्मिता येन सावस्तिः§ गौड़देशे महापुरी ॥
तस्माच्च वृहदश्वोऽभूत्तस्मात्कुवलयाश्वकः ।
धुन्धुमारः समभवत्¶ धुन्धुं हत्वा महासुरम् ॥

---

* यस्य इति B.

† प्राप्नुयाद्धार्म्मिकं सुतमित्यारभ्य आराधयन् हृषीकेशमित्यन्तं E, G, H पुस्तकेषु नास्ति ।

‡ श्रावस्तिरिति B, E and H. श्रावन्तिरिति G.

§ श्रावस्तिरिति B. श्रावन्तीति G.

Properly speaking S'rávasti is the real name. S'rávasti was the capital of Kośalá for a time, and is supposed to have been situated near Fyzabad. To place it in Gouḍa is to confound all geography. It can be affirmed confidently that, the kingdom of Gouḍa never comprised Oude within its jurisdiction. "It is situated north of the Ganges, and founded by king S'rávasti. It is said to have been the place where the merchant Anátha-pinḍada gave Buddha a house for his residence, and the delivery of his lectures. It is identified with Dharmapattana."

¶ धुन्धुमारत्वमगमदिति B and D.

धुन्धुमारस्य तनयास्त्रयः प्रोक्ता द्विजोत्तमाः ।
दृढ़ाश्वश्चैव दण्डाश्वः कपिलाश्वस्तथैव च ॥
दृढ़ाश्वस्य प्रमोदस्तु* हर्य्यश्वस्तस्य चात्मजः† ।
हर्य्यश्वस्य निकुम्भस्तु निकुम्भात्संहताश्वकः ॥
कृताश्वोऽथ रणाश्वश्च संहिताश्वस्य वै सुतौ ।
युवनाश्वो रणाश्वस्य शक्रतुल्यबलो युधि ॥
कृत्वा तु वारुणीमिष्टिं‡मृषीणां वै प्रसादतः ।
लेभे त्वप्रतिमं पुत्रं विष्णुभक्तमनुत्तमम् ॥
मान्धातारं महाप्राज्ञं सर्व्वशस्त्रभृतां वरम् ।
मान्धातुः पुरुकुत्सोऽभूदम्बरीषश्च वीर्य्यवान् ॥
मुचुकुन्दश्च पुण्यात्मा सर्व्वे शक्रसमा युधि ।
अम्बरीषस्य दायादो युवनाश्वोऽपरः स्मृतः ॥
हरितो युवनाश्वस्य हारितस्तत्सुतोऽभवत् ।
पुरुकुत्सस्य दायादस्त्रसदस्युर्म्महायशाः ॥
नर्म्मदायां समुत्पन्नः सम्भूतिस्तत्सुतः स्मृतः ।
विष्णुवृद्धः सुतस्तस्य त्वनरण्योऽभवत्ततः§ ॥
बृहदश्वोऽनरण्यस्य हर्य्यश्वस्तत्सुतोऽभवत् ॥
सोऽतीव धार्म्मिको राजा कर्द्दमस्य प्रजापतेः ।

---

* प्रमेयस्तु इति H. प्रमोदिस्तु इति D, प्रमेहस्तु इति E.

† हर्य्यश्वस्तस्य चात्मज इत्यारभ्य युवनाश्वो रणाश्वस्य इत्यन्तं B पुस्तके नास्ति ।

‡ वारुणीमिष्टिं—वरुणदेवताकं यागमित्यर्थः ।

§ ऽभवत्परः इति B.

प्रसादाद्धार्म्मिकं पुत्रं लेभे सूर्य्यपरायणम् ॥
स तु सूर्य्यं समभ्यर्च्य राजा वसुमनाः शुभम्।
लेभे त्वप्रतिमं पुत्रं त्रिधन्वानमरिन्दमम् ॥
अयजच्चाश्वमेधेन शत्रूञ्जित्वा द्विजोत्तमाः।
स्वाध्यायवान्दानशीलस्तितीर्षुर्द्धर्मतत्परः* ॥
ऋषयस्तु समाजग्मुर्यज्ञवाटं महात्मनः।
वसिष्ठकश्यपमुखा देवाश्चेन्द्रपुरोगमाः ॥
तान् प्रणम्य महाराजः पप्रच्छ विनयान्वितः।
समाप्य विधिवद्यज्ञं वसिष्ठादीन्द्विजोत्तमान् ॥

वसुमना उवाच।

किं हि श्रेयस्करतरं लोकेऽस्मिन् ब्राह्मणर्षभाः।
यज्ञस्तपो वा सन्यासो ब्रूत मे सर्व्ववेदिनः ॥

वसिष्ठ उवाच।

अधीत्य वेदान्विधिवत्सुतांश्चोत्पाद्य यत्नतः।
इष्ट्वा यज्ञेश्वरं यज्ञैर्गच्छेद्वनमथात्मवान् ॥

पुलस्त्य उवाच।

आराध्य तपसा देवं योगिनम्परमेश्वरम्†।
प्रव्रजेद्विधिवद्यज्ञैरिष्ट्वा पूर्व्वं सुरोत्तमान् ॥

पुलह उवाच।

यमाहुरेकं पुरुषं पुराणम्परमेश्वरम्।

---

* तितिक्षुर्धर्म्मतत्परः इति B.

† परमेष्ठिनमिति B.

तमाराध्य सहस्रांशुन्तपसो* मोक्षमाप्नुयात् ॥

जमदग्निरुवाच ।

अजो विश्वस्य कर्त्ता यो जगद्बीजं सनातनः ।
अन्तर्य्यामी च भूतानां स देवस्तपसेज्यते ॥

विश्वामित्र उवाच ।

योऽग्निः सर्व्वात्मकोऽनन्तः स्वयम्भूर्विश्वतोमुखः ।
स रुद्रस्तपसोग्रेण पूज्यते नेतरैर्म्मखैः ॥

भरद्वाज उवाच ।

यो यज्ञैरिज्यते देवो वासुदेवः† सनातनः ।
स सर्व्वदैवततनुः पूज्यते परमेश्वरः ॥

अत्रिरुवाच ।

यतः सर्व्वमिदं जातं यस्यापत्यं प्रजापतिः ।
तपः सुमहदास्थाय पूज्यते स महेश्वरः ॥

गौतम उवाच ।

यतः प्रधानपुरुषौ यस्य शक्तिरिदं‡ जगत् ।
स देवदेवस्तपसा पूजनीयः सनातनः ॥

कश्यप उवाच ।

सहस्रनयनो देवः साक्षी शम्भुः प्रजापतिः ।
प्रसीदति महायोगी पूजितस्तपसा परः ॥

---

* तमस इति B.

† जातवेदा इति B.

‡ शक्तिमयमिति B and D.

क्रतुरुवाच।

प्राप्ताध्ययनयज्ञस्य लब्धपुत्रस्य चैव हि।
नान्तरेण तपः कश्चिद्धर्म्मः शास्त्रेषु दृश्यते॥
इत्याकर्ण्य स राजर्षिस्तान् प्रणम्यातिहृष्टधीः।
विसर्जयित्वा* संपूज्य त्रिधन्वानमथाब्रवीत्॥
आराधयिष्ये तपसा देवमेकाक्षराह्वयम्।
प्राणं बृहन्तं पुरुषमादित्यान्तरसंस्थितम्॥
त्वन्तु धर्म्मरती नित्यं पालयैतदतन्द्रितः।
चातुर्वर्ण्यसमायुक्तमशेषं क्षितिमण्डलम्॥
एवमुक्त्वा स तद्राज्यं निधायात्मभवे नृपः।
जगामारण्यमनघस्तपस्तप्तुमनुत्तमम्॥
हिमवच्छिखरे रम्ये देवदारुवनाश्रये।
कन्दमूलफलाहारैरुत्पन्नैरयजत्सुरान्॥
संवत्सरशतं साग्रन्तपोनिर्द्धूतकिल्विषः†।
जजाप मनसा देवीं सावित्रीं वेदमातरम्‡॥
तस्यैवन्तपतो§ देवः स्वयम्भूः परमेश्वरः।
हिरण्यगर्भो विश्वात्मा¶ तं देशमगमत्स्वयम्॥

---

* विसर्जयित्वा इति आर्षम्।

† कल्मष इति B.

‡ देवमातरमिति B.

§ जपत इति B.

¶ भगवानिति B.

दृष्ट्वा देवं समायान्तं ब्रह्माणं विश्वतोमुखम् ।
ननाम शिरसा तस्य पादयोर्नाम कीर्त्तयन् ॥
नमो देवाधिदेवाय ब्रह्मणे परमात्मने ।
हिरण्यमूर्त्तये तुभ्यं सहस्राक्षाय वेधसे ॥
नमो धात्रे विधात्रे च नमो देवात्ममूर्त्तये ।
सांख्ययोगाधिगम्याय नमस्ते ज्ञानमूर्त्तये ॥
नमस्त्रिमूर्त्तये तुभ्यं स्रष्ट्रे सर्व्वार्थवेदिने ।
पुरुषाय पुराणाय योगिनां गुरवे नमः ॥
ततः प्रसन्नो भगवान्विरिञ्चो विश्वभावनः ।
वरं वरय भद्रन्ते वरदोऽस्मीत्यभाषत ॥

राजोवाच ।

जपेयन्देवदेवेश गायत्रीं वेदमातरम् ।
भूयो वर्षशतं साग्रन्तावदायुर्भवेन्मम ॥
वाढ़मित्याह विश्वात्मा समालोक्य नराधिपम् ।
स्पृष्ट्वा कराभ्यां सुप्रीतस्तत्रैवान्तरधीयत ॥
सोऽपि लब्धवरः श्रीमाञ्जजापातिप्रसन्नधीः ।
शान्तस्त्रिषवणस्नायी कन्दमूलफलाशनः ॥
तस्य पूर्णे वर्षशते भगवानुग्रदीधितिः ।
प्रादुरासीन्महायोगी भानोर्मण्डलमध्यगः* ॥
तं दृष्ट्वा वेदवपुषं† मण्डलस्थं सनातनम् ।

---

* मध्यत इति B.

† देवदेवेशमिति B.

स्वयम्भुवमनाद्यन्तं ब्रह्माणं विस्मयङ्गतः ॥
तुष्टाव वैदिकैर्म्मन्त्रैः सावित्र्या च विशेषतः ।
क्षणादपश्यत्पुरुषं तमेव परमेश्वरम् ॥
चतुर्म्मुखं जटामौलिमष्टहस्तं त्रिलोचनम् ।
चन्द्रावयवलक्ष्माणं नरनारीतनुं हरम् ॥
भासयन्तं जगत्कृत्स्नं नीलकण्ठं स्वरश्मिभिः ।
रक्ताम्बरधरं रक्तं रक्तमाल्यानुलेपनम् ॥
तद्भावभावितो दृष्ट्वा सद्भावेन परेण हि ।
ननाम शिरसा रुद्रं सावित्र्या तेन* चैव हि ॥
नमस्ते नीलकण्ठाय भास्वते परमेष्ठिने ।
त्रयीमयाय रुद्राय कालरूपाय हेतवे ॥
तदा प्राह महादेवो राजानं प्रीतमानसः ।
इमानि मे रहस्यानि नामानि शृणु चानघ ॥
सर्व्ववेदेषु गीतानि संसारशमनानि तु ।
नमः कुरुष्व नृपते† एभिर्म्मां सततं शुचिः ॥
अधीष्व शतरुद्रीयं यजुषां सारमुद्धृतम् ।
जपस्वानन्यचेतस्कोऽ‡ मय्यासक्तमना नृप ॥
ब्रह्मचारी निराहारो भस्मनिष्ठः समाहितः ।
जपेदामरणाद्रुद्रं स याति परमं पदम् ॥

---

* सावित्र्यानेनेति B.

† नमस्कुरुष्व सततमिति B.

‡ जपस्व इत्यार्षमात्मनेपदम् ।

इत्युक्त्वा भगवान्रुद्रो भक्तानुग्रहकाम्यया ।
पुनः संवत्सरशतं राज्ञे ह्यायुरकल्पयत् ॥
दत्त्वास्मै तत्परं ज्ञानं वैराग्यं परमेश्वरः ।
क्षणादन्तर्द्दधे रुद्रस्तदद्भुतमिवाभवत् ॥
राजापि तपसा रुद्रं जजापानन्यमानसः ।
भस्मच्छन्नस्त्रिषवणं* स्नात्वा शान्तः समाहितः ॥
जपतस्तस्य नृपतेः पूर्णे वर्षशते पुनः ।
योगप्रवृत्तिरभवत्कालात्कालपरं† पदम् ॥
विवेशैतद्वेदसारं‡ स्थानं वै परमेष्ठिनः ।
भानोः समण्डलं§ शुभ्रं ततो यातो महेश्वरम् ॥
यः पठेच्छृणुयाद्वापि राज्ञश्चरितमुत्तमम् ।
सर्व्वपापविनिर्मुक्तो ब्रह्मलोके महीयते ॥

इति श्रीकूर्म्मपुराणे राजवंशकीर्त्तने विंशोऽध्यायः ।

---

* भस्मच्छन्नं त्रिषवणमिति B.

† कालात्मकमिति B. कालान्तकमिति D and E. कालात्कालात्परं पदमिति G and H.

‡ विवेश तद्वेदसारमिति B.

§ श्रीमण्डलमिति B.

एकविंशोऽध्यायः ।

सूत उवाच ।

त्रिधन्वा राजपुत्रस्तु धर्म्मेणापालयन्महीम् ।
तस्य पुत्रोऽभवद्विद्वांस्त्रय्यारुण इति श्रुतः ॥
तस्य सत्यव्रतो नाम कुमारोऽभून्महाबलः ।
भार्य्या सत्यधना नाम हरिश्चन्द्रमजीजनत् ॥
हरिश्चन्द्रस्य पुत्रोऽभूद्रोहितो नाम* वीर्य्यवान् । †
रोहितस्य‡ वृकः पुत्रस्तस्माद्बाहुरजायत ॥
सगरस्तस्य पुत्रोऽभूद्राजा परमधार्म्मिकः ।
द्वे भार्य्ये सगरस्यापि प्रभा भानुमती तथा ॥
ताभ्यामाराधितो वह्निः प्रददौ§ वरमुत्तमम् ॥
एकं भानुमती पुत्रमगृह्णादसमञ्जसम् ।
प्रभा षष्टिसहस्रन्तु पुत्राणां जगृहे शुभा ॥

---

* कुरुकी नाम इति A.

† अतः परं B पुस्तके वक्ष्यमाणमतिरिक्तं दृश्यते—

हरितो रोहितस्याथ धुन्धुस्तस्य सुतोऽभवत् ।
विजयश्च सुदेवश्च धुन्धुपुत्रौ बभूवतुः ॥
विजयस्याभवत्पुत्रः कारुकोनाम वीर्य्यवान् ।

‡ कुरुकस्य इति A, D, E and H.

§ ताभ्यामाराधितः प्रादादौर्व्वोऽग्निरिति B. ताभ्यामाराधितः प्रादात्पुराग्निरिति D.

असमञ्जसपुत्त्रोऽभूदंशुमान्नाम* पार्थिवः ।
तस्य पुत्त्रो दिलीपस्तु दिलीपात्तु भगीरथः ॥
येन भागीरथी गङ्गा तपः कृत्वावतारिता ।
प्रसादाद्देवदेवस्य महादेवस्य धीमतः ॥
भगीरथस्य तपसा देवः प्रीतमना हरः । †
बभार शिरसा गङ्गां सोमान्ते सोमभूषणः ॥
भगीरथसुतश्चापि श्रुतो नाम बभूव ह ।
नाभागस्तस्य दायादः सिन्धुद्वीपस्ततोऽभवत्‡ ॥
अयुतायुः सुतस्तस्य ऋतुपर्णो महाबलः§ ।
ऋतुपर्णस्य पुत्त्रोऽभूत्सुदासो नाम धार्म्मिकः ॥
सौदासस्तस्य तनयः ख्यातः¶ कल्माषपादकः ॥
वसिष्ठस्तु महातेजाः क्षेत्रे काल्माषपादके‖ ।
अश्मकं जनयामास तमिक्ष्वाकुकुलध्वजम् ।
अश्मकस्योत्कलायान्तु** नकुलो नाम पार्थिवः ॥

---

* असमञ्जसस्य तनयो ह्यंशुमान्नाम इति B. असमञ्जस्य पुत्त्रोभूदंशुमान्नाम इति D, E and H.

† तस्य पुत्त्रो दिलीपस्तु इत्यारभ्य प्रीतमना हरइत्यन्तं B पुस्तके नास्ति ।

‡ सिन्धुद्वीपसमोऽभवदिति G and H.

§ ऋतुपर्णस्तु तत्सुतः इति B.

¶ ततः इति D.

‖ कल्माषपादक इति D, E and H.

** अश्मकस्योत्तरायान्तु इति B.

स हि रामभयाद्राजा* वनं प्राप सुदुःखितः ।
दधत्† सनारीकवचं तस्माच्छतरथोऽभवत् ॥
तस्माद्दिलिविलिः‡ श्रीमान् वृद्धशर्म्मा च तत्सुतः§ ।
तस्माद्विश्वसहस्तस्मात्खट्वाङ्ग इति¶ विश्रुतः ॥
दीर्घबाहुः सुतस्तस्माद्रघुः स्तस्मादजायत ।
रघोरजः समुत्पन्नो राजा दशरथस्ततः ॥
रामो दाशरथिर्व्वीरो धर्म्मज्ञो लोकविश्रुतः ।
भरतो लक्ष्मणश्चैव शत्रुघ्नश्च महाबलः ॥
सर्व्वे शक्रसमा युद्धे विष्णुशक्तिसमन्विताः ।
जज्ञे रावणनाशार्थं विष्णुरंशेन विश्वभुक्‖ ॥
रामस्य भार्य्या सुभगा जनकस्यात्मजा सुता ।
सीता त्रिलोकविख्याता** शीलौदार्य्यगुणान्विता ॥
तपसा तोषिता देवी जनकेन गिरीन्द्रजा ।
प्रायच्छज्जानकीं सीतां राममेवाश्रितां पतिम् ॥
प्रीतश्च भगवानीशस्त्रिशूली नीललोहितः ।
प्रददौ शत्रुनाशार्थं जनकायाद्भुतं धनुः ॥

---

* कामभयादिति D.

† बिभ्रदिति B.

‡ दिलिविल इति D.

§ तस्माद्दिलिविलिः श्रीमान् वृद्धधर्म्मा च तत्सुत इति B.

¶ वट्वाङ्ग इति D. वेट्वङ्ग इति G. वट्वङ्ग इति E and H.

‖ विश्वहदिति B.

** सीतेति लोकविख्याता इति B.

स राजा जनको धीमान्* दातुकामः सुतामिमाम् ।
अघोषयदमित्रघ्नो लोकेऽस्मिन्द्विजपुङ्गवाः ॥
इदं धनुः समादातुं यः शक्नोति जगत्त्रये ।
देवो वा दानवो वापि स सीतां लब्धुमर्हति ॥
विज्ञाय रामो बलवाञ्जनकस्य गृहं प्रभुः ।
भञ्जयामास चादाय गत्वासौ लीलयैव हि ॥
उद्ववाहाथ† तां कन्यां पार्व्वतीमिव शङ्करः ।
रामः परमधर्म्मात्मा सेनामिव च षण्मुखः ॥
ततो बहुतिथे काले राजा दशरथः स्वयम् ।
रामं ज्येष्ठसुतं वीरं राजानं कर्त्तुमारभत्‡ ॥
तस्याथ पत्नी सुभगा कैकेयी चारुहासिनी§ ।
निवारयामास पतिं प्राह सम्भ्रान्तमानसा ॥
मत्सुतं भरतं वीरं राजानं कर्त्तुमर्हसि ।
पूर्व्वमेव वरो यस्माद्दत्तो मे भवता यतः¶ ॥
स तस्या वचनं श्रुत्वा राजा दुःखितमानसः ।
वाढ़मित्यब्रवीद्वाक्यं तथा रामोऽपि धर्म्मवित् ॥
प्रणम्याथ पितुः पादौ लक्ष्मणेन सहाच्युतः ।

---

* विद्वानिति B.

† उदुवाह इति तु वक्तव्ये उद्ववाह इत्यार्षम् ।

‡ कर्त्तुमारभदित्यत्र परस्मैपदमार्षम् ।

§ चारुभाषिणीति B.

¶ भवता च यदिति B.

यया वनं सपत्नीकः कृत्वा समयमात्मवान् ॥
संवत्सराणां चत्वारि दश चैव महाबलः।
उवास तत्र भगवान्* लक्ष्मणेन सह प्रभुः ॥
कदाचिद्वसतोऽरण्ये रावणो नाम राक्षसः।
परिव्राजकवेषेण सीतां हृत्वा ययौ पुरीम् ॥
अदृष्ट्वा लक्ष्मणो रामः सीतामाकुलितेन्द्रियौ।
दुःखशोकाभिसन्तप्तौ बभूवतुररिन्दमौ ॥
ततः कदाचित्कपिना सुग्रीवेण द्विजोत्तमाः।
वानराणामभूत्सख्यं रामस्याक्लिष्टकर्म्मणः ॥
सुग्रीवस्यानुगो वीरो हनूमान्नाम वानरः।
वायुपुत्रो महातेजा रामस्यासीत्प्रियः सदा ॥
स कृत्वा परमं धैर्य्यं रामाय कृतनिश्चयः।
आनयिष्यामि तां सीतामित्युक्त्वा विचचार ह ॥
महीं सागरपर्य्यन्तां सीतादर्शनतत्परः।
जगाम रावणपुरीं लङ्कां सागरसंस्थिताम् ॥
तत्राथ निर्ज्जने देशे वृक्षमूले शुचिस्मिताम्।
अपश्यदमलां सीतां राक्षसीभिः समावृताम्।
अश्रुपूर्णेक्षणां हृद्यां संस्मरन्तीमनिन्दिताम्।
राममिन्दीवरश्यामं लक्ष्मणञ्चात्मसंस्थितम् ॥

---

* मतिमानिति B.

निवेदयित्वा* चात्मानं सीतायै रहसि प्रभुः† ।
असंशयाय प्रददावस्यै रामाङ्गुलीयकम् ॥
दृष्ट्वाङ्गुलीयकं सीता पत्युः परमशोभनम् ।
मेने समागतं रामं प्रीतिविस्फुरितेक्षणा ॥
समाश्वास्य तदा सीतां दृष्ट्वा रामस्य चान्तिकम् ।
नयिष्ये त्वां महाबाहुमुक्त्वा रामं ययौ पुनः ॥
निवेदयित्वा रामाय सीतादर्शनमात्मवान् ।
तस्थौ रामेण पुरतो लक्ष्मणेन च पूजितः ॥
ततः स रामो बलवान्सार्द्धं हनुमता स्वयम् ।
लक्ष्मणेन च युद्धाय बुद्धिञ्चक्रे हि रक्षसा‡ ॥
कृत्वाथ वानरशतैर्लङ्कामार्गं महोदधेः ।
सेतुम्परमधर्मात्मा रावणं हतवान्प्रभुः ।
सपत्नीकं हि§ ससुतं सभ्रातृकमरिन्दमः ॥
आनयामास तां सीतां वायुपुत्रसहायवान् ॥
सेतुमध्ये महादेवमीशानङ्कृत्तिवाससम् ।
स्थापयामास लिङ्गस्थं¶ पूजयामास राघवः ॥
तस्य देवो महादेवः पार्वत्या सह शङ्करः ।

---

* निवेदयित्वा इत्यार्षं, निवेद्य इति साधु ।

† स्वयमिति B.

‡ चक्रेतिराक्षसमिति A, E and H.

§ सपत्नीकञ्चेति B.

¶ लिङ्गञ्चेति B.

प्रत्यक्षमेव भगवान्दत्तवान्वरमुत्तमम् ॥
यत्त्वया स्थापितं लिङ्गं* द्रक्ष्यन्तीदं द्विजातयः ।
महापातकसंयुक्तास्तेषां पापं विनंक्ष्यति ॥
अन्यानि चैव पापानि स्नातस्यात्र महोदधौ ।
दर्शनादेव लिङ्गस्य नाशं यान्ति न संशयः ॥
यावत्स्थास्यन्ति गिरयो यावदेषा च मेदिनी ।
यावत्सेतुश्च तावच्च स्थास्याम्यत्र तिरोहितः† ॥
स्नानं दानं तपः श्राद्धं सर्वम्भवतु चाक्षयम्‡ ।
स्मरणादेव लिङ्गस्य दिनपापम्प्रणश्यति§ ॥
इत्युक्त्वा भगवाञ्छम्भुः परिष्वज्य तु राघवम् ।
सनन्दी सगणो रुद्रस्तत्रैवान्तरधीयत ॥
रामोऽपि पालयामास राज्यन्धर्मपरायणः ।
अभिषिक्तो महातेजा भरतेन महाबलः ॥
विशेषाद्ब्राह्मणान्सर्वान्पूजयामास चेश्वरम् ।
यज्ञेन यज्ञहन्तारमश्वमेधेन शङ्करम् ॥
रामस्य तनयो जज्ञे कुश इत्यभिविश्रुतः ।
लवश्च सुमहाभागः सर्वतत्त्वार्थवित्सुधीः ॥
अतिथिस्तु कुशाज्जज्ञे निषधस्तत्सुतोऽभवत् ।

---

* तत्र इति B.

† स्थास्यन्त्यत्र तिरोहिता इति B.

‡ भविष्यत्यक्षयम्महदिति B.

§ नाशं यान्ति न संशय इति B.

नलस्य निषधस्यासीत्* नभास्तस्मादजायत ॥
नभसः पुण्डरीकाक्षः क्षेमधन्वा तु तत्सुतः ।
तस्य पुत्त्रोऽभवद्वीरो देवानीकः प्रतापवान् ॥
अहीनगुस्तस्य सुतो महस्वांस्†तत्सुतोऽभवत्‡ ।
तस्माच्चन्द्रावलोकस्तु ताराधीशश्च§ तत्सुतः ॥
ताराधीशाच्चन्द्रगिरिर्भानुवित्तस्ततोऽभवत् ।
श्रुतायुरभवत्तस्मादेते चेक्ष्वाकुवंशजाः ।
सर्वे प्राधान्यतः प्रोक्ताः समासेन द्विजोत्तमाः ॥
य इमं शृणुयान्नित्यमिक्ष्वाकोर्वंशमुत्तमम् ।
सर्वपापविनिर्मुक्तो देवलोके महीयते ॥

इति श्रीकूर्म्मपुराणे इक्ष्वाकुवंशे एकविंशोऽध्यायः ।

---

* नलस्तु निषधस्याभूदिति B.

† सहस्र इति D. सहस्वानिति H.

‡ सहस्वांश्च सुतोऽभवदिति B.

§ तारापीड़स्तु इति B.

द्वाविंशोऽध्यायः ।

सूत उवाच ।*

ऐलः पूरूरवाश्चाथ राजा राज्यमपालयत् ।
तस्य पुत्रा बभूवुर्हि षड़िन्द्रसमतेजसः† ॥
आयुर्मायुरमायुश्च विश्वायुश्चैव वीर्यवान् ।
शतायुश्च श्रुतायुश्च दिव्याश्चैवोर्वशीसुताः ॥
आयुषस्तनया वीराः पञ्चैवासन्महौजसः ।
स्वर्भानुतनयायां वै प्रभायामिति नः श्रुतम् ॥
नहुषः प्रथमस्तेषां धर्म्मज्ञो लोकविश्रुतः ॥
नहुषस्य तु दायादाः पञ्चेन्द्रोपमतेजसः‡ ।
उत्पन्नाः पितृकन्यायां विरजायां महाबलाः ॥
यातिर्ययातिः§ संयातिरायातिः पञ्चमोऽश्वकः ।
तेषां ययातिः पञ्चानां महाबलपराक्रमः ॥
देवयानीमुशनसः सुतां भार्य्यामवाप सः ।
शर्मिष्ठामासुरीञ्चैव तनयां वृषपर्वणः ॥

---

* रोमहर्षण उवाचेति B.

† षड़िन्द्रोपमतेजस इति G.

‡ पञ्चासन्नमितौजस इति D. षड़िन्द्रोपमतेजस इति B, E and H.

§ यतिरिति B.

यदुञ्च तुर्वशुञ्चैव देवयानी व्यजायत* ।
द्रुह्युञ्चानुञ्च पूरुञ्च शर्म्मिष्ठा चाप्यजीजनत् ॥
सोऽभ्यषिञ्चदतिक्रम्य ज्येष्ठं यदुमनिन्दितम् ।
पूरुमेव कनीयांसम्पितुर्वचनपालकम् ॥
दिशि दक्षिणपूर्वस्यान्तुर्वशुं पुत्रमादिशत् ।
दक्षिणापरयो† राजा यदुं श्रेष्ठं न्ययोजयत् ॥
प्रतीच्यामुत्तरायाञ्च द्रुह्युञ्चानुमकल्पयत् ।
तैरियं पृथिवी सर्व्वा धर्म्मतः परिपालिता ॥
राजापि दारसहितो वनं प्राप महायशाः ।
यदोरप्यभवन् पुत्राः पञ्च देवसुतोपमाः ॥
सहस्रजित्तथा श्रेष्ठः क्रोष्टुर्नीलो जिनो रघुः ।
सहस्रजित्सुतस्तद्वच्छतजिन्नाम पार्थिवः ॥
सुताः शतजितोऽप्यासंस्त्रयः परमधार्म्मिकाः ।
हैहयश्च हयश्चैव राजा वेणुहयश्च यः ॥
हैहयस्याभवत्पुत्रो धर्म्म इत्यभिविश्रुतः ।
तस्य पुत्रोऽभवद्विप्रा धर्म्मनेत्रः प्रतापवान् ॥
धर्म्मनेत्रस्य कीर्त्तिस्तु सञ्जित‡स्तत्सुतोऽभवत् ।
महिष्मः§ सञ्जितस्याभूद्भद्रश्रेण्यस्तदन्वयः ॥

---

* अत्र अन्तर्भूतण्यर्थत्वादजनयदित्येवार्थः ।

† दक्षिणापरयोः—दक्षिणस्यामपरस्याञ्च (पश्चिमायां) दिशि इत्यर्थः ।

‡ संज्ञित इति B.

§ महिष्मानिति B.

भद्रश्रेण्यस्य दायादो दुर्द्दमो नाम पार्थिवः।
दुर्द्दमस्य सुतो धीमानन्धको नाम वीर्य्यवान्॥
अन्धकस्य तु दायादाश्चत्वारो लोकसम्मताः।
कृतवीर्य्यः कृताग्निश्च कृतवर्म्मा च तत्सुतः* ॥
कृतौजाश्च चतुर्थोऽभूत्कार्त्तवीर्य्यस्तथार्जुनः† ।
सहस्रबाहुर्द्युतिमान्धनुर्वेदविदां वरः॥
तस्य रामोऽभवन्मृत्युर्जामदग्न्यो जनार्द्दनः।
तस्य पुत्रशतान्यासन्पञ्च तत्र महारथाः॥
कृतास्त्रा बलिनः शूराः धर्म्मात्मानो मनस्विनः।
शूरश्च सुरसेनश्च कृष्णो धृष्णस्तथैव च।
जयध्वजश्च बलवान्नारायणपरो नृपः॥
शूरसेनादयः पूर्वे चत्वारः प्रथितौजसः।
रुद्रभक्ता महात्मानः पूजयन्ति स्म शङ्करम्॥
जयध्वजस्तु मतिमान्देवं नारायणं हरिम्।
जगाम शरणं विष्णुं दैवतन्धर्म्मतत्परः॥
तमूचुरितरे पुत्रा नायं धर्म्मस्तवानघ।
ईश्वराराधनरतः पितास्माकमिति श्रुतिः॥
तानब्रवीन्महातेजा ह्येष धर्मः परो मम।
विष्णोरंशेन सम्भूता राजानो ये महीतले॥
राज्यं पालयितावश्यम्भगवान्पुरुषोत्तमः।

---

* तथैव च इति B.

† कार्त्तवीर्य्यार्जुनोऽभवदिति B.

पूजनीयोऽजितो* विष्णुः पालको जगतां हरिः ॥
सात्विकी राजसी चैव तामसी च स्वयं प्रभुः† ।
तिस्रस्तु मूर्त्तयः प्रोक्ताः सृष्टिस्थित्यन्तहेतवः ॥
सत्त्वात्मा भगवान्विष्णुः संस्थापयति सर्व्वदा ।
सृजेद्ब्रह्मा रजोमूर्त्तिः संहरेत्तामसी हरः ॥
तस्मान्महीपतीनान्तु राज्यम्पालयतामिदम् ।
आराध्यो भगवान्विष्णुः केशवः केशिमर्द्दनः ॥
निशम्य तस्य वचनं भ्रातरोऽन्ये मनस्विनः ।
प्रोचुः संहारकोरुद्रः‡ पूजनीयो मुमुक्षुभिः ॥
अयं हि भगवान्रुद्रः सर्व्वं जगदिदं शिवः ।
तमोगुणं समाश्रित्य कालान्ते संहरेत्प्रभुः ॥
या सा घोरतमा मूर्त्तिरस्य तेजोमयी परा ।
संहरेद्विद्यया पूर्व्वं§ संसारं शूलभृत्तया ॥
ततस्तानब्रवीद्राजा विचिन्त्यासौ जयध्वजः ।
सत्त्वेन मुच्यते जन्तुः सत्त्वात्मा भगवान्हरिः ॥
तमूचुर्भ्रातरो रुद्रः सेवितः सात्त्विकैर्जनैः ।
मोचयेत्सत्त्वसंयुक्तः पूजयेत्सततं हरम् ॥

---

* पूजनीयश्च य इति B.

† स्वयम्भुव इति B.

‡ संहारकृद्रुद्रः इति B.

§ सर्व्वमिति B.

अथाब्रवीद्राजपुत्रः प्रहसन्वै* जयध्वजः ।
स्वधर्म्मो मुक्तये युक्तो† नान्यो मुनिभिरिष्यते ॥
तथाच वैष्णवीं शक्तिं नृपाणान्दधतां सदा ।
आराधनम्परो धर्म्मो मुरारेरमितौजसः ॥
तमब्रवीद्राजपुत्रः कृष्णो मतिमतां वरः ।
यदर्जुनोऽस्मज्जनकः स धर्म्मं कृतवानिति ॥
एवं विवादे वितते शूरसेनोऽब्रवीद्वचः ।
प्रमाणमृषयो ह्यत्र ब्रूयुस्ते तत्तथैव‡ तत् ॥
ततस्ते राजशार्दूलाः पप्रच्छुर्ब्रह्मवादिनः ।
गत्वा सर्व्वे सुसंरब्धाः सप्तर्षीणां तदाश्रमम्§ ॥
तानब्रुवंस्ते मुनयो वसिष्ठाद्या यथार्थतः ।
या यस्याभिमता पुंसः सा हि तस्यैव देवता ॥
किन्तु कार्य्यविशेषेण पूजिता चेष्टदा नृणाम् ।
विशेषात्सर्व्वदा नायन्नियमो ह्यन्यथा नृपाः ॥
नृपाणां दैवतं विष्णुस्तथैशश्च¶ पुरन्दरः ।
विप्राणामग्निरादित्यो ब्रह्मा चैव पिनाकधृक्‖ ॥

---

* सह सत्वैरिति D.

† पन्था इति B and D. अधर्म्ममुक्तये मुक्त इति E and H.

‡ यत्तथैव इति B.

§ तदाश्रयमिति B.

¶ तथैव चेति B.

‖ त्रिशूलभृदिति B.

देवानां दैवतं विष्णुर्दानवानां त्रिशूलधृक् ।
गन्धर्व्वाणां तथा सोमो यक्षाणामपि कथ्यते ॥
विद्याधराणां वाग्देवी सिद्धानां भगवान् हरिः ।
रक्षसां शङ्करो रुद्रः किन्नराणाञ्च पार्व्वती ॥
ऋषीणां भगवान् ब्रह्मा महादेवस्त्रिशूलभृत् ।
मान्या स्त्रीणामुमा* देवी तथा विष्णुशभास्कराः ॥
गृहस्थानाञ्च सर्व्वे स्युर्ब्रह्म वै ब्रह्मचारिणाम् ।
वैखानसानामर्कः स्याद्यतीनाञ्च महेश्वरः† ॥
भूतानां भगवान्रुद्रः कूष्माण्डानां विनायकः ।
सर्व्वेषां भगवान् ब्रह्मा देवदेवः प्रजापतिः ॥
इत्येवं भगवान् ब्रह्मा स्वयं देवो ह्यभाषत ।
तस्माज्जयध्वजो नूनं‡ विष्णाराधनमर्हति ॥§
सम्प्रणम्याथ¶ ते जग्मुः पुरीम्परमशोभनाम् ।
पालयाञ्चक्रिरे पृथ्वीञ्जित्वा सर्व्वान्रिपून्रणे ॥
ततः कदाचिद्विप्रेन्द्रा विदेहो नाम दानवः ।

---

* मनूनां स्यादुमा इति B and D.

† विष्णुः सभास्करः इति B.

‡ नामेति B.

§ अतः परं B पुस्तके वक्ष्यमाणमधिकं दृश्यते—

किन्तु रुद्रेण तादात्म्यं बुद्धा पूज्यो हरिर्नरैः ।
अन्यथा नृपतेः शत्रुं न हरिः संहरेद्यतः ॥

¶ तान् प्रणम्याथ इति B and D.

भीषणः सर्व्वसत्त्वानां पुरीं* तेषां समाययौ ॥
दंष्ट्राकरालो दीप्तात्मा युगान्तदहनोपमः ।
शूलमादाय सूर्याभं नादयन्वै दिशो दश ॥
तन्नादश्रवणान्मर्त्त्यास्तत्र ये निवसन्ति ते† ।
तत्यजुर्ज्जीवितं त्वन्ये दुद्रुवुर्भयविह्वलाः ॥
ततः सर्व्वे सुसंयत्ताः कार्त्तवीर्य्यात्मजास्तदा‡ ।
शूरसेनादयः पञ्च राजानस्तु महाबलाः ।
युद्धाय कृतसंरम्भा विदेहन्त्वभिदुद्रुवुः ॥
शूरोऽस्त्रं प्राहिणोद्रौद्रं शूरसेनस्तु वारुणम् ।
प्राजापत्यं तथा कृष्णो वायव्यं धृष्ण एव च ॥
जयध्वजश्च कौवेरमैन्द्रमाग्नेयमेव च ।
भञ्जयामास शूलेन तान्यस्त्राणि स दानवः ॥
ततः कृष्णो महावीर्य्यो गदामादाय भीषणाम् ।
स्पृष्टमात्रेण§ तरसा चिक्षेप च ननाद च ॥
सम्प्राप्य सा गदास्योरो विदेहस्य शिलोपमम् ।
न दानवञ्चालयितुं शशाकान्तकसन्निभम् ॥

---

* पुरमिति B.

† वै इति B.

‡ कार्त्तवीर्य्यार्ज्जुनात्मजा इति B. अतः परं B पुस्तकेऽधिकं दृश्यते—
युयुधुर्दानवं शक्तिगिरिकूटासिमुद्गरैः ।
तान् सर्व्वान् सहि विप्रेन्द्राः शूलेन प्रहसन्निव ।
वारयामास घोरात्मा कल्पान्ते भैरवो यथा ॥ इति D पुस्तकेऽप्यस्ति ।

§ स्पृष्टा मन्त्रेण इति B and D.

दुद्रुवुस्ते भयग्रस्ता दृष्ट्वा तस्यातिपौरुषम् ॥
जयध्वजस्तु मतिमान् सस्मार जगतः पतिम् ।
विष्णुं जयिष्णुं लोकादिमप्रमेयमनामयम् ।
त्रातारं पुरुषं पूर्व्वं* श्रीपतिम्पीतवाससम् ॥
ततः प्रादुरभूच्चक्रं सूर्य्यायुतसमप्रभम् ।
आदेशाद्वासुदेवस्य भक्तानुग्रहणात्तदा† ॥
जग्राह जगतां योनिं स्मृत्वा नारायणं नृपः ।
प्राहिणोद्वै विदेहाय दानवेभ्यो यथा हरिः ॥
सम्प्राप्य तस्य घोरस्य स्कन्धदेशं सुदर्शनम् ।
पृथिव्यां पातयामास शिरोऽद्रिशिखराकृति ॥‡
तस्मिन् हते देवरिपौ शूराद्या भ्रातरो नृपाः ।
समाययुः पुरीं रम्यां भ्रातरञ्चाप्यपूजयन् ॥
श्रुत्वाजगाम भगवाञ्जयध्वजपराक्रमम्§ ।
कार्त्तवीर्य्यसुतं द्रष्टुं विश्वामित्रो महामुनिः ॥
तमागतमथो दृष्ट्वा राजा सम्भ्रान्तलोचनः¶ ।

---

* सर्व्वमिति B.

† भक्तानुग्रहकारणादिति B and D.

‡ अतः परं B पुस्तके श्लोकोऽयं दृश्यते—

तद्धि चक्रं पुरा विष्णुस्तपसाराध्य शङ्करम् ।
यस्मादवाप तत्तस्मादसुराणां विनाशकम् ॥

§ कृत्वा जयपराक्रममिति E and H.

¶ सम्भ्रान्तमानस इति B and D.

समाविश्यासने रम्ये पूजयामास भावतः ॥
उवाच भगवन् घोरः प्रसादाद्भवतोऽसुरः ।
निपातितो मया सोऽथ* विदेहो दानवेश्वरः ॥
त्वद्वाक्याच्छिन्नसन्देहो विष्णुं सत्यपराक्रमम् ।
प्रपन्नः शरणं तेन प्रसादो मे कृतः शुभः ॥
यक्ष्यामि परमेशानं विष्णुं पद्मदलेक्षणम् ।
कथङ्केन विधानेन† सम्पूज्यो हरिरीश्वरः ॥
कोऽयन्नारायणो देवः किंप्रभावश्च सुव्रत ।
सर्व्वमेतन्ममाचक्ष्व परङ्कौतूहलं हि मे ॥

विश्वामित्र उवाच ।

यतः प्रवृत्तिर्भूतानां यस्मिन्सर्व्वं यतो जगत् ।
स विष्णुः सर्व्वभूतात्मा तमाश्रित्य विमुच्यते ॥
यमक्षरात्परतरात्परं प्राहुर्गुहाश्रयम्‡ ।
आनन्दं परमं व्योम स वै नारायणः स्मृतः§ ॥
नित्योदितो निर्विकल्पो नित्यानन्दो निरञ्जनः ।
चतुर्व्यूहधरो विष्णुरव्यूहः प्रोच्यते स्वयम् ॥
परमात्मा परन्धाम परं व्योम परं पदम् ।

---

* संख्ये इति B. मयास्त्रेण इति D.

† प्रकारेण इति B.

‡ गुहाश्रया इति B. गुहाश्रयमिति D. गुहा मनीषिणां परिशुद्धा बुद्धिरिति शङ्करभाष्ये ।

§ स वै नारायण इत्यारभ्य परमात्मा परन्धाम इत्यन्तं B पुस्तके नास्ति ।

त्रिपादमक्षरं ब्रह्म तमाहुर्ब्रह्मवादिनः ॥
स वासुदेवो विश्वात्मा योगात्मा पुरुषोत्तमः ।
यस्यांशसम्भवो ब्रह्मा रुद्रोऽपि परमेश्वरः ॥
स्ववर्णाश्रमधर्म्मेण* पुंसायं पुरुषोत्तमः ।
अकामाद्व्रतभावेन† समाराध्यो न चान्यथा ॥
एतावदुक्त्वा भगवान्विश्वामित्रो महातपाः ।
शूराद्यैः पूजितो विप्रो जगामाथ स्वमाश्रमम् ॥
अथ शूरादयो देवमयजन्त महेश्वरम् ।
यज्ञेन यज्ञगम्यन्तं निष्कामा रुद्रमव्ययम् ॥
तान्वसिष्ठस्तु भगवान्याजयामास धर्म्मवित् ।
गौतमोऽगस्तिरत्रिश्च सर्व्वे रुद्रपराक्रमाः‡ ॥
विश्वामित्रस्तु भगवाञ्जयध्वजमरिन्दमम् ।
याजयामास भूतादिमादिदेवं जनार्द्दनम् ॥§
तस्य यज्ञे महायोगी साक्षाद्देवः स्वयं हरिः ।
आविरासीत्स भगवांस्तदद्भुतमिवाभवत् ॥

---

* सवर्णाश्रमधर्म्मेण इति D.

† रुद्रस्यायं परा मूर्त्तिरिति B. अकामहतभावेन इति D. अकामाहतभावेन इति E and H.

‡ रुद्रपरायणा इति B and D.

§ अतः परं B पुस्तके श्लोकोऽधिको दृश्यते—

जयध्वजोऽपि तं विष्णुं रुद्रस्य परमां तनुम् ।
इत्येवं सर्व्वदा बुद्ध्वा यज्ञेनायजदच्युतम् ॥

य इमं शृणुयान्नित्यं जयध्वजपराक्रमम् ।
सर्व्वपापविनिर्मुक्तो विष्णुलोकं स गच्छति ॥

इति श्रीकूर्म्मपुराणे सोमवंशानुकीर्तने द्वाविंशोऽध्यायः ।

—:—

त्रयोविंशोऽध्यायः ।

सूत उवाच ।

जयध्वजस्य पुत्रोऽभूत्तालजङ्घ इति स्मृतः ।
शतं पुत्रास्तु तस्यासन्तालजङ्घा इति स्मृताः* ॥
तेषां ज्येष्ठो महावीर्यो वीतिहोत्रोऽभवन्नृपः ।
वृषप्रभृतयश्चान्ये यादवाः पुण्यकर्म्मिणः ॥
वृषो† वंशकरस्तेषां तस्य पुत्रोऽभवन्मधुः ।
मधोः पुत्रशतं त्वासीद्वृषण‡स्तस्य वंशभाक् ॥
वीतिहोत्रसुतश्चापि§ विश्रुतोऽनन्त इत्यतः¶ ।
दुर्ज्जयस्तस्य पुत्रोऽभूत्सर्व्वशास्त्रविशारदः ॥

---

* प्रकीर्त्तिता इति B and D.

† वृषा इति B. वृषाद्वंशकर इति D.

‡ कर्षण इति D. वृषश इति H.

§ सुतश्चासीदिति B.

¶ ऽवनिरचक इति D. इत्युत इति E and H.

तस्य भार्य्या रूपवती गुणैः सर्व्वैरलङ्कृता ।
पतिव्रतासीत्यतिना स्वधर्म्मपरिपालिका ॥
स कदाचिन्महाराजः* कालिन्दीतीरसंस्थिताम् ।
अपश्यदुर्व्वशीं देवीं गायन्तीं मधुरश्रुतिम्† ॥
ततः कामाहतमनास्तत्समीपमुपेत्य वै ।
प्रोवाच सुचिरङ्कालं देवि रन्तुं मयार्हसि ॥
सा देवी नृपतिं दृष्ट्वा रूपलावण्यसंयुतम् ।
रेमे तेन चिरङ्कालं कामदेवमिवापरम् ॥
कालात्प्रबुद्धो राजा तामुर्व्वशीं‡ प्राह शोभनाम् ।
गमिष्यामि पुरीं रम्यां हसन्तीत्यब्रवीद्वचः ॥
न ह्येतेनोपभोगेन§ भवती राजसुन्दर ।
प्रीतिः सञ्जायते मह्यं स्थातव्यं वत्सरं पुनः ॥
तामब्रवीत्स मतिमान् गत्वा शीघ्रतरं पुरीम् ।
आगमिष्यामि भूयोऽत्र तन्मेऽनुज्ञातुमर्हसि ॥
तमब्रवीत्सा सुभगा तथा कुरु विशाम्पते ।
नान्ययाप्सरसा तावद्रन्तव्यम्भवता पुनः ॥
ओमित्युक्त्वा ययौ तूर्णं पुरीं परमशोभनाम् ।
गत्वा पतिव्रतां पत्नीं दृष्ट्वा भीतोऽभवन्नृपः ॥

---

* कदाचिन्महाभागः इति B.

† मधुरस्वरामिति B.

‡ राजासावुर्व्वशीमिति B.

§ न ह्यनेनोपभोगेनेति B.

संप्रेक्ष्य सा गुणवती भार्य्या तस्य पतिव्रता ।
भीतं प्रसन्नया प्राह* वाचा पीनपयोधरा ॥
स्वामिन् किमत्रभवतो भीतिरद्य प्रवर्त्तते ।
तद्ब्रूहि मे यथातत्त्वं† न राज्ञां‡ कीर्त्तये त्विदम् ॥
स तस्या वाक्यमाकर्ण्य लज्जावनतमानसः ।
नोवाच किञ्चिन्नृपतिर्ज्ञानदृष्ट्या विवेद सा ॥
न भेतव्यं त्वया राजन् कार्य्यं पापविशोधनम् ।
भीते त्वयि महाराज राष्ट्रन्ते नाशमेष्यति ॥
ततः§ स राजा द्युतिमान्निर्गत्य तु पुरात्ततः ।
गत्वा कण्वाश्रमं पुण्यं दृष्ट्वा तत्र महामुनिम् ।
निशम्य¶ कण्ववदनात्प्रायश्चित्तविधिं शुभम् ।
जगाम हिमवत्पृष्ठं समुद्दिष्टं‖ महाबलः ॥
सोऽपश्यत्पथि** राजेन्द्रो गन्धर्व्ववरमुत्तमम् ।
भ्राजमानं श्रिया व्योम्नि भूषितं दिव्यमालया ॥
वीक्ष्य†† मालामभिघ्नः सस्माराप्सरसं वराम् ।

---

* भीतं प्राह प्रसन्नेवेति A, E and H.

† तद्ब्रवीहि यथातत्त्वमिति A.

‡ रागादिति B.

§ तदेति B.

¶ निर्दिश्य इति A, E and H.

‖ हिमवत्पार्श्वं समुद्दिश्य इति B and D.

** सोऽपश्यदथ इति E, G and H.

†† वीक्ष्यमाणो ह्यभिघ्न इति E and H.

उर्व्वशीन्तां मनश्चक्रे तस्या एवेयमर्हति ॥
सोऽतीव कामुको राजा गन्धर्व्वेणाथ तेन हि ।
चकार सुमहद्युद्धं मालामादातुमुद्यतः ॥
विजित्य समरे मालां गृहीत्वा दुर्ज्जयो द्विजाः ।
जगाम तामप्सरसङ्कालिन्दीन्द्रष्टुमादरात् ॥
अदृष्ट्वाप्सरसं तत्र कामवाणाभिपीड़ितः ।
बभ्राम सकलां पृथ्वीं सप्तद्वीपसमन्विताम् ॥
आक्रम्य हिमवत्पार्श्वमुर्व्वशीदर्शनोत्सुकः ।
जगाम शैलप्रवरं हेमकूटमिति श्रुतम्* ॥
तत्र तत्राप्सरोवर्य्या दृष्ट्वा तं सिंहविक्रमम् ।
कामं सन्दधिरे घोरं भूषितं चित्रमालया ॥
संस्मरन्नुर्व्वशीवाक्यं तस्यां संसक्तमानसः ।
न पश्यति स्म ताः सर्व्वा गिरेः शृङ्गाणि जग्मिवान् ॥
तत्राप्यप्सरसन्दिव्यामदृष्ट्वा कामपीड़ितः ।
देवलोकं महामेरुं ययौ देवपराक्रमः ॥
स तत्र मानसं नाम सरस्त्रैलोक्यविश्रुतम् ।
भेजे शृङ्गमतिक्रम्य† स्वबाहुवलभावितः ॥
तस्य तीरेषु‡ सुभगाञ्चरन्तीमतिलालसाम् ।
दृष्टवाननवद्याङ्गीं तस्यै मालान्ददौ पुनः ॥

---

* स्मृतमिति A, D, E and H.

† शृङ्गाण्यतिक्रम्य इति B.

‡ स तस्य तीरे इति B.

स मालया तदा देवीं भूषितां प्रेक्ष्य मोहितः।
रेमे* कृतार्थमात्मानं जानानः सुचिरन्तया† ॥
अथोर्व्वशी राजवर्य्यं रतान्ते वाक्यमब्रवीत्।
किं कृतं भवता वीर पुरीङ्गत्वा तदा‡ नृप ॥
स तस्यै सर्व्वमाचष्ट पत्न्या यत्समुदीरितम्।
कण्वस्य दर्शनञ्चैव मालापहरणं तथा ॥
श्रुत्वैतद्वराहतन्तेन गच्छेत्याह हितैषिणी।
शापन्दास्यति§ ते कण्वो ममापि भवतः प्रिया ॥
तयासकृन्महाराजः प्रोक्तोऽपि मदमोहितः।
न च तत्कृतवान्वाक्यं¶ तत्र संन्यस्तमानसः ॥
तदोर्व्वशी कामरूपा राज्ञे स्वं रूपमुत्कटम्।
सुरोमशम्पिङ्गलाक्षं दर्शयामास सर्व्वदा ॥
तस्यां विरक्तचेतस्कः स्मृत्वा कण्वाभिभाषितम्।
धिङ्मामिति विनिश्चित्य तपः कर्त्तुं‖ समारभत् ॥
संवत्सरद्वादशकं कन्दमूलफलाशनः।
भूय एव द्वादशकं वायुभक्षोऽभवन्नृपः ॥

---

* मेने इति B.

† नभः सुरुचिरं यथा इति D.

‡ व्रथा इति B.

§ शापन्ददातीति A, D, E and H.

¶ न तत्याजाथ तत्पार्श्वमिति B and D.

‖ विनिश्चित्य तपः कर्त्तुं ततः कर्त्तुमिति A. समारभत इति साधु।

गत्वा कण्वाश्रमं भीत्या* तस्मै सर्व्वं न्यवेदयत् ।
वासमप्सरसा भूयस्तपोयोगमनुत्तमम् ॥
वीक्ष्य तं राजशार्दूलं प्रसन्नो भगवानृषिः ।
कर्त्तुकामो हि निर्व्वीजं तस्याघमिदमब्रवीत् ॥

कण्व उवाच ।

गच्छ वाराणसीं दिव्यामीश्वराध्युषितां पुरीम् ।
आस्ते मोचयितुं लोकं तत्र देवो महेश्वरः ॥
स्नात्वा सन्तर्प्य विधिवद्गङ्गायां देवताः पितॄन् ।
दृष्ट्वा विश्वेश्वरं लिङ्गं किल्विषान्मोक्ष्यसे क्षणात् ॥
प्रणम्य शिरसा कण्वमनुज्ञाप्य च दुर्ज्जयः ।
वाराणस्यां हरं† दृष्ट्वा पापान्मुक्तोऽभवत्ततः ॥
जगाम स्वपुरीं शुभ्रां‡ पालयामास मेदिनीम्§ ।
याजयामास तं कण्वो याचितो घृणया मुनिः ॥
तस्य पुत्रोऽथ मतिमान् सुप्रतीक इति स्मृतः¶ ।
बभूव जातमात्रं तं राजानमुपतस्थिरे ॥
उर्व्वश्याञ्च महावीर्याः सप्त देवसुतोपमाः ।
कन्या जगृहिरे सर्व्वा गन्धर्व्वी दयिता द्विजाः ॥

---

* प्रीत्येति B.

† शिवमिति B.

‡ रम्यामिति B.

§ धर्म्मत इति B.

¶ सुप्रीत इति विश्रुत इति B.

एष वः कथितः सम्यक्सहस्रजितउत्तमः।
वंशः पापहरो नृणां क्रोष्टोरपि निबोधत॥

इति श्रीकूर्म्मपुराणे राजवंशानुकीर्त्तने त्रयोविंशोऽध्यायः।

चतुर्विंशोऽध्यायः।

सूत उवाच।*

क्रोष्टोरेकोऽभवत्पुत्रो वज्रवानिति विश्रुतः।
तस्य पुत्रोऽभवच्छान्तिः कुशिक†स्तत्सुतोऽभवत्॥
कुशिकादभवत्पुत्रो नाम्ना चित्ररथो बली।
अथ चैत्ररथिर्लोके शशविन्दुरिति‡ स्मृतः॥
तस्य पुत्रः पृथुयशा राजाभूद्धर्म्मतत्परः।
पृथुकर्म्मा§ च तत्पुत्रः तस्मात्पृथुजयोऽभवत्॥
पृथुकीर्त्तिरभूत्तस्मात्पृथुदानस्ततोऽभवत्।
पृथुश्रवास्तस्य पुत्रस्तस्यासीत्पृथुसत्तमः॥
उशनास्तस्य पुत्रोऽभूच्छ्रतेषुस्तत्सुतोऽभवत्।

---

* एतत् A पुस्तके नास्ति।

† कुशङ्कुरिति D.

‡ शशिविन्दुरिति E, G and H.

§ पृथुवर्म्मा इति H.

तस्माद्वै* रुक्मकवचः परावृत्तश्च तत्सुतः ॥
परावृत्तसुतो जज्ञे यामघो लोकविश्रुतः ।
तस्माद्विदर्भः सञ्जज्ञे विदर्भात्क्रथकौशिकौ ।
लोमपाद†स्तृतीयस्तु बभ्रुस्तस्यात्मजो नृपः‡ ॥
धृतिस्तस्याभवत्पुत्रः श्वेत§स्तस्याप्यभूत्सुतः ।
श्वेतस्य¶ पुत्रो बलवान्नाम्ना विश्वसहः स्मृतः‖ ॥
तस्य पुत्रो महावीर्य्यः प्रभावात्कौशिकः स्मृतः** ।
अभूत्तस्य सुतो धीमान् सुमन्तश्च ततोऽनलः†† ॥
अनलस्य‡‡ सुतः श्वेनिः श्वेनेरन्येऽभवन्सुताः ।
तेषां प्रधानो द्युतिमान्वपुष्मान्तत्सुतोऽभवत् ॥
वपुष्मतो वृहन्मेधाः श्रीदेवस्तत्सुतोऽभवत् ।
तस्य वीतरथो विप्रा रुद्रभक्तो महाबलः ॥
क्रथस्याप्यभवत्कुन्ति§§र्वृष्णिस्तस्याभवत्सुतः ।

---

* तस्याभूदिति B.

† रोमपाद इति D.

‡ रोमपादसुतो यस्तु बभ्रुस्तस्यात्मजोऽभवदिति B.

§ सन्त इति B. शत इति D.

¶ सन्तस्य इति B.

‖ शुभ इति B.

** प्रजावान् कौशिकस्तत इति B.

†† सुमन्तुस्तत्सुतोऽनल इति B. ततोऽमल इति E, G and H.

‡‡ अमलस्य इति E, G and H.

§§ कुम्भी इति E and H.

तस्मान्नवरथो नाम बभूव सुमहाबलः ॥
कदाचिन्मृगयां यातो दृष्ट्वा राक्षसमूर्ज्जितम्।
दुद्राव महताविष्टो भयेन मुनिपुङ्गवाः ॥
अन्वधावत संक्रुद्धो राक्षसस्तं महाबलः।
दुर्य्योधनोऽग्निसंकाशः शूलासक्तमहाकरः ॥
राजा नवरथो भीतो नातिदूरादवस्थितम्।
अपश्यत्परमं स्थानं सरस्वत्याः सुगोपितम् ॥
स तद्वेगेन महता सम्प्राप्य मतिमान्नृपः।
ववन्दे शिरसा दृष्ट्वा साक्षाद्देवीं सरस्वतीम् ॥
तुष्टाव वाग्भिरिष्टाभिर्बद्धाञ्जलिरमित्रजित्।
पपात दण्डवद्भूमौ त्वामहं शरणङ्गतः ॥
नमस्यामि महादेवीं साक्षाद्देवीं सरस्वतीम्।
वाग्देवतामनाद्यन्तामीश्वरीं ब्रह्मचारिणीम् ॥
नमस्ये जगतां योनिं योगिनीं परमां कलाम्।
हिरण्यगर्भसम्भूतां* त्रिनेत्रां चन्द्रशेखराम् ॥
नमस्ये परमानन्दाञ्चित्कलां ब्रह्मरूपिणीम्।
पाहि मां परमेशानि भीतं शरणमागतम् ॥
एतस्मिन्नन्तरे क्रुद्धो राजानं राक्षसेश्वरः।
हन्तुं समागतः स्थानं यत्र देवी सरस्वती ॥

---

* हिरण्यगर्भमहिषीमिति B and D.

समुद्यम्य तथा* शूलं प्रविष्टो बलगर्व्वितः† ।
त्रिलोकमातुर्हि स्थानं शशाङ्कादित्यसन्निभम् ॥
तदन्तरे महद्भूतं युगान्तादित्यसन्निभम् ।
शूलेनोरसि निर्भिद्य पातयामास तम्भुवि ॥
गच्छेत्याह महाराज न स्थातव्यं त्वया पुनः ।
इदानीं निर्भयस्तूर्णं स्थानेऽस्मिन्राक्षसो हतः ॥
ततः प्रणम्य हृष्टात्मा राजा नवरथः परम् ।
पुरीं जगाम विप्रेन्द्राः पुरन्दरपुरोपमाम् ॥
स्थापयामास देवेशीन्तत्र भक्तिसमन्वितः ।
ईजे च विविधैर्यज्ञैर्होमैर्देवीं सरस्वतीम् ॥
तस्य चासीद्दशरथः पुत्रः परमधार्म्मिकः ।
देव्या भक्तो महातेजाः शकुनिस्तस्य चात्मजः ॥
तस्मात्करम्भः सम्भूतो देवरातोऽभवत्ततः ।
ईजे स चाश्वमेधेन देवक्षत्रश्च‡ तत्सुतः ॥
मधुस्तस्य तु दायादस्तस्मात्कुरुरजायत§ ।
पुत्रद्वयमभूत्तस्य सुत्रामा चानुरेव च ॥
अनोस्तु प्रियगोत्रोऽभूत्¶ अंशुस्तस्य च रिक्थभाक् ।

---

* तदा इति B. महाशूलमिति D.

† बलदर्पित इति B.

‡ देवक्षेत्रश्च इति B.

§ तस्मात्कुरुवशोऽभवदिति B.

¶ कुरुकुत्सोऽभूदिति B and D.

अथांशोरन्धको* नाम विष्णुभक्तः प्रतापवान् ।
महात्मा दाननिरतो धनुर्व्वेदविदां वरः ॥
स नारदस्य वचनाद्वासुदेवार्च्चने रतः ।
शास्त्रं प्रवर्त्तयामास कुण्डगोलादिभिः श्रुतम् ॥
तस्य नाम्ना तु विख्यातं सात्वतानाञ्च शोभनम् ।
प्रवर्त्तते महच्छास्त्रं कुण्डादीनां हितावहम् ॥
सात्वतस्तस्य पुत्रोऽभूत्सर्व्वशास्त्रविशारदः ।
पुण्यश्लोको महाराजस्तेन वै तत्प्रवर्त्तितम् ॥
सात्वतान्सत्वसम्पन्नान्कौशल्या सुषुवे सुतान् ॥†
अन्धकं वै महाभोजं वृष्णिन्देवावृधं नृपम् ।
ज्येष्ठञ्च भजमानाख्यं धनुर्वेदविदां वरम् ॥
तेषां देवावृधो राजा चचार परमन्तपः ।
पुत्रः सर्व्वगुणोपेतो मम भूयादिति प्रभुः ॥
तस्य बभ्रुरिति ख्यातः पुण्यश्लोकोऽभवन्नृपः ।
धार्म्मिको रूपसम्पन्नस्तत्त्वज्ञानरतः सदा ॥
भजमानाः श्रियन्दिव्यां‡ भजमानाद्विजज्ञिरे ।
तेषां प्रधानौ विख्यातौ निमिः क्रकण एव च§ ॥
महाभोजकुले जाता भोजा वैमातृकास्तथा ।

---

* अथांशोः सात्वत इति B. सत्वतो नाम इति D. साधक इति E.

† सात्वतात्सत्वसम्पन्नं कौशल्या सुषुवे सुतमिति G.

‡ भजमानस्य सृञ्जय्यामिति B. भजमानस्य संज्ञायामिति D.

§ शनिः क्रकश एव च इति G. क्रतक इति D.

वृष्णेः* सुमित्रो बलवाननमित्रस्तिमिस्तथा ॥
अनमित्रादभून्निघ्नो निघ्नस्य द्वौ बभूवतुः ।
प्रसेनस्तु महाभागः सत्राजिन्नाम चोत्तमः ॥
अनमित्राच्छिनि†र्ज्जज्ञे कनिष्ठो वृष्णिनन्दनात् ।
सत्यवाक् सत्यसम्पन्नः सत्यकस्तत्सुतोऽभवत् ॥
सात्यकिर्युयुधानस्तु तस्यासङ्गोऽभवत्सुतः‡ ।
कुणिस्तस्य§ सुतो धीमांस्तस्य पुत्रो युगन्धरः ॥
माद्र्यां वृष्णेः सुतो जज्ञे वृष्णेर्वै यदुनन्दनः ।
जज्ञाते तनयौ वृष्णेः श्वफल्कश्चित्रकस्तु हि ॥
श्वफल्कः काशिराजस्य सुतां भार्य्यामविन्दत ।
तस्यामजनयत्पुत्रमक्रूरं नाम धार्म्मिकम् ॥
उपमङ्गुं तथा मङ्गुम्¶ अन्ये च बहवः सुताः ।
अक्रूरस्य स्मृतः पुत्रो‖ देववानिति विश्रुतः ॥
उपदेवश्च देवात्मा** तयोर्विश्वप्रमाथिनौ ।
चित्रकस्याभवत्पुत्रः पृथुर्विपृथुरेव च ॥

---

* वृष्णेस्तु पुत्र इति D. विष्णोस्तु मित्र इति E. विष्णोस्तु पुत्र इति H.

† च्छिनिरिति D. च्छनिरिति E and H.

‡ तस्याश्टाङ्ग इति E and H.

§ कालस्तस्येति B. कुलिस्तस्य इति D.

¶ उपमङ्गुस्तथा मङ्गुरिति B.

‖ सुतोजज्ञे इति B.

** पुण्यात्मा इति B.

अश्वग्रीवः सुबाहुश्च सुधाश्वकगवेचकौ* ।
अन्धकस्य सुतायान्तु† लेभे च चतुरः सुतान् ॥
कुकुरं भजमानञ्च शमीकं बलगर्व्वितम् ।
कुकुरस्य सुतो वृष्णिर्वृष्णेस्तु‡ तनयोऽभवत् ॥
कपोतरोमा विख्यातस्तस्य पुत्रो विलोमकः§ ।
तस्यासीत्तुम्बुरुसखा विद्वान्पुत्रस्तमः¶ किल ।
तमस्याप्यभवत्पुत्रस्तथैवानकदुन्दुभिः ॥
स गोवर्द्धनमासाद्य तताप विपुलन्तपः ।
वरन्तस्मै ददौ देवो ब्रह्मा लोकमहेश्वरः ॥
वंशस्ते चाक्षया कीर्त्तिर्ज्ञानयोगस्तथोत्तमः ।
गुरोरप्यधिकं विप्राः कामरूपित्वमेव च ॥
स लब्ध्वा वरमव्यग्रो वरेण्याद्वृषवाहनम् ।
पूजयामास गानेन स्थाणुं त्रिदशपूजितम् ॥
तस्य गानरतस्याथ|| भगवानम्बिकापतिः ।
कन्यारत्नं ददौ देवो दुर्लभं त्रिदशैरपि ॥
तया स सङ्गतो राजा गानयोगमनुत्तमम् ।

---

* सुपार्श्वकगवेषणौ इति B.

† अन्धकात्काश्यदुहिता इति B and D.

‡ धृष्णिर्धृष्णेस्तु इति E, G and H.

§ कपोतनामा विपुलस्तस्य पुत्रो विलोपकः इति B.

¶ पुत्रोनलः इति B and D.

|| तस्य गानेन वश्योऽथ इति B.

अश्विच्चयदमितघ्नः प्रियान्तां भ्रान्तलोचनाम् ॥
तस्यामुत्पादयामास सुभुजं नाम शोभनम् ।
रूपलावण्यसम्पन्नां ह्रीमतीमिति* कन्यकाम् ॥
ततस्तं जननी पुत्रं बाल्ये वयसि शोभनम् ।
शिक्षयामास विधिवज्ज्ञानविद्याञ्च कन्यकाम् ॥
कृतोपनयनो वेदानधीत्य विधिवद्गुरोः ।
उद्वाहात्मजां कन्यां गन्धर्व्वाणान्तु मानसीम् ॥
तस्यामुत्पादयामास पञ्च पुत्राननुत्तमान् ।
वीणावादनतत्त्वज्ञान् गानशास्त्रविशारदान् ॥
पुत्रैः पौत्रैः सपत्नीको राजा गानविशारदः ।
पूजयामास गानेन देवं त्रिपुरनाशनम् ॥
ह्रीमतीञ्चारुसर्व्वाङ्गीं श्रीमिवायतलोचनाम्† ।
सुबाहुनामा गन्धर्व्वस्तामादाय ययौ पुरीम् ॥
तस्यामप्यभवन् पुत्रा गन्धर्व्वस्य सुतेजसः ।
सुषेणधीरसुग्रीवसुभोजनरवाहनाः ॥
अथासीदभिजित्पुत्रश्चन्दनोदकदुन्दुभिः‡ ।
पुनर्वसुश्चाभिजितः सम्बभूवाहुकस्ततः§ ॥
आहुकस्योग्रसेनश्च देवकश्च द्विजोत्तमाः ।

---

* ह्रीमतीमपीति B.

† ह्रीमती चापि या कन्या श्रीरिवायतलोचना इति B and D.

‡ वीरस्थानकदुन्दुभिरिति B.

§ सम्बभूवाहुकः सुत इति B.

देवकस्य सुता वीरा जज्ञिरे त्रिदशोपमाः।
देववानुपदेवश्च सुदेवो देवरक्षितः॥
तेषां स्वसारः सप्तासन्वसुदेवाय ता ददौ।
धृतदेवोपदेवा* च तथान्या देवरक्षिता।
श्रीदेवा शान्तिदेवा च सहदेवा च सुव्रता।
देवकी चापि तासान्तु वरिष्ठाभूत्सुमध्यमा॥
उग्रसेनस्य पुत्रोऽभून्न्यग्रोधः कंस एव च।
सुभूमी† राष्ट्रपालश्च तुष्टिमाञ्छङ्कुरेव‡ च॥
भजमानादभूत्पुत्रः प्रख्यातोऽसौ विदूरथः।
तस्य सूरसमस्तस्मात्प्रतिक्षत्रश्च तत्सुतः§॥
स्वयं भोजस्ततस्तस्माद्धार्दीकः शत्रुतापनः।
कृतवर्म्माथ तत्पुत्रः शूरसेनः सुतोऽभवत्¶॥
वसुदेवोऽथ तत्पुत्रो नित्यं धर्म्मपरायणः॥||
वसुदेवान्महाबाहुर्वासुदेवो जगद्गुरुः।
बभूव देवकीपुत्रो देवैरभ्यर्थितो हरिः॥
रोहिणी च महाभागा वसुदेवस्य शोभना।

---

* वृकदेव्युपदेवीति B. वृकदेवोपदेशीति G.

† सुसीमा इति B.

‡ चक्षुरेव इति B.

§ प्रतिक्षत्रस्ततोऽभवदिति B.

¶ देवलस्तत्सुतः स्मृत इति B.

|| स शूरस्तत्सुतो धीमान्वसुदेवोऽथ तत्सुत इति B.

असूत पत्नी सङ्कर्षं रामं ज्येष्ठं हलायुधम् ॥
स एव परमात्मासौ वासुदेवो जगन्मयः ।
हलायुधः स्वयं साक्षाच्छेषः सङ्कर्षणः प्रभुः ॥
भृगुशापच्छलेनैव मानयन्मानुषीं तनुम् ।*
बभूव तस्यां देवक्यां रोहिण्यामपि माधवः ॥
उमादेहसमुद्भूता† योगनिद्रा च कौशिकी ।
नियोगाद्वासुदेवस्य यशोदातनया त्वभूत् ॥
ये चान्ये वसुदेवस्य वासुदेवाग्रजाः सुताः ।
प्रागेव कंसस्तान्सर्व्वाञ्जघान मुनिसत्तमाः‡ ॥
सुषेणश्च ततो दायी भद्रसेनो§ महाबलः ।
वज्रदम्भो भद्रसेनः¶ कीर्त्तिमानपि पूजितः‖ ॥
हतेष्वेतेषु सर्व्वेषु रोहिणी वसुदेवतः ।
असूत रामं लोकेशं बलभद्रं हलायुधम् ॥
जातेऽथ रामे देवानामादिमात्मानमच्युतम् ।
असूत देवकी कृष्णं श्रीवत्साङ्कितवक्षसम्** ॥

---

* एतच्चरणद्वयं B पुस्तके न दृश्यते ।

† उमा देवी समुद्भूता इति B.

‡ मुनिपुङ्गवा इति B.

§ तथोदापिर्भद्रसेन इति B.

¶ ऋजुदासो भद्रदासः इति B.

‖ पूर्व्वज इति B.

** श्रीवत्सकृतलक्षणमिति B.

रेवती नाम रामस्य भार्य्यासीत्सुगुणान्विता।
तस्यामुत्पादयामास पुत्रौ द्वौ निशितोल्मुकौ* ॥
षोड़शस्त्रीसहस्राणि कृष्णस्याक्लिष्टकर्म्मणः।
बभूवुश्चात्मजास्तासु शतशोऽथ सहस्रशः ॥
चारुदेष्णः सुचारुश्च चारुवेषो यशोधरः।
चारुश्रवाश्चारुयशाः प्रद्युम्नः साम्बएव च ॥
रुक्मिण्यां वासुदेवस्य महाबलपराक्रमाः।
विशिष्टाः सर्व्वपुत्राणां सम्बभूवुरिमे सुताः ॥
तान्दृष्ट्वा तनयान्वीरान्रौक्मिणेयाञ्जनार्द्दनात्।
जाम्बवत्यब्रवीत्कृष्णं भार्य्या तस्य शुचिस्मिता ॥
मम त्वं पुण्डरीकाक्ष विशिष्टगुणवत्तरम्†।
सुरेशसम्मितं‡ पुत्रं देहि दानवसूदन ॥
जाम्बवत्या वचः श्रुत्वा जगन्नाथः स्वयं हरिः।
समारेभे तपः कर्त्तुं तपोनिधिररिन्दमः ॥
तच्छृणुध्वं मुनिश्रेष्ठा यथासौ देवकीसुतः।
दृष्ट्वा लेभे सुतं रुद्रं तप्त्वा तीव्रम्महत्तपः ॥

इति श्रीकूर्म्मपुराणे यदुवंशानुकीर्त्तने चतुर्विंशोऽध्यायः।

---

* निशथोल्मुकौ इति D. निषधोल्मुकौ इति E.

† विशिष्टं गुणवत्तरमिति B.

‡ सुरेशसदृशमिति B.

पञ्चविंशोऽध्यायः ।

सूत उवाच ।

अथ देवो हृषीकेशो भगवान्पुरुषोत्तमः ।
तताप घोरं पुत्रार्थं निधानं तपसस्तपः* ॥
स्वेच्छयाप्यवतीर्णोऽसौ कृतकृत्योऽपि विश्वसृक्† ।
चचार स्वात्मनो मूलं बोधयन्परमेश्वरम्‡ ॥
जगाम योगिभिर्जुष्टं नानापक्षिसमाकुलम् ।
आश्रमन्तूपमन्योर्वै मुनीन्द्रस्य महात्मनः ।
पतत्रिराजमारूढः सुपर्णमतितेजसम् ।
शङ्खचक्रगदापाणिः श्रीवत्साङ्कितलक्षणः ।
नानाद्रुमलताकीर्णं नानापुष्पोपशोभितम्§ ॥
ऋषीणामाश्रमैर्जुष्टं वेदघोषनिनादितम् ।
सिंहर्क्षशरभाकीर्णं शार्दूलगजसंयुतम् ।¶
विमलस्वादुपानीयैः सरोभिरुपशोभितम् ।
आरामैर्विविधैर्जुष्टं देवतायतनैः शुभैः ।
ऋषिभिर्ऋषिपुत्रैश्च महामुनिगणैस्तथा ।

---

* तपसान्तप इति B.

† विश्वधृगिति B.

‡ भावमैश्वरमिति B.

§ शार्दूलगजसङ्कुलमिति B.

¶ एष श्लोकः B पुस्तके नास्ति ।

वेदाध्ययनसम्पन्नैः सेवितञ्चाग्निहोत्रिभिः ।
योगिभिर्ध्याननिरतैर्नासाग्रन्यस्तलोचनैः ।
उपेतं सर्व्वतः पुण्यं ज्ञानिभिस्तत्त्वदर्शिभिः ।
नदीभिरभितोजुष्टं जापकैर्ब्रह्मवादिभिः ।
सेवितं तापसैः पुण्यैरीशाराधनतत्परैः ।
प्रशान्तैः सत्यसङ्कल्पैर्निःशोकैर्निरुपद्रवैः* ।
भस्मावदातसर्व्वाङ्गैः रुद्रजाप्यपरायणैः ।
मुण्डितैर्जटिलैः शुद्धैस्तथान्यैश्च शिखाजटैः ।
सेवितं तापसैर्नित्यं ज्ञानिभि†र्ब्रह्मवादिभिः ॥
तत्राश्रमवरे‡ रम्ये सिद्धाश्रमविभूषिते ।
गङ्गा भगवती§ नित्यं वहत्येवाघनाशिनी ॥
स तत्र वीक्ष्य¶ विश्वात्मा तापसान्वीतकल्मषान् ।
प्रणामेनाथ वचसा पूजयामास माधवः ॥
तन्ते दृष्ट्वा जगद्योनिं शङ्खचक्रगदाधरम् ।
प्रणेमुर्भक्तिसंयुक्ता योगिनां परमं गुरुम् ॥
स्तुवन्ति वैदिकैर्म्मन्त्रैः कृत्वा हृदि सनातनम् ।
प्रोचुरन्योन्यमव्यक्तमादिदेवं महामुनिम् ॥

---

* निरुपप्लवैरिति E and H.

† न्यासिभिरिति B.

‡ तदाश्रमवरे इति B.

§ भागीरथीति B.

¶ स तानुद्दिश्य इति B.

अयं स भगवानेकः साक्षी नारायणः परः ।
आगच्छत्यधुना देवः प्रधानपुरुषः* स्वयम् ॥
अयमेवाव्ययः स्रष्टा संहर्त्ता चैव रक्षकः ।
अमूर्त्तोमूर्त्तिमान् भूत्वा मुनीन्द्रष्टुमिहागतः ॥
एष धाता विधाता च समागच्छति सर्व्वगः ।
अनादिरक्षयोऽनन्तो महाभूतो महेश्वरः ॥
श्रुत्वा बुद्ध्वा हरिस्तेषां वचांसि वचनातिगः ।
ययौ स तूर्णं गोविन्दः† स्थानं तस्य महात्मनः ॥
उपस्पृश्याथ भावेन तीर्थे तीर्थे स यादवः ।
चकार देवकीसूनुर्देवर्षिपितृतर्पणम् ॥
नदीनां तीरसंस्थानि स्थापितानि मुनीश्वरैः ।
लिङ्गानि पूजयामास शम्भोरमिततेजसः ॥
दृष्ट्वा दृष्ट्वा समायान्तं यत्र यत्र‡ जनार्द्दनम् ।
पूजयाञ्चक्रिरे पुष्पैरक्षतैस्तन्निवासिनः ॥
समीक्ष्य वासुदेवन्तं शार्ङ्गशङ्खासिधारिणम् ।
तस्थिरे निश्चलाः सर्व्वे शुभाङ्गा§ यतमानसाः¶ ॥
यानि तत्रारुरुक्षूणां मानसानि जनार्द्दनम् ।

---

* पुराणः पुरुष इति B, E and H.

† भगवानिति B.

‡ तत्र तत्र इति B.

§ शुभाङ्गावनताननाः इति E and H.

¶ शुभाङ्गं तन्निवासिन इति B and D.

दृष्ट्वा समाहितान्यासन्निष्क्रामन्ति पुरा हरिम् ॥
अथावगाह्य गङ्गायां कृत्वा देवर्षितर्पणम् ।
आदाय पुष्पवर्य्याणि मुनीन्द्रस्याविशद्गृहम् ॥
दृष्ट्वा तं योगिनां श्रेष्ठं भस्मोद्धूलितविग्रहम् ।
जटाचीरधरं शान्तं ननाम शिरसा मुनिम्* ॥
आलोक्य कृष्णमायान्तं पूजयामास तत्त्ववित् ।
आसने वासयामास† योगिनां‡ प्रथमातिथिम् ॥
उवाच वचसां योनिर्ज्ञानीमः परमम्पदम् ।
विष्णुमव्यक्तसंस्थानं शिष्यभावेन संस्थितम् ॥
स्वागतन्ते हृषीकेश सफलानि तपांसि नः ।
यत्साक्षादेव विश्वात्मा मद्गेहं विष्णुरागतः ॥
त्वां न पश्यन्ति§ मुनयो यतन्तो¶ऽपीह योगिनः ।
तादृशस्यात्रभवतः‖ किमागमनकारणम् ॥
श्रुत्वोपमन्योस्तद्वाक्यं भगवान्देवकीसुतः** ।
व्याजहार महायोगी प्रसन्नं†† प्रणिपत्य तम् ॥

---

* महीमिति B.

† चासयामास इति E and H.

‡ योगिनमिति E and H.

§ त्वां नमस्यन्तीति B.

¶ यतन्त इत्यार्षं, यतमाना इति साधु ।

‖ तादृशस्याय भवत इति B. तावदाख्याहि भवत इति D.

** केशिमर्द्दन इति B.

†† वचनमिति B.

कृष्ण उवाच ।

भगवन्द्रष्टुमिच्छामि गिरीशं कृत्तिवाससम् ।
सम्प्राप्तो भवतः स्थानं भगवद्दर्शनोत्सुकः ॥
कथं स भगवानीशो दृश्यो योगविदां वरः ।
मयाचिरेण कुत्राहं* द्रक्ष्यामि तमुमापतिम् ॥
प्रत्याह† भगवानुक्तो दृश्यते परमेश्वरः ।
भक्त्यैवोग्रेण तपसा तत्कुरुष्वेह संयतः‡ ॥
इहेश्वरं देवदेवं मुनीन्द्रा ब्रह्मवादिनः ।
ध्यायन्त्याराधयन्त्येनं योगिनस्तापसाश्च ये§ ॥
इह देवः सपत्नीको भगवान्वृषभध्वजः ।
क्रीड़ते विविधैर्भूतैर्योगिभिः परिवारितः ॥
इहाश्रमे पुरा रुद्रं तपस्तप्त्वा सुदारुणम् ।
लेभे महेश्वराद्योगं वसिष्ठो भगवानृषिः ॥
इहैव भगवान्व्यासः कृष्णद्वैपायनः स्वयम् ।
दृष्ट्वा तं परमेशानं¶ लब्धवान् ज्ञानमैश्वरम्‖ ॥

---

* पुत्रार्थमिति D.

† इत्याह इति B, E and H. वनेह भगवान् रुद्र इति D.

‡ यत्नत इति B.

§ ध्यायन्त आसते देवं योगिनस्तापसाश्च ये इति B.

¶ परमं ज्ञानमिति B, E and H.

‖ लब्धवानीश्वरेश्वरमिति B, E and H.

इहाश्रमपदे* रम्ये तपस्तप्त्वा कपर्द्दिनः† ।
अविन्दन्पुत्रकानुद्रात्सूरयो भक्तिसंयुताः ॥
इह देवा महादेवीं भवानीञ्च महेश्वरीम् ।
संस्तुवन्तो महादेवं‡ निर्भया निर्वृतिं ययुः ॥
इहाराध्य महादेवं सावर्णिस्तपतां वरः ।
लब्धवान्परमं योगं ग्रन्थकारत्वमुत्तमम् ॥
प्रवर्त्तयामास स तां§ कृत्वा वै संहितां शुभाम्¶ ।
द्विजः पौराणिकीं पुण्यां प्रसादेन‖ द्विजोत्तमैः ।**
इहैव ख्यापितं शिष्यैर्वैशम्पायनभाषितम् ॥
याज्ञवल्क्यो महायोगी दृष्ट्वात्र तपसा हरम् ।
चकार तन्नियोगेन योगशास्त्रमनुत्तमम् ॥

---

* इहाश्रमवरे इति B.

† कपर्द्दिनमिति B.

‡ इहैव देवताः पूर्व्वं कालाद्गीता महेश्वरम् । दृष्टवन्तो हरं देवमिति B. इहैव देवताः पूर्व्वं कालाग्निं वा महेश्वरमिति D.

§ शुभामिति B.

¶ द्विज इति B.

‖ पौराणिकीं सुपुण्यार्थं सच्छिष्येष्विति B and D.

** अतः परं B पुस्तकेऽधिकं दृश्यते—

इहैव संहितां दृष्ट्वा कामो यः शशिपायिनः ।
महादेवश्चकारेमां पौराणीं तन्नियोगतः ॥
द्वादशैव सहस्राणि श्लोकानां पुरुषोत्तम ।
इह प्रवर्त्तिता पुण्या द्वात्सहस्रिकोत्तरा ॥
वायवीयोत्तरं नाम पुराणं वेदसम्मतम् । इति

इहैव भृगुणा पूर्व्वं तप्तापूर्व्वं महातपः* ।
शुक्रो महेश्वरात्पुत्रो लब्धो योगविदां वरः ॥
तस्मादिहैव देवेश तपस्तप्ता सुदुश्चरम् ।†
द्रष्टुमर्हसि विश्वेशमुग्रम्भीमङ्कपर्द्दिनम् ॥
एवमुक्ता ददौ ज्ञानमुपमन्युर्महामुनिः ।
व्रतं पाशुपतं योगं कृष्णायाक्लिष्टकर्म्मणे ॥
स तेन मुनिवर्य्येण व्याहृतो मधुसूदनः ।
तत्रैव तपसा देवं रुद्रमाराधयत्प्रभुः ‡ ॥
भस्मोद्धूलितसर्व्वाङ्गो मुण्डो वल्कलसंयुतः ।
जजाप रुद्रमनिशं शिवैकाहितमानसः ॥
ततो बहुतिथे काले सोमः§ सोमार्द्धभूषणः ।
अदृश्यत महादेवो व्योम्नि देव्या महेश्वरः ॥
किरीटिनं गदिनञ्चित्रमालं
पिनाकिनं शूलिनन्देवदेवम् ।
शार्दूलचर्म्माम्बरसंवृताङ्गं
देव्या महादेवमसौ ददर्श¶ ॥

---

* तप्ता वै परमं तपः इति B. तप्तापूर्व्वमित्यारभ्य तस्मादिहैव देवेश इत्यन्तं G पुस्तके नास्ति ।

† शुक्र इत्यारभ्य सुदुश्चरमित्यन्तं श्लोकार्द्धद्वयं H पुस्तके नास्ति ।

‡ प्रभुमिति B.

§ सौम्यः इति E and H.

¶ एष श्लोकः B पुस्तके अनन्तरश्लोकात्परं दृश्यते ।

प्रभुम्पुराणं पुरुषं पुरस्ता-
त्सनातनं योगिनमीशितारम् ।
अणोरणीयांसमनन्तशक्तिं
प्राणेश्वरं शम्भुमसौ ददर्श ॥
परश्वधासक्तकरं त्रिनेत्रं
नृसिंहचर्मावृतभस्मगात्रम् ।
समुद्गिरन्तं प्रणवं बृहन्तं
सहस्रसूर्य्यप्रतिमन्ददर्श ॥
न यस्य देवा न पितामहोऽपि
नेन्द्रो न चाग्निर्वरुणो न मृत्युः ।
प्रभावमद्यापि वदन्ति* रुद्रं
तमादिदेवं पुरतो† ददर्श ॥
तदान्वपश्यद्गिरिशस्य वामे
स्वात्मानमव्यक्तमनन्तरूपम् ।
स्तुवन्तमीशं बहुभिर्वचोभिः
शङ्खासिचक्रान्वित‡हस्तमाद्यम् ॥
कृताञ्जलिं दक्षिणतः सुरेशं
हंसाधिरूढं पुरुषं ददर्श ।
स्तुवानमीशस्य परम्प्रभावं

---

* विदन्ति इति D.

† प्रयत इति B.

‡ चक्रार्पित इति E and H.

पितामहं लोकगुरुं दिविस्थम् ॥
गणेश्वरानर्क*सहस्रकल्पा-
न्नन्दीश्वरादीनमितप्रभावान् ।
त्रिलोकभर्त्तुः पुरतोऽन्वपश्य-
त्कुमारमग्निप्रतिमं गणेशम्† ॥
मरीचिमत्रिम्पुलहम्पुलस्त्य-
म्प्रचेतसन्दक्षमथापि कण्वम् ।
पराशरन्तत्पुरतोवसिष्ठं
स्वायम्भुवञ्चापि मनुन्ददर्श ॥
तुष्टाव मन्त्रैरमरप्रधानं
बद्धाञ्जलिर्विष्णुरुदारबुद्धिः ।
प्रणम्य देव्या गिरिशं स्वभक्त्या
स्वात्मन्यथात्मानमसौ विचिन्त्य ॥

कृष्ण उवाच ।

नमोऽस्तु ते शाश्वत सर्व्वयोग‡
ब्रह्मादयस्त्वामृषयो§ वदन्ति ।
तमश्च सत्त्वञ्च रजस्त्वयञ्च¶

---

* गणेश्वरानिक इति E and H.

† विशाखमिति B.

‡ विश्वयोने इति B. सर्व्वयोने इति D.

§ ब्रह्माधिपत्वामृषय इति B.

¶ तपश्च सत्त्वञ्च रजस्तमश्च इति B. त्वमेव सत्त्वं रजस्तमश्च इति D.

त्वामेव सर्व्वं प्रवदन्ति सन्तः ॥
त्वं ब्रह्मा हरिरथ विश्वकर्त्ता*
संहर्त्ता दिनकरमण्डलाधिवासः ।
प्राणस्त्वं हुतवहवासवादिभेदः
त्वामेकं शरणमुपैमि देवमीशम् ॥
साङ्ख्यास्त्वामगुणमथाहुरेकरूपं
योगस्थं सततमुपासते हृदिस्थम् ।
वेदास्त्वामभिदधतीह रुद्रमीड्यं†
त्वामेकं शरणमुपैमि देवमीशम् ॥
त्वत्पादे कुसुममथापि पत्रमेकं
दत्त्वासौ भवति विमुक्तविश्वबन्धः ।
सर्व्वाघं प्रणुदति सिद्धयोगिजुष्टं
स्मृत्वा ते पदयुगलं भवत्प्रसादात् ॥

यस्याशेषविभागहीनममलं हृद्यन्तरावस्थितं
तं त्वां योनि‡मनन्तमेकमचलं सत्यं परं सर्व्वगम् ।
स्थानं प्राहुरनादिमध्यनिधनं यस्मादिदं जायते
नित्यं त्वाहमुपैमि सत्यविभवं विश्वेश्वरन्तं शिवम् ॥
ओंनमो नीलकण्ठाय त्रिनेत्राय च रंहसे ।
महादेवाय ते नित्यमीशानाय नमो नमः ॥

---

* विश्वयोनिरिति B. त्वमेव सत्वं रजस्तमश्च इति D.

† रुद्रमग्निमिति B.

‡ तत्त्वं ज्योतिरिति B. यस्य ज्योतिरिति D.

नमः पिनाकिने तुभ्यं नमो मुण्डाय दण्डिने ।
नमस्ते वज्रहस्ताय दिग्वस्त्राय कपर्द्दिने ॥
नमो भैरवनादाय कालरूपाय दंष्ट्रिणे ।
नागयज्ञोपवीताय नमस्ते वह्निरेतसे* ॥
नमोऽस्तु ते गिरीशाय स्वाहाकाराय ते नमः ।
नमो मुक्ताट्टहासाय भीमाय च नमो नमः ॥
नमस्ते कामनाशाय नमः कालप्रमाथिने ।
नमो भैरववेषाय हराय च निषङ्गिणे ॥
नमोऽस्तु ते त्र्यम्बकाय नमस्ते कृत्तिवाससे ।
नमोऽम्बिकाधिपतये पशूनां† पतये नमः ॥
नमस्ते व्योमरूपाय व्योमाधिपतये नमः ।
नरनारीशरीराय साङ्ख्ययोगप्रवर्त्तिने ॥
नमो भैरवनाथाय देवानुगतलिङ्गिने ।
कुमारगुरवे तुभ्यं‡ देवदेवाय ते नमः ॥
नमो यज्ञाधिपतये नमस्ते ब्रह्मचारिणे ।
मृगव्याधाय महते ब्रह्माधिपतये नमः ॥
नमो हंसाय§ विश्वाय मोहनाय नमो नमः ।
योगिने योगगम्याय योगमायाय ते नमः ॥

---

* ब्रह्मरेतसे इति G and H. चार्करेतसे इति D.

† वसूनामिति A, E and H.

‡ नित्यमिति B.

§ मोहाय इति B.

नमस्ते प्राणपालाय घण्टानादप्रियाय च।
कपालिने नमस्तुभ्यं ज्योतिषां पतये नमः॥
नमो नमोऽस्तु ते तुभ्यं भूय एव नमो नमः।
मह्यं सर्व्वात्मना कामान् प्रयच्छ परमेश्वर॥

सूत उवाच।*

एवं हि भक्त्या देवेशमभिष्टूय† स माधवः।
पपात पादयोर्विप्रा देवदेवस्य दण्डवत्॥
उत्थाप्य भगवान् सोमः कृष्णं केशिनिषूदनम्।
बभाषे मधुरं वाक्यं मेघगम्भीरनिःस्वनः॥
किमर्थं पुण्डरीकाक्ष तप्यते भवता तपः‡।
त्वमेव दाता सर्व्वेषां कामानां कर्म्मणामिह§॥
त्वं हि सा परमा मूर्त्तिर्मम नारायणाह्वया।
न विना त्वां जगत्सर्व्वं¶ विद्यते पुरुषोत्तम॥
वेत्थ नारायणानन्तमात्मानं परमेश्वरम्‖।
महादेवं महायोगं स्वेन** योगेन केशव॥
श्रुत्वा तद्वचनं कृष्णः प्रहसन्वै वृषध्वजम्।

---

* एतत् B पुस्तके नास्ति।

† अभिसंस्तुत्य इति E and H.

‡ तपस्तप्तं त्वयाव्यय इति B.

§ कामिनामिह इति B.

¶ नानवाप्तं त्वया तात इति B.

‖ पुरुषोत्तममिति B.

** येन इति B.

उवाचान्वीक्ष्य विश्वेशन्देवीञ्च हिमशैलजाम् ॥
ज्ञातं हि भवता सर्व्वं स्वेन योगेन शङ्कर ।
इच्छाम्यात्मसमं पुत्रं त्वद्भक्तन्देहि शङ्कर ॥
तथास्त्वित्याह विश्वात्मा प्रहृष्टमनसा हरः ।
देवीमालोक्य गिरिजां केशवं परिषस्वजे ॥
ततः सा जगतां माता शङ्करार्द्धशरीरिणी ।
व्याजहार हृषीकेशं देवी हिमगिरीन्द्रजा ॥
अहं* जाने तवानन्त निश्चलां सर्व्वदाच्युत ।
अनन्यामीश्वरे भक्तिमात्मन्यपि च केशव ॥
त्वं हि नारायणः साक्षात्सर्व्वात्मा पुरुषोत्तमः ।
प्रार्थितो दैवतैः पूर्व्वं सञ्जातो देवकीसुतः ॥
पश्य त्वमात्मनात्मानमात्मानं मम सम्प्रति† ।
नावयोर्व्विद्यते भेद एकं पश्यन्ति सूरयः ॥
इमानिह वरानिष्टान्मत्तो गृह्णीष्व केशव ।
सर्व्वज्ञत्वं तथैश्वर्यं ज्ञानं तत्पारमेश्वरम् ।
ईश्वरे निश्चलां भक्तिमात्मन्यपि परं बलम् ॥
एवमुक्तस्तया कृष्णो महादेव्या जनार्द्दनः ।
आदेशं‡ शिरसा गृह्य देवोऽप्याह तथेश्वरम्§ ॥

---

* वत्स जाने तवानन्तामिति B.

† अमलं पदमिति B. परमं पदमिति E.

‡ आशिष इति B.

§ देवः प्राह महेश्वर इति B.

प्रगृह्य कृष्णं भगवानथेशः*
करेण देव्या सह देवदेवः ।
सम्पूज्यमानो मुनिभिः सुरेशै-
र्जगाम कैलासगिरिं गिरीशः ॥

इति श्रीकूर्म्मपुराणे यदुवंशानुकीर्त्तने कृष्णतपश्चरणे पञ्चविंशोऽध्यायः ।

—०—

षड्विंशोऽध्यायः ।

सूत उवाच ।

प्रविश्य मेरुशिखरं कैलासं कनकप्रभम् ।*
ररामं† भगवान्सोमः केशवेन महेश्वरः ॥
अपश्यंस्ते महात्मानं कैलासगिरिवासिनः ।
पूजयाञ्चक्रिरे कृष्णं देवदेवमिवाच्युतम् ॥
चतुर्बाहुमुदाराङ्गं कालमेघसमप्रभम् ।
किरीटिनं शार्ङ्गपाणिं श्रीवत्साङ्कितवक्षसम् ॥

---

* भगवानपीश इति B.

---

* इतः परं श्लोकद्वयं B पुस्तके न दृश्यते ।

† रराम इति परस्मैपदमार्षम् ।

दीर्घबाहुं विशालाक्षं पीतवाससमच्युतम् ।
दधानमुरसा मालां वैजयन्तीमनुत्तमाम् ।
भ्राजमानं श्रिया देव्या युवानमतिकोमलम् ।
पद्माङ्घ्रिं पद्मनयनं सस्मितं सद्गतिप्रदम् ॥
कदाचित्तत्र लीलार्थं देवकीनन्दवर्द्धनः ।
भ्राजमानः श्रिया कृष्णश्चचार गिरिकन्दरम्* ॥
गन्धर्वाप्सरसां मुख्या नागकन्याश्च कृत्स्नशः ।
सिद्धा यक्षाश्च गन्धर्व्वा देवास्तत्र जगन्मयम् ।
दृष्ट्वाश्चर्य्यम्परं गत्वा हर्षादुत्फुल्ललोचनाः ।
मुमुचुः पुष्पवर्षाणि तस्य मूर्ध्नि महात्मनः ॥
गन्धर्व्वकन्यका दिव्यास्तद्वदप्सरसो† वराः ।
दृष्ट्वा चकमिरे कृष्णं सुस्तुतं शुचिभूषणाः‡ ॥
काश्चिद्गायन्ति विविधं गानं§ गीतविशारदाः ।
सम्प्रेक्ष्य देवकीसूनुं सुन्दरं काममोहिताः ॥
काश्चिद्विलासबहुला नृत्यन्ति स्म तदग्रतः ।
सम्प्रेक्ष्य सस्मितं काश्चित्पपुस्तद्वदनामृतम् ॥
काश्चिद्भूषणवर्याणि स्वाङ्गादादाय सादरम् ।

---

* गिरिकन्दरे इति B.

† अप्सरसामिति B.

‡ सत्सवस्त्रविभूषणा इति B.

§ विविधा गीतीरिति B.

भूषयाञ्चक्रिरे कृष्णं कन्या लोकविभूषणम्* ॥
काश्चिद्भूषणवर्य्याणि समादाय तदङ्गतः।
स्वात्मानं भूषयामासुः स्वात्मकैरपि माधवम् ॥
काचिदागत्य कृष्णस्य समीपं काममोहिता।
चुचुम्ब वदनाम्भोजं हरेर्मुग्धमृगेक्षणा ॥
प्रगृह्य काचिद्गोविन्दं† करेण भवनं स्वकम्।
प्रापयामास लोकादिं मायया तस्य मोहिता ॥
तासां स भगवान् कृष्णः कामान् कमललोचनः।
बहूनि कृत्वा रूपाणि पूरयामास लीलया ॥
एवं वै‡ सुचिरं कालन्देवदेवपुरे हरिः।
रेमे नारायणः श्रीमान्मायया मोहयञ्जगत् ॥
गते बहुतिथे काले द्वारवत्याः§ निवासिनः।
बभूवुर्विकला भीता गोविन्दविरहे जनाः ॥
ततः सुपर्णो बलवान्पूर्व्वमेव विसर्ज्जितः।
स कृष्णं मार्गमाणस्तु हिमवन्तं ययौ गिरिम्¶ ॥
अदृष्ट्वा तत्र गोविन्दं प्रणम्य शिरसा मुनिम्।
आजगामोपमन्युं तं पुरीं द्वारवतीं पुनः ॥

---

* कामिन्यो लोकभूषणमिति B.

† चापि गोविन्दमिति B.

‡ तु इति B.

§ द्वारावत्यामिति B.

¶ नगमिति B.

तदन्तरे महादैत्या राक्षसाश्चातिभीषणाः ।
आजग्मुर्द्वारकां शुभ्रां भीषयन्तः सहस्रशः ॥
स तान्सुपर्णो बलवान्* कृष्णतुल्यपराक्रमः ।
हत्वा युद्धेन महता रक्षति स्म पुरीं शुभाम् ॥
एतस्मिन्नेव काले तु नारदोभगवानृषिः ।
दृष्ट्वा कैलासशिखरे कृष्णं द्वारवतीं गतः ॥
ते† दृष्ट्वा नारदमृषिं सर्व्वे तत्र निवासिनः ।
प्रोचुर्नारायणो नाथः कुत्रास्ते भगवान्हरिः ॥
स तानुवाच भगवान्कैलासशिखरे हरिः ।
रमतेऽद्य महायोगी तं दृष्ट्वाहमिहागतः ॥
तस्योपश्रुत्य वचनं सुपर्णः पततां वरः ।
जगामाकाशगो विप्राः कैलासं गिरिमुत्तमम् ॥
ददर्श देवकीसूनुं भवने रत्नमण्डिते ।
तत्रासनस्थं‡ गोविन्दं देवदेवान्तिके हरिम् ।
उपास्यमानममरैर्दिव्यस्त्रीभिः समन्ततः ।
महादेवगणैः सिद्धैर्योगिभिः परिवारितम् ॥
प्रणम्य दण्डवद्भूमौ सुपर्णः शङ्करं शिवम् ।
निवेदयामास हरिं प्रवृत्तं द्वारकापुरे ॥
ततः प्रणम्य शिरसा शङ्करं नीललोहितम् ।

---

* भगवानिति B.

† तमिति B.

‡ वरासनस्थमिति B.

आजगाम पुरीं कृष्णः सोऽनुज्ञातो हरेण तु ॥
आरुह्य कश्यपसुतं स्त्रीगणैरभिपूजितः ।
वचोभिरमृतास्वादैर्मानितो मधुसूदनः ॥
वीक्ष्य यान्तमभिन्नघ्नं गन्धर्व्वाप्सरसां वराः* ।
अन्वगच्छन्महायोगं शङ्खचक्रगदाधरम् ॥
विसर्ज्जयित्वा विश्वात्मा सर्व्वा एवाङ्गना हरिः ।
ययौ स तूर्णं गोविन्दो दिव्यां द्वारवतीं पुरीम् ॥
गते देवेऽसुररिपौ न कामिन्यो मुनीश्वराः ।†
निशेव चन्द्ररहिता विना तेन चकाशिरे ॥
श्रुत्वा पौरजनास्तूर्णं कृष्णागमनमुत्तमम् ।
मण्डयाञ्चक्रिरे दिव्यां पुरीं द्वारवतीं शुभाम् ॥
पताकाभिर्विशालाभिर्ध्वजैरन्तर्वह्निःकृतैः‡ ।
मालादिभिः§ पुरीं रम्यां भूषयाञ्चक्रिरे जनाः ॥
अवादयन्त विविधान्वादित्रान्मधुरस्वनान् ।
शङ्खान् सहस्रशो दध्मुर्वीणावादान्वितेनिरे ॥
प्रविष्टमात्रे गोविन्दे पुरीं द्वारवतीं शुभाम् ।
अगायन्मधुरं गानं स्त्रियो यौवनशोभिताः¶ ॥

---

* गन्धर्व्वाप्सरसां गणः इति B.

† गतेऽसुररिपौ नैव कामिन्यो मुनिपुङ्गवा इति B.

‡ ध्वजैरत्नपरिष्कृतैरिति B and D.

§ लाजादिभिरिति B, E and H.

¶ यौवनपालिता इति B.

दृष्ट्वा ननृतुरीशानं स्थिताः प्रासादमूर्द्धसु ।
मुमुचुः पुष्पवर्षाणि वसुदेवसुतोपरि ॥
प्रविश्य भगवान्* कृष्णस्त्वाशीर्व्वादाभिवर्द्धितः ।
वरासने महायोगी भाति देवीभिरन्वितः ॥
सुरम्ये मण्डपे शुभ्रे शङ्खाद्यैः परिवारितः ।
आत्मजैरभितो मुख्यैः स्त्रीसहस्रैश्च संवृतः ॥
तत्रासनवरे रम्ये जाम्बवत्या सहाच्युतः ।
भ्राजते चोमया देवो यथा देव्या समन्वितः ॥
आजग्मुर्द्देवगन्धर्वा द्रष्टुं लोकादिमव्ययम् ।
महर्षयः पूर्व्वजाता मार्कण्डेयादयो द्विजाः ॥
ततः स भगवान् कृष्णो† मार्कण्डेयं समागतम् ।
ननामोत्थाय शिरसा स्वासनञ्च ददौ हरिः‡ ॥
संपूज्य तानृषिगणान् प्रणामेन सहानुगः ।§
विसर्जयामास हरिर्दत्त्वा तदभिवाञ्छितान्¶ ॥
तदा मध्याह्नसमये देवदेवः स्वयं हरिः ।
स्नातः‖ शुक्लाम्बरो भानुमुपतिष्ठन्** कृताञ्जलिः ।

---

* भवनमिति B.

† विष्णुरिति B.

‡ त्वासनं प्रददौ पुनरिति B.

§ संपूज्यर्षिगणान् सर्व्वान् प्रणामेन महाभुज इति B.

¶ दत्त्वा तदभिवाञ्छितानित्यत्र पुंस्त्वमार्षं, सामान्यत्वात् क्लीवत्वमेवोचितम् ।

‖ स्नात्वा इति B.

** उपतिष्ठन्नित्यार्षम्. उपतिष्ठमान इति साधु ।

जजाप जाप्यं विधिवत्प्रेक्षमाणो दिवाकरम् ॥
तर्पयामास देवेशो देवान् पितृगणान्मुनीन् ॥
प्रविश्य देवभवनं मार्कण्डेयेन चैव हि ।
पूजयामास लिङ्गस्थं भूतेशम्भूतिभूषणम् ॥
समाप्य नियमं सर्व्वं नियन्ता स स्वयं नृणाम्* ।
भोजयित्वा मुनिवरं ब्राह्मणानभिपूज्य च ।
कृत्वात्मयोगं विप्रेन्द्रा मार्कण्डेयेन चाच्युतः ।
कथाम्पौराणिकीं पुण्यां चक्रे पुत्रादिभिर्वृतः ॥
अथैतत्सर्व्वमखिलं दृष्ट्वा कर्म्म महामुनिः ।
मार्कण्डेयो हसन्कृष्णं बभाषे मधुरं वचः ॥

मार्कण्डेय उवाच ।

कः समाराध्यते देवो भवता कर्म्मभिः शुभैः ।
ब्रूहि त्वं कर्म्मभिः पूज्यो योगिनां ध्येय एव च ॥
त्वं हि तत्परमं ब्रह्म निर्वाणममलम्पदम्† ।
भारावतरणार्थाय जातो वृष्णिकुले प्रभुः‡ ॥
तमब्रवीन्महाबाहुः§ कृष्णो ब्रह्मविदां वरः ।
शृण्वतामेव पुत्राणां सर्व्वेषां प्रहसन्निव ॥

---

* नियन्तासौ नृणां स्वयमिति B.

† निर्वाणममलं परमिति B.

‡ हरिरिति B.

§ महातेजा इति B.

श्रीभगवानुवाच ।*

भवता कथितं सर्व्वं तथ्यमेव न संशयः ।
तथापि देवमीशानं पूजयामि सनातनम् ॥
न मे विप्रास्ति कर्त्तव्यं नानवाप्तं कथञ्चन ।
पूजयामि तथापीशञ्जानन्वै परमं शिवम् ॥
न वै पश्यन्ति ते देवं मायया मोहिता जनाः ।
ततश्चैवात्मनो मूलं† ज्ञापयन् पूजयामि तम्‡ ॥
न च लिङ्गार्चनात्पुण्यं लोके दुर्गतिनाशनम्§ ।
तथा¶ लिङ्गे हितायैषां लोकानां पूजयेच्छिवम् ॥
योऽहन्तल्लिङ्गमित्याहुर्वेदवादविदो जनाः ।
ततोऽहमात्म‖मीशानं पूजयाम्यात्मनैव तत् ॥
तस्यैव परमा मूर्त्तिस्तन्मयोऽहं न संशयः ।
नावयोर्विद्यते भेदो वेदेष्वितन्न संशयः** ॥
एष देवो महादेवः सदा संसारभीरुभिः ।
याज्यः†† पूज्यश्च वन्द्यश्च ज्ञेयो लिङ्गे महेश्वरः ॥

---

* कृष्ण उवाच इति B.

† ततोऽहं स्वात्मनो मूलमिति B.

‡ ज्ञापयामि च तं शिवमिति B.

§ लोकेऽस्मिन् भीतिनाशनमिति B.

¶ विप्र इति B.

‖ आत्ममात्मस्वरूपं, स्वरूपार्थे षण् ततो मलोपः ।

** वेदेष्वेवं विनिश्चय इति B.

†† ध्येय इति B.

मार्कण्डेय उवाच ।

किं तल्लिङ्गं सुरश्रेष्ठ लिङ्गे संपूज्यते च कः ।
ब्रूहि कृष्ण विशालाक्ष गहनं ह्येतदुत्तमम् ॥

श्रीभगवानुवाच ।

अव्यक्तं लिङ्गमित्याहुरानन्दं ज्योतिरक्षयम्* ।
वेदा महेश्वरन्देवमाहुर्लिङ्गिनमव्ययम् ॥
पुरा चैकार्णवे घोरे नष्टे स्थावरजङ्गमे ।
प्रबोधार्थं ब्रह्मणो मे प्रादुर्भूतो महाशिवः ॥
तस्मात्कालात्समारभ्य ब्रह्मा चाहं सदैव हि ।
पूजयावो महादेवं लोकानां हितकाम्यया ॥

मार्कण्डेय उवाच ।

कथं लिङ्गमभूत्पूर्वमैश्वरं परमम्पदम् ।
प्रबोधार्थं स्वयं कृष्ण वक्तुमर्हसि साम्प्रतम् ॥

श्रीभगवानुवाच ।

आसीदेकार्णवं घोरमविभागं तमोमयम् ।
मध्ये चैकार्णवे तस्मिञ्छङ्खचक्रगदाधरः ।
सहस्रशीर्षा भूत्वाहं सहस्राक्षः सहस्रपात् ।
सहस्रबाहुः पुरुषः† शयितोऽहं सनातनः ॥
एतस्मिन्नन्तरे दूरे पश्यामि ह्यमितप्रभम् ।
कोटिसूर्य्यप्रतीकाशं भ्राजमानं श्रियावृतम् ॥

---

* ज्योतिरक्षरमिति B.

† युक्तात्मा इति B.

चतुर्वक्त्रं महायोगं पुरुषं कारणं प्रभुम्* ।
कृष्णाजिनधरन्देवमृग्यजुःसामभिः स्तुतम् ॥
निमिषमात्रेण स† मामाप्तो योगविदां वरः ।
व्याजहार स्वयं ब्रह्मा स्मयमानो महाद्युतिः ॥
कस्त्वं कुतो वा किञ्चेह तिष्ठसे वद मे प्रभो ।
अहं कर्त्ता हि लोकानां स्वयम्भूः प्रपितामहः ॥
एवमुक्तस्तदा तेन ब्रह्मणाहमुवाच ह‡ ।
अहं कर्त्तास्मि लोकानां संहर्त्ता च पुनः पुनः ॥
एवं विवादे वितते मायया परमेष्ठिनः ।
प्रबोधार्थं परं लिङ्गं प्रादुर्भूतं शिवात्मकम् ।
कालानलसमप्रख्यं ज्वालामालासमाकुलम् ।
क्षयवृद्धिविनिर्मुक्तमादिमध्यान्तवर्ज्जितम् ॥
ततो मामाह भगवानधो गच्छ त्वमाशु वै ।
अन्तमस्य विजानीव§ ऊर्द्धं गच्छेऽहमित्यजः ॥
तदाशु समयं कृत्वा गतावूर्द्धमधश्च तौ ।
पितामहोऽप्यहन्नान्तं ज्ञातवन्तौ समेत्य तौ¶ ॥
ततो विस्मयमापन्नौ भीतौ देवस्य शूलिनः ।

---

* काञ्चनप्रभमिति B.

† तु इति B.

‡ तमिति B.

§ विजानीया इति B.

¶ समाः शतमिति B.

मायया मोहितौ तस्य ध्यायन्तौ विश्वमीश्वरम् ॥
प्रोच्चरन्तौ महानादमोङ्कारं परमं पदम् ।
तं प्राञ्जलिपुटौ भूत्वा शम्भुं तुष्टुवतुः परम् ॥

ब्रह्मविष्णू ऊचतुः ।

अनादिमूलसंसाररोगवैद्याय शम्भवे ।
नमः शिवाय शान्ताय ब्रह्मणे लिङ्गमूर्त्तये ॥
प्रलयार्णवसंस्थाय प्रलयोद्भूतिहेतवे ।
नमः शिवाय शान्ताय ब्रह्मणे लिङ्गमूर्त्तये ॥
ज्वालामालाप्रतीकाय* ज्वलनस्तम्भरूपिणे† ।
नमः शिवाय शान्ताय ब्रह्मणे लिङ्गमूर्त्तये ॥
आदिमध्यान्तहीनाय स्वभावामलदीप्तये‡ ।
नमः शिवायानन्ताय ब्रह्मणे लिङ्गमूर्त्तये ॥
प्रधानपुरुषेशाय व्योमरूपाय वेधसे ।
नमः शिवाय शान्ताय ब्रह्मणे§ लिङ्गमूर्त्तये ॥
निर्विकाराय सत्याय नित्यायातुलतेजसे¶ ।
वेदान्तसाररूपाय कालरूपाय ते नमः ॥
नमः शिवाय शान्ताय ब्रह्मणे लिङ्गमूर्त्तये ॥

---

* हुताङ्गाय इति B.

† स्तम्भमूर्त्तये इति B.

‡ इदं पादद्वयं B पुस्तके प्रागेव लिखितम् ।

§ एतत्पर्य्यन्तं E, G, H पुस्तकेषु नास्ति ।

¶ नित्यायामलमूर्त्तये इति B.

एवं संस्तूयमानस्तु व्यक्तो भूत्वा महेश्वरः ।
भाति देवो* महायोगी सूर्य्यकोटिसमप्रभः ।
वक्त्रकोटिसहस्रेण ग्रसमान इवाम्बरम् ।
सहस्रहस्तचरणः सूर्य्यसोमाग्निलोचनः ।
पिनाकपाणिर्भगवान् कृत्तिवासास्त्रिशूलधृक् ।
व्यालयज्ञोपवीतश्च मेघदुन्दुभिनिःस्वनः ॥
अथोवाच महादेवः प्रीतोऽहं सुरसत्तमौ ।
पश्यतं† मां महादेवं भयं सर्व्वं प्रमुच्यताम् ॥
युवां प्रसूतौ गात्रेभ्यो मम पूर्व्वं सनातनौ ।
अयं मे दक्षिणे पार्श्वे ब्रह्मा लोकपितामहः‡ ॥
वामपार्श्वे च मे§ विष्णुः पालको हृदये हरः ।
प्रीतोऽहं युवयोः सम्यग्वरन्दद्मि¶ यथेप्सितम् ॥
एवमुक्ताथ‖ मान्देवो महादेवः स्वयं शिवः ।
आलिङ्ग्य देवं ब्रह्माणं प्रसादाभिमुखोऽभवत् ॥
ततः प्रहृष्टमनसौ प्रणिपत्य महेश्वरम् ।
ऊचतुः प्रेक्ष्य तद्वक्त्रं नारायणपितामहौ ॥

---

* आदिदेव इति B.

† पश्यतमिति B.

‡ लोककरः प्रभुरिति B.

§ वामे पार्श्वे चैव इति B.

¶ दद्मीति आर्षं, ददामीति साधु ।

‖ एवमुक्त्वा तु इति B.

यदि प्रीतिः समुत्पन्ना यदि देयो वरो हि नः।
भक्तिर्भवतु नो नित्यं त्वयि* देव महेश्वरे॥
ततः स भगवानीशः प्रहसन्परमेश्वरः।
उवाच मां महादेवः प्रीतं प्रीतेन चेतसा॥

देव उवाच।

प्रलयस्थितिसर्गाणां कर्त्ता त्वं धरणीपते।
वत्स वत्स हरे विश्वम्पालयैतच्चराचरम्॥†
द्विधा भिन्नोऽस्म्यहं विष्णो ब्रह्मविष्णुहराख्यया‡।
सर्गरक्षालयगुणैर्निर्गुणोऽपि निरञ्जनः॥
संमोहन्त्यज भो विष्णो पालयैनं पितामहम्।
भविष्यत्येव भगवांस्तव पुत्रः सनातनः॥
अहञ्च भवतो§ वक्त्रात्कल्पादौ सुररूपधृक्¶।
शूलपाणिर्भविष्यामि क्रोधजस्तव पुत्रकः॥
एवमुक्त्वा महादेवो ब्रह्माणं मुनिसत्तम।
अनुगृह्य च मान्देवस्तत्रैवान्तरधीयत॥
ततःप्रभृति लोकेषु लिङ्गार्चा सुप्रतिष्ठिता।

---

* भुवि इति B.

† एतत्पादद्वयं G पुस्तके नास्ति।

‡ भिन्नाख्यया इति B.

§ अहं प्रभवतो वक्त्रादिति E and H.

¶ कल्पान्ते घोररूपधृगिति B.

लिङ्गन्तत्तु यतो* ब्रह्मन् ब्रह्मणः परमं वपुः ॥
एतल्लिङ्गस्य माहात्म्यं भाषितं ते मयानघ।
एतद्बुध्यन्ति योगज्ञा न देवा न च दानवाः ॥
एतद्धि परमं ज्ञानमव्यक्तं शिवसंज्ञितम्।
येन सूक्ष्ममचिन्त्यं तत्पश्यन्ति ज्ञानचक्षुषः† ॥
तस्मै भगवते नित्यं नमस्कारं प्रकुर्म्महे।
महादेवाय देवाय‡ देवदेवाय शृङ्गिणे§ ॥
नमो वेदरहस्याय नीलकण्ठाय वै नमः।
विभीषणाय शान्ताय स्थाणवे हेतवे¶ नमः ॥
ब्रह्मणे वामदेवाय‖ त्रिनेत्राय महीयसे।
शङ्कराय महेशाय गिरीशाय शिवाय च ॥
नमः कुरुष्व सततन्ध्यायस्व च महेश्वरम्**।
संसारसागरादस्मादचिराद्धुद्धरिष्यसि ॥
एवं स वासुदेवेन व्याहृतो मुनिपुङ्गवः।
जगाम मनसा देवमीशानं विश्वतोमुखम् ॥

---

* लिङ्गं त्वन्नयनादिति D, E and H.

† ज्ञानचक्षुषेति D, E and H.

‡ रुद्राय इति B.

§ लिङ्गिने इति B.

¶ योगिने इति B.

‖ देवदेवाय इति B.

** मनसा हरमिति B.

प्रणम्य शिरसा कृष्ण*मनुज्ञातो महामुनिः।
जगाम चेप्सितं शम्भुन्देवदेवन्त्रिशूलिनम्† ॥
य इमं श्रावयेन्नित्यं लिङ्गाध्यायमनुत्तमम्।
शृणुयाद्वा पठेद्वापि सर्व्वपापैः प्रमुच्यते ॥
श्रुत्वा सकृदपि ह्येतत्तपश्चरणमुत्तमम्।
वासुदेवस्य विप्रेन्द्राः पापं मुञ्चति मानवः‡ ॥
जपेद्वाहरहर्नित्यं ब्रह्मलोके महीयते।
एवमाह महायोगी कृष्णद्वैपायनः प्रभुः ॥

इति श्रीकूर्म्मपुराणे यदुवंशानुकीर्त्तने लिङ्गोत्पत्तौ षड्विंशोऽध्यायः।

—o—

सप्तविंशोऽध्यायः।

सूत उवाच।

ततो लब्धवरः कृष्णो जाम्बवत्यां महेश्वरात्।
अजीजनन्महात्मानं शाम्बमात्मजमुत्तमम्* ॥
प्रद्युम्नस्य ह्यभूत्पुत्रो ह्यनिरुद्धो महाबलः।

---

* विष्णुमिति B.

† देशं देवदेवञ्च शूलिनमिति B and D.

‡ मुञ्चन्ति मानवा इति B.

---

* शाम्बमात्मजसत्तममिति B.

तावुभौ गुणसम्पन्नौ कृष्णस्यैवापरे तनू ॥
हत्वा च कंसं नरकमन्यांश्च शतशोऽसुरान् ।
विजित्य लीलया शक्रञ्जित्वा बाणं महासुरम् ॥
स्थापयित्वा जगत्कृत्स्नं लोके धर्म्मांश्च* शाश्वतान् ।
चक्रे नारायणो गन्तुं स्वस्थानं बुद्धिमुत्तमाम् ॥
एतस्मिन्नन्तरे विप्राः भृग्वाद्याः कृष्णमीश्वरम् ।
आजग्मुर्द्वारकां द्रष्टुं कृतकार्य्यं सनातनम् ॥
स तानुवाच विश्वात्मा प्रणिपत्याभिपूज्य च ।
आसनेषूपविष्टान्वै सह रामेण धीमता ॥
गमिष्यामि परं स्थानं स्वकीयं विष्णुसंज्ञितम् ।
कृतानि सर्व्वकार्य्याणि प्रसीदध्वं† मुनीश्वराः ॥
इदं कलियुगं घोरं सम्प्राप्तमधुनाऽशुभम् ।
भविष्यन्ति जनाः सर्वे ह्यस्मिन्पापानुवर्त्तिनः ॥
प्रवर्त्तयध्वं विज्ञानमज्ञानाच्च‡ हितावहम् ।
येनेमे कलिजैः पापैर्मुच्यन्ते हि§ द्विजोत्तमाः ॥
ये मां जनाः संस्मरन्ति कलौ सकृदपि प्रभुम् ।
तेषां नश्यति¶ तत्पापं भक्तानां पुरुषोत्तमे ॥

---

* लोकधर्म्मांश्च इति B.

† आर्षमात्मनेपदम् ।

‡ वै ज्ञानं ब्राह्मणानामिति B.

§ वै इति B.

¶ नश्यतु इति B.

येऽर्चयिष्यन्ति मां भक्त्या नित्यं कलियुगे द्विजाः।
विधिना वेददृष्टेन ते गमिष्यन्ति तत्पदम्॥
ये ब्राह्मणा वंशजाता युष्माकं वै सहस्रशः।
तेषां नारायणे भक्तिर्भविष्यति कलौ युगे॥
परात्परतरं यान्ति नारायणपरा जनाः।
न ते तत्र गमिष्यन्ति ये द्विषन्ति महेश्वरम्॥
ध्यानं योगः*स्तपस्तप्तं ज्ञानं यज्ञादिको विधिः।
तेषां विनश्यति क्षिप्रं ये निन्दन्ति महेश्वरम्†॥
यो मां समर्चयेन्नित्यमेकान्तं भावमाश्रितः।
विनिन्दन्देवमीशानं स याति नरकायुतम्॥
तस्मात्संपरिहर्त्तव्या‡ निन्दा पशुपतेर्द्विजाः।
कर्म्मणा मनसा वाचा मद्भक्तेष्वपि यत्नतः॥
ये च§ दक्षाध्वरे शप्ता दधीचेन द्विजोत्तमाः।
भविष्यन्ति कलौ भक्तैः परिहार्य्याः प्रयत्नतः॥
द्विषन्तो देवमीशानं युष्माकं वंशसम्भवाः।
शप्ताश्च गौतमेनोर्व्यां न सम्भाष्या द्विजोत्तमैः¶॥
एवमुक्ताश्च‖ कृष्णेन सर्वे ते वै महर्षयः।

* हीन इति B.

† पिनाकिनमिति B.

‡ तस्मात्सा परिहर्त्तव्या इति B.

§ तु इति B.

¶ द्विजोत्तमाः इति B.

‖ इत्येवमुक्ताः इति B.

ओमित्युक्त्वा ययुस्तूर्णं स्वानि स्थानानि सत्तमाः॥
ततो नारायणः कृष्णो लीलयैव जगन्मयः।
संहृत्य स्वकुलं सर्वं ययौ तत्परमं पदम्॥
इत्येष वः समासेन राज्ञां वंशः सुकीर्त्तितः*।
न शक्यो विस्तराद्वक्तुं किं भूयः श्रोतुमिच्छथ॥
यः पठेच्छृणुयाद्वापि वंशानां कथनं शुभम्।
सर्वपापविनिर्मुक्तः स्वर्गलोके महीयते॥

इति श्रीकूर्म्मपुराणे राजवंशानुकीर्त्तने सप्तविंशोऽध्यायः।

अष्टाविंशोऽध्यायः।

ऋषय ऊचुः।

कृतं त्रेता द्वापरञ्च कलिश्चेति चतुर्युगम्।
एषां प्रभावं* सूताद्य कथयस्व समासतः॥

सूत उवाच।

गते नारायणे कृष्णे स्वमेव परमं पदम्।
पार्थः परमधर्म्मात्मा पाण्डवः शत्रुतापनः॥

---

* वंशोऽनुकीर्त्तितः इति B.

—:—

* स्वभावमिति B.

कृत्वा चैवोत्तरविधिं शोकेन महतावृतः ।
अपश्यत्पथि गच्छन्तं कृष्णद्वैपायनं मुनिम् ॥
शिष्यैः प्रशिष्यैरभितः संवृतं ब्रह्मवादिनम् ।
पपात दण्डवद्भूमौ त्यक्त्वा शोकं तदार्जुनः ॥
उवाच परमप्रीत्या* कस्मादेतन्महामुने† ।
इदानीं गच्छसि क्षिप्रं कं वा देशं‡ प्रति प्रभो ॥
सन्दर्शनाद्वै भवतः शोको मे विपुलो गतः ।
इदानीं मम यत्कार्य्यं ब्रूहि पद्मदलेक्षण ॥
तमुवाच महायोगी कृष्णद्वैपायनः स्वयम् ।
उपविश्य नदीतीरे शिष्यैः परिवृतो मुनिः ॥

इति श्रीकूर्म्मपुराणे अष्टाविंशोऽध्यायः ।

ऊनत्रिंशोऽध्यायः ।

व्यास उवाच ।

इदं कलियुगं घोरं सम्प्राप्तं पाण्डुनन्दन ।
ततो गच्छामि देवस्य पुरीं वाराणसीं शुभाम्* ॥

---

* परमप्रीतः इति B and D.

† कस्माद्देशान्महामुने इति B and D.

‡ गङ्गादेशमिति E and H.

---

* वाराणसीं महापुरीमिति B, E and H.

अस्मिन् कलियुगे घोरे लोकाः पापानुवर्त्तिनः ।
भविष्यन्ति महाबाहो* वर्णाश्रमविवर्ज्जिताः ॥
नान्यत्पश्यामि जन्तूनां मुक्त्वा† वाराणसीं पुरीम् ।
सर्वपापोपशमनं‡ प्रायश्चित्तं कलौ युगे ॥
कृतं त्रेता द्वापरञ्च सर्वेष्वेतेषु ते§ नराः ।
भविष्यन्ति महात्मानो धार्म्मिकाः सत्यवादिनः ॥
त्वं हि लोकेषु विख्यातो धृतिमाञ्जनवत्सलः ।
पालयाद्य परं धर्म्मं स्वकीयं मुच्यसे भयात् ॥
एवमुक्तो भगवता पार्थः परपुरञ्जयः ।
पृष्टवान्प्रणिपत्यासौ युगधर्मान्द्विजोत्तमाः ॥
तस्मै प्रोवाच सकलं मुनिः सत्यव्रतीसुतः ।
प्रणम्य देवमीशानं युगधर्मान्सनातनान् ॥

व्यास उवाच ।

वक्ष्यामि ते समासेन युगधर्मान्नरेश्वर ।
न शक्यते मया राजन्विस्तरेणाभिभाषितुम् ॥
आद्यं कृतयुगं प्रोक्तं ततस्त्रेतायुगं बुधैः ।
तृतीयं द्वापरं पार्थ चतुर्थं कलिरुच्यते ॥

---

* महापापा इति B.

† त्यक्त्वा इति B.

‡ सर्व्वपापप्रशमनमिति B.

§ वै इति B.

ध्यानं तपः* कृतयुगे त्रेतायां ज्ञानमुच्यते† ।
द्वापरे यज्ञमेवाहुर्दानमेकं‡ कलौ युगे ॥
ब्रह्मा कृतयुगे देवस्त्रेतायां भगवान्रविः ।
द्वापरे दैवतं विष्णुः कलौ देवो§ महेश्वरः ॥
ब्रह्मा विष्णुस्तथा सूर्यः सर्वं एव कलिष्वपि ।
पूज्यन्ते भगवानुद्रश्चतुर्ष्वपि पिनाकधृक् ॥
आद्ये कृतयुगे धर्मश्चतुष्पादः प्रकीर्त्तितः¶ ।
त्रेतायुगे त्रिपादः स्याद्द्विपादो द्वापरे स्थितः ।
त्रिपादहीनस्तिष्ठेत्तु सत्तामात्रेण तिष्ठति ॥
कृते तु मिथुनोत्पत्तिर्वृत्तिः साक्षादलोलुपा ।
प्रजास्तृप्ताः सदा सर्वाः सर्वानन्दाश्च भोगिनः‖ ॥
अधमोत्तमत्वं नास्त्यासां निर्विशेषाः पुरञ्जय** ।
तुल्यमायुः सुखं रूपं तासु†† तस्मिन् कृते युगे ॥
विशोकास्तत्त्वबहुला‡‡ एकान्तबहुलास्तथा ।

---

* परमिति B.

† ज्ञानमध्वर इति B.

‡ दानमेव इति B.

§ रुद्र इति B.

¶ सनातन इति B.

‖ भोगिन्य इति वक्तव्ये भोगिन इति आर्षम् ।

** सदानन्दाः पुरन्धय इति D.

†† तासामिति B.

‡‡ सत्त्वबहुला इति B.

ध्याननिष्ठास्तपोनिष्ठा महादेवपरायणाः ॥
ता वै निष्कामचारिण्यो* नित्यं मुदितमानसाः ।
पर्व्वतोदधिवासिन्यो ह्यनिकेताः परन्तप ॥
रसोल्लासः कालयोगात्त्रेताख्ये† नश्यति द्विजाः ।‡
तस्यां सिद्धौ प्रनष्टायामन्या सिद्धिरवर्त्तत ॥
अपां सौख्ये प्रतिहते§ तदा मेघात्मना तु वै ।
मेघेभ्यस्तनयित्नुभ्यः प्रवृत्तं वृष्टिसर्ज्जनम् ॥
सकृदेव तया वृष्ट्या संयुक्ते¶ पृथिवीतले ।
प्रादुरासंस्तथा तासां वृक्षा वै गृहसंज्ञिताः ॥
सर्व्वः प्रत्युपयोगस्तु तासान्तेभ्यः प्रजायते ।
वर्त्तयन्ति स्म तेभ्यस्तास्त्रेतायुगमुखे प्रजाः ॥
ततः कालेन महता तासामेव विपर्य्ययात्‖ ।
रागलोभात्मको** भावस्तदा ह्याकस्मिकोऽभवत् ॥
विपर्य्ययेण तासान्तु†† तेन तत्कालभाविता: ।

---

* भावेन कामचारिण्य इति B.

† आलस्यात्कालयोगाच्च इति D. रसोल्लासः कलायोगादिति E and H.

‡ नश्यते तत इति B.

§ प्रतिगते इति B.

¶ संपृक्ते इति B.

‖ विपर्य्यये इति B.

** भोगात्मक इति B.

†† नाशाच्च इति B.

प्रणश्यन्ति ततः सर्वे वृक्षास्ते गृहसंज्ञिताः॥
ततस्तेषु प्रनष्टेषु विभ्रान्ता मैथुनोद्भवाः।
अभिध्यायन्ति तां सिद्धिं सत्याभिध्यानत*स्तदा॥
प्रादुर्बभूवुस्तासान्तु वृक्षास्ते गृहसंज्ञिताः।
वस्त्राणि ते प्रसूयन्ते फलान्याभरणानि च॥
तेष्वेव जायते तासां गन्धवर्णरसान्वितम्।
अमाक्षिकं महावीर्यं पुटके पुटके मधु॥
तेन ता वर्त्तयन्ति स्म त्रेतायुगमुखे प्रजाः।
हृष्टास्तुष्टास्तया सिद्धया सर्व्वा वै विगतज्वराः॥
पुनः† कालान्तरेणैव ततो‡ लोभावृतास्तदा।
वृक्षांस्तान् पर्य्यगृह्णन्त मधु वा माक्षिकं बलात्॥
तासान्तेनापचारेण पुनर्लोभकृतेन वै।
प्रनष्टा मधुना सार्द्धं कल्पवृक्षाः क्वचित् क्वचित्॥
शीतवर्षातपैस्तीव्रै§स्तास्ततो¶ दुःखिता भृशम्।
द्वन्द्वैः संपीड्यमानास्तु चक्रुरावरणानि च॥
कृत्वा द्वन्द्वविनिर्घातान्‖ वार्त्तोपायमचिन्तयन्।

---

* सत्याभिध्यायिन इति B.

† तत इति B and D.

‡ पुनरिति B and D.

§ तीक्ष्णैरिति B.

¶ ततस्ता इति B and D.

‖ द्वन्द्वप्रतीकारानिति B. प्रतीघातानिति D.

नष्टेषु मधुना सार्द्धं कल्पवृक्षेषु वै तदा ॥
ततः प्रादुरभूत्तासां* सिद्धिस्त्रेतायुगे पुनः ।
वार्त्तायाः साधिका ह्यन्या वृष्टिस्तासान्निकामतः ॥
तासां वृष्ट्युदकानीह यानि निम्नैर्गतानि तु ।
अभवन्† वृष्टिसन्तत्या स्रोतःस्थानानि निम्नगाः ॥
यदा आपो बहुतरा‡ आपन्नाः पृथिवीतले ।
अपाम्भूमेश्च संयोगादोषध्यस्तास्तदाभवन् ॥
अफालकृष्टाश्चानुप्ता ग्राम्यारण्याश्चतुर्द्दश ।
ऋतुपुष्पफलैश्चैव वृक्षगुल्माश्च जज्ञिरे ॥
ततः प्रादुरभूत्तासां रागो लोभश्च सर्व्वशः ।
अवश्यम्भावितार्थेन त्रेतायुगवशेन वै§ ॥
ततस्ताः पर्य्यगृह्णन्त नदीक्षेत्राणि पर्व्वतान् ।
वृक्षगुल्मौषधीश्चैव प्रसह्य तु यथाबलम् ॥
विपर्य्ययेण तासान्ताः¶ ओषध्यो विविशुर्म्महीम् ।
पितामहनियोगेन दुदोह पृथिवीं पृथुः ॥
ततस्ता जगृहुः सर्व्वा ह्यन्योन्यं क्रोधमूर्च्छिताः ।

---

* प्रादुर्बभूवाथेति E and H.

† अवहन्निति B.

‡ ये पुनस्तदपां स्रोका इति B and D.

§ तु इति B.

¶ नाशाश्च इति E and H.

सदाचारे विनष्टे तु* बलात्कालबलेन च ॥
मर्य्यादायाः प्रतिष्ठार्थं† ज्ञात्वैतद्भगवानजः ।
ससर्ज क्षत्रियान्ब्रह्मा ब्राह्मणानां हिताय वै ॥
वर्णाश्रमव्यवस्थाञ्च त्रेतायां कृतवान्प्रभुः ।
यज्ञप्रवर्त्तनञ्चैव पशुहिंसाविवर्ज्जितम् ॥
द्वापरेऽप्यथ विद्यन्ते मतिभेदास्तथा नृणाम्‡ ।
रागो लोभस्तथा युद्धं मत्वा बुद्धिविनिश्चयम् ॥
एको वेदश्चतुष्पादस्त्रिधा त्विह विभाव्यते ।§
वेदव्यासैश्चतुर्द्धा च न्यस्यते द्वापरादिषु ॥
ऋषिपुत्रैः पुनर्वेदा भिद्यन्ते दृष्टिविभ्रमैः ।
मन्त्रब्राह्मणविन्यासैः स्वरवर्णविपर्य्ययैः ॥
संहिता ऋग्यजुःसाम्नां प्रोच्यन्ते परमर्षिभिः¶ ।
सामान्योद्भावना चैव‖ दृष्टिभेदैः क्वचित्क्वचित् ॥
ब्राह्मणं कल्पसूत्राणि ब्रह्मप्रवचनानि च ।
इतिहासपुराणानि धर्म्मशास्त्राणि सुव्रत ॥

---

* आत्मदारधनाद्यास्तु इति B.

† प्रतिष्ठानमिति B and D.

‡ तत्त्वानामविनिश्चय इति B.

§ एको वेदश्चतुष्पादस्त्रेतास्त्विह विधीयते इति B and D.

¶ संह्रियन्ते श्रुतर्षिभिरिति B and D.

‖ सामान्यादैकृताश्चैव इति B and D.

अवृष्टिर्मरणञ्चैव तथैवान्ये ह्युपद्रवाः* ।
वाङ्मनःकायजैर्दोषैः† निर्वेदो जायते नृणाम् ॥
निर्वेदाज्जायते तेषां दुःखमोक्षविचारणा ।
विचारणाच्च वैराग्यं वैराग्याद्दोषदर्शनम् ॥
दोषाणां दर्शनाच्चैव द्वापरे ज्ञानसम्भवः ।
एषा रजस्तमोयुक्ता वृत्तिर्वै द्वापरे द्विजाः ॥
आद्ये कृते तु धर्म्मोऽस्ति स त्रेतायां प्रवर्त्तते ।
द्वापरे व्याकुलीभूत्वा‡ प्रणश्यति कलौ युगे ॥

इति श्रीकूर्म्मपुराणे युगवंशानुकीर्त्तने एकोनत्रिंशोऽध्यायः ।

त्रिंशोऽध्यायः ।

व्यास उवाच ।

तिष्ये मायामसूयाञ्च वधञ्चैव* तपस्विनाम् ।
साधयन्ति नरा नित्यं तमसा व्याकुलीकृताः ॥

---

* तथैव व्याध्युपद्रवा इति B and D.

† दुःखैरिति B and D.

‡ व्याकुलीभूय इति साधु ।

---

* वधञ्चैव इति E and H.

कलौ प्रमारको रोगः सततं क्षुद्भयन्तथा ।
अनावृष्टिभयं घोरं देशानाञ्च विपर्य्ययः ॥
अधार्म्मिका निराहारा महाकोपाल्पतेजसः ।
अनृतं ब्रुवते लुब्धास्तिष्ये जाताः सुदुष्प्रजाः ॥
दुरिष्टैर्दुरधीतैश्च दुराचारैर्दुरागमैः ।
विप्राणां कर्म्मदोषैश्च प्रजानां जायते भयम् ॥
नाधीयते तदा वेदान्* न यजन्ति द्विजातयः ।
यजन्ति यज्ञान्वेदांश्च† पठन्ते चाल्पबुद्धयः ॥
शूद्राणां मन्त्रयोगैश्च‡ सम्बन्धो ब्राह्मणैः सह ।
भविष्यति कलौ तस्मिञ्छयनासनभोजनैः ॥
राजानः शूद्रभूयिष्ठा ब्राह्मणान्बाधयन्ति च ।
भ्रूणहत्या वीरहत्या प्रजायेत नरेश्वरे§ ॥
स्नानं होमं जपं दानं देवतानां तथार्चनम् ।
तथान्यानि च¶ कर्म्माणि न कुर्व्वन्ति द्विजातयः ॥
विनिन्दन्ति महादेवं ब्राह्मणान् पुरुषोत्तमम् ।
आम्नायधर्म्म‖शास्त्राणि** पुराणानि कलौ युगे ॥

---

* नाधीयन्ते कलौ वेदा इति B and D.

† यजन्त्यन्यायतो वेदानिति B. जपन्त्यन्यायतोवेदानिति D.

‡ मन्त्रमौनैश्च इति B.

§ स जायेते नरेश्वर इति B.

¶ अन्यानि चैव इति B and D.

‖ सर्व्व इति B.

** स्मृतिशास्त्राणीति D.

कुर्व्वन्त्यवेददृष्टानि कर्म्माणि विविधानि तु।
स्वधर्म्मे तु रुचिर्नैव ब्राह्मणानां प्रजायते॥
कुशीलचर्या पाषण्डैर्वृथारूपैः समावृताः।
बहुयाचनका लोका भविष्यन्ति परस्परम्॥
अट्टशूला जनपदाः शिवशूलाश्चतुष्पथाः।
प्रमदाः केशशूलाश्च भविष्यन्ति कलौ युगे॥
शुक्लदन्ताजिनाख्याश्च मुण्डाः काषायवाससः।
शूद्रा धर्म्मञ्चरिष्यन्ति युगान्ते समुपस्थिते॥
शस्यचौरा भविष्यन्ति तथा चैलाभिमर्शिनः।
चौराच्चौराश्च हर्त्तारो* हर्त्तुर्हन्ता तथापरः॥
दुःखप्रचुर†मल्पायुर्देहोत्सादः सरोगता।
अधर्म्माभिनिवेशत्वात्तमोवृत्तं कलौ स्मृतम्॥
काषायिणोऽथ निर्ग्रन्थास्तथा कापालिकाश्च ये।
वेदविक्रयिणश्चान्ये तीर्थविक्रयिणः परे॥‡
आसनस्थान्द्विजान्दृष्ट्वा चालयन्त्यल्पबुद्धयः।
ताड़यन्ति द्विजेन्द्रांश्च शूद्रा राजोपजीविनः॥
उच्चासनस्थाः शूद्राश्च§ द्विजमध्ये परन्तप।

---

* चौराश्चौरस्य इति B and D.

† प्रचुरताल्पायुरिति D and E.

‡ एतत्पादद्वयं B पुस्तके नास्ति।

§ शूद्रास्तु इति B and D.

द्विजामानकरो* राजा कलौ कालबलेन तु ॥
पुष्पैश्च भूषणैश्चैवं† तथान्यैर्मङ्गलैर्द्विजाः।
शूद्रान्परिचरन्त्यल्प‡श्रुतभाग्यबलान्विताः ॥
न प्रेचन्तेऽर्चितांश्चापि शूद्रान्द्विजवरान्नृप।
सेवावसरमालोक्य द्वारे तिष्ठन्ति च द्विजाः ॥
वाहनस्थान्समावृत्य शूद्राञ्छूद्रोपजीविनः।
सेवन्ते ब्राह्मणास्तांसु स्तुवन्ति स्तुतिभिः§ कलौ ॥
अध्यापयन्ति वै वेदाञ्छूद्राञ्छूद्रोपजीविनः।
एवं निर्वैदकानर्थान्नास्तिक्यं घोरमाश्रिताः ॥
तपोयज्ञकलानान्तु विक्रेतारो द्विजोत्तमाः।
यतयश्च भविष्यन्ति शतशोऽथ सहस्रशः ॥
नाशयन्तः¶ स्वकन्धर्म्मन्नाधिगच्छन्ति तत्पदम्‖।
गायन्ति लौकिकैर्गानैर्दैवतानि नराधिप ॥
वाम**पाशुपताचारास्तथा वै पाञ्चरात्रिकाः।
भविष्यन्ति कलौ तस्मिन्ब्राह्मणाः चत्रियास्तथा ॥

---

* ज्ञाला न हिंसिते इति B and D.

† हसितैश्चैव इति B and D.

‡ शूद्रानभ्यर्चयन्त्यल्प इति B and D.

§ श्रुतिभिरिति B and D.

¶ नाशयन्ति ह्यधीतानि इति B and D.

‖ चानघ इति B.

** वामाः इति B.

ज्ञाने* कर्म्मण्यपगते लोके निष्क्रियताङ्गते।
कीटमूषिकसर्पाश्च धर्षयिष्यन्ति मानुषान्† ॥
कुर्व्वन्ति चावताराणि ब्राह्मणानां कुलेषु वै।
देवीशापविनिर्द्दग्धाः‡ पुरा दक्षाध्वरे द्विजाः ॥
निन्दन्ति च महादेवं तमसाविष्टचेतसः।
वृथा धर्म्मञ्चरिष्यन्ति कलौ तस्मिन्युगान्तिके ॥
ये चान्ये शापनिर्द्दग्धा गौतमस्य महात्मनः।
सर्व्वे तेऽवतरिष्यन्ति§ ब्राह्मणास्तासु योनिषु ॥¶
विनिन्दन्ति हृषीकेशं ब्राह्मणा ब्रह्मवादिनः।
वेदबाह्यव्रताचारा दुराचारा वृथाश्रमाः ॥
मोहयन्ति जनान् सर्व्वान्दर्शयित्वा फलानि च।
तमसाविष्टमनसो वैड़ालव्रतिकाधमाः ॥
कलौ रुद्रो महादेवो लोकानामीश्वरः परः।
तदेव साधयेन्नृणां‖ देवतानाञ्च दैवतम् ॥
करिष्यत्यवताराणि** शङ्करो नीललोहितः।
श्रौतस्मार्त्तप्रतिष्ठार्थं भक्तानां हितकाम्यया ॥

---

* ज्ञान इति B, E and H.

† मानवानिति B and D.

‡ दधीचशापनिर्द्दग्धाः इति B and D.

§ ते च भविष्यन्तीति E and H.

¶ सर्व्वे वीरा भविष्यन्ति ब्राह्मणाद्याः स्वजातिषु इति B.

‖ न देवता भवेन्नृणामिति B and D.

** क्लीवत्वमार्षम्।

उपदेक्ष्यति तज्ज्ञानं शिष्याणां ब्रह्मसंज्ञितम्।
सर्व्ववेदान्तसारं हि धर्म्मान्वेदनिदर्शितान्* ॥
ये तत्प्रीता† निषेवन्ते येन केनोपचारतः।
विजित्य कलिजान्दोषान्यान्ति ते परमम्पदम् ॥
अनायासेन सुमहत्पुण्यमाप्नोति मानवः।
अनेकदोषदुष्टस्य कलेरेको महान् गुणः ॥
तस्मात्सर्व्वप्रयत्नेन प्राप्य माहेश्वरं युगम्।
विशेषाद्ब्राह्मणोरुद्रमीशानं शरणं व्रजेत् ॥
ये नमन्ति विरूपाक्षमीशानं कृत्तिवाससम्।
प्रसन्नचेतसो रुद्रं ते यान्ति‡ परमम्पदम् ॥
यथा रुद्रनमस्कारः सर्व्वकामफलो ध्रुवः।
अन्यदेवनमस्कारान्न तत्फलमवाप्नुयात् ॥
एवंविधे कलियुगे दोषाणामेव शोधनम्।
महादेवनमस्कारो ध्यानं दानमिति श्रुतिः§ ॥
तस्मादनीश्वरानन्यान्¶ त्यक्त्वा देवं महेश्वरम्।
समाश्रयेद्विरूपाक्षं यदीच्छेत्परमम्पदम् ॥
नार्चयन्तीह ये रुद्रं शिवं त्रिदशवन्दितम्।

---

* सर्ववर्णान् समुद्दिश्य स्वधर्म्मा ये निदर्शिता इति D. निदर्शनानिति E and H.

† ये विप्रास्तानिति D.

‡ यान्ति ते इति B.

§ दानं परा गतिरिति B.

¶ तस्मादधीश्वरानन्यानिति B and D.

तेषां दानं तपो यज्ञो वृथा जीवितमेव च ॥
नमो रुद्राय महते देवदेवाय शूलिने ।
त्र्यम्बकाय त्रिनेत्राय योगिनां गुरवे नमः ॥
नमोऽस्तु देवदेवाय* महादेवाय वेधसे ।
शम्भवे स्थाणवे नित्यं शिवाय परमेष्ठिने ॥
नमः सोमाय रुद्राय महाग्रासाय हेतवे† ।
प्रपद्येऽहं विरूपाक्षं शरण्यं ब्रह्मचारिणम् ॥
महादेवं महायोगमीशानञ्चाम्बिकापतिम् ।
योगिनां योगदातारं योगमायासमावृतम् ॥
योगिनां गुरुमाचार्य्यं‡ योगिगम्यम्पिनाकिनम् ।
संसारतारणं रुद्रं ब्रह्माणं ब्रह्मणोऽधिपम् ॥
शाश्वतं सर्व्वगं शान्तं ब्रह्मण्यं ब्राह्मणप्रियम् ।
कपर्द्दिनं कालमूर्त्तिममूर्त्तिम्परमेश्वरम्§ ॥
एकमूर्त्तिं महामूर्त्तिं वेदवेद्यन्दिवस्पतिम् ।
नीलकण्ठं विश्वमूर्त्तिं व्यापिनं विश्वरेतसम्¶ ॥
कालाग्निङ्कालदहनं कामदङ्कामनाशनम् ।

---

* वामदेवाय इति B and D.

† महाग्रासाभिहेतवे इति B.

‡ परमाचार्य्यमिति B.

§ ममरेश्वरमिति B and D.

¶ विश्वचेतसमिति B.

नमस्ये* गिरिशं देवं चन्द्रावयवभूषणम्† ॥
विलोहितं लेलिहानमादित्यम्परमेष्ठिनम् ।
उग्रम्पशुपतिं भीमं भास्करं परमन्तपः‡ ॥
इत्येतल्लक्षणं प्रोक्तं युगानां वै समासतः ।
अतीतानागतानां वै यावन्मन्वन्तरक्षयः ॥
मन्वन्तरेण चैकेन सर्व्वाण्येवान्तराणि वै ।
व्याख्यातानि न सन्देहः कल्पः कल्पेन चैव हि§ ॥
मन्वन्तरेषु चैतेषु अतीतानागतेषु वै ।
तुल्याभिमानिनः सर्व्वे नामरूपैर्भवन्त्युत ॥
एवमुक्तो भगवता किरीटी श्वेतवाहनः ।
बभार परमां भक्तिमीशानेऽव्यभिचारिणीम् ॥
नमश्चकार तमृषिं कृष्णद्वैपायनं प्रभुम् ।
सर्व्वज्ञं सर्व्वकर्त्तारं साक्षाद्विष्णुं व्यवस्थितम् ॥
तमुवाच पुनर्व्यासः पार्थं परपुरञ्जयम् ।
कराभ्यां सुशुभाभ्याञ्च संस्पृश्य प्रणतं मुनिः ॥
धन्योऽस्यनुगृहीतोऽसि¶ त्वादृशोऽन्यो न विद्यते ।
त्रैलोक्ये शङ्करे नूनं भक्तः परपुरञ्जयः ॥

---

* नमस्ये—नमस्करोमि । आर्षमात्मनेपदम् ।

† भूषितमिति B.

‡ तमसः परमिति B and D.

§ कल्पे कल्पे तथैव हि इति G and H.

¶ धन्योऽस्म्यनुगृहीतोऽस्मीति A.

दृष्टवानसि तन्देवं विश्वाक्षं विश्वतोमुखम्।
प्रत्यक्षमेव सर्व्वेषां* रुद्रं सर्व्वजगन्मयम्† ॥
ज्ञानं तदैश्वरं‡ दिव्यं यथावद्विदितं त्वया।
स्वयमेव हृषीकेशः§ प्रीत्योवाच सनातनः ॥
गच्छ गच्छ स्वकं स्थानं न शोकं कर्त्तुमर्हसि।
व्रजस्व परया भक्त्या शरण्यं शरणं शिवम् ॥
एवमुक्त्वा स भगवाननुगृह्यार्ज्जुनं प्रभुः¶।
जगाम शङ्करपुरीं समाराधयितुं भवम्‖ ॥
पाण्डवेयोऽपि** तद्वाक्यात्संप्राप्य शरणं शिवम्।
सन्त्यज्य सर्व्वकर्म्माणि ज्ञात्वा तत्परमोऽभवत्†† ॥
नार्ज्जुनेन समः शम्भोर्भक्त्या भूतो भविष्यति।
मुक्त्वा सत्यवतीसूनुं कृष्णं वा देवकीसुतम् ॥
तस्मै भगवते नित्यं नमः शान्ताय धीमते।

---

* सर्व्वेशमिति B and D.

† सर्व्वजगद्धरमिति B and D.

‡ तच्चैश्वरमिति B and D.

§ हृषीकाणामिन्द्रियाणामीशः जितेन्द्रिय इत्यर्थः, सनातनः चिरजीवी, व्यास इत्यर्थः। अथवा हृषीकेशस्य अवतारत्वाद्व्यासो हृषीकेश इत्युक्तः, तथाच "व्यासो नारायणः स्वयम्" इति। गुडाकेशमिति E, G and H.

¶ प्रतीति E and H.

‖ हरमिति B.

** पाण्डवोऽपि च इति B.

†† तद्भक्तिपरमोऽभवदिति B.

पाराशर्य्याय मुनये व्यासायामिततेजसे ॥
कृष्णद्वैपायनः साक्षाद्विष्णुरेव सनातनः।
को ह्यन्यस्तत्त्वतो रुद्रं वेत्ति तं परमेश्वरम् ॥
नमः कुरुध्वं* तमृषिं कृष्णं सत्यवतीसुतम्।
पाराशर्य्यं महात्मानं योगिनं विष्णुमव्ययम् ॥
एवमुक्ता तु मुनयः सर्व्वे एव समाहिताः।
प्रणेमुस्तं महात्मानं व्यासं सत्यवतीसुतम् ॥

इति श्रीकूर्म्मपुराणे व्यासार्जुनसंवादे युगधर्मे त्रिंशोऽध्यायः।

एकत्रिंशोऽध्यायः।

ऋषय ऊचुः।

प्राप्य वाराणसीन्दिव्यां कृष्णद्वैपायनो मुनिः।
किमकार्षीन्महाबुद्धिः श्रोतुं कौतूहलं हि नः ॥

सूत उवाच।

प्राप्य वाराणसीन्दिव्यामुपस्पृश्य महामुनिः।
पूजयामास जाह्नव्यां देवं विश्वेश्वरं शिवम् ॥

---

* नमामि रुद्रमिति B.

तमागतं मुनिं दृष्ट्वा तत्र ये निवसन्ति च*।
पूजयाञ्चक्रिरे व्यासं मुनयो मुनिपुङ्गवम्॥
पप्रच्छुः प्रणताः सर्व्वे कथां पापप्रणाशिनीम्†।
महादेवाश्रयाम्पुण्यां मोक्षधर्म्मान्सनातनान्॥
स चापि कथयामास सर्व्वज्ञो भगवानृषिः।
माहात्म्यं देवदेवस्य धर्म्यं वेदनिदर्शनात्‡॥
तेषां मध्ये मुनीन्द्राणां व्यासशिष्यो महामुनिः।
पृष्टवाञ्जैमिनिर्व्यासं गूढ़मर्थं सनातनम्॥

जैमिनिरुवाच।

भगवन् संशयञ्चैकं छेत्तुमर्हसि सर्व्ववित्§।
न विद्यते ह्यविदितं भवतः परमर्षिणः॥
केचिद्ध्यानं प्रशंसन्ति धर्म्ममेवापरे जनाः।
अन्ये साङ्ख्यं तथा योगं तपश्चान्ये¶ महर्षयः॥
ब्रह्मचर्य्यमथो नूनमन्ये‖ प्राहुर्म्महर्षयः।
अहिंसां सत्यमप्यन्ये सन्न्यासमपरे विदुः॥
केचिद्दयां प्रशंसन्ति दानमध्ययनं तथा।

---

* वै इति B.

† कथाः पापविनाशिनीरिति B and D.

‡ धर्म्मान्वेदनिदर्शितानिति B and D.

§ तत्त्वविदिति B and D.

¶ तपस्त्वन्ये इति B.

‖ मौनमन्ये इति B.

तीर्थयात्रां तथा केचिदन्ये चेन्द्रियनिग्रहम् ॥
किमेषाञ्च* भवेच्छ्रेयः प्रब्रूहि मुनिपुङ्गव ।
यदि वा विद्यतेऽप्यन्यद्गुह्यं तद्वक्तुमर्हसि ॥
श्रुत्वा स जैमिनेर्वाक्यं कृष्णद्वैपायनो मुनिः ।
प्राह गम्भीरया वाचा प्रणम्य वृषकेतनम् ॥

श्रीभगवानुवाच ।

साधु साधु महाभाग यत्पृष्टं भवता मुने ।
वक्ष्ये गुह्यतमाद्गुह्यं शृण्वन्त्वन्ये महर्षयः ॥
ईश्वरेण पुरा प्रोक्तं ज्ञानमेतत्सनातनम् ।
गूढमप्राज्ञविद्विष्टं सेवितं सूक्ष्मदर्शिभिः ॥
नाश्रद्दधाने दातव्यं नाभक्ते परमेष्ठिनः ।
नावेदविदुषे देयं† ज्ञानानां ज्ञानमुत्तमम् ॥
मेरुशृङ्गे महादेवमीशानं त्रिपुरद्विषम् ।
देवासनगता देवी महादेवमपृच्छत ॥

श्रीदेव्युवाच ।

देव देव महादेव भक्तानामार्त्तिनाशन ।
कथन्त्वां पुरुषो देवमचिरादेव पश्यति ॥
साङ्ख्ययोगस्तपो‡ ध्यानं कर्म्मयोगश्च§ वैदिकः ।

---

* किमेतेषामिति D.

† न वेदविदुषी ज्ञेयमिति E, G and H.

‡ तथा इति B and D.

§ योगोऽथ इति B and D.

40

आयासबहुलान्याहुर्यानि चान्यानि शङ्कर॥
येन विभ्रान्तचित्तानां विज्ञानां योगिनामपि*।
दृश्यो हि भगवान्सूक्ष्मः सर्व्वेषामपि देहिनाम्॥
एतद्गुह्यतमं ज्ञानं गूढं ब्रह्मादिसेवितम्।
हिताय सर्वभक्तानां ब्रूहि कामाङ्गनाशन॥

ईश्वर उवाच।

अवाच्यमेतद्गूढार्थं† ज्ञानमज्ञैर्वहिष्कृतम्।
वक्ष्ये तव यथातत्त्वं यदुक्तं परमर्षिभिः॥
परं गुह्यतमं क्षेत्रं मम वाराणसी पुरी।
सर्वेषामेव भूतानां संसारार्णवतारिणी॥
तस्मिन्‡ भक्ता महादेवि मदीयं व्रतमास्थिताः।
निवसन्ति महात्मानः परं नियममास्थिताः॥
उत्तमं सर्वतीर्थानां स्थानानामुत्तमञ्च यत्§।
ज्ञानानामुत्तमं ज्ञानमविमुक्तं परं मम॥
स्थानान्तरे पवित्राणि तीर्थान्यायतनानि च।
श्मशाने संस्थितान्येव दिवि भूमिगतानि¶ च॥
भूर्लोके नैव संलग्नमन्तरीक्षे ममालयम्।

---

* योगिनां कर्म्मिणामपीति B and D. स्वकर्म्मकर्म्मिणामपीति E, G and H.

† विज्ञानमिति B and D.

‡ तत्र इति B and D.

§ तदिति B.

¶ दिव्येति B and D.

अविमुक्ता न पश्यन्ति मुक्ताः पश्यन्ति चेतसा ॥
श्मशानमेतद्विख्यातमविमुक्तमिति स्मृतम्* ।
कालो भूत्वा जगदिदं संहराम्यत्र सुन्दरि ॥
देवीदं सर्वगुह्यानां स्थानं प्रियतमं मम ।
मद्भक्ता यत्र† गच्छन्ति मामेव प्रविशन्ति ते ॥
दत्तं जप्तं हुतञ्चेष्टं तपस्तप्तं कृतञ्च यत् ।
ध्यानमध्ययनं ज्ञानं सर्वं तत्राक्षयं भवेत् ॥
जन्मान्तरसहस्रेषु यत्पापं पूर्वसञ्चितम् ।
अविमुक्ते प्रविष्टस्य तत्सर्व्वं व्रजति क्षयम् ॥
ब्राह्मणाः क्षत्रिया वैश्याः शूद्रा ये वर्णसङ्कराः ।
स्त्रियोम्लेच्छाश्च ये चान्ये सङ्कीर्णाः‡ पापयोनयः ॥
कीटाः पिपीलिकाश्चैव ये चान्ये मृगपक्षिणः ।
कालेन निधनं प्राप्ता अविमुक्ते वरानने ॥
चन्द्रार्द्धमौलयस्त्र्यक्षा महावृषभवाहनाः ।
शिवे मम पुरे देवि जायन्ते तत्र मानवाः ॥
नाविमुक्ते मृतः कश्चिन्नरकं याति किल्बिषी ।
ईश्वरानुगृहीता हि सर्व्वे यान्ति पराङ्गतिम् ॥
मोक्षं सुदुर्लभं ज्ञात्वा§ संसारञ्चातिभीषणम् ।

---

* श्रुतमिति B and D.

† तत्र इति B, E and H.

‡ सङ्कीर्णाः—अनुलोमप्रतिलोमभ्यां सङ्करजातीया इत्यर्थः ।

§ मत्वा इति B.

अश्मना चरणौ हत्वा वाराणस्यां वसेन्नरः ॥
दुर्लभा तपसोऽवाप्तिर्भूतस्य* परमेश्वरि ।
यत्र तत्र विपन्नस्य गतिः संसारमोचणी ॥
प्रसादाद्दह्यते ह्येनो† मम शैलेन्द्रनन्दिनि ।
अत्राबुधा‡ न पश्यन्ति मम मायाविमोहिताः ॥
अविमुक्तं न पश्यन्ति§ मूढ़ा ये तमसावृताः ।
विण्मूत्ररेतसां मध्ये संविशन्ति पुनः पुनः ॥
हन्यमानोऽपि यो देवि¶ विशेद्विघ्नशतैरपि ।
स याति परमं स्थानं यत्र गत्वा न शोचति ॥
जन्ममृत्युजरामुक्तं परं याति शिवालयम् ।
अपुनर्मरणानां हि सा गतिर्मोक्षकाङ्क्षिणाम् ॥
यां प्राप्य कृतकृत्यः स्यादिति मन्येत पण्डितः‖ ।
न दानैर्न तपोभिश्च न यज्ञैर्नापि विद्यया ॥
प्राप्यते गतिरुत्कृष्टा या विमुक्ते तु लभ्यते ।
नानावर्णा विवर्णाश्च चण्डालाद्या जुगुप्सिताः ॥
किल्बिषैः पूर्णदेहा ये प्रकृष्टैस्तापकैस्तथा** ।

---

* तपसा चापि पूतस्य इति B and D.

† जायते ह्येतदिति B.

‡ अपि बुद्धा इति B. अविद्वांस इति D.

§ सेवन्ते इति B and D.

¶ विद्वानिति B and D. पुमान्देवि विद्वानिति E and H.

‖ मन्यन्ति पण्डिता इति B and D.

** विशिष्टे पातकैरिति D.

भेषजम्परमं तेषामविमुक्तं विदुर्बुधाः ॥
अविमुक्तं परं ज्ञानमविमुक्तं परं पदम् ।
अविमुक्तं परन्तत्त्वमविमुक्तं परं शिवम् ॥
कृत्वा वै नैष्ठिकीन्दीक्षामविमुक्ते वसन्ति ये ।
तेषां तत्परमं ज्ञानं ददाम्यन्ते परं पदम् ॥
प्रयागं नैमिषं* पुण्यं श्रीशैलोऽथ हिमालयः ।
केदारं भद्रकर्णञ्च गया पुष्करमेव च ॥
कुरुक्षेत्रं रुद्रकोटिर्नर्मदा हाटकेश्वरम् ।
शालिग्रामञ्च पुष्पाग्रं वंशं कोकामुखं तथा ॥
प्रभासं विजयेशानं गोकर्णं शङ्कुकर्णकम् ।
एतानि पुण्यस्थानानि त्रैलोक्ये विश्रुतानि च ।
यास्यन्ति परमं† मोक्षं वाराणस्यां यथा मृताः ॥
वाराणस्यां विशेषेण गङ्गा त्रिपथगामिनी ।
प्रविष्टा‡ नाशयेत्पापं जन्मान्तरशतैः कृतम् ॥
अन्यत्र सुलभा गङ्गा श्राद्धं दानं तथा§ जपः ।
व्रतानि सर्व्वमेवैतद्वाराणस्यां सुदुर्लभम् ॥

---

* नैमिषं—In Oude, about 15 miles from Unau station on the Oude and Rohilkhand Railway.

† न यास्यन्ति परमिति B.

‡ प्रवेशादिति B.

§ तपः इति B and D.

यजेत्तु जुहुयान्नित्यं ददात्यर्च्चयतेऽपरान्* ।
वायुभक्षश्च सततं वाराणस्यां स्थितो नरः ॥
यदि पापो यदि शठो यदि चाधार्म्मिको† नरः ।
वाराणसीं समासाद्य पुनाति स कुलत्रयम्‡ ॥
वाराणस्यां महादेवं ये स्तुवन्त्यर्च्चयन्ति च§ ।
सर्व्वपापविनिर्मुक्तास्ते विज्ञेया गणेश्वराः ॥
अन्यत्र योगाज्ज्ञानाद्वा सन्न्यासादथवान्यतः ।
प्राप्यते तत्परं¶ स्थानं सहस्रेणैव जन्मना ॥
ये भक्ता‖ देवदेवेशे वाराणस्यां वसन्ति वै ।
ते विन्दन्ति परं मोक्षमेकेनैव तु जन्मना ॥
यत्र योगस्तथा ज्ञानं मुक्तिरेकेन जन्मना ।
अविमुक्तं समासाद्य नान्यद्गच्छेत्तपोवनम् ॥
यतो मया न मुक्तन्तदविमुक्तमिति स्मृतम् ।
तदेव गुह्यं गुह्यानामेतद्विज्ञाय मुच्यते** ॥
ज्ञानध्याननिविष्टानां†† परमानन्दमिच्छताम् ।

---

* ऽमरानिति B, D, E and H.

† वाधार्म्मिक इति B.

‡ सकलं कुलमिति B.

§ येऽर्च्चयन्ति स्तुवन्ति च इति B.

¶ परममिति B.

‖ भक्त्या इति B and D.

** मेतद्विज्ञानमुच्यते इति B.

†† ज्ञानध्यानाभिनिष्टानामिति B.

या गतिर्विहिता सुभ्रु साविमुक्ते मृतस्य तु ॥*
यानि कान्यविमुक्तानि देवैरुक्तानि नित्यशः।
पुरी वाराणसी तेभ्यः स्थानेभ्योऽप्यधिका शुभा ॥
यत्र साक्षान्महादेवो देहान्तेऽक्षय्यमीश्वरः† ।
व्याचष्टे तारकं ब्रह्म तथैव‡ ह्यविमुक्तकम् ॥
यत्तत्परतरन्तत्त्वमविमुक्तमिति स्मृतम् ।
एकेन जन्मना देवि वाराणस्यां तदाप्यते§ ॥
भ्रूमध्ये नाभिमध्ये च हृदयेऽपि च मूर्द्धनि ।
यथाविमुक्तमादित्ये वाराणस्यां व्यवस्थितम् ॥
वरणायास्तथा ह्यस्या¶ मध्ये वाराणसी पुरी ।
तत्रैव संस्थितन्तत्त्वं नित्यमेवाविमुक्तिकम् ॥
वाराणस्याः परं स्थानं न भूतं न भविष्यति ।
यथा नारायणोदेवो महादेवादिवेश्वरात् ॥
तत्र देवाः सगन्धर्व्वाः सयक्षोरगराक्षसाः ।
उपासते मां सततं देवदेवः पितामहः ॥
महापातकिनोये च ये तेभ्यः पापकृत्तमाः ।
वाराणसीं समासाद्य ते यान्ति परमां गतिम् ॥

---

* योगान्ते विहिता मुक्तिः साविमुक्तमृतस्य तु इति B.

† स्वयमीश्वरः इति B.

‡ तत्रैव इति B.

§ तदाप्नुयादिति B.

¶ चास्या इति B.

तस्मान्मुमुक्षुर्नियतो वसेच्चामरणान्तिकम् ।
वाराणस्यां महादेवि ज्ञानं लब्ध्वा विमुच्यते ॥
किन्तु विघ्ना भविष्यन्ति पापोपहतचेतसाम् ।
ततो नैव चरेत्पापं कायेन मनसा गिरा ॥
एतद्रहस्यं वेदानां पुराणानां द्विजोत्तमाः* ।
अविमुक्ताश्रयं ज्ञानं न कश्चिद्वेत्ति तत्परम्† ॥
देवतानामृषीणाञ्च शृण्वतां परमेष्ठिनाम् ।
देव्यै देवेन कथितं सर्व्वपापविनाशनम्‡ ॥
यथा नारायणः श्रेष्ठो देवानां पुरुषोत्तमः ।
यथेश्वराणां गिरिशः स्थानानाञ्चैतदुत्तमम् ॥
यैः समाराधितो रुद्रः पूर्व्वस्मिन्नेव जन्मनि ।
ते विन्दन्ति परं क्षेत्रमविमुक्तं शिवालयम् ॥
कलिकल्मषसम्भूता येषामुपहता मतिः ।
न तेषां वीक्षितुं§ शक्यं स्थानं तत्परमेष्ठिनः ॥
ये स्मरन्ति सदा कालं विन्दन्ति¶ च पुरीमिमाम् ।
तेषां विनश्यति क्षिप्रमिहामुत्र च पातकम् ॥
यानि चेह प्रकुर्व्वन्ति पातकानि कृतालयाः ।

---

* पुरुषाणाञ्च सुव्रता इति B.

† कश्चिद्वेत्ति तत्त्वत इति B.

‡ प्रणाशनमिति B.

§ वेदितुमिति B and D.

¶ वदन्तीति B and D.

नाशयेत्तानि सर्व्वाणि तेन* कालतनुः शिवः ॥
आगच्छतामिदं स्थानं सेवितुं मोक्षकाङ्क्षिणाम् ।
मृतानां वै† पुनर्जन्म न भूयो भवसागरे ॥
तस्मात्सर्व्वप्रयत्नेन वाराणस्यां वसेन्नरः ।
योगी वाप्यथवायोगी पापी वा पुण्यकृत्तमः ॥
न लोकवचनात्पित्रोर्न चैव गुरुवादतः ।
मतिरुत्क्रमणीया स्यादविमुक्तागतिं प्रति ॥

सूत उवाच ।

एवमुक्त्वाथ‡ भगवान्व्यासो वेदविदां वरः ।
सहैव शिष्यप्रवरैर्वाराणस्याञ्चचार ह ॥

इति श्रीकूर्म्मपुराणे वाराणसीमाहात्म्ये एकत्रिंशोऽध्यायः ।

द्वात्रिंशोऽध्यायः ।

सूत उवाच ।

स शिष्यैः संवृतो धीमान् गुरुर्द्वैपायनो मुनिः ।
जगाम विपुलं* लिङ्गमोङ्कारं मुक्तिदायकम् ॥

---

* देवः इति B and D.

† चेति B.

‡ इत्येवमुक्त्वा इति B.

* विमलमिति B and D.

तत्राभ्यर्च्च्य महादेवं शिष्यैः सह महामुनिः।
प्रोवाच तस्य माहात्म्यं मुनीनां भावितात्मनाम्॥
इदं तद्विमलं लिङ्गमोङ्कारं नाम शोभनम्।
अस्य स्मरणमात्रेण मुच्यते सर्व्वपातकैः॥
अत्र* तत्परमं ज्ञानं पञ्चायतनमुत्तमम्।
अर्च्चितं† मुनिभिर्न्नित्यं वाराणस्यां विमोक्षदम्॥
अत्र साक्षान्महादेवः पञ्चायतनविग्रहः।
रमते‡ भगवान्रुद्रो जन्तूनामपवर्गदः॥
यत्तत्पाशुपतं ज्ञानं पञ्चार्थमिति कथ्यते§।
तदेव विमलं लिङ्गमोङ्कारं समवस्थितम्॥
शान्त्यतीता परा¶ शान्तिर्विद्या चैव यथाक्रमम्।
प्रतिष्ठा च निवृत्तिश्च पञ्चार्थं लिङ्गमैश्वरम्॥
पञ्चानामपि देवानां ब्रह्मादीनां यदाश्रयम्‖।
ओङ्कारबोधितं** लिङ्गं पञ्चायतनमुच्यते††॥

---

* एतदिति B and D.

† सेवितमिति B and D.

‡ वसते इति B.

§ शक्यते इति B.

¶ तथा इति B.

‖ सदाश्रयमिति B and D.

** ओङ्कारबोधकमिति B.

†† मव्ययमिति B.

संस्मरेदीश्वरं लिङ्गं पञ्चायतनमव्ययम्।*
देहान्ते तत्परं ज्योतिरानन्दं विशते पुनः† ॥
अत्र देवर्षयः पूर्व्वं सिद्धा ब्रह्मर्षयस्तथा।
उपास्य देवमीशानं प्राप्तवन्तः परम्पदम् ॥
मत्स्योदर्यास्तटे पुण्यं स्थानं गुह्यतमं शुभम्।
गोचर्म्ममात्रं विप्रेन्द्रा ओङ्कारेश्वरमुत्तमम् ॥
कृत्तिवासेश्वरं लिङ्गं मध्यमेश्वरमुत्तमम्।
विश्वेश्वरं तथोङ्कारं कपर्द्दीश्वरमुत्तमम् ॥
एतानि गुह्यलिङ्गानि वाराणस्यां द्विजोत्तमाः।
न कश्चिदिह जानाति विना शम्भोरनुग्रहात् ॥
एवमुक्का ययौ कृष्णः पाराशर्य्यो महामुनिः।
कृत्तिवासेश्वरं लिङ्गं द्रष्टुं देवस्य शूलिनः ॥
समभ्यर्च्य सदा‡ शिष्यैर्माहात्म्यं कृत्तिवाससः।
कथयामास विप्रेभ्यो भगवान् ब्रह्मवित्तमः ॥
अस्मिन् स्थाने पुरा दैत्यो हस्ती भूत्वा भवान्तिकम्।
ब्राह्मणान् हन्तुमायातो येऽत्र§ नित्यमुपासते ॥
तेषां लिङ्गान्महादेवः प्रादुरासीत्त्रिलोचनः।
रक्षणार्थं द्विजश्रेष्ठा भक्तानां भक्तवत्सलः ॥

---

* एतत्पादद्वयं B पुस्तके नास्ति।

† बुधः इति B.

‡ तथा इति B.

§ येनेति B.

हत्वा गजाकृतिं दैत्यं शूलेनावज्ञया हरः ।
वासस्तस्याकरोत्कृत्तिं कृत्तिवासेश्वरस्ततः ॥
अत्र* सिद्धिम्परां प्राप्ता मुनयो मुनिपुङ्गवाः ।
तेनैव च शरीरेण प्राप्तास्तत्परमम्पदम् ॥
विद्या विद्येश्वरा रुद्राः शिवा ये वः† प्रकीर्त्तिताः ।
कृत्तिवासेश्वरं लिङ्गं नित्यमावृत्य संस्थिताः ॥
ज्ञात्वा कलियुगं घोरमधर्म्मबहुलज्जनाः ।
कृत्तिवासं न मुञ्चन्ति कृतार्थास्ते न संशयः ॥
जन्मान्तरसहस्रेण मोक्षोऽन्यत्राप्यते न वा ।
एकेन जन्मना‡ मोक्षः कृत्तिवासे तु लभ्यते ॥
आलयः सर्व्वसिद्धानामेतत्स्थानं वदन्ति हि ।
गोपितन्देवदेवेन महादेवेन शम्भुना ॥
युगे युगे ह्यत्र दान्ता ब्राह्मणा वेदपारगाः ।
उपासते महादेवं जपन्ति शतरुद्रियम् ॥
स्तुवन्ति सततं देवं महादेवं त्रियम्बकम्§ ।
ध्यायन्तो¶ हृदये नित्यं स्थाणुं सर्वान्तरं‖ शिवम् ॥

---

* तत्र इति B.

† च इति B.

‡ वसता इति E and H.

§ त्र्यम्बकं कृत्तिवाससमिति B.

¶ ध्यायन्तीति B and D.

‖ सर्व्वोत्तरमिति B.

गायन्ति सिद्धाः किल गीतकानि
ये वाराणस्यां निवसन्ति विप्राः* ।
तेषामथैकेन भवेन मुक्तिः
ये कृत्तिवासं शरणं प्रपन्नाः ॥
सम्प्राप्य लोके जगतामभीष्टं
सुदुर्लभं विप्रकुलेषु जन्म ।
ध्यानं† समादाय जपन्ति रुद्रं
ध्यायन्ति चित्ते यतयो महेशम्‡ ॥
आराधयन्ति प्रभुमीशितारं
वाराणसीमध्यगता मुनीन्द्राः ।
यजन्ति यज्ञैरभिसन्धिहीनाः
स्तुवन्ति रुद्रं प्रणमन्ति शम्भुम् ॥
नमो भवायामलभाव§धाम्ने
स्थाणुं प्रपद्ये गिरिशं पुराणम् ।
स्मरामि रुद्रं हृदये निविष्टं
जाने महादेवमनेकरूपम् ॥

इति श्रीकूर्म्मपुराणे वाराणसीमाहात्म्ये द्वात्रिंशोऽध्यायः ।

---

* वाराणसीं ये निवसन्ति विप्राः इति B.

† काले इति B.

‡ ध्यायन्ति ये चित्तगतं महेशमिति E, D and G.

§ योग इति B.

त्रयस्त्रिंशोऽध्यायः ।

सूत उवाच ।

समाभाष्य मुनीन्धीमान्देवदेवस्य शूलिनः ।
जगाम लिङ्गं तद्द्रष्टुं कपर्द्दीश्वरमव्ययम् ॥
स्नात्वा तत्र विधानेन तर्पयित्वा पितॄन्द्विजाः ।
पिशाचमोचने तीर्थे पूजयामास शूलिनम् ॥
तत्राश्चर्य्यमपश्यंस्ते मुनयो गुरुणा सह ।
मेनिरे क्षेत्रमाहात्म्यं प्रणेमुर्गिरिशं हरम् ॥
कश्चिदभ्याजगामेमं शार्द्दूलो घोररूपधृक् ।
मृगीमेकां भक्षयितुं कपर्द्दीश्वरमुत्तमम् ॥
तत्र सा भीतहृदया कृत्वा कृत्वा प्रदक्षिणम् ।
धावमाना सुसम्भ्रान्ता* व्याघ्रस्य वशमागता ॥
तां विदार्य्य नखैस्तीक्ष्णैः शार्द्दूलः सुमहाबलः ।
जगाम चान्यद्विजनं स दृष्ट्वा तान्मुनीश्वरान्† ॥
मृतमात्रा च सा बाला कपर्द्दीशाग्रतो मृगी ।
अदृश्यत महाज्वाला व्योम्नि सूर्य्यसमप्रभा ॥
त्रिनेत्रा नीलकण्ठा च‡ शशाङ्काङ्कितशेखरा§ ।

---

* वारयामास सम्भ्रान्ता इति B.

† देशं दृष्ट्वा मुनीश्वरमिति B and D.

‡ नीलखट्वाङ्गा इति E and H.

§ मूर्द्धजा इति B.

वृषाधिरूढ़ा पुरुषैस्ताद्दशैरेव संयता ॥
पुष्पवृष्टिं विमुञ्चन्ति खेचरास्तस्य मूर्द्धनि।
गणेश्वरः स्वयं भूत्वा न दृष्टस्तत्क्षणात्ततः ॥
दृष्ट्वैतदाश्चर्य्यवरं* जैमिनिप्रमुखास्तदा।
कपर्द्दीश्वरमाहात्म्यं पप्रच्छुर्गुरुमच्युतम् ॥
तेषां प्रोवाच भगवान्देवाग्रे चोपविश्य सः।
कपर्द्दीशस्य माहात्म्यं प्रणम्य वृषभध्वजम् ॥
इदं देवस्य तल्लिङ्गं कपर्द्दीश्वरमुत्तमम्।†
पूजितव्यं प्रयत्नेन स्तोतव्यं वैदिकैः स्तवैः ॥
ध्यायतामत्र नियतं योगिनां शान्तचेतसाम्।
जायते योगसिद्धिश्च‡ षण्मासेन न संशयः ॥
ब्रह्महत्यादिपापानि विनश्यन्त्यस्य पूजनात्।
पिशाचमोचने कुण्डे स्नातस्यात्र समीपतः ॥
अस्मिन् क्षेत्रे पुरा विप्रास्तपस्वी शंसितव्रतः।
शङ्कुकर्ण इति ख्यातः पूजयामास शूलिनम् ॥

---

* तरमिति B.

† अतः परं B पुस्तके

स्मृत्वैवाशेषपापौघं क्षिप्रमस्य विनश्यति।
कामक्रोधादयो दोषा वाराणस्यां निवासिनः।
विप्राः सर्व्वे विनश्यन्ति कपर्द्दीश्वरपूजनात्।
तस्मात्सदैव द्रष्टव्यं कपर्द्दीश्वरमुत्तमम्।

इत्यधिकं दृश्यते।

‡ सिद्धिः सा इति B and D.

जजाप रुद्रमनिशं प्रणवं रुद्ररूपिणम्।
पुष्पधूपादिभिः स्तोत्रैर्नमस्कारैः प्रदक्षिणैः॥
उवास तत्र योगात्मा कृत्वा दीक्षान्तु नैष्ठिकीम्।
कदाचिदागतं प्रेतं पश्यति स्म क्षुधान्वितम्।
अस्थिचर्म्मपिनद्धाङ्गं निःश्वसन्तं मुहुर्मुहुः॥
तं दृष्ट्वा स मुनिश्रेष्ठः कृपया परया युतः।
प्रोवाच को भवान् कस्माद्देशाद्देशमिमङ्गतः॥
तस्मै पिशाचः क्षुधया पीड्यमानोऽब्रवीद्वचः॥
पूर्व्वजन्मन्यहं विप्रो धनधान्यसमन्वितः।
पुत्रपौत्रादिभिर्युक्तः कुटुम्बभरणोत्सुकः॥
न पूजिता मया देवा गावोऽप्यतिथयस्तथा।
न कदाचित्कृतं पुण्यमल्पं वा स्वल्पमेव वा॥
एकदा भगवान्रुद्रो* गोवृषेश्वरवाहनः।
विश्वेश्वरो वाराणस्यां दृष्टः स्पृष्टो नमस्कृतः॥
तदाचिरेण कालेन पञ्चत्वमहमागतः।
न दृष्टं तन्महाघोरं यमस्य वदनं मुने॥
ईदृशीं योनिमापन्नः पैशाचीं क्षुधयार्दितः।
पिपासया परिक्रान्तो† न जानामि हिताहितम्॥
यदि कञ्चित्समुद्धर्त्तुमुपायं पश्यसि प्रभो।
कुरुष्व तं नमस्तुभ्यं त्वामहं शरणं गतः॥

---

* देव इति B.

† पिपासयाधुनाक्रान्त इति B.

इत्युक्तः शङ्कुकर्णोऽथ पिशाचमिदमब्रवीत् ।
त्वादृशो नहि लोकेऽस्मिन्विद्यते पुण्यकृत्तमः ।
यत्त्वया भगवान् पूर्व्वं दृष्टो विश्वेश्वरः शिवः ॥
संस्पृष्टो वन्दितोभूयः कोऽन्यस्त्वत्सदृशो भुवि ।
तेन कर्म्मविपाकेन देशमेतं समागतः ॥
स्नानं कुरुष्व शीघ्रं त्वमस्मिन् कुण्डे समाहितः ।
येनेमां कुत्सितां योनिङ्क्षिप्रमेव प्रहास्यसि ॥

स एवमुक्तो मुनिना पिशाचो
दयावता देववरं विनेत्वम् ।
स्मृत्वा कपर्द्दीश्वरमीशितारं
चक्रे समाधाय मनोऽवगाहम् ॥
तदावगाहान्मुनि*सन्निधाने
ममार दिव्याभरणोपपन्नः ।
अदृश्यतार्कप्रतिमे विमाने
शशाङ्कचिह्नाङ्कितचारुमौलिः ॥
विभाति रुद्रैरुदितो दिविस्थैः
समावृतो योगिभिरप्रमेयैः ।
स बालखिल्यादिभिरेष देवो
यथोदये भानुरशेषदेवः ॥
स्तुवन्ति सिद्धा दिवि देवसङ्घा
नृत्यन्ति दिव्याप्सरसोऽभिरामाः ।

* तदावगाढोमुनि इति B and D. तदावगाह्य इति H.

मुञ्चन्ति वृष्टिं कुसुमालिमिश्रां
गन्धर्व्वविद्याधरकिन्नराद्याः॥
संस्तूयमानोऽथ मुनीन्द्रसङ्घै-
रवाप्य बोधं भगवत्प्रसादात्।
समाविशन्मण्डलमेवमग्र्यं*
त्रयीमयं यत्र विभाति रुद्रः॥
दृष्ट्वा विमुक्तं स पिशाचभूतं
मुनिः प्रहृष्टो मनसा महेशम्।
विचिन्त्य रुद्रङ्कविमेवमग्र्यं
प्रणम्य तुष्टाव कपर्द्दिनं तम्॥

शङ्कुकर्ण उवाच।

नमामि नित्यं† परतः परस्ता-
द्गोप्तारमेकं पुरुषं पुराणम्।
व्रजामि योगेश्वरमीशितार-
मादित्यमग्निं कपिलाधिरूढ़म्॥
त्वां ब्रह्मपारं हृदि सन्निविष्टं
हिरण्मयं योगिनमादिहीनम्‡।
व्रजामि रुद्रं शरणं दिविस्थं

---

* मेतदग्र्यमिति B.

† कपर्द्दिनं त्वामिति B.

‡ भोगिनमादिमन्तमिति A, E and H.

महामुनिं ब्रह्मपरं* पवित्रम् ॥
सहस्रपादाक्षिशिरोऽभियुक्तं
सहस्रबाहुं† तमसः परस्तात् ।
त्वां ब्रह्मपारं प्रणमामि शम्भुं‡
हिरण्यगर्भाधिपतिं त्रिनेत्रम् ॥
यतः प्रसूतिर्जगतो विनाशो
येनाहृतं सर्वमिदं शिवेन ।
तं ब्रह्मपारं भगवन्तमीशं
प्रणम्य नित्यं शरणं प्रपद्ये ॥
अलिङ्गमालोकविहीनरूपं§
स्वयंप्रभुश्चित्प्रतिमैकरुद्रम् ।
तं ब्रह्मपारं परमेश्वरं त्वां
नमस्करिष्ये न यतोऽन्यदस्ति ॥
यं योगिनस्त्यक्तसवीजयोगा-
ल्लब्ध्वा समाधिम्परमात्मभूताः ।
पश्यन्ति देवं प्रणतोऽस्मि नित्यं¶
तद्ब्रह्मपारं भवतः स्वरूपम् ॥

---

* ब्रह्ममयमिति B.

† सहस्ररूपमिति B.

‡ रुद्रमिति B.

§ अलिङ्गमित्यारभ्य स्वयंभुवं त्वां शरणं प्रपद्ये इत्यन्तं G पुस्तके नास्ति ।

¶ अतः परं स्वयम्भुवं त्वां शरणं प्रपद्ये इत्यन्तं B पुस्तके नास्ति ।

न यत्र नामानि* विशेषक्लृप्ति-
र्न संदृशे तिष्ठति यत्स्वरूपम्† ।
तं ब्रह्मपारं प्रणतोऽस्मि नित्यं
स्वयम्भुवं त्वां शरणं प्रपद्ये ॥
यद्वेदवेदाभिरता‡ विदेहं
स ब्रह्मविज्ञानमभेदमेकम् ।
पश्यन्त्यनेकं भवतः स्वरूपं
तद्ब्रह्मपारं प्रणमामि§ नित्यम् ॥
यतः प्रधानं पुरुषः पुराणो
विवर्त्तते यं प्रणमन्ति देवाः¶ ।
नमामि तं ज्योतिषि संनिविष्टं
कालं बृहन्तभवतः स्वरूपम् ॥
व्रजामि नित्यं शरणं महेशं‖
स्थाणुं प्रपद्ये गिरिशं पुराणम् ।
शिवं प्रपद्ये हरमिन्दुमौलिं

---

* मानादीति D. नामादीति E.

† यस्य रूपमिति E.

‡ वेदवेदाभिरताः—वेदानां वेदः ज्ञानं तस्मिन् रताः । ब्रह्मवादाभिरताः इति B. यद्वेदवाक्यादिभिरादिदेवमिति D.

§ प्रणतोऽस्मीति B.

¶ वेदाः इति A, E and H.

‖ गृहेशमिति B. गुहेशमिति D.

पिनाकिनं त्वां शरणं व्रजामि* ॥
स्तुत्वैवं शङ्कुकर्णोसौ भगवन्तङ्कपर्दिनम् ।
पपात दण्डवद्भूमौ प्रोच्चरन्प्रणवं शिवम्† ॥
तत्क्षणात्परमं लिङ्गं प्रादुर्भूतं शिवात्मकम् ।
ज्ञानमानन्दमद्वैतं कोटिकालाग्निसंन्निभम् ॥
शङ्कुकर्णोऽथ स तदा मुनिः सर्वात्मकोऽमलः‡ ।
निलिम्पे§ विमले लिङ्गे तदद्भुतमिवाभवत् ॥
एतद्रहस्यमाख्यातं माहात्म्यं च¶ कपर्दिनः ।
न कश्चिद्वेत्ति तमसा विद्वानप्यत्र मुह्यति ॥
य इमां शृणुयान्नित्यं कथां पापप्रणाशिनीम् ।
भक्तः पापविमुक्तात्मा‖ रुद्रसामीप्यमाप्नुयात् ॥
पठेच्च सततं शुद्धो ब्रह्मपारं महास्तवम् ।
प्रातर्मध्याह्नसमये स योगं प्राप्नुयान्नरः** ॥
इहैव नित्यं वत्स्यामोदेवदेवं कपर्द्दिनम् ।
द्रक्ष्यामः सततं देवं पूजयामस्त्रिलोचनम्†† ॥

---

* नमामीति A.

† परमिति B.

‡ मुक्तात्मा धर्मात्मा सर्वगोऽमलः इति B.

§ निनिन्ये इति B.

¶ वः इति B.

‖ त्यक्तपापविमुक्तात्मा इति B.

** परमिति B.

†† पूजयामोऽथ शूलिनमिति B.

इत्युक्ता भगवान्व्यासः शिष्यैः सह महाद्युतिः* ।
उवास तत्र युक्तात्मा पूजयन्वै कपर्द्दिनम् ॥

इति श्रीकूर्म्मपुराणे वाराणसीमाहात्म्ये चयस्त्रिंशोऽध्यायः।

चतुस्त्रिंशोऽध्यायः ।

सूत उवाच ।

उषित्वा तत्र भगवान् कपर्द्दीशान्तिके पुनः ।
ययौ द्रष्टुं मध्यमेशं* बहुवर्षगणान्प्रभुः ॥
तत्र मन्दाकिनीं पुण्यामृषिसङ्घनिषेविताम् ।
नदीं विमलपानीयां दृष्ट्वा हृष्टोऽभवन्मुनिः ॥
स तामन्वीक्ष्य मुनिभिः सह द्वैपायनः प्रभुः ।
चकार भावपूतात्मा स्नानं स्नानविधानवित् ॥
सन्तर्प्य विधिवद्देवानृषीन् पितृगणांस्तथा† ।

---

* महामुनिरिति B.

---

* मध्यदेशमिति B.

† विविधान्देवानृषीन् पितृगणान् स्वयमिति B. अतः परं B पुस्तके
पूजयामास लोकादिं पुष्पैर्नानाविधैर्भवम् ।
प्रविश्य शिष्यप्रवरैः सार्द्धं सत्यवतीसुतः ॥
इत्यधिकं दृश्यते, तथा D पुस्तकेऽपि ।

मध्यमेश्वरमीशानमर्च्चयामास शूलिनम् ॥
ततः पाशुपताः शान्ता भस्मोद्धूलितविग्रहाः।
द्रष्टुं समागता रुद्रं मध्यमेश्वरमीश्वरम् ॥
ओङ्कारासक्तमनसो वेदाध्ययनतत्पराः।
जटिला मुण्डिताश्चापि शुद्ध*यज्ञोपवीतिनः ॥
कौपीनवसनाः केचिदपरे चाप्यवाससः† ।
ब्रह्मचर्य्यरताः शान्ता दान्ता वै ज्ञानतत्पराः‡ ॥
दृष्ट्वा द्वैपायनं विप्राः शिष्यैः परिवृतं मुनिम्।
पूजयित्वा यथान्यायमिदं वचनमब्रुवन् ॥
कोभवान् कुत आयातः सह शिष्यैर्म्महामुने।
प्रोचुः पैलादयः§ शिष्यास्तानृषीन्धर्म्मभावितान् ॥
अयं सत्यवतीसूनुः कृष्णद्वैपायनः प्रभुः¶ ।
व्यासः स्वयं हृषीकेशो येन वेदाः पृथक्कृताः ॥
यस्य देवो महादेवः साक्षाद्देवः पिनाकधृक्।
अंशांशेनाभवत्पुत्रो नाम्ना शुक इति प्रभुः ॥
यो वै‖ साक्षान्महादेवं सर्व्वभावेन शङ्करम्।

---

* शुक्लेति D, E and H.

† चान्यवाससः इति B.

‡ वेदान्तध्यानतत्पराः इति B. वेदान्तज्ञानतत्परा इति D.

§ शैलादयः इति B.

¶ मुनिरिति B.

‖ स इति B.

प्रपन्नः परया भक्त्या यस्य तज्ज्ञानमैश्वरम् ॥
ततः पाशुपताः सर्वे ते च हृष्टतनूरुहाः* ।
ऊचु†रव्यग्रमनसो व्यासं‡ सत्यवतीसुतम् ॥
भगवन् भवता ज्ञातं विज्ञानं परमेष्ठिनः ।
प्रसादाद्देवदेवस्य यत्तन्माहेश्वरं परम्§ ॥
तद्वदास्माकमव्यग्रं¶ रहस्यं गुह्यमुत्तमम् ।
क्षिप्रं पश्येम तं देवं श्रुत्वा भगवतो मुखात् ॥
विसर्जयित्वा‖ ताञ्छिष्यान् सुमन्तुप्रमुखांस्तदा ।**
प्रोवाच तत्परं ज्ञानं योगिभ्यो†† योगवित्तमः ॥
तत्क्षणादेव विमलं सम्भूतं ज्योतिरुत्तमम् ।
लीनास्तत्रैव ते विप्राः क्षणादन्तरधीयत ॥
ततः शिष्यान् समाहूय‡‡ भगवान् ब्रह्मवित्तमः§§ ।

---

* हृष्टसर्व्वतनूरुहाः इति B.

† नेमुरिति B.

‡ प्रोचुरिति B.

§ पदमिति B.

¶ मव्यक्तमिति B.

‖ समाभाष्य च इति G. विसर्जयित्वा इत्यार्षम् ।

** स्वयम्भूप्रमुखांस्ततः इति B.

†† योगिन इति B.

‡‡ समाहूयेति B.

§§ प्रोवाच तत्परमित्यारभ्य ब्रह्मवित्तम इत्यन्तं E, H पुस्तकयोर्न दृश्यते ।

प्रोवाच मध्यमे शस्यमाहात्म्यं पैलपूर्व्वकान्* ॥
अस्मिन् स्थाने स्वयं देवो देव्या सह महेश्वरः ।
रमते भगवान्नित्यं रुद्रैश्च परिवारितः ॥
अत्र पूर्व्वं हृषीकेशो विश्वात्मा देवकीसुतः ।
उवास वत्सरं कृष्णः सदा पाशुपतैर्वृतः ॥
भस्मोद्धूलितसर्व्वाङ्गो रुद्राराधनतत्परः† ।
आराधयन् हरिः शम्भुं कृत्वा पाशुपतं व्रतम् ॥
तस्य वै‡ बहवः शिष्या ब्रह्मचर्य्यपरायणाः ।
लब्ध्वा तद्वचनात्§ ज्ञानं दृष्टवन्तो महेश्वरम् ॥
तस्य देवो महादेवः प्रत्यक्षं नीललोहितः ।
ददौ कृष्णस्य भगवान्वरदो वरमुत्तमम् ॥
येऽर्च्चयिष्यन्ति गोविन्दं मद्भक्ता विधिपूर्व्वकम् ।
तेषां तदैश्वरं ज्ञानमुत्पत्स्यति¶ जगन्मय ॥
त्वमीशो‖ऽर्च्चयितव्यश्च ध्यातव्यो मत्परैर्जनैः ।
भविष्यसि** न सन्देहो मत्प्रसादाद्द्विजातिभिः†† ॥

---

* शैलपूर्व्वकानिति B.

† रुद्राध्ययनतत्पर इति B.

‡ ते इति B.

§ तद्वदनादिति B.

¶ परस्मैपदमार्षम् ।

‖ नमस्यो इति B.

** भजिष्यन्तीति B.

†† द्विजातयः इति B.

ये च* द्रक्ष्यन्ति देवेशं ध्यात्वा देवं† पिनाकिनम् ।
ब्रह्महत्यादिकं पापं तेषामाशु विनश्यति ॥
प्राणांस्त्यजन्ति ये विप्राः‡ पापकर्म्मरता अपि ।
ते यान्ति परमं§ स्थानं नात्र कार्य्या विचारणा¶ ॥
धन्यास्तथ्यन्तु ते‖ विप्रा मन्दाकिन्यां कृतोदकाः ।
अर्च्चयन्ति महादेवं मध्यमेश्वरमुत्तमम् ॥
स्नानं दानं तपः श्राद्धं पिण्डनिर्व्वपणन्त्विह ।
एकैकशः कृतं विप्राः पुनात्यासप्तमं कुलम् ॥
सन्निहत्यामुपस्पृश्य राहुग्रस्ते दिवाकरे ।
यत्फलं लभते मर्त्त्यस्तस्माद्दशगुणन्त्विह ॥
एवमुक्त्वा महायोगी मध्यमेशान्तिके प्रभुः ।
उवास सुचिरङ्कालं पूजयन्वै महेश्वरम् ॥

इति श्रीकूर्म्मपुराणे वाराणसीमाहात्म्ये चतुस्त्रिंशोऽध्यायः ।

---

* येऽत्र इति B.

† ज्ञात्वा रुद्रमिति B.

‡ मर्त्त्या इति B.

§ तत्परमिति B.

¶ कार्य्यविचारणा इति B.

‖ धन्यास्तु खलु मे इति B.

पञ्चत्रिंशोऽध्यायः ।

सूत उवाच ।

ततः* सर्व्वाणि गुह्यानि तीर्थान्यायतनानि च ।
जगाम भगवान्व्यासो जैमिनिप्रमुखैर्वृतः ॥
प्रयागं परमं तीर्थं प्रयागादधिकं† शुभम् ।
विश्वरूपं तथा तीर्थं कालतीर्थमनुत्तमम् ॥
आकाशाख्यं महातीर्थं तीर्थञ्चैवानुषं‡ परम् ।
स्वर्लीनञ्च महातीर्थं गौरीतीर्थमनुत्तमम्§ ॥
प्राजापत्यं तथा¶ तीर्थं स्वर्गद्वारं‖ तथैव च ।
जम्बुकेश्वरमित्युक्तं चर्म्माख्यं तीर्थमुत्तमम् ॥
गयातीर्थं महातीर्थं तीर्थञ्चैव महानदी ।
नारायणं परं तीर्थं वायुतीर्थमनुत्तमम् ॥**
ज्ञानतीर्थं परं गुह्यं वाराहन्तीर्थमुत्तमम् ।

---

* श्रुत्वा इति B.

† प्रयागादधिकमित्यारभ्य गयातीर्थं महातीर्थमित्यन्तं E H पुस्तकयोर्न दृश्यते ।

‡ चैवार्षभमिति B.

§ केदारं तीर्थमुत्तममिति B.

¶ परमिति B.

‖ स्वर्गतीर्थमिति B.

** अतः परं G पुस्तके विश्वरूपं तथा तीर्थं तालतीर्थमनुत्तममिति अधिकं दृश्यते ।

यमतीर्थं महापुण्यं तीर्थं संवर्त्तकं परम्* ॥
अग्नितीर्थं द्विजश्रेष्ठाः कालकेश्वरमुत्तमम्† ।
नागतीर्थं सोमतीर्थं सूर्य्यतीर्थं तथैव च ॥
पर्व्वताख्यं महापुण्यं‡ मणिकर्णमनुत्तमम् ।
घटोत्कचं तीर्थवरं श्रीतीर्थञ्च पितामहम् ॥
गङ्गातीर्थन्तु देवेशं तथा तत्तीर्थमुत्तमम् ।
कापिलञ्चैव सोमेशं§ ब्रह्मतीर्थमनुत्तमम्¶ ॥||
भूतेश्वरं तथा तीर्थं तीर्थं धर्म्मसमुद्भवम् ।
गन्धर्व्वतीर्थं सुशुभं वाह्नेयन्तीर्थमुत्तमम् ॥
दौर्वासिकं ह्योमतीर्थं** चन्द्रतीर्थं द्विजोत्तमाः ।

---

* शुभमिति B.

† कलसेश्वरमुत्तममिति B and G.

‡ महागुह्यमिति B.

§ देवीशमिति B.

¶ ययातेस्तीर्थमुत्तममिति B and G.

|| अतः परं B पुस्तके

यत्र लिङ्गं पूजनीयं स्नातुं ब्रह्मा यदागतः ।
तदानीं स्थापयामास विष्णुस्तल्लिङ्गमैश्वरम् ॥
ततः स्नात्वा समागत्य ब्रह्मा प्रोवाच तं हरिम् ।
मयानीतमिदं लिङ्गं कस्मात्स्थापितवानसि ॥
तमाह विष्णुस्त्वत्तोऽपि रुद्रे भक्तिर्दृढ़ा यतः ।
तस्मात्प्रतिष्ठितं लिङ्गं नाम्ना तत्र भविष्यति ॥

इत्यधिकं दृश्यते ।

** व्योमतीर्थमिति B, G, E and H.

चित्राङ्गदेश्वरं पुण्यं पुण्यं विद्याधरेश्वरम्॥
केदारं तीर्थमुख्याख्यं कालञ्जर*मनुत्तमम्।
सारस्वतं प्रभासञ्च खेटकर्णं हरं† शुभम्॥
लौकिकाख्यं महातीर्थं तीर्थञ्चैव हिमालयम्।
हिरण्यगर्भं गोप्रख्यं तीर्थञ्चैव वृषध्वजम्॥
उपशान्तं शिवञ्चैव व्याघ्रेश्वरमनुत्तमम्।
त्रिलोचनं महातीर्थं लोलार्कञ्चोत्तराह्वयम्॥
कपालमोचनं तीर्थं ब्रह्महत्याविनाशनम्।
शुक्रेश्वरं‡ महापुण्य§मानन्दपुरमुत्तमम्॥
एवमादीनि तीर्थानि प्राधान्यात्कथितानि तु।
न शक्या विस्तराद्वक्तुं तीर्थसंख्या द्विजोत्तमाः॥
तेषु सर्व्वेषु तीर्थेषु स्नात्वाभ्यर्च्य सनातनम्¶।
उपोष्य तत्र तत्रासौ पाराशर्य्यो महामुनिः।
तर्पयित्वा पितॄन्देवान् कृत्वा पिण्डप्रदानकम्।
जगाम पुनरेवापि यत्र विश्वेश्वरः शिवः॥
स्नात्वाभ्यर्च्य महालिङ्गं‖ शिष्यैः सह महामुनिः।

---

* कालिञ्जरमिति G.

† भद्रकर्णं फलमिति B.

‡ शक्रेश्वरमिति B.

§ महातीर्थमिति B.

¶ पिनाकिनमिति B.

‖ परं लिङ्गमिति B, D, E and H.

उवाच शिष्यान्धर्म्मात्मा यथेष्टं गन्तुमर्हथ ॥
ते प्रणम्य महात्मानं जग्मुः पैलादयो द्विजाः ।
वासञ्च तत्र नियतो वाराणस्यां चकार सः ॥
शान्तो दान्तस्त्रिषवणं स्नात्वाभ्यर्च्य पिनाकिनम् ।
भैक्षाहारी विशुद्धात्मा ब्रह्मचर्य्यपरायणः ॥
कदाचित्तत्र वसता* व्यासेनामिततेजसा ।
भ्रममाणेन भिक्षा वै† नैव लब्धा द्विजोत्तमाः ॥
ततः क्रोधावृततनुर्नराणामिह वासिनाम् ।
विघ्नं सृजामि सर्व्वेषां येन सिद्धिर्हि हीयते ॥
तत्क्षणात्सा महादेवी शङ्करार्द्धशरीरिणी ।
प्रादुरासीत्स्वयं प्रीत्या वेषं कृत्वा तु मानुषम् ॥
भो भो व्यास महाबुद्धे शप्तव्या न त्वया पुरी‡ ।
गृहाण भिक्षां मत्तस्त्वमुक्त्वैवं प्रददौ शिवा ॥
उवाच च महादेवी क्रोधनस्त्वं यतो मुने§ ।
इह क्षेत्रे न वस्तव्यं कृतघ्नोऽसि यतः सदा ॥
एवमुक्तः स भगवान्ध्यात्वा¶ ज्ञात्वा परां शिवाम् ।
उवाच प्रणतो भूत्वा स्तुत्वा च प्रवरैः स्तवैः ॥

---

* कदाचिद्वसता तत्रेति B.

† तु इति B.

‡ भवता नहीति A.

§ भवान्यत इति B and D.

¶ ध्यानादिति B.

चतुर्दश्यामथाष्टम्यां प्रवेशं देहि शङ्करि ।
एवमस्त्वित्यनुज्ञाय देवी चान्तरधीयत ॥
एवं स भगवान्व्यासो महायोगी पुरातनः ।
ज्ञात्वा क्षेत्रगुणान् सर्व्वान् स्थितस्तस्याथ पार्श्वतः* ॥
एवं व्यासं स्थितं ज्ञात्वा क्षेत्रं सेवन्ति† पण्डिताः ।
तस्मात्सर्व्वप्रयत्नेन वाराणस्यां वसेन्नरः ॥

सूत उवाच ।

यः पठेदविमुक्तस्य माहात्म्यं शृणुयादथ‡ ।
श्रावयेद्वा द्विजाञ्छान्तान् स याति परमाङ्गतिम्§ ॥
श्राद्धे वा दैविके कार्य्ये रात्रावहनि वा द्विजाः¶ ।
नदीनां चैव तीरेषु देवतायतनेषु च ॥
स्नात्वा‖ समाहितमनाः कामक्रोधविवर्जितः** ।
जपेदीशं नमस्कृत्य स याति परमाङ्गतिम् ॥

इति श्रीकूर्म्मपुराणे वाराणसीमाहात्म्ये पञ्चत्रिंशोऽध्यायः ।

वाराणसीमाहात्म्यं समाप्तम् ।

---

* अपार्श्वत इति A. पार्श्वभिन्ने देशे इत्यर्थः । अतिपार्श्वत इति E, G and H.

† सेवन्तीति परस्मैपदमार्षम् ।

‡ शृणुयादपीति B.

§ सोऽपि याति परं पदमिति B.

¶ यात्रायां वा द्विजोत्तमा इति E, G and H.

‖ स्नात्वा इति B.

** दम्भमात्सर्य्यवर्जित इति B and D.

षट्त्रिंशोऽध्यायः ।

ऋषय ऊचुः ।

माहात्म्यमविमुक्तस्य यथावत्समुदीरितम् ।
इदानीञ्च* प्रयागस्य माहात्म्यं ब्रूहि सुव्रत† ॥
यानि तीर्थानि तत्रैव विश्रुतानि महान्ति वै ।
इदानीं कथयास्माकं सूत सर्व्वार्थविद्भवान् ॥

सूत उवाच ।

शृणुध्वमृषयः‡ सर्व्वं विस्तरेण ब्रवीमि वः ।
प्रयागस्य च माहात्म्यं यत्र देवः पितामहः ॥
मार्कण्डेयेन कथितं कौन्तेयाय महात्मने ।
यथा युधिष्ठिरायैतत्तद्वक्ष्ये भवतामहम् ॥
निहत्य कौरवान्सर्व्वान्भ्रातृभिः सह पार्थिवः ।
शोकेन महताविष्टो मुमोह स युधिष्ठिरः ॥
अचिरेणाथ कालेन मार्कण्डेयो महातपाः ।
सम्प्राप्तो हास्तिनपुरं राजद्वारे स तिष्ठति ॥
द्वारपालोऽपि तं दृष्ट्वा राज्ञः कथितवान्द्रुतम् ।
मार्कण्डेयो द्रष्टुमिच्छं§स्त्वामास्ते द्वार्य्यसौ मुनिः ॥

---

* इदानीन्तु इति B.

† सत्तम इति B.

‡ शृणुध्वं मुनय इति B.

§ द्रष्टुमिच्छुरिति B.

त्वरितो धर्म्मपुत्रस्तु द्वारमभ्येत्य सत्वरम्* ।
द्वारमभ्यागतस्येह† स्वागतन्ते महामुने ॥
अद्य मे सफलं जन्म अद्य मे तारितं कुलम् ।
अद्य मे पितरस्तुष्टास्त्वयि तुष्टे सदा‡ मुने ॥
सिंहासनमुपस्थाप्य पादशौचार्चनादिभिः ।
युधिष्ठिरो महात्मेति पूजयामास तं मुनिम् ॥
मार्कण्डेयस्तु संपृष्टः§ प्रोवाच स युधिष्ठिरम् ।
किमर्थं मुह्यसे विद्वन् सर्व्वं ज्ञात्वा समागतः¶ ॥
ततो युधिष्ठिरो राजा प्रणम्य शिरसाब्रवीत्‖ ।
कथयस्व** समासेन येन मुच्यामि किल्विषम्†† ॥
निहता बहवो युद्धे पुंसो निरपराधिनः ।
अस्माभिः कौरवैः सार्द्धं प्रसङ्गान्मुनिसत्तम‡‡ ॥
येन हिंसासमुद्भूताज्जन्मान्तरकृतादपि ।

* द्वारमित्याह तत्पर इति B.

† स्वागतं ते महाप्राज्ञ इति B.

‡ महा इति B and D.

§ ततस्तुष्ट इति B.

¶ ज्ञात्वाहमागत इति B and D.

‖ प्रणम्याह महामुनिमिति B.

** कथय त्वमिति B.

†† मुच्येय किल्विषैरिति B and D.

‡‡ पुङ्गव इति B.

मुच्येम* पातकादद्य तद्भवान्वक्तुमर्हति ॥

मार्कण्डेय उवाच।

शृणु राजन्महाभाग यन्मां पृच्छसि भारत।
प्रयागगमनं श्रेष्ठं नराणां पापनाशनम् ॥
तत्र देवो महादेवो रुद्रोऽवात्सीन्नरेश्वर।
समास्ते भगवान् ब्रह्मा स्वयम्भुः सह दैवतैः ॥

युधिष्ठिर उवाच।

भगवाञ्छ्रोतुमिच्छामि प्रयागगमने फलम्।
मृतानां का गतिस्तत्र स्नातानाञ्चैव किम्फलम् ॥
ये वसन्ति प्रयागे तु† ब्रूहि तेषान्तु‡ किम्फलम्।
भवतो विदितं ह्येतत्तन्मे ब्रूहि नमोऽस्तु ते ॥

मार्कण्डेय उवाच।

कथयिष्यामि ते वत्स प्रयागस्नानजं फलम्§।
पुरा महर्षिभिः सम्यक्कथ्यमानं मया श्रुतम् ॥
एतत्प्रजापतेः क्षेत्रन्त्रिषु लोकेषु विश्रुतम्।
अत्र¶ स्नात्वा दिवं यान्ति ये मृतास्तेऽपुनर्भवाः ॥
तत्र‖ ब्रह्मादयो देवा रक्षां कुर्व्वन्ति सङ्गताः।

---

* मुच्यते इति B and D.

† च इति B.

‡ च इति B.

§ या चेष्टा यच्च तत्फलमिति B and D. यच्च ते फलमिति G.

¶ अत्रेत्यारभ्य सार्द्धैकादश श्लोकाः E, G, H पुस्तकेषु न दृश्यन्ते।

‖ अत्रेति B.

बह्वन्यन्यानि तीर्थानि सर्व्वपापापहानि तु ॥
कथितुं नेह शक्नोमि बहुवर्षशतैरपि ।
सङ्क्षेपेण प्रवक्ष्यामि प्रयागस्येह कीर्त्तनम् ॥
षष्टिर्धनुःसहस्राणि तानि रक्षन्ति जाह्नवीम् ।
यमुनां रक्षति सदा सविता सप्तवाहनः ॥
प्रयागे तु विशेषेण स्वयं वसति वासवः ।
मण्डलं रक्षति हरिः सर्व्वदेवैश्च सम्मितम्* ॥
न्यग्रोधं रक्षते नित्यं शूलपाणिर्महेश्वरः ।
स्थानं रक्षन्ति वै देवाः सर्व्वपापहरं शुभम् ॥
स्वकर्म्मणा हता लोका नैव गच्छन्ति तत्पदम् ।
स्वल्पमल्पतरं पापं यस्य चास्ति† नराधिप ॥
प्रयागं स्मरमाणस्य सर्वमायाति सङ्क्षयम् ।
दर्शनात्तस्य तीर्थस्य नामसङ्कीर्त्तनादपि ॥
मृत्तिकालम्भनाद्वापि नरः पापात्प्रमुच्यते ।
पञ्च कुण्डानि राजेन्द्र येषां मध्ये तु जाह्नवी ॥
प्रयागं विशतः पुंसः पापं नश्यति तत्क्षणात् ।
योजनानां सहस्रेषु गङ्गां स्मरति यो‡ नरः ॥
अपि§ दुष्कृतकर्म्मासौ लभते परमाङ्गतिम् ।

---

* सम्मित इति B.

† यदा तस्येति B.

‡ यः स्मरते इति B.

§ अपीत्यारभ्य भवसागरः इत्यन्तं B पुस्तके नास्ति ।

कीर्त्तनान्मुच्यते पापाद्दृष्ट्वा भद्राणि पश्यति ॥
तथोपस्पृश्य राजेन्द्र सुरलोके महीयते ।
व्याधितो यदि वा दीनः क्रुद्धो वापि भवेन्नरः ॥
पितॄणां तारकञ्चैव सर्व्वपापप्रणाशनम् ।
यैः प्रयागे कृतो वास उत्तीर्णो भवसागरः ॥
गङ्गायमुन*मासाद्य त्यजेत्प्राणान्प्रयत्नतः ।†
ईप्सितांल्लभते कामान्वदन्ति मुनिपुङ्गवाः ॥
दीप्तकाञ्चनवर्णाभैर्व्विमानैर्भानुवर्त्तिभिः‡ ।
सर्व्वरत्नमयैर्द्दिव्यैर्नानाध्वजसमाकुलैः ।
वराङ्गनासमाकीर्णैर्मोदते शुभलक्षणः ।
गीतवादित्रनिर्घोषैः प्रसुप्तः प्रतिबुध्यते ॥
यावन्न स्मरते§ जन्म तावत्स्वर्गे महीयते ।
तस्मात्स्वर्गात्परिभ्रष्टः क्षीणकर्म्मा नरोत्तमः ॥¶
हिरण्यरत्नसम्पूर्णे समृद्धे जायते कुले ।
तदेव‖ स्मरते तीर्थं स्मरणात्तत्र गच्छति ॥
देशे वा यदि वारण्ये विदेशे यदि वा गृहे ।

---

* गङ्गायमुनमित्यत्र समाहारद्वन्द्वः ।

† अतः परमेव दीप्तकाञ्चनेति पादद्वयं B G पुस्तकयोर्दृश्यते ।

‡ वर्णिभिरिति B. वह्निभैरिति A.

§ यावन्नागमते इति B. यावन्न लभते इति D.

¶ एतत्पादद्वयं B पुस्तके नास्ति ।

‖ तदेवेत्यारभ्य यदि वा गृहे इत्यन्तं B पुस्तके नास्ति ।

प्रयागं स्मरमाणस्तु यस्तु प्राणान्परित्यजेत्।
ब्रह्मलोक*मवाप्नोति वदन्ति मुनिपुङ्गवाः॥
सर्वकामफला वृक्षा मही यत्र हिरण्मयी।†
ऋषयो मुनयः सिद्धास्तत्र लोके‡ स गच्छति॥
स्त्रीसहस्राकुले रम्ये मन्दाकिन्यास्तटे शुभे।
मोदते मुनिभिः सार्द्धं स्वकृतेनेह§ कर्म्मणा॥
सिद्धचारणगन्धर्वैः पूज्यते देवदानवैः¶।
ततः स्वर्गात्परिभ्रष्टो जम्बुद्वीपपतिर्भवेत्॥
ततः शुभानि कर्म्माणि चिन्तयानः पुनः पुनः।
गुणवान्वित्तसम्पन्नो भवतीत्यनुशुश्रुम‖॥
कर्म्मणा मनसा वाचा सत्ये धर्म्मे प्रतिष्ठितः**।
गङ्गायमुनयोर्म्मध्ये यस्तु ग्रासं†† प्रयच्छति।
सुवर्णमथ मुक्तां वा तथैवान्यत्परिग्रहम्‡‡।

---

* शिवलोकमिति G.

† एतत्पादद्वयं B पुस्तके नास्ति।

‡ सिद्धाः शिवलोके इति E and H.

§ सुकृतेनेहेति B.

¶ दिवि दैवतैरिति B and D.

‖ भवतीह न संशय इति B and D.

** सत्यधर्म्मप्रतिष्ठित इति B and D.

†† ग्रामभिति B. ग्राममिति D.

‡‡ तस्मै वान्यत्प्रतिग्रहमिति G. प्रतिग्रहमिति क्लीवत्वमार्षम्।

स्वकार्य्ये पितृकार्य्ये वा तीर्थे योऽभ्यर्च्चयेन्नरः।
निष्फलं तस्य तत्तीर्थं यावत्तत्फलमश्नुते॥
अतस्तीर्थेन गृह्णीयात्पुण्येष्वायतनेषु च।
निमित्तेषु च सर्व्वेषु अप्रमत्तो द्विजो भवेत्॥
कपिलां पाटलां धेनुं यस्तु कृष्णां प्रयच्छति।
स्वर्णशृङ्गीं* रौप्यखुराञ्चैलकर्णीं पयस्विनीम्॥
तस्या यावन्ति लोमानि सन्ति गात्रेषु सत्तम।
तावद्वर्षसहस्राणि रुद्रलोके महीयते॥

इति श्रीकूर्म्मपुराणे प्रयागमाहात्म्ये षट्त्रिंशोऽध्यायः।

सप्तत्रिंशोऽध्यायः।

मार्कण्डेय उवाच।

कथयिष्यामि ते वत्स तीर्थयात्राविधिक्रमम्।
आर्षेण तु विधानेन यथा दृष्टं यथा श्रुतम्॥
प्रयागतीर्थयात्रार्थी* यः प्रयाति नरः क्वचित्।
बलीवर्द्दं समारूढः† शृणु तस्यापि यत्फलम्॥

---

* स्वर्णशृङ्गामिति B.

---

* प्रयागतीर्थं यात्रार्थीति B.

† बलीवर्द्दसमारूढ़ इति B and D.

नरके वसते घोरे समाः कल्पशतायुतम् ॥
ततो* निवर्त्तितो घोरी गवां क्रोधः सुदारुणः† ।
सलिलञ्च न गृह्णन्ति पितरस्तस्य देहिनः ॥‡
यस्तु पुत्रांस्तथा बालानन्नहीनान्प्रमुञ्चति ।
यथात्मानं तदा सर्व्वं दानं विप्रेषु दापयेत् ॥
ऐश्वर्य्याल्लोभमोहाद्वा गच्छेद्यानेन यो नरः ।
निष्फलं तस्य तत्तीर्थं तस्माद्यानं विवर्ज्जयेत् ॥
गङ्गायमुनयोर्मध्ये यस्तु कन्यां प्रयच्छति ।
आर्षेण तु विधानेन यथा विभवविस्तरम् ।
न स पश्यति तं घोरं नरकन्तेन कर्म्मणा ।
उत्तरान् स कुरून् गत्वा मोदते कालमव्ययम् ॥
वटमूलं समाश्रित्य यस्तु प्राणान्परित्यजेत् ।
स्वर्गलोकानतिक्रम्य रुद्रलोकं स गच्छति ॥
यत्र ब्रह्मादयो देवा दिशश्च सदिगीश्वराः ।
लोकपालाश्च पितरः सर्व्वे ते लोकसंस्थिताः§ ॥
सनत्कुमारप्रमुखास्तथा ब्रह्मर्षयोऽपरे ।
नागाः सुपर्णाः सिद्धाश्च तथा नित्यं समासते ।

---

* यत इति B.

† क्रोधोहि दारुण इति B and D.

‡ अतः परं B पुस्तके पादषट्कं नास्ति ।

§ लोकसम्मता इति B and D.

हरिश्च भगवानास्ते प्रजापतिपुरस्कृतः॥
गङ्गायमुनयोर्मध्यं पृथिव्या जघनं स्मृतम्।
प्रयागं राजशार्दूल त्रिषु लोकेषु विश्रुतम्॥
तत्राभिषेकं यः कुर्य्यात्सङ्गमे शंसितव्रतः।
तुल्यं फलमवाप्नोति राजसूयाश्वमेधयोः॥
न मातृवचनात्तात न लोकवचनादपि।
मतिरुत्क्रमणीया ते प्रयागगमनं प्रति॥
षष्टि*तीर्थसहस्राणि षष्टिकोट्यस्तथापराः।
तेषां सान्निध्यमत्रैव तीर्थानां कुरुनन्दन॥
या गतिर्योगयुक्तस्य सन्न्यस्तस्य मनीषिणः।
सा गतिस्त्यजतः प्राणान् गङ्गायमुनसङ्गमे॥
न ते जीवन्ति लोकेऽस्मिन्यत्र तत्र युधिष्ठिर।
ये प्रयागं न सम्प्राप्तास्त्रिषु लोकेषु वञ्चिताः†॥
एवं दृष्ट्वा तु तत्तीर्थं प्रयागं परमं पदम्।
मुच्यते सर्वपापेभ्यः शशाङ्क इव राहुणा॥
कम्बलाश्वतरौ नागौ यमुनादक्षिणे तटे।
तत्र स्नात्वा च पीत्वा च मुच्यते सर्व्वपातकैः॥
तत्र गत्वा नरः स्नानं‡ महादेवस्य धीमतः।

---

* दशेति B and D.

† विश्रुतमिति B and D.

‡ नवस्थानमिति B. नरः स्थानमिति D.

समस्तांस्तारयेत्* पूर्व्वान् दशातीतान्दशावरान्† ॥
कृत्वाभिषेकन्तु नरः सोऽश्वमेधफलं लभेत्‡ ।
स्वर्गलोकमवाप्नोति यावदाभूतसंप्लवम्§ ॥
पूर्व्वपार्श्वे तु गङ्गायास्त्रैलोक्ये याति मानवः¶ ।
अवटः सर्वसामुद्रः प्रतिष्ठानञ्च विश्रुतम् ॥
ब्रह्मचारी जितक्रोधस्त्रिरात्रं यदि तिष्ठति ।
सर्वपापविशुद्धात्मा सोऽश्वमेधफलं लभेत् ॥
उत्तरेण प्रतिष्ठानं भागीरथ्यास्तु सव्यतः ।
हंसप्रपतनं नाम तीर्थं त्रैलोक्यविश्रुतम् ॥
अश्वमेधफलं तत्र स्मृतमात्रे तु|| जायते ।
यावच्चन्द्रश्च सूर्य्यश्च तावत्स्वर्गे महीयते ॥
उर्वशीपुलिने रम्ये विपुले हंसपाण्डुरे ।
परित्यजति यः प्राणाञ्छृणु तस्यापि यत्फलम् ॥
षष्टिवर्षसहस्राणि षष्टिवर्षशतानि च ।
आस्ते स पितृभिः सार्द्धं स्वर्गलोके नराधिप ॥
अथ सन्ध्यावटे रम्ये ब्रह्मचारी समाहितः ।

---

* आत्मना तारयेदिति B and D.

† अतीतानूर्द्धतनान्, अवरानधस्तनान् ।

‡ परस्मैपदमार्षम् ।

§ आभूतसंप्लवं यावत्प्रलयपर्य्यन्तमित्यर्थः ।

¶ ख्यातिमान्नृप इति B and D.

|| स्मृतमात्रात्तु इति B and D.

नरः शुचिरुपासीत ब्रह्मलोकमवाप्नुयात् ॥
कोटितीर्थं समासाद्य* यस्तु प्राणान् परित्यजेत् ।
कोटिवर्षसहस्राणि स्वर्गलोके महीयते ॥
यत्र गङ्गा महाभागा बहुतीर्थतपोवना† ।
सिद्धं क्षेत्रं हि तज्ज्ञेयं नात्र कार्य्या विचारणा ॥
क्षितौ तारयते मर्त्त्यान्नागांस्तारयतेऽप्यधः ।
दिवि तारयते देवांस्तेन सा त्रिपथा स्मृता ॥
यावदस्थीनि गङ्गायां तिष्ठन्ति पुरुषस्य तु‡ ।
तावद्वर्षसहस्राणि स्वर्गलोके महीयते ॥
तीर्थानां परमं तीर्थं नदीनां परमा नदी ।
मोक्षदा सर्व्वभूतानां महापातकिनामपि ॥
सर्व्वत्र सुलभा गङ्गा त्रिषु स्थानेषु दुर्लभा ।
गङ्गाद्वारे प्रयागे च गङ्गासागरसङ्गमे ॥
सर्व्वेषामेव भूतानां पापोपहतचेतसाम् ।
गतिमन्वेषमाणानां नास्ति गङ्गासमा गतिः ॥
पवित्राणां पवित्रं यन्मङ्गलानाञ्च मङ्गलम् ।
महेश्वरात्परिभ्रष्टा सर्वपापहरा शुभा ॥
कृते तु नैमिषं तीर्थं त्रेतायां पुष्करं वरम्§ ।

---

* समाश्रित्य इति B.

† बहुतीर्थतपोवना — बहूनि तीर्थानि तपोवनानि च यत्र सा ।

‡ हीति B.

§ परमिति B. Pushkara is near Ajmere celebrated to the present day.

द्वापरे तु कुरुक्षेत्रं कलौ गङ्गा विशिष्यते ॥
गङ्गामेव निषेवन्ते प्रयागे तु विशेषतः।
नान्यत्कलियुगे रौद्रे भेषजन्नृप विद्यते* ॥
अकामो वा सकामो वा गङ्गायां यो विपद्यते।
स मृतो जायते स्वर्गे नरकञ्च न पश्यति ॥

इति श्रीकूर्मपुराणे प्रयागमाहात्म्ये सप्तत्रिंशोऽध्यायः।

अष्टात्रिंशोऽध्यायः।

मार्कण्डेय उवाच।

षष्टिस्तीर्थ*सहस्राणि षष्टिस्तीर्थ†शतानि च।
माघमासे गमिष्यन्ति गङ्गायमुनसङ्गमे‡ ॥
गवां शतसहस्रस्य सम्यग्दत्तस्य यत्फलम्।
प्रयागे माघमासे तु त्र्यहं स्नातस्य तत्फलम् ॥
गङ्गायमुनयोर्मध्ये करीषाग्निञ्च साधयेत्§।

---

* नान्यत्कलियुगोद्भूतं मलं हन्तुं सुदुष्करमिति B and D.

---

* षष्टितीर्थेति B.

† षष्टितीर्थेति B.

‡ सङ्गममिति B.

§ कामाग्निं यस्तु धारयेदिति B.

अहीनाङ्गो ह्यरोगश्च पञ्चेन्द्रियसमन्वितः ॥
यावन्ति रोमकूपाणि तस्य गात्रेषु भूमिप ।
तावद्वर्षसहस्राणि स्वर्गलोके महीयते ॥
ततः स्वर्गात्परिभ्रष्टो जम्बूद्वीपपतिर्भवेत् ।*
भुक्त्वा स विपुलान्भोगांस्तत्तीर्थं लभते† पुनः ॥
जलप्रवेशं यः कुर्य्यात्सङ्गमे लोकविश्रुते ।‡
राहुग्रस्तो यथा सोमो विमुक्तः सर्वपातकैः ॥
सोमलोकमवाप्नोति सोमेन सह मोदते ।
षष्टिवर्षसहस्राणि षष्टिवर्षशतानि च ॥
स्वर्गतः शक्रलोकेऽसौ मुनिगन्धर्व्वसेविते ।
ततो भ्रष्टस्तु राजेन्द्र समृद्धे जायते कुले§ ॥
अधःशिरास्तु यो धारामूर्द्ध्वपादः पिबेन्नरः ।¶
शतवर्षसहस्राणि स्वर्गलोके महीयते ॥
तस्माद्भ्रष्टस्तु राजेन्द्र अग्निहोत्री भवेन्नरः ।
भुक्त्वाथ‖ विपुलान्भोगांस्तत्तीर्थं भजते पुनः ॥**

---

* एतत्पादद्वयं B पुस्तके नास्ति ।

† व्रजते इति B.

‡ एतत्पादद्वयं B पुस्तके नास्ति ।

§ पुनरिति B.

¶ एतत्पादद्वयं B पुस्तके न दृश्यते ।

‖ भुक्त्वा तु इति B.

** एष श्लोकः G पुस्तके नास्ति ।

यः शरीरं विकर्त्तित्वा* शकुनिभ्यः प्रयच्छति।
विहङ्गैरुपभुक्तस्य शृणु तस्यापि यत्फलम्॥
शतं वर्षसहस्राणां सोमलोके महीयते।
ततस्तस्मात्परिभ्रष्टो राजा भवति धार्म्मिकः॥
गुणवान्रूपसम्पन्नो विद्वांस्तु प्रियवाक्यवान्†।
भोगान् भुक्त्वाथ दत्त्वा च‡ तत्तीर्थं भजते पुनः॥
उत्तरे यमुनातीरे प्रयागस्य च दक्षिणे।
ऋणप्रमोचनं नाम तीर्थन्तु परमं स्मृतम्॥
एकरात्रोषितः स्नात्वा ऋणात्तत्र§ प्रमुच्यते।
स्वर्गलोक¶मवाप्नोति अनृणश्च सदा भवेत्॥

इति श्रीकूर्म्मपुराणे प्रयागमाहात्म्ये अष्टात्रिंशोऽध्यायः।

---

* विकर्त्तित्वा इति आर्षम्, विकृत्य इति साधु।

† विद्वान् सुप्रियवाक्यवानिति B.

‡ भुक्त्वा तु विपुलान् भोगानिति B.

§ ऋणैस्तत्रेति B. ऋषिदेवपितॄणैरित्यर्थः।

¶ सूर्य्यलोक इति B.

एकोनचत्वारिंशोऽध्यायः।

मार्कण्डेय उवाच।

तपनस्य सुता देवी त्रिषु लोकेषु विश्रुता।
समागता महाभागा यमुना यत्र निम्नगा॥
येनैव निःसृता गङ्गा तेनैव यमुना गता।
योजनानां सहस्रेषु कीर्त्तनात्पापनाशिनी॥
तत्र स्नात्वा च पीत्वा च यमुना यत्र निम्नगा*।
सर्व्वपापविनिर्मुक्तः पुनात्या सप्तमं कुलम्॥
प्राणांस्त्यजति यस्तत्र स याति परमां गतिम्।
अग्नितीर्थमिति ख्यातं यमुनादक्षिणे तटे॥
पश्चिमे धर्म्मराजस्य तीर्थन्त्वनरकं स्मृतम्।
तत्र स्नात्वा दिवं यान्ति ये मृतास्तेऽपुनर्भवाः॥
कृष्णपक्षे चतुर्द्दश्यां स्नात्वा सन्तर्प्य वै शुचिः।
धर्म्मराजं महापापैर्मुच्यते नात्र संशयः॥
दशतीर्थसहस्राणि दश†कोट्यस्तथापराः।
प्रयागसंस्थितानि स्युरेवमाहुर्मनीषिणः॥
तिस्रः कोट्योऽर्द्धकोटिश्च तीर्थानां वायुरब्रवीत्।
दिवि भूम्यन्तरीक्षे च तत्सर्वं जाह्नवी स्मृता॥
यत्र गङ्गा महाभागा स देशस्तत्तपोवनम्।

---

* यमुनायां युधिष्ठिर इति B and D.

† विंशदिति B.

सिद्धक्षेत्रन्तु तज्ज्ञेयं गङ्गातीरं समाश्रितम्* ॥
यत्र देवो महादेवो माधवेन† महेश्वरः।
आस्ते देवेश्वरो‡ नित्यं तत्तीर्थं तत्तपोवनम् ॥
इदं सत्यं द्विजातीनां साधूनामात्मजस्य च।
सुहृदाञ्च जपेत्कर्णे शिष्यस्यानुगतस्य च ॥
इदं धन्यमिदं स्वर्ग्यमिदं मेध्यमिदं शुभम्।
इदं पुण्यमिदं रम्यं पावनं धर्म्ममुत्तमम् ॥
महर्षीणामिदं गुह्यं सर्वपापप्रमोचनम्।
अत्राधीत्य द्विजोऽध्यायं निर्म्मलत्वमवाप्नुयात् ॥
यश्चेदं शृणुयान्नित्यं तीर्थं पुण्यं सदा शुचिः।
जातिस्मरत्वं लभते नाकपृष्ठे च मोदते ॥
प्राप्यन्ते तानि तीर्थानि सद्भिः शिष्टानुदर्शिभिः।
स्नाहि तीर्थेषु कौरव्य मा च वक्रमतिर्भव ॥
एवमुक्त्वा स भगवान्मार्कण्डेयो महामुनिः।
तीर्थानि कथयामास पृथिव्यां यानि कानिचित्§ ॥
भूसमुद्रादिसंस्थानं ग्रहाणां ज्योतिषां स्थितिम्¶।
पृष्टः प्रोवाच सकलमुक्त्वाथ प्रययौ मुनिः ॥

---

* गङ्गातीरसमाश्रितमिति B.

† देव्या सहेति B and D.

‡ वटेश्वर इति B and D.

§ कानि चेति B.

¶ ग्रहाणं ज्योतिषां स्मृतिमिति B. ग्रहाणं ज्योतिषां स्थितिमिति D.

सूत उवाच।

य इदं कल्पमुत्थाय शृणोति पठतेऽथवा।
मुच्यते सर्वपापैस्तु* रुद्रलोकं स गच्छति॥

इति श्रीकूर्म्मपुराणे प्रयागमाहात्म्ये एकोनचत्वारिंशोऽध्यायः।

चत्वारिंशोऽध्यायः।

मुनय ऊचुः।

एवमुक्तास्तु मुनयो नैमिषीया महामुनिम्*।
पप्रच्छुरुत्तरं† सूतं पृथिव्यादिविनिर्णयम्॥‡

ऋषय ऊचुः।

कथितो भवता सर्गः§ मनुः¶ स्वायम्भुवः शुभः‖।
इदानीं श्रोतुमिच्छामस्त्रिलोकस्यास्य मण्डलम्॥

---

* सर्व्वपापेभ्य इति B.

---

* महामतिमिति B.

† उत्तरं सर्गात्परवर्तिनम्, प्रतिसर्गान्तर्गतं पृथिव्यादिविनिर्णयं सूतं पप्रच्छुरित्यर्थः॥

‡ मुनय ऊचुरित्यारभ्य विनिर्णयमित्यन्तं D पुस्तके नास्ति।

§ सूत इति B.

¶ सर्ग इति B.

‖ शुभ इति E and H.

यावन्तः सागर*द्वीपास्तथा वर्षाणि पर्वताः ।
वनानि सरितः सूर्यो ग्रहाणां स्थितिरेव च ॥
यदाधारमिदं सर्व्वं येषां पृथ्वी पुरा त्वियम् ।†
नृपाणां तत्समासेन तत्तद्वक्तु‡मिहार्हसि ॥

सूत उवाच ।

वक्ष्ये देवाधिदेवाय विष्णवे प्रभविष्णवे ।
नमस्कृत्याप्रमेयाय यदुक्तं तेन धीमता ॥
स्वायम्भुवस्यास्य§ मनोः प्रागुक्तो यः प्रियव्रतः ।
पुत्रस्तस्याभवन्पुत्राः प्रजापतिसमा दश ॥
आग्नीध्रश्चाग्निबाहुश्च वपुषान्द्युतिमांस्तथा ।
मेधा मेधातिथिर्हव्यः सवनः पुत्र एव च ।¶
ज्योतिष्मान्दशमस्तेषां महाबलपराक्रमः ।
धार्म्मिको दाननिरतः सर्व्वभूतानुकम्पकः‖ ॥
मेधाग्निबाहुपुत्रास्तु त्रयो योगपरायणाः ।
जातिस्मरा महाभागा न राज्ये दधिरे मतिम् ॥

---

* सागरा इति B and D.

† एतत्पादद्वयं B पुस्तके नास्ति ।

‡ सूत वक्तु इति B.

§ स्वायम्भुवस्य तु इति B.

¶ एष श्लोकः B पुस्तके नास्ति ।

‖ कम्पन इति H.

प्रियव्रतोऽभ्यषिञ्चद्वै सप्तद्वीपेषु सप्त तान्।*
जम्बुद्वीपेश्वरं पुत्रमाग्नीध्रमकरोन्नृपः॥
प्लक्षद्वीपेश्वरश्चैव तेन मेधातिथिः कृतः।
शाल्मलीशं वपुष्मन्तं नरेन्द्रमभिषिक्तवान्॥
ज्योतिष्मन्तं कुशद्वीपे राजानं कृतवान् प्रभुः।
द्युतिमन्तञ्च राजानं क्रौञ्चद्वीपे समादिशत्॥
शाकद्वीपेश्वरञ्चापि हव्यं†चक्रे प्रियव्रतः।
पुष्कराधिपतिञ्चक्रे सवनञ्च प्रजापतिः॥‡
पुष्करेश्वरतश्चापि महावीतः§ सुतोऽभवत्।
धातकिश्चैव द्वावेतौ पुत्रौ पुत्रवतां वरौ॥
महावीतं स्मृतं वर्षं तस्य स्यात्तु महात्मनः।¶
नाम्ना वै‖ धातकेश्चापि धातकीखण्डमुच्यते॥
शाकद्वीपेश्वरस्यापि हव्यस्या**प्यभवन् सुताः।
जलदश्च कुमारश्च सुकुमारो मणीचकः††॥

---

* एतत्पादद्वयं B पुस्तके नास्ति।

† भव्यमिति B and D.

‡ एतत्पादद्वयं E, G, H पुस्तकेषु नास्ति।

§ महीवीत इति B.

¶ एतत्पादद्वयं B पुस्तके नास्ति।

‖ तु इति B.

** भव्यस्या इति B and D.

†† मणीवक इति B and D.

कुशोत्तरोऽथ मोदाकिः सप्तमः* स्यान्महाद्रुमः।†
जलदं जलदस्याथ वर्षं प्रथममुच्यते॥
कुमारस्य तु कौमारं तृतीयं सुकुमारकम्।
मणीचकचतुर्थञ्च पञ्चमञ्च कुशोत्तरम्‡॥
मोदाकं षष्ठ§मित्युक्तं सप्तमन्तु महाद्रुमम्।
क्रौञ्चद्वीपेश्वरस्यापि सुता द्युतिमतोऽभवन्॥
कुशलः प्रथमस्तेषां द्वितीयस्तु मनोहरः।
उष्णस्तृतीयः सम्प्रोक्तश्चतुर्थः पीवरः¶ स्मृतः॥
अन्धकारो मुनिश्चैव दुन्दुभिश्चैव सप्त वै‖।
तेषां स्वनामभिर्देशाः क्रौञ्चद्वीपाश्रयाः शुभाः॥
ज्योतिष्मतः कुशद्वीपे सप्तैवासन्महौजसः।
उद्भिदो वेणुमांश्चैवाश्वरथो लम्बनो धृतिः॥
षष्ठः प्रभाकरश्चापि सप्तमः कपिलः स्मृतः।
स्वनामचिह्नतस्यात्र** तथा वर्षाणि सुव्रताः॥

---

* सप्तम इत्यारभ्य सप्तमन्तु महाद्रुममित्यन्तं G पुस्तके नास्ति।

† एतत्पादद्वयं B पुस्तके नास्ति। सप्तमः स्यादित्यारभ्य महाद्रुममित्यन्तं E, H पुस्तकयोर्न दृश्यते।

‡ पञ्चमं कुसुमोत्तरमिति B.

§ मोदकं षष्ठमिति B.

¶ प्रवर इति B and D.

‖ दुन्दुभिश्चेति सप्तम इति B.

** स्वनामचिह्निता यत्र इति B and D.

ज्ञेयानि च तथान्येषु द्वीपेष्वेवन्नयो मतः* ।
शाल्मलिद्वीपनाथस्य सुताश्चासन्वपुष्मतः ॥†
श्वेतश्च हरितश्चैव जीमूतो रोहितस्तथा ।
वैद्यतो‡ मानसश्चैव सप्तमः सुप्रभो मतः ॥
प्लक्षद्वीपे§श्वरस्यापि सप्त मेधातिथेः सुताः ।
ज्येष्ठः शान्तमय¶स्तेषां शिशिरस्तु सुखोदयः ॥
आनन्दश्च शिवश्चैव‖ क्षेमकश्च ध्रुवस्तथा ।
प्लक्षद्वीपादिके ज्ञेया** शाकद्वीपान्तिकेषु च ॥
वर्णानाञ्च†† विभागेन स्वधर्म्मो मुक्तये मतः‡‡ ।
जम्बुद्वीपेश्वरस्यापि पुत्राश्चासन्महाबलाः ॥
आग्नीध्रस्य द्विजश्रेष्ठास्तन्नामानि निबोधत ।
नाभिः किम्पुरुषश्चैव तथा हरिरिलावृतः ॥
रम्यो हिरण्वांश्च कुरुर्भद्राश्वः केतुमालकः ।

---

* द्वीपेष्वेतानि नामत इति B and D.

† एतत्पाददयं B पुस्तके नास्ति ।

‡ वैद्युत इति B. विद्युत इति E, G and H.

§ कुशद्वीपेति E and H.

¶ शान्तभय इति E and H.

‖ आनन्दश्चामरश्चैव इति B.

** सप्तद्वीपादिषु शेष इति B.

†† वर्णाश्रम इति B and D.

‡‡ द्विजा इति B.

जम्बुद्वीपेश्वरो राजा स चाग्नीध्रो महामतिः* ॥
विभज्य नवधा तेभ्यो यथान्यायं ददौ पुनः।
नाभेस्तु दक्षिणे वर्षे† हिमाह्वं प्रददौ पिता ॥
हेमकूटन्ततो वर्षन्ददौ किम्पुरुषाय सः।
तृतीयं नैषधं वर्षं हरये दत्तवान् पिता ॥
इलावृताय प्रददौ मेरुमध्यमिलावृतम्।
नीलाद्रेराश्रितं‡ वर्षं रम्याय प्रददौ पिता ॥
श्वेतं यदुत्तरं वर्षं पित्रा दत्तं हिरण्वते।
यदुत्तरं शृङ्गवतो वर्षं तत्कुरवे ददौ ॥
मेरोः पूर्वेण यद्वर्षं भद्राश्वाय न्यवेदयत्।
गन्धमादनवर्षन्तु केतुमालाय दत्तवान् ॥
वर्षेष्वेतेषु तान्पुत्रानभ्यषिञ्चन्नराधिपः§।
संसारासारतां¶ ज्ञात्वा तपस्तप्तुं वनङ्गतः ॥
हिमाह्वयन्तु यद्वर्षं‖ नाभेरासीन्महात्मनः।
तस्यर्षभोऽभवत्पुत्रो मरुदेव्यां महाद्युतिः ॥
ऋषभाद्भरतो जज्ञे वीरः** पुत्रशताग्रजः ॥

---

* महामुनिरिति E and H.

† दक्षिणं वर्षमिति B.

‡ नीलाचलाश्रयमिति B and D.

§ अभिषिच्य नराधिप इति B.

¶ संसारकष्टतामिति B and D.

‖ यस्यैतदिति B.

** धीर इति B.

सोऽभिषिच्यर्षभः पुत्रं भरतं पृथिवीपतिः ।
वानप्रस्थाश्रमं गत्वा तपस्तेपे यथाविधि ॥
तपसा धर्षितो*ऽत्यर्थं कृशोऽयमनिशन्ततः† ।
ज्ञानयोगरतो भूत्वा महापाशुपतोऽभवत् ॥
सुमतिर्भरतस्यापि‡ पुत्रः परमधार्म्मिकः ॥
सुमतेस्तैजसस्तस्मादिन्द्रद्युम्नो महाद्युतिः ।
परमेष्ठी सुतस्तस्मात्प्रतीहारस्तदन्वयः ॥
प्रतिहर्त्तेति विख्यात उत्पन्नस्तस्य चात्मजः ।
भवस्तस्मादथोद्गीथः प्रस्तावस्तत्सुतोऽभवत् ॥
पृथुस्ततस्ततो नक्तो नक्तस्यापि गयः स्मृतः§ ।
नरो गयस्य तनयस्तस्य भूयो¶ विराडभूत् ॥
तस्य पुत्रो महावीर्य्यो धीमांस्तस्मादजायत ।
धीमतोऽपि ततश्चाभूद्भौवण‖स्तत्सुतोऽभवत् ॥
त्वष्टा त्वष्टुश्च विरजो रजस्तस्मादभूत्सुतः ।
शतजिद्रथजित्तस्य जज्ञे पुत्रशतं द्विजाः ॥
तेषां प्रधानो बलवान्विश्वज्योतिरिति स्मृतः ।

---

* कर्षित इति B and D.

† धमनिसन्तत इति B and D.

‡ भरतस्याभूदिति B.

§ सुत इति B.

¶ पुत्र इति B.

‖ भौवन इति B.

आराध्य देवं ब्रह्माणं क्षेमकं नाम पार्थिवम् ।
असूत पुत्रं धर्म्मज्ञं महाबाहुमरिन्दमम् ॥
एते पुरस्ताद्राजानो महासत्त्वा महौजसः ।
एषां वंशप्रसूतैस्तु* भुक्तेयं पृथिवी पुरा ॥

इति श्रीकूर्म्मपुराणे भुवनविन्यासे चत्वारिंशोऽध्यायः ।

—○:○—

एकचत्वारिंशोऽध्यायः ।

सूत उवाच ।

अतः परं प्रवक्ष्यामि संक्षेपेण द्विजोत्तमाः ।
त्रैलोक्यस्यास्य मानं वो न शक्यं विस्तरेण तु ॥
भूर्लोकोऽथ भुवर्लोकः स्वर्लोकोऽथ महस्तथा ।
जनस्तपश्च सत्यञ्च लोकास्त्वण्डोद्भवास्तथा* ॥
सूर्य्याचन्द्रमसौ यावत्किरणैरेव भासतः ।†
तावद्भूर्लोक आख्यातः पुराणे द्विजपुङ्गवाः ॥‡

---

* प्रसूतैश्च इति B.

---

* मता इति B.

† एतत्पादद्वयं B पुस्तके नास्ति ।

‡ एतत्पादद्वयं E, G, H पुस्तकेषु नास्ति ।

यावत्प्रमाणो भूर्लोको विस्तरात्परिमण्डलात्।
भुवर्लोकोऽपि तावत्स्यान्मण्डलाद्भास्करस्य तु॥
ऊर्द्ध्वं यन्मण्डलं व्योम्नि ध्रुवो यावद्व्यवस्थितः।
स्वर्गलोकः* समाख्यातस्तत्र वायोस्तु नेमयः॥
आवहः प्रवहश्चैव तत्रैवानुवहः पुनः†।
संवहो विवहश्चैव‡ तदूर्द्ध्वं स्यात्परावहः॥
तथा परिवहश्चैव§ वायोर्वै सप्तनेमयः।
भूमेर्योजनलक्षे तु भानोर्वै मण्डलं स्थितम्॥
लक्षे दिवाकरस्यापि मण्डलं शशिनः स्मृतम्।
नक्षत्रमण्डलं कृत्स्नं तल्लक्षेण प्रकाशते॥
द्विलक्षे ह्यन्तरे¶ विप्रा बुधो नक्षत्रमण्डलात्‖।
तावत्प्रमाणभागे तु बुधस्याप्युशना स्थितः॥
अङ्गारकोऽपि शुक्रस्य तत्प्रमाणे व्यवस्थितः।
लक्षद्वयेन भौमस्य स्थितो देवपुरोहितः॥
सौरिर्द्विलक्षेण गुरोर्ग्रहाणामथ मण्डलात्।
सप्तर्षिमण्डलं तस्माल्लक्षमात्रे प्रकाशते॥

---

* सुरलोक इति D.

† पर इति B.

‡ विवहश्चाथ इति B.

§ परिवहश्चोर्द्धमिति B.

¶ द्वे लक्षेऽप्युत्तरे इति B, D, E and H.

‖ बुधोनक्षत्र इत्यारभ्य गुरोरित्यन्तं B, D पुस्तकयोर्नास्ति।

ऋषीणाम्मण्डलादूर्द्ध्वं लक्षमात्रे स्थितो ध्रुवः*।
तत्र धर्मः स भगवान्विष्णुर्नारायणः स्थितः ॥
नवयोजनसाहस्रो विष्कम्भः† सवितुः स्मृतः।
त्रिगुणस्तस्य विस्तारो मण्डलस्य प्रमाणतः ॥
द्विगुणः सूर्य‡विस्ताराद्विस्तारः शशिनः स्मृतः।
तुल्यस्तयोस्तु स्वर्भानुर्भूत्वा तानुपसर्पति§ ॥
उद्धृत्य पृथिवीच्छायां निर्म्मितोमण्डलाकृतिः।
स्वर्भानोस्तु बृहत्स्थानं तृतीयं यत्तमोमयम् ॥
चन्द्रस्य षोड़शो भागोभार्गवस्य विधीयते।
भार्गवात्पादहीनस्तु विज्ञेयो वै बृहस्पतिः ॥
बृहस्पतेः पादहीनौ भौमसौरावुभौ स्मृतौ।¶
विस्ताराम्मण्डलाच्चैव पादहीनस्तयोर्बुधः ॥‖
तारानक्षत्ररूपाणि वपुष्मन्तीह यानि वै।
बुधेन तानि तुल्यानि विस्ताराम्मण्डलात्तथा ॥
तारानक्षत्ररूपाणि हीनानि तु परस्परम्।
शतानि पञ्चचत्वारि त्रीणि द्वे चैव योजने ॥

---

* मेधीभूतसमस्तस्य ज्योतिश्चक्रस्य वै ध्रुव इत्यधिकं B पुस्तके दृश्यते। मेचीभूत-इति D, E, H पुस्तकेषु दृश्यते। मेचीभूतः मेधीभूतो वा केन्द्रीभूत इत्यर्थः।

† विष्कम्भ Means a diameter.

‡ तस्य इति B.

§ भूत्वाधस्तात्प्रसर्पतीति B and D.

¶ एतत्पादद्वयं B पुस्तके नास्ति।

‖ एतत्पादद्वयं E, G, H पुस्तकेषु नास्ति।

पूर्वापरानुकृष्टानि तारकामण्डलानि तु ।
योजनाद्यर्द्धमात्राणि तेभ्योह्रस्वं न विद्यते ॥
उपरिष्टात्त्रयस्तेषां* ग्रहा वै दूरसर्पिणः ।
सौरोऽङ्गिराश्च वक्रश्च ज्ञेयोमन्दविचारणः† ॥
तेभ्योऽधस्ताच्च चत्वारः पुनरन्ये महाग्रहाः ।
सूर्य्यः सोमोबुधश्चैव भार्गवश्चैव शीघ्रगाः‡ ॥
दक्षिणायनमार्गस्थो यदा चरति रश्मिमान् ।
तदा पूर्वग्रहाणां वै सूर्य्योऽधस्तात्प्रसर्पति ॥
विस्तीर्णं मण्डलं कृत्वा तस्योर्द्धं चरते शशी ।
नक्षत्रमण्डलं कृत्स्नं सोमादूर्द्धं प्रसर्पति ॥
नक्षत्रेभ्यो बुधश्चोर्द्धं बुधादूर्द्धं तु भार्गवः ।
वक्रस्तु§ भार्गवादूर्द्धं वक्रादूर्द्धं बृहस्पतिः ॥
तस्माच्छनैश्चरोऽप्यूर्द्धन्तस्मात्सप्तर्षिमण्डलम् ।
ऋषीणाञ्चैव सप्तानां ध्रुवश्चोर्द्धं व्यवस्थितः ॥
योजनानां सहस्राणि भास्करस्य रथो नव ।
ईषादण्डस्तथा तस्य¶ द्विगुणो द्विजसत्तमाः ॥
सार्द्धकोटिस्तथा सप्त नियुतान्यधिकानि तु ।

---

* उपरिष्टाच्च तेषां ये इति E, G and H.

† ज्ञेया मन्दविचारिण इति B. एतत्पादद्वयं G पुस्तके नास्ति ।

‡ शुक्रः शीघ्रगादक्षिणायने इति E, G and H.

§ शनिस्तु इति G.

¶ तथैव स्यादिति B.

योजनानान्तु तस्याचस्तत्र चक्रं प्रतिष्ठितम् ॥
त्रिनाभिमति* पञ्चारे षण्णेमिन्यक्षयात्मके ।†
संवत्सरमयं कृत्स्नं कालचक्रं प्रतिष्ठितम् ॥
चत्वारिंशत्सहस्राणि द्वितीयाक्षो‡ व्यवस्थितः§ ।
पञ्चाशयानि¶ सार्द्धानि योजनानि द्विजोत्तमाः ॥
अक्षप्रमाणमुभयोः प्रमाणं तद्युगार्द्धयोः‖ ।
ह्रस्वोऽक्षस्तद्युगार्द्धेन** ध्रुवाधारो रथस्य तु†† ॥
द्वितीयेऽक्षे तु तच्चक्रं संस्थितं मानसाचले ।
हयाश्च सप्त छन्दांसि तन्नामानि निबोधत ॥
गायत्री च बृहत्युष्णिक् जगती पंक्तिरेव च ।
अनुष्टुब्त्रिष्टुबप्युक्ता छन्दांसि हयो हरेः‡‡ ॥
मानसोपरि माहेन्द्री प्राच्यां दिशि महापुरी ।

---

* त्रिनाभिमति इति D.

† एतत्पादद्वयं B पुस्तके नास्ति ।

‡ द्वितीयोऽपि विवस्वत इति D.

§ विवस्वत इति B.

¶ पञ्चान्यानि तु सार्द्धानि स्यन्दनस्य द्विजोत्तमाः ।
लक्षप्रमाणमुभयोः प्रमाणं तद्युगार्द्धयोरिति D.

‖ तत्परार्द्धयोरिति B.

** भूयोऽचस्तद्युगार्द्धे तु इति D.

†† वै इति B.

‡‡ रवेरिति B.

दक्षिणायां* यमस्याथ वरुणस्य तु पश्चिमे ॥
उत्तरेषु† च सोमस्य तन्नामानि निबोधत।
अमरावती संयमनी‡ सुखा चैव विभावरी ॥
काष्ठागतोदक्षिणतः क्षिप्तेषुरिव सर्पति।
ज्योतिषां चक्रमादाय देवदेवः पितामहः ॥
दिवसस्य रविर्मध्ये सर्वकालं व्यवस्थितः।
सर्पद्वीपेषु विप्रेन्द्रा निशार्द्धस्य च सम्मुखः ॥
उदयास्तमने चैव सर्वकालं तु सम्मुखे।
दिशास्वशेषासु तथा विप्रेन्द्रा विदिशासु च ॥
कुलालचक्रपर्यन्तं भ्रमत्येष यथेश्वरः।
करोत्येष यथा¶ रात्रिं विमुञ्चन्मेदिनीन्द्विजाः ॥
दिवाकरकरैरेतत्पूरितं भुवनत्रयम्।
त्रैलोक्यं कथितं सद्भिर्लोकानां मुनिपुङ्गवाः ॥
आदित्यमूलमखिलं त्रैलोक्यं नात्र संशयः।
भवत्यस्माज्जगत्सर्वं‖ सदेवासुरमानुषम्।
रुद्रेन्द्रोपेन्द्रचन्द्राणां विप्रेन्द्राणां दिवौकसाम्।
द्युतिमान्द्युतिमत्कृत्स्नमजयत्सार्वलौकिकम्** ॥

---

* दक्षिणेन इति B.

† उत्तरेण तु इति B.

‡ अत्र नवाक्षरः पादः।

¶ करोत्यहस्तथा इति B.

‖ कृत्स्नमिति B.

** द्युतिर्द्युतिमतां कृत्स्नं यत्तेज इति B and D.

सर्वात्मा सर्वलोकेशो महादेवः प्रजापतिः।
सूर्य एष तु लोकस्य* मूलं परमदैवतम्॥
द्वादशान्ये तथादित्या देवास्ते येऽधिकारिणः।
निर्वहन्ति वदन्त्यस्य† तदंशा विष्णुमूर्त्तयः॥

सर्वे नमस्यन्ति सहस्रबाहुं
गन्धर्वयक्षोरगकिन्नराद्याः।
यजन्ति यज्ञैर्विविधैर्मुनीन्द्राः‡
छन्दोमयं ब्रह्ममयं पुराणम्।

इति श्रीकूर्म्मपुराणे ज्योतिषां सन्निवेशे एकचत्वारिंशोऽध्यायः।

द्वाचत्वारिंशोऽध्यायः।

सूत उवाच।

सरथोऽधिष्ठितो देवैरादित्यैर्मुनिभि*स्तथा।
गन्धर्वैरप्सरोभिश्च ग्रामणीसर्पराक्षसैः॥

---

* त्रिलोकस्य इति B and D.

† पदं तस्य इति D.

‡ द्विजेन्द्रा इति B.

---

* वसुभिरिति B.

धातार्यमा च* मित्रश्च वरुणः शक्र एव च।
विवस्वानथ पूषा च पर्ज्जन्यश्चांशुरेव च† ॥
भगस्त्वष्टा च विष्णुश्च द्वादशैते दिवाकराः।
आप्याययति वै भानुर्वसन्तादिषु वै क्रमात् ॥
पुलस्त्यः पुलहश्चात्रिर्वसिष्ठश्चाङ्गिरा भृगुः।
भरद्वाजो गौतमश्च कश्यपः क्रतुरेव च ॥
जमदग्निः कौशिकश्च मुनयो ब्रह्मवादिनः।
स्तुवन्ति देवं विविधैश्छन्दोभिस्ते यथाक्रमम् ॥
रथकृच्च रथौजाश्च रथचित्रः सुबाहुकः।
रथस्वनोऽथ वरुणः सुषेणः सेनजित्तथा ॥
तार्क्ष्यश्चारिष्टनेमिश्च क्रतजित्‡ सत्यजित्तथा।
ग्रामण्यो देवदेवस्य कुर्व्वतेऽभीशुसंग्रहम् ॥
अथ हेतिः प्रहेतिश्च पौरुषेयो वधस्तथा।
सर्पोव्याघ्रस्तथा पश्च वातोविद्युद्दिवाकरः ॥
ब्रह्मोपेतश्च विप्रेन्द्रा यज्ञोपेतस्तथैव च।
राक्षसप्रवरा ह्येते प्रयान्ति पुरतः क्रमात् ॥
वासुकिः कङ्कनीलश्च§ तक्षकः सर्पपुङ्गवः।

---

* धातार्यमाथ इति B.

† पर्य्यन्यश्चांश्च एव चेति B and D.

‡ रथजिदिति B.

§ कङ्कीनरश्चेति B and D.

एलापत्रः* शङ्खपालस्तथैरावतसंज्ञितः ॥
धनञ्जयो महापद्मस्तथा कर्कोटकोद्विजाः।
कम्बलो†ऽश्वतरश्चैव वहन्त्येनं यथाक्रमम् ॥
तुम्बुरुर्नारदो हाहा हूहूर्विश्वावसुस्तथा।
उग्रसेनोऽथ सुरुचिरर्वावसुस्तथापरः ॥
चित्रसेनस्तथोर्णायुर्धृतराष्ट्रो द्विजोत्तमाः।
सूर्य्यवर्चा द्वादशैते गन्धर्व्वा गायना वराः‡ ॥
गायन्ति गानैर्विविधैर्भानुं षड्जादिभिः§ क्रमात्।
ऋतुस्थलाप्सरोवर्य्या¶ तथान्या पुञ्जिकस्थला ॥
मेनका सहजन्या च प्रम्लोचा च द्विजोत्तमाः।
अनुम्लोचा च विश्वाची घृताची‖ चोर्वशी तथा ॥
अन्या च पूर्व्वचित्तिः स्याद्रम्भाचैव तिलोत्तमा।
ताण्डवैर्विविधैरेनं वसन्तादिषु वै क्रमात् ॥
तोषयन्ति महादेवं भानुमात्मानमव्ययम् ॥
एवं देवा वसन्त्यर्कें द्वौ द्वौ मासौ क्रमेण तु।
सूर्य्यमाप्याययन्त्येते तेजसा तेजसां निधिम् ॥

---

* एलपत्र इति E and H.

† कलम्ब इति B.

‡ गायतां वरा इति B and D.

§ विविधैर्गानैर्भानुं षड्जर्षभैरिति B. षड्धातुषु क्रमादिति D.

¶ क्रतस्थला इति D. क्रतुस्थला इति E and H.

‖ घृताची च विश्वाचीति B.

ग्रथितैस्तैर्वचोभिस्तु स्तुवन्ति मुनयो रविम् ।
गन्धर्व्वाप्सरसश्चैनं नृत्यगेयैरुपासते ॥
ग्रामणीयक्षभूतानि कुर्व्वतेऽभीशुसंग्रहम् ।
सर्पा वहन्ति देवेशं यातुधानाः प्रयान्ति च* ॥
वालखिल्या नयन्त्यस्तं परिवार्य्योदयाद्रविम् ।
एते तपन्ति वर्षन्ति भान्ति वान्ति सृजन्ति तु† ॥
भूतानामशुभं कर्म्म व्यपोहन्तीति कीर्त्तिताः ।
एते सहैव सूर्य्येण भ्रमन्ति दिवि भानुगाः‡ ॥
विमाने च स्थिता नित्यं कामगे वातरंहसि ।
वर्षन्तश्च तपन्तश्च ह्लादयन्तश्च वै क्रमात्§ ।
गोपायन्तीह भूतानि सर्व्वाणीह युगक्रमात्¶ ॥
एतेषामेव देवानां यथावीर्य्यं यथातपः ।
यथायोगं यथासत्वं स एष तपति प्रभुः ॥
अहोरात्रव्यवस्थानकारणं स प्रजापतिः ।
पितृदेव‖मनुष्यादीन्स सदाप्याययद्रविः** ॥

---

* वै इति B.

† च इति B.

‡ सानुषु इति B. सानुगा इति D.

§ प्रजाः इति B.

¶ युगचयादिति B.

‖ पितृदेव इत्यारभ्य परमेष्ठी प्रजापतिरित्यन्तं G पुस्तके नास्ति। एतदपि E, H पुस्तकयोर्न दृश्यते ।

** प्यायते रविरिति B.

तत्र देवी महादेवो भास्वान्साक्षान्महेश्वरः ।
भासते वेदविदुषां नीलग्रीवः सनातनः ॥
स एष देवो भगवान्परमेष्ठी प्रजापतिः ॥
स्थानं तद्विदुरादित्ये वेदज्ञा वेदविग्रहम्* ॥

इति श्रीकूर्म्मपुराणे द्विचत्वारिंशोऽध्यायः ।

—०:०—

त्रिचत्वारिंशोऽध्यायः ।

सूत उवाच ।

एवमेष महादेवो देवदेवः पितामहः ।
करोति नियतं कालं कालात्मा ह्यैश्वरी तनुः ॥
तस्य ये रश्मयो विप्राः सप्त*लोकप्रदीपकाः ।
तेषां श्रेष्ठाः पुनः† सप्तरश्मयो गृहमेधिनः‡ ॥
सुषुम्नो हरिकेशश्च विश्वकर्म्मा तथैव च ।§
विश्वश्रवाः पुनश्चान्यः संयद्वसुरतः परः ॥

---

* वेदविग्रहाः इति B.

---

* सर्व्व इति B.

† पुनश्चण्ड इति D.

‡ ग्रहयोनयः इति B and D.

§ अतः परवर्त्ती श्लोकः B पुस्तके नास्ति ।

अर्व्वावसुरिति ख्यातः स्वरकः सप्त कीर्त्तिताः ।
सुषुम्नः सूर्य्यरश्मिस्तु पुष्णाति शिशिरद्युतिम् ॥
तिर्य्यगूर्द्धप्रचारोऽसौ सुषुम्नः परिपठ्यते* ।
हरिकेशस्तु यः प्रोक्तो रश्मिर्नक्षत्रपोषकः ॥
विश्वकर्म्मा तथा रश्मिर्बुधं पुष्णाति सर्व्वदा ।
विश्वश्रवास्तु† यो रश्मिः शुक्रं पुष्णाति नित्यदा ॥
संयद्वसुरिति ख्यातो यः पुष्णाति स लोहितम् ।
बृहस्पतिं प्रपुष्णाति‡ रश्मिरर्व्वावसुः प्रभुः ॥
शनैश्चरं प्रपुष्णाति सप्तमस्तु स्वरस्तथा§ ॥
एवं सूर्य्यप्रभावेण सर्व्वा नक्षत्रतारकाः ।
वर्द्धन्ते वर्द्धिता नित्यं नित्यमाप्याययन्ति च ॥
दिव्यानां पार्थिवानाञ्च नैशानाञ्चैव नित्यशः¶ ।
आदानान्नित्यमादित्यस्तेजसां तमसामपि ॥‖
आदत्ते सतु नाड़ीनां सहस्रेण समन्ततः ।
नादेयं चैव सामुद्रं कौप्यं चैव सहस्रदृक् ।**

---

* परिवर्णितः इति B. परिगीयते इति D.

† विश्ववाचास्तु इति B.

‡ सुपुष्णातीति B.

§ सुराट् ततः इति B and D.

¶ सर्व्वशः इति B.

‖ एतत्पादद्वयं B पुस्तके नास्ति ।

** नादेयांश्चैव सामुद्रान् कूप्यांश्चैव सहस्रधृगिति B.

स्थावरं जङ्गमश्चैव यदा* कुल्यादिकं पयः ॥
तस्य रश्मिसहस्रन्तु शीतवर्षोष्णनिस्रवम् ।
तासाञ्चतुःशता नाड्यो वर्षन्ते चित्रमूर्त्तयः ॥
चन्द्रगाश्चैव गाह्याश्च काञ्चनाः शातनास्तथा† ।
अमृता नामतः‡ सर्वा रश्मयोवृष्टिसर्जनाः ॥
हिमोद्वताश्च§ तानाड्यो रश्मयो निःसृताः¶ पुनः ।
रेध्यो मेध्यश्च वास्यश्च‖ ह्रादिन्यः सर्जनास्तथा ॥
चन्द्रास्ता नामतः सर्वाः पीतास्ताः सुगभस्तयः ।
शुक्लाश्च कुङ्कुमाश्चैव** गावोविश्वभृतस्तथा ॥
शुक्लास्ता नामतः सर्वास्त्रिविधा घर्म्मसर्जनाः ।
समं बिभर्त्ति ताभिः समनुष्यपितृदेवताः ॥
मनुष्यानौषधेनेह स्वधया च पितृनपि ।
अमृतेन सुरान्सर्वांस्त्रींस्त्रिभिस्तर्पयत्यसौ ॥
वसन्ते ग्रीष्मके चैव षड्भिः स तपति प्रभुः ।

---

* यद्वेति B.

† चन्द्रगाश्चैव याम्याश्च केतनाः पूतनास्तथा इति B. चन्दनाश्चैव जाताश्च कीतला भूतलास्तथा इति D.

‡ नाम ताः इति B and D.

§ हिमोद्वाहाश्च इति B and D.

¶ त्रिंशतमिति B and D.

‖ रम्यो मेध्यश्च पौष्यश्च इति B. रसग्रो मेध्यश्च पौष्यश्च इति D.

** ककुभश्चैव इति B and D.

शरद्यपि च वर्षासु चतुर्भिः संप्रवर्षति* ॥
हेमन्ते शिशिरे चैव हिममुत्सृजति त्रिभिः ।
वरुणो माघमासे तु सूर्य्यः पूषा तु† फाल्गुने ॥
चैत्रे मासे स देवेशो धाता वैशाखतापनः ।
ज्यैष्ठे मासे भवेदिन्द्रः‡ आषाढ़े तपते रविः§ ॥
विवस्वान् श्रावणे मासि प्रौष्ठपद्याम्भगः स्मृतः ।
पर्ज्जन्योऽश्वयुजे¶ मासि कार्त्तिके मासि भास्करः‖ ॥
मार्गशीर्षे भवेन्मित्रः पौषे विष्णुः सनातनः ।
पञ्चरश्मिसहस्राणि** वरुणस्यार्ककर्म्मणि ॥
षड्भिः सहस्रैः पूषा तु देवेशः†† सप्तभिस्तथा ।
धाताष्टभिः सहस्रैस्तु नवभिश्च शतक्रतुः ॥
विवस्वान्दशभिः पाति पात्येकादशभिर्भगः ।
सप्तभिस्तपते मित्रस्त्वष्टा चैवाष्टभि‡‡स्तपेत् ॥

---

* अवर्षिभिरिति B.

† च इति B.

‡ ज्येष्ठामूले पतेदिन्द्रः इति B.

§ सविता रविरिति B and G.

¶ पर्जन्यश्चाश्विने त्वष्टा इति B. पर्ज्जन्योऽश्वयुजि त्वष्टा इति D.

‖ भार्गवः इति B.

** परं रश्मिसहस्राणीति B.

†† देवोऽंशः इति B and D.

‡‡ वै चाष्टभिरिति B.

अर्य्यमा दशभिः पाति पर्जन्योनवभिस्तथा* ।
षड्भी रश्मिसहस्रैस्तु विष्णुस्तपति विश्वधृक् ॥
वसन्ते कपिलः सूर्य्यो ग्रीष्मे काञ्चनसप्रभः ।
श्वेतो वर्षासु विज्ञेयः† पाण्डुरः‡ शरदि प्रभुः ॥
हेमन्ते ताम्रवर्णः स्याच्छिशिरे लोहितो रविः ।
ओषधीषु कलान्धत्ते§ स्वधामपि पितृष्वथ ॥
सूर्योऽमरेष्वमृतन्तु¶ त्रयं त्रिषु‖ नियच्छति ।
अन्ये चाष्टौ ग्रहाज्ञेयाः सूर्य्येणाधिष्ठिता** द्विजाः ॥
चन्द्रमाः सोमपुत्रश्च शुक्रश्चैव वृहस्पतिः ।
भौमो††मन्दस्तथा राहुः केतुमानपि चाष्टमः ॥
सर्व्वे ध्रुवे निबद्धा वै ग्रहास्ते वातरश्मिभिः ।
भ्राम्यमाणा यथायोगं भ्रमन्त्यनुदिवाकरम् ॥
अलातचक्रवद्यान्ति वातचक्रेरितास्तथा‡‡ ।
यस्माद्वहति तान्वायुः प्रवहस्तेन स स्मृतः ॥

---

* तपेदिति B.

† वर्णेन इति B.

‡ पाण्डरः इति B and D.

§ बलं धत्ते इति B.

¶ सूर्य्योऽमरत्वममृते इति B.

‖ तेष्विति B.

** सूर्य्येणाधिकृता इति B. सूर्य्येणाधिगता इति D.

†† भानुरिति B.

‡‡ द्विजा इति B.

रथस्त्रिचक्रः सोमस्य कुन्दाभास्तस्य वाजिनः।
वामदक्षिणतो युक्ता दश ते न क्षपाकरः* ॥
वीथ्याश्रयाणि चरति नक्षत्राणि रविर्य्यथा।
ह्रासवृद्धी तु विप्रेन्द्रा ध्रुवाधाराणि सर्व्वदा† ॥
स सोमः शुक्लपक्षे तु भास्करे परतः स्थिते।
आपूर्य्यते परस्यान्ते सततञ्चैव ताः प्रभाः‡ ॥
क्षीणम्पीतं§ सुरैः सोममाप्याययति नित्यदा।
एकेन रश्मिना विप्राः सुषुम्नाख्येन भास्करः ॥
एषा सूर्य्यस्य वीर्य्येण सोमस्याप्यायिता तनुः।
पौर्णमास्यां स दृश्येत सम्पूर्णो दिवसक्रमात् ॥
सम्पूर्णमर्द्धमासेन तं सोमममृतात्मकम्।
पिबन्ति देवता विप्रा यतस्तेऽमृतभोजनाः ॥
ततः पञ्चदशे भागे किञ्चिच्छिष्टे कलात्मके।
अपराह्णे पितृगणा जघन्यं पर्य्युपासते ॥
पिबन्ति द्विलवं¶ कालं शिष्टा तस्य कला तु या।
सुधामृतमयीं पुण्यां तामिन्दोरमृतात्मिकाम् ॥
निःसृतं तदमावास्यां गभस्तिभ्यः स्वधामृतम्।

---

* निशाकर इति B.

† रश्मीनां सूर्य्यवत्स्मृत इति B.

‡ सततं दिवसक्रमादिति B and D.

§ क्षीणाधितमिति B.

¶ त्रिकलमिति B. द्विकलमिति D.

मासत्तृप्तिमवाप्स्यन्ति* पितरः सन्ति निर्वृताः ॥
न सोमस्य विनाशः स्यात्सुधा चैव सुपीयते† ।
एवं सूर्यनिमित्तोऽस्य क्षयोवृद्धिश्च सत्तमाः ॥
सोमपुत्रस्य चाष्टाभिर्वाजिभिर्वायुवेगिभिः ।
वारिजैः‡ स्यन्दनो युक्तस्तेनासौ याति सर्वतः ॥
शुक्रस्य भूमिजैरश्वैः स्यन्दनो दशभिर्वृतः ।
अष्टाभिश्चापि भौमस्य रथोहैमः सुशोभनः ॥
वृहस्पतेरथोऽष्टाश्वः स्यन्दनो हैमनिर्मितः ।
रथो रूप्यमयोऽष्टाश्वो मन्दस्यायसनिर्मितः ॥§
स्वर्भानोर्भास्करारेश्च तथाष्टाभि¶र्हयैर्वृतः ।
एते महाग्रहाणां|| वै समाख्याता रथाश्च वै** ॥
सर्वे ध्रुवे महाभागा निबद्धावायुरश्मिभिः†† ।

---

* मवाप्स्यामिति B and D. ममावस्यामिति E and H.

† देवैस्तु पीयते इति B and D.

‡ वाजिभिरिति D. वायुभिरिति H.

§ एतत्पादद्वयं B पुस्तके नास्ति ।

¶ षड्भिरिति B. तथा षष्टिहयैरिति D.

|| मया ग्रहाणामिति B.

** नव इति B and D.

†† वातरश्मिभिरिति B and D. निबद्धाम्बुदरश्मिभिरिति E and H. निबद्धा अम्बुदरश्मिभिरत्र सन्धिः सोढव्य आर्षत्वात् ।

ग्रहर्चताराधिष्ण्यानि ध्रुवे बद्धान्यशेषतः॥
भ्रमन्ति भ्रामयन्त्येनं सर्व्वाण्यनिलरश्मिभिः॥*

इति श्रीकूर्म्मपुराणे भुवनकोशे त्रिचत्वारिंशोऽध्यायः।

—•◎•—

चतुश्चत्वारिंशोऽध्यायः।

सूत उवाच।

ध्रुवादूर्द्ध्वं महर्लोकः कोटियोजनविस्तृतः।
कल्पाधिकारिणस्तत्र संस्थिता द्विजपुङ्गवाः॥
जनलोको महर्लोकात्तथा कोटिद्वयात्मकः।
सनकाद्यास्तथा तत्र* संस्थिता ब्रह्मणः सुताः॥
जनलोकात्तपोलोकः कोटित्रयसमन्वितः।
वैराजास्तत्र वै देवाः स्थिता दाहविवर्जिताः॥
प्राजापत्यात्सत्यलोकः कोटिषट्केन संयुतः।
अपुनर्मारको नाम† ब्रह्मलोकस्तु स स्मृतः॥

---

* एष श्लोकः B पुस्तके नास्ति।

* सनन्दनादयस्तत्रेति B and D.

† अपुनर्नरकास्तत्र इति B.

अत्र* लोकगुरुर्ब्रह्मा विश्वात्मा विश्वभावनः† ।
आस्ते स योगिभिर्नित्यं पीत्वा योगामृतं परम् ॥
वसन्ति‡ यतयः शान्ता नैष्ठिका§ ब्रह्मचारिणः ।
योगिनस्तापसाः सिद्धा जापकाः परमेष्ठिनः ॥
द्वारं¶ तद्योगिनामेकं गच्छतां परमं पदम् ।
तत्र गत्वा न शोचन्ति स विष्णुः स च शङ्करः ॥
सूर्यकोटिप्रतीकाशं पुरन्तस्य दुरासदम् ।
न मे वर्णयितुं शक्यं ज्वालामालासमाकुलम् ॥
तत्र नारायणस्यापि भवनं ब्रह्मणः पुरे ।
शेते तत्र हरिः श्रीमान्योगी‖ मायामयः परः ॥
स विष्णुलोकः कथितः पुनरावृत्तिवर्जितः ।
यान्ति तत्र महात्मानो ये प्रपन्ना जनार्द्दनम् ॥
ऊर्द्ध्वं तद्ब्रह्म** सदनात्पुरं ज्योतिर्मयं शुभम् ।
वह्निना च परिक्षिप्तं तत्रास्ते भगवान् हरः†† ॥

---

* तत्र इति B.

† विश्वतोमुखः इति B.

‡ विशन्तीति B.

§ आस्तिका इति B.

¶ ज्ञानमिति B.

‖ मायी इति D, E and H.

** ऊर्द्ध्वन्तु ब्रह्मसदनादिति B.

†† भव इति B.

देव्या सह महादेवश्चिन्त्यमानो मनीषिभिः ।
योगिभिः शतसाहस्रैर्भूतैरुद्रैश्च संवृतः ॥
तत्र ते* यान्ति निरता†भक्ता‡ वै ब्रह्मचारिणः ।
महादेवपराः शान्तास्तापसाः सत्यवादिनः§ ॥
निर्म्ममा निरहङ्काराः कामक्रोधविवर्ज्जिताः ।
द्रक्ष्यन्ति ब्राह्मणायुक्ता¶ रुद्रलोकः स वै स्मृतः ॥
एते सप्त महालोकाः पृथिव्याः‖ परिकीर्त्तिताः ।
महातलादयश्चाधः पातालाः सन्ति वै द्विजाः ॥
महातलं च पातालं** सर्व्वरत्नोपशोभितम् ।
प्रासादैर्विविधैः शुभ्रैर्देवतायतनैर्युतम् ॥
अनन्तेन च संयुक्तं मुचुकुन्देन धीमता ।
नृपेण बलिना चैव पातालं स्वर्गवासिना†† ॥
शैलं रसातलं विप्राः शार्करं हि तलातलम् ।
पीतं सुतलमित्युक्तं नितलं विद्रुमप्रभम् ॥

---

* शै इति B.

† नियता इति B.

‡ द्विजा इति B.

§ ब्रह्मवादिन इति B.

¶ मुक्ता इति B.

‖ पृथिव्यामिति B.

** महातलं हेमतलमिति B and D.

†† स्वर्गवासिनामिति B.

सितं च* वितलं प्रोक्तं तलञ्चैव सितेतरम्।
सुपर्णेन मुनिश्रेष्ठास्तथा वासुकिना शुभम्॥
रसातलमिति ख्यातं तथान्यैश्च निषेवितम्।
विरोचनहिरण्याचतारकाद्यैश्च† सेवितम्॥
तलातलमिति ख्यातं सर्वशोभासमन्वितम्।
वैनतेयादिभिश्चैव कालनेमिपुरोगमैः॥
पूर्वदेवैः समाकीर्णं सुतलञ्च तथापरैः।
नितलं यवनाद्यैश्च तारकाग्निमुखैस्तथा॥‡
जम्भकाद्यैस्तथा नागैः§ प्रह्लादेनासुरेण च।
वितलं चैव विख्यातं कम्बलाहीन्द्रसेवितम्॥
महाजम्भेन वीरेण हयग्रीवेण धीमता।
शङ्कुकर्णेन सम्भिन्नं तथा नमुचिपूर्वकैः॥
तथान्यैर्विविधैर्नागैस्तलञ्चैव सुशोभनम्।
तेषामधस्तान्नरकाः कूष्माण्डाद्याः¶ परिकीर्त्तिताः॥
पापिनस्तेषु पच्यन्ते न ते वर्णयितुं क्षमाः।
पातालानामधश्चास्ते शेषाख्या वैष्णवी तनुः॥
कालाग्निरुद्रो योगात्मा नारसिंहोऽपि माधवः।

---

* हीति B.

† तचकाद्यैश्च इति B.

‡ एतत्पादद्वयं B पुस्तके नास्ति।

§ महान्तकाद्यैर्नागैश्च इति B.

¶ मायाद्या इति B, D and H.

योऽनन्तः पठ्यते देवो नागरूपी जनार्द्दनः ।
तदाधारमिदं सर्व्वं स कालाग्निं समाश्रितः* ॥
तमाविश्य† महायोगी कालस्तद्वदनोषितः‡ ।
विषज्वालामयश्चेशो जगत्संहरति स्वयम् ॥
सहस्रमारिप्रतिमः§ संहर्त्ता शङ्करो भवः ।
तामसी शाम्भवी मूर्त्तिः कालो लोकप्रकालनः ॥

इति श्रीकूर्म्मपुराणे भुवनविन्यासे चतुश्चत्वारिंशोऽध्यायः ।

पञ्चचत्वारिंशोऽध्यायः ।

सूत उवाच ।

एतद्ब्रह्माण्डमाख्यातञ्चतुर्द्दशविधम्महत् ।
अतःपरम्प्रवक्ष्यामि भूर्लोकस्यास्य निर्णयम् ॥
जम्बूद्वीपः प्रधानोऽयं प्लक्षः शाल्मलिरेव च* ।

---

* कालाग्निसमाश्रित इति B.

† तदाविश्येति B.

‡ वदनोत्थित इति B and D.

§ सहस्रमायोऽप्रतिम इति B, D and E.

---

* शाल्मलएव चेति B and D.

कुशः क्रौञ्चश्च शाकश्च पुष्करश्चैव* सप्तमः ॥
एते सप्त महाद्वीपाः समुद्रैः सप्तभिर्वृताः ।
द्वीपाद्द्वीपो महानुक्तः सागराच्चापि† सागरः ॥
क्षारोदेक्षुरसोदश्च सुरोदश्च घृतोदकः‡ ।
दध्योदः क्षीरसलिलः स्वादूदश्चेति सागराः ॥
पञ्चाशत्कोटिविस्तीर्णा ससमुद्रा धरा स्मृता ।
द्वीपैश्च सप्तभिर्युक्ता योजनानां समन्ततः§ ॥
जम्बूद्वीपः समस्तानां मध्ये चैव व्यवस्थितः¶ ।
तस्य मध्ये महामेरुर्विश्रुतः कनकप्रभः ॥
चतुरशीतिसाहस्रो योजनैस्तस्य चोच्छ्रयः ।
प्रविष्टः षोड़शाधस्ताद्द्वात्रिंशन्मूर्द्ध्नि विस्तृतः ॥
मूले षोड़शसाहस्रो विस्तारस्तस्य सर्व्वतः ।
भूपद्मस्यास्य शैलोऽसौ कर्णिकात्वेन संस्थितः ॥
हिमवान् हेमकूटश्च निषधश्चास्य दक्षिणे ।
नीलः श्वेतश्च शृङ्गी च उत्तरे वर्षपर्व्वताः ॥
लक्षप्रमाणौ द्वौ मध्ये दशहीनास्तथापरे ।

---

* पुष्कलश्चैवेति B.

† सागरादपीति B.

‡ क्षीरोदेक्षुरसश्चैव सुरोदकघृतोदक इति B and D.

§ समासत इति D.

¶ द्वीपानां मध्यमः शुभ इति B. मध्यत शुभ इति D.

सहस्रद्वितयोच्छ्रायास्तावद्विस्तारिणश्च ते ॥*

भारतम्प्रथमं† वर्षन्ततः किम्पुरुषं स्मृतम् ।

हरिवर्षं तथैवान्यत्‡ मेरोर्द्दक्षिणतो द्विजाः ॥

रम्यकञ्चोत्तरं वर्षं तस्यैवानु§ हिरण्मयम् ।

उत्तरे¶ कुरवश्चैव यथैते भारतास्तथा ॥

नवसाहस्रमेकैकमेतेषां द्विजसत्तमाः ।‖

इलावृतञ्च तन्मध्ये तन्मध्ये मेरुरुच्छ्रितः ॥

मेरोश्चतुर्द्दिशन्तत्र नवसाहस्रविस्तरम्** ।

इलावृतं महाभागाश्चत्वारस्तत्र पर्व्वताः ।

विष्कम्भा रचितामेरोर्योजनायुतमुच्छ्रिताः ॥

पूर्व्वेण मन्दरो नाम दक्षिणे गन्धमादनः ।

विपुलः पश्चिमे पार्श्वे†† सुपार्श्वश्चोत्तरः‡‡ स्मृतः ॥

कदम्बस्तेषु जम्बूश्च पिप्पलो वट एव च ।

---

* एतच्चरणद्वयं B पुस्तके नास्ति ।

† दक्षिणमिति B.

‡ तथैवान्ये इति B and D.

§ तथैवानु इति B.

¶ उत्तरा इति B and D.

‖ एतच्चरणद्वयं B पुस्तके नास्ति ।

** विस्तृतमिति B and D.

†† भागे इति B and D.

‡‡ पार्श्वश्चोत्तरत इति B.

जम्बूद्वीपस्य सा जम्बूर्नामहेतुर्महर्षय: ॥
महागजप्रमाणानि जम्ब्वास्तस्या: फलानि च।
पतन्ति भूभृत: पृष्ठे शीर्य्यमाणानि सर्व्वत: ॥
रसेन तस्या: प्रख्याता तत्र जम्बूनदी गिरौ*।
सरित्प्रवर्त्तते चापि पीयते तत्र वासिभि: ॥
न स्वेदो न च दौर्गन्ध्यन्न जरा नेन्द्रियच्चय:।
न ताप: स्वच्छमनसान्नासौख्यं† तत्र जायते ॥
तत्तीरमृद्रसम्प्राप्य वायुना सुविशोषितम्।‡
जाम्बूनदाख्यम्भवति सुवर्णं सिद्धभूषणम् ॥
भद्राश्व: पूर्व्वतो मेरो: केतुमालश्च पश्चिमे।
वर्षे द्वे तु मुनिश्रेष्ठास्तयोर्मध्ये इलावृतम् ॥
वनञ्चैत्ररथम्पूर्व्वं दक्षिणङ्गन्धमादनम्।
वैभ्राजम्पश्चिमं विद्यादुत्तरं§ सवितुर्व्वनम् ॥
अरुणोदम्महाभद्रमसितोदञ्च मानसम्।
सरांस्येतानि चत्वारि देवभोग्यानि सर्व्वदा ॥
सितान्तश्च कुमुद्वांश्च कुररी माल्यवांस्तथा।
वैकङ्को मणिशैलश्च वृक्षवांश्चाचलोत्तम: ¶॥

---

* नदीति वै इति B and D.

† तत्पानात्सुस्थमनसां नराणामिति B and D.

‡ एतच्चरणद्वयं B पुस्तके नास्ति।

§ विन्ध्यादुत्तरे इति B.

¶ ऋक्षेति B and D.

महानीलोऽथ रुचकः सविन्दुर्मन्दरस्तथा ।
वेणुमांश्चैव मेघश्च* निषधो देवपर्व्वतः ॥
इत्येते देवरचिताः† सिद्धावासाः प्रकीर्त्तिताः ॥
अरुणोदस्य सरसः पूर्व्वतः केसराचलः‡ ।
त्रिकूटः सशिरश्चैव§ पतङ्गो रुचकस्तथा ॥
निषधो वसुधारश्च¶ कलिङ्गस्त्रिशिखः स्मृतः‖ ।
समूलो वसुवेदिश्च** कुरुश्चैव सानुमान् ॥
ताम्रातश्च विशालश्च कुमुदो वेणुपर्व्वतः ।
एकशृङ्गो महाशैलो गजशैलश्च पिञ्जकः†† ॥
पञ्चशैलोऽथ कैलासो हिमवांश्चाचलोत्तमः ।
इत्येते देवचरिता उत्कटाः पर्व्वतोत्तमाः ॥
महाभद्रस्य सरसो दक्षिणे केसराचलः‡‡ ।
शिखिवासाश्च वैदूर्य्यः कपिलो गन्धमादनः ॥

---

* वेणुमांश्च समेघश्चेति B and D.

† देवचरिता इति B and D.

‡ केशवाचल इति B.

§ त्रिकूटः शिखरश्चैव इति B and D. शशिरांश्चैव इति E and H.

¶ वसुमारश्चेति B and D.

‖ शुभ इति B.

** वसुधारश्चेति B. वसुधीरश्चेति D.

†† गजशैलः पिशाचक इति B and D.

‡‡ केशवाचल इति B.

जारुधिश्च सुराम्बुश्च* सर्व्वगन्धाचलोत्तमः।
सुपार्श्वश्च सुपक्षश्च कङ्कः कपिल एव च॥
विरजो भद्रजालश्च सुसकश्च† महाबलः।
अञ्जनो मधुमांस्तद्वच्चित्रशृङ्गो महालयः‡॥
कुमुदो मुकुटश्चैव§ पाण्डुरः कृष्ण एव च।
पारिजातो महाशैलस्तथैव कपिलाचलः¶॥
सुषेणः पुण्डरीकश्च महामेघस्तथैव च।
एते पर्व्वतराजानः‖ सिद्धगन्धर्व्वसेविताः॥
असितोदस्य सरसः** पश्चिमे केसराचलः††।
शङ्खकूटोऽथ वृषभो हंसो नागस्तथैव च‡‡॥
कालाञ्जनः शुक्र§§शैलो नीलः कमल¶¶ एव च।

---

* जारुधितः सुगन्धश्चेति B. सुगन्धश्च श्रीशृङ्गश्चाचलोत्तम इति D.

† पिञ्जलो भद्रशैलश्च सुरसश्चेति B.

‡ कुमुदो मुकुटस्तथा इति B.

§ सहस्रशिखरश्चैव इति B and D.

¶ कपिलोदर इति B.

‖ पर्व्वतराजान इति आर्षं, पर्व्वतराजाः इति साधु।

** पारिख इति B and D.

†† केशवाचल इति B.

‡‡ तथापर इति B.

§§ कलिञ्जरः शक्रेति B.

¶¶ कनक इति B.

पारिजातो महाशैलः शैलः कनक एव च ॥*
पुष्पकश्च सुमेघश्च वाराही विरजास्तथा ।
मयूरः कपिलश्चैव महाकपिल एव च ॥
इत्येते देवगन्धर्व्वसिद्धयक्षैश्च सेविताः† ।
सरसो मानसश्चेह उत्तरे केसराचलः‡ ॥
एतेषां शैलमुख्यानामन्तरेषु यथाक्रमम् ।
सन्ति चैवान्तरद्रोण्यः सरांसि च वनानि च ॥
वसन्ति तत्र मुनयः सिद्धा वै§ ब्रह्मभाविताः ।
प्रसन्ना शान्तरजसः सर्व्वदुःखविवर्ज्जिताः ॥

इति श्रीकूर्म्मपुराणे भुवनकोशे पर्व्वतसंख्याने पञ्चचत्वारिंशोऽध्यायः ।

षट्चत्वारिंशोऽध्यायः ।

सूत उवाच ।

चतुर्द्दशसहस्राणि* योजनानाम्महापुरी ।
मेरोरुपरि विख्याता देवदेवस्य वेधसः ॥

---

* एतच्चरणद्वयं B पुस्तके नास्ति ।

† सिद्धसङ्घनिषेविता इति B and D.

‡ केशवाचल इति B.

§ सिद्धाश्चेति B and D.

---

* सहस्राणामिति B.

तत्रास्ते भगवान् ब्रह्मा विश्वात्मा विश्वभावनः।
उपास्यमानो योगीन्द्रैर्मुनीन्द्रोपेन्द्रशङ्करैः॥
तत्र देवेश्वरेशानं विश्वात्मानम्प्रजापतिम्।
सनत्कुमारो भगवानुपास्ते नित्यमेव हि॥
स सिद्धऋषिगन्धर्व्वैः पूज्यमानः सुरैरपि।
समास्ते योगयुक्तात्मा पीत्वा तत्परमामृतम्॥
तत्र देवाधिदेवस्य* शम्भोरमिततेजसः।
दीप्तमायतनं शुभ्रम्पुरस्ताद्ब्रह्मणः स्थितम्॥
दिव्यकान्तिसमायुक्तञ्चतुर्द्वारं सुशोभनम्।
महर्षिगणसङ्कीर्णं ब्रह्मविद्भिर्निषेवितम्॥
देव्या सह महादेवः शशाङ्कार्काग्निलोचनः।
रमते तत्र विश्वेशः प्रमथैः प्रमथेश्वरः॥
तत्र वेदविदः शान्ता मुनयो ब्रह्मचारिणः।
पूजयन्ति महादेवन्तपसा सत्यवादिनः॥
तेषां साक्षान्महादेवो मुनीनां भावितात्मनाम्†।
गृह्णाति पूजां शिरसा पार्व्वत्या परमेश्वरः॥
तत्रैव पर्व्वतवरे शक्रस्य परमा पुरी।
नाम्नामरावती पूर्व्वं सर्व्वशोभासमन्विता॥
तत्र चाप्सरसः सर्व्वा गन्धर्व्वाः सिद्धचारणाः‡।

---

* देवादिदेवस्येति B ; देवातिदेवस्य इति D.

† ब्रह्मवादिनामिति B and D.

‡ गीततत्परा इति B. गीततत्परमिति D.

उपासते सहस्राचं देवास्तत्र सहस्रशः ॥
ये धार्म्मिका वेदविदो यागहोमपरायणाः ।
तेषान्तत्परमं स्थानं देवानामपि दुर्लभम् ॥
तस्माद्दचिण*दिग्भागे वह्नेरमिततेजसः ।
तेजोवती नाम पुरी दिव्याश्चर्य्यसमन्विता ॥
तत्रास्ते भगवान्वह्निर्भ्राजमानः स्वतेजसा ।
जपिनां होमिनां स्थानं दानवानां दुरासदम् ॥
दचिणे पर्व्वतवरे यमस्यापि† महापुरी ।
नाम्ना संयमनी दिव्या सर्व्वशोभासमन्विता‡ ॥
तत्र वैवस्वतं देवं देवाद्याः पर्य्युपासते ।
स्थानं तत्सत्यसन्धानां लोके पुण्यकृतां नृणाम् ॥
तस्यास्तु पश्चिमे भागे निर्ऋतेस्तु महात्मनः ।
रचोवती नाम पुरी राचसैः संवृता तु या§ ॥
तत्र ते¶ नैर्ऋतं देवं राचसाः पर्य्युपासते ।
गच्छन्ति तां धर्म्मरता ये तु‖ तामसवृत्तयः ॥
पश्चिमे पर्व्वतवरे वरुणस्य महापुरी ।

---

* तस्य दचिणेति B and D.

† यमस्य तु इति B.

‡ सिद्धगन्धर्व्वसेविता इति B and D.

§ सर्व्वतो वृता इति B and D.

¶ तमिति B and D.

‖ धर्म्मवतां ये वै इति B.

नाम्ना शुद्धवती पुण्या सर्व्वकामर्द्धिसंयुता ॥
तत्राप्सरोगणैः सिद्धैः सेव्यमानोऽमराधिपैः* ।
आस्ते स वरुणो राजा तत्र गच्छन्ति येऽम्बुदाः† ॥
तस्या उत्तरदिग्भागे वायोरपि महापुरी ।
नाम्ना गन्धवती पुण्या तत्रास्तेऽसौ प्रभञ्जनः ॥
अप्सरोगणगन्धर्व्वैः सेव्यमानो महान् प्रभुः‡ ।
प्राणायामपरा विप्राः§ स्थानं तद्यान्ति शाश्वतम्¶ ॥
तस्याः पूर्व्वे तु दिग्भागे सोमस्य परमा पुरी ।
नाम्ना कान्तिमती शुभ्रा तस्यां‖ सोमो विराजते ॥
तत्र ये धर्म्मनिरताः** स्वधर्म्मं पर्य्युपासते ।
तेषां तदुचितं स्थानं नानाभोगसमन्वितम् ॥
तस्यास्तु पूर्व्वदिग्भागे शङ्करस्य महापुरी ।
नाम्ना यशोवती पुण्या सर्व्वेषां सा†† दुरासदा ॥
तत्रेशानस्य भवनं रुद्रेणाधिष्ठितं‡‡ शुभम् ।

---

* अमराधिपः इति B. नराधिपैरिति E and H.

† ये मुदा इति B and D.

‡ सेव्यमानोऽमरः प्रभुरिति D.

§ मर्त्त्याः इति B and D. प्राणायामरता मर्त्त्याः इति G.

¶ शोभनमिति B and D.

‖ तत्र इति B.

** भोगनिरताः इति B and D.

†† सु इति B and D.

‡‡ रुद्रं विष्णुतनोरिति B and D.

गणेश्वरस्य विपुलं तत्रास्ते स गणावृतः* ॥
तत्र भोगादिलिप्सूनां भक्तानां परमेष्ठिनः ।
निवासः कल्पितः पूर्व्वं देवदेवेन शूलिना ॥
विष्णुपादाद्विनिष्क्रान्ता प्लावयित्वेन्दुमण्डलम् ।
समन्ताद्ब्रह्मणः पुर्य्यां गङ्गा पतति वै ततः† ॥
सा तत्र पतिता दिक्षु चतुर्द्धा ह्यभवद्द्विजाः ।
सीता चालकनन्दा च सुचक्षुर्भद्रनामिका ॥
पूर्व्वेण शैलाच्छैलन्तु‡ सीता यात्यन्तरिक्षगा§ ।
ततश्च पूर्व्ववर्षेण भद्राश्वाद्याति चार्णवम् ॥
तथैवालकनन्दा च दक्षिणादेत्य भारतम् ।
प्रयाति सागरं भित्त्वा सप्तभेदाद्द्विजोत्तमाः ॥
सुचक्षुः पश्चिमगिरीनतीत्य सकलांस्तथा ।
पश्चिमं केतुमालाख्यं वर्षं गत्वैति चार्णवम् ॥
भद्रा तथोत्तरगिरीनुत्तरांश्च तथा कुरून् ।
अतीत्य चोत्तराम्भोधिं समभ्येति महर्षयः ॥
आनीलनिषधायामौ माल्यवद्गन्धमादनौ ।
तयोर्मध्यं गतो¶ मेरुः कर्णिकाकारसंस्थितः ॥

---

* गणैर्वृतः इति B.

† दिवः इति B and D.

‡ सीता शैलात्तु इति B.

§ शैले यात्यन्तरीक्षतः इति B and D.

¶ तयोर्मध्यगतः इति B and D.

भारताः* केतुमालाश्च भद्राश्वाः कुरवस्तथा ।
पत्राणि लोकपद्मस्य मर्य्यादाशैलवाह्यतः† ॥
जठरो देवकूटश्च मर्य्यादापर्व्वतावुभौ ।
दक्षिणोत्तरमायातावानीलनिषधायतौ ॥
गन्धमादनकैलासौ पूर्व्वपश्चायतावुभौ ।
अशीतियोजनायामावर्णवान्तर्व्यवस्थितौ ॥
निषधः पारिपात्रश्च मर्य्यादापर्व्वताविमौ ।
मेरोः पश्चिमदिग्भागे यथापूर्व्वं व्यवस्थितौ ॥
त्रिशृङ्गो जारुधिस्तद्वदुत्तरे वर्षपर्व्वतौ ।
तावदायामविस्तारौ‡ अर्णवान्तर्व्यवस्थितौ ॥
मर्य्यादापर्व्वताः प्रोक्ता अष्टाविह मया द्विजाः ।
जठराद्याः स्थिताः मेरोश्चतुर्द्दिक्षु महर्षयः ॥

इति श्रीकूर्म्मपुराणे भुवनविन्यासे षट्चत्वारिंशोऽध्यायः ।

---

* तारकाः इति B.

† मर्य्यादाः शैलवाह्यतः इति B.

‡ पूर्व्वपश्चायतावेतौ इति B and D.

सप्तचत्वारिंशोऽध्यायः।

सूत उवाच।

केतुमाले नराः काकाः सर्व्वे पनसभोजनाः।
स्त्रियश्चोत्पलपत्राभा*स्ते जीवन्ति वर्षायुतम् ॥†
भद्राश्वे पुरुषाः शुक्लाः‡ स्त्रियश्चन्द्रांशुसन्निभाः।
दशवर्षसहस्राणि जीवन्ते§ चान्नभोजनाः¶ ॥
रम्यके पुरुषा नार्य्यो रमन्ति|| रजतप्रभाः** ।
दशवर्षसहस्राणि शतानि दश पञ्च च।
जीवन्ति चैव सत्वस्था न्यग्रोधफलभोजनाः ॥
हिरण्मये हिरण्याभाः सर्व्वे श्रीफलभोजनाः।
एकादशसहस्राणि शतानि दश पञ्च च।
जीवन्ति पुरुषा नार्य्यो देवलोकस्थिता इव ॥
त्रयोदशसहस्राणि शतानि दश पञ्च च।
जीवन्ति कुरुवर्षे तु श्यामाङ्गाः क्षीरभोजनाः।

---

* पत्राढ्यः इति E, G and H.

† ते जीवन्ति वर्षायुतमित्यत्र छन्दःपतनम्।

‡ शुभाः इति B.

§ जीवन्ते इत्यार्षमात्मनेपदम्।

¶ वायुभोजनाः इति B and D.

|| रमन्तीति परस्मैपदमार्षम्।

** एतत्पादद्वयं B पुस्तके नास्ति।

सर्व्वे मिथुनजाताश्च नित्यं सुखनिषेविताः ॥
चन्द्रद्वीपे महादेवं यजन्ति सततं शिवम् ।
तथा किंपुरुषे विप्रा मानवा हेमसन्निभाः ।
दशवर्षसहस्राणि जीवन्ति प्लक्षभोजनाः ॥
यजन्ति सततं देवं चतुःशीर्षं चतुर्भुजम्* ।
ध्याने मनः समाधाय सादरं भक्तिसंयुताः ॥
तथा च हरिवर्षे तु† महारजतसन्निभाः ।
दशवर्षसहस्राणि जीवन्तीक्षुरसाशिनः ॥
तत्र नारायणं देवं विश्वयोनिं सनातनम् ।
उपासते सदा विष्णुं मानवा विष्णुभाविताः ॥
तत्र चन्द्रप्रभं शुभ्रं शुद्धस्फटिकसन्निभम् ।
विमानं वासुदेवस्य पारिजातवनाश्रितम् ॥
चतुर्द्वारमनौपम्यं चतुस्तोरणसंयुतम् ।
प्राकारैर्दशभिर्युक्तं दुराधर्षं सुदुर्गमम् ॥
स्फाटिकैर्मण्डपैर्युक्तं देवराजगृहोपमम् ।
सुवर्णस्तम्भसाहस्रैः‡ सर्व्वतः समलङ्कृतम् ॥
हेमसोपानसंयुक्तं नानारत्नोपशोभितम् ।
दिव्यसिंहासनोपेतं सर्व्वशोभासमन्वितम् ॥

---

* चतुर्मूर्त्तिं चतुर्मुखमिति B.

† हरिवर्षेऽपि इति B.

‡ स्वर्णस्तम्भसहस्रैश्च इति B and D. सुवर्णशतसाहस्रैः पर्व्वतैः समलङ्कृतमिति E, G and H.

सरोभिः स्वादुपानीयैर्नदीभिश्चोपशोभितम्।
नारायणपरैः शुद्धैर्वेदाध्ययनतत्परैः॥
योगिभिश्च समाकीर्णं ध्यायद्भिः पुरुषं हरिम्।
स्तुवद्भिः सततं मन्त्रैर्नमस्यद्भिश्च माधवम्॥
तत्र देवाधिदेवस्य* विष्णोरमिततेजसः।
राजानः सर्व्वकालन्तु महिमानं प्रकुर्व्वते॥
गायन्ति चैव नृत्यन्ति विलासिन्यो मनोहराः।
स्त्रियो यौवनशालिन्यः सदा मण्डनतत्पराः॥
इलावृते पद्मवर्णा जम्बूरसफलाशिनः†।
त्रयोदशसहस्राणि वर्षाणाञ्च‡ स्थिरायुषः॥
भारतेषु स्त्रियः पुंसो§ नानावर्णाः प्रकीर्त्तिताः।
नानादेवार्च्चने युक्ता नानाकर्म्माणि कुर्व्वते॥
परमायुः स्मृतं तेषां शतं वर्षाणि सुव्रताः।
नवयोजनसाहस्रं वर्षमेतत्प्रकीर्त्तितम्॥
कर्म्मभूमिरियं विप्रा नराणामधिकारिणाम्।
महेन्द्रो मलयः सह्यः शुक्तिमानृक्षपर्व्वतः॥
विन्ध्यश्च पारियात्रश्च¶ सप्तात्र कुलपर्व्वताः।

---

* देवादिदेवस्य इति B and D.

† जम्बूफलरसाशिनः इति B and D.

‡ वर्षानां वै इति B and D.

§ पुंस इति आर्षं, पुमांस इति साधु।

¶ पारिपात्रश्च इति B and D.

इन्द्रद्वीपः* कसेरुमान्† ताम्रपर्णो‡ गभस्तिमान्॥
नागद्वीपस्तथा सौम्यो गन्धर्व्वस्त्वथ वारुणः।
अयन्तु नवमस्तेषां द्वीपः सागरसंस्थितः॥
योजनानां सहस्रन्तु द्वीपोऽयं दक्षिणोत्तरः।
पूर्व्वे किरातास्तस्यान्ते पश्चिमे यवनास्तथा॥
ब्राह्मणाः क्षत्त्रिया वैश्याः मध्ये शूद्रास्तथैव च।
इज्यायुद्धवणिज्याभिर्वर्त्तयन्त्यत्र मानवाः§॥
स्रवन्ते पावना नद्यः पर्व्वतेभ्यो विनिःसृताः¶।
शतद्रुश्चन्द्रभागा च सरयूर्यमुना तथा॥
इरावती वितस्ता च विपाशा देविका‖ कुहूः।
गोमती धूतपापा च बाहुदा** च दृषद्वती॥
कौशिकी लोहिनी†† चेति हिमवत्पादनिःसृताः।
वेदस्मृतिर्वेदवती‡‡ व्रतघ्नी त्रिदिवा तथा॥

---

* इन्द्रद्युम्नः इति B and D.

† कसेरुमान् इति D.

‡ ताम्रवर्णः इति B and D.

§ वर्त्तयन्त्यत्र मानवः इति B.

¶ अस्य श्लोकार्द्धस्य परिवर्त्ते स्वधर्म्मनिरता विष्णुमर्पयन्त्यत्र मानवा इति D पुस्तके दृश्यते।

‖ द्रैविका इति B.

** बहुदा इति E, G and H.

†† लोहिता इति B and D.

‡‡ वेदरता इति B.

वर्णाशा चन्दना* चैव सचर्म्मण्वती सुरा† ।
विदिशा वेत्रवत्यापि पारियात्राश्रयाः स्मृताः ॥
नर्म्मदा सुरसा शोणो दशार्णा च महानदी ।‡
मन्दाकिनी चित्रकूटा तामसी च पिशाचिका ॥
चित्रोत्पला विशाला§ च मञ्जुला बालुवाहिनी¶ ।
ऋक्षवत्पादजा नद्यः सर्व्वपापहरा नृणाम् ॥
तापी पयोष्णी निर्विन्ध्या शीघ्रोदा च महानदी ।
विन्ना|| वैतरणी चैव बलाका च कुमुद्वती ॥
तथा चैव महागौरी दुर्गा चान्तःशिला तथा ।
विन्ध्यपादप्रसूतास्तु नद्यः पापहरा नृणाम्** ॥
गोदावरी भीमरथी कृष्णा वेणा च वञ्जता†† ।
तुङ्गभद्रा सुप्रयोगा कावेरी च द्विजोत्तमाः ।
दक्षिणापथनद्यस्तु सह्यपादाद्विनिःसृताः ॥

---

* पर्णा साबन्धना इति B. पर्णाशा बन्धना चैव इति D. पर्णाशा चन्दना चैवेति E.

† सदानीरा मनोरमा चर्म्मखती तथा सूर्या विदिशा वेत्रवत्यपि इति B and D.

‡ एतत्पादद्वयं B पुस्तके नास्ति। अस्मात्परं दक्षिणापथनद्यस्तु इत्यन्तं G पुस्तके नास्ति।

§ विपाशा च इति D, E and H.

¶ रत्नवाहिनीति B.

|| वेण्या इति B and D. चिन्ना इति E.

** पुण्यजलाः शुभाः इति B and D.

†† वर्णा च वत्सरी इति E.

ऋतुमाला ताम्रपर्णी पुष्पवत्युत्पलावती ।
मलयान्निःसृता नद्यः सर्व्वाः शीतजलाः स्मृताः ॥
ऋषिकुल्या त्रिसामा च गन्धमादनगामिनी ।
क्षिप्रा* पलाशिनी चैव ऋषीका वंशधारिणी† ।
शुक्तिमत्पादसञ्जाताः सर्व्वपापहरा नृणाम् ॥
आसां नद्युपनद्यश्च शतशो द्विजपुङ्गवाः ।
सर्व्वपापहराः‡ पुण्याः स्नानदानादिकर्म्मसु ॥
तास्विमे कुरुपाञ्चाला मध्यदेशादयो जनाः ।
पूर्व्वदेशादिकाश्चैव कामरूपनिवासिनः ॥
पुण्ड्राः§ कलिङ्गा मगधा दाक्षिणात्याश्च कृत्स्नशः ।
तथापरान्ताः सौराष्ट्रशूद्रा हीना¶स्तथार्वुदाः ॥
मालका मलपाश्चैव‖ पारियात्रनिवासिनः ।
सौवीराः सैन्धवा हूणा माल्या बाल्यानिवासिनः** ॥
माद्रा रामास्तथैवान्ध्राः पारसीकास्तथैव च ।
आसां पिवन्ति सलिलं वसन्ति सरितां सदा ॥

---

* रूपा इति B and D.

† वलकारिणीति B. रसकारिणी इति D.

‡ सर्व्वाः पापहराः इति B.

§ पुण्ड्रा इत्यारभ्य पारियात्रनिवासिन इत्यन्तं B पुस्तके इतः श्लोकाष्टकात्पूर्व्वं दृश्यते ।

¶ शूद्राभीरा इति B.

‖ मलद्रा इति E and H.

** कूणाः शाल्वाः कल्पनिवासिन इति D.

चत्वारि भारते वर्षे युगानि कवयोऽब्रुवन्।
कृतं त्रेता द्वापरञ्च कलिश्चान्यत्र न क्वचित्॥
यानि किम्पुरुषाद्यानि वर्षाण्यष्टौ महर्षयः।
न तेषु शोको नायासो नोद्वेगः क्षुद्भयं न च॥
स्वस्थाः प्रजा निरातङ्काः सर्वदुःखविवर्ज्जिताः।
रमन्ते विविधैर्भावैः सर्वाश्च स्थिरयौवनाः॥

इति श्रीकूर्म्मपुराणे भुवनकोशवर्णने सप्तचत्वारिंशोऽध्यायः।

अष्टचत्वारिंशोऽध्यायः।

सूत उवाच।

हेमकूटगिरेः शृङ्गे महाकूटं सुशोभनम्।
स्फाटिकं देवदेवस्य विमानं परमेष्ठिनः॥
तत्र देवाधिदेवस्य* भूतेशस्य त्रिशूलिनः।
देवाः सर्षिगणाः सिद्धाः† पूजां नित्यं प्रकुर्वते॥
स देव्याः‡ गिरिशः सार्द्धं महादेवो§ महेश्वरः।

---

* देवादिदेवस्य इति B.

† सिद्धगणा यक्षाः इति B and D.

‡ देवः इति B and D.

§ महादेव्या इति B and D..

भूतैः परिवृतो नित्यं भाति तत्र पिनाकधृक् ॥
विभक्तचारुशिखरः कैलासो यत्र पर्वतः।
निवासः कोटियक्षाणां कुवेरस्य च धीमतः ॥
तत्रापि देवदेवस्य भवस्यायतनं महत्।
मन्दाकिनी तत्र पुण्या* रम्या सुविमलोदका ॥
नदी नानाविधैः पद्मैरनेकैः समलङ्कृता।
देवदानवगन्धर्व्वयक्षराक्षसकिन्नरैः ॥
उपस्पृष्टजला नित्यं सुपुण्या सुमनोरमा।
अन्याश्च नद्यः शतशः स्वर्णपद्मैरलङ्कृताः ॥
तासां कूले तु देवस्य स्थानानि परमेष्ठिनः।
देवर्षिगणजुष्टानि तथा नारायणस्य तु† ॥
तस्यापि शिखरे शुभ्रे‡ पारिजातवनं शुभम्।
तत्र शक्रस्य विपुलं भवनं रत्नमण्डितम् ॥
स्फाटिकस्तम्भसंयुक्तं हेमगोपुरशोभितम्§।
तत्राथ देवदेवस्य विष्णोर्विश्वात्मनः प्रभोः¶ ॥
पुण्यञ्च‖ भवनं रम्यं सर्वरत्नोपशोभितम् ॥

---

* दिव्या इति B.

† च इति B.

‡ सिताभशिखरे चापि इति B. सितान्तशिखरे चापि इति D.

§ संयुतमिति B.

¶ विश्वानरैश्चितुरिति B.

‖ सुपुण्यमिति B and D.

तत्र नारायणः श्रीमान् लक्ष्म्या सह जगत्पतिः।
आस्ते सर्वेश्वरः श्रेष्ठः* पूज्यमानः सनातनः॥
तथाच वसुधारे तु वसूनां रत्नमण्डितम्।
स्थानानामुत्तमं पुण्यं दुराधर्षं सुरद्विषाम्॥
रत्नधारे गिरिवरे सप्तर्षीणां महात्मनाम्।
सप्ताश्रमाणि पुण्यानि सिद्धावासैर्युतानि च†॥
तत्र हैमं चतुर्द्वारं वज्रनीलादिमण्डितम्।
सुपुण्यं सद्वस्थानं‡ ब्रह्मणोऽव्यक्तजन्मनः॥
तत्र देवर्षयो विप्राः सिद्धा ब्रह्मर्षयोऽपरे।
उपासते देवदेवं§ पितामहमजं परम्॥
सर्वैः सम्पूजितो नित्यं देव्या सह चतुर्मुखः।
आस्ते हिताय लोकानां शान्तानां परमा गतिः॥
तस्यैकशृङ्गशिखरे महापद्मैरलङ्कृते।
स्वच्छामृतजलं पुण्यं सुगन्धं¶ सुमहत्सरः।
जैगीषव्याश्रमं पुण्यं योगीन्द्रैरुपसेवितम्‖॥

---

* सर्व्वामरश्रेष्ठः इति B and D.

† सिद्धावासयुतानि चेति B.

‡ सुमहत्स्थानमिति B and D.

§ सदा देवमिति B.

¶ सुगन्धमार्षं, सुगन्धि।

‖ शोभितमिति B.

तत्रास्ते* भगवान्नित्यं सर्व्वशिष्यैः† समावृतः।
प्रशान्तदोषैरक्षुद्रैर्ब्रह्मविद्भिर्महात्मभिः॥
शङ्खो मनोहरश्चैव कौशिकः कृष्ण एव च।
सुमना वेदवादश्च शिष्यास्तस्य प्रसादतः‡॥
सर्वयोगरताः शान्ता भस्मोद्धूलितविग्रहाः।
उपासते महाचार्य्या§ ब्रह्मविद्यापरायणाः॥
तेषामनुग्रहार्थाय यतीनां शान्तचेतसाम्।
सान्निध्यं कुरुते भूयो देव्या सह महेश्वरः॥
अनेकान्याश्रमाणि¶ स्युस्तस्मिन् गिरिवरोत्तमे।
मुनीनां युक्तमनसां|| सरांसि सरितस्तथा॥
तेषु योगरता विप्रा** जापकाः संयतेन्द्रियाः।
ब्रह्मण्यासक्तमनसो रमन्ते ज्ञानतत्पराः॥
आत्मन्यात्मानमाधाय शिखान्ते पर्य्यवस्थितम्††।
ध्यायन्ति देवमीशानं येन सर्व्वमिदं ततम्॥

---

* तत्रास्ते इति B and D.

† आस्ते शिष्यैरिति B and D.

‡ प्रधानतः इति B and D.

§ महावीर्य्या इति B and D.

¶ अन्यानि चाश्रमाणीति B and D.

|| योगनिरतचित्तानामित्यर्थः।

** वैद्या इति E and H.

†† शिखान्तान्तरमाश्रितमिति B and D.

सुमेघं* वासवस्थानं सहस्रादित्यसन्निभम्।
तत्रास्ते भगवानिन्द्रः शच्या सह सुरेश्वरः॥
गजशैले तु दुर्गाया भवनं मणितोरणम्।
आस्ते भगवती दुर्गा तत्र साक्षान्महेश्वरी।
उपास्यमाना विविधैः शक्तिभेदैरितस्ततः॥
पीत्वा योगामृतं लब्ध्वा साक्षादमृतमैश्वरम्†।
सुलीलस्य‡ गिरेः शृङ्गे§ नानाधातुसमुज्ज्वले॥
राक्षसानां पुराणि स्युः सरांसि शतशो द्विजाः।
तथा पुरशतं विप्राः शतशृङ्गे महाचले॥
स्फाटिकस्तम्भसंयुक्तं यक्षाणाममितौजसाम्।
श्वेतोदरगिरेः शृङ्गे सुपर्णस्य महात्मनः॥
प्राकारगोपुरोपेतं मणितोरणमण्डितम्।
स तत्र गरुड़ः श्रीमान् साक्षाद्विष्णुरिवापरः॥
ध्यात्वा तत्परमं ज्योतिरात्मन्येवमथाव्ययम्¶।
अन्यच्च भवनं पुण्यं श्रीशृङ्गे मुनिपुङ्गवाः॥
श्रीदेव्याः सर्वरत्नाढ्यं हैमं समणितोरणम्।

---

* सुमेघे इति B. अमोघमिति D.

† साक्षादानन्दमैश्वरमिति B and D.

‡ सुनीलस्य इति B, D and E.

§ मूर्ध्नि इति B. नानाधातु इत्यादिपादाष्टकं B पुस्तके नास्ति।

¶ ध्यात्वास्ते तत्परं ज्योतिरात्मानं विष्णुमव्ययमिति B and D.

तत्र सा परमा शक्तिर्विष्णोरतिमनोरमा ॥
अनन्तविभवा लक्ष्मीर्जगत्संमोहनोत्सुका।
अध्यास्ते देवगन्धर्वसिद्धचारणवन्दिता॥
विचिन्त्या जगतो योनिः स्वशक्तिकिरणोज्ज्वला।
तत्रैव देवदेवस्य विष्णोरायतनं महत्॥
सरांसि तत्र चत्वारि विचित्रकमलाशयाः।
तथा सहस्रशिखरे विद्याधरपुराष्टकम्॥
रत्नसोपानसंयुक्तं सरोभिश्चोपशोभितम्।
नद्यो विमलपानीयाश्चित्रनीलोत्पलाकराः॥
कर्णिकारवनं दिव्यं* तत्रास्ते शङ्करः स्वयम्†।
पारिजाते महालक्ष्म्याः पर्वते तु‡ पुरं शुभम्॥
रम्य§प्रासादसंयुक्तं घण्टाचामरभूषितम्।
नृत्यद्भिरप्सरःसङ्घैरितश्चेतश्च शोभितम्॥
मृदङ्गपणवोद्घुष्टं¶ वेणुवीणा‖निनादितम्।
गन्धर्व्वकिन्नराकीर्णं संवृतं सिद्धपुङ्गवैः॥

---

* तत्र इति B.

† शङ्करोऽम्बया इति B.

‡ परिपार्श्वे महाशैले महालक्ष्म्याः इति B.

§ रम्यमिति B.

¶ मुरजोद्घुष्टमिति B.

‖ वीणावेणु इति B.

भास्वद्भिर्भृगमायुक्तं* महाप्रासादसङ्कुलम्।
महागणेश्वरैर्जुष्टं† धार्म्मिकानां सुदर्शनम्॥
तत्र सा वसते‡ देवी नित्यं योगपरायणा।
महालक्ष्मीर्महादेवी त्रिशूलवरधारिणी॥
त्रिनेत्रा सर्वशक्त्यौघसंवृता सा च तन्मयी§।
पश्यन्ति तत्र मुनयः सिद्धा ये ब्रह्मवादिनः॥
सुपार्श्वस्योत्तरे भागे सरस्वत्याः पुरोत्तमम्।
सरांसि सिद्धजुष्टानि देवभोग्यानि सत्तमाः॥
पाण्डुरस्य गिरेः शृङ्गे विचित्रद्रुमसङ्कुलम्¶।
गन्धर्व्वाणां पुरशतं दिव्यस्त्रीभिः समावृतम्॥
तेन नित्य‖मदोत्सिक्ता नरा नार्य्यस्तथैव च।
क्रीड़न्ति मुदिता नित्यं विलासैर्भोगतत्पराः॥
अञ्जनस्य** गिरेः शृङ्गे नारीपुरमनुत्तमम्।
वसन्ति तत्राप्सरसो रम्भाद्या रतिलालसाः॥
चित्रसेनादयो यत्र समायान्त्यर्थिनः सदा।

---

* भास्वद्भित्तिसमाकीर्णमिति B and D.

† गणेश्वरादिना युक्तमिति B. गणेश्वराङ्गनाजुष्टमिति D.

‡ वसते इत्यार्षमात्मनेपदम्।

§ सन्मयीति D, E and H.

¶ सङ्कुले इति B.

‖ ते तु नित्यमिति B.

** इतः प्रभृति प्रथवर्णैर्युता इत्यन्तं B पुस्तके नास्ति।

सा पुरी सर्वरत्नाढ्या नैकप्रस्रवणैर्युता ॥
अनेकानि पुराणि स्युः कौमुदे चापि सत्तमाः* ।
रुद्राणां शान्तरजसामीश्वरासक्तचेतसाम्† ॥
तेषु रुद्रा महायोगा महेशान्तरचारिणः ।
समासते पुरं ज्योतिरारूढ़ाः स्थानमैश्वरम्‡ ॥
पिञ्जरस्य गिरेः शृङ्गे गणेशानां पुरत्रयम् ।
नदीश्वरस्य कपिला तत्रास्ते स महामतिः ॥
तथा च जारुधेः शृङ्गे देवदेवस्य धीमतः ।
दीप्तमायतनं पुण्यं§ भास्करस्यामितौजसः ।
तस्यैवोत्तरदिग्भागे चन्द्रस्थानमनुत्तमम् ।
वसते¶ तत्र रम्यात्मा भगवान् शान्त‖दीधितिः ॥
अन्यत्र भवनं दिव्यं हंसशैले महर्षयः ।
सहस्रयोजनायामं सुवर्णमणितोरणम् ॥
तत्रास्ते भगवान् ब्रह्मा सिद्धसङ्घैरभिष्टुतः ।
सावित्र्या सह विश्वात्मा वासुदेवादिभि**र्युतः ॥

---

* सुव्रताः इति B.

† मीश्वरार्पितचेतसामिति B.

‡ स्थानमुत्तममिति B.

§ रम्यमिति B.

¶ रमते इति B.

‖ शीत इति B and D.

** वामदेवादिभिरिति B and D.

तस्य दक्षिणदिग्भागे सिद्धानां पुरमुत्तमम्* ।
सनन्दनाद्यो यत्र वसन्ति मुनिपुङ्गवाः ॥
पञ्चशैलस्य शिखरे दानवानां पुरत्रयम् ।
नातिदूरेण तस्माच्च† दैत्याचार्य्यस्य धीमतः ।
सुगन्धशैलशिखरे सरिद्भिरुपशोभितम् ।
कर्द्दमस्याश्रमं पुण्यं तत्रास्ते भगवानृषिः ॥
तस्यैव पूर्व्वदिग्भागे किञ्चिद्वै दक्षिणाश्रिते ।
सनत्कुमारो भगवांस्तत्रास्ते ब्रह्मवित्तमः ॥
सर्व्वेष्वेतेषु शैलेषु तथान्येषु मुनीश्वराः ।
सरांसि विमला नद्यो देवानामालयानि‡ च ॥
सिद्धलिङ्गानि पुण्यानि मुनिभिः स्थापितानि च§ ।
तानि चायतनान्याशु¶ संख्यातुं नैव शक्यते‖ ॥
एष सङ्क्षेपतः प्रोक्तो जम्बूद्वीपस्य विस्तरः ।
न शक्यो विस्तराद्वक्तुं मया वर्षशतैरपि ॥

इति श्रीकूर्म्मपुराणे जम्बूद्वीपवर्णनं नाम अष्टचत्वारिंशोऽध्यायः ।

---

* पुरसत्तममिति A.

† तस्माथ इति B.

‡ अत्र क्लीवत्वमार्षम् ।

§ तु इति B.

¶ वन्यान्याश्रमवर्य्याणीति B and D.

‖ एकत्वमार्षम्, शक्यन्ते ।

ऊनपञ्चाशोऽध्यायः।

सूत उवाच।

जम्बूद्वीपस्य विस्ताराद्द्विगुणेन समन्ततः।
संवेष्टयित्वा* क्षीरोदं प्लक्षद्वीपो व्यवस्थितः॥
प्लक्षद्वीपे च विप्रेन्द्राः सप्तासन्कुलपर्व्वताः।
सिद्धायुताः† सुपर्वाणः सिद्धसङ्घनिषेविताः॥
गोमेदः‡ प्रथमस्तेषां द्वितीयश्चन्द्र उच्यते।
नारदो दुन्दुभिश्चैव मणिमान्मेघनिस्वनः§।
वैभ्राजः सप्तमस्तेषां¶ ब्रह्मणोऽत्यन्तवल्लभः॥
तत्र देवर्षिगन्धर्व्वैः सिद्धैश्च भगवानजः।
उपास्यते स विश्वात्मा साक्षी सर्व्वस्य विश्वदृक्‖।
तेषु पुण्या जनपदा आधयो व्याधयो न च।
न तत्र** पापकर्त्तारः पुरुषा वै कथञ्चन॥
तेषां नद्यश्च सप्तैव वर्षाणान्तु समुद्रगाः।

---

* संवेष्टयित्वा इत्यार्षम्, संवेष्ट्य इति साधु।

† ऋज्वायताः इति B and D.

‡ गोमेद्ध इति D.

§ सोमस्य ऋषभस्तथेति B and D.

¶ सप्तमः प्रोक्तः इति B.

‖ विश्वधृक् इति B and D.

** चात्र इति B.

तासु ब्रह्मर्षयो नित्यं पितामहमुपासते ॥
अनुतप्ताशिखे चैव विपापा त्रिदिवा कृता ।
अमृता सुकृता चैव नामतः परिकीर्त्तिताः ॥
क्षुद्रनद्यस्तु विख्याताः सरांसि च बहून्यपि* ।
न चैतेषु युगावस्था पुरुषा वै चिरायुषः ॥
आर्य्यकाः कुरराश्चैव विदेहा† भाविनस्तथा ।
ब्रह्मक्षत्रियविट्शूद्रास्तस्मिन्द्वीपे प्रकीर्त्तिताः ॥
इज्यते भगवानीशो‡ वर्णैस्तत्र निवासिभिः ।
तेषाञ्च सोमसाम्राज्यं§ सारूप्यं मुनिपुङ्गवाः ॥
सर्व्वे धर्म्मरता नित्यं सर्व्वे¶ मुदितमानसाः ।
पञ्चवर्षसहस्राणि जीवन्ति च निरामयाः ॥
प्लक्षद्वीपप्रमाणन्तु द्विगुणेन समन्ततः ।
संवेष्ट्येक्षुरसाम्भोधिं शाल्मलिः संव्यवस्थितः ॥
सप्तवर्षाणि तत्रापि सप्तैव कुलपर्व्वताः ।‖
ऋज्वायताः सुपर्वाणः सप्तनद्यश्च सुव्रताः ॥
कुमुदश्चानदश्चैव तृतीयश्च वलाहकः ।

---

* संख्याताः सरांसि सुबहून्यपि इति B.

† विदशा इति B.

‡ भगवान् सोमः इति B and D.

§ सोमसायुज्यमिति B, D, E, G and H.

¶ नित्यमिति B.

‖ एतच्चरणद्वयं A, E, H पुस्तकेषु नास्ति ।

द्रोणः कंसस्तु* महिषः ककुद्मान् सप्तमस्तथा† ॥
योनी तोया वितृष्णा च चन्द्रा शुक्ला विमोचनी ।
निवृत्तिश्चेति ता नद्यः स्मृताः पापहरा नृणाम् ॥
न तेषु विद्यते लोभः क्रोधो वा द्विजसत्तमाः ।
न चैवास्ति युगावस्था जना जीवन्त्यनामयाः ॥
यजन्ति सततं तत्र वर्णा वायुं सनातनम् ।
तेषां तत्साधनं युक्तं‡ सारूप्यञ्च सलोकता ॥
कपिला ब्राह्मणाः प्रोक्ता राजानश्चारुणास्तथा ।
पीता वैश्याः स्मृताः कृष्णा द्वीपेऽस्मिन् वृषला द्विजाः ॥
शाल्मलस्य तु विस्ताराद्द्विगुणेन समन्ततः ।
संवेष्ट्य तु सुरोदाब्धिं कुशद्वीपो व्यवस्थितः ॥
विद्रुमश्चैव हेमश्च§ द्युतिमान् पुष्पवांस्तथा ।
कुशेशयो हरिश्चैव मन्दरः सप्त¶ पर्व्वताः ॥
धुतपापा शिवा चैव पवित्रा सम्मिता तथा ।
तथा विद्युत्प्रभा रामा महानद्यश्च सप्त वै‖ ॥
अन्याश्च शतशो विप्रा नद्यो मणिजलाः शुभाः ।

---

* कङ्कस्तु इति B, D and E.

† सप्तपर्व्वतानिति B.

‡ तेषां तस्याथ सायुज्यमिति B and D.

§ हेमश्च इति B.

¶ हरिश्चाथ मन्दरः सन्तु इति B.

‖ विद्युदन्ता मही चेति नद्यस्तत्र जलावहाः इति B and D.

तासु ब्रह्माणमीशानं देवाद्याः पर्य्युपासते ॥
ब्राह्मणा द्रविणो विप्राः क्षत्रियाः शुष्मिणस्तथा ।
वैश्यास्तोभासु* मन्देहाः शूद्रास्तत्र प्रकीर्त्तिताः ॥
मर्त्येऽपि ज्ञानसम्पन्ना† मैत्रादिगुणसंयुताः ।
यथोक्तकारिणः सर्व्वे सर्व्वे भूतहिते रताः ॥
यजन्ति यज्ञैर्विविधै‡र्ब्रह्माणं परमेष्ठिनम् ।
तेषाञ्च ब्रह्मसायुज्यं सारूप्यञ्च सलोकता ॥
कुशद्वीपस्य विस्ताराद्द्विगुणेन समन्ततः ।
क्रौञ्चद्वीपः स्थितो§ विप्रा वेष्टयित्वा घृतोदधिम् ॥
क्रौञ्चो वामनकश्चैव तृतीयश्चाधिकारिकः ।
देवाब्दश्च त्रिविदश्च¶ पुण्डरीकस्तथैव च ।
नाम्ना च सप्तमः प्रोक्तः पर्वतो दुन्दुभिस्वनः ॥
गौरी कुमुद्वती चैव सन्ध्या रात्रिर्मनोजवा ।
कोभिश्च‖ पुण्डरीकाद्या नद्यः प्राधान्यतः स्मृताः ॥
पुष्कलाः पुष्करा धन्यास्तिष्या वर्णाः** क्रमेण वै ।

---

* वैश्याः स्नेहास्तु इति B.

† मर्त्ते विज्ञानसम्पन्ना इति B.

‡ विविधैर्यज्ञैरिति B.

§ क्रौञ्चद्वीपस्ततः इति B.

¶ दिवावृत्तगिरीन्द्रश्च इति B. देवपूर्वोगिरीन्द्रश्च इति D.

‖ ख्यातिश्च इति B and D.

** तिष्यान्तस्य इति B. तिष्यास्तत्र इति D.

ब्राह्मणाः क्षत्रिया वैश्याः शूद्राश्चैव द्विजोत्तमाः ॥
अर्च्चयन्ति महादेवं यज्ञदानशमादिभिः।
व्रतोपवासैर्व्विविधैर्होमैश्च पितृतर्पणैः* ॥
तेषां वै रुद्रसायुज्यं सारूप्यञ्चातिदुर्ल्लभम्।
सलोकता च सामीप्यं जायते तत्प्रसादतः ॥
क्रौञ्चद्वीपस्य विस्ताराद्द्विगुणेन समन्ततः।
शाकद्वीपः स्थितो विप्रा आवेष्ट्य दधिसागरम् ॥
उदयो रैवतश्चैव श्यामकाष्ठ†गिरिस्तथा।
आम्बिकेयस्तथा रम्यः केसरी चेति पर्व्वताः ॥
सुकुमारी कुमारी च नलिनी वेणुका तथा।
इक्षुका धेनुका चैव गभस्तिश्चेति निम्नगाः ॥
आसां पिबन्तः सलिलं जीवन्ति तत्र मानवाः।
अनामयाश्चाशोकाश्च‡ रागद्वेषविवर्ज्जिताः ॥
मृगाश्च§ मगधाश्चैव मानसा मन्दगास्तथा।
ब्राह्मणाः क्षत्रिया वैश्याः शूद्राश्चात्र क्रमेण तु ॥
यजन्ति सततं देवं सर्व्वलोकैकसाक्षिणम्।
व्रतोपवासैर्व्विविधैर्द्देवदेवं दिवाकरम् ॥

---

* होमैः स्वाध्यायतर्पणैरिति B and D.

† श्यामाकास्त इति B.

‡ अनामया ह्यशोकाश्च इति B.

§ मगाश्च इति D, E, G and H.

तेषां वै सूर्य्यसायुज्यं* सामीप्यञ्च सरूपता।
सलोकता च विप्रेन्द्रा जायते तत्प्रसादतः॥
शाकद्वीपं समावृत्य क्षीरोदः सागरः स्थितः।
श्वेतद्वीपञ्च तन्मध्ये नारायणपरायणाः।
तत्र पुण्या जनपदा नानाश्चर्य्यसमन्विताः।
श्वेतास्तत्र नरा नित्यं जायन्ते विष्णुतत्पराः॥
नाधयो व्याधयस्तत्र जरामृत्युभयं न च।
क्रोधलोभविनिर्म्मुक्ता मायामात्सर्य्यवर्ज्जिताः॥
नित्यपुष्टा निरातङ्का नित्यानन्दाश्च भोगिनः।
नारायणसमाः सर्व्वे नारायणपरायणाः॥†
केचिद्ध्यानपरा नित्यं योगिनः संयतेन्द्रियाः।
केचिज्जपन्ति तप्यन्ति केचिद्विज्ञानिनोऽपरे॥
अन्ये निर्व्वीजयोगेन ब्रह्मभावेन भाविताः।
ध्यायन्ति तत्परं ब्रह्म वासुदेवं सनातनम्‡॥
एकान्तिनो निरालम्बा महाभागवताः परे।
पश्यन्ति तत्परं§ ब्रह्म विष्ण्वाख्यं तमसः परम्॥
सर्व्वे चतुर्भुजाकाराः शङ्खचक्रगदाधराः।

---

* तेषां सूर्य्येण सायुज्यमिति B.

† तत्र पुण्या इत्यादिश्लोकषट्कं A, D, E, H पुस्तकेषु नास्ति।

‡ परं पदमिति B.

§ परममिति B.

सुपीतवाससः सर्व्वे श्रीवत्साङ्कितवक्षसः ॥
अन्ये महेश्वरपरास्त्रिपुण्ड्राङ्कितमस्तकाः ।
सुयोगाङ्गतिकरणा* महागरुड़वाहनाः ॥
सर्व्वे शक्तिसमायुक्ता† नित्यानन्दाश्च निर्म्मलाः ।
वसन्ति तत्र पुरुषाः विष्णोरन्तरचारिणः ॥
तत्र नारायणस्यान्यं दुर्गमन्दुरतिक्रमम् ।
नारायणं नाम पुरं प्रासादै‡रुपशोभितम् ॥
हेमप्राकारसंयुक्तं स्फाटिकैर्मण्डपैर्युतम् ।
प्रभासहस्रकलिलन्दुराधर्षं सुशोभनम् ॥
हर्म्म्यप्रासाद§संयुक्तमट्टालक¶समाकुलम् ।
हेमगोपुरसाहस्रैर्नानारत्नोपशोभितैः ॥
शुभ्रास्तरणसंयुक्तै‖र्विचित्रैः समलङ्कृतम् ।
नन्दनैर्विविधाकारैः स्रवन्तीभिश्च शोभितम् ॥
सरोभिः सर्व्वतो युक्तं वीणावेणुनिनादितम् ।
पताकाभिर्विचित्राभिरनेकाभिश्च शोभितम् ॥
वीथीभिः सर्व्वतो युक्तं सोपानैः रत्नभूषितैः ।

---

* सुयोगोङ्कृतकिरणाः इति B and D.

† सर्व्वशक्तिसमायुक्ताः इति B and D.

‡ व्यासाद्यैरिति B and D.

§ प्राकार इति B and D.

¶ महाट्टाल इति B and D.

‖ शुभ्रतोरणसंयुक्तमिति B.

नदी*शतसहस्राढ्यं दिव्यगाननिनादितम्† ॥
हंसकारण्डवाकीर्णं चक्रवाकोपशोभितम्।
चतुर्द्वारमनौपम्यमगम्यं देवविद्विषाम् ॥
तत्र तत्राप्सरःसङ्घैर्नृत्यद्भिरुपशोभितम्।
नानागीतविधानज्ञैर्देवानामपि दुर्लभैः‡ ॥
नानाविलाससम्पन्नैः कामुकैरतिकोमलैः।
प्रभूतचन्द्रवदनैर्नूपुरारावसंयुतैः ॥
ईषत्स्मितैः सुबिम्बोष्ठैर्बालमुग्धमृगीक्षणैः।
अशेषविभवोपेतैस्तनुमध्यविभूषितैः§ ॥
सुराजहंसचलनैः सुवेषैर्मधुरस्वनैः।
संलापालाप¶कुशलैर्दिव्याभरणभूषितैः।
स्तनभारविनम्रैश्च मधुघूर्णितलोचनैः ॥
नानावर्णविचित्राङ्गैर्नानाभोगरतिप्रियैः।
उत्फुल्लकुसुमोद्यानैस्तद्भूतशतशोभितम्‖ ॥
असंख्येयगुणं शुद्धमसंख्येयैस्त्रिदशैरपि।

---

* नारीति B and D.

† दिव्यगेयसमन्वितमिति B. दिव्यपेयसमन्वितमिति D.

‡ दुर्लभमिति B.

§ भूषितैस्तनुमध्यमैरिति B.

¶ संलापोल्लाप इति B.

‖ द्रुतश्चैतश्च शोभितमिति B.

श्रीमत्पवित्रन्देवस्य श्रीपतेरमितौजसः॥
तस्य मध्येऽतितेजस्कमुच्चप्राकार*तोरणम्।
स्थानं तद्वैष्णवं दिव्यं योगिनां सिद्धिदायकम्† ॥
तन्मध्ये भगवानेकः पुण्डरीकदलद्युतिः।
शेतेऽशेषजगत्सूतिः शेषाहिशयने हरिः॥
विचिन्त्यमानो योगीन्द्रैः सनन्दनपुरोगमैः।
स्वात्मानन्दामृतं पीत्वा पुरस्तात्तमसः परः॥
पीतवासा विशालाक्षो‡ महामायो महाभुजः।
क्षीरोदकन्यया नित्यं गृहीतचरणद्वयः॥
सा च देवी जगद्वन्द्या पादमूले हरिप्रिया।
समास्ते तन्मना नित्यं पीत्वा नारायणामृतम्॥
न तत्राधार्म्मिका यान्ति न च देवान्तरालयाः§।
वैकुण्ठं नाम तत्स्थानं त्रिदशैरपि वन्दितम्॥
न मे¶ प्रभवति प्रज्ञा कृत्स्नशास्त्र‖निरूपणे।
एतावच्छक्यते वक्तुं नारायणपुरं हि तत्॥
स एव परमं ब्रह्म वासुदेवः सनातनः।

---

* उच्चप्राकार इति B.

† योगिनामपि दुर्लभमिति B and D.

‡ सुपीतवसनोऽनन्तः इति B and D.

§ देवान्तराश्रयाः इति B.

¶ न मेऽत्र भवतीति D, E and H.

‖ कृष्णशास्त्र इति G.

शेते नारायणः श्रीमान्मायया मोहयञ्जगत्* ॥
नारायणादिदं जातं तस्मिन्नेव व्यवस्थितम् ।
तमाश्रयति† कालान्ते स एव परमा गतिः ॥

इति श्रीकूर्म्मपुराणे भुवनविन्यासे एकोनपञ्चाशोऽध्यायः ।

पञ्चाशोऽध्यायः ।

सूत उवाच ।

शाकद्वीपस्य विस्ताराद्द्विगुणेन व्यवस्थितः ।
क्षीरार्णवं समाश्रित्य* द्वीपं पुष्करसंज्ञितम् ॥
एक एवात्र विप्रेन्द्राः पर्वतो मानसोत्तरः ।
योजनानां सहस्राणि चोर्द्ध्वं पञ्चाशदुच्छ्रितः ॥
तावदेव च विस्तीर्णः सर्व्वतः पारिमण्डलः ।

---

* मोहितमिति B.

† तमेवाभ्येति इति B and G. तं समभ्येति कल्यान्ते इति D.

---

* समावृत्य इति B.

स एव द्वीपश्चार्द्धेन* मानसोत्तरसंस्थितः† ॥
एक एव महाभागः सन्निवेशो द्विधा‡ कृतः ।
तस्मिन्द्वीपे स्मृतौ द्वौ तु§ पुण्यौ जनपदौ शुभौ ।
अपरौ मानसस्याथ पर्व्वतस्यानुमण्डलौ ॥ ¶
महावीतं|| स्मृतं वर्षं धातकीखण्डमेव च ।
स्वादूदकेनोदधिना पुष्करः परिवारितः ॥
तस्मिन्द्वीपे महावृक्षो न्यग्रोधोऽमरपूजितः ।
तस्मिन्निवसति ब्रह्मा विश्वात्मा विश्वभावनः ॥
तत्रैव मुनिशार्दूलाः शिवनारायणालयः ।
वसत्यत्र महादेवो हरोर्द्धं हरिरव्ययः ॥
सम्पूज्यमानो ब्रह्माद्यैः कुमाराद्यैश्च योगिभिः ।
गन्धर्व्वैः किन्नरैर्यक्षैरीश्वरः कृष्णपिङ्गलः** ॥
स्वस्थास्तत्र प्रजाः सर्व्वा ब्राह्मणाः शतशस्त्विषः†† ।
निरामया विशोकाश्च रागद्वेषविवर्ज्जिताः ॥

---

* द्वीपः पश्चार्द्धे इति B, C and E.

† संश्रितः इति B and C.

‡ सन्निवेशाद्द्विधा इति B.

§ तु द्वौ इति B.

¶ एतत्पादद्वयं A, C, E, H पुस्तकेषु नास्ति ।

|| महावीतमिति B.

** कृष्णपिङ्गलैरिति B and C.

†† ब्राह्मणाः सहस्रत्विषः इति B. सहस्रायुषः इति C.

सत्यानृते न तत्रास्तां नोत्तमाधममध्यमाः ।
न* वर्णाश्रमधर्म्माश्च न नद्यो न च पर्व्वताः ॥
परेण पुष्करेणाथ समावृत्य स्थितो महान् ।
स्वादूदकसमुद्रस्तु समन्ताद्द्विजसत्तमाः ॥
परेण तस्य महती दृश्यते लोकसंस्थितिः ।
काञ्चनी द्विगुणा भूमिः सर्व्वैक†शिलोपमा ॥
तस्याः परेण शैलस्तु मर्य्यादा भानुमण्डलः‡ ।
प्रकाशश्चाप्रकाशश्च लोकालोकः स उच्यते ॥
योजनानां सहस्राणि दश तस्योच्छ्रयः स्मृतः ।
तावानेव च विस्तारो लोकालोकमहागिरेः ॥
समावृत्य तु तं शैलं सर्व्वतो वै समस्थितम् ।
तमश्चाण्डकटाहेन समन्तात्परिवेष्टितम् ॥
एते सप्त महालोकाः पातालाः सम्प्रकीर्त्तिताः§ ।
ब्रह्माण्डाशेष¶विस्तारः संक्षेपेण मयोदितः ॥
अण्डानामीदृशानान्तु कोट्यो ज्ञेयाः सहस्रशः ।
सर्व्वगत्वात्प्रधानस्य कारणस्याव्ययात्मनः ॥
अण्डेष्वेतेषु सर्व्वेषु भुवनानि चतुर्द्दश ।

---

* न इत्यारभ्य पादषट्कं B पुस्तके नास्ति ।

† सर्व्वचैव इति B. सर्व्वा चैव शिलोपमा इति C.

‡ स्थाणमण्डल इति C.

§ सप्त कीर्त्तिताः इति C, E and D.

¶ ब्रह्माण्डस्यैव इति B.

तत्र तत्र चतुर्वक्त्रा रुद्रा नारायणादयः ॥
दशोत्तरमथैकैकमण्डावरण*सप्तकम् ।
समन्तात्संस्थितं विप्रास्तत्र यान्ति मनीषिणः ॥
अनन्तमेवमव्यक्तमनादिनिधनं महत् ।
अतीत्य वर्त्तते सर्व्वञ्जगत्प्रकृतिरक्षरम् ॥
अनन्तत्वमनन्तस्य यतः सङ्ख्या न विद्यते ।
तदव्यक्तमिदं ज्ञेयं तद्ब्रह्म परमं ध्रुवम्† ॥
अनन्त एष सर्व्वत्र सर्व्वस्थानेषु पठ्यते ॥
तस्य पूर्व्वं मयाप्युक्तं यत्तन्माहात्म्यमुत्तमम् ।
स एष सर्वत्र गतः सर्वस्थानेषु पूज्यते‡ ॥
भूमौ रसातले चैव आकाशे पवनेऽनले ।
अर्णवेषु च सर्व्वेषु दिवि चैव न संशयः ॥
तथा तमसि तत्त्वे वा§प्येष एव महाद्युतिः ।
अनेकधा विभक्ताङ्गः¶ क्रीड़ते पुरुषोत्तमः ॥
महेश्वरः परोऽव्यक्तादण्डमव्यक्तसम्भवम् ।
अण्डाद्ब्रह्मा समुत्पन्नस्तेन सृष्टमिदं जगत् ॥

इति श्रीकूर्म्मपुराणे भुवनकोशे पञ्चाशोऽध्यायः ।

---

* वरक इति B.

† तदव्यक्तमिति प्रोक्तं ज्ञेयं तत्परमं पदमिति B.

‡ वर्त्तते इति B.

§ सत्त्वे च इति B.

¶ विभक्तश्च इति B.

एकपञ्चाशोऽध्यायः।

ऋषय ऊचुः।

अतीतानागतानीह यानि मन्वन्तराणि वै*।
तानि त्वं कथयास्माकं व्यासश्च द्वापरे युगे॥
वेदशाखाप्रणयिनो देवदेवस्य धीमतः।
धर्म्मार्थानां प्रवक्तारो ह्यीशानस्य† कलौ युगे॥
कियन्तो देवदेवस्य शिष्याः कलियुगेऽपि वै।
एतत्सर्व्वं समासेन सूत वक्तुमिहार्हसि॥

सूत उवाच।

मनुः स्वायम्भुवः पूर्व्वन्ततः स्वारोचिषो मतः‡।
उत्तमस्तामसश्चैव रैवतश्चाक्षुषस्तथा॥
षड़ेते मनवोऽतीताः साम्प्रतन्तु रवेः सुतः।
वैवस्वतोऽयं सप्तैतत्सप्तमं वर्त्तते परम्§॥
स्वायम्भुवन्तु कथितं कल्पादावन्तरं मया।
अत ऊर्द्ध्वं निबोधध्वं मनोः स्वारोचिषस्य तु॥
पारावताश्च तुषिता देवाः स्वारोचिषेऽन्तरे।

---

* तु इति B.

† तथावतारान्धर्म्मार्थमीशानस्य इति B and D.

‡ स्वारोचिषस्ततः इति B.

§ यस्यैतत्सप्तमी वर्त्ततेऽन्तरः इति B.

विपश्चिन्नाम देवेन्द्रो बभूवासुरमर्द्दनः* ॥
ऊर्ज्जस्तम्भस्तथा प्राणो दान्तोऽथ ऋषभस्तथा ।
तिमिरश्चार्वरीवांश्च सप्त सप्तर्षयोऽभवन् ॥
चैत्रकिम्पुरुषाद्यास्तु सुताः स्वारोचिषस्य तु ।
द्वितीयमेतदाख्यातमन्तरं शृणु चोत्तमम्† ॥
तृतीयेऽप्यन्तरे चैव उत्तमो नाम वै मनुः ।
सुशान्तिस्तत्र देवेन्द्रो बभूवामित्रकर्षणः ॥
सुधा‡ मानस्तथा सत्या शिवश्चाथ प्रतर्द्दनः ।
वशवर्त्तिनः पञ्चैते§ गणा द्वादशकाः स्मृताः ॥
रजोगात्रोर्द्ध्वबाहुश्च¶ सवनश्चानघस्तथा ।
सुतपाः शक्र‖ इत्येते सप्त सप्तर्षयोऽभवन् ॥
तामसस्यान्तरे देवाः सुरायासहरास्तथा** ।
सत्याश्च सुधियश्चैव सप्तविंशतिका गणाः ॥
शिविरिन्द्रस्तथैवासी††च्छतयज्ञोपलक्षणः ।

---

* सूदन इति B.

† चोत्तरमिति B.

‡ सुरा इति B.

§ यश्चैते इति B.

¶ रजोर्द्ध्वश्चोर्द्ध्वबाहुश्च इति B.

‖ शुक्र इति B and C.

** मृगवाङ्कवयस्तथा इति B. सुरायासहरास्तथा इति E.

†† तथाचासीदिति B.

बभूव शङ्करे भक्तो महादेवार्च्चने रतः॥
ज्योतिर्द्धाम पृथक्काव्यश्चैत्रोऽग्निवसनस्तथा*।
पीवरस्त्वृषयो† ह्येते सप्त तत्रापि चान्तरे॥
पञ्चमे चापि विप्रेन्द्रा रैवतो नाम नामतः।
मनुर्विभुश्च‡ तत्रेन्द्रो बभूवासुरमर्द्दनः॥
अमिता भूतयस्तत्र वैकुण्ठाश्च सुरोत्तमाः§।
एते देवगणास्तत्र चतुर्द्दश चतुर्द्दश॥
हिरण्यरोमा वेदश्री¶रूर्द्धबाहुस्तथैव च।
वेदबाहुः सुबाहुश्च सपर्ज्जन्यो‖ महामुनिः।
एते सप्तर्षयो विप्रास्तत्रासन्रैवतेऽन्तरे॥
स्वारोचिषश्चोत्तमश्च तामसो रैवतस्तथा।
प्रियव्रतान्विता ह्येते चत्वारो मनवः स्मृताः॥
षष्ठे मन्वन्तरे चापि** चाक्षुषस्तु मनुर्द्विजाः।
मनोजवस्तथैवेन्द्रो देवांश्चैव निबोधत॥

---

* ज्योतिर्धर्म्मा पृथुः काव्यश्चैत्रोऽग्निर्वरुणस्तथा इति B. ऽग्निसवनस्तथा इति C.

† पीवरश्चर्षयः इति B.

‡ वसुश्च इति B.

§ एतत्पादद्वयं B पुस्तके नास्ति।

¶ देवश्रीरिति B.

‖ देववाहुः सुधामा च पर्जन्यश्च इति B.

** चासीदिति B.

आद्याः प्रभूतभाव्याश्च प्रथनाश्च* दिवौकसः।
महानुभावा लेख्याश्च† पञ्च देवगणाः स्मृताः‡॥
विरजाश्च हविष्मांश्च सोमो मनुसमः स्मृतः§।
अविनामा¶ सविष्णुश्च सप्तासन्नृषयः शुभाः॥
विवस्वतः सुतो विप्राः श्राद्धदेवो महाद्युतिः।
मनुः संवर्त्तनो विप्राः‖ साम्प्रतं सप्तमेऽन्तरे॥
आदित्या वसवो रुद्रा देवास्तत्र मरुद्गणाः।
पुरन्दरस्तथैवेन्द्रो बभूव परवीरहा॥
वशिष्ठः कश्यप**श्चात्रिर्जमदग्निश्च गौतमः।
विश्वामित्रो भरद्वाजः सप्त सप्तर्षयोऽभवन्॥
विष्णुशक्तिरनौपम्या सत्त्वोद्रिक्ता स्थिताश्थितौ।
तदंशभूता राजानः सर्वे च त्रिदिवौकसः॥
स्वायम्भुवेऽन्तरे पूर्वं प्रकूत्यां†† मानसः सुतः।
रुचेः प्रजापतेर्जज्ञे तदंशेनाभवद्द्विजाः॥

---

* प्रसूता भव्याश्च पृथुगाश्च इति B.

† महान्धा बालखिल्याश्च इति B.

‡ पञ्चेति ह्यष्टका गणा इति B. पञ्चैतेऽप्यष्टका गणा इति C.

§ सुमेधा विरजाश्चैव हविष्मांश्च तमोमधुरिति B. हविष्मानुत्तमो मधुरिति C.

¶ अतिनामा इति B. अभिमानः सहिष्णुश्च इति C.

‖ मनुः स वर्त्तते धीमानिति B.

** काश्यप इति B.

†† माकुल्यामिति B.

ततः पुनरसौ देवः प्राप्ते स्वारोचिषेऽन्तरे ।
तुषितायां समुत्पन्नस्तुषितैः सह दैवतैः ॥
उत्तमे त्वन्तरे विष्णुः सत्यैः सह सुरोत्तमः* ।
सत्यायामभवत्सत्यः सत्यरूपो जनार्द्दनः ॥
तामसस्यान्तरे चैव सम्प्राप्ते पुनरेव हि ।
हर्य्यायां† हरिभिर्द्देवैर्हरिरेवाभवत्‡ हरिः ॥
रैवतेऽप्यन्तरे चैव सङ्कल्पान्मानसो हरिः§ ।
सम्भूतो मानसैः¶ सार्द्धं देवैः सह महाद्युतिः ॥
चाक्षुषेऽप्यन्तरे चैव वैकुण्ठः पुरुषोत्तमः ।
विकुण्ठायामसौ जज्ञे वैकुण्ठैर्दैवतैः सह ॥
मन्वन्तरे च‖ सम्प्राप्ते तथा वैवस्वतेऽन्तरे ।
वामनः कश्यपाद्विष्णुरदित्यां सम्बभूव ह ॥
त्रिभिः क्रमैः**रिमाँल्लोकाञ्जित्वा येन महात्मना ।
पुरन्दराय त्रैलोक्यं दत्तं निहतकण्टकम् ॥
इत्येतास्तनवस्तस्य सप्तमन्वन्तरेषु वै ।

---

* सुरोत्तमैरिति B, C, E and H.

† हर्षायामिति B and C.

‡ हरिरेषोऽभवदिति B.

§ संभूत्यां मानसोऽभवदिति B. सम्भूत्यां मानसो हरिरिति D.

¶ राजसैरिति B.

‖ ऽत्र इति B.

** त्रिविक्रमैरिति B.

सप्त चैवाभवन्विप्रा याभिः सङ्कर्षिताः प्रजाः* ॥
यस्माद्विश्वमिदं कृत्स्नं वामनेन महात्मना ।
तस्मात्सर्व्वैः स्मृतो नूनं देवैः सर्व्वेषु दैत्यहा† ॥
एष सर्व्वं सृजत्यादौ पाति हन्ति च केशवः ।
भूतान्तरात्मा भगवान्नारायण इति श्रुतिः ॥
एकांशेन जगत्सर्व्वं व्याप्य नारायणः स्थितः ।
चतुर्द्धा संस्थितो‡ व्यापी सगुणो निर्गुणोऽपि च§ ॥
एका भगवतो मूर्त्तिर्ज्ञानरूपा शिवामला ।
वासुदेवाभिधाना सा गुणातीता सुनिष्कला ॥
द्वितीया कालसंज्ञान्या¶ तामसी शिवसंज्ञिता‖ ।
निहन्त्री** सकलस्यान्ते वैष्णवी परमा तनुः ॥
सत्त्वोद्रिक्ता तृतीयान्या†† प्रद्युम्नेति च संज्ञिता‡‡ ।
जगत्संस्थापयेद्विश्वं§§ सा विष्णोः प्रकृतिर्ध्रुवा ॥

---

* एतत्पादद्वयं B पुस्तके नास्ति ।

† विष्णुर्विधिर्धाती: प्रवेशनादिति B. देवैः सर्व्वदेवेषु दैत्यहा इति G and H.

‡ चतुर्द्धारस्थितः इति B.

§ वा इति B.

¶ संज्ञाना इति B.

‖ तामसीशेन लक्षिता इति B.

** निहन्ति इति B and H.

†† तथैवान्या इति B.

‡‡ सम्मिता इति B.

§§ जगत्स्थापयते सर्व्वमिति B.

चतुर्थी वासुदेवस्य* मूर्त्तिर्ब्रह्मेति संज्ञिता† ।
राजसी सानिरुद्धस्य पुरुषसृष्टिकारिता ॥
यः स्वपित्यखिलं हत्वा प्रद्युम्नेन सह प्रभुः‡ ।
नारायणाख्यो ब्रह्मासौ प्रजासर्गं करोति सः ॥
यासौ नारायणतनुः प्रद्युम्नाख्या शुभा स्मृता§ ।
तया सम्मोहयेद्विश्वं सदेवासुरमानुषम्¶ ॥
ततः सैव जगन्मूर्त्तिः‖ प्रकृतिः परिकीर्त्तिता ।
वासुदेवो ह्यनन्तात्मा केवलो निर्गुणो हरिः ॥
प्रधानं पुरुषं कालः सत्त्वत्रयमनुत्तमम् ।
वासुदेवात्मकं नित्यमेतद्विज्ञाय मुच्यते** ॥
एकश्चेदं†† चतुष्पादं चतुर्द्धा पुनरच्युतः ।
बिभेद वासुदेवोऽसौ प्रद्युम्नो भगवान् हरिः ॥
कृष्णद्वैपायनो व्यासो विष्णुर्नारायणः स्वयम् ।
अवातरत्स सम्पूर्णं स्वेच्छया भगवान्‡‡ हरिः ॥

---

* चानिरुद्धाख्या इति B.

† प्रद्युम्नमूर्त्तिकारिका इति B.

‡ एतत्पादद्वयं B पुस्तके नास्ति ।

§ मुनीश्वराः इति B.

¶ मानवमिति B.

‖ सैव सर्व्वजगत्सूतिरिति B.

** विज्ञानमुच्यते इति B.

†† एकं देवमिति B.

‡‡ ह्यभवदिति B.

अनाद्यन्तं परं ब्रह्म न देवा ऋषयो* विदुः।
एकोऽयं वेद भगवान् व्यासो नारायणः प्रभुः॥
इत्येतद्विष्णुमाहात्म्यं कथितं मुनिसत्तमाः†।
एतत्सत्यं‡ पुनः सत्यमेवं ज्ञात्वा न मुह्यति॥

इति श्रीकूर्म्मपुराणे मन्वन्तरकीर्त्तने विष्णुमाहात्म्ये एकपञ्चाशोऽध्यायः।

द्वापञ्चाशोऽध्यायः।

सूत उवाच।

अस्मिन्मन्वन्तरे पूर्व्वं वर्त्तमाने महान् प्रभुः*।
द्वापरे प्रथमे व्यासो† मनुः स्वायम्भुवो मतः॥
बिभेद बहुधा वेदं नियोगाद्ब्रह्मणः प्रभोः।
द्वितीये द्वापरे चैव वेदव्यासः प्रजापतिः॥

---

* नर्षयः इति B.

† उक्तं वो मुनिपुङ्गवा इति B.

‡ एतत्सर्व्वमिति B.

---

* विभुरिति B.

† काल इति B.

तृतीये चोशना व्यासश्चतुर्थे स्याद्बृहस्पतिः।
सविता पञ्चमे व्यासः षष्ठे मृत्युः प्रकीर्त्तितः॥
सप्तमे च तथैवेन्द्रो वशिष्ठश्चाष्टमे मतः।
सारस्वतश्च* नवमे त्रिधामा दशमे मतः† ॥
एकादशे तु ऋषभः सुतेजा द्वादशे स्मृतः‡।
त्रयोदशे तथा धर्म्मः सुचक्षुस्तु चतुर्द्दशे॥
त्रय्यारुणिः§ पञ्चदशे षोड़शे तु धनञ्जयः।
कृतञ्जयः सप्तदशे ह्यष्टादशे ऋतञ्जयः॥
ततो व्यासो भरद्वाजस्तस्मादूर्द्ध्वन्तु गौतमः।
वाचश्रवाश्चैकविंशे तस्मान्नारायणः¶ परः॥
तृणविन्दुस्त्रयोविंशे वाल्मीकिस्तत्परः स्मृतः।
पञ्चविंशे तथा‖ प्राप्ते यस्मिन्वै द्वापरे द्विजाः।
पराशरसुतो व्यासः कृष्णद्वैपायनोऽभवत्॥

---

* वैवस्वतश्च इति B.

† स्मृतः इति B.

‡ एतत्पादद्वयं B पुस्तके नास्ति।

§ आरुणिर्वै इति B.

¶ तस्मात् शुष्मायणः इति B and F.

‖ इतः परं

शक्तिः षड्‌विंशे तु पराशरः।
सप्तविंशे तथा व्यासो जातूकर्णो महामुनिः॥
अष्टाविंशे पुनः

इत्यधिकं B, E, F, G पुस्तकेषु दृश्यते।

स एव सर्व्ववेदानां पुराणानां प्रदर्शकः।
पाराशर्य्यो महायोगी कृष्णद्वैपायनो हरिः॥
आराध्य देवमीशानं दृष्ट्वा स्तुत्वा* त्रिलोचनम्।
तत्प्रसादादसौ व्यासं वेदानामकरोत्प्रभुः॥
अथ शिष्यान् स जग्राह चतुरो वेदपारगान्।
जैमिनिञ्च सुमन्तुञ्च वैशम्पायनमेव च।
पैलं तेषां चतुर्थञ्च पञ्चमं मां महामुनिः॥
ऋग्वेदपाठकं† पैलं जग्राह स महामुनिः।
यजुर्व्वेदप्रवक्तारं वैशम्पायनमेव च॥
जैमिनिं सामवेदस्य पाठकं‡ सोऽन्वपद्यत।
तथैवाथर्व्ववेदस्य सुमन्तुमृषिसत्तमम्।
इतिहासपुराणानि प्रवक्तुं मामयोजयत्§॥
एक आसीद्यजुर्व्वेदस्तं चतुर्द्धा प्रकल्पयत्।
चतुर्होत्रमभूत्तस्मिंस्तेन यज्ञमथाकरोत्॥
आध्वर्य्यवं यजुर्भिः स्यादृग्भिर्होत्रं द्विजोत्तमाः।
औद्गात्रं सामभिश्चक्रे ब्रह्मत्वञ्चाप्यथर्व्वभिः॥
ततः सत्रे च उद्धृत्य ऋग्वेदं कृतवान् प्रभुः।

---

* श्रुत्वा इति E and H. साम्बमिति B.

† श्रावकमिति B.

‡ श्रावकमिति B.

§ व्यकल्पयदिति B.

यजूंषि तु* यजुर्व्वेदं सामवेदन्तु सामभिः† ॥
एकविंशतिभेदेन ऋग्वेदं कृतवान् पुरा ।
शाखानान्तु शतेनैव‡ यजुर्व्वेदमथाकरोत् ॥
सामवेदं सहस्रेण शाखानां प्रबिभेद§ सः ।
अथर्व्वाणमथो वेदं विभेद कुशकेतनः¶ ।
भेदैरष्टादशैर्व्यासः पुराणं कृतवान् प्रभुः‖ ॥
सोऽयमेकश्चतुष्पादो वेदः पूर्व्वं पुरातनः ।
ओङ्कारो ब्रह्मणो जातः सर्व्वदोषविशोधनः ॥
वेदविद्योऽथ** भगवान्वासुदेवः सनातनः ।
स गीयते परो वेदैर्यो वेदैनं स वेदवित् ॥
एतत्परतरं ब्रह्म ज्योतिरानन्दमुत्तमम् ।
वेदवाक्योदितन्तत्त्वं वासुदेवः परम्पदम् ॥
वेदविद्यमिमं†† वेत्ति वेदं वेदपरो मुनिः ।
अवेदं परमं वेत्ति वेदनिःश्वासकृत्परः‡‡ ॥

---

* च इति B.

† सामगमिति B.

‡ शतेनाथ इति B.

§ शाखानाञ्च बिभेद इति B.

¶ नवकेन तु इति B and H.

‖ पुनरिति B.

** हि इति B.

†† वेदविद्यामिमामिति B.

‡‡ वेदनिष्ठः सदेश्वरः इति B, वेदनिष्ठं सदेश्वरमिति F.

स वेदवेद्यो भगवान्वेदमूर्त्तिर्महेश्वरः ।
स एव वेद्यो वेदश्च तमेवाश्रित्य मुच्यते ॥
इत्येतदक्षरं वेद*मोङ्कारं वेदमव्ययम् ।
अवेदश्च विजानाति पाराशर्य्यो महामुनिः ॥

इति श्रीकूर्म्मपुराणे वेदशाखाप्रणयने द्वापञ्चाशोऽध्यायः ।

त्रिपञ्चाशोऽध्यायः ।

सूत उवाच ।
वेदव्यासावताराणि* द्वापरे कथितानि तु ।
महादेवावताराणि कलौ शृणुत सुव्रताः ॥
आद्ये† कलियुगे श्वेतो देवदेवो महाद्युतिः ।
नाम्ना हिताय विप्राणामभूद्वैवस्वतेऽन्तरे ॥
हिमवच्छिखरे रम्ये सकले पर्व्वतोत्तमे ।

---

* वेद्यमिति B.

---

* अत्र क्लीवत्वमार्षम् ।

† आदौ इति B.

तस्य शिष्याः प्रशिष्याश्च* बभूवुरमितप्रभाः ॥
श्वेतः श्वेतशिखश्चैव श्वेतास्यः श्वेतलोहितः ।
चत्वारस्ते महात्मानो ब्राह्मणा वेदपारगाः ॥
सुतारो मदनश्चैव† सुहोत्रः कङ्कणस्तथा ।
लोकाचिस्त्वथ योगीन्द्रो जैगीषव्योऽथ सप्तमे‡ ॥
अष्टमे दधिवाहः स्यान्नवमे ऋषभः प्रभुः ।
भृगुस्तु दशमे प्रोक्तस्तस्मादुग्रः परः स्मृतः ॥
द्वादशेऽतिसमाख्यातो बाली वाथ त्रयोदशे ।
चतुर्द्दशे गौतमस्तु वेददर्शी§ ततः परः ॥
गोकर्णश्चाभवत्तस्माद्गुहावासः शिखण्डधृक्¶ ।
यजमाल्यट्टहासश्च‖ दारुको लाङ्गली तथा** ॥
महायामो मुनिः†† शूली डिण्डमुण्डीश्वरः स्वयम्‡‡ ।

---

* शिखायुक्ता इति B and F.

† सुभावी दमनश्चाथ इति B.

‡ सप्तमः इति B.

§ वेदशीर्षा इति B, E, G and H.

¶ शिखण्डाग्र इति B.

‖ जटामाल्यश्चण्डहासः इति B.

** क्रमादिति B.

†† श्वेतः परस्तथा इति B.

‡‡ डिण्डी मुण्डी च वै क्रमादिति B. डिण्डिमुण्डीश्वरः इति G.

सहिष्णुः सोमशर्म्मा च नकुलीश्वर एव च* ॥
तत्र देवाधिदेवस्य चत्वारः सुतपोधनाः ।
शिष्या बभूवुस्तान्येषां प्रत्येकं मुनिपुङ्गवाः ॥
प्रसन्नमनसो दान्ता ऐश्वरीं भक्तिमास्थिताः† ।
क्रमेण तान्प्रवक्ष्यामि योगिनो योगवित्तमान्‡ ॥
दुन्दुभिः शतरूपश्च ऋचीकः केतुमांस्तथा ।
विशोकश्च§ विकेशश्च विशाखः¶ शापनाशनः ॥
सुमुखो दुर्मुखश्चैव दुर्द्दमो दुरतिक्रमः ।
सनकः‖ सनातनश्चैव तथैव च** सनन्दनः ॥

---

* अतः परं B पुस्तके

वैवस्वतेऽन्तरे शम्भोरवताराश्त्रिशूलिनः ।
अष्टविंशतिराख्याता ह्यन्ते कलियुगे प्रभोः ।
तीर्थे कायावतारे स्याद्देवेशो नकुलीश्वरः ।

इत्यधिकं दृश्यते ।

† भक्तिमाश्रिताः इति B.

‡ अतः परं B पुस्तके

श्वेतः श्वेतशिखश्चैव श्वेतास्यः श्वेतलोहितः ।

इत्यधिकं दृश्यते ।

§ विश्वकेशः इति B.

¶ विपापः इति B.

‖ सनः इति B.

** कुमारश्च इति B.

दालभ्यश्च* महायोगी धर्म्मात्मानो महौजसः† ।
सुधामा विरजाश्चैव शङ्खवाण्यज एव च ॥
सारस्वतस्तथा मेधो धनवाहः‡ सुवाहनः ।
कपिलश्चासुरिश्चैव वोढुः पञ्चशिखो मुनिः ॥
पराशरश्च गर्गश्च भार्गवश्चाङ्गिरास्तथा ।
चलबन्धु§र्निरामित्रः केतुशृङ्गस्तपोधनाः ॥
लम्बोदरश्च लम्बश्च विक्रोशो लम्बकः शुकः¶ ।
सर्व्वज्ञः समबुद्धिश्च साध्यासाध्यस्तथैव च‖ ॥
सुधामा काश्यपश्चाथ** वसिष्ठोवरिजास्तथा ।
अत्रिरुग्रस्तथा चैव श्रवणोऽथ सुवेद्यकः ॥
कुणिश्च कुणिबाहुश्च कुशरीरः कुनेत्रकः ।
कश्यपो ह्युशना चैव च्यवनोऽथ वृहस्पतिः ॥
उच्चास्यो†† वामदेवश्च महाकालो‡‡ महानिलिः§§ ।

---

* वाष्कलश्च इति E. G and H.

† एतत्पादद्वयं B पुस्तके नास्ति ।

‡ मेधो घनवाहः इति B.

§ बलबन्धुरिति B.

¶ लम्बाक्षो लम्बकेशकः इति B.

‖ साध्यः सत्यस्तथैव च इति B.

** काश्यपश्चैव इति B.

†† उतथ्य इति B and F.

‡‡ महाकायः इति B and G.

§§ महानिलः इति B.

वाजश्रवा* सुकेशश्च श्यावाश्वः सुपथीश्वरः ॥
हिरण्यनाभः कौशिल्योऽकाक्षुः कुथुमिधस्तथा† ।
सुमन्तवर्च्चसो विद्वान् कबन्धः कुषिकन्धरः ॥
प्लक्षो दर्वायणिश्चैव‡ केतुमान् गौतमस्तथा ।
भल्लाची मधुपिङ्गश्च श्वेतकेतुस्तपोधनः§ ॥
उषिधा¶ वृहद्रक्षश्च देवलः कविरेव च ।
शालहोत्राग्निवेश्यस्तु|| युवनाश्वः शरद्वसुः ॥
कुण्डलः** कुण्डकर्णश्च कुन्तश्चैव प्रवाहकः ।
उलूको विद्युतश्चैव शाद्वको ह्याश्वलायनः ॥
अक्षपादः कुमारश्च उलूको वसुवाहनः†† ।
कुणिकश्चैव गर्गश्च मित्रको रुरुरेव‡‡ च ॥
शिष्या एते महात्मानः सर्व्वावर्त्तेषु§§ योगिनाम् ।

---

* वाचःश्रवा इति B and F.

† लौकाचिः कुथुमिस्तथा इति B and F.

‡ दर्णायनिरिति E and H. दर्भायणिरिति F.

§ तपोनिधिरिति B.

¶ इलजः इति B. उषिजो वृहदश्वश्च इति F.

|| शालिहोत्रोऽग्निवेश्यश्च इति B.

** कुगलः इति B.

†† वत्स एव च इति B.

‡‡ ऋष्यएव इति B.

§§ सर्व्वावर्त्तेन इति B. सर्व्वेऽश्रेयाः सुयोगिनामिति F.

विमला ब्रह्मभूयिष्ठा ज्ञानयोगपरायणाः ॥
कुर्व्वन्ति चावताराणि ब्राह्मणानां हिताय च* ।
योगेश्वराणामादेशाद्वेदसंस्थापनाय वै ॥
ये ब्राह्मणाः संस्मरन्ति नमस्यन्ति च सर्व्वदा ।
तर्पयन्त्यर्च्चयन्त्येतान् ब्रह्मविद्यामवाप्नुयुः ॥
इदं वैवस्वतं प्रोक्तमन्तरं विस्तरेण तु ।
भविष्यति च सावर्णो दक्षसावर्ण एव च ॥
दशमो ब्रह्मसावर्णो धर्म्म एकादशः स्मृतः ।
द्वादशो रुद्रसावर्णो रौच्यनामा† त्रयोदशः ।
भौत्यश्चतुर्द्दशः प्रोक्तो भविष्या मनवः क्रमात् ॥
अयं वः कथितो ह्यंशः पूर्व्वो नारायणेरितः ।
भूतैर्भव्यैर्वर्त्तमानैराख्यानैरुपवृंहितः ॥
यः पठेच्छृणुयाद्वापि श्रावयेद्वा द्विजोत्तमान्‡ ।
सर्व्वपापविनिर्मुक्तो ब्रह्मलोके महीयते§ ॥
पठेद्देवालये स्नात्वा नदीतीरेषु चैव हि ।
नारायणं नमस्कृत्य भावेन पुरुषोत्तमम् ॥

---

* हि इति B.

† रौचमानः इति B and F.

‡ द्विजोत्तमाः इति B and F.

§ ब्रह्मणा सह मोदते इति B.

नमो देवाधिदेवाय* देवानां परमात्मने।
पुरुषाय पुराणाय विष्णवे प्रभविष्णवे† ॥

इति श्रीकूर्म्मपुराणे पूर्व्वविभागे त्रिपञ्चाशोऽध्यायः।

पूर्व्वविभागः समाप्तः।

---

* देवादिदेवाय इति B.

† कूर्म्मरूपिणे इति B.

उत्तरविभागः।

प्रथमोऽध्यायः।

ऋषय ऊचुः।

भवता कथितः सम्यक् सर्गः स्वायम्भुवः प्रभुः* ।
ब्रह्माण्डस्यादि† विस्तारो मन्वन्तरविनिश्चयः ॥
तत्रेश्वरेश्वरो देवो वर्णिभिर्धर्म्मतत्परैः ।
ज्ञानयोगरतैर्नित्यमाराध्यः कथितस्त्वया ॥
तत्त्वञ्चाशेषसंसारदुःखनाशमनुत्तमम्‡ ।
ज्ञानं ब्रह्मैकविषयं तेन§ पश्येम तत्परम् ॥
त्वं हि नारायणः साक्षात्कृष्णद्वैपायनात्प्रभो ।
अवाप्ताखिलविज्ञानस्त्त्वां पृच्छामहे¶ पुनः ॥
श्रुत्वा मुनीनां तद्वाक्यं कृष्णद्वैपायनात्प्रभुः ।
सूतः पौराणिकः श्रुत्वा भाषितुं ह्युपचक्रमे ॥

---

* ततः इति B. शुभ इति E, G and H.

† ब्रह्माण्डस्यास्य इति B.

‡ नाशनमुत्तममिति B.

§ येन इति B, E and H.

¶ अत्र आर्षमात्मनेपदम् ।

तथास्मिन्नन्तरे व्यासः कृष्णद्वैपायनः स्वयम् ।
आजगाम मुनिश्रेष्ठा यत्र सत्रं* समासते ॥
तं दृष्ट्वा वेदविद्वांसङ्कालमेघसमद्युतिम् ।
व्यासङ्कमलपत्राक्षं प्रणेमुर्द्विजपुङ्गवाः ॥
पपात दण्डवद्भूमौ दृष्ट्वासौ लोमहर्षणः ।
प्रणम्य शिरसा भूमौ प्राञ्जलिर्वशगोऽभवत्† ॥
पृष्टास्तेऽनामयं विप्राः शौनकाद्या महामुनिम् ।
समाहृत्यासनं‡ तस्मै तद्योग्यं समकल्पयन् ॥
अथैनानब्रवीद्वाक्यं पराशरसुतः प्रभुः ।
कच्चिन्न हानिस्तपसः§ स्वाध्यायस्य श्रुतस्य च ॥
ततश्च¶ सूतः स्वगुरुं प्रणम्याह महामुनिम् ।
ज्ञानं तद्ब्रह्मविषयं मुनीनां वक्तुमर्हसि ॥
इमे हि मुनयः शान्तास्तापसा धर्म्मतत्पराः ।
शुश्रूषा जायते चैषां‖ वक्तुमर्हसि तत्त्वतः ॥
ज्ञानं विमुक्तिदं दिव्यं यन्मे साक्षात्त्वयोदितम् ।
मुनीनां व्याहृतं पूर्व्वं विष्णुना कूर्म्मरूपिणा ॥

---

* यत्र इति B.

† प्रदक्षिणीकृत्य गुरुं प्राञ्जलिः पार्श्वतोऽभवदिति B. पार्श्वतोऽभवदिति F.

‡ समाश्वास्यासनमिति B.

§ तपसो हानिरिति B.

¶ ततः स इति B.

‖ चैव इति B.

श्रुत्वा सूतस्य वचनं मुनिः सत्यवतीसुतः।
प्रणम्य शिरसा रुद्रं वचः प्राह सुखावहम्॥

व्यास उवाच।

वक्ष्ये देवो महादेवः पृष्टो योगीश्वरैः पुरा।
सनत्कुमारप्रमुखैः स स्वयं* समभाषत॥
सनत्कुमारः सनकस्तथैव च सनन्दनः।
अङ्गिरा रुद्रसहितो भृगुः परमधर्म्मवित्॥
कणादः कपिलो गर्गो† वामदेवो महामुनिः।
शुक्रो वशिष्ठो भगवान् सर्व्वे संयतमानसाः॥
परस्परं विचार्य्यैते संयमाविष्टचेतसः‡।
तप्तवन्तस्तपो घोरं पुण्ये वदरिकाश्रमे॥
अपश्यंस्ते महायोगमृषिधर्म्मसुतं मुनिम्§।
नारायणमनाद्यन्तं नरेण सहितं तदा॥
संस्तूय विविधैः स्तोत्रैः सर्व्ववेदसमुद्भवैः।
प्रणेमुर्भक्तिसंयुक्ता योगिनो योगवित्तमम्॥
विज्ञाय वाञ्छितं तेषां भगवानपि सर्व्ववित्।
प्राह गम्भीरया वाचा किमर्थं तप्यते तपः॥
अब्रुवन् हृष्टमनसो विश्वात्मानं सनातनम्।

---

* स्वयं यदिति B.

† योगीति B and F.

‡ संशयाविष्टचेतसः इति B and F.

§ शुचिमिति B.

साक्षान्नारायणं देवमागतं सिद्धिसूचकम् ॥
वयं संयममापन्नाः* सर्वे वै ब्रह्मवादिनः।
भवन्तमेकं† शरणं प्रपन्नाः पुरुषोत्तमम् ॥
त्वं वेत्सि परमं गुह्यं सर्वन्तु भगवानृषिः।
नारायणः स्वयं‡ साक्षात्पुराणोऽव्यक्तपूरुषः ॥
नह्यन्यो विद्यते वेत्ता त्वामृते परमेश्वरम्।
स त्वमस्माकमचलं§ संशयं छेत्तुमर्हसि ॥
किं कारणमिदं कृत्स्नं को नु संसरते सदा।
कश्चिदात्मा च का मुक्तिः¶ संसारः किन्निमित्तकः ॥
कः संसार इतीशानः‖ को वा सर्वं प्रपश्यति।
किं तत्परतरं ब्रह्म सर्वं नो वक्तुमर्हसि ॥
एवमुक्त्वा तु मुनयः प्रापश्यन् पुरुषोत्तमम्।
विहाय तापसं वेषं** संस्थितं स्वेन तेजसा ॥
विभ्राजमानं विमलं प्रभामण्डलमण्डितम्।
श्रीवत्सवक्षसन्देवं तप्तजाम्बूनदप्रभम् ॥

---

* संशयमापन्नाः इति B and F.

† भवन्तमेव इति B.

‡ परः इति B.

§ शुश्रूषास्माकमखिलमिति B and F.

¶ सा मूर्त्तिरिति B.

‖ संसारपतीशान इति B, E and H.

** रूपमिति B.

शङ्खचक्रगदापाणिं शार्ङ्गहस्तं श्रिया वृतम् ।
न दृष्टस्तत्क्षणादेव नरस्तस्यैव तेजसा ॥
तदन्तरे महादेवः शशाङ्काङ्कितशेखरः ।
प्रसादाभिमुखो रुद्रः प्रादुरासीन्महेश्वरः ॥
निरीक्ष्य ते जगन्नाथं त्रिनेत्रं चन्द्रभूषणम् ।
तुष्टुवुर्हृष्टमनसो भक्त्या तं परमेश्वरम् ॥
जयेश्वर महादेव जय भूतपते शिव ।
जयाशेषमुनीशान तपसाऽभिप्रपूजित ॥
सहस्रमूर्त्ते विश्वात्मन् जगद्यन्त्रप्रवर्त्तक ।
जयानन्त जगज्जन्मत्राणसंहारकारक* ॥
सहस्रचरणेशान शम्भो योगीन्द्रवन्दित ।
जयाम्बिकापते देव नमस्ते परमेश्वर ॥
संस्तुतो भगवानीशस्त्र्यम्बको भक्तवत्सलः ।
समालिङ्ग्य हृषीकेशं प्राह गम्भीरया गिरा ॥
किमर्थं पुण्डरीकाक्ष मुनीन्द्रा ब्रह्मवादिनः ।
इमं समागता देशं किन्नु† कार्य्यं मयाच्युत‡ ॥
आकर्ण्य तस्य तद्वाक्यं देवदेवो जनार्द्दनः ।
प्राह देवो महादेवं प्रसादाभिमुखं स्थितम् ॥
इमे हि मुनयो देव तापसाः क्षीणकल्मषाः ।

---

* कारण इति B.

† किंवा इति B.

‡ ममाच्युत इति B.

अभ्यागतानां शरणं सम्यग्दर्शनकाङ्क्षिणाम् ॥
यदि प्रसन्नो भगवान्मुनीनां भावितात्मनाम् ।
सन्निधौ मम तज्ज्ञानं दिव्यं वक्तुमिहार्हसि ॥
त्वं हि वेत्थ स्वमात्मानं न ह्यन्यो विद्यते शिव ।
वद* त्वमात्मनात्मानं मुनीन्द्रेभ्यः प्रदर्शय ॥
एवमुक्त्वा हृषीकेशः प्रोवाच मुनिपुङ्गवान् ।
प्रदर्शयन्योगसिद्धिं निरीक्ष्य वृषभध्वजम् ॥
सन्दर्शनान्महेशस्य† शङ्करस्याथ शूलिनः ।
कृतार्थं स्वयमात्मानं ज्ञातुमर्हथ तत्त्वतः ॥
पूजामर्हथ देवेशं‡ प्रत्यक्षं पुरतः स्थितम् ।
ममैव सन्निधाने स§ यथावद्वक्तुमीश्वरः ॥
निशम्य विष्णोर्वचनं प्रणम्य वृषभध्वजम् ।
सनत्कुमारप्रमुखाः पृच्छन्ति स्म महेश्वरम् ॥
अथास्मिन्नन्तरे दिव्यमासनं विमलं शिवम् ।
किमप्यचिन्त्यं गगनादीश्वरार्थं समुद्बभौ ॥
तत्राससाद योगात्मा विष्णुना सह विश्वकृत्¶ ।
तेजसा पूरयन्विश्वं भाति देवो महेश्वरः ॥

---

* ततः इति B.

† सन्दर्शनादुमेशस्य इति B.

‡ द्रष्टुमर्हथ विश्वेशमिति B. देवेशं पूजामर्हथ देवेशं पूजयितुमर्हथेत्यर्थः ।

§ सन्निधावेव इति B. ईश्वरः शक्नोतीत्यर्थः ।

¶ विश्वविदिति B.

ततो देवाधिदेवेशं* शङ्करं ब्रह्मवादिनः ।
विभ्राजमानं विमले तस्मिन्ददृशुरासने ॥
तमासनस्थं भूतानामीशं ददृशिरे किल ।
यदन्तरा सर्वमेतद्यतोऽभिन्नमिदं जगत् ॥
सवासुदेवमीशानमीशं ददृशिरे परम्† ॥
प्रोवाच पृष्टो भगवान्मुनीनां परमेश्वरः ।
निरीक्ष्य पुण्डरीकाक्षं स्वात्मयोगमनुत्तमम् ॥
तच्छृणुध्वं यथान्यायमुच्यमानं‡ मयानघाः ।
प्रशान्तमनसः§ सर्व्वे विशुद्धं ज्ञानमैश्वरम्¶ ॥

इति श्रीकूर्म्मपुराणे ईश्वरगीतासु‖ प्रथमोऽध्यायः ।

---

* तं ते देवादिदेवेशमिति B and H.

† स वासुदेवमासीनं तमीशं ददृशुः किल इति B.

‡ याच्यमानमिति B.

§ प्रशान्तमानसाः इति B.

¶ ज्ञानमीश्वरभाषितमिति B and F.

‖ उपविभागे ईश्वरगीतासूपनिषत्सु इति B and F.

द्वितीयोऽध्यायः ।

ईश्वर उवाच ।

अवाच्यमेतद्विज्ञानं मम गुह्यं सनातनम् ।
यन्न देवा विजानन्ति यतन्तोऽपि* द्विजातयः ॥
इदं ज्ञानं समाश्रित्य ब्राह्मीभूता† द्विजोत्तमाः ।
न संसारं प्रपद्यन्ते‡ पूर्व्वेऽपि ब्रह्मवादिनः ॥
गुह्याद्गुह्यतमं साक्षाद्गोपनीयं प्रयत्नतः ।
वक्ष्ये भक्तिमतामद्य युष्माकं ब्रह्मवादिनाम् ॥
आत्मायं केवलः स्वच्छः शुद्धः§ सूक्ष्मः सनातनः ।
अस्ति सर्व्वान्तरः साक्षाच्चिन्मात्रस्तमसः¶ परः ॥
सोऽन्तर्य्यामी स पुरुषः स प्राणः स महेश्वरः ।
स कालोऽत्र‖ तदव्यक्तं स च वेद इति श्रुतिः ॥
अस्माद्विजायते विश्वमत्रैव प्रविलीयते ।
स मायी** मायया बद्धः करोति विविधास्तनूः ॥

---

* यतन्त इत्यार्षम्, यतमाना इति साधु ।

† ब्रह्मभूता: इति B, E, F and H.

‡ प्रपश्यन्तीति B.

§ सुस्थः शान्तः इति B. शान्तः सूक्ष्मः इति F.

¶ चिन्मयस्तामसः इति B. तन्मनाः परः इति F.

‖ स कालोऽग्निरिति B and F.

** अमायीति B

न चाप्ययं संसरति न संसारमयः प्रभुः* ।
नायं पृथ्वी न सलिलं न तेजः पवनो नभः ॥†
न प्राणो न मनोऽव्यक्तं न शब्दः स्पर्श एव च ।
न रूपं न रसो गन्धो‡ नायं कर्त्ता न वागपि ॥
न पाणिपादौ नो पायुर्न चोपस्थं द्विजोत्तमाः ।
न च कर्त्ता न भोक्ता वा§ न च प्रकृतिपूरुषौ ।
न माया नैव च प्राणा न चैव परमार्थतः¶ ॥
यथा प्रकाशतमसोः‖ सम्बन्धो नोपपद्यते ।
तद्वदैक्यं न सम्बन्धः प्रपञ्चपरमात्मनोः ॥
छायातपौ यथा लोके परस्परविलक्षणौ ।
तद्वत्प्रपञ्चपुरुषौ विभिन्नौ परमार्थतः ॥
तथात्मा मलिनः सृष्टो** विकारी स्यात्स्वरूपतः ।
न हि तस्य भवेन्मुक्तिर्जन्मान्तरशतैरपि ॥
पश्यन्ति मुनयो मुक्ताः स्वात्मानं परमार्थतः ।
विकारहीनं निर्द्वन्द्वमानन्दात्मानमव्ययम् ॥

---

* न च संसारयेत् प्रभुरिति E, F, G and H.

† एष श्लोकः B पुस्तके नास्ति ।

‡ न रूपरसगन्धाश्च इति B.

§ न कर्त्ता न च भोक्ता वा इति B.

¶ चैतन्यं परमार्थतः इति B. चैतन्ये परमार्थत इति F and H.

‖ न रागद्वेषतमसोरिति B.

** सुस्थः इति B.

अहं कर्त्ता सुखी दुःखी कृशः स्थूलेति* या मतिः।
सा चाहङ्कारकर्त्तृत्वादात्मन्यारोपिता जनैः॥
वदन्ति† वेदविद्वांसः साक्षिणं प्रकृतेः परम्।
भोक्तारमक्षरं शुद्धं सर्व्वत्र समवस्थितम्॥
तस्मादज्ञानमूलो हि‡ संसारः सर्व्वदेहिनाम्।
अज्ञानादन्यथा ज्ञानात्तत्त्वं प्रकृतिसङ्गतम्॥
नित्योदितं स्वयं ज्योतिः सर्व्वगः पुरुषः परः।
अहङ्काराविवेकेन कर्त्ताहमिति मन्यते॥
पश्यन्ति ऋषयो§ऽव्यक्तं नित्यं सदसदात्मकम्।
प्रधानं पुरुषं¶ बुद्धा कारणं ब्रह्मवादिनः॥
तेनायं‖ सङ्गतः स्वात्मा** कूटस्थोऽपि निरञ्जनः।
स्वात्मानमक्षरं ब्रह्म नावबुद्ध्येत तत्त्वतः॥
अनात्मन्यात्मविज्ञानं तस्माद्दुःखं†† तथेतरत्।
रागद्वेषादयो दोषाः सर्व्वे भ्रान्तिनिबन्धनाः॥

---

* कालेति B.

† विदन्तीति B.

‡ अज्ञानमूलोऽयमिति B.

§ ऋषय इति B.

¶ प्रकृतिमिति B. प्रकृतिं बुद्धेरिति F.

‖ तेनाच इति B.

** सङ्गतो ह्यात्मा इति B.

†† सुखमिति B.

कर्म्माण्यस्य महान्दोषः* पुण्यापुण्यमिति स्थितिः†।
तद्वशादेव सर्व्वेषां सर्व्वदेहसमुद्भवः॥
नित्यं सर्व्वत्र गुह्यात्मा‡ कूटस्थो दोषवर्ज्जितः।
एकः सन्तिष्ठते§ शक्त्या मायया न स्वभावतः॥
तस्माद्द्वैतमेवाहुर्मुनयः परमार्थतः।
भेदोऽव्यक्तस्वभावेन सा च मायात्मसंश्रया॥
यथा च¶ धूमसम्पर्क्कान्नाकाशो मलिनो भवेत्।
अन्तःकरणजैर्भावैरात्मा तद्वन्न लिप्यते॥
यथा स्वप्रभया भाति केवलः स्फटिकोपलः‖।
उपाधिहीनो विमलस्तथैवात्मा प्रकाशते॥
ज्ञानस्वरूपमेवाहुर्जगदेतद्विचक्षणाः।
अर्थस्वरूपमेवान्ये** पश्यन्त्यन्ये कुदृष्टयः॥
कूटस्थो निर्गुणो व्यापी चैतन्यात्मा स्वभावतः।
दृश्यते ह्यर्थरूपेण पुरुषैर्ज्ञानदृष्टिभिः॥
यथा स लक्ष्यते रक्तः केवलं स्फाटिको जनैः।

---

* भवेद्दोषः इति B and F.

† श्रुतिरिति B and H.

‡ नित्यः सर्व्वगो ह्यात्मा इति B, E, F and H.

§ स भिद्यते इति B, F and H.

¶ तथाहीति B.

‖ स्फाटिकोऽमलः इति B.

** अर्थस्वरूपं विज्ञानादिति B. मेवाज्ञा इति F.

रत्तिकाद्युपधानेन तद्वत्परमपूरुषः ॥
तस्मादात्माक्षरः शुद्धो नित्यः सर्व्वत्रगोऽव्ययः* ।
उपासितव्यो मन्तव्यः श्रोतव्यश्च मुमुक्षुभिः ॥
यदा मनसि चैतन्यं भाति सर्व्वत्र सर्व्वदा† ।
योगिनः श्रद्दधानस्य‡ तदा सम्पद्यते स्वयम् ॥
यदा सर्व्वाणि भूतानि स्वात्मन्येवाभिधीयते§ ।
सर्व्वभूतेषु चात्मानं ब्रह्म सम्पद्यते तदा ॥
यदा सर्व्वाणि भूतानि समाधिस्थो न पश्यति ।
एकीभूतः परेणासौ¶ तदा भवति केवलम्‖ ॥
यदा सर्व्वे प्रमुच्यन्ते कामा येऽस्य हृदि स्थिताः ।
तदासावमृतीभूतः क्षेमं गच्छति पण्डितः ॥
यदा भूतपृथग्भावमेकस्थमनुपश्यति ।
तत एव च विस्तारं** ब्रह्म सम्पद्यते सदा†† ॥
यदा पश्यति चात्मानं केवलं परमार्थतः ।

---

* सर्व्वगतोऽव्ययः इति B.

† सर्व्वत्रगं सदेति B and F.

‡ योगिनोऽव्यवधानेन इति B.

§ स्वात्मन्येवाभिपश्यतीति B.

¶ परेणादौ इति B.

‖ केवलः इति B and F.

** विस्तारः इति B.

†† तदा इति B and F.

मायामात्रं तदा सर्व्वं जगद्भवति* निर्वृतः ॥
यदा जन्मजरादुःखव्याधीनामेकभेषजम् ।
केवलं ब्रह्मविज्ञानं जायतेऽसौ तदा शिवः ॥
यथा नदीनदा लोके सागरेणैकतां ययुः ।
तद्वदात्माक्षरेणासौ निष्कलेनैकतां व्रजेत् ॥
तस्माद्विज्ञानमेवास्ति न प्रपञ्चो न संस्थितिः ।
अज्ञानेनावृतं लोके† विज्ञानं तेन मुह्यति‡ ॥
विज्ञानं निर्म्मलं सूक्ष्मं निर्व्विकल्पं तदव्ययम् ।
अज्ञानमितरत्सर्वं§ विज्ञानमिति तन्मतम्¶ ॥
एतद्वः कथितं‖ साङ्ख्यं भाषितं** ज्ञानमुत्तमम् ।
सर्ववेदान्तसारं हि योगस्तत्रैकचित्तता ॥
योगात्सञ्जायते ज्ञानं ज्ञानाद्योगः†† प्रवर्त्तते ।
योगज्ञानाभियुक्तस्य नावाप्यं विद्यते क्वचित् ॥
यदेव योगिनो यान्ति साङ्ख्यैस्तदतिगम्यते‡‡ ।

---

* जगत्कृत्स्नं तदाभवतीति B.

† अज्ञानेनावृतं लोकः इति B.

‡ मुह्यते इति B.

§ अज्ञानमिति तत्सर्व्वमिति B.

¶ मे मतमिति B.

‖ परममिति B and F.

** भावितमिति B.

†† ज्ञानान्मोक्षः इति B.

‡‡ तदधिगम्यते इति B and F. अभिगम्यते इति E and H.

एकं साङ्ख्यञ्च योगञ्च यः पश्यति स तत्त्ववित्॥
अन्ये हि योगिनो विप्रा ह्यैश्वर्य्यासक्तचेतसः।
मज्जन्ति तत्र तत्रैव ये चान्ये कुण्ठबुद्धयः॥
यत्तत्सर्वमतं* दिव्यमैश्वर्य्यममलं महत्।
ज्ञानयोगाभियुक्तस्तु देहान्ते तदवाप्नुयात्॥
एष आत्माहमव्यक्तो मायावी परमेश्वरः।
कीर्त्तितः सर्ववेदेषु सर्वात्मा सर्वतोमुखः॥
सर्वरूपः† सर्वरसः सर्वगन्धोऽजरोऽमरः।
सर्वतः पाणिपादोऽहमन्तर्यामी सनातनः॥
अपाणिपादो जवगो‡ ग्रहीता हृदि संस्थितः।
अचक्षु§रपि पश्यामि तथाकर्णः शृणोम्यहम्॥
वेदाहं सर्वमेवेदं न मां जानाति कश्चन।
प्राहुर्महान्तं पुरुषं मामेकं तत्त्वदर्शिनः॥
पश्यन्ति ऋषयो¶ हेतुमात्मनः सूक्ष्मदर्शिनः।
निर्गुणामलरूपस्य यदैश्वर्य्यमनुत्तमम्‖॥
यन्न देवा विजानन्ति मोहिता मम मायया।

---

* सर्व्वगतमिति B, F and H.

† सर्व्वकामः इति B.

‡ जवनः इति E, F and H.

§ विचक्षुरिति B.

¶ चर्षयः इति B.

‖ यत्तदैश्वर्य्यमुत्तमनिति B.

वक्ष्ये समाहिता यूयं शृणुध्वं ब्रह्मवादिनः ॥
नाहं प्रशस्तः सर्वस्य मायातीतः स्वभावतः ।
प्रेरयामि तथापीदं कारणं सूरयो विदुः ॥
यतो* गुह्यतमं देहं सर्वगं तत्त्वदर्शिनः ।
प्रविष्टा मम सायुज्यं लभन्ते योगिनोऽव्ययम् ॥
ये हि मायामतिक्रान्ता मम या† विश्वरूपिणी ।
लभन्ते परमं शुद्धं निर्वाणन्ते मया सह ॥
न तेषां परमावृत्तिः‡ कल्पकोटिशतैरपि ।
प्रसादान्मम योगीन्द्रा एतद्वेदानुशासनम् ॥
तत्पुत्रशिष्ययोगिभ्यो दातव्यं ब्रह्मवादिभिः ।
मदुक्तमेतद्विज्ञानं साङ्ख्यं योगसमाश्रयम् ॥

इति श्रीकूर्म्मपुराणे ईश्वरगीतासु§ द्वितीयोऽध्यायः ।

---

* यन्मे इति B.

† तेषां हि वशमापन्ना माया मे इति B and H.

‡ पुनरावृत्तिरिति B and F.

§ ईश्वरगीतासूपनिषत्सु इति B.

तृतीयोऽध्यायः ।

ईश्वर उवाच ।

अव्यक्तादभवत्कालः प्रधानं पुरुषः परः ।
तेभ्यः सर्वमिदं जातं तस्माद्ब्रह्ममयं जगत् ॥
सर्वतः पाणिपादान्तं सर्वतोऽक्षिशिरोमुखम् ।
सर्व्वतः श्रुतिमल्लोके सर्व्वमावृत्य तिष्ठति ॥
सर्व्वेन्द्रियगुणाभासं सर्व्वेन्द्रियविवर्ज्जितम् ।
सर्वाधारं सदानन्दमव्यक्तं द्वैतवर्ज्जितम् ॥
सर्वोपमानरहितं प्रमाणातीतगोचरम् ।
निर्व्विकल्पं निराभासं सर्वावासं परामृतम् ॥
अभिन्नं भिन्नसंस्थानं शाश्वतं ध्रुवमव्ययम् ।
निर्गुणं परमं ज्योतिस्तज्ज्ञानं सूरयो विदुः ॥
स आत्मा सर्व्वभूतानां स वाह्याभ्यन्तरः परः ।
सोऽहं सर्व्वगः शान्तो ज्ञानात्मा परमेश्वरः ॥
मया ततमिदं विश्वं जगत्स्थावरजङ्गमम्* ।
मत्स्थानि सर्व्वभूतानि यस्तं वेदविदो विदुः† ॥
प्रधानं पुरुषश्चैव तद्वस्तु समुदाहृतम् ।
तयोरनादिरुद्दिष्टः‡ कालः संयोगजः परः ॥

---

* जगदव्यक्तमूर्त्तिनेति B. जगदव्ययमूर्त्तिना इति F.

† यस्तं वेद स वेदविदिति B and F.

‡ तयोरनादिर्निर्दिष्टः इति B.

त्रयमेतदनाद्यन्तमव्यक्ते समवस्थितम्।
तदात्मकं तदन्यत्स्यात्तद्रूपं मामकं विदुः॥
महदाद्यं विशेषान्तं* सम्प्रसूतेऽखिलं जगत्।
या सा प्रकृतिरुद्दिष्टा मोहिनी सर्व्वदेहिनाम्॥
पुरुषः प्रकृतिस्थो वै† भुङ्क्ते यः प्राकृतान् गुणान्।
अहङ्कारविमुक्तत्वात्प्रोच्यते पञ्चविंशकः॥
आद्यो विकारः प्रकृतेर्महानिति च कथ्यते।
विज्ञातृशक्तिविज्ञानात्‡ ह्यहङ्कारस्तदुत्थितः॥
एक एव महानात्मा सोऽहङ्कारोऽभिधीयते।
स जीवः सोऽन्तरात्मेति गीयते तत्त्वचिन्तकैः॥
तेन वेदयते सर्व्वं सुखं दुःखञ्च जन्मसु।
स विज्ञानात्मकस्तस्य मनः स्यादुपकारकम्॥
तेनापि तन्मयस्तस्मात्§ संसारः पुरुषस्य तु।
स चाविवेकः प्रकृतौ सङ्गात्कालेन सोऽभवत्॥
कालः सृजति भूतानि कालः संहरते प्रजाः।
सर्व्वे कालस्य वशगाः न कालः कस्यचिद्वशे॥
सोऽन्तरा सर्व्वमेवेदं नियच्छति सनातनः।

---

* महदाद्यं विशेषान्तं—महत्तत्त्वादारभ्य विशेषपदार्थपर्य्यन्तमित्यर्थः। महत् प्रधानं, विशेषः वैशेषिकैरभ्युपेतः पदार्थः।

† ह्यीति B.

‡ विज्ञानशक्तिर्विज्ञाता इति B.

§ तेनाविवेकतस्तस्मादिति B.

प्रोच्यते भगवान्प्राणः सर्व्वज्ञः पुरुषोत्तमः ॥
सर्व्वेन्द्रियेभ्यः परमं मन आहुर्मनीषिणः ।
मनसश्चाप्यहङ्कारमहङ्कारान्महान्परः ॥
महतः परमव्यक्तमव्यक्तात्पुरुषः परः ।
पुरुषाद्भगवान् प्राणस्तस्य सर्व्वमिदं जगत् ॥
प्राणात्परतरं व्योम व्योमातीतोऽग्निरीश्वरः ।
सोऽहं ब्रह्माव्ययः* शान्तो मायातीतमिदं जगत्† ॥
नास्ति मत्तः परं भूतं माञ्च विज्ञाय मुच्यते‡ ।
नित्यं नास्तीति§ जगति भूतं स्थावरजङ्गमम् ।
ऋते मामेव¶मव्यक्तं व्योमरूपं महेश्वरम् ॥
सोऽहं सृजामि सकलं संहरामि सदा जगत् ।
मायी मायामयो देवः कालेन सह सङ्गतः ॥
मत्सन्निधावेष कालः करोति सकलं जगत् ।
नियोजयत्यनन्तात्मा ह्येतद्वेदानुशासनम् ॥

इति श्रीकूर्म्मपुराणे ईश्वरगीतासु तृतीयोऽध्यायः ।

---

* सर्व्वगः इति B.

† ज्ञानात्मा परमेश्वरः इति B.

‡ मां विज्ञाय विमुच्यते इति B.

§ नित्यं हि नास्ति इति B.

¶ मायिकमिति B.

चतुर्थोऽध्यायः।

ईश्वर उवाच।

वक्ष्ये समाहिता यूयं शृणुध्वं ब्रह्मवादिनः।
माहात्म्यं देवदेवस्य येन सर्व्वं प्रवर्त्तते* ॥
नाहं तपोभिर्विविधैर्न दानेन न चेज्यया।
शक्यो हि पुरुषैर्ज्ञातुमृते भक्तिमनुत्तमाम् ॥
अहं हि सर्व्वभूतानामन्तस्तिष्ठामि सर्वतः‡।
मां सर्वसाक्षिणं लोको न जानाति मुनीश्वराः ॥
यस्यान्तरा सर्वमिदं यो हि सर्वान्तकः परः।
सोऽहं धाता विधाता च कालोऽग्निर्§विश्वतोमुखः ॥
न मां पश्यन्ति मुनयः सर्व्वे पितृदिवौकसः।
ब्रह्मा च¶ मनवः शक्रो ये चान्ये प्रथितौजसः ॥
गृणन्ति सततं वेदा‖ मामेकं परमेश्वरम्।
यजन्ति विविधैर्यज्ञैः** ब्राह्मणा वैदिकैर्मखैः ॥

---

* येनेदं संप्रवर्त्तते इति B.

† भावानामिति B.

‡ सर्व्वगः इति B.

§ लोकेऽस्मिन्निति B.

¶ ब्रह्माद्याः इति B and F.

‖ देवा इति B.

** विविधैरग्निमिति B. विविधैरग्नौ इति F.

सर्व्वे लोका न पश्यन्ति* ब्रह्मा लोकपितामहः।
ध्यायन्ति योगिनो देवं भूताधिपतिमीश्वरम्॥
अहं हि सर्व्वहविषां भोक्ता चैव† फलप्रदः।
सर्व्वदेवतनुर्भूत्वा सर्वात्मा सर्व्वसंस्थितः‡।
मां पश्यन्तीह विद्वांसो धार्म्मिका वेदवादिनः॥
तेषां सन्निहितो नित्यं ये मां नित्यमुपासते§।
ब्राह्मणाः क्षत्रिया वैश्या धार्म्मिका मामुपासते।
तेषां ददामि तत्स्थानमानन्दं परमम्पदम्॥
अन्येऽपि ये स्वधर्म्मस्थाः शूद्राद्या नीचजातयः।
भक्तिमन्तः प्रमुच्यन्ते कालेनापि हि¶ सङ्गताः॥
मद्भक्ता न‖ विनश्यन्ति मद्भक्ता वीतकल्मषाः।
आदावेव** प्रतिज्ञातं न मे भक्तः†† प्रणश्यति॥
यो वै निन्दति तं मूढ़ो देवदेवं स निन्दति।

---

* नमस्यन्तीति B.

† चैक इति B and F.

‡ सर्व्वसंस्तुतः इति B and F.

§ ये भक्त्या मामुपासते इति B and F.

¶ कालेन मयीति B.

‖ न मद्भक्ता इति B.

** आदावैतदिति B.

†† मद्भक्तः इति B.

येा हि पूजयते* भक्त्या स पूजयति† मां सदा ॥
पत्रं पुष्पं फलं तोयं मदाराधनकारणात्।
येा मे ददाति नियतं स मे भक्तः प्रियेा मम ॥
अहं हि जगतामादौ ब्रह्माणं परमेष्ठिनम्।
विदधौ दत्तवान्वेदानशेषानात्मनिःसृतान् ॥
अहमेव हि सर्व्वेषां येागिनां गुरुरव्ययः।
धार्म्मिकाणाञ्च गेाप्ताहं निहन्ता वेदविद्विषाम् ॥
अहं हि‡ सर्व्वसंसारान्मोचको येागिनामिह।
संसारहेतुरेवाहं सर्व्वसंसारवर्ज्जितः ॥
अहमेव हि संहर्त्ता संस्रष्टा§ परिपालकः।
माया वै मामिका शक्तिर्माया लेाकविमेाहनी ॥
ममैव च परा शक्तिर्या सा विद्येति गीयते।
नाशयामि च तां मायां योगिनां हृदि संस्थितः ॥
अहं हि सर्वशक्तीनां प्रवर्त्तकनिवर्त्तकः।
आधारभूतः सर्व्वासां निधानममृतस्य च ॥
एका सर्व्वान्तरा शक्तिः करोति विविधञ्जगत्।¶

---

* यो हि तं पूजयेदिति B.

† स पूजयतीति B.

‡ वै इति B.

§ स्रष्टाहमिति B.

¶ अतः परं B पुस्तके

नाहं प्रेरयिता विप्राः परमं योगमाश्रिताः।

इत्यधिकं दृश्यते।

आस्थाय ब्रह्मणो रूपं मन्मयी मदधिष्ठिता ॥
अन्या च शक्तिर्विपुला संस्थापयति मे जगत्।
भूत्वा नारायणोऽनन्तो जगन्नाथो* जगन्मयः ॥
तृतीया महती शक्तिर्निहन्ति सकलं जगत्।
तामसी मे समाख्याता कालाख्या रुद्ररूपिणी ॥
ध्यानेन मां प्रपश्यन्ति केचिज्ज्ञानेन चापरे।
अपरे भक्तियोगेन कर्मयोगेन चापरे ॥
सर्व्वेषामेव भक्तानामिष्टः प्रियतमो मम।
यो हि ज्ञानेन मान्नित्यमाराधयति नान्यथा ॥
अन्ये च हरये† भक्ता मदाराधनकारिणः।
तेऽपि मां प्राप्नुवन्त्येव नावर्त्तन्ते च वै पुनः ॥
मया ततमिदं कृत्स्नं‡ प्रधानपुरुषात्मकम्।
मय्येव संस्थितं चित्तं मया सम्प्रेर्य्यते जगत् ॥
नाहं प्रेरयिता विप्राः परमं योगमास्थितः§।
प्रेरयामि जगत्कृत्स्नमेतद्यो वेद सोऽमृतः ॥
पश्याम्यशेषमेवेदं वर्त्तमानं स्वभावतः।
करोति कालो भगवान्महायोगेश्वरः स्वयम् ॥
योऽहं सम्प्रोच्यते योगी मायी शास्त्रेषु सूरिभिः।

---

* अहमेव हीति B.

† येऽच मे इति B.

‡ कृत्स्नमिति B.

§ योगमाश्रितः इति B.

योगेश्वरोऽसौ भगवान्महायोगेश्वरः स्वयम्* ॥
महत्त्वं सर्व्वसत्त्वानां वरत्वात्† परमेष्ठिनः ।
प्रोच्यते भगवान् ब्रह्मा महाब्रह्ममयोऽमलः ॥
यो मामेवं विजानाति महायोगेश्वरेश्वरम् ।
सोऽविकल्पेन योगेन युज्यते नात्र संशयः ॥
सोऽहं प्रेरयिता देवः परमानन्दसंश्रितः‡ ।
नृत्यामि योगी सततं यस्तद्वेद स योगवित्§ ॥
इति गुह्यतमं ज्ञानं सर्व्ववेदेषु निश्चितम्¶ ।
प्रसन्नचेतसे देयं धार्म्मिकायाहिताग्नये ॥

इति श्रीकूर्म्मपुराणे ईश्वरगीतासु चतुर्थोऽध्यायः ।

---

* महादेवो महाप्रभुरिति B, G and H.

† सर्व्वतत्त्वानां परत्वादिति B.

‡ माश्रितः इति B.

§ प्रेरयामि जगत्कृत्स्नं यस्तं वेद स वेदविदिति B.

¶ निष्ठितमिति B.

पञ्चमोऽध्यायः।

सूत उवाच*।

एतावदुक्त्वा भगवान्योगिनां परमेश्वरः।
ननर्त्त परमं भावमैश्वरं सम्प्रदर्शयन्॥
तं ते ददृशुरीशानं तेजसां परमं निधिम्।
नृत्यमानं† महादेवं विष्णुना गगनेऽमले॥
तं‡ विदुर्योगतत्त्वज्ञा योगिनो यतमानसाः।
तमीशं सर्व्वभूतानामाकाशे ददृशुः किल॥
यस्य मायामयं सर्वं येनेदं भ्रियते§ जगत्।
नृत्यमानः स्वयं विप्रैर्विश्वेशः खलु दृश्यते॥
यत्पादपङ्कजं स्मृत्वा पुरुषो ज्ञानजम्भयम्।
जहाति नृत्यमानन्तं भूतेशं ददृशुः किल॥
केचिन्निद्रा¶जितश्वासाः शान्ता भक्तिसमन्विताः।
ज्योतिर्म्मयं प्रपश्यन्ति स योगी दृश्यते किल॥
योऽज्ञानान्मोचयेत् क्षिप्रं प्रसन्नो भक्तवत्सलः।

---

* व्यास उवाच इति B and F.

† नृत्यमानमित्यार्षं, नृत्यन्तमिति साधु।

‡ यमिति B.

§ प्रेष्यते इति B. पूर्य्यते इति F.

¶ यं विनिद्रा इति B, E, F, and H.

तमेवं मोचनं* रुद्रमाकाशे ददृशुः परम्॥
सहस्रशिरसं देवं सहस्रचरणाकृतिम्।
सहस्रबाहुं जटिलं चन्द्रार्द्धकृतशेखरम्॥
वसानं चर्म्म वैयाघ्रं शूलासक्तमहाकरम्।
दण्डमात्रं† त्रयीनेत्रं सूर्य्यसोमाग्निलोचनम्॥
ब्रह्माण्डं तेजसा स्वेन सर्व्वमावृत्य धिष्ठितम्‡।
दंष्ट्राकरालं दुर्द्धर्षं सूर्य्यकोटिसमप्रभम्॥
सृजन्तमनलज्वालं दहन्तमखिलं जगत्।
नृत्यन्तन्ददृशुर्देवं विश्वकर्म्माणमीश्वरम्॥
महादेवं महायोगं देवानामपि दैवतम्।
पशूनां पतिमीशानं ज्योतिषां§ ज्योतिरव्ययम्॥
पिनाकिनं विशालाक्षं भेषजं भवरोगिणाम्।
कालात्मानं कालकालं¶ देवदेवं महेश्वरम्॥
उमापतिं विशालाक्षं योगानन्दमयं परम्।
ज्ञानवैराग्यनिलयं ज्ञानयोगं सनातनम्॥
शाश्वतैश्वर्य्यविभवं‖ धर्म्माधारं दुरासदम्।

---

* मोचयतीति मोचनस्तम्, नन्द्यादिरन:। तमेव मोचकमिति B.

† दण्डपाणिमिति B and F.

‡ अत्राधिरार्षोऽकारलोपः।

§ आनन्दमिति B.

¶ कलाकालमिति B and G. कलादिस्वरूपमित्यर्थः। कलाकारमिति F.

‖ विटपमिति B.

महेन्द्रोपेन्द्रनमितं महर्षिगणवन्दितम् ॥
योगिनां हृदि तिष्ठन्तं योगमायासमावृतम् ।
क्षणेन जगती योनिं नारायणमनामयम् ।
ईश्वरेणैक्यमापन्न*मपश्यन् ब्रह्मवादिनः ॥
दृष्ट्वा तदैश्वरं रूपं रुद्रं नारायणात्मकम् ।
कृतार्थं मेनिरे सन्तः स्वात्मानं ब्रह्मवादिनः ॥

सनत्कुमारः सनको भृगुश्च
सनातनश्चैव सनन्दनश्च ।
रैभ्योऽङ्गिरा वामदेवोऽथ शुक्रो
महर्षिरत्रिः कपिलोमरीचिः ॥
दृष्ट्वाथ† रुद्रं जगदीशितारं
तं पद्मनाभाश्रितवामभागम् ।
ध्यात्वा हृदिस्थं प्रणिपत्य मूर्द्ध्ना
कृत्वाञ्जलिं स्वेषु शिरःसु भूयः ॥
ओङ्कारमुच्चार्य्य विलोक्य देव-
मन्तःशरीरं निहितं गुहायाम्‡ ।
समस्तुवन् ब्रह्ममयैर्वचोभि-
रानन्दपूर्णाहितमानसा वै§ ॥

---

* ईश्वरेणैकतापन्नमिति B and F.

† दृष्ट्वा चेति B.

‡ मनीषायामित्यर्थः ।

§ मानसास्ते इति B.

मुनयः ऊचुः ।

त्वामेकमीशं पुरुषं पुराणं
प्राणेश्वरं रुद्रमनन्तयोगम् ।
नमाम सर्व्वे हृदि सन्निविष्टं
प्रचेतसं ब्रह्ममयं पवित्रम् ॥
पश्यन्ति त्वां मुनयो ब्रह्मयोनिं
दान्ताः शान्ता विमलं रुक्मवर्णम् ।
ध्यात्वात्मस्थमचलं* स्वे शरीरे
कविं परेभ्यः परमं परञ्च ॥
त्वत्तः प्रसूता जगतः प्रसूतिः
सर्वानुभूस्त्वं परमाणुभूतः† ।
अणोरणीयान्महतो महीयां-
स्त्वामेव सर्व्वे प्रवदन्ति सन्तः ॥
हिरण्यगर्भो जगदन्तरात्मा
त्वत्तोऽस्ति जातः पुरुषः पुराणः ।
सञ्जायमानो भवता निसृष्टो‡
यथाविधानं सकलं स सद्यः ॥

---

* ध्यात्वा सुस्थमनलमिति B. स्वप्रचलं—स्वेन आत्मना प्रचलतीति तथोक्तम् । ध्यात्वात्मसंस्थमचलमिति F. ध्यात्मस्थमचलमिति H.

† विष्णुरिति B.

† विश्वनाभिरिति B. विश्वनाभः इति G.

त्वत्तोवेदाः सकलाः संप्रसूता-
स्त्वय्येवान्ते संस्थितिं ते लभन्ते।
पश्यामस्त्वाञ्जगतो हेतुभूतं
नृत्यन्तं स्वे हृदये सन्निविष्टम्॥
त्वयैवेदं भ्राम्यते ब्रह्मचक्रं
मायावी त्वं जगतामेकनाथः।
नमामस्त्वां शरणं संप्रपन्ना*
योगात्मानं नृत्यन्तं† दिव्यनृत्यम्॥
पश्यामस्त्वां परमाकाशमध्ये
नृत्यन्तं ते महिमानं स्मरामः।
सर्व्वात्मानं बहुधा सन्निविष्टं
ब्रह्मानन्दमनुभूयानुभूय॥
ओङ्कारस्ते वाचको मुक्तिवीजं
त्वमक्षरं प्रकृतौ गूढ़रूपम्।
तत्त्वां‡ सत्यं प्रवदन्तीह सन्तः
स्वयम्प्रभं भवतो यत्प्रभावम्§॥
स्तुवन्ति त्वां सततं सर्व्ववेदा
नमन्ति त्वामृषयः क्षीणदोषाः।

---

* प्रपन्नाः इति B. प्रकृतेर्गुणाश्च इति F.

† चित्पतिमिति B. रुद्रमनन्तशक्तिमिति F.

‡ तं त्वामिति B.

§ स्वप्रकाशमिति B.

शान्तात्मानः सत्यसन्धं वरिष्ठं
विशन्ति त्वां* यतयो ब्रह्मनिष्ठाः॥
भुवो नाशो नादिमान्विश्वरूपः†
ब्रह्मा विष्णुः परमेष्ठी वरिष्ठः।
स्वात्मानन्दमनुभूय विशन्ते
स्वयं ज्योतिरचला नित्यमुक्ताः॥
एको रुद्रस्त्वं करोषीह विश्वं
त्वं पालयस्यखिलं विश्वरूपम्।
त्वामेवान्ते निलयं विन्दतीदं
नमामस्त्वां शरणं संप्रपन्नाः॥
एको वेदो बहुशाखो ह्यनन्त-
स्त्वामेवैकं बोधयत्येकरूपम्।
वन्द्यं‡ त्वां ये शरणं संप्रपन्ना
मायामेतां ते तरन्तीह विप्राः§॥
त्वामेकमाहुः कविमेकरुद्रं¶
ब्रह्म गृणन्तं हरिमग्निमीशम्।
रुद्रं नित्यमनिलं‖ चेकितानं

---

* त्वां विशन्तीति B.

† भवानीशो नादिमांस्तेजोराशिरिति B.

‡ वेद्यमिति B and F.

§ तेषां शान्तिः शाश्वती नेतरेषामिति B.

¶ परमञ्च रुद्रमिति B.

‖ इन्द्रं मृत्युमनलमिति B.

धातारमादित्यमनेकरूपम् ॥
त्वमक्षरं परमं वेदितव्यं
त्वमस्य विश्वस्य परं निधानम्।
त्वमव्ययः शाश्वतधर्म्मगोप्ता
सनातनस्त्वं पुरुषोत्तमोऽसि ॥
त्वमेव विष्णुश्चतुराननस्त्वं
त्वमेव रुद्रो* भगवानपीशः।
त्वं विश्वनाथः† प्रकृतिः प्रतिष्ठा
सर्वेश्वरस्त्वं परमेश्वरोऽसि ॥
त्वामेकमाहुः पुरुषं पुराण-
मादित्यवर्णं तमसः परस्तात्।
चिन्मात्रमव्यक्तमनन्तरूपं
खं ब्रह्म शून्यं प्रकृतिर्गुणाश्च‡ ॥
यदन्तरा सर्वमिदं विभाति
यदव्ययं निर्म्मलमेकरूपम्।
किमप्यचिन्त्यं तव रूपमेत-
त्तदन्तरा यत्प्रतिभाति तत्त्वम् ॥
योगेश्वरं भद्रमनन्तशक्तिं

---

* विष्णुरिति B.

† विश्वनाभ इति E, F and H.

‡ प्रकृतिर्निर्गुणश्चेति B.

परायणं ब्रह्मतनुं पुराणम् ।
नमाम सर्वे शरणार्थिनस्त्वां
प्रसीद भूताधिपते महेश ॥
त्वत्पादपद्मस्मरणादशेष-*
संसारवीजं निलयं प्रयाति ।
मनो नियम्य प्रणिधाय कायं†
प्रसादयामो वयमेकमीशम् ॥
नमो भवायाथ‡ भवोद्भवाय
कालाय सर्वाय हराय तुभ्यम् ।
नमोऽस्तु रुद्राय कपर्द्दिने ते
नमोऽग्नये देव नमः शिवाय ॥

ततः स भगवान्प्रीतः§ कपर्द्दी वृषवाहनः ।
संहृत्य परमं रूपं प्रकृतिस्थोऽभवद्भवः ॥
ते भवं भूतभव्येशं पूर्व्ववत्समवस्थितम् ।
दृष्ट्वा नारायणं देवं विस्मितं¶ वाक्यमब्रुवन् ॥
भगवन् भूतभव्येश गोवृषाङ्कितशासन ।

---

* अशेषमिति B.

† कार्य्यमिति F.

‡ भवायास्तु इति B.

§ देवः इति B.

¶ विस्मिताः इति B and F.

दृष्ट्वा ते परमं रूपं निवृत्ताः* स्मः सनातन ॥
भवत्प्रसादादमले परस्मिन्परमेश्वरे।
अस्माकं जायते भक्तिस्त्वय्येवाव्यभिचारिणी ॥
इदानीं श्रोतुमिच्छामो माहात्म्यं तव शङ्कर।
भूयोऽपि चैवं यन्नित्यं† याथात्म्यं परमेष्ठिनः ॥
स तेषां वाक्यमाकर्ण्य योगिनां योगसिद्धिदः‡।
प्राह गम्भीरया वाचा समालोक्य च माधवम् ॥

इति श्रीकूर्म्मपुराणे ईश्वरगीतासु पञ्चमोऽध्यायः।

षष्ठोऽध्यायः।

ईश्वर उवाच।

शृणुध्वमृषयः सर्वे यथावत्परमेष्ठिनः।
वक्ष्यामीशस्य माहात्म्यं यत्तद्वेदविदो विदुः ॥
सर्व्वलोकैकनिर्माता सर्व्वलोकैकरक्षिता।
सर्व्वलोकैकसंहर्त्ता सर्वात्माहं सनातनः।

---

* निर्वृताः इति B.

† तारयन्नित्यमिति B.

‡ योगसिद्धिदमिति B.

सर्व्वेषामेव वस्तूनामन्तर्यामी महेश्वरः*।
मध्ये चान्तः† स्थितं सर्व्वं नाहं सर्वत्र संस्थितः॥
भवद्भिरद्भुतं दृष्टं यत्स्वरूपञ्च मामकम्।
ममैषा ह्युपमा विप्रा माया वै‡ दर्शिता मया॥
सर्व्वेषामेव भावानामन्तरं समवस्थितः।
प्रेरयामि जगत्कृत्स्नं क्रियाशक्तिरियं§ मम॥
मयेदं चेष्टते विश्वं तद्वै भावानुवर्त्ति मे¶।
सोऽहं कालो जगत्कृत्स्नं प्रेरयामि कलात्मकम्॥
एकांशेन जगत्कृत्स्नं करोमि मुनिपुङ्गवाः।
संहराम्येकरूपेण स्थितावस्था‖ ममैव तु॥
आदिमध्यान्तनिर्मुक्तो मायातत्त्वप्रवर्त्तकः।
क्षोभयामि च सर्गादौ प्रधानपुरुषावुभौ॥
ताभ्यां सञ्जायते विश्वं संयुक्ताभ्यां परस्परम्।
महदादिक्रमेणैव मम तेजो विजृम्भते**॥

---

* पिता ह्यहमिति B.

† मध्येवान्ते इति B.

‡ मायर्येति B.

§ क्रियाशक्तिरित्यारभ्य जगत्कृत्स्नमित्यन्तं A पुस्तके नास्ति।

¶ ययेदं चेष्टते विश्वं तत्स्वभावानुवर्त्ति न इति E.
मयेदं चेष्टितं विश्वं मत्स्वभावानुवर्त्ति च इति F.

‖ द्विधावस्था ममैव तु इति B and F.

** विजृम्भितमिति B.

यो हि सर्व्वजगत्साक्षी कालचक्रप्रवर्त्तकः ।
हिरण्यगर्भो मार्त्तण्डः सोऽपि मद्देहसम्भवः ॥
तस्मै दिव्यं स्वमैश्वर्य्यं ज्ञानयोगं सनातनम् ।
दत्तवानात्मवान्वेदान्* कल्पादौ चतुरो द्विजाः ॥
स मन्नियोगतो† देवो ब्रह्मा मद्भावभावितः ।
दिव्यं तन्मामकैश्वर्य्यं सर्व्वदावगतः‡ स्वयम् ॥
स सर्व्वलोकनिर्माता मन्नियोगेन सर्ववित् ।
भूत्वा चतुर्मुखः सर्गं सृजत्येवात्मसम्भवः ॥
योऽपि नारायणोऽनन्तो लोकानां प्रभवोऽव्ययः ।
ममैव च परा§ मूर्त्तिः करोति परिपालनम् ॥
योऽन्तकः सर्व्वभूतानां रुद्रः कालात्मकः प्रभुः ।
मदाज्ञयासौ सततं संहरिष्यति मे तनुः ॥
हव्यं वहति देवानां कव्यं कव्याशिनामपि ।
पाकञ्च कुरुते वह्निः सोऽपि मच्छक्तिनोदितः ॥
भुक्तमाहारजातञ्च पचते तदहर्निशम्¶ ।
वैश्वानरोऽग्निर्भगवानीश्वरस्य नियोगतः ॥
योऽपि सर्व्वाम्भसां योनिर्वरुणो देवपुङ्गवः ।

---

* दत्तवानात्मजानेवेति B. दत्तवानात्मजान्वेदानिति F.

† मम नियोगत इति B.

‡ सर्व्वदा वहतीति B.

§ परमेति B.

¶ पचत्येतदहर्निशमिति B.

सोऽपि सञ्जीवयेत्कृत्स्नमीश्वरस्य नियोगतः॥
योऽन्तस्तिष्ठति भूतानां वहिर्देवः प्रभञ्जनः।
मदाज्ञयासौ भूतानां शरीराणि बिभर्त्ति हि॥
योऽपि सञ्जीवनो नृणां देवानाममृताकरः।
सोमः स मन्नियोगेन नोदितः किल वर्त्तते॥
यः स्वभासा जगत्कृत्स्नं प्रभासयति सर्वशः*।
सूर्य्यो वृष्टिं वितनुते स्वोत्स्नेणैव† स्वयम्भुवः॥
योऽप्यशेषजगच्छास्ता शक्रः सर्व्वामरेश्वरः।
यज्वनां फलदो देवो वर्त्तते स‡ मदाज्ञया॥
यः प्रशास्ता ह्यसाधूनां वर्त्तते नियमादिह।
यमो वैवस्वतो देवो देवदेवनियोगतः॥
योऽपि सर्व्वधनाध्यक्षो धनानां सम्प्रदायकः।
सोऽपीश्वरनियोगेन कुवेरो वर्त्तते सदा॥
यः सर्वरक्षसां नाथस्तामसानां§ फलप्रदः।
मन्नियोगादसौ देवो वर्त्तते निर्ऋतिः सदा॥
वेतालगणभूतानां स्वामी भोगफलप्रदः।¶
ईशानः किल भक्तानां सोऽपि तिष्ठेन्मदाज्ञया॥

---

* प्रकाशयति सर्वदा इति B.

† शास्त्रेणैवेति B, F and H.

‡ वर्त्ततेऽसौ इति B.

§ तापसानामिति B, F and H.

¶ मन्नियोगादित्यारभ्य पादचतुष्टयं A पुस्तके न दृश्यते।

यो वामदेवोऽङ्गिरसः शिष्यो रुद्रगणाग्रणीः।
रक्षको योगिनां नित्यं वर्त्ततेऽसौ मदाज्ञया॥
यश्च सर्व्वजगत्पूज्यो वर्त्तते विघ्ननायकः।
विनायको धर्म्मरतः* सोऽपि मद्वचनात्किल॥
योऽपि ब्रह्मविदां श्रेष्ठो देवसेनापतिः प्रभुः।
स्कन्दोऽसौ वर्त्तते नित्यं स्वयम्भूर्विधिनोदितः॥
ये च प्रजानां पतयो मरीच्याद्या महर्षयः।
सृजन्ति विविधं लोकं परस्यैव नियोगतः†॥
या च श्रीः सर्व्वभूतानान्ददाति विपुलां श्रियम्।
पत्नी नारायणस्यासौ वर्त्तते मदनुग्रहात्॥
वाचं ददाति विपुलां या च देवी सरस्वती।
सापीश्वरनियोगेन नोदिता‡ संप्रवर्त्तते॥
याशेषपुरुषान् घोरान्नरकात्तारयिष्यति।
सावित्री संस्मृता चापि§ मदाज्ञानुविधायिनी॥
पार्व्वती परमा देवी ब्रह्मविद्याप्रदायिनी।
यापि ध्याता विशेषेण सापि मद्वचनानुगा॥
योऽनन्तमहिमानन्तः शेषोऽशेषामरप्रभुः।

---

* धर्म्मनेता इति B.

† यस्यैव निलयो गतः इति A. स च पाठो न समीचीनः।

‡ पूजितेति A and H.

§ देवीति B.

दधाति शिरसा लोकं सोऽपि देवनियोगतः॥
योऽग्निः संवर्त्तको नित्यं बड़वारूपसंस्थितः।
पिबत्यखिलमम्भोधिमीश्वरस्य नियोगतः॥
ये चतुर्द्दश लोकेऽस्मिन्मनवः प्रथितौजसः।
पालयन्ति प्रजाः सर्वास्तेऽपि तस्य नियोगतः॥
आदित्या वसवो रुद्रा मरुतश्च तथाश्विनौ।
अन्याश्च देवताः सर्वाः शास्त्रेणैव विनिर्म्मिताः* ॥
गन्धर्वा गरुड़ाद्याश्च† सिद्धाः साध्याश्च चारणाः।
यक्षरक्षःपिशाचाश्च स्थिताः सृष्टाः स्वयम्भुवा॥
कला काष्ठा निमेषाश्च मुहूर्त्ता दिवसाः क्षपाः।
ऋतवः पक्षमासाश्च स्थिताः शास्त्रे प्रजापतेः॥§
युगमन्वन्तराण्येव मम तिष्ठन्ति शासने।
पराश्चैव परार्द्धाश्च कालभेदास्तथापरे॥
चतुर्विधानि भूतानि स्थावराणि चराणि च।
नियोगादेव¶ वर्त्तन्ते देवस्य परमात्मनः॥
पातालानि च सर्वाणि भुवनानि च शासनात्।
ब्रह्माण्डानि‖ च वर्त्तन्ते सर्व्वाण्येव स्वयम्भुवः॥

---

* महाखेणैव निष्ठिताः इति B मच्छास्त्रेनैव निष्ठिता इति F.

† गरुड़ा ऋचाः इति B. गरुड़ाः पचा ऽति F.

§ अयं श्लोकः A पुस्तके नास्ति।

¶ नियमादेवेति B.

‖ मर्यौढ़ानीति A and F. त्वर्यौढ़ानीति E.

अतीतान्यप्यसंख्यानि ब्रह्माण्डानि ममाज्ञया ।
प्रवृत्तानि पदार्थौघैः सहितानि समन्ततः ॥
ब्रह्माण्डानि भविष्यन्ति सह चात्मभि*रात्मगैः ।
करिष्यन्ति† सदैवाज्ञां परस्य परमात्मनः ॥
भूमिरापोऽनलो वायुः खं मनोबुद्धिरेव च ।
भूतादिरादिप्रकृतिर्नियोगे मम वर्त्तते ॥
याशेषजगतां योनिर्मोहिनी सर्व्वदेहिनाम् ।
माया विवर्त्तते नित्यं सापीश्वरनियोगतः ॥
यो वै‡ देहभृतान्देवः पुरुषः पठ्यते परः ।
आत्मासौ वर्त्तते नित्यमीश्वरस्य§ नियोगतः ॥
विधूय मोहकलिलं यया पश्यति तत्पदम् ।
सापि बुद्धि¶र्महेशस्य नियोगवशवर्त्तिनी ॥
बहुनात्र किमुक्तेन मम शक्त्यात्मकं जगत् ।
मयैव प्रेर्य्यते‖ कृत्स्नं मय्येव प्रलयं व्रजेत् ॥
अहं हि भगवानीशः स्वयं ज्योतिः सनातनः ।
परमात्मा परं ब्रह्म मत्तो ह्यन्यो न विद्यते ॥

---

* वस्तुभिरिति B and F.

† वहिष्यन्तीति B.

‡ ह्यीति B.

§ महेश्वरेति B.

¶ विद्या इति B.

‖ मय्येव युज्यते इति B.

इत्येतत्परमं ज्ञानं युष्माकं कथितं मया ।
ज्ञात्वा विमुच्यते जन्तुर्जन्मसंसारबन्धनात् ॥

इति श्रीकूर्मपुराणे ईश्वरगीतासु षष्ठोऽध्यायः ।

सप्तमोऽध्यायः ।

ईश्वर उवाच ।

शृणुध्वमृषयः सर्व्वे प्रभावं परमेष्ठिनः ।
यं ज्ञात्वा पुरुषो मुक्तो न संसारे पतेत्पुनः ॥
परात्परतरं ब्रह्म शाश्वतं ध्रुवमव्ययम्* ।
नित्यानन्दं निर्विकल्पं तद्धाम परमं मम ॥
अहं ब्रह्मविदां ब्रह्मा स्वयम्भूर्विश्वतोमुखः ।
मायाविनामहन्देवः पुराणो हरिरव्ययः ॥
योगिनामस्म्यहं शम्भुः स्त्रीणान्देवी गिरीन्द्रजा ।
आदित्यानामहं विष्णुर्वसूनामस्मि पावकः ॥
रुद्राणां शङ्करश्चाहं गरुड़ः पततामहम् ।
ऐरावतो गजेन्द्राणां रामः शस्त्रभृतामहम् ॥

---

* निष्कलं परमिति B.

ऋषीणाञ्च वसिष्ठोऽहं देवानाञ्च शतक्रतुः ।
शिल्पिनां विश्वकर्म्माहं प्रह्लादः सुरविद्विषाम्* ॥
मुनीनामप्यहं व्यासो गणानाञ्च विनायकः ।
वीराणां वीरभद्रोऽहं सिद्धानां कपिलो मुनिः ॥
पर्व्वतानामहं मेरुर्नक्षत्राणाञ्च चन्द्रमाः ।
वज्रम्प्रहरणानाञ्च व्रतानां सत्यमस्म्यहम् ॥
अनन्तो भोगिनान्देवः सेनानीनाञ्च पावकिः ।
आश्रमाणां गृहस्थोऽहमीश्वराणां महेश्वरः ॥
महाकल्पश्च कल्पानां युगानाङ्कृतमस्म्यहम्† ।
कुवेरः सर्व्वयक्षाणां तृणानाञ्चैव वीरुधः‡ ॥
प्रजापतीनान्दक्षोऽहं निर्ऋतिः सर्व्वरक्षसाम् ।
वायुर्बलवतामस्मि द्वीपानां पुष्करोऽस्म्यहम् ॥
मृगेन्द्राणाञ्च सिंहोऽहं यन्त्राणां धनुरेव च ।
वेदानां सामवेदोऽहं यजुषां शतरुद्रियम् ॥
सावित्री सर्व्वजप्यानां गुह्यानां प्रणवोऽस्म्यहम् ।
सूक्तानां पौरुषं सूक्तं ज्येष्ठसाम च सामसु ॥
सर्व्ववेदार्थविदुषां मनुः स्वायम्भुवोऽस्म्यहम् ।
ब्रह्मावर्त्तस्तु देशानां क्षेत्राणामविमुक्तकम् ॥

---

* प्रह्लादोऽस्म्यमरद्विषामिति B.

† B पुस्तके एतत्पादद्वयमुपरिस्थश्लोकात् प्रागेव दृश्यते ।

‡ गणेशानाञ्च वीरकः इति B.

विद्यानामात्मविद्याहं ज्ञानानामैश्वरं परम्* ।
भूतानामस्म्यहं व्योम तत्त्वानां मृत्युरेव च ॥
पाशानामस्म्यहं माया कालः कलयतामहम् ।
गतीनां मुक्तिरेवाहं परेषां परमेश्वरः ॥
यच्चान्यदपि लोकेऽस्मिन् सत्त्वं तेजोबलाधिकम् ।
तत्सर्व्वं प्रतिजानीध्वं मम तेजोविजृम्भितम्† ॥
आत्मानः पशवः प्रोक्ताः सर्व्वे संसारवर्त्तिनः ।
तेषां पतिरहन्देवः स्मृतः पशुपतिर्बुधैः ॥
मायापाशेन बध्नामि पशूनेतान् स्वलीलया ।
मामेव मोचकं प्राहुः पशूनां वेदवादिनः ॥
मायापाशेन बद्धानां मोचकोऽन्यो न विद्यते ।
मामृते परमात्मानं भूताधिपतिमव्ययम् ॥
चतुर्विंशतितत्त्वानि माया कर्म्म गुणा इति ।
एते पाशाः पशुपतेः क्लेशाश्च पशुबन्धनाः ॥
मनो बुद्धिरहङ्कारः खानिलाग्निजलानि भूः ।
एताः प्रकृतयस्त्वष्टौ विकाराश्च तथापरे ॥
श्रोत्रन्त्वक् चक्षुषी जिह्वा घ्राणञ्चैव तु पञ्चमम् ।
पायूपस्थं करौ पादौ वाक् चैव दशमी मता ॥
शब्दः स्पर्शश्च रूपञ्च रसो गन्धस्तथैव च ।

---

* ईश्वरः परमिति A.

† विजृम्भनमिति B.

त्रयोविंशतिरेतानि तत्त्वानि प्राकृतानि च ॥
चतुर्विंशकमव्यक्तं प्रधानं गुणलक्षणम्।
अनादिमध्यनिधनं कारणं जगतः परम्॥
सत्त्वं रजस्तमश्चेति गुणत्रयमुदाहृतम्।
साम्यावस्थितिमेतेषामव्यक्तां प्रकृतिं विदुः॥
सत्त्वं ज्ञानं तमो ज्ञानं राजसं समुदाहृतम्*।
गुणानां बुद्धिवैषम्याद्वैषम्यं कवयो विदुः॥
धर्म्माधर्म्माविति प्रोक्तौ पाशौ द्वौ कर्म्म†संज्ञितौ।
मय्यर्पितानि कर्म्माणि न बन्धाय विमुक्तये॥
अविद्यामस्मितां रागं द्वेषञ्चाभिनिवेशनम्।
क्लेशाख्यांस्तान् स्वयं प्राहुः पाशानात्मनिबन्धनात्॥
एतेषामेव पाशानां माया कारणमुच्यते।
मूलप्रकृतिरव्यक्ता सा शक्तिर्मयि तिष्ठति॥
स एव मूलप्रकृतिः प्रधानं पुरुषोऽपि च।
विकारा महदादीनि देवदेवः सनातनः॥

स एव बन्धः स च बन्धकर्त्ता
स एव पाशः पशुभृत्स‡ एव।

---

* रजोमिश्रमुदाहृतमिति B.

† बन्धेति B.

‡ पाशाः पशवः स इति B.

स वेद सर्व्वंन्न च तस्य वेत्ता
तमाहुराद्यं* पुरुषं पुराणम् ॥

इति श्रीकूर्म्मपुराणे ईश्वरगीतासु सप्तमोऽध्यायः ।

* तमाहुरग्र्यमिति B.

अष्टमोऽध्यायः ।

ईश्वर उवाच ।

अन्यद्गुह्यतमं ज्ञानं वक्ष्ये ब्राह्मणपुङ्गवाः ।
येनासौ तरते जन्तुर्घोरं* संसारसागरम् ॥
अयं† ब्रह्मा तमः शान्तः शाश्वतो निर्म्मलोऽव्ययः ।
एकाकी भगवानुक्तः केवलः परमेश्वरः ॥
मम योनिर्महद्ब्रह्म तत्र गर्भं दधाम्यहम् ।
मूलमायाभिधानन्तं‡ ततो जातमिदं जगत् ॥
प्रधानं पुरुषो ह्यात्मा महद्भूतादि§रेव च ।
तन्मात्राणि मनो¶ भूतानीन्द्रियाणि च जज्ञिरे ॥

* घोरेति B.

† अहमिति B. अहं ब्रह्ममयः इति F.

‡ तु इति B.

§ महान् भूतादिरिति B.

¶ महेति B.

ततोऽण्डमभवद्धैममर्क*कोटिसमप्रभम् ।
तस्मिञ्जज्ञे महाब्रह्मा मच्छक्त्या चोपवृंहितः ॥
ये चान्ये बहवो जीवास्तन्मयाः† सर्व एव ते ।
न मां पश्यन्ति पितरं मायया मम मोहिताः ॥
यासु‡ योनिषु ताः सर्व्वाः§ सम्भवन्तीह¶ मूर्त्तयः ।
तां मातरं परां योनिं|| मामेव पितरं विदुः ॥
यो मामेवं** विजानाति वीजिनं पितरं प्रभुम्††।
स वीरः‡‡ सर्व्वलोकेषु न मोहमधिगच्छति ॥
ईशानः सर्व्वविद्यानां भूतानां परमेश्वरः ।
ओङ्कारमूर्त्तिर्भगवानहं ब्रह्मा प्रजापतिः ॥
समं सर्व्वेषु भूतेषु तिष्ठन्तं परमेश्वरम् ।
विनश्यत्स्वविनश्यन्तं यः पश्यति स पश्यति ॥
समं पश्यन् हि सर्व्वत्र समवस्थितमीश्वरम् ।

---

* सूर्य्येति B.

† मन्मया इति B.

‡ याश्चेति B.

§ सर्व्वासु इति B.

¶ सम्भवन्ति हीति B.

|| तासां माया परा योनिरिति B.

** मायामेवमिति B.

†† विभुमिति B.

‡‡ धीर इति B.

न हिनस्त्यात्मनात्मानं ततो याति पराङ्गतिम्* ॥
विदित्वा सप्त सूक्ष्माणि षड़ङ्गञ्च महेश्वरम् ।
प्रधानविनियोगज्ञः परं ब्रह्माधिगच्छति ॥

सर्व्वज्ञता तृप्तिरनादिबोधः
स्वच्छन्दता† नित्यमलुप्तशक्तिः ।
अनन्तशक्तिश्च विभोर्विदित्वा
षड़ाहुरङ्गानि महेश्वरस्य ॥
तन्मात्राणि मन आत्मा च तानि
सूक्ष्माण्याहुः सप्त तत्त्वात्मकानि ।
या सा हेतुः प्रकृतिः सा प्रधानं‡
बन्धः प्रोक्तो विनयेनापि§ तेन ॥
या सा शक्तिः प्रकृतौ लीनरूपा
वेदेषूक्ता कारणं ब्रह्मयोनिः ।
तस्या एकः परमेष्ठी पुरस्ता-
न्माहेश्वरः पुरुषः सत्यरूपः ॥
ब्रह्मा योगी परमात्मा महीयान्
व्योमव्यापी वेदवेद्यः पुराणः ।

---

* परं पदमिति B.

† स्वतन्त्रता इति B and F.

‡ साधनमिति B.

§ विनियोगोऽपि इति B.

एको रुद्रो मृत्युमव्यक्तमेकं
वीजं विश्वं देव* एकः स एव ॥
तमेवैकं प्राहुरन्येऽप्यनेकं
त्वामेवात्मा† केचिदन्यं तमाहुः ।
अणोरणीयान्महतो महीया-
न्महादेवः प्रोच्यते विश्वरूपः‡ ॥
एवं हि यो वेद गुहाशयं परं§
प्रभुं¶ पुराणं पुरुषं विश्वरूपम् ।
हिरण्मयं बुद्धिमतां पराङ्गतिं
स बुद्धिमान्‖ बुद्धिमतीत्य तिष्ठति ॥

इति श्रीकूर्म्मपुराणे ईश्वरगीतासु अष्टमोऽध्यायः ।

——o——

---

* वेद इति A, E and H.

† त्वेकात्मानमिति B.

‡ वेदविद्भिरिति B.

§ प्रभुमिति B.

¶ परमिति B.

‖ अबुद्धिमानिति E and H.

नवमोऽध्यायः ।

ऋषय ऊचुः ।

निष्कलोनिर्म्मलो नित्यो निष्क्रियः परमेश्वरः ।
ततो वद* महादेव विश्वरूपः कथं भवान् ॥

ईश्वर उवाच ।

नाहं विश्वो न विश्वञ्च मामृते विद्यते द्विजाः ।
माया निमित्तमात्रास्ति सा चात्मनि मया श्रिता ॥
अनादिनिधना शक्तिर्माया व्यक्तिसमाश्रया† ।
तन्निमित्तः प्रपञ्चोऽयमव्यक्ताज्जायते खलु‡ ।
अव्यक्तं कारणं प्राहुरानन्दं ज्योतिरक्षरम् ॥
अहमेव परं ब्रह्म मत्तोह्यन्यन्न§ विद्यते ।
तस्मान्मे विश्वरूपत्वं निश्चितं ब्रह्मवादिभिः ॥
एकत्वे च पृथक्त्वे च¶ प्रोक्तमेतन्निदर्शनम् ।
अहं तत्परमं ब्रह्म परमात्मा सनातनः ॥
अकारणं द्विजाः प्रोक्ता न दोषोह्यात्मनस्तथा ।

---

* देव इति A.

† व्यक्तसमाश्रिता इति B. व्यक्तसमाश्रया इति F.

‡ मव्यक्तादभवत् खलु इति B.

§ मत्तोऽन्यद्धि इति B.

¶ एकत्वेन पृथक्त्वेन इति B.

अनन्ताः* शक्तयोऽव्यक्ता मायया संस्थिता ध्रुवाः ।
तस्मिन्दिविस्थितं नित्यमव्यक्तं भाति केवलम् ॥
अभिन्नं वच्यते भिन्नं ब्रह्माव्यक्तं सनातनम्† ।
एकया मायया युक्तमनादिनिधनं ध्रुवम् ॥
पुंसोऽन्याभूद्यथा भूतिरन्यया न तिरोहितम्‡ ।
अनादिमध्यन्तिष्ठन्तं चेष्टते विद्यया किल ॥
तदेतत्परमव्यक्तं प्रभामण्डलमण्डितम् ।
तदक्षरं परं ज्योतिस्तद्विष्णोः परमं पदम् ॥
तत्र सर्व्वमिदं प्रोतमोतं चैवाखिलं जगत् ।
तदेवेदं§ जगत्कृत्स्नं तद्विज्ञाय विमुच्यते ॥
यतोवाचो निवर्त्तन्ते अप्राप्य मनसा सह ।
आनन्दं ब्रह्मणो विद्वान् बिभेति न कुतश्चन¶ ॥
वेदाहमेतं पुरुषं महान्त-
मादित्यवर्णं पुरुषं पुरस्तात्‖ ।

---

* सुलभाः इति B.

† अभिन्नस्तु स्वभावतः इति B and F.

‡ तत्तिरोहितमिति E and H.

§ तदेव च इति B.

¶ न बिभेति कदाचनेति B.

‖ तमसः परस्तादिति B and F.

तं विज्ञाय परिमुच्येत विद्वा-
न्नित्यानन्दी भवति ब्रह्मभूतः* ॥
अस्मात्परं नापरमस्ति किञ्चि-
द्यज्ज्योतिषां ज्योतिरेकं दिविस्थम्† ।
तदेवात्मानं मन्यमानोऽथ विद्वा-
नात्मानन्दी भवति ब्रह्मभूतः ॥
तदप्यहं‡ कलिलं गूढ़देहं
ब्रह्मानन्दममृतं विश्वधामा§ ।
वदन्त्येवं ब्राह्मणा ब्रह्मनिष्ठा-
यत्र गत्वा न निवर्त्तेत भूयः ॥
हिरण्मये परमाकाशतत्त्वे
यद्वै दिवि¶ विप्रतिभातीव तेजः ।
तद्विज्ञाने‖ परिपश्यन्ति धीरा-
विभ्राजमानं विमलं व्योमधाम ॥

---

* ब्रह्मभूयः इति B.

† दिविष्ठमिति B.

‡ तदव्ययमिति B.

§ विश्वधाम इति B.

¶ यदर्चिषीति B.

‖ तद्विज्ञानेन इति B.

ततः* परम्परिपश्यन्ति धीरा-
आत्मन्यात्मानमनुभूय साक्षात्† ।
स्वयं प्रभुः परमेष्ठी महीयान्
ब्रह्मानन्दी भगवानीश‡ एषः ॥
एकोदेवः सर्व्वभूतेषु गूढ़ः
सर्व्वव्यापी सर्व्वभूतान्तरात्मा ।
तमेवैकं येऽनुपश्यन्ति धीरा-
स्तेषां शान्तिः शाश्वती नेतरेषाम् ॥
सर्व्वाननशिरोग्रीवः सर्व्वभूतगुहाशयः ।
सर्व्वव्यापी स भगवान्तस्मादन्यन्न विद्यते ॥
इत्येतदीश्वरज्ञानमुक्तं वो मुनिपुङ्गवाः ।
गोपनीयं विशेषेण योगिनामपि दुर्लभम् ॥

इति श्रीकूर्म्मपुराणे ईश्वरगीतासु नवमोऽध्यायः ।

---

* यतः इति B.

† अनुभूय इति B.

‡ भवानीश इति B.

दशमोऽध्यायः।

ईश्वर उवाच।

अलिङ्गमेकमव्यक्तलिङ्गं ब्रह्मेति निश्चितम्।
स्वयञ्ज्योतिः परन्तत्त्वं पूर्व्वे* व्योम्नि व्यवस्थितम्॥
अव्यक्तं कारणं यत्तदक्षरं परमं पदम्।
निर्गुणं सिद्धि†विज्ञानं तद्वै पश्यन्ति सूरयः॥
तन्निष्टस्वान्तसङ्कल्पा‡ नित्यं तद्भावभाविताः।
पश्यन्ति तत्परं ब्रह्म यत्तल्लिङ्गमिति श्रुतिः॥
अन्यथा न हि मां द्रष्टुं शक्यं वै मुनिपुङ्गवाः।
न हि तद्विद्यते ज्ञानं येन तज्ज्ञायते§ परम्॥
एतत्तत्परमं स्थानं¶ केवलं कवयो विदुः।
अज्ञानतिमिरं‖ ज्ञानं यस्मान्मायामयं जगत्॥
यज्ज्ञानं निर्म्मलं शुद्धं** निर्विकल्पन्निरञ्जनम्††।

---

* परे इति B and F.

† शुद्धेति B.

‡ तन्निष्ठाः शान्तसङ्कल्पा इति B, F and H.

§ यतस्तज्ज्ञायते इति B.

¶ ज्ञानमिति B.

‖ अज्ञानमितरं ज्ञानमिति F. इतरदिति साधु।

** सूक्ष्ममिति B.

†† यदव्ययमिति B.

ममात्मासौ तदेवैन*मिति प्राहुर्विपश्चितः ॥
येऽप्यनेकं प्रपश्यन्ति तत्परं परमं पदम्।
आश्रिताः परमान्निष्ठां बुद्धैक्यं† तत्त्वमव्ययम् ॥
ये पुनः परमन्तत्त्वमेकं वानेकमीश्वरम्।
भक्ता‡ मां सम्प्रपश्यन्ति विज्ञेयास्ते तदात्मकाः ॥
साक्षाद्देवं§ प्रपश्यन्ति स्वात्मानं परमेश्वरम्।
नित्यानन्दं निर्व्विकल्पं सत्यरूपमिति स्थितिः ॥
भजन्ते परमानन्दं सर्व्वगं जगदात्मकम्¶।
स्वात्मन्यवस्थिताः शान्ताः परे व्यक्तापरस्य|| तु ॥
एषा विमुक्तिः परमा मम सायुज्यमुत्तमम्।
निर्व्वाणं ब्रह्मणा चैक्यं कैवल्यं कवयो विदुः ॥
तस्मादनादिमध्यान्तं वस्त्वेकं परमं शिवम्**।
स ईश्वरो महादेवस्तं विज्ञाय प्रमुच्यते ॥
न तत्र सूर्यः प्रतिभातीह चन्द्रो
नक्षत्राणां गणो†† नोत विद्युत्।

---

* तदेवेदमिति B. एतदिति साधु।

† बुद्ध्यैकमिति B.

‡ भक्त्या इति B.

§ साक्षादेव इति B.

¶ यत्तदात्मकमिति B. यत्तदात्मकमिति G and H.

|| परव्यक्ते परस्य तु इति F.

** परमः शिवः इति B.

†† न नक्षत्राणि तपनः इति B. नक्षत्रतारातपनश्च विद्युदिति F.

तद्भासितं ह्यखिलम्भाति विश्व-
मतीव* भासममलन्तद्विभाति ॥
विश्वोदितन्निष्कलं† निर्व्विकल्पं
शुद्धं बृहत्परमं‡ यद्विभाति।
अत्रान्तरे ब्रह्मविदोऽथ नित्यं
पश्यन्ति तत्त्वमचलं यत्स ईशः ॥
नित्यानन्दममृतं सत्यरूपं
शुद्धं वदन्ति पुरुषं सर्व्ववेदाः।
प्राणानिति§ प्रणवेनेश्वितारं
ध्यायन्ति वेदैरिति निश्चितार्थाः¶ ॥
न भूमिरापो न मनो न वह्निः
प्राणोऽनिलो गगनं नोत बुद्धिः।
न चेतनोऽन्यत्परमाकाशमध्ये
विभाति देवः शिव एव केवलः ॥
इत्येतदुक्तं परमं रहस्यं
ज्ञानञ्चेदं‖ सर्व्ववेदेषु गीतम्**।

---

* तन्नित्येति B.

† नित्योदितं सामदमिति B.

‡ शुभं विशस्तं परममिति B. शुभं बृहत्परममिति F.

§ तमीमिति इति B.

¶ वेदार्थिविपश्चितार्थाः इति B. वेदार्थविनिश्चितार्थमिति F.

‖ ज्ञानामृतमिति B.

** गूढ़मिति B.

जानाति योगी विजनेऽथ देशे*
युञ्जीत योगं प्रयतो ह्यजस्रम् ॥

इति श्रीकूर्म्मपुराणे ईश्वरगीतासु दशमोऽध्यायः ।

एकादशोऽध्यायः ।

ईश्वर उवाच ।

अतः परं प्रवक्ष्यामि योगं परमदुर्लभम् ।
येनात्मानं प्रपश्यन्ति भानुमन्तमिवेश्वरम् ॥
योगाग्निर्दहति* क्षिप्रमशेषं पापपञ्जरम्† ।
प्रसन्नं जायते ज्ञानं साक्षान्निर्वाणसिद्धिदम् ॥
योगात्सञ्जायते ज्ञानं‡ ज्ञानाद्योगः प्रवर्त्तते ।
योगज्ञानाभियुक्तस्य प्रसीदति महेश्वरः ॥

---

* यदेवमिति A and H.

---

* दहतीति B.

† सञ्चयमिति B.

‡ ज्ञानमित्यन्तं पादद्वयं A, E, H पुस्तकेषु नास्ति ।

एककालं द्विकालं वा त्रिकालं नित्यमेव च* ।
ये युञ्जन्ति महायोगं ते विज्ञेया महेश्वराः ॥
योगस्तु द्विविधो† ज्ञेयो ह्यभावः प्रथमो मतः ।
अपरस्तु महा‡योगः सर्व्वयोगोत्तमोत्तमः ॥
शून्यं सर्व्वनिराभासं स्वरूपं यत्र चिन्त्यते ।
अभावयोगः स प्रोक्तो येनात्मानं प्रपश्यति ॥
यत्र पश्यति चात्मानं नित्यानन्दं निरञ्जनम् ।
मयैक्यं स मया योगो§ भाषितः परमः स्वयम्¶ ॥
ये चान्ये योगिनां योगाः श्रूयन्ते ग्रन्थविस्तरे ।
सर्व्वे ते ब्रह्मयोगस्य कलां नार्हन्ति षोड़शीम् ॥
यत्र साक्षात्प्रपश्यन्ति विमुक्ता विश्वमीश्वरम् ।
सर्व्वेषामेव योगानां स योगः परमो मतः ॥
सहस्रशोऽथ बहुशो‖ ये चेश्वरवहिष्कृताः ।
न ते पश्यन्ति मामेकं योगिनो यतमानसाः ॥
प्राणायामस्तथा ध्यानं प्रत्याहारोपधारणा** ।

---

* वा इति B.

† प्रथमः इति A, E and H.

‡ अनुफा सुनफा इति A, E and H.

§ महायोगः इति B.

¶ परमेश्वरः इति B.

‖ शतशः इति B.

** प्रत्याहारोऽथ धारणा इति B and G.

समाधिश्च मुनिश्रेष्ठा यमश्च नियमासने ॥
मय्येकचित्तता योगः प्रत्यन्तर*नियोगतः ।
तत्साधनानि चान्यानि युष्माकं कथितानि तु ॥
अहिंसा सत्यमस्तेयं ब्रह्मचर्य्यापरिग्रहौ ।
यमाः सङ्क्षेपतः प्रोक्ताश्चित्तशुद्धिप्रदा नृणाम् ॥
कर्म्मणा मनसा वाचा सर्व्वभूतेषु सर्व्वदा ।
अक्लेशजननं प्रोक्ता त्वहिंसा परमर्षिभिः ॥
अहिंसायाः परो धर्म्मो नास्त्यहिंसापरं सुखम् ।
विधिना या भवेद्धिंसा त्वहिंसैव प्रकीर्त्तिता† ॥
सत्येन सर्व्वमाप्नोति सत्ये सर्व्वं प्रतिष्ठितम् ।
यथार्थकथनाचारः सत्यम्प्रोक्तं द्विजातिभिः ॥
परद्रव्यापहरणं चौर्य्यादथ‡ बलेन वा ।
स्तेयं तस्यानाचरणादस्तेयं धर्म्मसाधनम् ॥
कर्म्मणा मनसा वाचा सर्व्वावस्थासु सर्व्वदा ।
सर्व्वत्र मैथुनत्यागं ब्रह्मचर्य्यम्प्रचक्षते ॥
द्रव्याणामप्यनादानमापद्यपि तथेच्छया ।
अपरिग्रहमित्याहुस्तं प्रयत्नेन पालयेत् ॥
तपः स्वाध्यायसन्तोषौ शौचमीश्वरपूजनम् ।

---

* वृत्तान्तर इति B and F.

† सा त्वहिंसैव कीर्त्तिता इति B.

‡ चौर्य्याद्वाथ इति B.

समासान्नियमाः प्रोक्ता योगसिद्धिप्रदायिनः ॥
उपवासपराकादिकृच्छ्रचान्द्रायणादिभिः ।
शरीरशोषणम्प्राहुस्तापसास्तप उत्तमम् ॥
वेदान्तशतरुद्रीय*प्रणवादिजपम्बुधाः ।
सत्त्वसिद्धिकरं पुंसां स्वाध्यायं परिचक्षते ॥
स्वाध्यायस्य त्रयो भेदा वाचिकोपांशुमानसाः ।
उत्तरोत्तरवैशिष्टं प्राहुर्वेदार्थवेदिनः ॥
यः शब्दबोधजननः परेषां शृखतां स्फुटम् ।
स्वाध्यायो वाचिकः प्रोक्त उपांशोरथ लक्षणम् ॥
ओष्ठयोः स्पन्दमात्रेण परस्याशब्दबोधकम् ।
उपांशुरेष निर्द्दिष्टः साध्वसौ वाचिकाज्जपात्† ॥
यत्पदाक्षरसङ्गत्या परिस्पन्दनवर्ज्जितम्‡ ।
चिन्तनं सर्व्वशब्दानां मानसं तज्जपं विदुः ॥
यदृच्छालाभतो वित्तं§ अलं पुंसो भवेदिति ।
प्राशस्त्यमृषयः प्राहुः सन्तोषं सुखलक्षणम् ॥
वाह्यमाभ्यन्तरं शौचं द्विधा प्रोक्तं द्विजोत्तमाः ।
मृज्जलाभ्यां स्मृतं वाह्यं मनःशुद्धिरथान्तरम् ॥

---

* A celebrated hymn and prayer of the यजुर्वेद occurring in the वाजसनेयी संहिता.

† सहस्रवाचिको जपः इति B.

‡ परिस्पन्दविवर्जितमिति B.

§ नित्यमिति B, E and H.

स्तुतिस्मरणपूजाभिर्वाङ्मनःकायकर्म्मभिः ।
सुनिश्चला शिवे भक्तिरेतदीशस्य* पूजनम् ॥
यमाश्च नियमाः प्रोक्ताः प्राणायामन्निबोधत ।
प्राणः स्वदेहजो वायुरायामस्तन्निरोधनम् ।†
उत्तमाधममध्यत्वात्त्रिधायं प्रतिपादितः ॥
य‡ एव द्विविधः प्रोक्तः सगर्भोऽगर्भ एव च ॥
मात्राद्वादशको मन्दश्चतुर्विंशतिमात्रकः ।
मध्यमः प्राणसंरोधः षट्त्रिंशन्मात्रिकोऽन्तकः§ ॥
यः स्वेदकम्पनोच्छ्वास¶जनकत्वं यथाक्रमम् ।
संयोगश्च मनुष्याणामानन्दाच्चोत्तमोत्तमः‖ ॥
सुनफाख्यं हि** तं योगं सगर्भविजय††म्बुधाः ।
एतद्वै योगिनां प्राहुः‡‡ प्राणायामस्य लक्षणम् ॥
सव्याहृतिं सप्रणवां गायत्रीं शिरसा सह ।

---

* ईश्वरेति B.

† एतत्पादद्वयं A पुस्तके नास्ति।

‡ स इति B, E and H.

§ मात्रिकोत्तम इति B, E and H.

¶ प्रस्वेदकम्पनोत्थान इति B. यः स्वेदकम्पनोत्थान इति G.

‖ मन्दमध्यमसुख्यानामानन्दादुत्तमोत्तमः इति B.

** सगर्भमाहुरिति B.

†† अगर्भविजपमिति B.

‡‡ एतद्धि योगिनामुक्तमिति B.

त्रिर्जपेद्दायतप्राणः प्राणायामोऽथ नामतः* ॥
रेचकः पूरकश्चैव प्राणायामोऽथ† कुम्भकः ।
प्रोच्यते सर्व्वशास्त्रेषु योगिभिर्यतमानसैः ॥
रेचको वाह्यनिश्वासः‡ पूरकस्तन्निरोधनः§ ।
साम्येन संस्थितिर्या सा कुम्भकः परिगीयते ॥
इन्द्रियाणां विचरतां विषयेषु स्वभावतः ।
निग्रहः प्रोच्यते सद्भिः प्रत्याहारस्तु सत्तमाः ॥
हृत्पुण्डरीके नाभ्यां वा मूर्द्ध्नि पर्व्वसु मस्तके ।
एवमादिषु देशेषु धारणा चित्तबन्धनम् ॥
देशावस्थितिमालम्ब्य ऊर्द्ध्वं¶ या वृत्तिसन्ततिः ।
प्रत्यन्तरैरसृष्टा या‖ तद्ध्यानं सूरयो विदुः ॥
एकाकारः समाधिः स्याद्देशालम्बनवर्ज्जितः ।
प्रत्ययो ह्यर्थमात्रेण योगशासन**मुत्तमम् ॥
धारणा द्वादशायामा ध्यानं द्वादश धारणाः ।
ध्यानं द्वादशकं यावत्समाधिरभिधीयते ॥

---

* प्राणायामः स उच्यते इति B.

† प्राणायामस्तु इति B.

‡ रेचकोऽजस्रनिश्वासादिति B.

§ निरोधतः इति B.

¶ बुद्धेरिति B, G, E and H.

‖ प्रत्यन्तरैरसंसृष्टा इति B. प्रत्यन्तरैरसंसृष्टा इति G.

** साधनेति B.

आसनं स्वस्तिकं प्रोक्तं पद्ममर्द्धासनन्तथा ।
साधनानाञ्च सर्व्वेषामेतत्साधनमुत्तमम् ॥
ऊर्व्वोरुपरि विप्रेन्द्राः कृत्वा पादतले उभे ।
समासीनात्मनः पद्ममेतदासनमुत्तमम् ॥
उभे कृत्वा पादतले जानूर्व्वोरन्तरेण हि ।
समासीनात्मनः प्रोक्तमासनं स्वस्तिकं परम् ॥
एकं पादमथैकस्मिन्विष्टभ्योरसि सत्तमाः ।
आसीनार्द्धासनमिदं योगसाधनमुत्तमम् ॥*
अदेशकाले योगस्य दर्शनं हि न विद्यते ।
अग्न्यभ्यासे जले वापि शुष्कपर्णचये तथा ॥
जन्तुव्याप्ते श्मशाने च जीर्णगोष्ठे चतुष्पथे ।
सशब्दे सभये† वापि चैत्यवल्मीकसञ्चये ॥
अशुभे दुर्जनाक्रान्ते मशकादिसमन्विते ।
नाचरेद्देहबाधे वा दौर्मनस्यादिसम्भवे ॥
सुगुप्ते सुशुभे देशे गुहायां पर्व्वतस्य च ।‡
नद्यास्तीरे पुण्यदेशे देवतायतने तथा ॥
गृहे वा सुशुभे देशे§ निर्ज्जने जन्तुवर्ज्जिते ।

---

* अयं श्लोकः B पुस्तके नास्ति ।

† सभये इति B.

‡ एतदन्तं पादचतुष्टयं A पुस्तके नास्ति ।

§ रम्ये इति B.

युञ्जीत योगं* सततमात्मानं तत्परायणः† ॥
नमस्कृत्याथ योगीन्द्राञ्छिष्यांश्चैव विनायकम् ।
गुरुञ्चैव च‡ मां योगी युञ्जीत सुसमाहितः ॥
आसनं स्वस्तिकं बद्धा पद्ममर्द्धमथापि वा ।
नासिकाग्रे समां दृष्टिमीषदुन्मीलितेक्षणः ॥
कृत्वाथ निर्भयः शान्तस्त्यक्त्वा मायामयं जगत् ।
स्वात्मन्यवस्थितन्देवं चिन्तयेत्परमेश्वरम् ॥
शिखाग्रे द्वादशाङ्गुल्ये कल्पयित्वाथ पङ्कजम् ।
धर्म्मकन्दसमुद्भूतं ज्ञाननालं सुशोभनम् ॥
ऐश्वर्य्याष्टदलं श्वेतं परं वैराग्यकर्णिकम् ।
चिन्तयेत्परमं कोशं कर्णिकायां हिरण्मयम् ॥
सर्व्वशक्तिमयं साक्षाद्यं प्राहुर्दिवमव्ययम् ।
ओङ्कारवाच्यमव्यक्तं रश्मिज्वाला§समाकुलम् ।
चिन्तयेत्तत्र विमलं परं ज्योतिर्यदक्षरम् ॥
तस्मिन्ज्योतिषि विन्यस्य स्वानन्दं मम भेदतः¶ ।
ध्यायीत कोश||मध्यस्थमीशं परमकारणम् ॥

---

* योगीति B.

† मत्परायण: इति B.

‡ गुरुञ्चैवाथ इति B and H.

§ ज्वालेति B.

¶ स्वात्मानं तदभेदतः इति B. स्वात्मानन्दमभेदतः इति G and H.

|| ध्यायीताकाशेति B and H. ध्यायीत--अत्र आत्मनेपदित्वमार्षम् ।

तदात्मा सर्व्वगो भूत्वा न किञ्चिदपि चिन्तयेत् ।
एतद्गुह्यतमं ज्ञानं ध्यानान्तरमथोच्यते ॥
चिन्तयित्वा तु पूर्व्वोक्तं हृदये पद्ममुत्तमम् ।
आत्मानमथ कान्तारं* तत्रानलसमत्विषम् ॥
मध्ये वह्निशिखाकारं पुरुषं पञ्चविंशकम् ।
चिन्तयेत्परमात्मानं तन्मध्ये गगनं परम् ॥
ओङ्कारबोधितं तत्त्वं शाश्वतं शिवमुच्यते† ।
अव्यक्तं‡ प्रकृतौ लीनं परं ज्योतिरनुत्तमम् ॥
तदन्तः परमं तत्त्वमात्माधारं निरञ्जनम् ।
ध्यायीत तन्मयो§ नित्यमेकरूपं महेश्वरम् ॥
विशोध्य सर्व्वतत्त्वानि प्रणवेनाथवा पुनः ।
संस्थाप्यमपि¶ चात्मानं निर्म्मले परमे पदे ॥
पावयित्वात्मनो‖ देहं तेनैव ज्ञानवारिणा ।
मदात्मा मन्मना** भस्म गृहीत्वा त्वाग्निहोत्रिकम्†† ॥

---

* कर्त्तारमिति B and F.

† शिवमच्युतमिति B, F and H.

‡ अनन्तमिति B.

§ तन्मना इति B.

¶ संस्थाप्य मयि इति B and H.

‖ प्लावयित्वात्मना इति B and H.

** मन्मयः इति B.

†† त्वग्निहोत्रजमिति B.

तेनोद्धूलितसर्व्वाङ्गमग्निरादित्य*मन्त्रतः ।
चिन्तयेत्स्वात्मनीशानं परं ज्योतिःस्वरूपिणम् ॥
एष पाशुपतो योगः पशुपाशविमुक्तये ।
सर्व्ववेदान्तमार्गोऽयं†मत्याश्रममिति‡ श्रुतिः ॥
एतत्परतरं गुह्यं मत्सायुज्यप्रदायकम्§ ।
द्विजातीनान्तु कथितं भक्तानां ब्रह्मचारिणाम् ॥
ब्रह्मचर्य्यमहिंसा च क्षमा शौचन्तपो दमः ।
सन्तोषः सत्यमास्तिक्यं व्रताङ्गानि विशेषतः ॥
एकेनाप्यथ हीनेन व्रतमस्य न¶ लुप्यते ।
तस्मादात्मगुणोपेतो मद्व्रतं‖ वोढुमर्हति ॥
वीतरागभयक्रोधा मन्मया मामुपाश्रिताः ।
बहवोऽनेन योगेन पूता मद्भावयोगतः** ॥
ये यथा मां प्रपद्यन्ते तांस्तथैव भजाम्यहम् ।
ज्ञानयोगेन मां तस्माद्यजेत परमेश्वरम् ॥
अथवा भक्तियोगेन वैराग्येण परेण तु ।

---

* मग्निरित्यादि इति B.

† सारोऽयमिति B and H.

‡ यत्याश्रम इति B.

§ मत्सायुज्योपपादकमिति B.

¶ तु इति B and F.

‖ तद्व्रतमिति B.

** मद्भावमागताः इति B.

चेतसा बोधयुक्तेन पूजयेन्मां सदा शुचिः ॥
सर्व्वकर्म्माणि संन्यस्य भिक्षाशी निष्परिग्रहः ।
प्राप्नोति मम सायुज्यं गुह्यमेतन्मयोदितम् ॥
अद्वेष्टा सर्व्वभूतानां मैत्रीकरुण एव च ।
निर्म्ममो निरहङ्कारो यो मद्भक्तः स मे प्रियः ॥
सन्तुष्टः सततं योगी यतात्मा दृढ़निश्चयः ।
मय्यर्पितमनोबुद्धिर्यो मद्भक्तः स मे प्रियः ॥
यस्मा*न्नोद्विजते लोको लोकान्नोद्विजते च यः ।
हर्षामर्षभयोद्वेगैर्मुक्तो यः सहि मे प्रियः ॥
अनपेक्षः शुचिर्दक्ष उदासीनो गतव्यथः ।
सर्व्वारम्भपरित्यागी भक्तिमान्यः स मे प्रियः ॥
तुल्यनिन्दास्तुतिर्मौनी सन्तुष्टो येन केनचित् ।
अनिकेतः स्थिरमतिर्मद्भक्तो मामुपैष्यति ॥
सर्व्वकर्म्माण्यपि सदा कुर्व्वाणो मत्परायणः ।
मत्प्रसादादवाप्नोति शाश्वतं परमं पदम् ॥
चेतसा सर्व्वकर्माणि मयि सन्न्यस्य मत्परः ।
निराशी निर्ममो भूत्वा मामेकं शरणं व्रजेत् ॥
त्यक्त्वा कर्म्मफलासङ्गं नित्यतृप्तो निराश्रयः ।
कर्म्मण्यपि प्रवृत्तोऽपि कर्म्मणा तेन बुध्यते† ॥

---

* यस्मादित्यादि सार्द्धश्लोकत्रयं A, E, H पुस्तकेषु नास्ति ।

† नैव तेन निबध्यते इति B and F.

निरागी यतचित्तात्मा* त्यक्तसर्व्वपरिग्रहः।
शारीरं केवलं कर्म्म कुर्व्वन्नाप्नोति तत्पदम्† ॥
यदृच्छालाभतुष्टस्य‡ द्वन्द्वातीतस्य§ चैव हि।
कुर्व्वतो मत्प्रसादार्थं कर्म्म संसारनाशनम् ॥
मन्मना मन्नमस्कारी मद्याजी मत्परायणः।
मामुपास्यति¶ योगीशो ज्ञात्वा मां परमेश्वरम् ॥
मामेवाहुः परं ज्योति‖र्बोधयन्तः परस्परम्।
कथयन्तश्च मां नित्यं मम सायुज्यमाप्नुयुः ॥
एवं नित्याभियुक्तानां मायेयं कर्म्म सात्त्वगम्।
नाशयामि तमः कृत्स्नं ज्ञानदीपेन भास्वता ॥
मद्बुद्धयो मां सततं पूजयन्तीह ये जनाः।
तेषां नित्याभियुक्तानां** योगक्षेमं वहाम्यहम् ॥
ये चान्ये भोगकर्म्मार्थां†† यजन्ते ह्यन्यदेवताः।
तेषां तदन्तं विज्ञेयं‡‡ देवतानुगतं फलम् ॥

---

* यतचिन्तात्मेति B. जितचित्तात्मेति G.

† किल्बिषमिति F and H.

‡ तुष्टस्येति B.

§ द्वन्द्वातीतस्य—द्वन्द्वं सुखदुःखशीतोष्णादिद्वन्द्वं तदतीतस्य इत्यर्थः।

¶ उपास्ते इति साधु। मामुपैष्यतीति B.

‖ मद्बुद्धयो मां सततमिति B.

** मायेयमित्यादि युक्तानामित्यन्तं A, H पुस्तकयोर्नास्ति।

†† येऽन्ये च कामभोगार्थमिति B.

‡‡ तदन्तरं ज्ञेयमिति B.

ये चान्य*देवताभक्ताः पूजयन्तीह देवताः ।
मद्भावनासमायुक्ता मुच्यन्ते तेऽपि मानवाः† ॥
तस्माद्विनश्वरा‡नन्यांस्त्यक्त्वा देवानशेषतः ।
मामेव संश्रयेदीशं स याति परमं पदम् ॥
त्यक्त्वा पुत्रादिषु स्नेहं निःशोको निष्परिग्रहः ।
यजेच्चामरणाल्लिङ्गं विरक्तः परमेश्वरम् ॥
येऽर्च्चयन्ति सदा लिङ्गं त्यक्त्वा भोगानशेषतः§ ।
एकेन जन्मना तेषां ददामि परमम्पदम् ॥
परात्मनः सदा¶ लिङ्गं केवलं रजतप्रभम्‖ ।
ज्ञानात्मकं सर्व्वगतं योगिनां हृदि संस्थितम्** ॥
ये चान्ये नियता†† भक्ता भावयित्वा विधानतः ।
यत्र क्वचन तल्लिङ्गमर्च्चयन्ति महेश्वरम् ॥
जले वा वह्निमध्ये वा व्योम्नि सूर्य्येऽप्यथान्यतः ।
रत्नादौ भावयित्वेशमर्च्चयेल्लिङ्गमैश्वरम् ॥

---

* वान्येति B.

† भावतः इति B and F.

‡ विश्वेश्वरेति B.

§ मामेवेति पादाष्टकं A, II पुस्तकेषु नास्ति ।

¶ परानन्दात्मकमिति B.

‖ सन्निरञ्जनमिति B.

** हृदये स्थितमिति B.

†† नियतमिति B.

सर्व्वलिङ्गमयं ह्येतत्सर्व्वं लिङ्गे* प्रतिष्ठितम् ।
तस्माल्लिङ्गेऽर्च्चयेदीशं यत्र क्वचन शाश्वतम् ॥
अग्नौ क्रियावतामप्सु व्योम्नि सूर्य्ये मनीषिणाम् ।
काष्ठादिष्वेव मूर्खाणां हृदि लिङ्गन्तु योगिनाम् ॥
यद्यनुत्पन्नविज्ञानो विरक्तः प्रीतिसंयुतः ।
यावज्जीवं जपेद्युक्तः प्रणवं ब्रह्मणो वपुः ॥
अथवा शतरुद्रीयं जपेदामरणाद्द्विजः ।
एकाकी जित†चित्तात्मा स याति परमम्पदम् ॥
वसेच्चामरणाद्विप्रा वाराणस्यां समाहितः ।
सोऽपीश्वरप्रसादेन याति तत्परमम्पदम् ॥‡
तत्रोत्क्रमणकाले हि सर्व्वेषामेव देहिनाम् ।
ददाति परमं§ ज्ञानं येन मुच्येत बन्धनात् ॥
वर्णाश्रमविधिङ्कृत्स्नङ्कुर्व्वाणो मत्परायणः ।
तेनैव जन्मना ज्ञानं लब्ध्वा याति शिवम्पदम् ॥
येऽपि तत्र वसन्तीह नीचा वै¶ पापयोनयः ।
सर्व्वे तरन्ति संसारमीश्वरानुग्रहाद्द्विजाः ॥

---

* सर्व्वलिङ्गे इति A.

† यतेति B.

‡ एष श्लोकः B पुस्तके नास्ति ।

§ तत्परमिति B.

¶ वेति B.

किन्तु विघ्ना* भविष्यन्ति पापोपहतचेतसाम्† ।
धर्म्मान्समाश्रयेत्तस्मान्मुक्तये सततं‡ द्विजाः ॥
एतद्रहस्यं वेदानां न देयं यस्य कस्यचित् ।
धार्म्मिकायैव दातव्यं भक्ताय ब्रह्मचारिणे ॥

व्यास उवाच ।

इत्येतदुक्त्वा भगवान् शाश्वतो योगमुत्तमम्§ ।
व्याजहार समासीनं नारायणमनामयम् ॥
मयैतद्भाषितं ज्ञानं हितार्थं ब्रह्मवादिनाम् ।
दातव्यं शान्तचित्तेभ्यः शिष्येभ्यो भवता शिवम् ॥
उक्त्वैवमर्थं¶ योगीन्द्रानब्रवीद्भगवानजः ।
हिताय|| सर्व्वभक्तानां द्विजातीनां द्विजोत्तमाः ॥
भवन्तोऽपि हि मज्ज्ञानं शिष्याणां विधिपूर्व्वकम् ।
उपदेक्ष्यन्ति भक्तानां सर्व्वेषां वचनान्मम ॥
अयं नारायणो योऽसावीश्वरो** नात्र संशयः ।
नान्तरं ये प्रपश्यन्ति तेषां देयमिदम्परम् ॥

---

* विप्रा इति B.

† चेतसः इति B.

‡ नियतमिति B.

§ आत्मयोगमनुत्तममिति B.

¶ उक्त्वैवमथेति B.

|| हितार्थमिति B.

** योऽहमीश्वरः इति B and F.

ममैषा परमा मूर्त्तिर्नारायणसमाह्वया ।
सर्व्वभूतात्मभूतस्था* शान्ता चाक्षरसंस्थिता ॥
येऽन्यथा मां† प्रपश्यन्ति लोके भेददृशो जनाः ।
न ते मुक्तिं प्रपश्यन्ति जायन्ते च पुनः पुनः ॥
ये त्वेनं विष्णुमव्यक्तं माञ्च देवं महेश्वरम् ।
एकीभावेन पश्यन्ति न तेषां पुनरुद्भवः ॥
तस्मादनादिनिधनं विष्णुमात्मानमव्ययम् ।
मामेव सम्प्रपश्यध्वं‡ पूजयध्वं तथैव च ॥
येऽन्यथा सम्प्रपश्यन्ति§ मत्वैवन्देवतान्तरम् ।
ते यान्ति नरकान् घोरान्नाहन्तेषु व्यवस्थितः ॥
मूर्खं वा पण्डितं वापि ब्राह्मणं वा मदाश्रयम् ।
मोचयामि श्वपाकं वा नारायणमनिन्दकम्¶ ॥
तस्मादेष‖ महायोगी मद्भक्तैः पुरुषोत्तमः ।
अर्च्चनीयो नमस्कार्य्यो मत्प्रीतिजननाय वै** ॥
एवमुक्त्वा वासुदेवमालिङ्ग्य स पिनाकधृक् ।

---

* सर्व्वभूतान्तर्भूता चेति B.

† ये त्वन्यथेति B.

‡ सम्प्रपश्यतेति साधु ।

§ मां प्रपश्यन्तीति B.

¶ न नारायणनिन्दकमिति B.

‖ तस्मादेवेति B.

** हीति B.

अन्तर्हितोऽभवत्तेषां सर्व्वेषामेव पश्यताम् ॥
नारायणोऽपि भगवांस्तापसं वेषमुत्तमम्।
जग्राह योगिनः सर्व्वांस्त्यक्त्वा वै परमं वपुः ॥
ज्ञानं भवद्भिरमलं प्रसादात्परमेष्ठिनः।
साक्षाद्देव*महेशस्य ज्ञानं संसारनाशनम् ॥
गच्छध्वं विज्वराः सर्व्वे विज्ञानं परमेष्ठिनः।
प्रवर्त्तयध्वं शिष्येभ्यो धार्म्मिकेभ्यो मुनीश्वराः ॥
इदं भक्ताय शान्ताय धार्म्मिकायाहिताग्नये।
विज्ञानमैश्वरं देयं ब्राह्मणाय विशेषतः ॥
एवमुक्त्वा स विश्वात्मा योगिनां योगवित्तमः† ।
नारायणो महायोगी जगामादर्शनं स्वयम् ॥
ऋषयस्तेऽपि देवेशं‡ नमस्कृत्य महेश्वरम्।
नारायणञ्च भूतादिं स्वानि स्थानानि लेभिरे§ ॥
सनत्कुमारो भगवान् संवर्त्ताय महामुनिः।
दत्तवानैश्वरं ज्ञानं सोऽपि सत्यव्रमायथौ¶ ॥
सनन्दनोऽपि योगीन्द्रः पुलहाय‖ महर्षये।

---

* साक्षाद्देवेति B.

† योगमुत्तममिति B.

‡ तेऽपि देवाधिदेवेशमिति B.

§ भेजिरे इति B and F.

¶ सत्यव्रताय तु इति B and F.

‖ पुलस्त्यायेति B.

प्रददौ गौतमायाथ* पुलहोऽपि प्रजापतिः ॥
अङ्गिरा वेदविदुषे भारद्वाजाय दत्तवान्।
जैगीषव्याय कपिलस्तथा पञ्चशिखाय च ॥
पराशरोऽपि सनकात्पिता मे सर्व्वतत्त्वदृक्।
लेभे तत्परमं ज्ञानं तस्माद्वाल्मीकिराप्तवान् ॥
ममोवाच पुरा देवः सतीदेहभवाङ्गजः।
वामदेवो महायोगी रुद्रः काल†पिनाकधृक् ॥
नारायणोऽपि भगवान्देवकीतनयो हरिः।
अर्जुनाय स्वयं साक्षाद्दत्तवानिदमुत्तमम् ॥
यदाहं‡ लब्धवान्रुद्राद्वामदेवादनुत्तमम्।
विशेषाद्गिरिशे भक्तिस्तस्मादारभ्य मेऽभवत् ॥
शरण्यं गिरिशं रुद्रं प्रपन्नोऽहं विशेषतः।
भूतेशं गिरिशं स्थाणुं देवदेवं त्रिशूलिनम् ॥
भवन्तोऽपि हि तं देवं शम्भुं गोवृषवाहनम्।
प्रपद्यन्तां सपत्नीकाः सपुत्राः शरणं शिवम् ॥
वर्त्तध्वन्तत्प्रसादेन कर्म्मयोगेन शङ्करम्।
पूजयध्वं महादेवं गोपतिं व्याल§भूषणम् ॥

---

* गौतमायाश्च इति B.

† किलेति B, E, F and H.

‡ यदापीति B.

§ भूतीति B.

एवमुक्ते पुनस्ते तु* शौनकाद्या महेश्वरम् ।
प्रणेमुः शाश्वतं स्थाणुं व्यासं सत्यवतीसुतम् ॥
अब्रुवन् हृष्टमनसः कृष्णद्वैपायनं प्रभुम्† ।
साक्षाद्देवं‡ हृषीकेशं शिवं लोकमहेश्वरम् ॥
भवत्प्रसादादचला शरण्ये गोवृषध्वजे ।
इदानीं जायते भक्तिर्या देवैरपि दुर्लभा§ ॥
कथयस्व मुनिश्रेष्ठ कर्म्मयोगमनुत्तमम् ।
येनासौ¶ भगवानीशः समाराध्यो मुमुक्षुभिः ॥
त्वत्सन्निधावेव सूतः शृणोतु भगवद्वचः ।
तद्वदखिललोकानां रक्षणं धर्म्मसंग्रहम् ॥
यदुक्तं देवदेवेन विष्णुना कूर्म्मरूपिणा ।
पृष्टेन मुनिभिः सर्व्वं शक्रेणामृतमन्थने ॥
श्रुत्वा सत्यवतीसूनुः कर्म्मयोगं सनातनम् ।‖
मुनीनां भाषितं कृत्स्नं प्रोवाच सुसमाहितः ॥
य इमं पठते नित्यं संवादं कृत्तिवाससः ।
सनत्कुमारप्रमुखैः सर्व्वपापैः प्रमुच्यते ॥

---

* एवमुक्ते तु मुनयः इति B.

† मुनिमिति B.

‡ साक्षाद्देवमिति B.

§ वल्लभेति B.

¶ येनासावित्यादि द्वादशपादाः A पुस्तके न सन्ति ।

‖ येनासौ भगवानित्यारभ्य कर्म्मयोगं सनातनमित्यन्तं E, H पुस्तकयोर्नास्ति ।

श्रावयेद्वा द्विजान् शुद्धान् ब्रह्मचर्य्यपरायणान्।
यो वा विचारयेदर्थं स याति परमाङ्गतिम्॥
यश्चैतच्छृणुयान्नित्यं भक्तियुक्तो दृढव्रतः।
सर्व्वपापविनिर्मुक्तो ब्रह्मलोके महीयते॥
तस्मात्सर्व्वप्रयत्नेन पठितव्यो मनीषिभिः।
श्रोतव्यश्चानु*मन्तव्यो विशेषाद्ब्राह्मणैः सदा॥

इति श्रीकूर्म्मपुराणे षट्साहस्र्यां संहितायां उत्तरभागे ईश्वरगीतासु एकादशोऽध्यायः। ईश्वरगीता समाप्ता।

द्वादशोऽध्यायः।

व्यास उवाच।

शृणुध्वमृषयः सर्व्वं वक्ष्यमाणं* सनातनम्।
कर्म्मयोगं ब्राह्मणानामात्यन्तिकफलप्रदम्॥
आम्नायसिद्धमखिलं ब्राह्मणानां प्रदर्शितम्†।

---

* श्रोतव्यश्चार्थेति B.

---

* ब्रह्मयोगमिति A, E and H.

† ब्रह्मणा सूपदर्शितमिति B.

ऋषीणां शृखतां पूर्व्वं मनुराह प्रजापतिः॥
सर्व्वपापहरं पुण्यं ऋषिसङ्घैर्निषेवितम्।
समाहितधियो यूयं शृणुध्वङ्गदतो मम॥
कृतोपनयनो वेदानधीयीत द्विजोत्तमाः*।
गर्भाष्टमेऽष्टमे वाब्दे स्वसूत्रोक्त†विधानतः॥
दण्डी च मेखली सूत्री कृष्णाजिनधरी मुनिः।
भिक्षाचारी ब्रह्मचारी स्वाश्रमे निवसन् सुखम्‡॥
कार्पासमुपवीतार्थं निर्म्मितं ब्रह्मणा पुरा।
ब्राह्मणानां त्रिवृत्सूत्रं कौशं वा वस्त्रमेव वा॥
सदोपवीती चैव स्यात्सदा बद्धशिखो द्विजः§।
अन्यथा यत्कृतं कर्म्म तद्भवत्ययथाकृतम्॥
वसेदविकृतं वासः कार्पासं वा कषायकम्।
तदेव परिधानीयं शुक्लमच्छिद्रमुत्तमम्॥
उत्तरन्तु समाख्यातं वासः कृष्णाजिनं शुभम्।
अभावे दिव्यमजिनं रौरवं वा विधीयते॥
उद्धृत्य दक्षिणं बाहुं सव्ये बाहौ¶ समर्पितम्।

---

* द्विजोत्तमः इति B.

† स्वगृह्योक्तेति B and F.

‡ भिक्षाहारी गुरुहितो वीक्षमाणो गुरोर्मुखमिति B and F.

§ द्विजाः इति A.

¶ सव्यबाहाविति B.

उपवीतं* भवेन्नित्यं निवीतं कण्ठसज्जने† ॥
सव्यं‡ बाहुं समुद्धृत्य दक्षिणे तु धृतं द्विजाः ।
प्राचीनावीतमित्युक्तं पैत्रे कर्म्मणि योजयेत् ॥
अग्न्यागारे गवां गोष्ठे होमे जप्ये तथैव च ।
स्वाध्याये भोजने नित्यं ब्राह्मणानाञ्च सन्निधौ ।
उपासने गुरूणाञ्च सन्ध्ययोः साधुसङ्गमे ।
उपवीती भवेन्नित्यं विधिरेष सनातनः ॥
मौञ्जी त्रिवृत्समा श्लक्ष्णा कार्य्या विप्रस्य मेखला ।
कुशेन निर्म्मिता विप्रा§ ग्रन्थिनैकेन वा त्रिभिः ॥
धारयेद्वैल्वपालाशौ दण्डौ केशान्तकौ¶ द्विजः‖ ।
यज्ञार्हवृक्षजं वाथ सौम्यमव्रणमेव च ॥
सायं प्रातर्द्विजः सन्ध्यामुपासीत समाहितः ।
कामाल्लोभाद्भयान्मोहात्त्यक्त्वैनां पतितो भवेत् ॥
अग्निकार्य्यं ततः कुर्य्यात्सायम्प्रातर्यथाविधि** ।

---

* उपवीतमित्यादि द्वादशपादाः A पुस्तके न सन्ति ।

† विधिरेष सनातन इति E and H.

‡ सव्यमित्यारभ्य उपवीती भवेन्नित्यमित्यन्तं E, H पुस्तकयोर्नास्ति ।

§ मुञ्जाभावे कुशेनाहुरिति B.

¶ केशान्तिकाविति B.

‖ द्विजाः इति A.

** प्रसन्नधीरिति B.

स्नात्वा सन्तर्पयेद्देवानृषीन् पितृगणांस्तथा ॥
देवताभ्यर्च्चनं कुर्य्यात्पुष्पैः पत्रेण चाम्बुना* ।
अभिवादनशीलः स्यान्नित्यं वृद्धेषु धर्म्मतः ॥
असावहं भो नामेति सम्यक् प्रणतिपूर्व्वकम् ।
आयुरारोग्यसान्निध्यं† द्रव्यादिपरिवर्ज्जितम्‡ ॥
आयुष्मान् भव सौम्येति वाच्यो विप्रोऽभिवादने ।
आकार§श्चास्य नाम्नोऽन्ते वाच्यः पूर्व्वाक्षरप्लुतः ॥
न कुर्य्याद्योऽभिवादस्य¶ द्विजः प्रत्यभिवादनम् ।
नाभिवाद्यः स विदुषा यथा शूद्रस्तथैव सः ॥
विन्यस्तपाणिना‖ कार्य्यमुपसंग्रहणं गुरोः ।
सव्येन सव्यः स्प्रष्टव्यो दक्षिणेन तु** दक्षिणः ॥
लौकिकं वैदिकञ्चापि†† तथाध्यात्मिकमेव वा ।
आददीत यतो ज्ञानं तं पूर्व्वमभिवादयेत् ॥
नोदकन्धारयेद्भैक्ष्यं पुष्पाणि समिधन्तथा‡‡ ।

---

* पत्रैरथाम्बुभिरिति B.

† सिद्धार्थमिति B. आयुरारोग्यमन्विच्छन्निति F.

‡ तन्वादिपरिवर्ज्जितः इति B.

§ अकार इति B.

¶ येन वेत्त्यभिवादस्येति B.

‖ स व्यस्तपाणिनेति B.

** चेति B.

†† वैदिकं वापीति B.

‡‡ समिधस्तथेति B.

एवंविधानि चान्यानि न दैवाद्येषु कर्म्मसु ॥
ब्राह्मणं* कुशलं पृच्छेत्क्षत्रबन्धुमनामयम् ।
वैश्यं क्षेमं समागत्य† शूद्रमारोग्यमेव च‡ ॥
उपाध्यायः पिता ज्येष्ठो भ्राता चैव महीपतिः ।
मातुलः श्वशुरश्चैव मातामहपितामहौ ॥
वर्णज्येष्ठः§ पितृव्यश्च सर्व्वे ते¶ गुरवः स्मृताः ।
माता मातामही गुर्व्वी पितुर्मातुश्च सोदराः ॥
श्वश्रूः पितामही ज्येष्ठा भ्रातृजाया गुरुः‖ स्त्रियः ।
इत्युक्तो गुरुवर्गोऽयं मातृतः पितृतस्तथा** ।
अनुवर्त्तनमेतेषां मनोवाक्कायकर्म्मभिः ॥
गुरुं†† दृष्ट्वा समुत्तिष्ठेदभिवाद्य कृताञ्जलिः ।
नैतैरुपविशेत्सार्द्धं विवदेतार्थकारणात्‡‡ ॥
जीवितार्थमपि द्वेषाद्गुरुभिर्नैव भाषणम् ।

---

* ब्राह्मणानिति B.

† समागम्येति B.

‡ त्विति B.

§ वर्योज्येष्ठ इति B.

¶ पुंसोऽत्वेति B.

‖ धात्री च गुरवः इति B.

** पितृतो द्विजाः इति B.

†† गुरूनिति B.

‡‡ विवदेन्नाच कारणादिति B.

उदितोऽपि गुणैरन्यैर्गुरुद्वेषी पतत्यधः ॥
गुरूणामपि सर्व्वेषां पूज्याः पञ्च विशेषतः ।
तेषामाद्यास्त्रयः श्रेष्ठास्तेषां माता सुपूजिता ॥
यो भावयति या सूते येन विद्योपदिश्यते ।
ज्येष्ठो भ्राता च भर्त्ता च पञ्चैते गुरवः स्मृताः ॥
आत्मनः सर्व्वयत्नेन प्राणत्यागेन वा पुनः ।
पूजनीया विशेषेण पञ्चैते भूतिमिच्छता ॥
यावत्पिता च माता च द्वावेतौ निर्व्विकारिणौ ।
तावत्सर्व्वं परित्यज्य पुत्रः स्यात्तत्परायणः ॥
पिता माता च सुप्रीतौ स्यातां पुत्रगुणैर्यदि ।
स पुत्रः सकलं धर्म्ममाप्नुयात्तेन कर्म्मणा ॥
नास्ति मातृसमो देवो* नास्ति तात†समो गुरुः ।
तयोः प्रत्युपकारो हि‡ न कथञ्चन विद्यते ॥
तयोर्नित्यं प्रियं कुर्य्यात्कर्म्मणा मनसा गिरा ।
न ताभ्यामननुज्ञातो धर्म्ममन्यं समाचरेत्§ ॥
वर्ज्जयित्वा मुक्तिफलं नित्यं नैमित्तिकं तथा ।
धर्म्मः सारः समुद्दिष्टः प्रेत्यानन्त¶फलप्रदः ॥

---

* मातृसमं देवमिति B.

† पितृ इति B.

‡ प्रत्युपकारोऽपीति B.

§ समाश्रयेदिति B.

¶ प्रेत्यानन्देति B.

सम्यगाराध्य वक्तारं विसृष्टस्तदनुज्ञया ।
शिष्यो विद्याफलं भुङ्क्ते प्रेत्य वा पूज्यते दिवि* ॥
यो भ्रातरं पितृसमं ज्येष्ठं मूर्खोऽवमन्यते† ।
तेन दोषेण स प्रेत्य‡ निरयङ्घोरमृच्छति ॥
पुंसां वर्त्मनि तिष्ठेत§ पूज्यो भर्त्ता च¶ सर्व्वदा ।
अपि मातरि लोकेऽस्मिन्नुपकाराद्धि गौरवम् ॥
ये नरा भर्त्तृपिण्डार्थं स्वान्प्राणान् सन्त्यजन्ति हि‖ ।
तेषामथाक्षयाँल्लोकान् प्रोवाच भगवान्मनुः ॥
मातुलांश्च पितृव्यांश्च श्वशुरानृत्विजो गुरून् ।
असावहमिति ब्रूयुः प्रत्युत्थाय यवीयसः ॥
अवाच्यो दीक्षितो नाम्ना यवीयानपि यो भवेत् ।
भो भवत्पूर्व्वकत्वेन अभिभाषेत धर्म्मवित् ॥
अभिवाद्यश्च पूज्यश्च शिरसा वन्द्य एव च ।
ब्राह्मणः क्षत्रियाद्यैश्च श्रीकामैः सादरं सदा ॥
नाभिवाद्यास्तु विप्रेन्द्रैः** क्षत्रियाद्याः कथञ्चन ।

---

* चापद्यते दिवमिति B.

† मूढ़ो न मन्यते इति B.

‡ संप्रेत्येति A.

§ चेष्टेतेति B.

¶ त्विति B.

‖ वै इति B.

** विप्रेणेति B.

ज्ञानकर्म्मगुणोपेता ये यजन्ति* बहुश्रुताः॥
ब्राह्मणः सर्व्ववर्णानां स्वस्ति कुर्य्यादिति श्रुतिः।
सवर्णेषु† सवर्णानां काम्यमेवाभिवादनम्॥
गुरुरग्निर्द्विजातीनां वर्णानां ब्राह्मणो गुरुः।
पतिरेव‡ गुरुः स्त्रीणां सर्व्वस्या§भ्यागतो गुरुः॥
विद्या कर्म्म तपो¶ बन्धुर्वित्तं भवति पञ्चमम्।
मान्यस्थानानि पञ्चाहुः पूर्व्वं पूर्व्वं गुरूत्तरात्॥
एतानि‖ त्रिषु वर्णेषु भूयांसि बल**वन्ति च।
यत्र स्युः सोऽत्र†† मानार्हः शूद्रोऽपि दशमीं गतः॥
पन्था देयो ब्राह्मणाय स्त्रियै राज्ञे ह्यचक्षुषे।
वृद्धाय भारभुग्नाय‡‡ रोगिणे दुर्बलाय च॥
भिक्षामाहृत्य शिष्टानां§§ गृहेभ्यः प्रयतोऽन्वहम्।

---

* यदाप्येति इति B and F.

† सवर्णेनेति B.

‡ पतिरेकः इति B.

§ सर्व्वत्रेति B.

¶ वय इति B, F and G. मनुसंहितायामेव यव इति पाठो दृश्यते।

‖ पञ्चानामिति B.

** वशेति B.

†† स्त्रीवेति E, F and H.

‡‡ भग्नायेति A, E and H. मग्नाय इति F.

§§ शिष्याणामिति B. स्पष्टानामिति F.

निवेद्य गुरवेऽश्नीयादाग्यत*स्तदनुज्ञया ॥
भवत्पूर्व्वञ्चरेद्भैक्षमुपनीतो द्विजोत्तमः ।
भवन्मध्यन्तु राजन्यो वैश्यस्तु भवदुत्तरम् ॥
मातरं वा स्वसारं वा मातुर्वा भगिनीन्निजाम् ।
भिक्षेत भिक्षां प्रथमं या चैनं न विमानयेत् ॥
स्वजातीयगृहेष्वेव सार्व्ववर्णिकमेव वा† ।
भैक्षस्य चरणं‡ युक्तं पतितादिषु वर्ज्जितम्§ ॥
वेदयज्ञैरहीनानां प्रपन्नानां¶ स्वकर्म्मसु ।
ब्रह्मचारी हरेद्भैक्षं गृहेभ्यः प्रयतोऽन्वहम् ॥
गुरोः कुले न भिक्षेत न ज्ञातिकुलबन्धुषु ।
अलाभे त्वन्यगेहानां पूर्व्वं पूर्व्वं विवर्ज्जयेत् ॥
सर्व्वं वा विचरेद्ग्रामं पूर्व्वोक्तानामसम्भवे ।
नियम्य प्रयतो वाचं दिशस्त्वनवलोकयन् ॥
समाहृत्य‖ तु तद्भैक्ष्यं पचेदन्नममायया ।
भुञ्जीत प्रयतो नित्यं वाग्यतोऽनन्यमानसः ॥

---

* वाग्यत इति B.

† चेति B.

‡ भैक्षस्याचरणमिति B.

§ पतितादिविवर्ज्जितः इति B.

¶ प्रशस्तानामिति B.

‖ समाहृत्येति दशपादाः A पुस्तके न सन्ति । तत आरभ्य पञ्चपादाः E, H पुस्तकयोर्न सन्ति ।

भैक्षेण वर्त्तयेन्नित्यमेकान्नादी भवेद्व्रती।
भैक्षेण व्रतिनो वृत्तिरुपवाससमा स्मृता॥
पूजयेदनसन्नित्यमद्याच्चैतदकुत्सयन्।
दृष्ट्वा हृष्येत्प्रसीदेच्च ततो भुञ्जीत वाग्यतः* ॥
अनारोग्यमनायुष्यमस्वर्ग्यञ्चातिभोजनम्।
अपुण्यं लोकविद्विष्टं तस्मात्तत्परिवर्ज्जयेत्॥
प्राङ्मुखोऽन्नानि भुञ्जीत सूर्य्याभिमुख एव वा।
नाद्यादुदङ्मुखो नित्यं विधिरेष सनातनः॥
प्रक्षाल्य पाणिपादौ च भुञ्जानो द्विरुपस्पृशेत्।
शुचौ देशे समासीनो भुक्त्वा च द्विरुपस्पृशेत्॥

इति श्रीकूर्म्मपुराणे उत्तरविभागे व्यासगीतासु द्वादशोऽध्यायः।

---

* प्रतिनन्देच्च सर्व्वशः इति B.

त्रयोदशोऽध्यायः ।

व्यास उवाच ।

भुक्त्वा पीत्वा च सुप्त्वा च स्नात्वा रथ्योपसर्पणे* ।
ओष्ठौ विलोमकौ स्पृष्ट्वा वासो विपरिधाय च ॥
रेतोमूत्रपुरीषाणामुत्सर्गेऽयुक्तभाषणे ।
ष्ठीवित्वाध्ययनारम्भे कासश्वासागमे तथा ॥
चत्वरं वा श्मशानं वा समागम्य द्विजोत्तमः† ।
सन्ध्ययोरुभयोस्तद्वदाचान्तोऽप्याचमेत्पुनः ॥
चण्डालम्लेच्छसम्भाषे स्त्रीशूद्रोच्छिष्टभाषणे ।
उच्छिष्टं पुरुषं स्पृष्ट्वा भोज्यञ्चापि तथाविधम् ।
आचामेदश्रुपाते वा लोहितस्य तथैव च ॥
भोजने सन्ध्ययोः स्नात्वा त्यागे‡ मूत्रपुरीषयोः ।
आचान्तोऽप्याचमेत्सुप्त्वा सकृत्सकृदथाव्ययः§ ॥
अग्नेर्गवामथालम्भे स्पृष्ट्वा प्रयतमेव च¶ ।
स्त्रीणामथात्मनः स्पर्शे‖ नीवीं वा परिधाय च ।

---

* रथ्यावसर्पणे इति B.

† द्विजोत्तमाः इति A.

‡ भोजनेन च सन्ध्यायाः स्नात्वेति B.

§ दयान्यतः इति B.

¶ चेति B.

‖ स्त्रीणमथात्मसंस्पर्शे इति B.

उपस्पृशेज्जलश्चान्तः* तृणं वा भूमिमेव च† ॥
केशानाञ्चात्मनः स्पर्शं वाससोऽक्षालितस्य च।
अनुष्णाभिरफेनाभिर्विशुद्धाद्भिश्च वाग्यतः‡।
शौचेऽप्सु सर्व्वदाचामेदासीनः प्रागुदङ्मुखः॥
शिरः प्रावृत्य कण्ठं वा मुक्तकच्छ§शिखोऽपि वा।
अकृत्वा पादयोः शौचमाचान्तोऽप्यशुचिर्भवेत्¶॥
सोपानत्को जलस्थो वा नोष्णीषी चाचमेद्बुधः।
न चैव वर्षधाराभिर्हस्तोच्छिष्टे तथा बुधः‖।
नैकहस्तार्पितजलैर्विना सूत्रेण वा पुनः।
न पादुकासनस्थो वा वहिर्जानुकरोऽपि** वा।
विट्शूद्रादिकरामुक्तैर्न चोच्छिष्टैस्तथैव च।††
न चैवाङ्गुलिभिः शस्तं प्रकुर्व्वन्नन्यमानसः‡‡॥
न वर्णरसदुष्टाभिर्न चैवाप्रचुरोदकैः§§।

---

* जलं वार्द्रमिति B.

† वेति B.

‡ अदुष्टाभिश्च धर्म्मतः इति B.

§ केशेति B.

¶ न शुचिर्भवेदिति B.

‖ न तिष्ठन्नोद्यतो जलैरिति B.

** जानुरथापीति B.

†† एतत्पादद्वयं B पुस्तके नास्ति।

‡‡ न कुर्य्यान्नान्यमानसः इति B.

§§ न चैव प्रदरोदकैरिति B.

न पाणिक्षुभिताभिर्वा न वह्निष्कृत एव वा॥
हृद्गाभिः पूयते विप्रः कण्ठगाभिः क्षत्रियः शुचिः।
प्राशिताभिस्तथा वैश्यः स्त्रीशूद्रौ स्पर्शतोऽम्भसः* ॥
अङ्गुष्ठमूलरेखायां तीर्थं ब्राह्ममिहोच्यते† ।
प्रदेशिन्याश्च यन्मूलं पितृतीर्थमनुत्तमम्‡ ।
कनिष्ठामूलतः पश्चात्प्राजापत्यं प्रचक्षते॥
अङ्गुल्यग्रे स्मृतं दैवं तद्दैवार्थं§ प्रकीर्त्तितम्।
मूले वा दैवमादिष्टमाग्नेयं¶ मध्यतः स्मृतम्।
तदेव सौमिकं तीर्थमेवं ज्ञात्वा न मुह्यति॥
ब्राह्मेणैव तु तीर्थेन द्विजो नित्यमुपस्पृशेत्।
कायेन वाथ दैवेन चाथाचान्ते शुचिर्भवेत्‖ ॥
त्रिराचामेदपः** पूर्व्वं ब्राह्मणः प्रयतस्ततः।
संहृताङ्गुष्ठमूलेन†† मुखं वै समुपस्पृशेत्॥
अङ्गुष्ठानामिकाभ्यान्तु स्पृशेन्नेत्रद्वयं ततः।
तर्ज्जन्यङ्गुष्ठयोगेन स्पृशेन्नासापुटद्वयम्॥

---

* स्पर्शतोऽन्ततः इति B.

† अङ्गुष्ठमूलान्तरितरेखायां ब्राह्ममुच्यते इति B.

‡ अङ्गुष्ठान्तप्रदेशिन्योः पितॄणां तीर्थमुत्तममिति B.

§ तद्देवार्थमिति B.

¶ दैवमादिष्टमाग्नेयमिति B.

‖ न तु पैत्रेण वै द्विजाः इति B.

** त्रिः प्राश्नीयादपः इति B.

†† संहृत्याङ्गुष्ठमूलेनेति B.

कनिष्ठाङ्गुष्ठयोगेन श्रवणे समुपस्पृशेत् ।
सर्व्वाङ्गुलीभिर्बाह्व च* हृदयन्तु तलेन वा ।
नाभिः शिरश्च सर्व्वाभिरङ्गुष्ठेनाथ† वा द्वयम् ॥
त्रिः प्राश्नीयात्तदम्भस्तु सुप्रीतास्तेन देवताः‡ ।
ब्रह्मा विष्णुर्महेशश्च भवन्तीत्यनुशुश्रुम ॥
गङ्गा च यमुना चैव प्रीयेते परिमार्ज्जनात् ।
संस्पृष्टयोर्लोचनयोः प्रीयेते शशिभास्करौ ॥
नासत्यदस्रौ प्रीयेते स्पृष्टे नासापुटद्वये ।
श्रोत्रयोः§ स्पृष्टयोस्तद्वत्प्रीयेते चानिलानलौ ॥
संस्पृष्टे हृदये चास्य¶ प्रीयन्ते सर्व्वदेवताः ।
मूर्द्ध्नि संस्पर्शनादेव प्रीतस्तु‖ पुरुषो भवेत् ॥
नोच्छिष्टं कुर्व्वते नित्यं** विप्रुषोऽङ्गं नयन्ति याः ।
दन्तान्तर्दन्त††लग्नेषु जिह्वोष्ठैरशुचिर्भवेत्‡‡ ॥

---

* सर्व्वासामथ योगेनेति B.

† स्पृशेद्वै शिरसस्तद्वदङ्गुष्ठेनाथेति B.

‡ प्रीतास्तेनाव्यदेवताः इति B.

§ कर्णयोरिति B.

¶ चास्येति B.

‖ संस्पर्शनादेकः प्रीतः स इति B.

** मुख्याः इति B.

†† दन्तवद्दन्तीति B.

‡‡ जिह्वास्पर्शेऽशुचिर्भवेदिति B.

स्पृशन्ति विन्दवः पादौ य आचामयतः परान् ।
भूमिकास्ते* समाज्ञेया न तैरप्रयतो भवेत् ॥
मधुपर्क्के च सोमे च ताम्बूलस्य च भक्षणे ।
फले मूलेक्षुदण्डे च† न दोषम्प्राह वै मनुः ॥
प्रचुरान्नोदपानेषु यद्युच्छिष्टो‡ भवेद्द्विजः ।
भूमौ निक्षिप्य तद्द्रव्यमाचम्याभ्युक्षिपेत्ततः§ ॥
तैजसं वा¶ समादाय यद्युच्छिष्टो भवेद्द्विजः ।
भूमौ निक्षिप्य तद्द्रव्यमाचम्याक्षियते‖ तु तत् ॥
यद्यमन्त्रं** समादाय भवेदुच्छेषणान्वितः ।
अनिधायैव तद्द्रव्यमाचान्तः शुचितामियात् ।
वस्त्रादिषु विकल्पः स्यान्न स्पृष्ट्वा चैवमेव हि†† ॥
अरण्येऽनुदके रात्रौ चौरव्याघ्राकुले पथि ।
कृत्वा मूत्रं पुरीषं वा द्रव्यहस्तो न दुष्यति ॥
निधाय दक्षिणे कर्णे ब्रह्मसूत्रमुदङ्मुखः ।

---

* भूमिगैस्तैरिति B and F.

† फलमूलेक्षुदण्डेनेति A.

‡ द्रव्यहस्त इति B.

§ माचम्याभ्युक्षयेत्ततः इति B.

¶ वै इति B.

‖ माचम्याभ्युक्षयेदिति B.

** यदा स्रुवमिति B.

†† तत्संस्पृश्याचमेदिहेति B.

अह्नि कुर्य्याच्छकृन्मूत्रं रात्रौ चेद्दक्षिणामुखः* ॥
अन्तर्द्धाय महीं काष्ठैः पत्रैर्लोष्टैस्तृणेन वा ।
प्रावृत्य च शिरः कुर्य्याद्विण्मूत्रस्य विसर्ज्जनम् ॥
छायाकूपनदीगोष्ठचैत्यान्तःपथि भस्मसु ।
अग्नौ वेश्म†श्मशाने च विण्मूत्रे न समाचरेत् ॥
न गोपथे न कृष्टे‡ वा महावृक्षे न शाड्वले ।
न तिष्ठन्वा न निर्वासा न च पर्व्वतमस्तके ॥
न जीर्णदेवायतने न वल्मीके कदाचन ।
न ससत्त्वेषु गर्त्तेषु§ नागच्छन्वा समाचरेत् ॥
तुषाङ्गारकपालेषु राजमार्गे तथैव च ।
न क्षेत्रे विमले चापि¶ न तीर्थे न चतुष्पथे ॥
नोद्याने न समीपे‖ वा नोषरे न पराशुचौ ।
न सोपानत्पादुको वा गन्ता यानान्तरिक्षगः** ॥
न चैवाभिमुखं स्त्रीणां गुरुब्राह्मणयोर्न च†† ।

---

* एतत्पादद्वयं A, H पुस्तकयोर्नास्ति ।

† चैवेति B.

‡ न गोमये न कुम्भे इति B.

§ गच्छन्वा इति A.

¶ न क्षेत्रे न विले नापीति B.

‖ नोद्यानोपसमीपे इति B. नो नद्यादिसमीपे वा इति F.

** न छत्री नान्तरीचके इति B.

†† गवामिति B, E and H.

न देवदेवालययोर्नद्यामपि* कदाचन ॥
नदीं ज्योतींषि वीक्षित्वा† न वार्य्यभिमुखोऽथ वा ।
प्रत्यादित्यं प्रत्यनलं प्रतिसोमं तथैव च ॥
आहृत्य मृत्तिकां कूलाल्लेपगन्धापकर्षणात्‡ ।
कुर्य्यादतन्द्रितः शौचं विशुद्धैरुद्धृतोदकैः ॥
नाहरेन्मृत्तिकां विप्रः पांशुलान्न च कर्द्दमान्§ ।
न मार्गान्नोषरादेशाच्छौचोच्छिष्टा तथैव च¶ ॥
न देवायतनात्कूपाद्ग्रामादन्तर्ज्जलात्तथा‖ ।
उपस्पृशेत्ततो नित्यं पूर्व्वोक्तेन विधानतः ॥

इति श्रीकूर्म्मपुराणे उत्तरविभागे त्रयोदशोऽध्यायः ।

---

* अपामपीति B and G.

† वीक्ष्येति साधु ।

‡ गन्धापकर्षणमिति B.

§ कर्द्दमादिति B.

¶ शौचशिष्टां परस्य तु इति B. शौचोच्छिष्टां परस्य चेति E, G and H.

‖ ग्रामान्न च जलात्तथेति B.

चतुर्द्दशोऽध्यायः ।

व्यास उवाच ।

एवं दण्डादिभिर्युक्तः शौचाचारसमन्वितः ।
आहूतोऽध्ययनं कुर्य्याद्वीक्षमाणो* गुरोर्मुखम् ॥
नित्यमुद्धृत†पाणिः स्यात्सन्ध्याचार‡समन्वितः ।
आस्यतामिति चोक्तः सन्नासीताभिमुखं गुरोः ॥
प्रतिश्रवणसम्भाषे शयानो न समाचरेत् ।
आसीनो न च तिष्ठन्वा उत्तिष्ठन्वा§ पराङ्मुखः ॥
न च शय्यासनञ्चास्य¶ सर्व्वदा गुरुसन्निधौ ।
गुरोश्च|| चक्षुर्विषये न यथेष्टासनो भवेत् ॥
नोदाहरेदस्य नाम परोक्षमपि केवलम् ।
न चैवास्यानुकुर्व्वीत गतिभाषितचेष्टितम् ॥
गुरोर्यत्र प्रतीवादो** निन्दा चापि प्रवर्त्तते ।
कर्णौ तत्र पिधातव्यौ गन्तव्यं वा ततोऽन्यतः ॥

---

* कुर्य्यादीक्षमाणः इति B.

† उद्यतेति B, E and H.

‡ साध्वाचारेति B.

§ नासीनो न च भुञ्जानो न तिष्ठन्निति B.

¶ नीचशय्यासनञ्चास्येति B.

|| गुरोस्तु इति B.

** परीवाद इति B and F.

दूरस्थो नार्च्चयेदेनं न क्रुद्धो नान्तिके स्त्रियाः ।
न चैवास्योत्तरं ब्रूयात् स्थिते नासीत* सन्निधौ ॥
उदकुम्भं कुशान् पुष्पं समिधोऽस्याहरेत्सदा ।
मार्ज्जनं लेपनं नित्यमङ्गानां वा समाचरेत् ॥
नास्य निर्माल्यशयनं पादुकोपानहावपि ।
आक्रमेदासनं छायामासन्दीं† वा कदाचन ॥
साधयेद्दन्तकाष्ठादीन् कृत्यञ्चास्मै‡ निवेदयेत् ।
अनापृच्छ्य न गन्तव्यं भवेत्प्रियहिते रतः ॥
न पादौ सारयेदस्य सन्निधाने कदाचन ।
जृम्भाहास्यादिकञ्चैव§ कण्ठप्रावरणं तथा ॥
वर्ज्जयेत्सन्निधौ नित्यमथास्फोटनमं वचः¶ ।
यथाकालमधीयीत यावन्न विमनाः गुरुः ॥
आसीताथ गुरोरूर्द्धे‖ फलके वा समाहितः ।
आसने शयने याने नैकस्तिष्ठेत्कदाचन** ।
धावन्तमनुधावेत्तं गच्छन्तञ्चानुगच्छति ॥

---

* स्थितो वासीतेति B.

† आसन्दी—चतुष्पादासनविशेषः। आक्रमेदासनं चास्य छायादीनिति B.

‡ लब्धञ्चास्मै इति B.

§ जृम्भितं हसितञ्चैवेति B.

¶ अवस्फोटनमेव चेति B. बाहुस्फोटनमेव चेति F.

‖ आसीताधो गुरोर्गच्छेदिति B. आसीताधो गुरोः कूर्चे इति F.

** नैव तिष्ठेत्कथञ्चनेति B.

गोऽश्वोष्ट्रयानप्रासादप्रस्तरेषु कटेषु च।
नासीत गुरुणा सार्द्धं शिलाफलकनौषु च॥
जितेन्द्रियः स्यात्सततं वश्यात्मा क्रोधनः शुचिः।
प्रयुञ्जीत सदा वाचं मधुरां हितभाषिणीम्*॥
गन्धमाल्यं रसभव्यं शुक्लं†प्राणिविहिंसनम्।
अभ्यङ्गञ्चाञ्जनोपानच्छत्रधारणमेव च।
कामं लोभं भयं निद्रां गीतवादित्रनर्त्तनम्।
द्यूतञ्जन‡परीवादं स्त्रीप्रेक्षालम्भनं तथा।
परोपघातं पैशुन्यं प्रयत्नेन विवर्ज्जयेत्॥
उदकुम्भं सुमनसो गोशकृन्मृत्तिकाकुशान्।
आहरेद्यावदर्थानि भैक्षञ्चाहरहश्चरेत्॥
कृतञ्च लवणं सर्व्वं वर्ज्यं पर्य्युषितञ्च यत्।
अनृत्यदर्शी सततं भवेद्गीतादिनिस्पृहः॥
नादित्यं वै समीक्षेत न चरे§द्दन्तधावनम्।
एकान्तमशुचिस्त्रीभिः शूद्रान्त्यैरभिभाषणम्॥
गुरुप्रियार्थं सर्व्वं हि¶ प्रयुञ्जीत न कामतः।

---

* हितकारिणीमिति B.

† शुक्लं—धौतधवलदुकूलमित्यर्थः। रसं कन्यां शुक्तमिति B.

‡ आतर्ज्जनमिति B.

§ नाचरेदिति B.

¶ गुरूच्छिष्टं भेषजार्थमिति B.

मलापकर्षणं स्नानमाचरेद्वै कथञ्चन* ॥
न कुर्य्यान्मानसं विप्रो गुरोस्त्यागे कदाचन† ।
मोहाद्वा यदि वा लोभात्त्यक्तेन पतितो भवेत् ॥
लौकिकं वैदिकञ्चापि‡ तथाध्यात्मिकमेव च§ ।
आददीत यतो ज्ञानं न तं द्रुह्येत्कदाचन ॥
गुरोरप्यवलिप्तस्य कार्य्याकार्य्यमजानतः ।
उत्पथप्रतिपन्नस्य मनुस्त्यागं समब्रवीत् ॥
गुरोर्गुरौ सन्निहिते गुरुवद्भक्तिमाचरेत्¶ ।
न चातिसृष्टो गुरुणा स्वान् गुरूनभिवादयेत् ॥
विद्यागुरुष्वेतदेव नित्या वृत्तिः स्वयोनिषु ।
प्रतिषेधत्सु चाधर्म्माद्धितं चोपदिशत्स्वपि ॥
श्रेयस्तु गुरुवद्वृत्तिं नित्यमेव समाचरेत् ।
गुरुपुत्रेषु दारेषु गुरोश्चैव स्वबन्धुषु ॥
बालः समानजन्मा वा‖ शिष्यो वा यज्ञकर्म्मणि** ।
अध्यापयन् गुरुसुतो गुरुवन्मानमर्हति ॥

---

* नाचरेद्धि कदाचनेति B.

† कथञ्चनेति B.

‡ वापीति B.

§ वेति B.

¶ गुरुवद्वृत्तिमिति B.

‖ सम्मानयन्मान्यानिति B.

** जपकर्म्मणीति B.

उत्सादनं वै* गात्राणां स्नापनोच्छिष्टभोजने ।
न कुर्य्याद्गुरुपुत्रस्य पादयोः शौचमेव च ॥
गुरुवत्परिपूज्यास्तु† सवर्णा गुरुयोषितः ।
असवर्णास्तु सम्पूज्याः प्रत्युत्थानाभिवादनैः ॥
अभ्यञ्जनं स्नापनञ्च गात्रोत्सादनमेव च ।
गुरुपत्न्या न कार्य्याणि केशानाञ्च प्रसाधनम् ॥
गुरुपत्नी तु युवती नाभिवाद्येह पादयोः ।
कुर्व्वीत वन्दनं भूमा‡वसावहमिति ब्रुवन् ॥
विप्रोष्य§ पादग्रहणमन्वहञ्चाभिवादनम् ।
गुरुदारेषु सर्व्वेषु¶ सतां धर्म्ममनुस्मरन् ।
मातृ‖ष्वसा मातुलानी श्वश्रूश्चाथ पितृष्वसा ।
संपूज्या गुरुपत्नी च** समस्ता गुरुभार्य्यया ॥
भ्रातुर्भार्य्योप††संग्राह्या सवर्णाहन्यहन्यपि ।
विप्रस्य तूपसंग्राह्या ज्ञातिसम्बन्धियोषितः ॥

---

* चेति B.

† स्त्विति B.

‡ भूम्यामिति B.

§ विप्रोऽथेति A.

¶ कुर्व्वीतेति B.

‖ मातुरिति B.

** गुरुपत्नीवेति B.

†† भार्य्या चेति B.

पितुर्भगिन्यां मातुश्च ज्यायस्यां च स्वसर्य्यपि।
मातृवद्वृत्तिमातिष्ठेन्माता ताभ्यो गरीयसी॥
एवमाचारसंपन्नमात्मवन्तमदाम्भिकम्।
वेदमध्यापयेद्धर्म्मं पुराणाङ्गानि* नित्यशः॥
संवत्सरोषिते शिष्ये गुरुर्ज्ञानमनिर्द्दिशन्।
हरते दुष्कृतं तस्य शिष्यस्य वसतो† गुरुः॥
आचार्य्यपुत्रः शुश्रूषुर्ज्ञानदो धार्म्मिकः शुचिः।
सूक्तार्थदोऽरसः‡ साधुः§ स्वाध्याय्यादशधर्म्मतः¶॥
कृतघ्नश्च तथाद्रोही मेधावी तूपकृन्नरः‖।
आप्तः प्रियोऽथ विधिवत् षड़ध्याप्या द्विजातयः॥
एतेषु ब्रह्मणो**दानमन्यत्र च यथोदितान्।

---

* पुराणानि अङ्गानि च।
"शिक्षा कल्पो व्याकरणं निरुक्तं ज्योतिषां गणः।
छन्दसां निचितिश्चैव षड़ङ्गो वेद इष्यते॥"

† दुष्कृतः इति B.

‡ अरसः—शृङ्गारादिरसहीनः रागहीन इत्यर्थः।

§ शक्तोऽन्नदोऽर्थदः साधुरिति B.

¶ स्वाध्याय्यादशधर्म्मतः—स्वाध्यायी—वेदाध्ययनरतः।
आदशधर्म्मतः—दशविधधर्म्मपर्य्यन्तम्।
"धृतिः क्षमा दमोऽस्तेयं शौचमिन्द्रियनिग्रहः।
धीर्विद्या सत्यमक्रोधो दशकं धर्म्मलक्षणम्॥"

‖ शुभकृन्नर इति B and F.

** ब्राह्मण इति B, E and H.

आचम्य संयतोनित्यमधीयीत ह्युदङ्मुखः ॥
उपसंगृह्य तत्पादौ वीक्षमाणो गुरोर्मुखम्।
अधीष्व भो इति ब्रूयाद्विरामस्त्विति नारभेत्* ॥
अनुकूलं समासीनः† पवित्रैश्चैव पावितः।
प्राणायामैस्त्रिभिः पूतस्ततओंकारमर्हति ॥
ब्राह्मणः प्रणवङ्कुर्यादन्ते च‡ विधिवद्द्विजः।
कुर्यादध्ययनं नित्यं ब्रह्माञ्जलिकरस्थितः ॥
सर्व्वेषामेव भूतानां वेदश्चक्षुः सनातनम्।
अधीयीताप्ययं नित्यं ब्राह्मण्याच्चयवतेऽन्यथा ॥
योऽधीयीत ऋचोनित्यं क्षीराहुत्या सदेवताः।
प्रीणाति तर्प्पयन्त्येनं कामैस्तृप्ताः सदैव हि§ ॥
यजूंष्यधीते नियतं दध्ना प्रीणाति देवताः।
सामान्यधीते प्रीणाति घृताहुतिभिरन्वहम् ॥
अथर्वाङ्गिरसोनित्यं मध्वा¶ प्रीणाति देवताः।
वेदाङ्गानि‖ पुराणानि मांसैश्च तर्पयेत्सुरान्** ॥

---

* चारभेदिति B. वारयेदिति F.

† प्राक्कूलं पर्य्युपासीनः इति B. प्राक्कूले इति F.

‡ दन्तेऽपीति B.

§ सदेवताः इति B.

¶ मधुना इति साधु।

‖ धर्म्माङ्गानीति B and F.

** मांसैस्तर्पयते सुरानिति B.

अपां समीपे नियतो*नैत्यिकं विधिमाश्रितः ।
गायत्रीमप्यधीयीत गत्वारण्यं समाहितः ॥
सहस्रपरमान्देवीं शतमध्यां दशावराम्† ।
गायत्रीं वै जपेन्नित्यं जपयज्ञः प्रकीर्त्तितः ॥
गायत्रीञ्चैव वेदांस्तु‡ तुलयातोलयत्प्रभुः ।
एकतश्चतुरो वेदान् गायत्रीञ्च तथैकतः ॥
ओङ्कारमादितः कृत्वा व्याहृतीस्तदनन्तरम् ।
ततोऽधीयीत सावित्रीमेकाग्रः श्रद्धयान्वितः ॥
पुराकल्पे समुत्पन्ना भूर्भुवः स्वः सनातनाः ।
महाव्याहृतयस्तिस्रः सर्व्वाशुभनिवर्हणाः ॥
प्रधानं पुरुषः कालो विष्णुर्ब्रह्मा महेश्वरः ।
सत्वं रजस्तमस्तिस्रः क्रमाद्व्याहृतयः स्मृताः ॥
ओङ्कारस्तत्परं ब्रह्म सावित्री स्यात्तदक्षरम् ।
एष मन्त्रोमहायोगः सारात्सार उदाहृतः ॥
योऽधीतेऽहन्यहन्येतां गायत्रीं§ वेदमातरम् ।
विज्ञायार्थं ब्रह्मचारी स याति परमाङ्गतिम् ॥
गायत्री वेदजननी गायत्री लोकपावनी ।
न गायत्र्याः परं जप्यमेतद्विज्ञाय मुच्यते ॥

---

* प्रयतः इति B and F.

† दशापरामिति B.

‡ वेदांश्चेति B.

§ सावित्रीमिति B.

श्रावणस्य तु मासस्य पौर्णमास्यां द्विजोत्तमाः ।
आषाढ्यां प्रोष्ठपद्यां वा वेदोपाकरणं स्मृतम् ॥
उत्सृज्य ग्रामनगरं मासान्विप्रोर्द्धपञ्चमान्* ।
अधीयीत शुचौ देशे ब्रह्मचारी समाहितः ॥
पुष्ये तु छन्दसाङ्कुर्य्याद्बहिरुत्सर्जनन्द्विजाः ।
माघशुक्लस्य वा प्राप्ते पूर्व्वाह्णे प्रथमेऽहनि ॥
छन्दसां प्रीणनं कुर्य्यात्† स्वेषु ऋक्षेषु‡ वै द्विजाः ।
वेदाङ्गानि पुराणानि कृष्णपक्षे च मानवः ॥
इमान्नित्यमनध्यायानधीयानो विवर्ज्जयेत् ।
अध्यापनं प्र§कुर्व्वाणो ह्यनध्यायान्विवर्ज्जयेत् ॥
कर्णश्रवेऽनिले रात्रौ¶ दिवापांशुसमूहने ।
विद्युत्स्तनितवर्षेषु|| महोल्कानाञ्च संप्लवे ।
आकालिकमनध्यायमेतेष्वाह प्रजापतिः ॥
निर्घाते भूमिचलने ज्योतिषाञ्चोपसर्ज्जने ।
एतानाकालिकान्विद्यादनध्यायानृतावपि ॥

---

* विप्रोर्द्धपञ्चमान्—हे विप्राः । सन्धिरार्षः ।

† छन्दांस्यूर्द्धमथोदस्येति B. छन्दांस्यूर्द्धमतोऽभ्यसेच्छुक्लपक्षेषु वै द्विजाः इति F.

‡ शुक्लपक्षेषु इति A and B.

§ चेति B.

¶ विद्युत्स्तनितनिस्वने इति E and H. इतः परं पादचतुष्टयं भीक्षपुस्तकयोर्नास्ति ।

|| इतः परं नव पादाः A पुस्तके न सन्ति ।

प्रादुष्कृतेष्वग्निषु तु विद्युत्स्तनितनिस्वने।
सज्योतिः स्यादनध्यायमनृतौ चात्र दर्शने॥
नित्यानध्याय एव स्याद्ग्रामेषु नगरेषु च।
धर्म्मनैपुण्यकामानां पूतिगन्धेन नित्यशः॥
अन्तःशवगते ग्रामे वृषलस्य च सन्निधौ।
अनध्यायो भुज्यमाने* समवाये जनस्य च॥
उदके मध्यरात्रे च विण्मूत्रे च विवर्ज्जयेत्।
उच्छिष्टः श्राद्धभुक् चैव मनसापि न चिन्तयेत्॥
प्रतिगृह्य द्विजो विद्वानेकोद्दिष्टस्य केतनम्।
त्र्यहं न कीर्त्तयेद्ब्रह्म राज्ञो राहोश्च सूतके† ॥
यावदेकोऽनुद्दिष्टस्य स्नेहोगन्धश्च‡ तिष्ठति।
विप्रस्य विपुले§ देहे तावद्ब्रह्म न कीर्त्तयेत्॥
शयानः प्रौढ़पादश्च कृत्वा वै चावसिक्थकाम्।
नाधीयीतामिषं जग्ध्वा सूतकाद्यन्नमेव च॥
नीहारपाते शब्दे च¶ सन्ध्ययोरुभयोरपि।
अमावास्यां चतुर्द्दश्यां पौर्णमास्यष्टमीषु च॥

---

* रुद्यमाने इति B. नुद्यमाने इति F.

† राज्ञः सूतके—राज्ञः पुत्रादिजननाशौचे; राहोः सूतके—राहुग्रहणात् परमकाले इत्यर्थः।

‡ लेपश्चेति B.

§ विदुषः इति B.

¶ नीहारे बाणपाते चेति B.

उपाकर्म्मणि चोत्सर्गे त्रिरात्रं क्षपणं स्मृतम् ।
अष्टकासु त्वहोरात्रमृत्वन्तासु च रात्रिषु ॥
मार्गशीर्षे तथा पौषे माघमासे तथैव च ।
तिस्रोऽष्टकाः समाख्याताः कृष्णपक्षे तु सूरिभिः ॥
श्लेष्मान्तकस्य च्छायायां शाल्मलेर्म्मधुकस्य च ।
कदाचिदपि नाध्येयं कोविदारकपित्थयोः ॥
समानविद्ये च मृते तथा सब्रह्मचारिणि ।
आचार्य्ये संस्थिते वापि त्रिरात्रं क्षपणं स्मृतम् ॥
छिद्राण्येतानि विप्राणां येऽनध्यायाः प्रकीर्त्तिताः ।
हिंसन्ति राक्षसास्तेषु तस्मादेतान्विसर्ज्जयेत्* ॥
नैत्यिके नास्त्यनध्यायः सन्ध्योपासन एव च ।
उपाकर्म्मणि कर्म्मान्ते† होममन्त्रेषु चैव हि ॥
एकामृचमथैकं वा यजुः सामाथ वा पुनः ।
अष्टकाद्यास्वधीयीत मारुते चातिवायति ॥
अनध्यायस्तु नाङ्गेषु नेतिहासपुराणयोः ।
न धर्म्मशास्त्रेष्वन्येषु पर्वाण्येतानि वर्ज्जयेत् ॥
एष धर्म्मः समासेन कीर्त्तितो ब्रह्मचारिणाम् ।
ब्रह्मणाभिहितः पूर्व्वमृषीणां भावितात्मनाम् ॥
योऽन्यत्र कुरुते यत्नमनधीत्य श्रुतिं द्विजाः‡ ।

---

* विवर्ज्जयेदिति B.

† होमान्ते इति B.

‡ द्विज इति B.

स संमूढ़ो न सम्भाष्यो वेदवाह्यो द्विजातिभिः॥
न वेदपाठमात्रेण सन्तुष्येदेष वै द्विजः*।
एवमाचारहीनस्तु† पङ्के गौरिव सीदति॥
योऽधीत्य विधिवद्वेदं वेदार्थं न विचारयेत्।
सचान्धः शूद्रकल्पस्तु‡ पदार्थं न प्रपद्यते॥
यदि चा§त्यन्तिकं वासं कर्त्तुमिच्छति वै गुरौ।
युक्तः परिचरेदेनमाशरीराभिघातनात्¶॥
गत्वा वनं वा विधिवज्जुहुयाज्जातवेदसम्।
अभ्यसेत्स‖ तदा नित्यं ब्रह्मनिष्ठः समाहितः॥
सावित्रीं शतरुद्रीयं वेदाङ्गानि** विशेषतः।
अभ्यसेत्सततं युक्तो भस्मस्नानपरायणः॥
एतद्विधानं परमं पुराणं
वेदाङ्गतः सम्यगिहेरितञ्च††।

---

* सन्तुष्टो वै द्विजोत्तमः इति B.

† पाठमात्रावसन्नस्तु इति B.

‡ स सान्वयः शूद्रकल्पः इति B and F.

§ वेति B.

¶ माशरीरविमोक्षणादिति B. माशरीरनिपातनादिति F.

‖ अधीयीतेति B and H.

** वेदान्तांश्चेति B and F.

†† वेदागमे सम्यगिहेरितं वः इति B and F.

पुरा महर्षिप्रवरानुपृष्टः*
स्वायम्भुवो यन्मनुराह देवः ॥
एवमीश्वरसमर्पितान्तरो
योऽनुतिष्ठति विधिं विधानवत्† ।
मोहजालमपहाय सोऽमृतं‡
याति तत्पदमनामयं शिवम् ॥

इति श्रीकूर्म्मपुराणे उत्तरभागे चतुर्द्दशोऽध्यायः ।

पञ्चदशोऽध्यायः ।

व्यास उवाच ।

वेदं वेदौ तथा वेदान्विन्द्याद्वा चतुरो द्विजाः* ।
अधीत्य चाभिगम्यार्थं ततः स्नायाद्द्विजोत्तमाः† ॥

---

* प्रवराभिपृष्टः इति B.

† विधानविदिति B.

‡ सोऽमृतः इति B.

---

* वेदाङ्गांश्चतुरोऽन्यथा इति B. साङ्गांन्वै चतुरो द्विजः इति F.

† द्विजोत्तमः इति B.

गुरवे तु धनं दत्त्वा स्नायीत* तदनुज्ञया ।
चीर्णव्रतोऽथ युक्तात्मा स शक्तः† स्नातुमर्हति ॥
वैणवीन्धारयेद्यष्टिमन्तर्वासं तथोत्तरम् ।
यज्ञोपवीतद्वितयं सोदकञ्च कमण्डलुम् ॥
छत्रं चोष्णीषममलं पादुके चाप्युपानहौ ।
रौक्मे च कुण्डले वेदं व्युप्त‡केशनखः शुचिः ॥
स्वाध्याये नित्ययुक्तः स्याद्बहिर्माल्यं न धारयेत् ।
अन्यत्र काञ्चनाद्विप्रः न रक्तां बिभृयात्स्रजम् ॥
शुक्लाम्बरधरोनित्यं सुगन्धः प्रियदर्शनः ।
नजीर्णमलवद्वासा भवेद्वै वैभवे§ सति ॥
न रक्तमुल्वणञ्चान्यधृतं वासोन कुण्डिकाम् ।
नोपानहौ स्रजं वाथ पादुके न प्रयोजयेत् ॥
उपवीतकरान्¶ दर्भांस्तथा कृष्णाजिनानि च ।
नापसव्यं परीदध्याद्वासोन विकृतञ्च यत् ॥
आहरेद्विधिवद्दारान् सदृशानात्मनः शुभान्|| ।
रूपलक्षणसंयुक्तान्योनिदोषविवर्ज्जितान् ॥

---

* स्नायादिति साधु ।

‡ तीर्णव्रतोऽथ मुक्तात्मा शक्तो वेति B. चीर्णे व्रते सुयुक्तात्मा इति F.

‡ कृत्तेति B, E, F and H.

§ विभवे इति B, E, F and H.

¶ उपवीतमलङ्कारमिति B, E, F and H.

|| समानिति A, E, F and H.

अमातृ*गोत्रप्रभवामसमानर्षिगोत्रजाम् ।
आहरेद्ब्राह्मणो भार्य्यां शीलशौचसमन्विताम् ॥
ऋतुकालाभिगामी स्याद्यावत्पुत्रोऽभिजायते ।
वर्जयेत्प्रतिषिद्धानि दिनानि तु प्रयत्नतः† ॥
षष्ठ्यष्टमीं पञ्चदशीं द्वादशीं च चतुर्द्दशीम् ।
ब्रह्मचारी भवेन्नित्यं ब्राह्मणः संयतेन्द्रियः‡ ॥
आदधीतावसथ्याग्निं जुहुयाज्जातवेदसम् ।
व्रतानि स्नातको नित्यं पावनानि च पालयेत् ॥
वेदोदितं स्वकं कर्म्म नित्यं कुर्य्यादतन्द्रितः ।
अकुर्वाणः पतत्याशु नरकान्याति भीषणान्§ ॥
अभ्यसेत्प्रयती वेदं महायज्ञांश्च भावयेत्¶ ।
कुर्य्याद्गृह्याणि कर्माणि सन्ध्योपासनमेव च ॥
सख्यं समाधिकैः कुर्य्यादर्च्चयेदीश्वरं‖ सदा ।
दैवतान्यधिगच्छेत** कुर्य्याद्भार्याविभूषणम्†† ॥

---

* अनत्रीति A. अमन्त्रीति H. आमन्त्रीति E.

† वर्ज्जयेत्तां प्रयत्नेन प्रतिषिद्धदिनानि तु इति B.

‡ तद्वज्जन्मनयाहनीति B and F.

§ नरकानतिभीषणानिति B.

¶ महायज्ञान्न हापयेदिति B and F.

‖ उपेयादीश्वरमिति B, E, F and H.

** दैवतान्यभिगच्छेतेति B.

†† भार्य्याभिपोषणमिति B and F.

न धर्म्मं ख्यापयेद्विद्वान्न पापं गूहयेदपि ।
कुर्व्वीतात्महितं नित्यं* सर्व्वभूतानुकम्पनम्† ॥
वयसः कर्म्मणोऽर्थस्य श्रुतस्याभिजनस्य च ।
वेद‡वाग्बुद्धिसारूप्यमाचरेद्विहरेत्सदा ॥
श्रुतिस्मृत्युदितः सम्यक् साधुभिर्यश्च सेवितः ।
तमाचारं निषेवेत नेहेतान्यत्र कुत्रचित्§ ॥
येनास्य पितरो याता येन याताः पितामहाः ।
तेन यायात्सतां मार्गं तेन गच्छन्तरिष्यति¶ ॥
नित्यं स्वाध्यायशीलः स्यान्नित्यं यज्ञोपवीतवान् ।
सत्यवादी जितक्रोधो ब्रह्मभूयाय कल्पते ॥
सन्ध्यास्नानपरो नित्यं ब्रह्मयज्ञपरायणः ।
अनसूयी मृदुर्दान्तो गृहस्थः प्रेत्य वर्द्धते ॥
वीतरागभयक्रोधो लोभमोहविवर्ज्जितः ।
सावित्रीजापनिरतः श्राद्धकृन्मुच्यते गृही‖ ॥
मातापित्रोर्हिते युक्तो गोब्राह्मणहिते रतः ।

---

* सर्व्वमिति B.

† भूतानुकम्पकः इति B.

‡ देशेति B. वेषेति F.

§ कर्हिचिदिति B.

¶ गच्छन्न दुष्यतीति B.

‖ श्राद्धकृन्मुच्यते गृही इति B, E and H. श्राद्धं कुर्व्वन् प्रमुच्यते इति F.

दान्तो* यज्वा देवभक्तो ब्रह्मलोके महीयते ॥
त्रिवर्गसेवी सततन्देवतानाञ्च पूजनम्।
कुर्य्यादहरहर्नित्यं नमस्येत्प्रयतः सुरान् ॥
विभागशीलः† सततं क्षमायुक्तो दयालुकः।
गृहस्थस्तु समाख्यातो न गृहेण गृही भवेत् ॥
क्षमा दया च विज्ञानं सत्यञ्चैव दमः शमः।
अध्यात्मनिरतं‡ज्ञानमेतद्ब्राह्मणलक्षणम् ॥
एतस्मा§न्न प्रमाद्येत विशेषेण द्विजोत्तमः।
यथाशक्ति चरेत्कर्म्म निन्दितानि विवर्ज्जयेत् ॥
विधूय मोहकलिलं लब्ध्वा योगमनुत्तमम्।
गृहस्थो मुच्यते बन्धान्नात्र कार्य्या विचारणा ॥
विगर्हातिक्रमाक्षेपहिंसाबन्धवधात्मनाम्।
अन्यमन्युसमुत्थानां दोषाणां मर्षणं क्षमा ॥
स्वदुःखेष्विव कारुण्यं परदुःखेषु सौहृदात्।
दयेति मुनयः प्राहुः साक्षाद्धर्म्मस्य साधनम् ॥
चतुर्द्दशानां विद्यानां धारणं हि यथार्थतः।
विज्ञानमिति तद्विद्याद्येन धर्म्मो विवर्द्धते ॥

---

* दातेति B and F.

† विभागशीलः—रात्रिन्दिवं विभज्य धर्म्मार्थकामसेवीत्यर्थः।

‡ शीलतेति B.

§ एकस्मादिति B.

अधीत्य विधिवद्वेदानर्थञ्चैवोपलभ्य तु ।
धर्म्मकार्य्यान्निवृत्तश्चेन्न तद्विज्ञानमिष्यते ॥
सत्येन लोकान्* जयति सत्यं तत्परमं पदम् ।
यथाभूतप्रवादन्तु सत्यमाहुर्म्मनीषिण: ॥
दम: शरीरोपरम: शम: प्रज्ञाप्रसादज: ।
अध्यात्ममक्षरं विद्याद्यत्र गत्वा न शोचति ॥
यया स देवो भगवान्विद्यया वेद्यते पर: ।
साक्षाद्देवो महादेवस्तज्ज्ञानमिति कीर्त्तितम् ॥
तन्निष्ठस्तत्परो विद्वान्नित्यमक्रोधन: शुचि: ।
महायज्ञपरो विद्वान्न भवेत्तदनुत्तमम्† ॥
धर्म्मस्यायतनं यत्नाच्छरीरं प्रतिपालयेत् ।
न च देहं विना रुद्रो विद्यते पुरुषै:‡ पर: ॥
नित्यधर्म्मार्थकामेषु युज्येत नियतो द्विज: ।§
न धर्म्मवर्ज्जितं काममर्थं वा मनसा स्मरेत् ॥
सीदन्नपि हि धर्म्मेण न त्वधर्म्मं समाचरेत् ।
धर्म्मो हि भगवान्देवो गति: सर्व्वेषु जन्तुषु ॥
भूतानां प्रियकारी स्यान्न परद्रोहकर्म्मधी: ।

---

* लोकमिति B.

† लभ्यते तनुमुत्तमामिति B. लभते तत्त्वमुत्तममिति F.

‡ पुरुषैर्विद्यते इति B.

§ एतत्पादद्वयं B पुस्तके नास्ति ।

न वेददेवतानिन्दां कुर्य्यात्तैश्च न संवदेत् ॥
यस्त्विमं नियतं विप्रो धर्म्माध्यायं पठेच्छुचिः ।
अध्यापयेच्छ्रावयेद्वा ब्रह्मलोके महीयते ॥

इति श्रीकूर्म्मपुराणे उत्तरभागे पञ्चदशोऽध्यायः ।

षोड़शोऽध्यायः ।

व्यास उवाच ।

न हिंस्यात्सर्व्वभूतानि नानृतं वा वदेत्क्वचित् ।
नाहितं नाप्रियं ब्रूयान्न स्तेनः स्यात्कथञ्चन ॥
तृणं वा यदि वा शाकं मृदं वा जलमेव च* ।
परस्यापहरञ्जन्तुर्नरकं प्रतिपद्यते ॥
न राज्ञः प्रतिगृह्णीयान्न शूद्रात्पतितादपि ।
नान्यस्माद्याचकत्वञ्च† निन्दिताद्वर्ज्जयेद्बुधः ॥
नित्यं याचनको न स्यात्पुनस्तन्नैव‡ याचयेत् ।

---

* वेति B.

† न चान्यस्मादशक्तश्चेति B.

‡ पुनस्तं नैवेति B.

प्राणानपहरन्त्येष* याचकस्तस्य दुर्म्मतिः† ॥
न देवद्रव्यहारी स्याद्विशेषेण द्विजोत्तमाः‡ ।
ब्रह्मस्वं वा नापहरेदापद्यपि कदाचन ॥
न विषं विषमित्याहुर्ब्रह्मस्वं विषमुच्यते§ ।
देवस्वं चापि यत्नेन सदा परिहरेत्ततः ॥
पुष्पे शाकोदके काष्ठे तथा मूले तृणे फले¶ ।
अदत्तादानमस्तेयं मनुः प्राह प्रजापतिः ॥
गृहीतव्यानि पुष्पाणि देवार्चनविधौ द्विजैः‖ ।
नैकस्मादेव नियतमननुज्ञाय केवलम् ॥
तृणं काष्ठं फलं पुष्पं प्रकाशं वै हरेद्बुधः ।
धर्म्मार्थं केवलं विप्रा** ह्यन्यथा पतितो भवेत् ॥
तिलमुद्गयवादीनां मुष्टिर्ग्राह्या पथिस्थितैः ।
क्षुधार्त्तैर्नान्यथा विप्रा धर्म्मविद्भिरिति स्थितिः†† ॥
न धर्म्मस्यापदेशेन पापं कृत्वा व्रतं चरेत् ।

---

* एवमिति B.

† दुर्म्मतेरिति B.

‡ द्विजोत्तमः इति B.

§ विषमिष्यते इति B.

¶ फले तृणे इति B.

‖ द्विजाः इति B.

** ग्राह्यमिति B. विप्र इति F.

†† श्रुतिरिति B. स्थितमिति F.

व्रतेन पापं प्रच्छाद्य कुर्व्वन् स्त्रीशूद्रदम्भनम्* ॥
प्रेत्येह चेदृशो विप्रोगर्ह्यते ब्रह्मवादिभिः।
छद्मना चरितं यच्च व्रतं रक्षांसि गच्छति ॥
अलिङ्गी लिङ्गिवेशेन यो वृत्तिमुपजीवति।
स लिङ्गिनां हरेदेनस्तिर्य्यग्योनौ च जायते ॥†
वैड़ालव्रतिनः‡ पापा लोके धर्म्मविनाशकाः।
सद्यः पतन्ति पापेषु कर्म्मणस्तस्य तत्फलम् ॥
पाषण्डिनोविकर्म्मस्थान्वामाचारांस्तथैव च।
पञ्चरात्रान्§ पाशुपतान्¶ वाङ्मात्रेणापि नार्चयेत् ॥
वेदनिन्दारतान्‖ मर्त्यान्देवनिन्दारतांस्तथा।
द्विजनिन्दारतांश्चैव मनसापि न चिन्तयेत् ॥
याजनं योनिसम्बन्धं सहवासञ्च भाषणम्।
कुर्व्वाणः पतते जन्तुस्तस्माद्यत्नेन वर्जयेत् ॥
देवद्रोहाद्गुरुद्रोहः कोटिकोटिगुणाधिकः।
ज्ञानापवादोनास्तिक्यं तस्मात्कोटिगुणाधिकम् ॥
गोभिश्च दैवतैर्विप्रैः कृष्या राजोपसेवया।

---

* लम्बनमिति B. लम्भनमिति F.

† छद्मनेति पादषट्कं A पुस्तके नास्ति। छद्मनेति पादत्रयं E H पुस्तकयोर्न दृश्यते।

‡ चण्डालव्रतिन इति E and H.

§ पञ्चरात्रान् पञ्चरात्रनामकग्रन्थानुसारिणो वैष्णवविशेषान्।

¶ पाशुपतान्—शैवविशेषान्।

‖ परानिति B.

कुलान्यकुलतां यान्ति यानि हीनानि वृत्तत:* ॥
कुविवाहै: क्रियालोपैर्वेदानध्ययनेन च ।
कुलान्यकुलतां यान्ति ब्राह्मणातिक्रमेण च ॥
अनृतात्पारदार्य्याच्च तथाऽभक्षस्य भक्षणात् ।
अश्रौतधर्म्माचरणात्क्षिप्रं नश्यति वै कुलम् ॥
अश्रोत्रियेषु वै दानाद्वृषलेषु तथैव च ।
विहिताचारहीनेषु क्षिप्रं नश्यति वै कुलम् ॥
नाधार्म्मिकैर्वृते ग्रामे न व्याधिबहुले भृशम् ।
न शूद्रराज्ये निवसेन्न पाषण्डजनैर्वृते ॥
हिमवद्विन्ध्ययोर्मध्ये पूर्व्वपश्चिमयो: शुभम् ।
मुक्त्वा समुद्रयोर्द्देशं नान्यत्र निवसेद्द्विज: ॥
कृष्णो वा यत्र चरति मृगो नित्यं स्वभावत: ।
पुण्याश्च विश्रुता नद्यस्तत्र वा निवसेद्द्विज: ॥
अर्द्धक्रोशान्नदीकूलं वर्जयित्वा द्विजोत्तम: ।
नान्यत्र निवसेत्पुण्यां नान्त्यजग्रामसन्निधौ ॥
न संवसेच्च पतितैर्न चण्डालैर्न पुक्कशै: ।
न मूर्खैर्नावलिप्तैश्च नान्त्यैर्नान्त्यावसायिभि: ॥
एकशय्यासनम्पङ्क्तिर्भाण्डपक्वान्नमिश्रणम् ।
याजनाध्यापनं योनिस्तथैव सहभोजनम् ॥
सहाध्यायस्तु दशम: सहयाजनमेव च ।

---

* धर्म्मत: इति B. सर्व्वत इति F.

एकादशैते निर्द्दिष्टाः* दोषाः सङ्कर†संज्ञिताः ॥
समीपे वाप्यवस्थानात्पापं सङ्क्रमते नृणाम् ।
तस्मात्सर्व्वप्रयत्नेन सङ्करं वर्ज्जयेद्बुधः ॥
एकपंक्त्युपविष्टा ये न स्पृशन्ति परस्परम् ।
भस्मना कृतमर्यादा न तेषां सङ्करो भवेत् ॥
अग्निना भस्मना चैव सलिलेन विशेषतः ।
द्वारेण स्तम्भमार्गेण षड्भिः पंक्तिर्विभिद्यते ॥
न कुर्य्याद्दुःखवैराणि‡ विवादं चैव पैशुनम्§ ।
परक्षेत्रे गां चरन्तीं न चाचक्षीत कस्यचित् ॥
न संवसेत्सूतकिना¶ न कञ्चिन्मर्म्मणि स्पृशेत् ।
न सूर्य्यपरिवेशं वा नेन्द्रचापं शवाग्निकम् ॥
परस्मै कथयेद्विद्वाञ्छशिनं वा कदाचन‖ ।
न कुर्य्याद्बहुभिः सार्द्धं विरोधं वा कदाचन** ॥
आत्मनः प्रतिकूलानि परेषां न समाचरेत् ।
तिथिं पक्षस्य न ब्रूयान्नक्षत्राणि विनिर्द्दिशेत् ॥

---

* एकादश समुद्दिष्टाः इति B.

† साङ्कर्य्येति B.

‡ शुष्कवैराणीति B, F and H.

§ न च पैशुनमिति B.

¶ न संवदेत्सूतकेनेति B.

‖ कथञ्चनेति B.

** बन्धुभिस्तथेति B. बन्धुभिः सह इति F.

नोदक्यामभिभाषेत नाशुचिं वा द्विजोत्तमः* ।
न देवगुरुविप्राणां दीयमानन्तु वारयेत् ॥
न चात्मानं प्रशंसेद्वा परनिन्दाञ्च वर्ज्जयेत् ।
वेदनिन्दान्देवनिन्दां प्रयत्नेन विवर्ज्जयेत् ॥
यस्तु देवानृषीन् विप्रान्† वेदान्वा निन्दति द्विजः ।
न तस्य निष्कृतिर्दृष्टा शास्त्रेष्विह मुनीश्वराः ॥
निन्दयेद्वै गुरून्देवान्वेदं वा सोपबृंहणम्‡ ।
कल्पकोटिशतं साग्रं रौरवे पच्यते नरः ॥
तूष्णीमासीत निन्दायां न ब्रूयात्किञ्चिदुत्तरम् ।
कर्णौ पिधाय गन्तव्यं न चैतानवलोकयेत् ॥
वर्ज्जयेद्वै रहस्यञ्च§ परेषां गूहयेद्बुधः ।
विवादं स्वजनैः सार्द्धं न कुर्य्याद्वै कदाचन ॥
न पापं पापिनं ब्रूयादपापं वा द्विजोत्तमम्¶ ।
स तेन तुल्यदोषः स्यान्मिथ्यादिदोषवान् भवेत् ॥
यानि मिथ्याभिशस्तानां पतन्त्यश्रूणि रोदनात् ।
तानि पुत्रान् पशून् घ्नन्ति तेषां मिथ्याभिशंसिनाम् ॥

---

* द्विजोत्तमाः इति B.

† चैवेति B.

‡ सोपबृंहणं—उपबृंहणान्वितम्। उपबृंहणं—संग्रहेण वर्द्धनम्, संहिताकारेण निबद्धम्। वेदव्यासोपबृंहणमिति B and F.

§ रहस्यानीति B.

¶ द्विजोत्तमाः इति B and F.

ब्रह्महत्यासुरापाने स्तेयगुर्वङ्गनागमे ।
दृष्टं विशोधनं सद्भिः* नास्ति मिथ्याभिशंसने ॥
नेक्षेतोद्यन्तमादित्यं शशिनञ्चानिमित्ततः† ।
नास्तं यातं न वारिस्थं नोपसृष्टं न मध्यगम् ॥
तिरोहितं वाससा वा‡ नादर्शान्तरगामिणम्§ ।
न नग्नां स्त्रियमीक्षेत पुरुषं वा कदाचन ॥
न च मूत्रं पुरीषं वा न च संसृष्टमैथुनम्¶ ।
नाशुचिः सूर्य्यसोमादीन् ग्रहानालोकयेद्बुधः ॥
पतितव्यङ्गचण्डालानुच्छिष्टान्नावलोकयेत् ।
नाभिभाषेत च परमुच्छिष्टो वावगर्व्वितः‖ ॥
न स्पृशेत्प्रेतसंस्पर्शं न क्रुद्धस्य गुरोर्मुखम् ।
न तैलोदकयोश्छायां न पत्नीं भोजने सति ।
नियुक्त**बन्धनाङ्गां वा नोन्मत्तं मत्तमेव वा†† ॥

---

* दृष्टं वै शोधनं वृद्धैरिति B. वृद्धैरिति F.

† शशिनं वानिमित्ततः इति B. वानिमित्तक इति F.

‡ वा संसारादिति B.

§ नादर्शाद्यनुगामिनमिति B. न दृश्याद्यनुगामिनमिति F.

¶ संस्पृश्येति B.

‖ वावगुण्ठितः इति B, E, G and H.

** नामुक्तेति B. न मुक्तेति F.

†† चेति B.

नाश्नीयाद्भार्य्यया सार्द्धं नैनामीक्षेत मेहनीम्* ।
क्षुवन्तीं जृम्भमाणां वा नासनस्थां यथासुखम् ॥
नोदके चात्मनोरूपं न कूलं श्वभ्रमेव वा† ।
न लङ्घयेच्च मूत्रं वा‡ नाधितिष्ठेत्कदाचन ॥
न शूद्राय मतिन्दद्यात्कृशरं पायसन्दधि ।
नोच्छिष्टं वा घृतमधु न च कृष्णाजिनं हविः ॥
न चैवास्मै व्रतन्दद्यान्न§ च धर्म्मं वदेद्बुधः ।
न च क्रोधवशङ्गच्छेद्द्वेषं रागञ्च¶ वर्ज्जयेत् ॥
लोभं दम्भं तथा वर्ज्ज्यं‖ यात्नावि**ज्ञानकुत्सनम् ।
मानं मोहं तथा क्रोधं द्वेषञ्च†† परिवर्ज्जयेत् ॥
न कुर्य्यात्कस्यचित्पीड़ां सुतं शिष्यञ्च ताड़येत् ।
न हीनानुपसेवेत न च तीक्ष्णमतीन्‡‡ क्वचित् ॥
नात्मानञ्चावमन्येत दैन्यं यत्नेन वर्ज्जयेत् ।

---

* चाशुचिमिति B.

† शुभं वाशुभमेव वेति B.

‡ मतिमानिति B.

§ ब्रूयान्नेति B.

¶ रोषञ्चेति B.

‖ यत्नादिति B.

** असूयामिति B.

†† ईर्षां मदन्तथा शोकं मोहञ्चेति B.

‡‡ तीक्ष्णां मतिमिति B.

न चाशिष्यं* न सत्कुर्य्यान्नात्मानं शंसयेद्बुधः† ॥
न नखैर्व्विलिखेद्भूमिं‡ गां च संवेशयेन्न हि ।
न नदीषु नदीं ब्रूयात्पर्व्वते न च पर्व्वतान्§ ॥
आवसेत्तेन नैवापि¶ न त्यजेत्सहयायिनम्‖ ।
नावगाहेदपो** नग्नो वह्निञ्चापि व्रजेत्पदा†† ॥
शिरोऽभ्यङ्गावशिष्टेन तैलेनाङ्गं न लेपयेत् ।
न शस्त्रसर्पैः‡‡ क्रीड़ेत न स्वानि खानि च स्पृशेत् ॥
रोमाणि च रहस्यानि नाशिष्टेन सह व्रजेत् ।
न पाणिपादावग्नौ च चापलानि समाश्रयेत् ॥
न शिश्नोदरयोर्न्नित्यं§§ न च श्रवणयोः क्वचित् ।
न चाङ्गनखवादं वै कुर्य्यान्नाञ्जलिना पिबत् ॥

---

* न विशिष्टानिति B and F. न च शिष्टानिति E and G. न चाशिष्टानिति H.

† वा शपेद्बुधः इति B.

‡ न नखेन लिखेद्भूमिमिति B.

§ नदीस्थितः नदीविषयिकां कथां तथाच पर्व्वतारूढ़ः पर्व्वतसम्बन्धिनीं कथां नापि प्रस्तुयात् ।

¶ तेन तादृशेन नद्यां नदीं पर्व्वते पर्व्वतं निर्द्दिशता जनेन सह नैवोत्तरेत् । आवासे भोजने वापीति B.

‖ सह पापिनामिति B.

** अवगाहेतेति साधु ।

†† वह्निं नापि व्रजेत्तदेति B.

‡‡ सर्पशस्त्रैरिति B and F.

§§ न शिश्नोदरचापल्यमिति B.

नाभिहन्याज्जलं पद्भ्यां पाणिना वा कदाचन ।
न शातयेदिष्टकाभिः फलानि न फलेन च* ॥
न म्लेच्छभाषणं शिक्षेन्नाकर्षेच्च पदासनम् ।
न भेदनमधिस्फोटं† छेदनं वा विलेपनम्‡ ॥
कुर्य्याद्विमर्द्दनं धीमान्नाकस्मादेव निष्फलम् ।
नोत्सङ्गे भक्षयेद्भक्ष्यान् वृथाचेष्टाञ्च नाचरेत् ॥
न नृत्येदथवा गायेन्न वादित्राणि वादयेत् ।
न संहिताभ्यां पाणिभ्यां कण्डूयेदात्मनः शिरः ॥
न लौकिकैस्तवैर्देवांस्तोषयेद्बेषजैरपि§ ।
नाक्षैः क्रीड़ेन्न धावेत नाप्सु विण्मूत्रमाचरेत् ॥
नोच्छिष्टः संविशेन्नित्यं न नग्नः स्नानमाचरेत् ।
न गच्छन्न पठेद्वापि न चैव स्वशिरः स्पृशेत् ॥
न दन्तैर्नखरोमाणि छिन्द्यात्सुप्तं न बोधयेत् ।
न बालातपमासेवेत्¶ प्रेतधूमं विवर्ज्जयेत् ॥
नैकः सुप्याच्छून्यगृहे स्वयं नोपानहौ हरेत् ।
नाकारणाद्वा निष्ठीवेन्न बाहुभ्यां नदीं तरेत् ॥
न पादक्षालनं कुर्य्यात्पादेनैव कदाचन ।

---

* सफलानि चेति B.

† नखभेदनमास्फोटमिति B and F.

‡ विलेखनमिति B.

§ वाक्यजैरपीति B. वाह्यजैरपीति F.

¶ आसेतेवेति साधु ।

नाग्नौ प्रतापयेत्पादौ* न कांस्ये धावयेद्बुधः ॥
नाभिप्रतारयेद्देवं† ब्राह्मणान् गामथापि वा।
वाय्वग्निगुरु‡विप्रान्वा सूर्य्यं वा शशिनं प्रति ॥
अशुद्धः शयनं यानं स्वाध्यायं स्नानभोजनम्।
वहिर्निष्क्रमणञ्चैव न कुर्व्वीत कथञ्चन ॥
स्वप्नमध्ययनं यानमुच्चारं§ भोजनं गतिम्।
उभयोः सन्ध्ययोर्नित्यं मध्याह्ने तु¶ विवर्ज्जयेत् ॥
न स्पृशेत्पाणिनोच्छिष्टो विप्रो गोब्राह्मणाऽनलान्।
न चैवान्नं‖ पदा वापि न देवप्रतिमां स्पृशेत् ॥
नाशुद्धोऽग्निं परिचरेन्न देवान् कीर्त्तयेदृषीन्।
नावगाहेदगाधाम्बु धारयेन्नाग्निमेकतः** ॥
न वामहस्तेनोद्धृत्य पिवेद्वक्त्रेण वा जलम्।
नोत्तरेदनुपस्पृश्य नाप्सु रेतः समुत्सृजेत् ॥
अमेध्यलिप्तमन्यद्वा लोहितं वा विषाणि वा।
व्यतिक्रमेन्न स्रवन्तीर्नाप्सु मैथुनमाचरेत् ॥

---

* प्रदापयेत्पादाविति B.

† नातिप्रसारयेदिति B and F.

‡ नृपेति B.

§ स्नानमुद्वर्त्तमिति B.

¶ चेति B.

‖ चात्मानमिति B.

** धारयेद्वानिमित्ततः इति B.

चैत्यं वृक्षं* न वै छिन्द्यान्नाप्सु ष्ठीवनमुत्सृजेत्† ।
नास्थिभस्मकपालानि न केशान्न च कण्टकान् ।
औषाङ्गारकरीषं वा नाधितिष्ठेत्कदाचन‡ ॥
न चाग्निं लङ्घयेद्धीमान्नोपदध्यादधः क्वचित् ।
न चैनं पादतः कुर्य्यान्मुखेन न धमेद्बुधः ॥
न कूपमवरोहेत नावेक्षेताशुचिः§ क्वचित् ।
अग्नौ न प्रक्षिपेदग्निं नाद्भिः प्रशमयेत्तथा ॥
सुहृन्मरणमार्त्तिं वा न स्वयं श्रावयेत्परान् ।
अपण्यमथ पण्यं¶ वा विक्रये न प्रयोजयेत् ॥
न वह्निं मुखनिश्वासैर्ज्वालयेन्नाशुचिर्बुधः ।
पुण्यस्नानोदकस्थाने सीमान्तं वा कृषेन्न तु‖ ॥
न भिन्द्यात्पूर्व्वसमयं** सत्योपेतं†† कदाचन ।
परस्परं पशून् व्यालान् पक्षिणो नावबोधयेत् ॥
परबाधां न कुर्व्वीत जलपानायनादिभिः‡‡ ।

---

* चैत्यवृक्षमिति B. चैत्यवृक्षानिति F.

† माचरेदिति B.

‡ एतत्पादद्वयं A, E, H पुस्तकेषु नास्ति ।

§ नावेक्षेताशुचिमिति B and F.

¶ कूटपण्यमिति B. कृतपण्यं चेति F.

‖ चाग्रसेन्न तु इति B. न कृषेत्—नातिक्रम्य गच्छेदित्यर्थः ।

** पूर्व्वसमयं पूर्व्वनियमबन्धमित्यर्थः ।

†† अभ्युपेतमिति B and F.

‡‡ जलवातातपादिभिरिति B and F.

कारयित्वा सुकर्म्माणि कारून् पश्चान्न वर्ज्जयेत्।
सायं प्रातर्गृहद्वारान् भिक्षार्थं नावघाटयेत्॥
वहिर्माल्यं वहिर्गन्धं* भार्य्यया सह भोजनम्।
विगृह्य वादं† कुद्वारप्रवेशञ्च विवर्ज्जयेत्॥
न खादन् ब्राह्मणस्तिष्ठेन्न जल्पन्‡ हसन् बुधः।
स्वमग्निं नैव हस्तेन§ स्पृशेन्नाप्सु चिरं वसेत्॥
न पक्षकेणोपधमेन्न शूर्पेण न पाणिना।
मुखेनैव धमेदग्निं मुखादग्निरजायत॥
परस्त्रियं न भाषेत नायाज्यं याजयेद्बुधः¶॥
नैकश्चरेत्सभां विप्रः समवायञ्च वर्ज्जयेत्‖।
देवतायतनं गच्छेत्कदाचिन्नाप्रदक्षिणम्॥
न वीजयेद्वा वस्त्रेण न देवायतने स्वपेत्।
नैकोऽध्वानं प्रपद्येत नाधार्म्मिकजनैः सह॥
न व्याधिदूषितैर्वापि न शूद्रैः पतितैर्न वा।
नोपानद्वर्ज्जितोऽध्वानं** जलादिरहितस्तथा॥

---

* सुगन्धञ्चेति B.

† वाटमिति B. विसृज्य द्वारमिति F.

‡ न जपेद्वा इति B.

§ हस्तेनैकेनेति A and H.

¶ याजयेद्विजः इति B.

‖ न देवायतनं गच्छेत्कदाचिद्वाप्रदक्षिणमिति B.

** वाथेति B.

न रात्रावरिणा सार्द्धं न विना च कमण्डलुम्।
नाग्निगोब्राह्मणादीनामन्तरेण व्रजेत्कचित्॥
न वत्स्यन्तीं न विनतामतिक्रामेद्द्विजोत्तमाः।
न निन्देद्योगिनः सिद्धान् गुणिनोवा* यतींस्तथा॥
देवतायतने प्राज्ञो न देवानाञ्च सन्निधौ†।
नाक्रामेत्कामतश्छायां ब्राह्मणानाङ्गवामपि‡॥
स्वान्तु नाक्रमयेच्छायां पतिताद्यैर्न रोगिभिः।
नाङ्गारभस्मकेशादिष्वधितिष्ठेत्कदाचन॥
वर्जयेन्मार्जनीरेणुं स्नानवस्त्रघटोदकम्।
न भक्षयेदभक्ष्याणि नापेयञ्चापिवेद्द्विजाः॥

इति श्रीकूर्म्मपुराणे उत्तरभागे षोड़शोऽध्यायः।

---

* व्रतिनोवेति B.

† देवतायतनं प्राज्ञोदेवानाञ्चैव मन्त्रिणामिति B.

‡ ब्राह्मणानाञ्च गोरपीति B.

सप्तदशोऽध्यायः ।

व्यास उवाच ।

नाद्याच्छूद्रस्य विप्रोऽन्नं मोहाद्वा यदि कामतः* ।
स शूद्रयोनिं व्रजति यस्तु भुंक्ते ह्यनापदि ॥
षण्मासान्यो द्विजो भुंक्ते शूद्रस्यान्नं विगर्हितम् ।
जीवन्नेव भवेच्छूद्रो मृतएवाभिजायते† ॥
ब्राह्मणक्षत्रियविशां शूद्रस्य च मुनीश्वराः ।
यस्यान्नेनोदरस्थेन मृतस्तद्योनिमाप्नुयात् ॥
नटान्नं‡ नर्त्तकान्नञ्च तक्ष्णोऽन्नं कर्म्मकारिणः§ ।
गणान्नङ्गणिकान्नञ्च षड़न्नानि च वर्ज्जयेत् ॥
चक्रोपजीविरजकतस्करध्वजिनान्तथा ।
गन्धर्व्वलोहकारान्नं सूतकान्नञ्च वर्ज्जयेत्¶ ॥
कुलालचित्रकर्म्मान्नं वार्द्धुषेः पतितस्य च‖ ।
सुवर्णकारशैलूषव्याधबद्धातुरस्य च** ॥

---

* वान्यतः इति B and F.

† मृतः श्वा चाभिजायते इति B and F.

‡ राजान्नमिति B.

§ चर्म्मकारिण इति B and F.

¶ सूतकान्नं विवर्ज्जयेदिति B.

‖ पौनर्भवशस्त्रकर्त्तॄरभिशस्तस्य चैव हि इति E and H.

** व्याधितस्यातुरस्य च इति F.

चिकित्सकस्य चैवान्नं पुंश्चल्या दण्डकस्य* च ।
स्तेननास्तिकयोरन्नन्देवतानिन्दकस्य च ॥
सोमविक्रयिणश्चान्नं श्वपाकस्य विशेषतः ।
भार्य्याजितस्य चैवान्नं यस्य चोपपतिर्गृहे ॥
उच्छिष्टस्य कदर्य्यस्य तथैवोच्छिष्टभोजिनः ।
अपङ्क्त्यनञ्च संघान्नं† शस्त्रजीवस्य चैव हि ॥
क्लीवसन्न्यासिनश्चान्नं मत्तोन्मत्तस्य चैव हि ।‡
भीतस्य रुदितस्यान्नमवक्रुष्टं परिग्रहम्§ ॥
ब्रह्मद्विषः पापरुचेः श्राद्धान्नं सूतकस्य च ।
वृथापाकस्य चैवान्नं शठान्नं चतुरस्य¶ च ॥
अप्रजानान्तु नारीणां भृतकस्य‖ तथैव च ।
कारुकान्नं विशेषेण शस्त्रविक्रयिणस्तथा ॥
शौण्डान्नं घातिकान्नञ्च** भिषजामन्नमेव च ।
विद्धप्रजननस्यान्नं परिवेत्तन्नमेव च†† ॥

---

* दाम्भिकस्येति B. दण्डिकस्य च इति F.

† सङ्घान्नमिति B.

‡ एतत्पादचतुष्टयं A G पुस्तकयोर्नास्ति ।

§ परिच्युतमिति B. अवक्रुद्धं परिच्युतमिति F.

¶ असुरस्येति B. शवान्नं भासुरस्य च इति F.

‖ कृतघ्नस्येति B.

** शौण्डिकान्नं घाटिकान्नमिति B, E and F.

†† एतत्पादद्वयं B पुस्तके नास्ति ।

पुनर्भुवो विशेषेण तथैव दिधिषूपतेः।
अवज्ञातं चावधूतं सरोषं विस्मयान्वितम्॥
गुरोरपि न भोक्तव्यमन्नं संस्कारवर्ज्जितम्।
दुष्कृतं हि मनुष्यस्य सर्व्वमन्ने व्यवस्थितम्॥
यो यस्यान्नं समश्नाति स तस्याश्नाति किल्बिषम्।
आर्द्धिकः* कुलमित्रश्च स्वगोपालश्च नापितः†॥
कुशीलवः कुम्भकारः क्षेत्रकर्म्मक एव च।‡
एते शूद्रेषु भोज्यान्नं दत्त्वा स्वल्पं पणं बुधैः।
पायसं स्नेहपक्वं यत्§ गोरसञ्चैव सक्तवः॥
पिण्याकञ्चैव तैलञ्च शूद्राद्ग्राह्यं तथैव च¶।
वृन्ताकञ्जालिका‖ शाकं कुसुम्भाश्मन्तकं तथा॥
पलाण्डुं लसुनं शुक्तं निर्य्यासञ्चैव वर्ज्जयेत्।
छत्राकं विड्वराहञ्च शेलं पीयूषमेव** च॥

---

* आर्त्तिजः इति B.

† गोपालो दासनापितौ इति B.

‡ एतत्पादद्वयं A, E, H पुस्तकेषु नास्ति।

§ चेति B.

¶ शूद्रादग्राह्यं द्विजातिभिरिति B.

‖ नालिकेति B.

** पीलूषमेवेति B. विड्वराहञ्च शेलं पेयुषमेव च इति H. विड्वराहञ्च शेलूषपेयूषमेव च इति F.

विलयं सुमुखञ्चैव कवकानि* च वर्ज्जयेत्† ।
गृञ्जनं किंशुकञ्चैव कुक्कुटञ्च‡ तथैव च ॥
उदुम्बरमलावुञ्च जग्ध्वा पतति वै द्विजः ।
वृथाकृशरसं यावं पायसापूपमेव च ॥
अनुपाकृतमांसञ्च देवान्नानि हवींषि च ।
यवागूं मातुलिङ्गञ्च मत्स्यानप्यनुपाकृतान् ॥
नीपं कपित्थं प्लक्षञ्च प्रयत्नेन विवर्ज्जयेत् ।
पिण्याकञ्चोद्धृतस्नेहं दिवाधाना§स्तथैव च ॥
रात्रौ च तिलसम्बद्धं प्रयत्नेन दधि त्यजेत् ।
नाश्नीयात्पयसा तक्रं न वीजान्युपजीवयेत् ॥
क्रियादुष्टं भावदुष्टमसत्सङ्गं विवर्ज्जयेत् ।
केशकीटावपन्नञ्च स्वभूल्लेखञ्च¶ नित्यशः ॥
श्वाघ्रातञ्च पुनः सिद्धं चण्डालावेक्षितं तथा ।
उदक्यया च पतितैर्गवा चाघ्रातमेव च‖ ॥
अनर्च्चितं पर्य्युषितं पर्य्याभ्रान्तञ्च नित्यशः ।
काककुक्कुटसंस्पृष्टं कृमिभिश्चैव संयुतम् ॥

---

* करकाणीति B.

† विवर्जयेदिति B.

‡ ककुभञ्चेति B.

§ देवधान्यमिति B.

¶ सुहृल्लेखञ्चेति B.

‖ वेति B.

मनुष्यैरथवा घ्रातं कुष्ठिना स्पृष्टमेव च* ।
न रजस्वलया दत्तं न पुंश्चल्या सरोषकम्† ॥
मलवद्वाससा चापि परया चोपयोजयेत्‡ ।
विवत्सायाश्च गोः क्षीरमौष्ट्रं वा निर्दशस्य च§ ॥
आविकं सन्धिनीक्षीरमपेयं¶ मनुरब्रवीत् ।
बलाकं हंसदात्यूहं कलविंकं शुकं तथा ॥
तथा कुररवल्लूरं‖ जालपादञ्च कोकिलम् ।
चाषांश्च खञ्जरीटांश्च श्येनं गृध्रं तथैव च ॥
उलूकं चक्रवाकञ्च भासं पारावतं तथा** ।
कपोतं टिट्टिभञ्चैव ग्रामकुक्कुटमेव च ॥
सिंहं व्याघ्रञ्च मार्जारं श्वानं कुक्कुरमेव च†† ।
शृगालं मर्कटञ्चैव गर्द्दभञ्च न भक्षयेत् ।
न भक्षयेत्सर्व्वमृगानन्यान्वनचरान्द्विजान्‡‡ ॥
जलेचरान् स्थलचरान् प्राणिनश्चेति धारणा ।

---

* अनर्चितमित्यादि पादषट्कं B पुस्तके नास्ति ।

† सरोमश्चेति B.

‡ परवासोऽथ वर्जयेदिति B.

§ वानिर्दशस्यथेति B.

¶ सन्धिनीक्षीरमदेयमिति B.

‖ कुररञ्च चकोरञ्चेति B.

** लपीति B.

†† एतत्पादद्वयं A, E, H पुस्तकेषु नास्ति ।

‡‡ पक्षिणोऽन्यान्वनेचरानिति B.

गोधा कूर्म्मः शशः श्वावित्* सल्लकी चेति सत्तमाः ॥
भक्ष्याः पञ्चनखा नित्यं मनुराह प्रजापतिः ।
मत्स्यान् सशल्कान् भुञ्जीयान्मांसं रौरवमेव च ॥
निवेद्य देवताभ्यस्तु ब्राह्मणेभ्यस्तु† नान्यथा ।
मयूरन्तित्तिरञ्चैव कपिञ्जलकमेव च‡ ॥
वार्ध्रीणसन्द्वीपिनञ्च भक्ष्यानाह प्रजापतिः ।
राजीवान् सिंहतुण्डांश्च§ तथा पाठीनरोहितौ ॥
मत्स्येष्वेते¶ समुद्दिष्टा भक्षणीया मुनीश्वराः ।
प्रोक्षितं भक्षयेदेषां मांसञ्च द्विजकाम्यया ॥
यथाविधि नियुक्तञ्च प्राणानामपि चात्यये ।
भक्षयेदेव मांसानि शेषभोजी न लिप्यते ॥
औषधार्थमशक्तौ वा नियोगाद्यं न कारयेत्‖ ।
आमन्त्रितस्तु यः श्राद्धे दैवे वा मांसमुत्सृजेत् ।
यावन्ति पशुरोमाणि तावतो नरकान् व्रजेत् ॥
अदेयं वाप्यपेयञ्च** तथैवास्पृश्यमेव च ।

---

* खड्गीति B.

† चेति B.

‡ कपोतञ्च कपिञ्जलमिति B.

§ शेखरं सिंहतुण्डञ्चेति B.

¶ मत्स्याश्चैते इति B.

‖ नियोगाद्यज्ञकारणादिति B.

** अपेयं वापि पेयञ्चेति B.

द्विजातीनां समालोच्यं* नित्यं मद्यमिति स्थितिः॥
तस्मात्सर्व्वप्रयत्नेन† मद्यं नित्यञ्च वर्ज्जयेत्‡।
पीत्वा पतितः§ कर्म्मभ्यो न सम्भाष्यो भवेद्विजैः¶॥
भक्षयित्वा ह्यभक्ष्याणि‖ पीत्वापेयान्यपि द्विजः।
नाधिकारी भवेत्तावद्यावत्तन्न व्रजत्यधः॥
तस्मात्परिहरेन्नित्यमभक्ष्याणि प्रयत्नतः।
आरोप्य याति चैवैको तथा वै याति रौरवम्**॥

इति श्रीकूर्म्मपुराणे भक्ष्याभक्ष्यनिर्णये व्यासगीतासु
सप्तदशोऽध्यायः।

---

* द्विजातीनामनालोक्यमिति B.

† प्रकारेणेति B.

‡ नित्यं विवर्जयेदिति B.

§ पततीति B.

¶ असम्भाष्यो भवेद्द्विजः इति B.

‖ भक्षयित्वाप्यभक्ष्याणीति B.

** अपेयानि च विप्रा वै तथा चेद्याति रौरवमिति B.

अष्टादशोऽध्यायः।

ऋषयः ऊचुः।

अहन्यहनि कर्त्तव्यं ब्राह्मणानां महामुने।
तदाचक्ष्वाखिलं कर्म्म येन मुच्येत बन्धनात्॥

व्यास उवाच।

वक्ष्ये* समाहिता यूयं शृणुध्वङ्गदतो मम।
अहन्यहनि कर्त्तव्यं ब्राह्मणानां क्रमाद्विधिः†॥
ब्राह्मे मुहूर्त्ते तूत्थाय धर्म्ममर्थञ्च चिन्तयेत्।
कायक्लेशञ्च यन्मूलं‡ ध्यायेत मनसेश्वरम्॥
उषाकाले§ऽथ सम्प्राप्ते कृत्वा चावश्यकं बुधः।
स्नायान्नदीषु शुद्धासु शौचङ्कृत्वा यथाविधि॥
प्रातःस्नानेन पूयन्ते येऽपि पापकृतो जनाः।
तस्मात्सर्व्वप्रयत्नेन प्रातःस्नानं समाचरेत्॥
प्रातस्स्नानं प्रशंसन्ति दृष्टादृष्टकरं हि तत्¶।
ऋषीणामृषिता नित्यं प्रातःस्नानान्न संशयः॥‖

---

* विप्रा इति B.

† क्रमाद्विधिमिति B.

‡ कायक्लेशं तदुद्भूतमिति B and F.

§ उषःकाले इति B.

¶ शुभमिति B.

‖ एतत्पादद्वयं A, E, H पुस्तकेषु नास्ति।

मुखे सुप्तस्य सततं लाला याः संस्रवन्ति हि।
ततो नैवाचरेत्कर्म्म अकृत्वा स्नानमादिमम्* ॥
अलक्ष्मको जलं किञ्चित्† दुःस्वप्नं दुर्विचिन्तितम्।
प्रातःस्नानेन पापानि पूयन्ते नात्र संशयः ॥
अतः‡ स्नानं विना पुंसां पापित्वं§ कर्म्मसु स्मृतम्।
होमे जप्ये विशेषेण तस्मात्स्नानं समाचरेत् ॥
अशक्तावशिरस्कं वा स्नानमस्य विधीयते।
आर्द्रेण वाससा वाथ मार्ज्जनं पावनं¶ स्मृतम् ॥
आयत्ये वै‖ समुत्पन्ने स्नानमेव** समाचरेत्।
ब्राह्मादीनामथाशक्तौ स्नानान्याहुर्म्मनीषिणः ॥
ब्राह्ममाग्नेयमुद्दिष्टं वायव्यं दिव्यमेव च।
वारुणं यौगिकं यच्च†† षोढ़ा स्नानं समासतः‡‡ ॥
ब्राह्मन्तु मार्ज्जनं§§ मन्त्रैः कुशैः सोदकविन्दुभिः।

---

* कर्म्माण्यकृत्वा स्नानमादितः इति B.

† अलक्ष्मीः कालकर्णी चेति B.

‡ न चेति B.

§ पावनमिति B.

¶ कायिकमिति B.

‖ असामर्थ्ये इति B.

** स्नानमेवमिति B.

†† तद्वदिति B.

‡‡ प्रकीर्त्तितमिति B.

§§ मार्जनैरिति B.

आग्नेयं भस्मनापादमस्तकाद्देहधूलनम् ॥
गवां हि रजसा प्रोक्तं वायव्यं स्नानमुत्तमम् ।
यत्तु* सातपवर्षेण स्नानं तद्दिव्यमुच्यते ॥
वारुणञ्चावगाहस्तु मानसं स्वात्मवेदनम् ।
योगिनां† स्नानमाख्यातं योगे विश्वादिचिन्तनम्‡ ॥
आत्मतीर्थमिति ख्यातं सेवितं ब्रह्मवादिभिः ।
मनःशुद्धिकरं पुंसां नित्यं तत्स्नानमाचरेत् ॥
शक्तश्चेद्वारुणं विद्वान् प्रायश्चित्ते§ तथैव च ॥
प्रक्षाल्य दन्तकाष्ठं वै भक्षयित्वा विधानतः ।
आचम्य प्रयतो नित्यं स्नानं प्रातः¶ समाचरेत् ॥
मध्याङ्गुलिसमस्थौल्यं द्वादशाङ्गुलसम्मितम् ।
सत्वचं दन्तकाष्ठं स्यात्तदग्रेण तु धावयेत् ॥
क्षीरवृक्षसमुद्भूतं मालतीसम्भवं शुभम् ।
अपामार्गञ्च विल्वञ्च करवीरं विशेषतः ॥
वर्ज्जयित्वा निन्दितानि गृहीत्वैकं यथोदितम् ।
परिहृत्य दिनं पापं भक्षयेद्वै विधानवित् ॥

---

* यत्त्वेति A.

† यौगिकमिति B.

‡ योगाद्विष्णुविचिन्तनमिति B.

§ प्राजापत्यमिति B.

¶ प्रातःस्नानमिति B.

नोत्पाटयेद्दन्तकाष्ठं* नाङ्गुल्यग्रेण धारयेत्† ।
प्रक्षाल्य भंक्त्वा तज्जह्याच्छुचौ देशे समाहितः ॥
स्नात्वा सन्तर्प्पयेद्देवानृषीन् पितृगणांस्तथा ।
आचम्य मन्त्रविन्नित्यं‡ पुनराचम्य वाग्यतः ॥
सम्मार्ज्ज्य मन्त्रैरात्मानं कुशैः सोदकविन्दुभिः ।
आपो हिष्ठाव्याहृतिभिः सावित्र्या वारुणैः शुभैः ॥
ओङ्कारव्याहृतियुतां गायत्रीं वेदमातरम्§ ।
जप्त्वा जलाञ्जलिं दद्याद्भास्करं प्रति तन्मनाः ॥
प्राक्कूलेषु ततः स्थित्वा¶ दर्भेषु सुसमाहितः ।
प्राणायामत्रयङ्कृत्वा ध्यायेत्सन्ध्यामिति स्मृतिः‖ ॥
या च सन्ध्या** जगत्सूतिर्मायातीता हि निष्कला ।
ऐश्वरी केवला†† शक्तिस्तत्त्वत्रयसमुद्भवा ॥
ध्यात्वार्कमण्डलगतां सावित्रीं वै जपेद्बुधः ।
प्राङ्मुखः सततं विप्रः सन्ध्योपासनमाचरेत् ॥
सन्ध्याहीनोऽशुचिर्नित्यमनर्हः सर्व्वकर्म्मसु ।
यदन्यत्कुरुते किञ्चिन्न तस्य फलमाप्नुयात् ॥
अनन्यचेतसः शान्ता ब्राह्मणा वेदपारगाः ।
उपास्य विधिवत्सन्ध्यां प्राप्ताः पूर्व्वेऽपरां गतिम् ॥

---

* नोत्पाटयेदिति B. † नाङ्गुल्या धारयेत् क्वचिदिति B. ‡ मन्त्रवन्नित्यमिति H. § देवमातरमिति B. ¶ प्राक्कूलेषु समासीनः इति B, E and G. ‖ श्रुतिरिति B. ** या सन्ध्या येति B. †† ऐश्वरी तु परेति B.

योऽन्यत्र कुरुते यत्नं धर्म्मकार्य्यें द्विजोत्तमः।
विहाय सन्ध्याप्रणतिं स याति नरकायुतम्॥
तस्मात्सर्व्वप्रयत्नेन सन्ध्योपासनमाचरेत्।
उपासितो भवेत्तेन देवो योगतनुः परः॥
सहस्रपरमां नित्यं शतमध्यां दशावराम्।
सावित्रीं वै तपेद्विद्वान् प्राङ्मुखः प्रयतः स्थितः॥
अथोपतिष्ठेदादित्यमुदयन्तं समाहितः।
मन्त्रैस्तु विविधैः सौरैः ऋग्यजुःसामसम्भवैः॥
उपस्थाय महायोगं देवदेवं दिवाकरम्।
कुर्व्वीत प्रणतिं भूमौ मूर्द्ध्ना तेनैव* मन्त्रतः॥
ओङ्खोल्काय† शान्ताय कारणत्रयहेतवे।
निवेदयामि चात्मानं नमस्ते विश्वरूपिणे‡॥
नमस्ते घृणिने तुभ्यं सूर्य्याय ब्रह्मरूपिणे।§
त्वमेव ब्रह्म परममापोज्योतीरसोऽमृतम्।
भूर्भुवः स्वस्त्वमोङ्कारः शर्व्वो रुद्रः सनातनः॥
पुरुषः सन्महोऽन्तस्थं प्रणमामि कपर्द्दिनम्।
त्वमेव विश्वम्बहुधा जातं यज्जायते¶ च यत्॥
नमो रुद्राय सूर्य्याय त्वामहं शरणं गतः।
प्रचेतसे नमस्तुभ्यं नमो मीढुष्टमाय च‖॥

---

* नित्यञ्चेति B. † शुष्कोष्कलायेति B. ओं खद्योताय इति F. ‡ ज्ञानरूपिणे इति B and F. § एतत्पादद्वयं A, E, H पुस्तकेषु नास्ति। ¶ सदसत्सूयते इति B. ‖ ते इति B.

नमो नमस्ते रुद्राय त्वामहं शरणङ्गतः।
हिरण्यबाहवे तुभ्यं हिरण्यपतये नमः॥
अम्बिकापतये तुभ्यमुमायाः पतये नमः *
नमोऽस्तु नीलग्रीवाय नमस्तुभ्यं पिनाकिने॥
विलोहिताय भर्गाय सहस्राक्षाय ते नमः।
तमोऽपहाय ते† नित्यमादित्याय नमोऽस्तु ते॥
नमस्ते वज्र‡हस्ताय त्र्यम्बकाय नमो नमः।
प्रपद्ये त्वां विरूपाक्षं महान्तं§ परमेश्वरम्॥
हिरण्मये गृहे गुप्तमात्मानं सर्व्वदेहिनाम्।
नमस्यामि परं ज्योतिर्ब्रह्माणन्त्वां परामृतम्¶॥
विश्वं पशुपतिं भीमं नरनारीशरीरिणम्।
नमः सूर्य्याय रुद्राय भास्वते परमेष्ठिने॥
उग्राय सर्व्वतक्षाय‖ त्वां प्रपद्ये सदैव हि।
एतद्वै सूर्य्यहृदयं जप्ता स्तवमनुत्तमम्॥
प्रातःकालेऽथ मध्याह्ने नमस्कुर्य्याद्दिवाकरम्।
इदं पुत्राय शिष्याय धार्म्मिकाय द्विजातये॥
प्रदेयं सूर्य्यहृदयं ब्रह्मणा तु प्रदर्शितम्** ।
सर्व्वपापप्रशमनं वेदसारसमुद्भवम्।

---

* एतत्पादद्वयं B पुस्तके नास्ति। † नम उमापतये इति B. ‡ बहु इति B. § दहन्तमिति B. ¶ परां गतिमिति B. ‖ सर्व्वभक्षाय इति B and F. ** ब्रह्मणस्तु प्रसादतः इति B.

ब्राह्मणानां हितं पुण्यमृषिसङ्घैः*निषेवितम् ॥†

अथागम्य गृहं विप्रः समाचम्य यथाविधि ।
प्रज्वाल्य वह्निं विधिवज्जुहुयाज्जातवेदसम् ॥

ऋत्विक् पुत्रोऽथ पत्नी वा शिष्यो वापि सहोदरः ।
प्राप्यानुज्ञां विशेषेण ह्यध्वर्युर्वा यथाविधि ।
पवित्रपाणिः पूतात्मा शुक्लाम्बरधरः शुचिः‡ ।
अनन्यमनसा नित्यं§ जुहुयात्संयतेन्द्रियः ॥

विना दर्भेण यत्कर्म्म विना सूत्रेण वा¶ पुनः ।
राक्षसं तद्भवेत्सर्व्वन्नामुत्रेह फलप्रदम् ॥

दैवतानि नमस्कुर्य्यादुपहारान्निवेदयेत्‖ ।
दद्यात्पुष्पादिकन्तेषां वृद्धांश्चैवाभिवादयेत् ॥

गुरुञ्चैवाप्युपासीत हितञ्चास्य समाचरेत् ।
वेदाभ्यासन्ततः कुर्य्यात्प्रयत्नाच्छक्तितो द्विजाः** ॥

जपेदध्यापयेच्छिष्यान्धारयेद्वै†† विचारयेत् ।
अवेक्षेताथ‡‡ शास्त्रेण धर्म्मादीनि द्विजोत्तमाः ॥

वैदिकांश्चैव निगमान्वेदाङ्गानि च सर्व्वशः§§ ।
उपेयादीश्वरं वाथ¶¶ योगक्षेमप्रसिद्धये ॥

---

* सङ्घैरिति F. † एतत्पादचतुष्टयं A पुस्तके न दृश्यते । ‡ शुक्लाम्बरधरोत्तर इति E and F. § अनन्यमनसो वह्निमिति B. ¶ मन्त्रेण यदीति B. ‖ देवसारान्निवेदयेदिति B. ** द्विजः इति B. †† श्रावयेच्चेति B. ‡‡ अवेक्षेत चेति B. अवेक्ष्य तत्र शास्त्राणि इति F. §§ विशेषतः इति B and E. ¶¶ उपेयादीश्वरञ्चाथेति B and H.

साधयेद्विविधानर्थान् कुटुम्बार्थे द्विजोत्तमः* ।
ततो मध्याह्नसमये स्नानार्थं मृदमाहरेत् ॥
पुष्पाक्षतान् कुशतिलान् गोशकृच्छुद्धमेव वा† ।
नदीषु देवखातेषु तड़ागेषु सरःसु च ।
स्नानं समाचरेन्नित्यं गर्त्तप्रस्रवणेषु च ॥
परकीयनिपानेषु न स्नायाद्वै कदाचन ।
पञ्चपिण्डान्समुद्धृत्य स्नायाद्वासम्भवे पुनः ॥
मृदैकया शिरः चाल्यं द्वाभ्यां नाभेस्तथोपरि ।
अधस्तु‡ तिसृभिः कायः§ पादौ षड्भिस्तथैव च ॥
मृत्तिका च समुद्दिष्टा सार्द्रा¶मलकमात्रिका ।
गोमयस्य प्रमाणन्तु‖ तेनाङ्गं लेपयेत्पुनः** ॥
लेपयित्वा तीरसंस्थं†† तल्लिङ्गैरेव मन्त्रतः‡‡ ।
प्रक्षाल्याचम्य विधिवत्ततः स्नायात्समाहितः ॥
अभिमन्त्र्य जलं मन्त्रैस्तल्लिङ्गैर्वारुणैः शुभैः ।
भावपूतस्तदव्यक्तं धारयेद्विष्णु§§मव्ययम् ॥
आपो नारायणोद्भूतास्ता¶¶ एवास्यायनं पुनः ।
तस्मान्नारायणन्देवं स्नानकाले स्मरेद्बुधः ॥

---

* ततो द्विजः इति B. † गोमयं शुद्धमेव चेति B, E and F. ‡ अधश्चेति B. § कायमिति B, E and F. ¶ त्वार्द्रा इति B. ‖ प्रमाणन्तदिति B. ** लेपयेत्ततः इति B. †† लेपयित्वा च तीरस्थमिति B and E; तीरस्थः सलिङ्गैः इति F. ‡‡ तल्लिङ्गेनैवेति B. §§ ध्यायन्वै विष्णुमिति B and E. धारयन्निति F. ¶¶ नारायणोद्भूतास्ता इति B, E and F.

प्रेक्ष्य* सोङ्कारमादित्यं त्रिर्निमज्जेज्जलाश्रये† ॥
आचान्तः पुनराचामेत्‡ मन्त्रेणानेन मन्त्रवित् ॥
अन्तश्चरसि भूतेषु गुहायां विश्वतोमुखः ।
त्वं यज्ञस्त्वं वषट्कार आपो ज्योती रसोऽमृतम् ॥
द्रुपदां वा त्रिरभ्यस्येद्व्याहृतिप्रणवान्विताम् ।
सावित्रीं वा जपेद्विद्वांस्तथा चैवाघमर्षणम् ॥
ततः सम्मार्ज्जनं कार्य्यम्§ आपो हिष्ठा मयो भुवः ।
इदमापः प्रवहतो व्याहृतिभिस्तथैव च ॥
तथाभिमन्त्र्य तत्तोयमापो हिष्ठादिभिस्त्रिकैः¶ ।
अन्तर्जलगतो मग्नो जपेत्त्रिरघमर्षणम् ॥
द्रुपदां‖ वाथ सावित्रीं तद्विष्णोः परमम्पदम् ।
आवर्त्तयेच्च** प्रणवं देवं वा संस्मरेद्धरिम् ॥
द्रुपदादिव यो मन्त्रो यजुर्वेदे प्रतिष्ठितः ।
अन्तर्जले त्रिरावर्त्त्य सर्व्वपापैः प्रमुच्यते ॥
अपः पाणौ समादाय जप्त्वा वै मार्ज्जने कृते ।
विन्यस्य मूर्द्ध्नि तत्तोयं मुच्यते सर्व्वपातकैः ॥
यथाश्वमेधः क्रतुराट् सर्व्वपापापनोदनः ।
तथाघमर्षणम्प्रोक्तं†† सर्व्वपापापनोदनम् ॥

---

* प्रोच्येति B. † जलाश्रये इति B. ‡ पुनः पुनस्तथाचामेदिति B and E. § कुर्य्यादिति B and E. ¶ हिष्ठादिमन्त्रकैरिति E and F. ‖ त्रिपथामिति B त्रिपदामिति E. ** आवर्त्तयेद्वा इति B and E. †† अथाघमर्षणं सूक्तमिति B, E and F.

अथोपतिष्ठेदादित्यमूर्द्ध्वं पुष्पाक्षतान्वितम्* ।
प्रक्षिप्यालोकयेद्देवमूर्द्ध्वं यस्तमसः परः† ॥
उदुत्यं चित्रमित्येते तच्चक्षुरिति मन्त्रतः ।
हंसः शुचिषदन्त्येन सावित्र्या सविशेषतः‡ ॥
अन्यैश्च वैदिकैर्मन्त्रैः सौरैः पापप्रणाशनैः ।
सावित्रीं वै जपेत्पश्चाज्जपयज्ञः स वै स्मृतः ॥
विविधानि पवित्राणि§ गुह्यविद्यास्तथैव च ।
शतरुद्रीयं शिरसं सौरान्मन्त्रांश्च¶ सर्व्वतः ॥
प्राक्तेषु‖ समासीनः कुशेषु प्राङ्मुखः शुचिः ।
तिष्ठंश्च वीक्षमाणोऽर्कं** जप्यं कुर्य्यात्समाहितः ॥
स्फाटिकेन्द्राक्षरुद्राक्षैः पुत्रजीवसमुद्भवैः ।
कर्त्तव्या त्वक्षमाला स्यादुत्तरादुत्तमा स्मृता†† ॥
जपकाले न भाषेत व्यङ्गा न‡‡ प्रक्षयेद्बुधः ।
न कम्पयेच्छिरो ग्रीवां दन्तान्नैव प्रकाशयेत् ॥
गुह्यका राक्षसाः सिद्धा हरन्ति प्रसभं यतः ।
एकान्तेषु§§ शुचौ देशे तस्माज्जप्यं समाचरेत् ॥

---

* पुष्पाक्षताञ्जलिमिति B. पुष्पान्वितं जलमिति E. † उद्वयं तमसस्परि इति A, E and F. ‡ च विशेषत इति B, E and F. § च चित्राणीति B. ¶ शतरुद्रीयमाथर्व्वशिरः सौरांश्चेति B, E and F. ‖ प्राक्कूलेषु इति B, E, F and G. ** तिष्ठंश्चोद्वीक्षमाणोऽर्कमिति B and E. †† उत्कृष्टोत्तरोत्तरा इति A. ‡‡ नान्यानीति B, E and F. §§ सुशुभे इति E.

चण्डालाशौचिपतितान्* दृष्ट्वा चैव पुनर्ज्जपेत् ।
तैरेव भाषणं कृत्वा स्नात्वा चैव पुनर्ज्जपेत्† ॥
आचम्य प्रयतो नित्यं जपेदशुचिदर्शने ।
सौरान्मन्त्रान् शक्तितो वै पावमानीस्तु कामतः ॥
यदि स्यात् क्लिन्न‡वासा वै वारिमध्यं गतोऽपि वा ।
अन्यथा तु शुचौ भूम्यां दर्भेषु सुसमाहितः ॥
प्रदक्षिणं समावृत्य नमस्कृत्य ततः क्षितौ ।
आचम्य च यथाशास्त्रं शक्त्या§ स्वाध्यायमाचरेत् ॥
ततः सन्तर्पयेद्देवानृषीन् पितृगणांस्तथा¶ ।
आदावोङ्कारमुच्चार्य्य नामान्ते‖ तर्पयामि वः** ॥
देवान् ब्रह्मऋषींश्चैव तर्पयेदक्षतोदकैः ।
तिलोदकैः पितॄन् भक्त्या स्वसूत्रोक्त††विधानतः । ‡‡
देवर्षींस्तर्पयेद्धीमानुदकाञ्जलिभिः पितॄन् ॥
यज्ञोपवीती देवानां निवीती ऋषितर्पणे ।
प्राचीनावीती पैत्रेण§§ स्वेन तीर्थेन भावितः ॥
निष्पीड्य स्नानवस्त्रन्तु समाचम्य च वाग्यतः¶¶ ।
स्वैर्मन्त्रैरर्च्चयेद्देवान् पुष्पैः पत्रैरथाम्बुभिः ॥

---

* चाण्डालाशौचपतितानिति B and F. † जपेत्पुनरिति B and E. ‡ खिन्नेति B. § भक्त्या इति B. ¶ पितृगणान् क्रमादिति B. ‖ नमोऽन्ते इति B. नमोऽन्ते तर्पयामि च इति E and F. ** चेति B. †† स्वगृह्योक्त इति B. ‡‡ अन्वारब्धेन सव्येन पाणिना दक्षिणेन तु इत्यधिकः पाठः E and F. §§ पित्रेत्र तु इति B, E and F. ¶¶ एतत्पादद्वयं B पुस्तके नास्ति ।

ब्रह्माणं शङ्करं सूर्य्यं तथैव मधुसूदनम्।
अन्यांश्चाभिमतान्देवान् भक्त्याचारो नरोत्तमः* ॥
प्रदद्याद्वाथ पुष्पाणि सूक्तेन पौरुषेण† तु।
आपो वा देवताः सर्व्वास्तेन सम्यक् समर्च्चिताः ॥
ध्यात्वा प्रणवपूर्व्वं वै दैवतानि समाहितः।
नमस्कारेण पुष्पाणि विन्यसेद्वै पृथक् पृथक् ॥
विष्णोराराधनात्पुण्यं‡ विद्यते कर्म्म वैदिकम्।
तस्मादनादिमध्यान्तं नित्यमाराधयेद्धरिम् ॥
तद्विष्णोरिति मन्त्रेण सूक्तेन सुसमाहितः§।
न ताभ्यां¶ सदृशो मन्त्रो वेदेषूक्तश्चतुर्ष्वपि‖।
तदात्मा तन्मनाः शान्तस्तद्विष्णोरिति मन्त्रतः ॥
अथवा देवमीशानं भगवन्तं सनातनम्।
आराधयेन्महादेवं भावपूतो महेश्वरम् ॥
मन्त्रेण रुद्रगायत्र्या प्रणवेनाथवा पुनः।
ईशानेनाथवा रुद्रैस्त्र्यम्बकेन** समाहितः ॥
पुष्पैः पत्रैरथाद्भिर्वा चन्दनाद्यैर्महेश्वरम्।

* अन्यांश्चापि महादेवान् भक्त्या चाक्रोधनो नर इति B, E and F. † सूक्तेन पौरुषेण—पुरुषसूक्तेन "सहस्रशीर्षा पुरुष" इत्यादिमन्त्रेण। ‡ न विष्ण्वाराधनादिति E and F. § पुरुषेण तु इति B, E and F. ¶ नैताभ्यामिति B, E and F. ‖ अतः परं निवेदयेच्च स्वात्मानं विष्णवेऽमलतेजसे इति B, E, F पुस्तकेष्वधिकः पाठो दृश्यते। ** रुद्रे त्र्यम्बकेनेति A.

उक्त्वा* नमः शिवायेति मन्त्रेणानेन वा जपेत्† ॥
नमस्कुर्य्यान्महादेवं तं मृत्युञ्जयमीश्वरम्‡ ।
निवेदयीत स्वात्मानं यो ब्राह्मणमितीश्वरम् ॥
प्रदक्षिणं§ द्विजः कुर्य्यात्पञ्च वर्षाणि वै बुधः¶ ।
ध्यायीत‖ देवमीशानं व्योममध्यगतं शिवम् ॥
अथावलोकयेदर्क** हंसः शुचिषदित्यृचा ।
कुर्व्वन्†† पञ्च महायज्ञान् गृहङ्गत्वा समाहितः ॥
देवयज्ञं पितृयज्ञम्भूतयज्ञन्तथैव च‡‡ ।
मानुषं§§ ब्रह्मयज्ञञ्च पञ्च यज्ञान् प्रचक्षते ॥
यदि स्यात्तर्पणादर्वाक् ब्रह्मयज्ञः कृतो न हि ।
कृत्वा मनुष्ययज्ञं वै ततः स्वाध्यायमाचरेत् ॥
अग्नेः पश्चिमतो देशे भूतयज्ञान्त एव च¶¶ ।
कुशपुञ्जे समासीनः कुशपाणिः समाहितः ॥
शालाग्नौ लौकिके वाथ जले भूम्यामथापि वा ।
वैश्वदेवश्च कर्त्तव्यो‖‖ देवयज्ञः स वै स्मृतः ॥
यदि स्याल्लौकिके पक्षे ततोऽन्नं तत्र हूयते ।
शालाग्नौ तत्पचेदन्नं विधिरेष सनातनः ॥

---

* अथो इति B, E and F. † योजयेदिति B. ‡ ऋतं सत्यमितीश्वरमिति B and E. § प्रदक्षिणः इति A. ¶ जपन्निति B. पञ्च ब्रह्माणि वै जपन्निति E and F. ‖ ध्यायीत ध्यायेत्, आर्षः प्रयोगः । ** अथवालोकयेदिति B. †† कुर्य्यादिति B and F. ‡‡ ऋषियज्ञन्तथैव चेति B. §§ मानुष्यमिति B. ¶¶ वा इति B. ‖‖ वैश्वदेवनिमित्तमिति B.

देवेभ्यश्च हुतादन्नात्* शेषां†द्भूतबलिं हरेत्।
भूतयज्ञः स विज्ञेयो‡ भूतिदः§ सर्व्वदेहिनाम्॥
श्वभ्यश्च श्वपचेभ्यश्च पतितादिभ्यएव च।
दद्याद्भूमौ वहिश्चान्नम्पक्षिभ्यो द्विजसत्तमाः¶॥
सायञ्चान्नस्य|| सिद्धस्य पत्न्यमन्त्रं बलिं हरेत्।
भूतयज्ञस्त्वयन्नित्यं सायम्प्रातर्य्यथाविधि**॥
एकन्तु भोजयेद्विप्रं पितॄनुद्दिश्य सन्ततम्††।
नित्यश्राद्धं तदुद्दिष्टं‡‡ पितृयज्ञो गतिप्रदः॥
उद्धृत्य वा यथाशक्ति किञ्चिदन्नं समाहितः।
वेदतत्त्वार्थविदुषे§§ द्विजायैवोपपादयेत्॥
पूजयेदतिथिन्नित्यं नमस्येदर्च्चयेद्द्विजः¶¶।
मनोवाक्कर्म्मभिः शान्तः स्वागतं स्वगृहङ्गतः||||॥
अन्वारब्धेन सव्येन पाणिना दक्षिणेन तु***।
हन्तकारमथाग्रं वा भिक्षां वा शक्तितो द्विजः।
दद्यादतिथये नित्यम्बुध्येत परमेश्वरम्॥
भिक्षामाहुर्ग्रासमात्रामग्रं तत्स्याच्चतुर्गुणम्†††।

---

* देवेभ्यस्तु हुतान्दत्त्वा इति B. † शेषमिति F. ‡ वै ज्ञेय इति B. § भूतितइति B. ¶ बलिं त्वन्नं पक्षिभ्योऽथ द्विजोत्तमा इति B and E. || सायमन्नस्येति B. ** विधीयते इति B. †† सततमिति B and E. सततमिति F. ‡‡ यदुद्दिष्टमिति B. तदुद्दिष्टमिति E, F and H. §§ विज्ञायेति B. ¶¶ अर्च्चयेद्विभुमिति B. तथा इति F. |||| तत इति B, E and F. *** एतत्पादद्वयं B, E, F पुस्तकेषु नास्ति। ††† तस्माच्चतुर्गुणमिति B and H. तस्याश्चतुर्गुणमिति E and F.

पुष्कलं हन्तकारन्तु तच्चतुर्गुणमिष्यते* ॥
गोदोहकालमात्रं† वै प्रतीक्ष्यो ह्यतिथिः‡ स्वयम् ।
अभ्यागतान्यथाशक्ति पूजयेदतिथींस्सदा§ ॥
भिक्षां वै भिक्षवे दद्याद्विधिवद्ब्रह्मचारिणे ।
दद्यादन्नं यथाशक्ति ह्यर्थिभ्यो लोभवर्ज्जितः ॥
सर्व्वेषामप्यलाभे हि¶ त्वन्नङ्गोभ्यो निवेदयेत् ।
भुञ्जीत बहुभिः‖ सार्द्धं वाग्यतोऽन्नमकुत्सयन् ॥
अकृत्वा तु द्विजः पञ्च महायज्ञान्द्विजोत्तमाः ।
भुञ्जीत चेत्स मूढ़ात्मा तिर्य्यग्योनिं स गच्छति ॥
वेदाभ्यासोऽन्वहं शक्त्या महायज्ञक्रियाक्षमाः ।
नाशयन्त्याशु पापानि देवताभ्यर्च्चनन्तथा ॥
यो मोहादथवाज्ञानादकृत्वा** देवतार्च्चनम् ।
भुङ्क्ते स याति नरकं शूकरं नात्र संशयः†† ॥
तस्मात्सर्व्वप्रयत्नेन कृत्वा कर्म्माणि वै द्विजाः ।
भुञ्जीत स्वजनैः सार्द्धं स याति परमाङ्गतिम् ॥

इति श्रीकूर्म्मपुराणे‡‡ व्यासगीतासु अष्टादशोऽध्यायः ।

---

* मुच्यते इति B and F. † गोदोहमात्रं कालमिति B, E and H. ‡ प्रतीक्ष्योऽप्यतिथिरिति B. § यथेति B and E. तथेति F. ¶ चेति B. ‖ बन्धुभिरिति B, E and F. ** मोहादथ बालत्वादकृत्वा इति B and F. †† शूकरेष्वभिजायते इति B and F. ‡‡ उपविभागे इत्यधिकः पाठः B पुस्तके दृश्यते ।

ऊनविंशोऽध्यायः ।

व्यास उवाच ।

प्राङ्मुखोऽन्नानि भुञ्जीत सूर्य्याभिमुखएव* वा ।
आसीनः स्वासने शुद्धे भूम्यां पादौ निधाय च ॥
आयुष्यं प्राङ्मुखो भुङ्क्ते यशस्यं दक्षिणामुखः ।
श्रियम्प्रत्यङ्मुखो भुङ्क्ते ऋतम्भुङ्क्ते उदङ्मुखः ॥
पञ्चार्द्रो भोजनङ्कुर्य्याद्भूमौ पात्रं निधाय च ।
उपवासेन तत्तुल्यं मनुराह प्रजापतिः ॥
उपलिप्ते शुचौ देशे पादौ प्रक्षाल्य वै करौ ।
आचम्यार्द्राननोऽक्रोधः पञ्चार्द्रो भोजनञ्चरेत् ॥
महाव्याहृतिभिस्त्वन्नं परिधायोदकेन तु ।
अमृतोपस्तरणमसीत्यापोऽशान†क्रियाञ्चरेत् ॥
स्वाहाप्रणवसंयुक्तां प्राणायाद्याहुतिन्ततः ।
अपानाय ततो भुक्त्वा व्यानाय तदनन्तरम् ॥
उदानाय ततः कुर्य्यात्समानायेति पञ्चमीम्‡ ।
विज्ञाय तत्त्वमेतेषां जुहुयादात्मनि द्विजः ॥
शेषमन्नं यथाकामं§ भुञ्जीत व्यञ्जनैर्युतम् ।
ध्यात्वा तन्मनसा देवानात्मानं¶ वै प्रजापतिम् ॥

---

* सूर्य्याभिमुखमेवेति B and H. † आपःपानेति B. ‡ पञ्चममिति A and H. § यथोक्तञ्च इति B. ¶ देवमात्मानमिति B and F.

अमृतापिधानमसीत्युपरिष्टादपः पिवेत् ।
आचान्तः पुनराचामेदयङ्गौरिति मन्त्रतः ॥
द्रुपदां वा त्रिरावर्त्त्य सर्व्वपापप्रणाशनीम् ।
प्राणानाङ्ग्रन्थिरसीत्यालभेदुदरन्ततः* ॥
आचम्याङ्गुष्ठमात्रेण पादाङ्गुष्ठेन† दक्षिणे ।
निस्रावयेद्धस्तजलमूर्द्धहस्तः समाहितः ॥
कृता‡नुमन्त्रणं कुर्य्यात्सन्ध्यायामिति मन्त्रतः ।
अथ मन्त्रेण स्वात्मानं योजयेद्ब्राह्मणेति हि§ ॥
सर्व्वेषामेव योगानामात्मयोगः स्मृतः परः¶ ।
योऽनेन विधिना कुर्य्यात् स कविर्ब्राह्मणः स्वयम्‖ ॥
यज्ञोपवीती भुञ्जीत स्रग्गन्धालङ्कृतः शुचिः ।
सायम्प्रातर्नान्तरा** वै सन्ध्यायान्तु विशेषतः ॥
नाद्यात्सूर्य्यग्रहात्पूर्व्वं प्रतिसायं शशिग्रहात्†† ।
ग्रहकाले न चाश्नीयात्स्नात्वाश्नीयाद्विमुक्तये‡‡ ॥
मुक्ते शशिनि चाश्नीयाद्यदि§§ न स्यान्महानिशा ।
अमुक्तयोरस्तगयोरद्याद्दृष्ट्वा परेऽहनि ॥
नाश्नीयात्प्रेक्षमाणानामप्रदाय च¶¶ दुर्मतिः ।

---

* लभेत हृदयन्तत इति B. † पादाङ्गुष्ठेऽथेति B. ‡ हुता इति B. § अथाचरेण स्वात्मानं योजयेद्ब्रह्मणेति हीति B and E. अथ क्रमेणेति H. ¶ परः स्मृतइति B. ‖ स याति ब्रह्मणः क्षयमिति B and E. ** प्रातर्नान्तरेति B, H and G. †† अह्नि सायं प्रचक्षते इति B. अह्नि सायं शशिग्रहे इति E. ‡‡ स्नात्वाश्नीयात्तु मुक्तये इति B. §§ भुञ्जीत यदीति B. ¶¶ अप्रदायैव इति B.

यज्ञावशिष्टमर्यादा* न क्रुद्धो नान्यमानसः ॥
आत्मार्थं भोजनं यस्य रत्यर्थं यस्य मैथुनम् ।
वृत्त्यर्थं यस्य चाधीतं निष्फलं तस्य जीवितम् ॥
यद्भुङ्क्ते वेष्टितशिराः यच्च भुङ्क्ते विदिङ्मुखः† ।
सोपानत्कश्च यो भुङ्क्ते सर्व्वं विद्यात्तदासुरम् ॥
नार्द्धरात्रे न मध्याह्ने नाजीर्णे नार्द्रवस्त्रधृक् ।
न च भिन्नासनगतो न यानसंस्थितोऽपि वा‡ ॥
न भिन्नभाजने चैव न भूम्यां न च पाणिषु ।
नोच्छिष्टो घृतमादद्यात्§ न मूर्द्धानं स्पृशेदपि ॥
न ब्रह्म कीर्त्तयेच्चापि¶ न निःशेषं न भार्य्यया ।
नान्धकारे न सन्ध्यायां‖ न च देवालयादिषु ॥
नैकवस्त्रस्तु भुञ्जीत न यानशयनस्थितः** ।
न पादुकानिर्गतोऽथ†† न हसन्विलपन्नपि ॥
भुक्त्वा वै‡‡ सुखमास्थाय तदन्नम्परिणामयेत् ।
इतिहासपुराणाभ्यां वेदार्थानुपबृंहयेत्§§ ॥
ततः सन्ध्यामुपासीत पूर्व्वोक्तविधिना शुचिः¶¶ ।

---

* न यज्ञशिष्टादन्यद्वा इति B and E. † उदङ्मुखः इति B and E. ‡ न शयानः स्थितोऽपि वेति B. न शय्यान्तःस्थितोऽपि वा इति E. § आदद्यादिति आर्षः प्रयोगः, आददीत इति साधु। ¶ कीर्त्तयेद्वापीति B. ‖ न चाकाशे इति B and E. ** न शयानः स्थितोऽपि वेति B. †† न पादुकानुगतो वा इति B. ‡‡ भुक्त्वैवमिति B. §§ तदर्थोऽनुपबृंहयेदिति H. ¶¶ द्विज इति B and E.

आसीनश्च* जपेद्देवीं गायत्रीं पश्चिमाम्प्रति ॥
न तिष्ठति तु यः पूर्व्वांनास्ते† सन्ध्यान्तु पश्चिमाम् ।
स शूद्रेण समो लोके सर्व्वकर्म्म‡विवर्ज्जितः ॥
हुत्वाग्निं विधिवन्मन्त्रैर्भुक्त्वा यज्ञावशिष्टकम् ।
सभृत्य§बान्धवजनः स्वपेच्छुष्कपदो निशि ॥
नोत्तराभिमुखः स्वप्यात्पश्चिमाभिमुखो न च ।
न चाकाशे न नग्नो वा नाशुचिर्नासने क्वचित् ॥
न शीर्णायान्तु खट्वायां शून्यागारे न चैव हि ।
नानुवंशे¶ न पालाशे शयने वा कदाचन ॥
इत्येतदखिलेनोक्तमहन्यहनि वै मया ।
ब्राह्मणानाङ्कृत्यजात‖मपवर्गफलप्रदम् ॥
नास्तिक्यादथवालस्याद्ब्राह्मणो न करोति यः ।
स याति नरकान्घोरान् काकयोनौ च जायते ॥
नान्यो विमुक्तये पन्था मुक्त्वाश्रमविधिं स्वकम् ।
तस्मात्कर्म्माणि कुर्व्वीत तुष्टये परमेष्ठिनः ॥

इति श्रीकूर्म्मपुराणे उपविभागे व्यासगीतासु ऊनविंशोऽध्यायः ।

—

* आसीनस्तु इति B, E and F. † पूर्व्वां नापीति B. ‡ धर्म्मेति B. सर्व्व-कर्म्मबहिष्कृत इति F. § सहृद्येति B. ¶ नापि वीणे इति B. ‖ कृत्यतममिति B.

विंशोऽध्यायः ।

व्यास उवाच ।

अथ श्राद्धममावास्यां प्राप्य कार्य्यं द्विजोत्तमैः ।
पिण्डान्वाहार्य्यकम्भक्त्या भुक्तिमुक्तिफलप्रदम् ॥
पिण्डान्वाहार्य्यकं श्राद्धं क्षीणे राजनि* शस्यते ।
अपराह्णे द्विजातीनां प्रशस्तेनामिषेण च ॥
प्रतिपत्प्रभृति ह्यन्यास्तिथयः कृष्णपक्षके ।
चतुर्द्दशीं वर्ज्जयित्वा प्रशस्ता ह्युपरोधतः† ॥
अमावास्याष्टकास्तिस्रः पौषमासादिषु त्रिषु ।
तिस्रस्तास्त्वष्टकाः‡ पुण्या माघी पञ्चदशी तथा ॥
त्रयोदशी मघायुक्ता वर्षासु च विशेषतः ।
शस्यपाकः श्राद्धकालाः नित्याः§ प्रोक्ताः दिने दिने ॥
नैमित्तिकन्तु¶ कर्त्तव्यं ग्रहणे चन्द्रसूर्य्ययोः ।
बान्धवानां विस्तरेण‖ नारकी स्यादतोऽन्यथा ॥
काम्यानि** चैव श्राद्धानि शस्यन्ते ग्रहणादिषु ।
अयने विषुवे चैव व्यतीपाते त्वनन्तकम्†† ॥
संक्रान्त्यामक्षयं‡‡ श्राद्धं तथा जन्मदिनेष्वपि ।

---

* क्षीणे राजनि क्षययुक्ते चन्द्रे कृष्णपक्षे इत्यर्थः । † ह्यपरा यतः इति B. ह्युत्तरोत्तरे इति F. ‡ तिस्रश्चान्वाहार्य्यकमिति B. § नित्यमिति B. ¶ नैमित्तिकं हि इति B. ‖ ब्राह्मणानाञ्च मरणे इति B. बान्धवानाञ्च मरणे इति F. ** शस्यानीति B. †† व्यतीपातेऽप्यनन्तकमिति B. ‡‡ संक्रान्त्यामयने इति B.

नक्षत्रेषु च सर्व्वेषु कार्य्यङ्काम्यं* विशेषतः॥
स्वर्गञ्च लभते कृत्वा कृत्तिकासु द्विजोत्तमः।
अपत्यमथ रोहिण्यां सौम्ये तु ब्रह्मवर्च्चसम्॥
रौद्राणां कर्म्मणां सिद्धिमार्द्रायां शौर्य्यमेव च†।
पुनर्व्वसौ तथा भूमिं श्रियं पुष्ये तथैव च॥
सर्व्वान्कामांस्तथा सार्प्ये‡ पित्र्ये सौभाग्यमेव च।
अर्य्यम्णे तु धनं विन्द्येत्§ फाल्गुन्यां पापनाशनम्॥
ज्ञातिश्रैष्ठ्यं तथा हस्ते चित्रायाञ्च बहून् सुतान्।
वाणिज्यसिद्धिं स्वातौ तु विशाखासु सुवर्णकम्॥
मैत्रे बहूनि मित्राणि राज्यं शाक्रे तथैव च।
मूले कृषिं लभेज्ज्ञानं सिद्धिमाप्ये समुद्रतः॥
सर्व्वान् कामान्वैश्वदेवे श्रैष्ठ्यन्तु श्रवणे पुनः।
धनिष्ठायां तथा कामानम्बुपे¶ च परम्बलम्॥
अजैकपादे कुप्यं स्यादाहिर्बुध्ने गृहं शुभम्।
रेवत्याम्बहवो गावो ह्यश्विन्यान्तुरगांस्तथा।
याम्ये तु जीवितन्तु‖ स्याद्यः श्राद्धं सम्प्रयच्छति**॥
आदित्यवारेऽप्यारोग्यं†† चन्द्रे सौभाग्यमेव च।
कुजे सर्व्वञ्च विजयं सर्व्वान् कामान् बुधस्य तु॥

---

* काले इति B. † रौद्राणां सिद्धिमार्द्रायां कर्म्मणां सौख्यमेव चेति B. रौहिण्यां कर्म्मणां सिद्धिमिति F. ‡ सार्पे इति B. § विद्यादिति B and F. ¶ वारुणे इति B. शाविष्टायां तथा काम्यं वारुणे इति F. ‖ जीवनं तदिति B. ** यदि श्राद्धं प्रयच्छति इति B. †† त्वारोग्यमिति B, F and H.

विद्यामभीष्टान्तु गुरौ* धनं वै भार्गवे पुनः ।
शनैश्चरे लभेदायुः प्रतिपत्सु सुतान् शुभान् ॥
कन्यका† वै द्वितीयायां तृतीयायान्तु वेदिनः‡ ।
पशून् क्षुद्रांश्चतुर्थ्यां वै§ पञ्चम्यां शोभनान् सुतान् ॥
षष्ठ्यां द्युतं¶ कृषिञ्चापि सप्तम्याञ्च धनं नरः‖ ।
अष्टम्यामपि वाणिज्यं लभते श्राद्धदः सदा ॥
स्यान्नवम्यामेकखुरं दशम्यां द्विखुरं बहु ।
एकादश्यान्तथा रूप्यं ब्रह्मवर्च्चस्विनः सुतान् ॥
द्वादश्यां जातरूपञ्च रजतं कुप्यमेव च ।
ज्ञातिश्रैष्ठ्यं त्रयोदश्यां चतुर्दश्यान्तु कुप्रजाः ।
पञ्चदश्यां सर्व्वकामान् प्राप्नोति** श्राद्धदः सदा ॥
तस्माच्छ्राद्धं न कर्त्तव्यं चतुर्द्दश्यां द्विजातिभिः ।
शस्त्रेण तु हतानान्तु श्राद्धं†† तत्र प्रकल्पयेत् ॥
द्रव्यब्राह्मणसम्पत्तौ न कालनियमः कृतः ।
तस्माद्भोगापवर्गार्थं श्राद्धं कुर्युर्द्विजातयः ॥
कर्म्मारम्भेषु सर्व्वेषु कुर्य्यादभ्युदये‡‡ पुनः ।
पुत्रजन्मादिषु श्राद्धं पार्व्वणं पर्व्वसु स्मृतम् ॥
अहन्यहनि नित्यं स्यात्काम्यं नैमित्तिकं पुनः ।

* विद्यामभीष्टां जीवे तु इति B and F. † कन्यकामिति B and F. ‡ विन्दतीति B. नन्दित इति F. § तु इति B. ¶ द्युतिमिति B. दूतमिति F. ‖ सप्तम्यां लभते नरः इति B and F. ** कामानाप्नोतीति B, F and H. †† हतानां वै तत्र श्राद्धमिति B. ‡‡ कुर्य्यादाभ्युदयमिति B and F.

एकोद्दिष्टादि विज्ञेयं द्विधा श्राद्धन्तु* पार्व्वणम् ॥
एतत्पञ्चविधं श्राद्धं मनुना परिकीर्त्तितम्।
यात्रायां षष्ठमाख्यातं तत्प्रयत्नेन पालयेत् ॥
शुद्धये सप्तमं श्राद्धं ब्रह्मणा परिभाषितम्।
दैविकञ्चाष्टमं श्राद्धं† यत्कृत्वा मुच्यते भयात् ॥
सन्ध्या रात्रौ न कर्त्तव्यं राहोरन्यत्र दर्शनात्।
देशानान्तु विशेषेण भवेत्पुण्यमनन्तकम् ॥
गङ्गायामक्षयं श्राद्धं प्रयागेऽमरकण्टके‡।
गायन्ति पितरो गाथां नर्त्तयन्ति§ मनीषिणः ॥
एष्टव्या बहवः पुत्राः शीलवन्तो गुणान्विताः।
तेषान्तु समवेतानां यद्येकोऽपि गयां व्रजेत् ॥
गयां प्राप्यानुषङ्गेण यदि श्राद्धं समाचरेत्¶।
तारिताः पितरस्तेन स याति परमाङ्गतिम् ॥
वाराहपर्व्वते चैव गयायां वै विशेषतः।
वाराणस्यां विशेषेण यत्र देवः स्वयं हरः ॥
गङ्गाद्वारे प्रभासे तु बिल्वके नीलपर्व्वते।
कुरुक्षेत्रे च कुब्जाम्रे‖ भृगुतुङ्गे महालये ॥
केदारे फल्गुतीर्थे** च नैमिषारण्य†† एव च।

* वृद्धिश्राद्धन्तु इति B and F. † इतः परं पादषट्कं B पुस्तके नास्ति। ‡ मरकण्टके इति H. § गाथाः कीर्त्तयन्ति इति B, E and F. ¶ यः श्राद्धं समुपाचरेदिति B. ‖ कुब्जाङ्के इति A. कुब्जाह्वे इति H. कुब्जाम्रे इति B, E and F. ** फल्गुनीतीर्थे इति B, E and F. †† नैमिषारण्ययोरपि इति H.

सरस्वत्यां विशेषेण पुष्करे तु विशेषतः॥
नर्म्मदायां कुशावर्त्ते श्रीशैले कर्णभद्रके*।
वेत्रवत्यां विशाखायां† गोदावर्य्यां विशेषतः॥
एवमादिषु चान्येषु‡ तीर्थेषु पुलिनेषु च।
नदीनाञ्चैव तीरेषु तुष्यन्ति पितरः सदा॥
व्रीहिभिश्च यवैर्माषैरद्भिर्मूलफलेन वा।
श्यामाकैश्च यवैः काशैः§नीवारैश्च प्रियङ्गुभिः।
गोधूमैश्च तिलैर्मुद्गैर्मासं प्रीणयते पितॄन्॥
आम्रान् पाने रतानिक्षून् मृद्वीकांश्च सदाड़िमान्¶।
विदार्थ्यांश्च कुरण्डांश्च‖ श्राद्धकाले प्रदापयेत्॥
लाजा मधुयुता** दद्यात्सक्तून् शर्करया सह।
दद्याच्छ्राद्धे प्रयत्नेन†† शृङ्गाटककशेरुकान्‡‡॥
द्वौ मासौ मत्स्यमांसेन त्रीन्मासान् हरिणेन§§ तु।
औरभ्रेणाथ चतुरः शाकुनेनेह पञ्च तु।
षण्मासांश्छागमांसेन पार्षतेनेह¶¶ सप्त वै॥

---

* भद्रकर्णके इति B and E. नन्दकार्णवे इति F. † विपाशायामिति B. जैत्रवत्यां विशेषेण इति E. ‡ एवमादिष्वथान्येषु इति B. § शाकैरिति B and E. शुभैः शाकैरिति F. ¶ अम्रव्याने च तानिच्छान् मृत्तिकानिति A and H. ‖ विदारीश्च भरण्डांश्च इति B. विदार्थ्यांश्च मकैरण्डांश्च इति H. ** लाजान्मधुयुतानिति B. †† दद्याच्छ्राद्धे च यत्नेनेति B. ‡‡ शृङ्गानविशके पुमानिति A and H. शृङ्गाटविषकेवुकानिति F. §§ हारितेनेति B. हारिणेन तु इति F and H. ¶¶ पार्षतेनाथ इति B.

अष्टावेणस्य मांसेन रौरवेण नवैव तु* ।
दश मासांस्तु तृप्यन्ति† वराहमहिषामिषैः ॥
शशकूर्म्मयोर्मांसेन‡ मासानेकादशैव तु ।
संवत्सरन्तु गव्येन पयसा पायसेन तु§ ।
वार्ध्रीणसस्य मांसेन तृप्तिर्द्वादशवार्षिकी ॥
कालशाकं महाशल्कः खड्गलोहामिषं¶ मधु ।
आनन्त्यायैव कल्पन्ते मुन्यन्नानि च सर्व्वशः ॥
क्रीत्वा लब्ध्वा स्वयं वाथ मृतानाहृत्य वै द्विजः ।
दद्याच्छ्राद्धे प्रयत्नेन तदस्याक्षयमुच्यते ॥
पिप्पली रुचकञ्चैव‖ तथा चैव मसूरकम् ।
कुष्माण्डालावुवार्त्ताकभूतृणं सरसं** तथा ॥
कुसुम्भं पिण्डमूलं वै तन्दुलीयकमेव च ।
राजमाषांस्तथा क्षीरं माहिषाजं†† विवर्ज्जयेत् ॥
आढ़क्यः‡‡ कोविदारांश्च पालक्या§§ मरिचांस्तथा ।
वर्जयेत्सतत यत्नेन श्राद्धकाले द्विजोत्तमः¶¶ ॥

इति श्रीकूर्म्मपुराणे उपविभागे श्राद्धकल्पे विंशोऽध्यायः ।

---

* च इति B. † मासास्तु तृप्यन्ते इति B. ‡ शशकूर्म्मयोस्तु मांसेनेति B. § वा इति B. ¶ महाशल्कं खड्गं लोहामिषमिति B. ‖ पिप्पलीं क्रमुकञ्चैव इति B. क्षतकञ्चैव इति F. ** सरसमिति B and H. मसुरं चणकं तथा इति F. †† माहिषञ्च इति B and F. ‡‡ कोद्रवानिति B., कोद्रवः कोविदारश्च जलङ्गं मरिचं तथेति F. §§ पालङ्गामिति B. ¶¶ द्विजोत्तमाः इति B.

एकविंशोऽध्यायः ।

व्यास उवाच ।

स्नात्वा यथोक्तं सन्तर्प्य पितॄंश्चन्द्रक्षये द्विजः ।
पिण्डान्वाहार्यकं श्राद्धं कुर्य्यात्सौम्यमनाः शुचिः ॥
पूर्व्वमेव समीक्षेत* ब्राह्मणं वेदपारगम् ।
तीर्थं तद्धव्यकव्यानां प्रदानानाञ्च स स्मृतः† ॥
ये सोमपा विरजसो धर्म्मज्ञाः शान्तचेतसः ।
व्रतिनो नियमस्थाश्च ऋतुकालाभिगामिनः ॥
पञ्चाग्निरप्यधीयानो यजुर्वेदविदेव च ।
बह्वृचश्च त्रिसौपर्णस्त्रिमधुर्वा च योऽभवत् ॥
त्रिणाचिकेतच्छन्दोगो ज्येष्ठसामग एव च ।
अथर्वशिरसोऽध्येता रुद्राध्यायी विशेषतः ॥
अग्निहोत्रपरो विद्वान्न्यायविच्च षड़ङ्गवित् ।
मन्त्रब्राह्मणविच्चैव यश्च‡ स्याद्धर्म्मपाठकः ॥
ऋषिव्रती हृषीकश्च शान्तचेता जितेन्द्रियः§ ।
ब्रह्मदेयानुसन्तानो गर्भशुद्धः सहस्रदः ॥
चान्द्रायणव्रतचरः सत्यवादी पुराणवित् ।
गुरुदेवाग्निपूजासु प्रसक्तो ज्ञानतत्परः ॥

---

* परीक्षेत इति B. † प्रदाने चातिथिः स्मृतः इति B. अतः परं श्लोकत्रयं B, F पुस्तकयोः नास्ति । ‡ यस्तु इति B. § तथा द्वादशवार्षिकः इति B and F.

विमुक्तः सर्व्वतो धीरो ब्रह्मभूतो द्विजोत्तमः ।
महादेवार्च्चनरतो वैष्णवः पंक्तिपावनः ॥*
अहिंसानिरतो नित्यमप्रतिग्रहणस्तथा ।
सत्त्री† च दाननिरतो विज्ञेयः पंक्तिपावनः ॥‡
मातापित्रोर्हिते युक्तः प्रातःस्नायी तथा द्विजः ।
अध्यात्मविन्मुनिर्दान्तो विज्ञेयः पंक्तिपावनः ॥
ज्ञाननिष्ठो महायोगी वेदान्तार्थविचिन्तकः ।
श्रद्धालुः§ श्राद्धनिरतो ब्राह्मणः पंक्तिपावनः ॥
वेदविद्यारतः¶ स्नातो ब्रह्मचर्य्यपरः सदा ।
अथर्व्वणो मुमुक्षुश्च ब्राह्मणः पंक्तिपावनः‖ ॥
असमानप्रवरको ह्यसगोत्रस्तथैव च ।
ससम्बन्धी** च विज्ञेया ब्राह्मणाः पंक्तिपावनाः ॥
भोजयेद्योगिनं शान्तं†† तत्त्वज्ञानरतं यतः‡‡ ।
अभावे§§ नैष्ठिकं दान्तमुपकुर्व्वाणकन्तथा ॥
तदलाभे गृहस्थन्तु मुमुक्षुं सङ्गवर्ज्जितम् ।
सर्व्वालाभे साधकं वा गृहस्थमपि भोजयेत् ॥

---

* अतः परं श्लोकचतुष्टयं A पुस्तके नास्ति । † सत्रण इति F. ‡ युवानः श्रोत्रियाः स्वस्थाः महायज्ञपरायणाः । सावित्रीजापनिरतब्राह्मणाः पंक्तिपावनाः ॥ कुलानां श्रुतवन्तश्च शीलवन्तस्तपस्विनः । अग्निचित् स्नातको विप्रो विज्ञेयाः पंक्तिपावनाः ॥ इत्यधिकः पाठः F पुस्तके अस्ति । § श्राद्धार्थम् इति F. ¶ व्रत इति F. ‖ इतः पूर्व्वं श्लोकचतुष्टयं H पुस्तके नास्ति । ** असम्बन्धीति B and F. †† पूर्व्वमिति B and F. ‡‡ यतिमिति B. §§ अलाभे इति B and F.

प्रकृतेर्गुणतत्त्वज्ञो यस्याश्नाति यतिर्हविः ।
फलं वेदान्तवित्तस्य* सहस्रादतिरिच्यते ॥
तस्माद्यत्नेन योगीन्द्रमीश्वरज्ञानतत्परम् ।
भोजयेद्धव्यकव्येषु अलाभा†दितरान्द्विजान् ॥
एष वै प्रथमः कल्पः प्रदाने हव्यकव्ययोः ।
अनुकल्पस्त्वयं ज्ञेयः सदा सद्भिरनुष्ठितः ॥
मातामहं मातुलञ्च स्वस्रीयं श्वशुरं गुरुम् ।
दौहित्रं विट्पतिम्बन्धुमृत्विग्याज्यौ च भोजयेत् ॥
न श्राद्धे भोजयेन्मित्रं धनैः‡ कार्य्योऽस्य सङ्ग्रहः ।
पैशाची दक्षिणाश्रा हि नेहामुत्र§ फलप्रदा ॥
कामं श्राद्धेऽर्चयेन्मित्रं नाभिरूपमपि त्वरिम् ।
द्विषता हि हविर्भुक्तं भवति प्रेत्य निष्फलम् ॥
ब्राह्मणो ह्यनधीयानस्तृणाग्निरिव शाम्यति ।
तस्मै हव्यं न दातव्यं न हि भस्मनि हूयते ॥
यथोषरे¶ वीजमुप्त्वा न वप्ता लभते फलम् ।
तथाऽनृचे हविर्दत्त्वा न दानाल्लभते‖ फलम् ॥
यावतो ग्रसते पिण्डान्हव्यकव्येष्वमन्त्रवित् ।
तावतो ग्रसते प्रेत्य दीप्तान् स्थूलांस्त्वयोगुडान्** ॥

---

* वेदविदां तस्य इति B and F. † त्वलाभादिति B. ‡ अन्नैरिति B.
§ नैवामुत्रेति B. ¶ यथा विले इति B. ‖ दाता लभते इति B and F.
** दीप्तानलानयोगुडानिति B.

अपि विद्याकुलैर्युक्ता हीनवृत्ता नराधमाः ।
यत्रैते भुञ्जते हव्यं तद्भवेदासुरन्द्विजाः ॥
यस्य वेदश्च वेदी च विच्छिद्येते त्रिपूरुषम् ।
स वै दुर्ब्राह्मणो नार्हः श्राद्धादिषु कदाचन ॥
शूद्रप्रेष्यो भृतो राज्ञो* वृषलानाञ्च याजकः† ।
वधबन्धोपजीवी च षड़ेते ब्रह्मबन्धवः ॥
दत्त्वानुयोगो वृत्त्यर्थं‡ पतितान्मनुरब्रवीत् ।
वेदविक्रयिणो ह्येते श्राद्धादिषु विगर्हिताः ॥
सुत§विक्रयिणो ये तु परपूर्व्वासमुद्भवाः ।
असामान्यान्¶ यजन्ते ये पतितास्ते प्रकीर्त्तिताः ॥
असंस्कृताध्यापका ये भृत्यर्थेऽध्यापयन्ति ये ।
अधीयते तथा वेदान् पतितास्ते प्रकीर्त्तिताः ॥
वृद्धश्रावकनिर्ग्रन्थाः पञ्चरात्रविदो जनाः ।
कापालिकाः पाशुपताः पाषण्डा ये च तद्विधाः ॥
यस्याश्नन्ति हवींष्येते दुरात्मानस्तु तामसाः ।
न तस्य तद्भवेच्छ्राद्धं प्रेत्य चेह फलप्रदम् ॥
अनाश्रमी यो द्विजः स्यादाश्रमी वा निरर्थकः‖ ।
मिथ्याश्रमी च ते विप्रा विज्ञेयाः पङ्क्तिदूषकाः ॥
दुश्चर्म्मा कुनखी कुष्ठी श्वित्री च श्यावदन्तकः ।

---

* दूत राज्ञ इति A and H. शूद्रप्रेष्यो भृती राज्ञ इति F. † वृषली ग्रामयाजकः इति B and F. ‡ द्रव्यार्थमिति B. § श्रुतीति B. वेदविक्रयिण- इति F. ¶ असमानानिति B and F. ‖ निबन्धकः इति B.

विद्धप्रजननश्चैव स्तेनः क्लीवोऽथ नास्तिकः ॥

मद्यपो वृषलीसक्तो वीरहा दिधिषूपतिः।

अगारदाही कुण्डाशी सोमविक्रयिणो द्विजाः ॥

परिवेत्ता च हिंस्रश्च* परिवित्तिर्निराकृतिः।

पौनर्भवः कुसीदी च† तथा नक्षत्रसूचकः‡ ॥

गीतवादित्रशीलश्च§ व्याधितः काण एव च।

हीनाङ्गश्चातिरिक्ताङ्गो ह्यवकीर्णी तथैव च ॥ ¶

अन्नदूषी|| कुण्डगोलौ अभिशस्तोऽथ** देवलः।

मित्रध्रुक् पिशुनश्चैव नित्यं भार्यानुवर्त्तितः ॥

मातापित्रोर्गुरोस्त्यागी दारत्यागी तथैव च।

गोत्रस्पृक्†† भ्रष्टशौचश्च काण्डस्पृष्टस्तथैव च ॥

अनपत्यः‡‡ कूटसाक्षी याचको रङ्गजीवकः§§।

समुद्रयायी कृतहा तथा समयभेदकः ॥

वेदनिन्दारतश्चैव¶¶ देवनिन्दापरस्तथा||||।

द्विजनिन्दारतश्चैव वर्ज्याः श्राद्धादिकर्म्मणि*** ॥

कृतघ्नः पिशुनः क्रूरो नास्तिको वेदनिन्दकः।

मित्रध्रुक् कुहकश्चैव विशेषात्पंक्तिदूषकाः ॥

---

* तथा हिंस्रः इति B. † कुसीदश्च इति A, F and H. ‡ नक्षत्रदर्शकः इति B and F § गीतवादित्रनिरत इति B. ¶ अतः परं श्लोकद्वयं F पुस्तके नास्ति। || कान्तादूषीति B. ** ह्यभिशस्तोऽथ इति B. †† गोत्रभिदिति B. ‡‡ कृशाक्षी चक्रवन्दी च याजको रङ्गजीवन इति F. §§ पाचको रत्नजीवकः इति B. ¶¶ देवनिन्दापरश्चैव इति B. |||| वेदनिन्दारतस्तथेति B. *** कर्म्मसु इति B.

सर्व्वे पुनरभोज्यान्ना न दानार्हाः स्वकर्म्मसु* ।
ब्रह्महा चाभिशस्ताश्च† वर्ज्जनीयाः प्रयत्नतः ॥
शूद्रान्नरसपुष्टाङ्गः सन्ध्योपासनवर्ज्जितः ।
महायज्ञविहीनश्च ब्राह्मणः पङ्क्तिदूषकः ॥
अधीतनाशनश्चैव स्नानदान‡विवर्ज्जितः ।
तामसो राजसश्चैव ब्राह्मणः पङ्क्तिदूषकः ॥
बहुनात्र किमुक्तेन विहितान् ये न कुर्व्वते ।
निन्दितानाचरन्त्येते वर्ज्याः श्राद्धे§ प्रयत्नतः ॥

इति श्रीकूर्म्मपुराणे उपविभागे व्याससगीतासु श्राद्धकल्पे
एकविंशोऽध्यायः ।

द्वाविंशोऽध्यायः ।

व्यास उवाच ।
गोमयेनोदकैर्भूमिं शोधयित्वा समाहितः ।
सन्निमन्त्र्य* द्विजान् सर्व्वान् साधुभिः सन्निमन्त्रयेत्† ॥

---

* तदा नार्हाश्च कर्म्मसु इति B. † ब्रह्मभावान्निरस्ताश्चेति B. ‡ ह्रीमिति B and F. मौनेति H. § वर्ज्जनीयाः इति B.

---

* सन्निपात्य इति B. † सन्निवर्त्तयेदिति B.

श्वो भविष्यति मे श्राद्धं पूर्व्वेद्युरभिपूज्य च।
असम्भवे परेद्युर्वै* यथोक्तैर्लक्षणैर्युतान्॥
तस्य ते पितरः श्रुत्वा श्राद्धकालमुपस्थितम्।
अन्योऽन्यं मनसा ध्यात्वा सम्पतन्ति मनोजवाः॥
तैर्ब्राह्मणैः† सहाश्नन्ति पितरो ह्यन्तरिक्षगाः।
वायुभूतास्तु तिष्ठन्ति भुक्त्वा यान्ति पराङ्गतिम्॥
आमन्त्रिताश्च ते विप्राः श्राद्धकाल उपस्थिते।
वसेयुर्नियताः सर्व्वे ब्रह्मचर्य्यपरायणाः॥
अक्रोधनोऽत्वरोऽमत्तः सत्यवादी समाहितः।
भारं‡ मैथुनमध्वानं श्राद्धकृद्वर्ज्जयेद्ध्रुवम्§॥
आमन्त्रितो ब्राह्मणो वै¶ योऽन्यस्मै कुरुते क्षणम्।
स याति नरकं|| घोरं शूकरत्वम्प्रयाति च**॥
आमन्त्रयित्वा यो मोहादन्यच्चामन्त्रयेद्द्विजः††।
स तस्मादधिकः पापी विष्ठाकीटोऽभिजायते॥
श्राद्धे निमन्त्रितो विप्रो मैथुनं योऽधिगच्छति।
ब्रह्महत्यामवाप्नोति तिर्य्यग्योनौ विधीयते‡‡॥
निमन्त्रितस्तु यो विप्रो ह्यध्वानं याति दुर्म्मतिः§§।
भवन्ति पितरस्तस्य तन्मासं पांशुभोजनाः¶¶॥

---

* परेद्युर्वा इति B. † ब्राह्मणैस्तैरिति B. ‡ भावमिति B. § जपमिति B and F. ¶ वा इति B. || रौरवमिति B. ** हि इति B. †† परच्चामन्त्रयेद्द्विजमिति B. ‡‡ च जायते इति B. §§ ह्यध्वानमधिगच्छति इति B. ¶¶ पापभोजनाः इति B.

निमन्त्रितस्तु यः श्राद्धे कुर्य्याद्वै* कलहं द्विजः ।
भवन्ति पितरस्तस्य तन्मासं† मलभोजनाः ॥
तस्मान्निमन्त्रितः श्राद्धे नियतात्मा भवेद्द्विजः ।
अक्रोधनः शौचपरः कर्त्ता चैव जितेन्द्रियः ॥
श्वो भूते दक्षिणां गत्वा दिशं दर्भान्समाहितः ।
समूलानाहरेद्वारि दक्षिणाग्रान् सुनिर्म्मलान्‡ ॥
दक्षिणाप्रवणं स्निग्धं विभक्तं§ शुभलक्षणम् ।
शुचिन्देशं विविक्तञ्च गोमयेनोपलेपयेत् ॥
नदीतीरेषु तीर्थेषु स्वभूमौ¶ चैव नाम्बुषु‖ ।
विविक्तेषु च तुष्यन्ति दत्तेन पितरः सदा ॥
पारक्ये भूमिभागे तु** पितॄणां नैव निर्वपेत् ।
स्वामिभिस्तद्विहन्येत मोहाद्यत्†† क्रियते नरैः ॥
अटव्यः पर्व्वताः पुण्यास्तीर्थान्यायतनानि च ।
सर्व्वाण्यस्वामिकान्याहुर्न ह्येतेषु परिग्रहः ॥
तिलान्प्रविकिरेत्तत्र‡‡ सर्व्वतो बन्धयेदजम्§§ ।
असुरोपहतं सर्व्वं¶¶ तिलैः शुध्यत्यजेन तु‖‖ ॥
ततोऽन्नम्बहुसंस्कारं नैकव्यञ्जनमव्ययम्*** ।

---

* प्रकुर्य्यादिति B and F. करोतीति H. † भवन्ति तस्य तन्मासं पितरः- इति B. ‡ सुनिर्म्मलमिति B. § विविक्तमिति B. ¶ सुभूमौ इति B. ‖ सानुषु इति B and F. ** च इति B. †† मोहाय इति B. तन्मोघमिति F. ‡‡ विकिरयेत्तत्रेति B. तिलांस्तु विकिरेत्तत्र इति F. §§ बन्धयेदजानिति B. ¶¶ श्राद्धमिति F. ‖‖ वा इति B. *** व्यञ्जनमच्युतमिति B. व्यञ्जनव्यञ्जितमिति F.

चोष्यं पेयं संस्कृतञ्च* यथाशक्ति प्रकल्पयेत् ॥
ततो निवृत्ते मध्याह्ने लुप्तरोमनखान्द्विजान् ।
अवगम्य† यथामार्गं प्रयच्छेद्दन्तधावनम्‡ ॥
तैलमभ्यञ्जनं§ स्नानं स्नानीयञ्च पृथग्विधम् ।
पात्रैरौदुम्बरैर्दद्याद्वैश्वदेवत्यपूर्व्वकम् ॥
ततः स्नानान्निवृत्तेभ्यः प्रत्युत्थाय कृताञ्जलिः ।
पाद्यमाचमनीयञ्च सम्प्रयच्छेद्यथाक्रमम् ॥
ये चात्र विश्वदेवानां विप्राः पूर्व्वं निमन्त्रिताः¶ ।
प्राङ्मुखान्यासनान्येषां त्रिदर्भोपहतानि च‖ ॥
दक्षिणामुखमुक्तानि पितॄणामासनानि च । **
दक्षिणाग्रेषु दर्भेषु प्रोक्षितानि तिलोदकैः ॥
तेषूपवेशयेदेतानासनं संस्पृशन्नपि†† ।
आसध्वमिति सञ्जल्पन्नासीरंस्ते पृथक् पृथक् ॥
द्वौ दैवे प्राङ्मुखौ पित्र्ये त्रयश्चोदङ्मुखास्तथा ।
एकैकं तत्र दैवन्तु पितृमातामहेष्वपि‡‡ ॥
सत्क्रियां देशकालौ च शौचं ब्राह्मणसम्पदम् ।

---

* संस्कृतञ्चेति B and F. † अभिगम्य इति B ‡ अस्य श्लोकार्डस्य स्थाने F पुस्तके "आसद्ध्वमिति संजल्पन्नासीरन्ते पृथक् पृथक्" इति दृश्यते। § तैलेनाभ्यञ्जनमिति B. ¶ द्विजाः पूर्व्वनिमन्त्रिताः इति B and F. ‖ विदर्भोपहतानि च इति H. वैधर्म्मोपहतानि च इति F. ** एतत्पादद्वयं A पुस्तके नास्ति। एतत् श्लोकार्डकं H पुस्तके नास्ति। †† स्पृश्य स द्विजमिति B. ‡‡ एकैकं वा भवेत्तत्र देवमातामहेष्वपीति B. एकैकं भावयेत्तत्र एवं मातामहेष्वपीति H.

पञ्चैतान्विस्तरो हन्ति तस्मान्नेहेत विस्तरम् ॥
अपि वा भोजयेदेकं ब्राह्मणं वेदपारगम् ।
श्रुतशीलादिसम्पन्नमलक्षणविवर्ज्जितम् ॥
उद्धृत्य पात्रे चान्नं तत्सर्व्वस्मात्प्रकृतात्ततः* ।
देवतायतने वासौ† निवेद्यान्यत्प्रवर्त्तयेत् ॥
प्राश्येदन्नं तदग्नौ तु दद्याद्वै‡ ब्रह्मचारिणे ।
तस्मादेकमपि श्रेष्ठं विद्वांसं भोजयेद्द्विजम् ॥ §
भिक्षुको ब्रह्मचारी वा भोजनार्थमुपस्थितः ।
उपविष्टस्तु यः श्राद्धे कामं तमपि भोजयेत् ॥
अतिथिर्यस्य नाश्नाति न तच्छ्राद्धम्प्रशस्यते ।
तस्मात्प्रयत्नाच्छ्राद्धेषु पूज्या ह्यतिथयो द्विजैः ॥
आतिथ्यरहिते श्राद्धे भुञ्जते ये द्विजातयः ।
काकयोनिं व्रजन्त्येते दाता चैव न संशयः ॥
हीनाङ्गः पतितः कुष्ठी व्रणयुक्तस्तु नास्तिकः¶ ।
कुक्कुटः शूकरश्वानौ‖ वर्ज्याः श्राद्धेषु दूरतः ॥
बीभत्सुमशुचिं नग्नं मत्तन्धूर्त्तं रजस्वलाम् ।
नीलकाषायवसनपाषण्डांश्च विवर्ज्जयेत् ॥
यत्तत्र क्रियते कर्म्म पैतृके ब्राह्मणान्प्रति ।
तत्सर्व्वमेव कर्त्तव्यं वैश्वदैवत्यपूर्व्वकम् ॥

---

* पुनरिति B and F. † चासौ इति B. ‡ दद्याद्वा इति B. § एतत्-पादद्वयं A पुस्तके नास्ति । ¶ व्रणी पुक्कशनास्तिकौ इति B. ‖ कुक्कुटाः शूकराः श्वानः इति B.

यथोपविष्टान् सर्व्वांस्तानलङ्कुर्य्याद्विभूषणैः* ।
स्रग्दामभिः शिरोवेष्टैर्धूपवासोऽनुलेपनैः ॥
ततस्त्वावाहयेद्देवान् ब्राह्मणानामनुज्ञया ।
उदङ्मुखो यथान्यायं विश्वेदेवास इत्यृचा ॥
द्वे पवित्रे गृहीत्वास्य† भाजने चालिते पुनः ।
शन्नो देवी जलं चिप्त्वा यवोऽसीति यवांस्तथा ॥
या दिव्या इति मन्त्रेण हस्ते त्वर्घं‡ विनिचिपेत् ।
प्रदद्याद्गन्धमाल्यानि धूपादीनि च शक्तितः ॥
अपसव्यं ततः कृत्वा पितॄणां दचिणामुखः ।
आवाहनं ततः कुर्य्यादुशन्तस्त्वेत्यृचा बुधः ॥
आवाह्य तदनुज्ञातो जपेदायन्तु§ नस्ततः ।
शन्नो देव्योदकं पात्रे तिलोऽसीति तिलांस्तथा ॥
चिप्त्वा चार्घं यथापूर्व्वन्दत्त्वा हस्तेषु वा¶ पुनः ।
संस्रवांश्च ततः सर्व्वान् पात्रे कुर्य्यात्समाहितः ॥
पितृभ्यः स्थानमसीति‖ न्युब्जपात्रं निधापयेत् ।
अग्नौ करिष्यन्नादाय** पृच्छेदन्नं†† घृतप्लुतम् ।
कुरुष्वेत्यभ्यनुज्ञातो जुहुयादुपवीतवित्‡‡ ॥
यज्ञोपवीतिना होमः कर्त्तव्यः कुशपाणिना ।

---

* संस्कुर्य्याद्विभूषणैरिति B. † गृहीत्वाथ इति B. ‡ हस्तेष्वर्घमिति B and F. § जपेदायान्तु इति B. ¶ वै इति B and F. ‖ स्थानमेतच्च इति B and F. ** करिष्येत्यादायेति B and F. †† पृच्छत्यन्नमिति B. ‡‡ जुहुयादुपनीतवानिति B.

प्राचीनावीतिना पित्र्यं वैश्वदेवन्तु होमयेत्* ॥
दक्षिणं पातयेज्जानुन्देवान् परिचरन्सदा† ।
पितॄणां परिचर्य्यासु पातयेदितरं तथा ॥
सोमाय वै पितृमते‡ स्वधा नम इति ब्रुवन् ।
अग्नये कव्यवाहनाय स्वधेति जुहुयात्ततः ॥
अग्न्यभावे तु विप्रस्य पाणावेवोपपादयेत् ।
महादेवान्तिके वाथ गोष्ठे वा सुसमाहितः ॥
ततस्तैरभ्यनुज्ञातो गत्वा वै दक्षिणान्दिशम् ।
गोमयेनोपलिप्याथ§ स्थानङ्कुर्य्यात्ससैकतम् ॥
मण्डलं चतुरस्रं वा दक्षिणा¶प्रवणं शुभम् ।
त्रिरुल्लिखेत्तस्य मध्यं दर्भेणैकेन चैव हि ॥
ततः संस्तीर्य्य तत्स्थाने दर्भान्वै दक्षिणाग्रगान्‖ ।
त्रीन् पिण्डान्निर्वपेत्तत्र हविःशेषात्समाहितः ॥
उप्यपिण्डांस्तु तद्धस्तं निमृज्याल्लेपभोजिनान्** ।
तेषु दर्भेष्वथाचम्य त्रिराचम्य शनैरसून् ।
तदन्नन्तु†† नमस्कुर्य्यात्पितॄनेव च मन्त्रवित् ॥
उदकन्निनयच्छेषं शनैः पिण्डान्तिके पुनः ।
अवजिघ्रेच्च तान् पिण्डान् यथा न्युप्ता‡‡ समाहितः ॥

---

* होमविदिति B. होमवदिति F. † पुमानिति B. ‡ पितृगते इति B. § उपलिप्योर्व्वीमिति B and F. ¶ इतः परं चैव हि इत्यन्तः पाठः B पुस्तके न दृश्यते । ‖ दक्षिणाग्रकानिति F. ** लुप्तपिण्डांस्तु तं हस्तं विसृज्य लेपभागिनामिति B. †† षड्तूंश्च इति F. ‡‡ लुप्तानिति B.

अथ पिण्डाच्च शिष्टान्नं* विधिवद्भोजयेद्द्विजान् ।
मांसान् पूपांश्च विविधान्खाद्यकल्पांस्तु शोभनान्† ॥
ततो‡ऽन्नमुत्सृजेद्भुक्तेष्वग्रतो विकिरन्भुवि ।
पृष्ट्वा तदन्नमित्येव तृप्तानाचामयेत्ततः ॥
आचान्ताननुजानीयादभितो रम्यतामिति ।
स्वधास्त्विति च ते ब्रूयुर्ब्राह्मणास्तदनन्तरम् ॥
ततो भुक्तवतां तेषामन्नशेषं निवेदयेत् ।
यथा ब्रूयुस्तथा कुर्य्यादनुज्ञातस्तु तैर्द्विजैः ॥
पित्र्ये स्वदितमित्येव वाच्यं गोष्ठेषु सुश्रितम् ।
सम्पन्नमित्यभ्युदये दैवे सेवित§मित्यपि ॥
विसृज्य ब्राह्मणान् तान्वै पितृपूर्व्वन्तु वाग्यतः ।
दक्षिणान्दिशमाकाङ्क्षन्याचेतेमान्वरान् पितॄन् ॥
दातारो नोऽभिवर्द्धन्तां वेदाः सन्ततिरेव च ।
श्रद्धा च नो मा विगमद्बहुदेयञ्च नोऽस्त्विति ॥
पिण्डांस्तु गोऽजविप्रेभ्यो दद्यादग्नौ जलेऽपि वा ।
मध्यमन्तु ततः पिण्डमद्यात्पत्नी सुतार्थिनी ॥
प्रक्षाल्य हस्तावाचम्य ज्ञातिं शेषेण तोषयेत् ।
सूपशाकफलानीक्षून्¶ पयो दधि घृतं मधु ॥

---

* पिण्डावशिष्टान्नमिति B and F. † दद्यात्कृशरपायसमिति B and F. ‡ तत आरभ्य तोषयेदित्यन्ताः सार्द्धसप्तश्लोकाः B and F पुस्तकयोर्न दृश्यन्ते । § रोचित-मित्यपीति E and H. ¶ पुष्पशाकफलानीक्षु इति B.

अन्नञ्चैव यथाकामं विविधं भोज्य*पेयकम्।
यद्यदिष्टं† द्विजेन्द्राणां तत्सर्वं विनिवेदयेत्॥
धान्यांस्तिलांश्च विविधान् शर्करा विविधास्तथा।
उष्णमन्नं द्विजातिभ्यो दातव्यं श्रेय इच्छता।
अन्यत्र फलमूलेभ्यो पानकेभ्यस्तथैव च॥
न भूमौ पातयेज्जानुं न कुप्येन्नानृतं वदेत्।
न पादेन स्पृशेदन्नं न चैवमवधूनयेत्‡॥
क्रोधेनैव च यद्भुक्तं यद्भुक्तं त्वयथाविधि।
यातुधाना विलुम्पन्ति जल्पता चोपपादितम्॥
स्विन्नगात्रो न तिष्ठेत सन्निधौ च द्विजन्मनाम्§।
न च पश्येत काकादीन् पक्षिणः प्रतिलोमगान्¶।
तद्रूपाः पितरस्तत्र समायान्ति बुभुक्षवः‖॥
न दद्यात्तत्र हस्तेन प्रत्यक्षं** लवणं तथा।
न चायसेन पात्रेण न चैवाश्रद्धया पुनः॥
काञ्चनेन तु पात्रेण राजतोदुम्बरेण वा††।
दत्तमक्षयतां याति खड्गेन च विशेषतः॥
पात्रे तु मृण्मये यो वै श्राद्धे वै भोजयेद्विजान्‡‡।
स याति नरकं घोरं भोक्ता चैव पुरोधसः॥

---

* भक्ष्येति B and F. † यदुद्दिष्टमिति B. ‡ न चैतदवधूनयेदिति B § द्विजोत्तमानिति A, E and H. ¶ प्रतिषिधयेदिति B and F. ‖ क्षुतःचराः इति B. ** लक्षणमिति B. †† च इति B. ‡‡ श्राद्धे भोजयते पितॄनिति B. श्राद्धे वै भोजयेत् पितॄनिति E, F, G and F.

न पङ्क्त्यां विषमं दद्यान्न याचेत न* दापयेत्।
याचिता दापिता दाता नरकान्याति भीषणान्† ॥
भुञ्जीरन्नथतः श्रेष्ठं‡ न ब्रूयुः प्राकृतान् गुणान्।
तावद्धि पितरोऽश्नन्ति यावन्नोक्ता हविर्गुणाः ॥
नाग्रासनोपविष्टस्तु भुञ्जीत प्रथमं द्विजः।
बहूनां पश्यतां सोऽन्यः पङ्क्त्या हरति किल्बिषम् ॥
न किञ्चिद्वर्ज्जयेच्छ्राद्धे नियुक्तस्तु द्विजोत्तमः।
न मांसस्य निषेधेन§ न चान्यस्यान्नमीक्षयेत् ॥
यो नाश्नाति द्विजो मांसं नियुक्तः पितृकर्म्मणि।
स प्रेत्य पशुतां याति सम्भवानेकविंशतिम् ॥
स्वाध्यायं श्रावयेदेषां¶ धर्म्मशास्त्राणि चैव हि‖।
ज्ञातिष्वपि चतुर्थेषु स्वान् भृत्यान् भोजयेत्ततः ॥
पश्चात्स्वयञ्च पत्नीभिः शेषमन्नं समाचरेत्¶।
नोद्वासयेत्‖ तदुच्छिष्टं यावन्नास्तङ्गतो रविः ॥
ब्रह्मचारी भवेतान्तु दम्पती रजनीन्तु ताम्।
दत्त्वा श्राद्धं तथा भुक्त्वा सेवते यस्तु मैथुनम्।

---

* न याचेन्न चेति B. न याचेत च दापयेदिति F. † दारुणानिति B. नरकं याति भीषणमिति F. ‡ भुञ्जीरन्वाग्यताः शिष्याः इति B. वाग्यतां शिष्टा इति F. § न मांसं प्रतिषेधेत इति B. ¶ श्रावयेद्देवानिति B. ‖ अतः परं B F पुस्तकयोः इतिहासपुराणानि श्राद्धकल्पांश्च शोभनान्। ततोऽन्नमुत्सृजेद्भुक्त्वा साग्रतो विकिरन्भुवि ॥ पृष्ट्वा स्वदितमित्येवं तृप्तानाचामयेत्ततः। आचान्ताननुजानीयादभितो रम्यतामिति ॥ स्वधास्त्विति च तं ब्रूयुर्ब्राह्मणास्तदनन्तरम्। ततो भुक्तवतां तेषामन्नशेषं निवेदयेत् ॥ इत्यधिकः पाठो दृश्यते। ¶ समाहरेदिति B. ‖ निखनेच्च इति B. भूम्यां खनेदिति F.

महारौरवमासाद्य कीटयोनिं व्रजेत्पुनः ॥
शुचिरक्रोधनः शान्तः सत्यवादी समाहितः ।
स्वाध्यायञ्च तथाध्वानं कर्त्ता भोक्ता च वर्ज्जयेत् ॥
श्राद्धं कृत्वा* परश्राद्धे भुञ्जते ये द्विजातयः ।
महापातकिभिस्तुल्या यान्ति ते नरकान् बहून् ॥
एष वो विहितः सम्यक् श्राद्धकल्पः समासतः† ।
अनेन वर्त्तयेत्‡नित्यं§ ब्राह्मणो व्यसनान्वितः ॥
आमश्राद्धं यदा¶ कुर्य्याद्विधिज्ञः श्रद्धयान्वितः ।
तेनाग्नौकरणं कुर्य्यात्पिण्डांस्तेनैव निर्वपेत् ॥
योऽनेन विधिना श्राद्धं कुर्य्याद्वै शान्तमानसः‖ ।
व्यपेतकल्मषो नित्यं यतिनां** वर्त्तयेत्पदम्†† ॥
तस्मात्सर्व्वप्रयत्नेन श्राद्धं कुर्य्याद्द्विजोत्तमः ।
आराधितो भवेदीशस्तेन सम्यक् सनातनः ॥
अपि मूलैः फलैर्वापि प्रकुर्य्यान्निर्द्धनो द्विजः ।
तिलोदकैस्तर्पयित्वा पितॄन् स्नात्वा समाहितः ।
न जीवत्पितृको दद्याद्धोमान्तं वा विधीयते‡‡ ।
येषां वापि पिता दद्यात्तेषाञ्चैके प्रचक्षते ॥

---

* भुक्त्वा इति B and F. † सनातनः इति B and F. ‡ वर्द्धयेदिति F. § अतः परं B पुस्तके उदासीनोऽथ तत्त्ववित् । अनग्निरध्वगो वापि तथैव इत्यधिकः पाठो दृश्यते । ¶ द्विजः इति B and F. ‖ यतमानसः इति B and F. ** योगिनामिति B. †† वर्त्तते पदमिति B. योगिनामृच्छते पदमिति F. ‡‡ होमादा-द्याभिधीयते इति B.

पिता पितामहश्चैव तथैव प्रपितामहः ।
यो यस्य प्रीयते तस्मै देयं नान्यस्य तेन तु ॥
भोजयेद्वापि जीवन्तं यथाकामन्तु भक्तितः ।
न जीवन्तमतिक्रम्य ददाति श्रूयते श्रुतिः* ॥
द्व्यामुष्यायणिको दद्याद्वीजि† क्षेत्रिकयोः समम्‡ ।
अधिकारी भवेत्सोऽथ नियोगोत्पादितो यदि ॥
अनियुक्तात्सुतो§ यश्च¶ शुक्रतो जायते त्विह ।
प्रदद्याद्वीजिने पिण्डं क्षेत्रिणे तु ततोऽन्यथा ॥
द्वौ पिण्डौ निर्वपेत्ताभ्यां क्षेत्रिणे वीजिने तथा ।
कीर्त्तयेदथचैवास्मिन्‖ वीजिनं क्षेत्रिणं ततः ।
मृताहनि तु कर्त्तव्यमेकोद्दिष्टं विधानतः ॥
अशौचे स्वे परिक्षीणे कार्य्यं वै कामतः पुनः ।
पूर्व्वाह्णे चैव कर्त्तव्यं श्राद्धमभ्युदयार्थिना ॥
देववत्सर्व्वमेव स्यान्नैव** कार्य्या तिलैः क्रिया:†† ।
दर्भाश्च ऋजवः कार्य्या युग्मान्वै भोजयेद्द्विजान् ॥
नान्दीमुखास्तु पितरः प्रीयन्तामिति वाचयेत् ।
मातृश्राद्धन्तु पूर्व्वं स्यात्पितॄणां तदनन्तरम्‡‡ ॥

---

* प्रयतः शुचिरिति B. † वीजेति F and G. ‡ भ्रात्रन्तरेण दत्तकत्वेन गृहीतोऽपि स्वपितुर्दायादिभाक् पुत्रो द्वामुष्यायणिकः। अत्र तु क्षेत्रजः। वीजी जन्मदाता, क्षेत्रिकः यस्य क्षेत्रे उत्पन्नः। § ऋतुक्रयादर्द्धं समादद्यादिति B and F. ¶ यस्तु इति B. ‖ कीर्त्तयेदथ वैकस्मिन्निति B, E, F and H. ** यवैरिति B. न वै इति F. †† तिलक्रिया इति B and F. ‡‡ स्यादनन्तरमिति B.

ततो मातामहानान्तु* वृद्धौ श्राद्धत्रयं स्मृतम् ।
दैवपूर्व्वम्प्रदयाद्वै न कुर्य्यादप्रदक्षिणम् ॥
प्राङ्मुखो निर्वपेद्विद्वान्† उपवीती समाहितः ।
पूर्व्वन्तु‡ मातरः पूज्या भक्त्या वै सगणेश्वराः ॥
स्थण्डिलेषु विचित्रेषु§ प्रतिमासु द्विजातिषु ।
पुष्पैर्धूपैश्च नैवेद्यैर्भूषणैरपि पूजयेत्¶ ॥
पूजयित्वा मातृगणं कुर्य्याच्छ्राद्धत्रयं द्विजः‖ ।
अकृत्वा मातृयोगन्तु** यः श्राद्धन्तु निवेशयेत्†† ॥
तस्य क्रोधसमाविष्टा हिंसां गच्छन्ति‡‡ मातरः ।

इति श्रीकूर्म्मपुराणे उपविभागे व्यासगीतासु श्राद्धकल्पे
द्वाविंशोऽध्यायः ।

---

* मातामहानाञ्च इति B. † पिण्डानिति B, E, F, G and H. ‡ पूर्व्वं वै इति B. § पवित्रेषु इति B. ¶ गन्धाद्यैर्भूषणैरपीति B and F. ‖ बुधः इति B and F. ** मातृयागन्तु इति B and F. †† श्राद्धं परिवेशयेदिति B and F. ‡‡ इच्छन्तीति B and F.

त्रयोविंशोऽध्यायः ।

सूत उवाच ।*

दशाहमाहुराशौचं† सपिण्डेषु विधीयते‡ ।
मृतेषु वापि§ जातेषु ब्राह्मणानां द्विजोत्तमाः ॥
नित्यानि चैव कर्म्माणि काम्यानि च विशेषतः ।
न कुर्य्याद्विहितं किञ्चित्स्वाध्यायं मनसापि च ॥
शुचीनक्रोधनान् भूम्यान्¶ शालाग्नौ भावयेत्‖ द्विजान् ।
शुष्कान्नेन फलैर्व्वापि वैतानान्** जुहुयात्तथा ॥
न स्पृशेयुरिमानन्ये न च तेभ्यः समाहरेत् ।
चतुर्थे पञ्चमे वाह्नि संस्पर्शः†† कथितो बुधैः ॥
सूतके तु सपिण्डानां संस्पर्शो नैव दुष्यति‡‡ ।
सूतकं सूतिकाञ्चैव वर्ज्जयित्वा नृणां पुनः ॥
अधीयानस्तथा वेदान्§§ वेदविच्च पिता भवेत् ।
स्पृश्याः स्युः¶¶ सर्व्व एवैते स्नानान्माता दशाहतः ॥
दशाहं निर्गुणे प्रोक्तमाशौचं वातिनिर्गुणे‖‖ ।
एकद्वित्रिगुणैर्युक्तश्चतुस्त्र्येकदिनैः*** शुचिः ॥

* व्यास उवाच इति B and F. † अशौचमिति B. ‡ विपश्चितः इति B and F. § वाथेति B. ¶ शुचीननिधनानन्यानिति B. शान्तानिति F. ‖ हारयेदिति B. हारयेदिति F. ** Burnt offering presented to the fire daily by a Bráhmana. †† वह्निसंस्पर्शः इति B. ‡‡ न प्रदुष्यतीति B. §§ यज्वा इति B and F. ¶¶ संस्पृश्याः इति B. ‖‖ चातिनिर्गुणे इति B. *** चतुस्त्र्येकगुणैरिति B. चतस्त्र्येकदिनैरिति F. चतुर्द्व्येकदिनैरिति E and H.

दशाङ्गादपरं* सम्यक् अधीयीत जुहोति च ।
चतुर्थे तस्य संस्पर्शं मनुः प्राह प्रजापतिः ॥
क्रियाहीनस्य मूर्खस्य महारोगिण एव च ।
यथेष्टाचरणस्येह† मरणान्तमशौचकम् ॥
त्रिरात्रं दशरात्रं वा ब्राह्मणानामशौचकम् ।
प्राक्संवत्सरात्त्रिरात्रं दशरात्रं ततः परम्§ ॥
ऊनद्विवार्षिके प्रेते मातापित्रोस्तदिष्यते ।¶
जातदन्ते त्रिरात्रं स्याद्यदि स्यातान्तु निर्गुणौ‖ ॥
आदन्तजननात्सद्यः आचूड़ादेकरात्रकम् ।
त्रिरात्रमौपनयनात्सपिण्डानामशौचकम्** ॥
जातमात्रस्य बालस्य यदि स्यान्मरणम्पितिः†† ।
मातुश्च सूतकं तत्स्यात्पिता स्यात्स्पृश्य एव च‡‡ ॥
सद्यःशौचं§§ सपिण्डानां कर्त्तव्यं सोदरस्य तु ।
ऊर्द्धं दशाहादेकाहं सोदरो यदि निर्गुणः ॥
ततोर्द्धं¶¶ दन्तजननात्सपिण्डानामशौचकम् ।

---

* दशाहात्तु परमिति B and F. † यथेष्टाचरणस्याहुरिति B and F. § प्राक्संस्काराच्चिरात्रं स्यात्तस्मादूर्द्ध्वं दशाहकमिति B. प्राक्संस्कारात्त्रिरात्रं वै दशरात्रमतः परमिति F. ¶ B F पुस्तकयोः त्रिरात्रेण शुचिस्त्वन्यो यदि ह्यत्यन्तनिर्गुणः ॥ अदन्तजातमरणे पित्रोरेकाहमिष्यते । इत्यधिकः पाठो दृश्यते । ‖ यदि ह्यत्यन्तनिर्गुणौ इति B. ** सपिण्डानामुदाहृतमिति B and F. †† मरणम्पितुरिति B and F. ‡‡ चास्पृश्य एव चेति B. §§ सद्यः शौचमिति B and F. ¶¶ अथोर्द्धमिति B and F.

एकरात्रं निर्गुणानां* चौड़ादूर्द्धन्त्रिरात्रकम् ॥
अदन्तजातमरणं सम्भवेद्यदि सत्तमाः।
एकरात्रं सपिण्डानां यदि तेऽत्यन्तनिर्गुणाः† ॥
व्रतादेशात्सपिण्डानां गर्भस्रावात्स्वपाततः‡ ।§
गर्भच्युतादहोरात्रं¶ सपिण्डेऽत्यन्तनिर्गुणे।
यथेष्टाचरणे ज्ञातौ त्रिरात्रमिति निश्चयः ॥
यदि स्यात्सूतके सूतिर्मरणे वा मृतिर्भवेत्।
शेषेणैव भवेच्छुद्धिरहःशेषे द्विरात्रकम्|| ॥
मरणोत्पत्तियोगेन मरणेन समाप्यते** ।
आद्यं†† वृद्धिमदाशौचं तदा पूर्व्वेण शुद्ध्यति‡‡ ॥§§
देशान्तरगतं श्रुत्वा सूतकं शावमेव च¶¶।
तावदप्रयतो मर्त्त्यो यावच्छेषं समाप्यते|||| ॥

---

* एकाहं निर्गुणानान्तु इति B. † चात्यन्तनिर्गुण इति A and F. ‡ अनुस्नानं विधीयते इति B. अवाक् स्नानं विधीयते इति F. § सर्व्वेषामेव गुणिनामूर्द्धन्तु विषमः पुनः। अर्व्वाक् षण्मासतः स्त्रीणां यदि स्याद्गर्भसंस्रवः॥ तदा माससमैस्तासामशौचं दिवसैः स्मृतम्। तत ऊर्द्धन्तु पतने स्त्रीणां द्वादशरात्रिकम्॥ सद्यः शौचं सपिण्डानां गर्भस्रावाच्च धातुतः। इत्यधिकः पाठः B F पुस्तकयोः दृश्यते। ¶ गर्भच्युतावहोरात्रमिति B. || त्रिरात्रकमिति B. ** मरणोत्पत्तियोगे तु मरणाच्छुद्धिरिष्यते इति B. †† अयवृद्धीति B. आद्यवृद्धीति F. अग्रवृद्धीति E and H. ‡‡ ऊर्द्धश्चेत्तेन शुद्ध्यति इति B. §§ तथाच पञ्चमीरात्रिमतीत्य परतो भवेदित्यधिकः पाठः B पुस्तके दृश्यते। ¶¶ शावमेव तु इति B. शावं मरणाशौचमित्यर्थः। |||| तावत्स्यादशुचिर्विप्रो यावच्छेषः समाप्यते इति B.

वार्त्तान्ते* सूतके प्रोक्तं सपिण्डानां त्रिरात्रकम् ।†
अप्रदानात्त्रिरात्रं‡ स्याद्दशरात्रं ततः§ परम् ॥
मातामहानां मरणे त्रिरात्रं स्यादशौचकम् ।
एकादशानाञ्च तथा¶ सूतके चैतदेव हि ॥
पक्षिणी योनिसम्बन्धे बान्धवेषु तथैव च ।
एकरात्रं समुद्दिष्टं गुरौ सब्रह्मचारिणि‖ ॥
प्रेते राजनि सज्योतिर्यस्य स्याद्विषये स्थितः** ।
गृहे मृतासु सर्व्वासु कन्यासु च†† त्र्यहं पितुः ॥
परपूर्व्वासु सर्व्वासु‡‡ पुत्त्रेषु कृतकेषु च ।
त्रिरात्रं स्यात्तथाचार्य्यस्वभार्य्यास्वन्यगासु च ॥
आचार्य्यपुत्ते पत्न्याञ्च अहोरात्र§§मुदाहृतम् ।
एकाहं स्यादुपाध्याये स्वग्रामे¶¶ श्रोत्रियेऽपि च ॥
त्रिरात्रमसपिण्डेषु‖‖ स्वगृहे संस्थितेषु च ।

---

* अतीते इति B and F. † अथैव मरणे स्नानमूर्द्धं संवत्सरादपि । वेदार्थविद्याधीयानो योऽग्निवान्वृत्तिकर्षितः । सद्यः शौचं भवेत्तस्य सर्व्वावस्थासु सर्व्वदा । स्त्रीणामसंस्कृतानान्तु प्रदानात्परतः सदा । सपिण्डानां त्रिरात्रं स्यात्संस्कारे भर्त्तुरेव हि । अहस्त्वदत्तकन्यानामशौचं मरणं स्मृतम् । ऊनद्विवर्षामरणे सद्यः शौचमुदाहृतम् । आदन्तात्सोदरे सद्य आचूड़ादेकरात्रकम् । इत्यधिकः पाठः B F पुस्तकयोः दृश्यते । ‡ आप्रदानात्त्रिरात्रमिति B. § अतः इति B and F. ¶ एकोदकानां मरणे इति B. एकोदकानाञ्च तथेति F. ‖ गुरोः सब्रह्मचारिणामिति B. ** स्थितिरिति B and F. †† दत्तासु कन्यकासु इति B and F. ‡‡ भार्य्यासु इति B and F. §§ त्वहोरात्रमिति B. ¶¶ संग्रामे इति B. ‖‖ त्रिरात्रन्तु सपिण्डेषु इति B.

एकाहञ्चास्ववर्य्ये* स्यादेकरात्रं तदिष्यते† ॥
त्रिरात्रं श्वश्रूमरणात्‡ श्वशुरे चैतदेव हि ।
सद्यःशौचं समुद्दिष्टं स्वगोत्रे संस्थिते सति ॥
शुद्धेद्विप्रो दशाहेन द्वादशाहेन भूमिपः ।
वैश्यः पञ्चदशाहेन शूद्रो मासेन शुद्ध्यति ॥
क्षत्त्रविट्शूद्रदायादा ये स्युर्विप्रस्य बान्धवाः ।
तेषामशौचे§ विप्रस्य दशाहाच्छुद्धिरिष्यते ॥
राजन्यवैश्यावप्येवं हीनवर्णासु योनिषु ।
तमेव¶ शौचं कुर्य्यातां विशुद्ध्यात्म‖मसंशयम् ॥
सर्व्वे तूत्तरवर्णानामशौचं कुर्य्युरादृताः** ।
तद्वर्णविधिदृष्टेन स्वन्तु शौचं स्वयोनिषु ॥
षड्रात्रं तु त्रिरात्रं स्यादेकरात्रं क्रमेण तु†† ।
वैश्यक्षत्त्रियविप्राणां शूद्रेष्वाशौचमेव च‡‡ ॥
अर्द्धमासोऽथ षड्रात्रं त्रिरात्रं द्विजपुङ्गवाः ।
शूद्रक्षत्त्रियविप्राणां वैश्यस्याशौचमेव च§§ ॥
षड्रात्रं वै दशाहञ्च¶¶ विप्राणां वैश्यशूद्रयोः ।
अशौचं क्षत्त्रिये प्रोक्तं क्रमेण द्विजपुङ्गवाः ॥

---

* एकाहञ्च श्वशुर्य्ये इति B. एकाहं वा श्वशुर्य्ये इति F. † तु शिष्यते इति B and F. ‡ श्वश्रूमरणे इति B. § अशौचमिति A. ¶ स्वमेव इति B and F. ‖ विशुद्ध्यर्थमिति B and F. ** शौचं कुर्य्युरनर्च्चिताः इति B and F. †† हीति B. ‡‡ शूद्रेष्वाशौचमेव तु इति B. §§ वैश्येष्वशौचमिष्यते इति B. ¶¶ द्वादशाहञ्च इति B. द्वादशरात्रञ्च इति F.

शूद्रविट्क्षत्रियाणान्तु ब्राह्मणस्य तथैव च* ।
दशरात्रेण शुद्धिः स्यादित्याह कमलापतिः† ॥
असपिण्डं द्विजं प्रेतं विप्रो निर्हृत्य बन्धुवत् ।
अशित्वा‡ च सहोषित्वा दशरात्रेण शुद्ध्यति ॥
यद्यन्नमत्ति तेषान्तु त्रिरात्रेण ततः शुचिः ।
अनदंस्त्वन्नमह्ना तु§ न च तस्मिन् गृहे वसेत्¶ ॥
सोदकेऽथ तदेव स्यान्मातुराप्तेषु बन्धुषु ।
दशाहेन शवस्पर्शी सपिण्डश्चैव शुद्ध्यति ॥‖
यदि निर्हरति प्रेतं लोभादाक्रान्तमानसः** ।
दशाहेन द्विजः शुद्धेद्द्वादशाहेन भूमिपः ॥
अर्द्धमासेन वैश्यस्तु शूद्रो मासेन शुध्यति ।
षड्रात्रेणाथवा सर्व्वं त्रिरात्रेणाथवा पुनः ॥ ††
अनाथञ्चैव निर्हृत्य ब्राह्मणं धनवर्जितम् ।
स्नात्वा सम्प्राश्य च‡‡ घृतं शुध्यन्ति ब्राह्मणादयः ॥
अपर§§श्चेत्परं वर्णमपरञ्चापरे¶¶ यदि ।
अशौचे संस्पृशेत्स्नेहात्तदा शौचेन शुद्ध्यति ॥
प्रेतीभूतं द्विजं विप्रो ह्यनुगच्छेत‖‖ कामतः ।

---

* ब्राह्मणे संस्थिते सतीति B and F. † कमलोद्भवः इति B and F. ‡ आसन्ना इति B. § अनदन्नन्नमह्नैव इति B. अदन्नन्नमह्नि चैव न चैतस्मिन्मठे वसेदिति F. ¶ वसन्निति B. ‖ एष श्लोकः B पुस्तके नास्ति। ** प्रलोभाक्रान्तमानसः इति B. †† दशाहेनेत्यादि पादषट्कं A, E, H पुस्तकेषु नास्ति। ‡‡ तु इति B. §§ अवर- इति B. ¶¶ अधरश्चाधरः इति B. ‖‖ योऽनुगच्छतीति B and F.

स्नात्वा सचेलं स्पृष्ट्वाग्निं घृतं प्राश्य विशुध्यति ॥
एकाहात्क्षत्रिये शुद्धिर्वैश्ये स्याच्च द्व्यहेन तु।
शूद्रे दिनत्रयं प्रोक्तं प्राणायामशतं पुनः ॥
अनस्थिसञ्चिते शूद्रे रौति चेद्ब्राह्मणः स्वकैः।
त्रिरात्रं स्यात्तथा*शौचमेकाहं त्वन्यथा स्मृतम् ॥
अस्थिसञ्चयनादर्वागेकाहः क्षत्रवैश्ययोः।
अन्यथा चैव सज्योतिर्ब्राह्मणे स्नानमेव तु ॥
अनस्थिसञ्चिते विप्रो ब्राह्मणो रौति चेत्तदा।
स्नानेनैव भवेच्छुद्धिः सचेलेनात्र† संशयः ॥
यस्तैः सहाशनं कुर्य्याच्छयनादीनि चैव हि।
बान्धवो वापरो वापि स दशाहेन शुध्यति ॥
यस्तेषां सममश्नाति सकृदेवापि कामतः।
तदाशौचे निवृत्तेऽसौ स्नानं कृत्वा विशुध्यति ॥
यावत्तदन्नमश्नाति दुर्भिक्षाभिहतो‡ नरः।
तावन्त्यहान्यशौचं स्यात्प्रायश्चित्तं ततश्चरेत्§ ॥
दाहाद्यशौचं कर्त्तव्यं द्विजानामग्निहोत्रिणाम्।
सपिण्डानाञ्च¶ मरणे मरणादितरेषु च ॥
सपिण्डता च‖ पुरुषे सप्तमे विनिवर्त्तते।
समानोदकभावस्तु जन्मनाम्नोरवेदने ॥
पिता पितामहश्चैव तथैव प्रपितामहः।

---

* स्यादथा इति B. † सचेलेन न इति B and F. ‡ दुर्भिक्षोपहतः इति B.
§ ततः स्मरेदिति A. ¶ सपिण्डानान्तु इति B. ‖ तु इति B.

लेपभाजस्त्रयो ज्ञेयाः सापिण्ड्यं साप्तपौरुषम् ॥
अप्रत्तानां तथा स्त्रीणां सापिण्ड्यं साप्तपौरुषम् ।
तासान्तु भर्तृसापिण्ड्यं प्राह देवः पितामहः ॥
ये चैकजाता बहवो भिन्नयोनय एव च ।
भिन्नवर्णास्तु सापिण्ड्यं भवेत्तेषां त्रिपूरुषम् ॥*
कारवः शिल्पिनो वैद्या दासीदासास्तथैव च ।
दातारो नियमाच्चैव† ब्रह्मविद्ब्रह्मचारिणौ ।
सत्रिणो व्रतिनस्तावत्सद्यःशौचमुदाहृतम्‡ ॥
राजा चैवाभिषिक्तश्च§ अन्न¶सत्रिण एव च ।
यज्ञे विवाहकाले च दैवयोगे तथैव च ।
सद्यःशौचं समाख्यातं दुर्भिक्षे चाप्युपप्लवे ॥
सदाहव‖हतानाञ्च सर्पादिमरणेऽपि च** ।
सद्यःशौचं समाख्यातं स्वज्ञातिमरणे तथा ॥††
अग्निमरुत्प्रपतने‡‡ वीराध्वन्यप्यनाशके ।
गोब्राह्मणार्थे§§ सन्न्यस्ते सद्यःशौचं विधीयते ॥
नैष्ठिकानां वनस्थानां यतीनां ब्रह्मचारिणाम् ।
नाशौचं कीर्त्यते सद्भिः पतिते च तथा मृते ॥

---

* अयं प्रागुक्तश्च श्लोकः B पुस्तके न दृश्यते । † नियमी चैवेति B and F. ‡ सद्यःशौचा उदाहृताः इति B. § चैवाभियुक्तश्च इति F. ¶ प्राणेति B and F. ‖ डिम्बाहवेति B. विवाहवे इति F. ** विद्युता पार्थिवैर्द्विजैरिति B and F. †† एतच्छ्लोकार्द्धं A पुस्तके नास्ति । सर्पादिमरणे तथा इति E, F and H. ‡‡ अग्नौ मरुप्रपतने इति B. §§ ब्रह्मणार्थेन इति B.

पतितानान्न दाहः स्यान्नान्त्येष्टिर्नास्थिसञ्चयः।
नाश्रुपातो न* पिण्डो वा कार्य्यं श्राद्धादिकं क्वचित्॥
व्यापादयेत्तथात्मानं स्वयं योऽग्निविषादिभिः।
विहितं तस्य नाशौचं नाग्निर्नाप्युदकादिकम्॥
अथ किञ्चित्प्रमादेन† म्रियतेऽग्निविषादिभिः।
तस्याशौचं विधातव्यं कार्य्यञ्चैवोदकादिकम्‡॥
जाते कुमारे तदहः कामं कुर्य्यात्प्रतिग्रहम्।
हिरण्यधान्य§गोवासस्तिलांश्च¶ गुड़सर्पिषा॥
फलानि पुष्पं शाकञ्च लवणं काष्ठमेव च।
तोय‖न्दधि घृतं तैलमौषधं चीरमेव च**।
आशौचिनो†† गृहाद्ग्राह्यं शुष्कान्नञ्चैव नित्यशः॥
आहिताग्निर्यथान्यायं दग्धव्यस्त्रिभिरग्निभिः।
अनाहिताग्निर्गृह्येण लौकिकेनेतरो जनः॥
देहाभावात्पलाशैश्च‡‡ कृत्वा प्रतिकृतिम्पुनः।
दाहः कार्य्यो यथान्यायं सपिण्डैः श्रद्धयान्वितैः॥
सकृत्प्रसिञ्चेदुदकं§§ नामगोत्रेण वाग्यतः¶¶।
दशाहं बान्धवाः श्राद्धं सर्व्वे चैव सुसंयताः‖‖॥
पिण्डं प्रतिदिनन्दद्युः सायं प्रातर्यथाविधि।

* न चाश्रुपातः इति B. † कश्चित्प्रमादेन इति B. ‡ उदकादिभिरिति B. § माल्येति B. ¶ तिलान्नेति B and F. ‖ तक्रमिति F. ** चीरमैत्त्ववं तैलमेव च इति B. †† अशौचिनामिति B and F. ‡‡ पलाशैस्तु इति B. §§ सकृत्प्रसिञ्च-न्त्युदकमिति B. ¶¶ वाग्यताः इति B. ‖‖ चैवार्द्रवाससः इति B and F.

प्रेताय च गृहद्वारि चतुर्थे भोजयेद्द्विजान्॥
द्वितीयेऽहनि कर्त्तव्यं क्षुरकर्म्म सबान्धवैः।
चतुर्थे बान्धवैः सर्व्वैरस्थ्नां सञ्चयनं भवेत्।
पूर्व्वान्प्रयुञ्जयेद्विप्रान्* युग्मान्सुश्रद्धया शुचीन्॥
पञ्चमे नवमे चैव तथैवैकादशेऽहनि।
युग्मांश्च† भोजयेद्विप्रान्नवश्राद्धन्तु तद्विजाः‡॥
एकादशेऽह्नि कुर्वीत प्रेतमुद्दिश्य भावतः।
द्वादशे वाह्नि§ कर्त्तव्यं नवमेऽप्यथवाहनि¶।
एकं पवित्रमेकोऽर्घः पिण्डपात्रं तथैव च॥
एवं मृताह्नि कर्त्तव्यं प्रतिमासन्तु वत्सरम्।
सपिण्डीकरणं प्रोक्तं पूर्णे संवत्सरे पुनः‖॥
कुर्य्याच्चत्वारि पात्राणि प्रेतादीनां द्विजोत्तमाः।
प्रेतार्थे पितृपात्रेषु** पात्रमासेचयेत्ततः॥
ये समाना इति द्वाभ्यां पिण्डानप्येवमेव हि।
सपिण्डीकरणश्राद्धं देवपूर्व्वं विधीयते॥
पितॄनावाहयेत्तत्र पुनः प्रेतं विनिर्द्दिशेत्††।
ये सपिण्डीकृताः प्रेता न तेषां स्युः प्रतिक्रियाः‡‡।

---

* पूर्व्वन्तु भोजयेद्विप्रानिति B and F. प्रयुञ्जयेत्—प्रयोजयेत्, आर्षः प्रयोगः।
† अयुग्मानिति B and F. ‡ तद्विदः इति B and F. § वाथ इति B and F.
¶ अनिन्द्ये त्वथवाहनि इति B and F. ‖ संवत्सरेऽपि वेति B. ** प्रेतार्थेपितृपात्रेषु इति B. †† प्रेतञ्च निर्द्दिशेदिति B and F. ‡‡ न तेषान्तु प्रतिक्रिया इति B. न तेषां स्यात्प्रतिक्रिया इति F.

यस्तु कुर्य्यात्पृथक् पिण्डं पितृहा सोऽभिजायते ॥
मृते पितरि वै पुत्रः पिण्डानव्दं समावसेत्* ।
दद्याच्चान्नं† सोदकुम्भं प्रत्यहं प्रेतधर्म्मतः ॥
पार्व्वणेन विधानेन सांवत्सरिकमिष्यते ।
प्रतिसंवत्सरं कुर्य्याद्विधिरेष‡ सनातनः ॥
मातापित्रोः सुतैः कार्य्यम्पिण्डदानादिकञ्च यत्§ ।
पत्नी कुर्य्यात्सुताभावे पत्न्यभावे तु सोदरः¶ ॥
अनेनैव विधानेन जीवः श्राद्धं समाचरेत् ।
कृत्वा दानादिकं सर्व्वं श्रद्धायुक्तः समाहितः ॥ ||
एष वः कथितः सम्यग्गृहस्थानां क्रियाविधिः ।
स्त्रीणां भर्तृषु शुश्रूषा धर्म्मो नान्य इहेष्यते** ॥
स्वधर्म्मतत्परा†† नित्यमीश्वरार्पितमानसाः‡‡ ।
प्राप्नुवन्ति परं§§ स्थानं यदुक्तं वेदवादिभिः ॥

इति श्रीकूर्म्मपुराणे उपविभागे व्याससीतासु श्राद्धकल्पे

त्रयोविंशोऽध्यायः ।

---

* पिण्डमव्दं समाचरेदिति B and F. † दद्यादन्नमिति B. ‡ कार्य्यं विधिरेष इति B and F. § दानादिकं पुनरिति B. पिण्डदानादि किञ्चन इति F. ¶ सहोदर इति B. || एष श्लोकः A, E, F, H पुस्तकेषु नास्ति। ** इहोच्यते इति B. †† स्वधर्म्मतत्परः इति B. ‡‡ मानसः इति B. §§ प्राप्नोति तत्परमिति B.

चतुर्विंशोऽध्यायः ।

व्यास उवाच ।

अग्निहोत्रन्तु जुहुयात्सायम्प्रातर्यथाविधि* ।
दर्शे चैव हि तस्यान्ते नवशस्ये तथैव च† ॥
इष्ट्वा चैव यथान्यायमृत्वन्ते च‡ द्विजोऽध्वरैः ।
पशुना त्वयनस्यान्ते समान्ते सोऽग्निकैर्मखैः§ ॥
नानिष्ट्वा नवशस्येष्ट्या पशुना वाग्निमान्द्विजः¶ ।
न चान्नमद्यान्मांसं वा दीर्घमायुर्जिजीविषुः ॥
नवेनान्नेन चानिष्ट्वा‖ पशुहव्येन चाग्नयः ।
प्राणानेवात्तुमिच्छन्ति नवान्नामिषगृद्धिनः ॥
सावित्रान्शान्तिहोमांश्च कुर्य्यात्पर्व्वसु नित्यशः ।
पितॄंश्चैवाष्टकाः सर्व्वे नित्यमन्वष्टकासु च ॥
एष धर्म्मः परो नित्यमपधर्म्मोऽन्य उच्यते ।
त्रयाणामिह वर्णानां गृहस्थाश्रमवासिनाम् ॥
नास्तिक्यादथवालस्याद्योऽग्नीन्नाधातुमिच्छति** ।
यजेत वा न यज्ञेन स याति नरकान् बहून् ॥

---

* आद्यन्तेऽहर्निशोः सदा इति B. आद्यन्ते ह्यनिशं सदा इति F. † दर्शेन चैव पक्षान्ते पौर्णमासेन चैव हि इति B. दर्शेन चार्द्धमासान्ते पौर्णमासेन चैव हि इति F. ‡ शस्यान्ते नवशस्येन तथर्त्त्वन्ते इति B and F. § समान्तेऽसौमिकैर्मखैरिति B. ¶ चाग्निमान्द्विजा इति B and F. ‖ वानिष्ट्वा इति B. ** योऽग्निं नाधातुमिच्छतीति B.

तस्मात्* सर्व्वप्रयत्नेन ब्राह्मणो हि† विशेषतः ।
आधायाग्निं विशुद्धात्मा यजेत परमेश्वरम् ॥
अग्निहोत्रात्परो धर्म्मो द्विजानां नेह विद्यते ।
तस्मादाराधयेन्नित्यमग्निहोत्रेण शाश्वतम् ॥ ‡
यस्त्वाध्यायाग्निमांश्च स्यान्न यष्टुं देवमिच्छति ।
स संमूढ़ो न§ सम्भाष्यः किं पुनर्नास्तिको जनः ॥
यस्य त्रैवार्षिकभक्तं¶ पर्य्याप्तं भृत्यवृत्तये ।
अधिकं वा भवेद्यस्य|| स सोमं पातुमर्हति ॥
एष वै सर्व्वयज्ञानां सोमः प्रथम इष्यते ।
सोमेनाराधयेद्देवं सोमलोकमहेश्वरम् ॥**
पितामहेन विप्राणामादाय विहितः पशुः††।
धर्म्मो विमुक्तये साक्षाच्छ्रौतः स्मार्त्तो भवेत्पुनः‡‡ ॥
श्रौतस्त्रेताग्निसम्बन्धात्§§ स्मार्त्तः पूर्व्वं मयोदितः ।
श्रेयस्करतमः श्रौतस्तस्माच्छ्रौतं समाचरेत् ॥

---

* इतः पूर्व्वं B पुस्तके तामिस्रमन्धतामिस्रं महारौरवरौरवौ । कुम्भीपाकं वैतरणी मसिपत्रवनं तथा । अन्यांश्च नरकान् घोरान् सम्प्राप्नोति सुदुर्म्मतिः । अन्त्यजानां कुले विप्राः शूद्रयोनौ च जायते । इत्यधिकः पाठो दृश्यते । † वै इति B. ‡ एष श्लोकः A पुस्तकेषु नास्ति । § सोऽसौ मूढ़ः इति B and F. ¶ भुक्तमिति B. || अधिकञ्चाथ विद्येत इति B. ** इतः परं B पुस्तके न सोमयागादधिको महेशाराधनात्ततः । न सोमो विद्यते तस्मात्सोमेनाभ्यर्च्चयेत्परम् । इत्यधिकः पाठो दृश्यते । †† आदावभिहितः शुभः इति B and F. ‡‡ द्विधा पुनरिति B and F. §§ सम्बद्धः इति B and F.

उभावपि हितौ धर्म्मौ वेद वेदविनिःसृतौ ।
शिष्टाचारस्तृतीयः स्याच्छ्रुतिस्मृत्योरभावतः* ॥
धर्म्मेणाधिगतो यैस्तु वेदः सपरिवृंहणः ।
ते शिष्टा ब्राह्मणा ज्ञेया† नित्यमात्मगुणान्विताः ॥
तेषामभिमतो यः स्याच्चेतसा नित्यमेव हि ।
स धर्म्मः कथितः सद्भिर्नान्येषामिति धारणा ॥ ‡
पुराणं धर्म्मशास्त्राणि वेदानामुपवृंहणम् ।
एकस्माद्ब्रह्मविज्ञानं धर्म्मज्ञानं तथैकतः§ ॥
धर्म्मं जिज्ञासमानानां तत्प्रमाणतरं स्मृतम् ।
धर्म्मशास्त्रं पुराणानि ब्रह्मज्ञानेतराश्रमम्¶ ॥
नान्यतो जायते धर्म्मो ब्राह्मी‖ विद्या च वैदिकी ।
तस्माद्धर्म्मं पुराणञ्च श्रद्धातव्यं मनीषिभिः ॥**

इति श्रीकूर्म्मपुराणे उपरिविभागे व्यासगीतासु

चतुर्विंशोऽध्यायः ॥

---

* अलाभतः इति B. † ब्राह्मणाः प्रोक्ताः इति B. ‡ एष श्लोकः A, E, H पुस्तकेषु नास्ति । § तथैव चेति A. ¶ ब्रह्मज्ञानपरायणाः इति B. ‖ ब्रह्मविद्या च वैदिकी इति E, F and H. ** धर्म्मं जिज्ञासमानानामित्यादि श्लोकद्वयं B पुस्तके श्लोकत्रयात् प्रागेव दृश्यते ।

पञ्चविंशोऽध्यायः ।

व्यास उवाच ।

एष वोऽभिहितः कृत्स्नो गृहस्थाश्रमवासिनः ।
द्विजातेः परमो धर्म्मो वर्त्तनानि निबोधत ॥
द्विविधस्तु गृही ज्ञेयः साधकश्चाप्यसाधकः ।
अध्यापनं याजनञ्च पूर्व्वस्याहुः प्रतिग्रहम् ।
कुसीदकृषिवाणिज्यम्प्रकुर्व्वन्तः* स्वयङ्कृतम् ॥
कृषेरभावे वाणिज्यं तदभावे कुसीदकम् ।
आपत्कल्पस्त्वयं† ज्ञेयः पूर्व्वोक्तो मुख्य इष्यते ॥
स्वयं वा कर्षणङ्कुर्य्याद्वाणिज्यं वा कुसीदकम् ।
कष्टा पापीयसी वृत्तिः कुसीदन्तं विवर्ज्जयेत्‡ ॥
क्षात्त्र§वृत्तिम्पराम्प्राहुर्न स्वयङ्कर्षणं द्विजैः ।
तस्मात्क्षात्त्रेण वर्त्तेत वर्त्तते नापदि द्विजः ॥
तेन चावाप्य¶ जीवन्तु वैश्यवृत्तिः‖ कृषिं व्रजेत् ।
न कथञ्चन कुर्व्वीत ब्राह्मणः कर्म्म कर्षणम् ॥
लब्धलाभः पितॄन्देवान् ब्राह्मणांश्चापि पूजयेत् ।
ते तृप्तास्तस्य तं दोषं शमयन्ति न संशयः ॥
देवेभ्यश्च पितृभ्यश्च दद्याद्भागन्तु विंशकम् ।

---

* प्रकुर्व्वीत इति B and F. † आपत्कल्पो ह्ययमिति B. ‡ कुसीदं तद्विवर्जये-
दिति B. § चत्रेति B. ¶ चैवाप्य इति B. ‖ वैश्यवृत्तिमिति B and F.

त्रिषट्भागं* ब्राह्मणानां कृष्यङ्कुर्व्वन्न† दुष्यति ॥
वाणिज्ये द्विगुणं दद्यात्‡ कुसीदी त्रिगुणं पुनः ।
कृषिपालान्न§ दोषेण युज्यते¶ नात्र संशयः ॥
शिलोञ्छं वाप्याददीत‖ गृहस्थः साधकः पुनः ।
विद्याशिल्पादयस्त्वन्ये बहवो वृत्तिहेतवः ॥
असाधकस्तु यः प्रोक्तो गृहस्थाश्रमसंस्थितः ।
शिलोञ्छे तस्य कथिते द्वे वृत्ती परमर्षिभिः ॥
अमृतेनाथवा जीवेन्मृतेनाप्यथवा यदि** ।
अयाचितं स्यादमृतं मृतम्भैक्षन्तु याचितम् ॥
कुशूल††धान्यको‡‡ वा स्यात्कुम्भीधान्यक§§ एव च¶¶ ।
त्र्यहै‖‖हिको*** वापि भवेदश्वस्तनिक एव च ॥
चतुर्णामपि वै तेषां††† द्विजानां गृहमेधिनाम् ।
श्रेयान्परः परो ज्ञेयो धर्म्मतो लोकजित्तमः ॥
षट्कर्म्मको‡‡‡ भवेत्तेषां त्रिभिरन्यः प्रवर्त्तते ।
द्वाभ्यामेकश्चतुर्थस्तु ब्रह्मसत्त्रेण जीवति ॥

---

* त्रिंशद्भागमिति B and F. † कृषिं कुर्व्वन्न इति B and F. ‡ वणिक् प्रदद्याद्द्विगुणमिति B and F. § कृषीवलोऽत्र इति B. कृषीपालो न दोषेण इति F. ¶ दूष्यते इति B. ‖ शिलोञ्छनमाददीतेति B. ** अथवापदीति B. †† सिञ्चनेति B. ‡‡ A householder who has three year's grain in store. §§ A householder who preserves grain in store for six days (according to some), for a year (according to others). ¶¶ वेति B . ‖‖ त्र्यह्निको वा इति F. *** यहैहिकः इति B. ††† चैतेषामिति B. ‡‡‡ षट्कर्म्मैकः इति A.

वर्त्तयंस्तु शिलोञ्छाभ्यामग्निहोत्रपरायणः।
इष्टीः पार्व्वायणान्ता याः* केवला निर्व्वपेत्सदा॥
न लोकवृत्तं† वर्त्तेत वार्त्तान्ते वृत्तिहेतवे‡।
अजिह्मामशठां शुद्धां जीवेद्ब्राह्मणजीविकाम्॥
याचित्वा चाथ सद्भ्योऽन्नं§ पितॄन्देवांस्तु¶ तोषयेत्।
याचयेद्वा शुचीन्दान्तान्तेन तृप्येत्‖ स्वयं ततः॥
यस्तु द्रव्यार्ज्जनङ्कृत्वा गृहस्थां**स्तोषयेन्न तु।
देवान्पितॄंस्तु†† विधिना शुनां योनिं व्रजत्यधः‡‡॥
धर्म्मश्चार्थश्च कामश्च श्रेयो मोक्षश्चतुष्टयम्।
धर्म्माविरुद्धः कामः स्याद्ब्राह्मणानान्तु नेतरः॥
योऽर्थो धर्म्माय नात्मार्थं सोऽर्थो नार्थस्तथेतरः§§।
तस्मादर्थं समासाद्य दद्याद्वै जुहुयाद्द्विजः॥

इति श्रीकूर्म्मपुराणे उपविभागे व्यासगीतासु
पञ्चविंशोऽध्यायः।

---

* पार्व्वायणान्तीयाः इति A, E and H. † लोकवृत्तिमिति B. ‡ वृत्तिहेतोः कथञ्चनेति B and F. § सद्भ्योऽर्थमिति B. ¶ देवांश्च इति B. ‖ याचयित्वा शुचिर्दान्तं न तृप्येदिति B. न तु तृप्येदिति G. न तु तृप्येत् सयव्रत इति F. ** गृहस्थमिति B. †† पितॄंश्च इति B. ‡‡ व्रजत्यसौ इति B and F. §§ सोऽर्थोऽनर्थस्तथेतरः इति B and F.

षड्विंशोऽध्यायः ।

व्यास उवाच ।

अथातः सम्प्रवक्ष्यामि दानधर्म्ममनुत्तमम् ।
ब्रह्मणाभिहितं पूर्व्वमृषीणां ब्रह्मवादिनाम् ॥
अर्थानामुचिते* पात्रे श्रद्धया प्रतिपादनम् ।
दानमित्यभिनिर्द्दिष्टं भुक्तिमुक्तिफलप्रदम् ॥
यद्ददाति विशिष्टेभ्यः शिष्टेभ्यः श्रद्धया† युतः ।
तद्विचित्रमहम्मन्ये‡ शेषं कस्यापि रक्षति ॥
नित्यं नैमित्तिकङ्काम्यं त्रिविधं दानमुच्यते ।
चतुर्थं विमलम्प्रोक्तं सर्व्वदानोत्तमोत्तमम् ॥
अहन्यहनि यत्किञ्चिद्दीयतेऽनुपकारिणे ।
अनुद्दिश्य फलं§ तस्माद्ब्राह्मणाय तु नित्यकम् ॥
यत्तु¶ पापोपशान्त्यर्थं दीयते विदुषाङ्करे ।
नैमित्तिकन्तदुद्दिष्टं दानं सद्भिरनुष्ठितम्‖ ॥
अपत्यविजयैश्वर्य्यस्वर्गार्थं यत्प्रदीयते ।
दानं तत्काम्यमाख्यातमृषिभिर्द्धर्म्मचिन्तकैः ॥
यदीश्वरप्रीणनार्थं ब्रह्मवित्सु प्रदीयते ।

---

* उदिते इति A and F. उदिते—शास्त्रोक्ते इत्यर्थः । † श्रद्धया परया युत इति B and F. ‡ तद्वै वित्तमहं मन्ये इति B and F. § अनुद्देश्यफलमिति B. ¶ वह इति B. ‖ सद्भिरनुत्तममिति B and F.

चेतसा धर्म्मयुक्तेन दानं तद्विमलं शिवम् ॥
दानधर्म्मं निषेवेत पात्रमासाद्य शक्तितः ।
उत्पत्स्यते हि तत्पात्रं यत्तारयति सर्व्वतः ॥
कुटुम्बभक्तवसनाद्देयं* यदतिरिच्यते ।
अन्यथा दीयते यद्धि न तद्दानं फलप्रदम् ॥
श्रोत्रियाय कुलीनाय विनीताय तपस्विने ।
व्रतस्थाय† दरिद्राय यद्देयं‡ भक्तिपूर्व्वकम् ॥
यस्तु दद्यान्महीभक्त्या ब्राह्मणायाहिताग्नये ।
स याति परमं स्थानं यत्र गत्वा न शोचति§ ॥
इक्षुभिः सन्ततां भूमिं यवगोधूमशालिनीम् ।
ददाति वेदविदुषे यः स भूयो न जायते ॥
गोचर्म्ममात्रामपि वा यो भूमिं सम्प्रयच्छति ।
ब्राह्मणाय दरिद्राय सर्व्वपापैः प्रमुच्यते ॥
भूमिदानात्परं दानं विद्यते नेह किञ्चन ।
अन्नदानन्तेन तुल्यं विद्यादानं ततोऽधिकम् ॥
यो ब्राह्मणाय शुचये धर्म्मशीलाय शीलिने¶ ।
ददाति विद्यां विधिना ब्रह्मलोके महीयते ॥
दद्यादहरहस्त्वन्नं श्रद्धया ब्रह्मचारिणे ।

---

* भरणाद्देयमिति B.   † वृत्तस्थाय इति B and H. वृत्तस्थाय—सदाचार-सम्पन्नाय इत्यर्थः ।   ‡ प्रदेयमिति B and F   § शोचते इति B.   ¶ शान्ताय शुचये धर्म्मशालिने इति B and F.

सर्व्वपापविनिर्मुक्तो ब्राह्मणं स्थानमेष्यति* ॥
गृहस्थायान्नदानेन फलम्प्राप्नोति† मानवः ।
आगमे चास्य‡ दातव्यं दत्त्वाप्नोति पराङ्गतिम् ॥
वैशाख्यां पौर्णमास्यान्तु ब्राह्मणान्सप्त पञ्च वा ।
उपोष्य विधिना शान्ताञ्छुचीन्§ प्रयतमानसः ॥
पूजयित्वा तिलैः कृष्णैर्मधुना च विशेषतः ।
गन्धादिभिः समभ्यर्च्च वाचयेद्वा¶ स्वयं वदेत् ॥
प्रीयतां धर्म्मराजेति यद्वा मनसि वर्त्तते ।
यावज्जीवकृतम्पापं‖ तत्क्षणादेव नश्यति ॥
कृष्णाजिने तिलान् कृत्वा** हिरण्यं मधुसर्पिषी ।
ददाति यस्तु विप्राय सर्व्वं तरति दुष्कृतम् ॥
कृतान्नमुदकुम्भञ्च वैशाख्याञ्च†† विशेषतः ।
निर्द्दिश्य धर्म्मराजाय विप्रेभ्यो मुच्यते भयात् ॥
सुवर्णतिलयुक्तैस्तु ब्राह्मणान् सप्त पञ्च वा ।
तर्पयेदुदपात्राणि‡‡ ब्राह्मणेभ्यो§§ व्यपोहति¶¶ ॥
शुक्लाम्बरधरः कृष्णैस्तिलैर्हुत्वा हुताशनम् ।

---

* स्थानमाप्नुयादिति B. ब्राह्मणं—ब्रह्मणः सम्बन्धीयमित्यर्थः, स्थानं ब्रह्मलोकमित्यर्थः । † फलं नाप्नोतीति B. ‡ आममेवास्य इति B and F. § शान्तः शुचिरिति B and F. ¶ वाचयित्वा इति B. ‖ यावज्जीवन्तु तत्पापमिति B. ** दत्त्वा इति B. †† वैशाख्यान्तु इति B. ‡‡ तर्पयेदुदपात्रैश्च इति B. उदपात्रेण इति F. §§ ब्रह्महत्यामिति B and F. ¶¶ अतः परं B, F पुस्तकयोः माघमासे तमिस्रे तु द्वादश्यां समुपोषितः इत्यधिकः पाठो दृश्यते ।

प्रदद्याद्ब्राह्मणेभ्यस्तु विप्रेभ्यः सुसमाहितः* ।
जन्मप्रभृति यत्पापं सर्व्वं तरति वै द्विजः ॥
अमावास्यामनुप्राप्य† ब्राह्मणाय तपस्विने ।
यत्किञ्चिद्देवदेवेशं दद्याद्दोद्दिश्य‡ शङ्करम् ॥
प्रीयतामीश्वरः सोमो महादेवः सनातनः ।
सप्तजन्मकृतं पापं तत्क्षणादेव नश्यति ॥
यस्तु कृष्णचतुर्द्दश्यां स्नात्वा देवं पिनाकिनम् ।
आराधयेद्द्विजमुखे न तस्यास्ति§ पुनर्भवः ॥
कृष्णाष्टम्यां विशेषेण धार्म्मिकाय द्विजातये ।
स्नात्वाभ्यर्च्य यथान्यायं पादप्रक्षालनादिभिः ॥
प्रीयतां मे महादेवो दद्याद्द्रव्यं स्वकीयकम् ।
सर्व्वपापविनिर्मुक्तः प्राप्नोति परमां गतिम् ॥
द्विजैः कृष्णचतुर्द्दश्यां कृष्णाष्टम्यां विशेषतः ।
अमावास्यान्तु वै भक्तैः¶ पूजनीयस्त्रिलोचनः ॥
एकादश्यां निराहारो द्वादश्यां पुरुषोत्तमम् ।
अर्च्चयेद्ब्राह्मणमुखे स गच्छेत्परमम्पदम् ॥
एषा तिथिर्वैष्णवी स्याद्द्वादशी शुक्लपक्षके‖ ।
तस्यामाराधयेद्देवम्प्रयत्नेन जनार्द्दनम् ॥
यत्किञ्चिद्देवमीशानमुद्दिश्य ब्राह्मणे शुचौ ।

---

* तिलानेव समाहितः इति B and F. † अनुप्राप्तः इति B. ‡ दद्याच्चोद्दिश्य इति B. § तस्य नास्ति इति B. ¶ अमावस्यायां भक्तैस्तु इति B. ‖ शुक्लपक्षतः इति B.

दीयते विष्णवे वापि तदनन्तफलं स्मृतम्* ॥
यो हि यान्देवतामिच्छेत्समाराधयितुन्नरः ।
ब्राह्मणान् पूजयेद्विद्वान्† स तस्यास्तोषहेतुतः‡ ॥
द्विजानां वपुरास्थाय नित्यं तिष्ठन्ति देवताः ।
पूज्यन्ते ब्राह्मणालाभे प्रतिमादिष्वपि क्वचित्§ ॥
तस्मात्सर्वप्रयत्नेन तत्तत्फलमभीप्सुभिः¶ ।
द्विजेषु देवता नित्यं पूजनीया विशेषतः ॥
विभूतिकामः सततं पूजयेद्वै‖ पुरन्दरम् ।
ब्रह्म**वर्च्चसकामस्तु ब्रह्माणं ब्रह्म††कामुकः ॥
आरोग्यकामोऽथ रविं धेनु‡‡कामी हुताशनम् ।
कर्म्मणां सिद्धिकामस्तु पूजयेद्वै विनायकम् ॥
भोगकामस्तु शशिनं बलकामः समीरणम् ।
मुमुक्षुः सर्व्वसंसारात्प्रयत्नेनार्च्चयेद्धरिम्§§ ॥
यस्तु योगन्तथा मोक्षमिच्छेत्तज्ज्ञानमैश्वरम् ।
सोऽर्च्चयेद्वै¶¶ विरूपाक्षं प्रयत्नेन महेश्वरम्‖‖ ॥
यो वाञ्छति महायोगात्*** ज्ञानानि च महेश्वरम् ।

---

* तदनन्तफलप्रदमिति B. † यत्नादिति B ‡ स तस्यां तोषयेत्ततः इति B. § प्रतिमादिषु ते क्वचिदिति B. ¶ अभीप्सता इति B and F. ‖ पूजयेद्धि इति B. ** सर्व्वेति B. †† ज्ञानेति B and F. ‡‡ धनेति B and F. §§ प्रयत्ना-दर्च्चयेद्धरिमिति B and F. ¶¶ सोऽर्च्चयेद्धि इति B. ‖‖ प्रयत्नेनेश्वरेश्वरमिति B. प्रयत्नेनेश्वरं हरमिति F. *** ये वाञ्छन्ति महाभागानिति B and F.

स पूजयति* भूतेशङ्केशवञ्चापि भोगिनम्† ॥
वारिदस्तृप्तिमाप्नोति धन‡मक्षय्यमन्नदः ।
तिलप्रदः प्रजामिष्टान्दीपदश्चक्षुरुत्तमम् ॥
भूमिदः सर्व्वमाप्नोति दीर्घमायुर्हिरण्यदः ।
गृहदोऽग्र्याणि वेश्मानि रूप्यदो रूपमुत्तमम् ॥
वासोदश्चन्द्रसालोक्यमश्विसालोक्यमश्वदः§ ।
अनडुहः श्रियं पुष्टां¶ गोदो ब्रध्नस्य विष्टपम्‖ ॥
यानशय्याप्रदो भार्य्यामैश्वर्य्यमभयप्रदः ।
धान्यदः शाश्वतं सौख्यं ब्रह्मदो ब्रह्मसात्मताम्** ॥
धान्यान्यपि†† यथाशक्ति विप्रेषु प्रतिपादयेत् ।
वेदवित्सु विशिष्टेषु प्रेत्य स्वर्गं समश्नुते ॥
गवां वास‡‡प्रदानेन सर्व्वपापैः प्रमुच्यते ।
इन्धनानां प्रदानेन दीप्ताग्निर्जायते नरः ॥
फलमूलानि शाकानि भोज्यानि§§ विविधानि च ।
प्रदद्याद्ब्राह्मणेभ्यस्तु मुदा युक्तः स्वयम्भवेत्¶¶ ॥
औषधं स्नेहमाहारं रोगिणे‖‖ रोगशान्तये ।
ददानो रोगरहितः सुखी दीर्घायुरेव च ॥

---

* ते पूजयन्तीति B and F. † भोगिनः इति B. ‡ सुखमिति B and F. § अश्वदो यानमुत्तममिति B. ¶ अर्थदाता श्रियञ्चेष्टामिति B. ‖ पिष्टपमिति B. ** ब्रह्म शाश्वतमिति B and F. †† धनान्यपीति B. ‡‡ वसेति B. घीषेति F. §§ पर्णानि पानानीति B. ¶¶ सदा भवेदिति B and F. ‖‖ रोगिणः इति B and F.

असिपत्रवनन्दुर्गं* क्षुरधारासमन्वितम् ।
तीव्रतापञ्च† तरति छत्त्रोपानत्प्रदो नरः ॥
यद्यदिष्टतमं लोके यच्चापि‡ दयितं गृहे ।
तत्तद्गुणवते देयन्तदेवाक्षयमिच्छता ॥
अयने विषुवे चैव ग्रहणे चन्द्रसूर्य्ययोः ।
संक्रान्त्यादिषु कालेषु दत्तम्भवति चाक्षयम् ॥
प्रयागादिषु तीर्थेषु पुण्येष्वायतनेषु च ।
दत्त्वा चाक्षयमाप्नोति नदीषु च वनेषु§ च ॥
दानधर्म्मात्परो धर्म्मो भूतानान्नेह विद्यते ।
तस्माद्विप्राय दातव्यं श्रोत्रियाय द्विजातिभिः ॥
स्वर्गायुर्भूतिकामेन तथा पापोपशान्तये ।
मुमुक्षुणा च¶ दातव्यं ब्राह्मणेभ्यस्तथान्वहम् ॥
दीयमानन्तु यो मोहाद्गोविप्राग्निसुरेषु च ।
निवारयति पापात्मा तिर्य्यग्योनिं व्रजेत्तु सः ॥
यस्तु द्रव्यार्ज्जनङ्कृत्वा नार्च्चयेद्ब्राह्मणान् सुरान् ।
सर्व्वस्वमपहृत्यैनं राष्ट्राद्विप्रतिवासयेत्‖ ॥
यस्तु दुर्भिक्षवेलायामन्नाद्यं न प्रयच्छति ।
म्रियमाणेषु सत्त्वेषु ब्राह्मणः** स तु गर्हितः ॥

---

* मार्गमिति B and F. † तीक्ष्णातपञ्चेति B and F. ‡ यच्चास्य इति B. § नदेषु चेति B. ¶ मुमुक्षूणाञ्चेति B, E and H. ‖ राजा राष्ट्रात्प्रवासयेदिति B and F. ** विप्रेषु ब्रह्महा इति B and F. सत्त्वेषु ब्रह्महा इति E.

तस्मान्न प्रतिगृह्णीयान्न वै देयञ्च तस्य हि* ।
अङ्कयित्वा† स्वकाद्राष्ट्रात्तं राजा विप्रवासयेत् ॥
यस्तु सङ्गो ददातीह न द्रव्यं ब्रह्म‡साधनम् ।
स पूर्व्वाभ्यधिकः पापी नरके पच्यते नरः ॥
स्वाध्यायवन्तो ये विप्रा विद्यावन्तो जितेन्द्रियाः ।
सत्यसंयमसंयुक्तास्तेभ्यो दद्याद्द्विजोत्तमाः§ ॥
सुभुक्तमपि विद्वांसं धार्म्मिकम्भोजयेद्द्विजम् ।
न तु मूर्खमवृत्तस्थं¶ दशरात्रमुपोषितम् ॥
सन्निकृष्टमतिक्रम्य श्रोत्रियं यः प्रयच्छति ।
स तेन कर्म्मणा पापी दहत्यासप्तमङ्कुलम् ॥
यदि स्यादधिको विप्रः शीलविद्यादिभिः स्वयम् ।
तस्मै यत्नेन दातव्यमतिक्रम्यापि‖ सन्निधिम् ॥
योऽर्च्चितम्प्रतिगृह्णाति** दद्यात्यर्च्चितमेव वा†† ।
तावुभौ गच्छतः स्वर्गं नरकन्तु विपर्य्यये ॥
न वार्य्यपि प्रयच्छेत नास्तिके हैतुके‡‡ऽपि च ।
पाषण्डेषु च§§ सर्व्वेषु नावेदविदि धर्म्मवित् ॥

---

* न तस्मात्प्रतिगृह्णीयुर्न विशेयुश्च ते न हि इति B. न दृष्येयुश्च तेन हि इति F.
† अङ्कापयित्वेति B. ‡ धर्म्मेति B. यश्चासभ्यो ददातीह स्वधनं धर्म्मसाधकमिति F.
§ सत्यसंयमसंस्थेभ्यो दद्याद्विप्रो द्विजोत्तमाः इति A. ¶ मूर्खमवृत्तिस्थमिति B.
‖ अतिक्रम्य चेति B. ** प्रतिगृह्णीयादिति B. †† दद्यादर्च्चितमेव तु इति B.
‡‡ हैतुके—हेतुमन्विष्यतीति हैतुकः कुतर्की, श्रद्धाहीनः, तस्मिन् । §§ न पाषण्डेषु इति B and F.

अपूपञ्च हिरण्यञ्च गामश्वं पृथिवीन्तिलान् ।
अविद्वान्प्रतिगृह्णानो भस्मीभवति काष्ठवत् ॥
द्विजातिभ्यो धनं लिप्सेत्प्रशस्तेभ्यो द्विजोत्तमः ।
अपि वा जातिमात्रेभ्यो* न तु शूद्रात्कथञ्चन ॥
वृत्तिसङ्कोचनादिच्छेत्† नेहेत धनविस्तरम् ।
धनलाभे‡ प्रसक्तस्तु ब्राह्मण्यादेव हीयते ॥
वेदानधीत्य सकलान् यज्ञांश्चावाप्य सर्व्वशः ।
न तां गतिमवाप्नोति सङ्कोचाद्यामवाप्नुयात् ॥
प्रतिग्रह§रुचिर्न स्याद्यात्रार्थन्तु धनं हरेत् ।
स्थित्यर्थादधिकं गृह्णन् ब्राह्मणो यात्यधोगतिम् ॥
यस्तु स्याद्याचको¶ नित्यं न स स्वर्गस्य भाजनम् ।
उद्वेजयति भूतानि यथा चौरस्तथैव सः ॥
गुरून् भृत्यांश्चोज्जिहीर्षन्‖ अर्च्चिष्यन्देवतातिथीन् ।
सर्व्वतः प्रतिगृह्णीयान्न तु तृप्येत्स्वयन्ततः ॥
एवं गृहस्थो युक्तात्मा देवतातिथिपूजकः ।
वर्त्तमानः संयतात्मा याति तत्परमम्पदम् ॥
पुत्रे निधाय वा सर्व्वं गत्वारण्यन्तु तत्त्ववित् ।
एकाकी विचरेन्नित्यमुदासीनः समाहितः ॥

---

* अपि राजन्यवैश्याभ्यामिति B and F. † वृत्तिसङ्कोचमन्विच्छेदिति B and F. ‡ धनलोभे इति B. धनलोभप्रसक्तस्तु इति F. § प्रतिगृह्येति B. ¶ यस्तु याचनकः इति B and F. ‖ उज्जिहीर्षुरिति B.

एष वः कथितो धर्म्मो गृहस्थानां द्विजोत्तमाः।
ज्ञात्वा तु तिष्ठेन्नियतं तथानुष्ठापयेद्द्विजान्॥

इति देवमनादिमेकमीशं
गृहधर्म्मेण समर्च्चयेदजस्रम्।
समतीत्य स सर्व्वभूतयोनिं
प्रकृतिं परं न याति जन्म॥*

इति श्रीकूर्म्मपुराणे उपविभागे† व्यासगीतासु षड्विंशोऽध्यायः।

सप्तविंशोऽध्यायः।

व्यास उवाच।

एवं गृहाश्रमे स्थित्वा द्वितीयम्भागमायुषः।
वानप्रस्थाश्रमं गच्छेत्सदारः साग्निरेव वा* ॥
निक्षिप्य भार्य्यां पुत्त्रेषु गच्छेद्वनमथापि वा।
दृष्ट्वापत्यस्य चापत्यं जर्ज्जरीकृतविग्रहः॥
शुक्लपक्षस्य पूर्व्वाह्णे प्रशस्ते चोत्तरायणे।
गत्वारण्यं नियमवांस्तपः कुर्य्यात्समाहितः॥

---

* एष श्लोकः A पुस्तके नास्ति। † एतत्पदं A, E, H पुस्तकेषु न दृश्यते।

---

* चेति B, E and F.

फलमूलानि पूतानि नित्यमाहारमाहरेत् ।
यताहारो* भवेत्तेन पूजयेत्पितृदेवताः ॥
पूजयित्वातिथीन्नित्यं† स्नात्वा चाभ्यर्चयेत्सुरान् ।
गृहानागत्य चाश्नीयादष्टौ‡ ग्रासान् समाहितः ॥
जटां वै§ बिभृयान्नित्यं नखरोमाणि नोत्सृजेत् ।
स्वाध्यायं सर्व्वदा कुर्य्यान्नियच्छेद्वाचमन्यतः ॥
अग्निहोत्रञ्च जुहुयात्पञ्चयज्ञान् समाचरेत् ।
मुन्यन्नैर्व्विविधैर्व्वन्यैः¶ शाकमूलफलेन च ॥
चीरवासा भवेन्नित्यं स्नाति‖ त्रिषवणं शुचिः ।
सर्व्वभूतानुकम्पी स्यात्प्रतिग्रहविवर्ज्जितः ॥
स दर्शपौर्णमासेन** यजेत नियतं द्विजः ।
ऋक्षेष्वाग्रयणे†† चैव चातुर्मास्यानि चाहरेत्‡‡ ॥
उत्तरायणञ्च क्रमशो§§ दक्षस्यायनमेव च ।
वासन्तैः शारदैर्मेध्यैर्मुन्यन्नैः स्वयमाहृतैः ॥
पुरोडाशांश्चरूंश्चैव विविधं निर्व्वपेत्पृथक् ।
देवताभ्यश्च तद्धुत्वा वन्यं मेध्यतरं हविः ॥

---

* यदाहारः इति B and F. † पूजयेदतिथिं नित्यमिति B and F. ‡ गृहादादाय चाश्नीयादष्टौ इति B. गृहादाहृत्य इति F. § जटाश्च इति B and F. ¶ अनन्यैर्व्विविधैर्मेध्यैरिति B. मुन्यन्नैर्व्विविधैर्मेध्यैरिति E and F. ‖ स्नायादिति B and F. ** दर्शेन पौर्णमासेन इति B and F. †† आग्रयणे—The first Soma libation at the Agnishoma sacrifice. ‡‡ चाहरेदिति B. §§ उत्तरायणञ्चन्द्रमस इति H.

शेषं समुपभुञ्जीत लवणञ्च स्वयङ्कृतम्।
वर्ज्जयेन्मधुमांसानि भौमानि कवकानि* च ॥
भूस्तृणं शिशुकञ्चैव† श्लेष्मातकफलानि च।
न फालकृष्टमश्नीयादुत्सृष्टमपि केनचित् ॥
न ग्रामजातान्यार्त्तोऽपि पुष्पाणि च फलानि च। ‡
श्रावणेनैव विधिना वह्निं परिचरेत्सदा ॥
न द्रुह्येत्सर्व्वभूतानि निर्द्वन्द्वो निर्भयो भवेत्।
न नक्तञ्चैवमश्नीयात्§ रात्रौ ध्यानपरो भवेत् ॥
जितेन्द्रियो जितक्रोधस्तत्त्वज्ञानविचिन्तकः।
ब्रह्मचारी भवेन्नित्यं न पत्नीमपि संश्रयेत् ॥
यस्तु पत्न्या¶ वनं गत्वा मैथुनं कामतश्चरेत्।
तद्व्रतं तस्य लुप्येत प्रायश्चित्तीयते द्विजः ॥
तत्र‖ यो जायते गर्भो न संस्पृश्यो भवेद्विजः।
न च वेदेऽधिकारोऽस्य तद्वंशेऽप्येवमेव हि ॥
अधः शयीत नियतं** सावित्रीजपतत्परः।
शरण्यः सर्व्वभूतानां संविभागरतः†† सदा ॥
परिवादं मृषावादं निद्रालस्यं विवर्ज्जयेत्।
एकाग्निरनिकेतः स्यात्प्रोक्षितां भूमिमाश्रयेत् ॥

---

* करकाणीति B. † सियुकञ्चैवेति E and H. ‡ न फालेत्यादि पादचतुष्टयं A, E, H पुस्तकेषु नास्ति। § न नक्तं किञ्चिदश्नीयादिति B and F. ¶ पत्न्यामिति B and F. ‖ तस्येति A, E, F and H. ** सततमिति B. †† परः इति B.

मृगैः सह चरेद्वा यस्तैः* सहैव च संविशेत् ।
शिलायां वा शर्करायां† शयीत सुसमाहितः ॥
सद्यःप्रक्षालको वा स्यान्माससञ्चयको‡ऽपि वा ।
षण्मासनिचयो वा स्यात्§ समानिचय एव च ॥
त्यजेदाश्वयुजे मासि सम्पन्नं पूर्व्वचिन्तितम्¶ ।
जीर्णानि चैव वासांसि शाकमूलफलानि च ॥
दन्तोलूखलिको वा स्यात्कापोतीं वृत्तिमाश्रयेत् ।
अश्मकुट्टो भवेद्वापि कालपक्वभुगेव च‖ ॥
नक्तञ्चान्नं** समश्नीयाद्दिवा चाहृत्य†† शक्तितः‡‡ ।
चतुर्थकालिको वा स्यात्स्याद्वा चाष्टम§§कालिकः ॥
चान्द्रायणविधानैर्वा शुक्ले कृष्णे च वर्त्तयेत् ।
पक्षे पक्षे समश्नीयाद्द्विजाग्रयान् कथितान्¶¶ सकृत् ॥
पुष्पमूलफलैर्वापि केवलैर्वर्त्तयेत्सदा ।
स्वाभाविकैः स्वयं शीर्णैर्वैखानसमते स्थितः ॥
भूमौ वा परिवर्त्तेत तिष्ठेद्वा प्रपदैर्दिनम्‖‖ ।
स्थानासनाभ्यां*** विहरेन्न क्वचिद्धैर्य्यमुत्सृजेत् ॥

---

* चरेद्वासं तैरिति B. चरेद्वान्त इति F. † शर्करायां वा इति B. ‡ सञ्चयिकः इति B. सद्यःप्रस्थानक इति F. § वापीति B. ¶ मूलस्थं पूर्व्वसञ्चितमिति B. उत्पन्नं पूर्व्वसञ्चितमिति F. ‖ कालः पक्वभुगेव वा इति B. कालपक्वभुगेव वा इति F. ** नक्तं वान्नमिति B. †† वाहृत्य इति B. ‡‡ यव्रत इति F. §§ स्याद्वाप्यष्टमेति B. ¶¶ यवागूं कथितामिति B. यवागूः कथिताः इति F. ‖‖ दिवमिति B. *** स्नानाशनाभ्यामिति B.

ग्रीष्मे पञ्चतपास्तद्वद्वर्षास्वभ्रावकाशकः* ।
आर्द्रवासास्तु हेमन्ते क्रमशो वर्द्धयंस्तपः ॥
उपस्पृश्य त्रिषवणं† पितृदेवांश्च तर्पयेत् ।
एकपादेन तिष्ठेत मरीचीन्वा पिबेत्तदा‡ ॥
पञ्चाग्निर्धूमपो वा स्यादुष्मपः सोमपोऽथवा§ ।
पयः पिबेच्छुक्लपक्षे कृष्णपक्षे च गोमयम्¶ ॥
शीर्णपर्णाशनो वा स्यात्कृच्छ्रैर्वा वर्त्तयेत्सदा‖ ।
योगाभ्यासरतश्चैव** रुद्राध्यायी भवेत्सदा ॥
अथर्व्वशिरसोऽध्येता वेदान्ताभ्यासतत्परः ।
यमान्†† सेवेत सततं नियमांश्चाप्यतन्द्रितः ॥
कृष्णाजिनः‡‡ सोत्तरीयः शुक्लयज्ञोपवीतवान् ।
अथ चाग्नीन् समारोप्य स्वात्मनि ध्यानतत्परः ।
अनग्निरनिकेतः स्यान्मुनिर्मोक्षपरो भवेत् ॥§§
तापसेष्वेव विप्रेषु याचिकं भैक्षमाहरेत्¶¶ ॥
गृहमेधिषु चान्येषु द्विजेषु वनवासिषु‖‖ ।
ग्रामादाहृत्य चाश्नीयादष्टौ ग्रासान्वने वसन् ॥
प्रतिगृह्य पुटेनैव पाणिना शकलेन*** वा ।

---

* अभावकाशिकः इति B. † उपोष्य त्रिषवणञ्चापीति B. ‡ सदा इति B and F. § सोमपोऽपि वेति B. ¶ कृष्णपक्षे तु सोमपः इति B. ‖ कृच्छ्रैरापद्यते सदेति B. ** रतश्च स्यादिति B. †† इमानिति B. ‡‡ कृष्णाजिनीति B. §§ एष श्लोकः A, E, H पुस्तकेषु नास्ति । ¶¶ पात्रिकं भैक्ष्यमाचरेदिति B. ‖‖ वनचारिषु इति B. *** करकेणेति B. कलकेनेति F.

विविधाश्चोपनिषद आत्मसंसिद्धये* जपेत् ॥
विद्याविशेषान् सावित्रीं रुद्राध्यायं तथैव च ।
महाप्रस्थानिकं वासौ कुर्य्यादनशनन्तु वा† ।
अग्निप्रवेशमन्यद्वा ब्रह्मार्पणविधौ स्थित: ॥‡

इति श्रीकूर्म्मपुराणे उपविभागे व्यासगीतासु वानप्रस्थाश्रमधर्म्मो नाम सप्तविंशोऽध्याय: ।

अष्टाविंशोऽध्याय: ।

व्यास उवाच ।

एवं वनाश्रमे स्थित्वा तृतीयं भागमायुष: ।
चतुर्थमायुषो भागं सन्न्यासेन नयेत् क्रमात् ॥
अग्नीनात्मनि संस्थाप्य द्विज: प्रव्रजितो भवेत् ।
योगाभ्यासरत: शान्तो ब्रह्मविद्यापरायण: ॥
यदा मनसि सञ्जातं* वैतृष्णं सर्व्ववस्तुषु ।
तदा सन्न्यासमिच्छन्ति पतित: स्याद्विपर्य्यये ॥

---

* चौपनिषदीरात्मसंसिद्धये इति G. † अनशनं तथेति B. ‡ येन सम्यगिममाश्रमं शिवं संश्रयन्त्यशिवं पुञ्जताश्रमं । ते विशन्ति पदमैश्वरं पदं यान्ति यत्र गतोऽस्य संस्थिते: ॥ इत्यधिक: पाठ: F पुस्तके दृश्यते ।

---

* सम्पन्नमिति B.

प्राजापत्यान्निरूप्येष्टिमाग्नेयीमथवा पुनः।
दान्तः पक्वः कषायोऽसौ ब्रह्माश्रमसुपाश्रयेत्॥
ज्ञानसन्यासिनः केचिद्वेदसन्यासिनः परे*।
कर्म्मसन्यासिनस्त्वन्ये विविधाः परिकीर्त्तिताः॥
यः सर्व्वसङ्गनिर्मुक्तो निर्द्वन्द्वश्चैव निर्भयः।
प्रोच्यते ज्ञानसन्यासी स्वात्मन्येव व्यवस्थितः॥
वेदमेवाभ्यसेन्नित्यन्निर्द्वन्द्वो† निष्परिग्रहः।
प्रोच्यते वेदसन्यासी सुमत्तुर्विजितेन्द्रियः॥
यस्त्वग्नीनात्मसात्कृत्वा ब्रह्मार्पणपरो द्विजः।
स ज्ञेयः‡ कर्म्मसन्यासी महायज्ञपरायणः॥
त्रयाणामपि चैतेषां योगी§ त्वभ्यधिको मतः।
न तस्य विद्यते कार्य्यं न लिङ्गं वा विपश्चितः॥
निर्म्ममो निर्भयः शान्तो निर्द्वन्द्वो निष्परिग्रहः¶।
जीर्णकौपीनवासा स्यान्नग्नो वा ध्यानतत्परः॥
ब्रह्मचारी मितग्रासी‖ ग्रामात्त्वन्नं** समाहरेत्।
अध्यात्ममतिरासीत निरपेक्षो निरामिषः।
आत्मनैव सहायेन सुखार्थी विचरेदिह॥
नाभिनन्देत†† मरणं नाभिनन्देत जीवितम्‡‡।

---

* सन्यासिनोऽपरे इति B and F. † निराशीति B and F. ‡ ज्ञेयः स इति B and F. § ज्ञानीति B and F. ¶ पर्णभोजनः इति B and F. ‖ मिताहारः इति B and F. ** ग्रामान्नान्नमिति B. ग्रामादन्नं समाहरेदिति F. †† नाभिनन्देत इति आर्षमात्मनेपदम्। ‡‡ जीवनमिति B.

कालमेव प्रतीक्षेत निदेशम्भृतको यथा ॥
नाध्येतव्यं न वक्तव्यं न श्रोतव्यं* कदाचन ।
एवं ज्ञात्वा परो† योगी ब्रह्मभूयाय कल्पते ॥
एकवासाथवा‡ विद्वान् कौपीनाच्छादनस्तथा§ ।
मुण्डी¶ शिखी वाथ भवेत्त्रिदण्डी निष्परिग्रहः ॥
कषायवासाः सततन्ध्यानयोगपरायणः ।
ग्रामान्ते वृक्षमूले वा वसेद्देवालयेऽपि वा ॥
समः शत्रौ च मित्रे च‖ तथा मानापमानयोः ।
भैक्ष्येण वर्त्तयेन्नित्यन्नैकान्नादी भवेत्क्वचित् ॥
यस्तु मोहेन वान्यस्मादेकान्नादी** भवेद्यतिः ।
न तस्य निष्कृतिः काचिद्†† धर्म्मशास्त्रेषु कथ्यते ॥
रागद्वेषविमुक्तात्मा समलोष्टाश्मकाञ्चनः ।
प्राणिहिंसानिवृत्तश्च मौनी स्यात्सर्वनिस्पृहः ॥
दृष्टिपूतन्न्यसेत्पादं वस्त्रपूतं जलं पिबेत् ।
शास्त्रपूतां वदेद्वाणीं मनःपूतं समाचरेत् ॥
नैकत्र निवसेद्देशे वर्षाभ्योऽन्यत्र भिक्षुकः ।
स्नान‡‡शौचरतो नित्यं कमण्डलुकरः शुचिः ॥
ब्रह्मचर्य्यरतो नित्यं वनवासरतो भवेत् ।

---

* श्रोतव्यं न इति B. † ज्ञानपरः इति B and F. ‡ एकवासाथवा इत्यत्र सन्धिरार्षः एकवासाः अथवा इति पदच्छेदः । § कौपीनाच्छादनोऽपि वा इति B. ¶ मुण्डः इति B. ‖ समः शत्रौ तथा मित्रे इति B. ** एकान्नाशीति B. †† कार्य्या इति B. ‡‡ स्नालेति B.

मोक्षशास्त्रेषु निरतो ब्रह्मचारी* जितेन्द्रियः ॥
दम्भाहङ्कारनिर्मुक्तो निन्दापैशुन्यवर्जितः ।
आत्मज्ञानगुणोपेतो यतिर्मोक्षमवाप्नुयात् ॥
अभ्यसेत्सततन्देवं† प्रणवाख्यं सनातनम् ।
स्नात्वाचम्य विधानेन शुचिर्देवालयादिषु ॥
यज्ञोपवीती शान्तात्मा कुशपाणिः समाहितः ।
धौतकाषायवसनो भस्मच्छन्नतनूरुहः ॥
अधियज्ञं‡ ब्रह्म जपेदाधिदैविकमेव वा ।
आध्यात्मिकञ्च सततं वेदान्ताभिहितञ्च यत् ॥
पत्रेषु§ चाथ निवसन् ब्रह्मचारी यतिर्मुनिः ।
वेदमेवाभ्यसेन्नित्यं स याति परमाङ्गतिम् ॥
अहिंसा सत्यमस्तेयं ब्रह्मचर्य्यं ततः परम्¶ ।
क्षमा दया च सन्तोषो व्रतान्यस्य विशेषतः ॥
वेदान्तज्ञाननिष्णातान् पञ्चयज्ञान् समाहितान् ।
कुर्य्यादहरहः स्नात्वा भिक्षान्ते नैव तेन हि ॥ ‖
होममन्त्राञ्जपेन्नित्यं होमकाले** समाहितः ।
स्वाध्यायञ्चान्वहं कुर्य्यात्सावित्रीं सन्ध्ययोर्जपेत् ॥

---

* ब्रह्मसूत्रीति B and F. † वेदमिति B, E and F. ‡ आधियज्ञमिति B. § पुत्रेषु इति B, E, F, G and H. ¶ तपः परमिति B. ‖ वेदान्तज्ञाननिष्ठो वा पञ्चयज्ञान् समाहितः । ज्ञानध्यानसमायुक्तो भिक्षार्थं नैव तेन हि इति B. ** काले काले इति B and F.

ततो ध्यायीत तन्देव*मेकान्ते परमेश्वरम्।
एकान्ते† वर्ज्जयेन्नित्यं कामं क्रोधं परिग्रहम्॥
एकवासा द्विवासा वा शिखी यज्ञोपवीतवान्।
कमण्डलुधरो‡ विद्वान् त्रिदण्डी याति तत्परम्॥

इति श्रीकूर्म्मपुराणे उपविभागे व्यासगीतासु यतिधर्म्मो नाम अष्टाविंशोऽध्यायः।

ऊनत्रिंशोऽध्यायः।

व्यास उवाच।

एवं स्वाश्रमनिष्ठानां यतीनां नियतात्मनाम्।
भैक्ष्येण वर्त्तनं प्रोक्तं फलमूलैरथापि वा॥
एकं कालं* चरेद्भैक्षं न प्रसज्येत विस्तरे।
भैक्ष्यप्रसक्तो हि† यतिर्विषयेष्वपि सज्जति॥
सप्तागारां‡श्चरेद्भैक्षमलाभे तु पुनश्चरेत्।

---

* ध्यायीत सततं देवमिति B, E, F, G and H. आत्मनेपदमार्षम्।
† एकान्तमिति B and F. ‡ कमण्डलुकरः इति B and F.

---

* एककालमिति B and F. † भैक्ष्ये प्रसक्तो हीति B. भैक्ष्येषु सक्तो हीति F.
‡ सप्तागारमिति E, F and H.

प्रक्षाल्य पात्रे भुञ्जीत अद्भिः प्रक्षालयेत्पुनः* ॥
अथवाऽन्यदुपादाय पात्रे भुञ्जीत नित्यशः।
भुक्त्वा तत्संमृजेत्पात्रं यात्रामात्रमलोलुपः ॥
विधूमे सन्नमुसले व्यङ्गारे भुक्तवर्ज्जने।
वृत्ते शरावसम्पाते भिक्षान्नित्यं यतिश्चरेत् ॥
गोदोहमात्रं तिष्ठेत कालम्भिक्षुरधोमुखः।
भिक्षेत्युक्त्वा सकृत्तूष्णीमश्नीयाद्वाग्यतः शुचिः ॥
प्रक्षाल्य पाणी पादौ च समाचम्य यथाविधि।
आदित्ये दर्शयित्वान्नं भुञ्जीत प्राङ्मुखो नरः† ॥
हुत्वा प्राणाहुतीः पञ्च ग्रासानष्टौ समाहितः।
आचम्य देवं ब्रह्माणं ध्यायीत परमेश्वरम् ॥
अलाबुपात्रं दार्व्वञ्च‡ मृण्मयं वैणवन्ततः§।
चत्वार्येतानि पात्राणि मनुराह प्रजापतिः ॥
प्राग्रात्रे पररात्रे च मध्यरात्रे तथैव च।
सन्ध्यास्वग्निविशेषेण चिन्तयेन्नित्यमीश्वरम् ॥
कृत्वा हृत्पद्मनिलये विश्वाख्यं विश्वसम्भवम्।
आत्मानं सर्व्वभूतानां परस्तात्तमसि स्थितम् ॥
सर्व्वस्याधारभूतानां¶मानन्दं ज्योतिरव्ययम्।
प्रधानपुरुषातीतमाकाशकुहरं शिवम्‖ ॥

---

* भुञ्जीयादद्भिः प्रक्षालयेत्तु तदिति B. † प्राङ्मुखोत्तर इति B. प्राङ्मुखोत्वर इति F. ‡ अलाबुं दारुपात्रञ्च इति B and F. § तथा इति B. ¶ आधारम-व्यक्तमिति B and F. ‖ आकाशं दहनं शिवमिति B and F.

तदन्तः सर्व्वभावानामीश्वरं ब्रह्मरूपिणम् ।
ध्यायेदनादिमध्यान्तमानन्दाख्य*गुणालयम् ॥
महान्तं पुरुषं† ब्रह्म ब्रह्माणं‡ सत्यमव्ययम् ।
सितं सितेतराकारं§ महेशं विश्वरूपिणम्¶ ॥ ||
ओङ्कारेणाथ** चात्मानं संस्थाप्य परमात्मनि ।
आकाशे देवमीशानं ध्यायीताकाशमध्यगम् ॥
कारणं सर्व्वभावानामानन्दैकसमाश्रयम् ।
पुराणं पुरुषं शुभ्रं†† ध्यायन्मुच्येत बन्धनात् ॥
यद्वा‡‡ गुहायां प्रकृतं§§ जगत्सम्मोहनालये ।
विचिन्त्य परमं व्योम सर्व्वभूतैककारणम् ॥
जीवनं सर्व्वभूतानां यत्र लोकः प्रतीयते¶¶ ।
आनन्दं ब्रह्मणः सूक्ष्मं यत्पश्यन्ति मुमुक्षवः ॥
तन्मध्ये निहितं ब्रह्म केवलं ज्ञानलक्षणम् ।
अनन्तं सत्यमीशानं विचिन्त्यासीत संयतः ॥
गुह्याद्गुह्यतमं ज्ञानं यतीनामेतदीरितम् ।
योऽनुतिष्ठेन्महेशेन|||| सोऽश्नुते योगमैश्वरम् ॥
तस्माद्ध्यानरतो नित्यमात्मविद्यापरायणः ।

---

* आनन्दादीति B. † परममिति B. ‡ पुरुषमिति B. § सितेतरारुणाकारमिति B. ¶ विश्वकारिणमिति B. || इदं श्लोकार्द्धद्वयं F पुस्तके नास्ति । ** ओङ्कारान्तेऽथ इति B. †† शम्भुमिति B, E, F, G and H. ‡‡ यथेति B. §§ प्रकृतौ इति B and F. ¶¶ प्रलीयते इति B and F. |||| योऽन्न तिष्ठेन्महेशेन इति B. योऽवतिष्ठेत सततमिति F.

ज्ञानं स मन्यते ब्रह्म* येन मुच्येत बन्धनात् ॥
नत्वा† पृथक् स्वमात्मानं सर्व्वस्मादेव केवलम्।
आनन्दमजरं ज्ञानं ध्यायीत च पुनः परम्‡ ॥
तस्माद्भवन्ति भूतानि यद्गत्वा नेह जायते।
स तस्मादीश्वरो देवः परस्माद्योऽधितिष्ठति§ ॥
यदन्तरे तद्गमनं¶ शाश्वतं शिवमुच्यते‖।
यदाहु**स्तत्परो यः स्यात् स देवस्तु†† महेश्वरः ॥
व्रतानि यानि भिक्षूणां तथैवोपव्रतानि च।‡‡
एकैकातिक्रमे तेषां प्रायश्चित्तं विधीयते ॥
उपेत्य तु§§ स्त्रियं कामात्कृच्छ्रसंयतमानसः¶¶।
प्राणायामसमायुक्तः कुर्य्यात्सान्तपनं शुचिः ॥
ततश्चरेत नियमात् कृच्छ्रं संयतमानसः। ‖‖
पुनराश्रममागम्य चरेद्भिक्षुरतन्द्रितः ॥
न नर्मयुक्तमनृतं हिनस्तीति मनीषिणः।
तथापि च न कर्त्तव्यं प्रसङ्गो ह्येष दारुणः ॥
एकरात्रोपवासश्च*** प्राणायामशतं तथा।

---

* समभ्यसेद्ब्राह्ममिति B, E, F, G and H. † मत्वा इति B, E, F and H. ‡ पुनरिति B. § परस्माद्योऽधितिष्ठतीति B. परस्माद्यो विवस्वत इति F. ¶ तद्गगनमिति B. तत्कमलमिति F. ‖ शिवमव्ययमिति B and F. ** यदंश इति B. †† यस्तु स देवः स्यादिति B. ‡‡ एतत् पादद्वयं A, E, H पुस्तकेषु नास्ति। §§ चेति B. ¶¶ प्रायश्चित्तं समाहितः इति B and F. ‖‖ एष श्लोकः A पुस्तके नास्ति। *** वासस्तु इति B.

कर्त्तव्यं यतिना धर्म्मलिप्सुना वरमव्ययम्* ॥
गतेनापि न कार्य्यन्ते न कार्य्यं स्तैन्यमन्यतः† ।
स्तेयादभ्यधिकः कश्चिन्नास्त्यधर्म्म इति श्रुतिः‡ ॥
हिंसा चैषा परा दिष्टा§ या चात्मज्ञाननाशिका ।
यदेतद्द्रविणं नाम प्राणा ह्येते वहिश्चराः ॥
स तस्य हरति प्राणान्यो यस्य हरते धनम् ॥
एतत्कृत्वा सुदुष्टात्मा¶ भिन्नवृत्तो व्रताहतः‖ ।
भूयोनिर्वेदमापन्नश्चरेच्चान्द्रायणव्रतम्** ॥
विधिना शास्त्रदृष्टेन संवत्सरमिति†† श्रुतिः ।
भूयो निर्वेदमापन्नश्चरेद्भिक्षुरतन्द्रितः ॥
अकस्मादेव हिंसान्तु यदि भिक्षुः समाचरेत् ।
कुर्य्यात्कृच्छ्रातिकृच्छ्रन्तु चान्द्रायणमथापि वा ॥
स्कन्नमिन्द्रिय‡‡दौर्बल्यात् स्त्रियन्दृष्ट्वा यतिर्यदि ।
तेन धारयितव्या वै प्राणायामास्तु षोड़श ॥
दिवास्कन्ने त्रिरात्रं स्यात्प्राणायामशतं तथा ॥
एकान्ते मधुमांसे च नवश्राद्धे तथैव च ।

---

* उक्ता नूनं प्रकर्त्तव्यं यतिना धर्म्मलिप्सुना इति B. † परमापन्नतेनापि न कार्य्यं स्तेयमन्यतः इति B. अत्यन्तापन्नवेनापि न कार्य्यं स्तेयमन्यत इति F. ‡ स्मृतिरिति B. and F. § हिंसा चैवापरा दुष्टा इति B and F. ¶ एवं कृत्वा स दुष्टात्मा इति B and F. ‖ व्रतान्नुरतः इति B and F. ** चान्द्रायणं व्रतमिति B. †† संवत्सर इति B. ‡‡ स्कन्नेदिन्द्रियैति B and G.

प्रत्यक्षलवणे चोक्तं* प्राजापत्यं विशोधनम्† ॥
ध्याननिष्ठस्य सततं नश्यते सर्व्वपातकम्‡।
तस्मान्महेश्वरं ज्ञात्वा तद्ध्यानपरमो भवेत्§ ॥
यद्ब्रह्म परमं ज्योतिः प्रतिष्ठाक्षरमव्ययम्¶।
योऽन्तरा परमं‖ ब्रह्म स विज्ञेयो महेश्वरः ॥
एष देवो महादेवः केवलः परमः शिवः।
तदेवाक्षरमद्वैतन्तदादित्यान्तरं परम् ॥
यस्मान्महीयसो**देवः स्वधाम्नि ज्ञानसंस्थिते†† ।
आत्मयोगाह्वये तत्त्वे महादेवस्ततः स्मृतः ॥
नान्यन्देवं‡‡ महादेवाद्व्यतिरिक्तं प्रपश्यति।
तमेवात्मानमात्मेति§§ यः स याति परम्पदम् ॥
मन्यन्ते ये स्वमात्मानं विभिन्नं परमेश्वरात्।
न ते पश्यन्ति तन्देवं वृथा तेषां परिश्रमः ॥
एकं ब्रह्म परं ब्रह्म¶¶ ज्ञेयं तत्तत्त्वमव्ययम्।
स देवस्तु महादेवो नैतद्विज्ञाय बाध्यते‖‖ ॥
तस्माद्यजेत नियतं यतिः संयतमानसः।
ज्ञानयोगरतः शान्तो महादेवपरायणः ॥

---

* नोक्तमिति B. प्रत्यक्षलवणं प्रोक्तमिति F. † विशोधनादिति B. ‡ सर्व्वपातकै-रिति B. § ध्यात्वा तस्य ध्यानरतो भवेदिति B. ¶ प्रतिष्ठाक्षरमद्वयमिति B. ‖ योऽन्त-रात्र परमिति B. ** यस्मान्महीयते इति B and F. †† संज्ञिते इति B and E. संज्ञित इति F. ‡‡ नान्यदेवमिति B. §§ तमेवात्मानमन्वेतीति B and F. ¶¶ एकमेव परं ब्रह्मेति B and F. ‖‖ बध्यते इति B and F.

एष वः कथितो विप्रा यतीनामाश्रमः शुभः ।
पितामहेन विभुना मुनीनां* पूर्व्वमीरितम् ॥
नात्र शिष्यस्य† योगिभ्यो दद्यादिदमनुत्तमम् ।
प्रोक्तं स्वयम्भुवा ज्ञानं‡ यतिधर्म्माश्रयं शुभम्§ ॥

इति यतिनियमानामेतदुक्तं विधानं
पशुपतिपरितोषे यद्भवेदेकहेतुः ।
न भवति पुनरेषामुद्भवो वा विनाशः
प्रणिहितमनसा ये नित्यमेवाचरन्ति ॥

इति श्रीकूर्म्मपुराणे उपविभागे व्यासगीतासु ऊनत्रिंशोऽध्यायः ॥

यतिधर्म्मः समाप्तः ।

त्रिंशोऽध्यायः ।

व्यास उवाच ।

अतः परं प्रवक्ष्यामि प्रायश्चित्तविधिं शुभम् ।
हिताय सर्व्वविप्राणां* पापानामपनुत्तये† ॥

---

* मुनिनेति B. † नापुत्रशिष्येति B, E and F. सत्पुत्रशिष्येति F. ‡ ज्ञानं स्वयम्भुना प्रोक्तमिति B. § शिवमिति B, E and F.

---

* सर्व्वलोकानामिति B. † दोषाणामनुपत्तये इति B and G. दोषाणामपनुत्तये इति H.

अकृत्वा विहितं कर्म्म कृत्वा निन्दितमेव च।
दोषमाप्नोति पुरुषः प्रायश्चित्तं विशोधनम्॥
प्रायश्चित्तमकृत्वा तु न तिष्ठेद्ब्राह्मणः क्वचित्।
यद्ब्रूयुर्ब्राह्मणाः शान्ता विद्वांसस्तत्समाचरेत्॥
वेदार्थवित्तमः शान्तो धर्म्मकामोऽग्निमान्द्विजः।
स एव स्यात्परो धर्म्मो यमेकोऽपि व्यवस्यति॥
अनाहिताग्नयो विप्रास्त्रयो वेदार्थपारगाः।
यद्ब्रूयुर्धर्मकामास्ते तज्ज्ञानं* धर्म्मसाधनम्॥
अनेकधर्म्मशास्त्रज्ञा ऊहापोहविशारदाः।
वेदाध्ययनसम्पन्नाः सप्तैते परिकीर्त्तिताः॥
मीमांसाज्ञान†तत्त्वज्ञा वेदान्त‡कुशला द्विजाः।
एकविंशतिविख्याताः§ प्रायश्चित्तं वदन्ति वै॥
ब्रह्महा मद्यपः स्तेनो गुरुतल्पग एव च।
महापातकिनस्त्वेते यश्चैतैः सह संविशेत्¶॥
संवत्सरन्तु पतितैः संसर्गङ्कुरुते तु यः।
यानशय्यासनैर्नित्यं जानन्वै पतितो भवेत्॥
याजनं योनिसम्बन्धं तथैवाध्यापनं‖ द्विजः।
सद्यः कृत्वा पतत्येव** सह भोजनमेव च॥

---

* तज्ज्ञेयमिति B. तज्ज्ञानं धर्म्मशासनमिति E. तत्त्वमं धर्म्मसाधनमि ति F.
† न्यायेति B and F. ‡ वेदाङ्गेति B. § संख्याता इति B and F. ¶ संवसेदिति B. यश्च तैः सह सञ्चरेदिति F. ‖ तथैवाध्ययनमिति B. ** कृत्वा सद्यः पतेज्ज्ञानादिति B and F.

अविज्ञायाथ यो मोहात्कुर्य्यादध्यापनं द्विजः ।
संवत्सरेण पतति सहाध्ययनमेव च ॥
ब्रह्महा द्वादशाब्दानि कुटिं* कृत्वा वने वसेत् ।
भैक्षमात्मविशुद्ध्यर्थं† कृत्वा शवशिरोध्वजम् ॥
ब्राह्मणावसथान् सर्व्वान् देवागाराणि वर्ज्जयेत् ।
विनिन्दन् स्वयमात्मानं ब्राह्मणन्तञ्च संस्मरन् ॥
असङ्कल्पितयोग्यानि सप्तागाराणि संविशेत् ।
विधूमे शनकैर्नित्यं व्यङ्गारे भुक्तवर्ज्जने‡ ॥
एककालञ्चरेद्भैक्षन्दोषं विख्यापयन्नृणाम् ।
वन्यमूलफलैर्वापि वर्त्तयेद्वै समाश्रितः§ ॥
कपालपाणिः खट्वाङ्गी ब्रह्मचर्य्यपरायणः ।
पूर्णे तु द्वादशे वर्षे ब्रह्महत्यां व्यपोहति ॥
अकामतः कृते पापे प्रायश्चित्तमिदं शुभम् ।
कामतो मरणाच्छुद्धिर्ज्ञेया नान्येन केनचित् ॥
कुर्य्यादनशनं वाथ भृगोः पतनमेव वा ।
ज्वलितं¶ वा विशेदग्निं जलं वा प्रविशेत्स्वयम् ॥
ब्राह्मणार्थे गवार्थे वा सम्यक् प्राणान् परित्यजेत् ।
ब्रह्महत्यापनोदार्थमन्तरा वा मृतस्य तु ॥
दीर्घामयाविनं विप्रं कृत्वानामयमेव वा‖ ।

---

* द्वादशाब्दानि कुटीमिति B. † भिक्षेदात्मविशुद्ध्यर्थमिति B. भैक्ष्यायात्मविशुद्ध्यर्थमिति F. ‡ भृङ्गारे भुक्तवर्जिते इति B. § वर्जयेद्वैर्य्यमाश्रितः इति B. वर्त्तयेद्वैर्य्यमाश्रितः इति F. ¶ ज्वलन्तमिति B and F. ‖ तु इति B.

दत्त्वा चान्नं* सुविदुषे ब्रह्महत्यां व्यपोहति ॥†
अश्वमेधावभृथके स्नात्वा वै शुध्यते द्विजः।
सर्व्वस्वं वा वेदविदे ब्राह्मणाय प्रदाय च ॥
सरस्वत्यास्त्वरुणया सङ्गमे लोकविश्रुते।
शुध्येत्त्रिषवणस्नानात्त्रिरात्रोपोषितो द्विजः ॥
गत्वा रामेश्वरं पुण्यं स्नात्वा चैव महोदधौ।
ब्रह्मचर्य्यादिभिर्युक्तो दृष्ट्वा रुद्रं विमोचयेत् ॥
कपालमोचनं नाम तीर्थं देवस्य शूलिनः।
स्नात्वाभ्यर्च्च्य पितॄन् देवान् ब्रह्महत्यां व्यपोहति ॥
यत्र देवाधिदेवेन‡ भैरवेणा§मितौजसा।
कपालं स्थापितं पूर्व्वं ब्रह्मणः परमेष्ठिनः ॥
समभ्यर्च्च्य महादेवं तत्र भैरवरूपिणम्।
तर्पयित्वा पितॄन् स्नात्वा मुच्यते ब्रह्महत्यया ॥

इति श्रीकूर्म्मपुराणे उपविभागे ब्रह्महत्याप्रायश्चित्ते त्रिंशोऽध्यायः।

---

* कृत्वा चान्नमिति B. † अतः परं श्लोकचतुष्टयं B पुस्तके नास्ति। ‡ देवादिदेवेनेति B. § भैरवेण हतौजसा इति E and H.

एकत्रिंशोऽध्यायः ॥

ऋषय ऊचुः ।

कथन्देवेन रुद्रेण शङ्करेणातितेजसा ।
कपालं ब्रह्मणः पूर्व्वं स्थापितन्देहजम्भुवि ॥

सूत उवाच* ।

शृणुध्वमृषयः† पुण्यां कथां पापप्रणाशिनीम्‡ ।
माहात्म्यं देवदेवस्य महादेवस्य धीमतः ॥
पुरा पितामहन्देवं मेरुशृङ्गे महर्षयः ।
प्रोचुः प्रणम्य लोकादिङ्किमेकं तत्त्वमव्ययम् ॥
स मायया महेशस्य मोहितो लोकसम्भवः ।
अविज्ञाय परम्भावं स्वात्मानं प्राह धर्षिणम्§ ॥
अहन्धाता जगद्योनिः स्वयम्भू रुद्र ईश्वरः¶ ।
अनादि मत्परं ब्रह्म मामभ्यर्च्च विमुच्यते ॥
अहं हि सर्व्वदेवानां‖ प्रवर्त्तकनिवर्त्तकः ।
न विद्यते चाभ्यधिको मत्तो लोकेषु कश्चन ॥
तस्यैवं मन्यमानस्य जज्ञे नारायणाद्विभुः** ।

---

* व्यास उवाच इति B and F. † शृणुध्वं मुनयः इति B. ऋषयः सर्व्वे इति F. ‡ पापप्रणाशनीमिति E. and H. § आत्मानं प्राह चर्षिणामिति B. सुविज्ञाय परं भावं प्राह देवर्षिणां तदा इति F. ¶ स्वयम्भूरेक ईश्वरः इति B. अहं जातो जगद्योनिः स्वयम्भूरेक ईश्वर इति F. ‖ देवानामेकः इति A, G, H पुस्तकेषु दृश्यते । ** नारायणांशजः इति B. नारायणांशत इति F.

प्रोवाच प्रहसन्वाक्यं रोषितोऽयं त्रिलोचनः* ॥
किं कारणमिदं ब्रह्मन्वर्त्तते तव साम्प्रतम् ।
अज्ञानयोगयुक्तस्य न त्वेतत्त्वयि विद्यते† ॥
अहङ्कर्त्तादिलोकानां‡ यज्ञो नारायणात्प्रभोः§ ।
न¶ मामृतेऽस्य जगतो जीवनं सर्व्वदा क्वचित् ॥
अहमेव परं ज्योतिरहमेव परा गतिः ।
मत्प्रेरितेन भवता सृष्टं भुवनमण्डलम् ॥
एवं विवदतोर्मोहात्परस्परजयैषिणोः ।
आजग्मुर्यत्र तौ देवौ वेदाश्चत्वार एव हि‖ ॥
अन्वीक्ष्य देवं ब्रह्माणं यज्ञात्मानञ्च संस्थितम् ।
प्रोचुः संविग्नहृदया याथात्म्यं** परमेष्ठिनः ॥

ऋग्वेद उवाच ।

यस्यान्तःस्थानि भूतानि यस्मात्सर्व्वं प्रवर्त्तते ।
यदाहुस्तत्परन्तत्त्वं स देवः स्यान्महेश्वरः ॥

यजुरुवाच†† ।

यो यज्ञैरखिलैरीशो योगेन च समर्च्यते‡‡ ।

---

* रोषताम्रविलोचनः इति B. रोषवान् रविलोचन इति F. † न त्वेतदुचितं तवेति B. न वैतदुचितं तवेति F. ‡ अहन्धाता हि लोकानामिति B. अहं कर्त्ता हि लोकानामिति F. § यज्ञो नारायणः प्रभुरिति B and F. ¶ न इत्यारभ्य गतिरित्यन्तः श्लोकः A, E, H पुस्तकेषु नास्ति। ‖ चेति B. ** माहात्म्यमिति B. †† यजुर्वेद उवाच इति B and F. ‡‡ समय्यते इति B. समर्थ्यते इति F. समर्भ्यते इति G.

यमाहुरीश्वरन्देवं स देवः स्यात्पिनाकधृक्* ॥

साम उवाच† ।

येनेदम्भ्राम्यते‡ विश्वं यदाकाशान्तरं शिवम् ।
योगिभिस्त्विन्त्यते§ तत्त्वं महादेवः स शङ्करः ॥

अथर्व्व उवाच¶ ।

यम्प्रपश्यन्ति देवेशं यजन्ते‖ यतयः परम् ।
महेशं पुरुषं रुद्रं स देवो भगवान् भवः ॥
एवं स भगवान् ब्रह्मा वेदानामीरितं शुभम् ।
श्रुत्वा विहस्य विश्वात्मा ततश्चाह विमोहितः** ॥

पितामह उवाच†† ।

कथं तत्परमं ब्रह्म सर्व्वसङ्गविवर्जितम् ।
रमते भार्य्यया सार्द्धं प्रमथैश्चातिवर्द्धितम्‡‡ ॥
इतीरितेऽथ भगवान् प्रणवात्मा सनातनः ।
अमूर्त्तो मूर्त्तिमान् भूत्वा वचः प्राह पितामहम्§§ ॥

प्रणव उवाच ।¶¶

नह्येष भगवानीशः‖‖ स्वयञ्ज्योतिः सनातनः ।

---

* स्यान्महेश्वरः इति B. † सामवेद उवाच इति B and F. ‡ क्राम्यते इति B. भ्राम्यते चक्रमिति F. § विद्यते इति B. वेद्यते इति F. ¶ अथर्व्ववेद-उवाच इति B and F. ‖ यतन्तः इति B and F. ** श्रुत्वाह प्रहसन्वाक्यं विश्वात्मापि विमोहितः इति B and F. †† एष पाठः B, F पुस्तकयोर्नास्ति। ‡‡ चातिगर्व्वितैरिति B and F. चातिगर्व्वित इति E. §§ हितावहमिति B. ¶¶ एष पाठः B पुस्तके नास्ति। ‖‖ अत्र न ह्येष भगवान् पत्न्या स्वात्मनो व्यतिरिक्तया। कयाचिद्रमते रुद्रस्तादृशो हि महेश्वरः॥ स्वयं स भगवानीशः इत्यधिकः पाठः B, F पुस्तकयोर्दृश्यते।

स्वानन्दभूता कथिता देवी आगन्तुका* शिवा ॥
इत्येवमुक्तेऽपि तदा यज्ञमूर्त्तेरजस्य च ।
नाज्ञानमगमन्नाशमीश्वरस्यैव मायया ॥
तदन्तरे महाज्योतिर्विरिञ्चो विश्वभावनः ।
प्रादर्शयदद्भुतं दिव्यम्पूरयन् गगनान्तरम् ॥
तन्मध्यसंस्थितज्ज्योतिर्मण्डलं† तेजसोज्ज्वलम् ।
व्योममध्यगतं शम्भुं‡ प्रादुरासीद्द्विजोत्तमाः ॥
स दृष्ट्वा वदनं दिव्यमूर्द्धं§ लोकपितामहः ।
तैजसं मण्डलं घोरमलोकय¶दनिन्दितम् ॥
प्रजज्वालातिकोपेन ब्रह्मणः पञ्चमं शिरः ।
क्षणादपश्यत्स‖ महान् पुरुषो नीललोहितः ॥
त्रिशूलपिङ्गलोदेवो नागयज्ञोपवीतवान् ।
तं प्राह भगवान् ब्रह्मा शङ्करं नीललोहितम् ॥
ज्ञानाय पूर्व्वं भवतो** ललाटादद्य†† शङ्करम् ।
प्रादुर्भावं महेशान मामतः‡‡ शरणं व्रज ॥
श्रुत्वा सगर्व्ववचनं पद्मयोनेरथेश्वरः§§ ।
प्राहिणोत्पुरुषं कालं भैरवं लोकदाहकम् ॥

---

* नागन्तुका इति B. नन्दासिका इति F. † तन्मध्यसंस्थं विमलं मण्डलमिति B and F. ‡ दिव्यमिति B. § दिव्यं मूर्द्ध्नि इति B and F. ¶ मालोकार्थमिति H. ‖ क्षणाददृश्यतेति B and F. ** जानामि भगवान् पूर्व्वमिति B. जानामि पूर्व्वं भगवन्निति F. †† ललाटादेवेति B ललाटे देवशङ्कर इति F. ‡‡ मामेवेति B. §§ रुमेश्वर इति B.

स कृत्वा सुमहद्युद्धं* ब्रह्मणा कालभैरवः।
प्रचकर्त्तास्य† वदनं विरिञ्चस्याथ पञ्चमम्॥
निकृत्तवदनो देवो ब्रह्मा देवेन शम्भुना।
ममार चेशो योगेन जीवितं प्राप विश्वकृत्‡॥
अथान्वपश्यदीशानं§ मण्डलान्तरसंस्थितम्।
समासीनं महादेव्या महादेवं सनातनम्¶॥||
भुजङ्गराजवलयं चन्द्रावयवभूषणम्।
कोटिसूर्य्यप्रतीकाशञ्जटाजूटविराजितम्॥
शार्दूलचर्म्मवसनं दिव्यमालासमन्वितम्।
त्रिशूलपाणिं दुष्प्रेक्ष्यं योगिनं भूतिभूषणम्॥
यमन्तरा योगनिष्ठाः प्रपश्यन्ति हृदीश्वरम्।
तमादिमेकं ब्रह्माणं महादेवन्ददर्श ह॥
यस्य सा परमा देवी शक्तिराकाशसंज्ञिता।
सोऽनन्तैश्वर्य्ययोगात्मा महेशो दृश्यते किल॥
यस्याशेषजगद्बीजं विलयं याति मोहनम्।
सकृत्प्रणाममात्रेण स रुद्रः खलु दृश्यते॥
येऽथ नाचारनिरतास्तद्भक्ताश्चैव केवलम्।
विलोचयति** लोकात्मा नायको दृश्यते किल॥

---

* स कृत्वा तु महद्युद्धमिति B. † चकर्त्त तस्येति B and F. ‡ विश्वधृक् इति B. § अथान्वपश्यद्गिरिशमिति B and F. ¶ त्रिलोचनमिति B. || इतः परं महादेव्या सनातनमित्यन्ताः सार्द्धचतुर्द्दशश्लोकाः B पुस्तके न दृश्यन्ते। ** विमोचयतीति E, F, G and H.

यस्य ब्रह्मादयो देवा ऋषयो ब्रह्मवादिनः ।
अर्च्चयन्ति सदा लिङ्गं स शिवः खलु दृश्यते ॥
यस्याशेषजगत्सूतिर्विज्ञानतनुरीश्वरः ।
न मुञ्चति सदा पार्श्वं शङ्करोऽसौ च दृश्यते ॥
विद्यासहायो भगवान्यस्यासौ मण्डलान्तरम् ।
हिरण्यगर्भपुत्रोऽसौ ईश्वरो दृश्यते परः ॥
पुष्पं वा यदि वा पत्रं यत्पादयुगले जलम् ।
दत्त्वा तरति संसारं रुद्रोऽसौ दृश्यते किल ॥
तत्सन्निधाने सकलं नियच्छति सनातनः ।
कालङ्किल नियोगात्मा कालः कालो हि दृश्यते* ॥
जीवनं सर्व्वलोकानां त्रिलोकस्यैव भूषणम् ।
सोमः स दृश्यते देवः सोमो यस्य विभूषणम् ॥
देव्या सह सदा साक्षाद्यस्य योगस्वभावतः ।
गीयते परमा मुक्तिर्म्महादेवः स दृश्यते ॥
योगिनो योगतत्त्वज्ञा वियोगाभिमुखोऽनिशम् ।
योगन्ध्यायन्ति देव्यासौ स योगी दृश्यते किल ॥
सोऽनुवीक्ष्य महादेवं महादेव्या सनातनम् ।
वरासने समासीनमवाप परमां† स्मृतिम् ॥
लब्ध्वा माहेश्वरीं दिव्यां संस्मृतिं भगवानजः ।
तोषयामास वरदं सोमं सोमार्द्धभूषणम्‡ ॥

---

* ह्यदृश्यते इति E, F and H. † अवाप्तपरमामिति B. ‡ सोमविभूषणमिति B.

ब्रह्मोवाच।*

नमो देवाय महते महादेव्यै नमो नमः।
नमः शिवाय शान्ताय शिवायै सततं† नमः॥
ओं नमो ब्रह्मणे तुभ्यं विद्यायै ते‡ नमो नमः।
महेशाय नमस्तुभ्यं मूलप्रकृतये नमः§॥
नमो विज्ञानदेहाय चिन्तायै ते नमो नमः।
नमोऽस्तु¶ कालकालाय ईश्वरायै नमो नमः॥
नमो नमोऽस्तु‖ रुद्राय रुद्राण्यै ते** नमो नमः।
नमो नमस्ते कालाय मायायै ते†† नमो नमः॥
नियन्त्रे सर्व्वकार्य्याणां क्षोभिकायै नमो नमः।
नमोस्तु ते प्रकृतये नमो नारायणाय च॥
योगदाय‡‡ नमस्तुभ्यं योगिनां गुरवे नमः।
नमः संसारवासाय§§ संसारोत्पत्तये नमः॥
नित्यानन्दाय विभवे नमोऽस्त्वानन्दमूर्त्तये।
नमः कार्य्यविहीनाय विश्वप्रकृतये नमः॥
ओङ्कारमूर्त्तये तुभ्यं तदन्तःसंस्थिताय च।
नमस्ते व्योमसंस्थाय व्योमशक्त्यै नमो नमः॥

---

* एष पाठः A, E, F, H पुस्तकेषु नास्ति। † शान्त्यै इति B and F. ‡ चेति B. § मूलप्रकृतये तुभ्यं महेशाय नमो नमः इति B. नमोमूलप्रकृतये महेशाय नमोनम इति F. ¶ नमस्ते इति B and F. ‖ नमस्तु इति B. मालायै इति E. नमस्ते कालकालाय यमायै ते नमोनम इति F. कलायै इति H. ** रुद्रायै चेति B. †† चेति B. ‡‡ योगदायै इति B and F. §§ संसारनाशाय इति B and F.

इति सोमाष्टकेनेशं प्रणिपत्य* पितामहः।
पपात दण्डवद्भूमौ गृणन्वै शतरुद्रियम्॥
अथ देवो महादेवः प्रणतार्त्तिहरो हरः।
प्रोवाचोत्थाप्य† हस्ताभ्यां प्रीतोऽस्मि तव साम्प्रतम्॥
दत्त्वास्मै‡ परमं योगमैश्वर्य्यमतुलं महत्।
प्रोवाचाग्रस्थितं रुद्रं§ नीललोहितमीश्वरम्॥
एष ब्रह्मास्य जगतः संपूज्यः प्रथमः स्थितः।
आत्मना रक्षणीयस्ते गुरुज्येष्ठः पिता तव॥
अयम्पुराणः पुरुषो न हन्तव्यस्त्वयानघ।
स योगैश्वर्य्यमाहात्म्यान्मामेव परमङ्गतः॥¶
अयञ्च यज्ञो गर्वोऽसौ सगर्वो‖ भवतानघ।
शासितव्यो विरिञ्चस्य धारणीयं शिरस्त्वया॥
ब्रह्महत्यापनोदार्थं व्रतं लोके प्रदर्शयन्**।
चरस्व सततं भिक्षां संस्थापय सुरद्विजान्॥
इत्येतदुक्त्वा वचनं भगवान् परमेश्वरः।
स्थानं स्वाभाविकं दिव्यं ययौ तत्परमम्पदम्॥
ततः स भगवानीशः कपर्द्दी नीललोहितः।

---

* इति संसाराष्टकेन प्रणनाम इति B. † उत्थाप्येति A. ‡ दत्त्वासौ इति B. § प्रोवाचान्ते स्थितं देवमिति B. प्रोवाचाग्रेस्थितं रुद्रमिति E and F. प्रोवाचोग्रस्थितमिति H. ¶ एष श्लोकः B पुस्तके नास्ति। शरणं गत इति E and F. ‖ अयञ्च यज्ञो भगवान् सङ्गतः इति B. अयञ्च जज्ञे इति H. ** लोकाय दर्शयन्निति B.

ग्राहयामास वदनं ब्रह्मणः कालभैरवम्* ॥
चर त्वं पापनाशार्थं व्रतं लोके हितावहम्† ।
कपालहस्तो भगवान् भिक्षां गृह्णातु सर्व्वतः‡ ॥
उक्त्वैवं प्राहिणोत्कन्यां ब्रह्महत्येति विश्रुताम् ।
दंष्ट्राकरालवदनां ज्वालामालाविभूषणाम्§ ॥
यावद्वाराणसीं दिव्यां पुरीमेष गमिष्यति ।
तावद्विभीषणाकारा ह्यनुगच्छ त्रिशूलिनम्¶ ॥
एवमाभाष्य कालाग्निं प्राह लोकमहेश्वरम्‖ ।
अटस्व लोकानखिलान्** भैक्षार्थी मन्नियोगतः ॥
यदा द्रक्ष्यसि देवेशं नारायणमनामयम् ।
तदासौ वक्ष्यति†† स्पष्टमुपायं पाप‡‡शोधनम् ॥
स देवदेवतावाक्यमाकर्ण्य भगवान् हरः ।
कपालपाणिर्विश्वात्मा चचार भुवनत्रयम् ॥
आस्थाय विकृतं वेषन्दीप्यमानं स्वतेजसा ।
श्रीमत्पवित्रं रुचिरं§§ लोचनत्रयसंयुतम्¶¶ ॥
सहस्रसूर्य्यप्रतिमं सिद्धैः प्रमथपुङ्गवैः‖‖ ।

---

* कालभैरवः इति B. † लोकहितावहमिति B, E and F. ‡ गृह्णीत सव्यतः इति B. § समन्वितामिति B. मालातिभीषणामिति F. ¶ तावत्त्वं भीषणे कालमनुगच्छ त्रिलोचनमिति B. भीषणं कालमनुगच्छस्व शूलिनमिति F ‖ देवो महेश्वरः इति B. महेश्वर इति F. ** निखिलं लोकमिति B. †† रक्षतीति B. ‡‡ कार्येति B. §§ पवित्रमतुलमिति B. सुचिरमिति F. ¶¶ जटाजूटविराजितमिति B. ‖‖ कोटिसूर्य्यप्रतीकाशैः प्रमथैश्चातिगर्व्वितैरिति B.

भाति कालाग्निनयनो महादेवः समावृतः॥
पीत्वा तदमृतं दिव्यमानन्दम्परमेष्ठिनः।
लीलाविलासबहुलो लोकानागच्छतीश्वरः* ॥
तन्दृष्ट्वा कालवदनं शङ्करं कालभैरवम्।
रूपलावण्यसम्पन्नं नारीकुलमगादनु† ॥
गायन्ति गीतैर्विविधैः‡ नृत्यन्ति पुरतः प्रभोः।
सस्मितं प्रेक्ष्य वदनञ्चक्रुर्भ्रूभङ्गमेव च ॥
स देवदानवादीनान्देशानभ्येत्य शूलधृक्।
जगाम विष्णोर्भुवनं यत्रास्ते पुरुषोत्तमः॥
सम्प्राप्य दिव्यभवनं§ शङ्करो लोकशङ्करः¶ ।
सहैव भूतप्रवरैः प्रवेष्टुमुपचक्रमे ॥
अविज्ञाय परं भावं दिव्यं तत्पारमेश्वरम्।
न्यवारयत्त्रिशूलाङ्कं द्वारपालो महाबलः‖ ॥
शङ्खचक्रगदापाणिः पीतवासा महाभुजः।
विष्वक्सेन इति ख्यातो विष्णोरंशसमुद्भवः** ॥
भीषणो भैरवादेशात्कालवेग इति स्मृतः।
विजित्य तं कालवेगं क्रोधसंरक्तलोचनः।

---

* कालोऽत्रागच्छतीश्वरः इति B. लोकानां गतिरीश्वर इति F. † ह इति B. दय इति F. ‡ विविधं गीतमिति B and F. § निरीक्ष्य भवनं दिव्यमिति B. ¶ यत्रास्ते मधुसूदनः इति B. ‖ न्यवारयन् त्रिशूलाङ्का द्वारपाला महाबलाः इति B. ** "अथ तं शङ्करगणं युयुधे विष्णुसम्भवः" इति E and H पुस्तकयोः, तथा "अथ तं शङ्करगणो युयुधे विष्णुसम्भव"मिति F पुस्तके च अधिकं दृश्यते।

दुद्रावाभिमुखं रुद्रं चिक्षेप च सुदर्शनम् ॥
अथ देवो महादेवस्त्रिपुरारिस्त्रिशूलभृत् ।
तमापतन्तं सावज्ञ*मालोकयदमित्रजित् ॥
तदन्तरे महद्भूतं युगान्तदहनोपमम् ।
शूलेनोरसि निर्भिद्य पातयामास तं भुवि ॥
स शूलाभिहतोऽत्यर्थं† त्यक्त्वा स्वम्परमं बलम् ।
तत्याज जीवितं दृष्ट्वा मृत्युं व्याधिहता इव ॥‡
निहत्य विष्णुपुरुषं सार्द्धं प्रमथपुङ्गवैः ।
विवेश चान्तरगृहं समादाय कलेवरम् ॥
वीक्ष्य तं§ जगतो हेतुमीश्वरं भगवान्हरिः ।
शिरां¶ ललाटात्सम्भिद्य रक्तधारामपातयत् ॥
गृहाण भिक्षां भगवन्‖ मदीयाममितद्युते** ।
न विद्यतेऽन्या ह्युचिता†† तव त्रिपुरमर्द्दन ॥
न सम्पूर्णं कपालं तद्ब्रह्मणः‡‡ परमेष्ठिनः ।
दिव्यं वर्षसहस्रन्तु सा च धारा प्रवाहिता ॥§§
अथाब्रवीत्कालरुद्रं हरिर्नारायणः प्रभुः¶¶ ।
संस्तूय विविधैर्भावैः‖‖ बहुमानपुरःसरम् ॥

---

* सारङ्गमिति B. † दृष्ट्वा इति B. ‡ "मृगीव्याधहती यथा" इति F. § निरीक्ष्य इति B and F. ¶ शिरः इति B. ‖ भगवन् भिक्षामिति B. ** अमृतद्युते इति B. †† न विद्यते नाभ्युदिता इति B. न विद्यतेऽन्यदुचितमिति F. ‡‡ असम्पूर्णं कपालञ्च ब्रह्मणः इति B. §§ एतत्पादद्वयं B पुस्तके नास्ति। ¶¶ स्वयमिति B. ‖‖ संस्तूय वैदिकैर्मन्त्रैरिति B.

किमर्थमेतद्वदनं ब्रह्मणो* भवता धृतम् ।
प्रोवाच वृत्तमखिलं देवदेवो महेश्वरः ॥
समाहूय हृषीकेशो ब्रह्महत्यामथाच्युतः ।
प्रार्थयामास भगवान्† विमुञ्चेति त्रिशूलिनम् ॥
न तत्याजाथ सा पार्श्वं‡ व्याहृतापि मुरारिणा ।
चिरन्ध्यात्वा जगद्योनिं§ शङ्करं प्राह सर्व्ववित् ॥
व्रजस्व दिव्यां भगवन्¶ पुरीं वाराणसीं शुभाम् ।
यत्राखिलजगद्दोषान्|| क्षिप्रन्नाशयतीश्वरः ॥
ततः सर्वाणि गुह्यानि** तीर्थान्यायतनानि च ।
जगाम लीलया देवो लोकानां हितकाम्यया ॥
संस्तूयमानः प्रमथैर्महायोगैरितस्ततः ।
नृत्यमानो महायोगी हस्तन्यस्तकलेवरः ॥
तमभ्यधावद्भगवान् हरिर्नारायणः प्रभुः††।
समास्थाय परं रूपं नृत्यदर्शनलालसः‡‡ ॥
निरीक्षमाणो गोविन्दं वृषेन्द्राङ्कितशासनः ।
सस्मयो§§ऽनन्तयोगात्मा नृत्यति स्म पुनः पुनः ॥
अनु चानुचरो रुद्रं स हरिर्द्धर्म्मवाहनः¶¶ ।

---

* इतः परं समाहूयेत्यन्तः पाठः B पुस्तके न दृश्यते। † देवेशः इति B. ‡ न तत्याज तदा पार्श्वमिति B. § जगद्‌ज्योतिरिति B. ¶ भजस्व भगवन्दिव्यामिति B. || जगत्स्रोऽयमिति B. ** भूतानीति B. †† स्वयमिति B. ‡‡ अथास्थायापरं रूपं रुद्रं दर्शनलालसमिति B. §§ सस्मितः इति B and F. ¶¶ अथ सानुचरो देवः ससहायः सवाहनः इति B. अथ सानुचरो रुद्रः स हरिर्धर्म्मवाहन इति F.

भेजे महादेवपुरीं वाराणसीति विश्रुताम् ॥
प्रविष्टमात्रे विश्वेशे* ब्रह्महत्या कपर्द्दिने† ।
हाहेत्युक्त्वा सनादं वै पातालं प्राप‡ दुःखिता ॥
प्रविश्य परमं स्थानं कपालं ब्रह्मणो हरः ।
गणानामग्रतो देवः स्थापयामास शङ्करः ॥
स्थापयित्वा महादेवो ददौ तच्च कलेवरम् ।
उक्त्वा स जीवमस्त्वीति§ विष्णवेऽसौ घृणानिधिः ॥
ये स्मरन्ति ममाजस्रङ्कापालं वेषमुत्तमम् ।
तेषां विनश्यति क्षिप्रमिहामुत्र च पातकम् ॥
आगम्य तीर्थप्रवरे¶ स्नानं कृत्वा विधानतः ।
तर्पयित्वा पितॄन्देवान्मुच्यते ब्रह्महत्यया ॥
अशाश्वतञ्जगज्ज्ञात्वा व्रजध्वं परमाम्पुरीम्‖ ।
देहान्ते तत्परं ज्ञानं ददाति परमम्पदम् ॥
इतीदमुक्त्वा** भगवान् समालिङ्ग्य जनार्द्दनम् ।
सहैव प्रमथेशानैः क्षणादन्तरधीयत ॥
स लब्ध्वा भगवान् कृष्णो विष्वक्सेनं त्रिशूलिनः ।
स्वन्देशमगमत्तूर्णीं†† गृहीत्वा परमं बुधः‡‡ ॥
एतद्वः कथितं पुण्यं§§ महापातकनाशनम् ।

---

* देवेशे इति B. † कपर्द्दिनीति B, F and H. ‡ सर्व्वाणि साऽन्यतः सम्प्राप इति B. § उक्त्वा सजीवनस्त्वीशः इति B. ¶ आसने तीर्थप्रवरे इति B. ‖ येऽस्मिन् स्थाने वसन्ति वै इति B and F. ** इत्येतदुक्त्वा इति B. †† स्वस्थानमगमत्तूर्ण-मिति B. ‡‡ वपुरिति B and F. §§ दिव्यमिति B.

कपालमोचनन्तीर्थं स्थाणोः प्रियतरं* शुभम् ॥
य इमं पठतेऽध्यायं ब्राह्मणानां समीपतः ।
मानसैर्वाचिकैः† पापैः कायिकैश्च प्रमुच्यते‡ ॥

इति श्रीकूर्मपुराणे उपविभागे कपालमोचनमाहात्म्यं नाम§ एकत्रिंशोऽध्यायः ।

द्वात्रिंशोऽध्यायः ।

व्यास उवाच ।

सुरापस्तु सुरां तप्तामग्निवर्णाम्पिवेत्तदा* ।
निर्दग्धकायः स तया मुच्यते च द्विजोत्तमः† ॥
गोमूत्रमग्निवर्णं वा गोशकृद्रसमेव वा ।
पयो घृतं जलं वाथ मुच्यते पातकात्ततः ॥
जलार्द्रवासाः प्रयतो ध्यात्वा नारायणं हरिम् ।
ब्रह्महत्याव्रतञ्चाथ चरेत्कृत्योपशान्तये‡ ॥

---

* प्रियकरमिति B. † वाचिकैर्मानसैरिति B. ‡ विमुच्यते इति B. § कपालमोची नाम इति B.

---

* स्वयं पिबेदिति B. † तया स काये निर्दग्धे मुच्यते तु द्विजोत्तमा इति B. ‡ पापप्रशान्तये इति B. पापोपशान्तये इति F.

सुवर्णस्तेयकृद्विप्रो* राजानमभिगम्य† तु।
स्वकर्म्म ख्यापयन्ब्रूयान्माम्भवाननुशास्त्विति॥
गृहीत्वा मुसलं राजा सकृद्धन्यात्तु तं‡ स्वयम्।
वधे तु§ शुद्ध्यते स्तेनो ब्राह्मणस्तपसाथवा¶॥
स्कन्धेनादाय मुसलं लकुचं‖ वापि खादिरम्।
शक्तिञ्चादाय तीक्ष्णाग्रामायसन्दण्डमेव वा॥
राजा तेन च गन्तव्यो मुक्तकेशेन धावता।
आचक्षाणेन तत्पापमेतत्कर्म्मास्मि शाधि माम्॥
शासनाद्वा विमोक्षाद्वा स्तेनः स्तेयाद्विमुच्यते।
अशासित्वा तु तं राजा स्तेनस्याप्नोति किल्विषम्॥
तपसापनोत्तुमिच्छंस्तु** सुवर्णस्तेयजं मलम्††।
चीरवासा द्विजोऽरण्ये चरेद्ब्रह्महणो व्रतम्‡‡॥
स्नात्वाश्वमेधावभृथे पूतः स्यादथवा द्विजः।
प्रदद्याद्वाथ विप्रेभ्यः स्वात्मतुल्यं§§ हिरण्यकम्॥
चरेद्वा वत्सरङ्कृच्छ्रं ब्रह्मचर्य्यपरायणः।
ब्राह्मणः स्वर्णहारी तु तत्पापस्यापनुत्तये॥
गुरोर्भार्य्यां समारुह्य¶¶ ब्राह्मणः काममोहितः।

---

* स्तेयकृद्वीरः इति B. † राजानमधिगम्य इति B. ‡ सकृद्धन्यात्ततः इति B.
§ वधेनेति B and F. ¶ तपसैव वेति B. इतः परं श्लोकत्रयं B पुस्तके नास्ति।
‖ लगुड़मिति E. लुकुटमिति H. ** तपसापनयेत् सुस्तु इति F. †† मनुमिति B.
‡‡ ब्रह्मगणाहृते इति B. §§ स्वार्थतुल्यमिति B. ¶¶ समारोप्य इति B. समागम्य इति F.

आलिङ्गयेत्*स्त्रियन्तप्तां दीप्ताङ्गारार्णायसीङ्कृताम् ॥
स्वयं वा शिश्नवृषणावुत्कृत्याधाय चाञ्जलौ ।
अभिगच्छेद्दक्षिणाशा†मानिपातादजिह्मगः ॥
गुर्व्वङ्गनागमः शुद्ध्यै चरेद्ब्रह्महणो व्रतम् ।
शाखां वा कण्टकोपेतां परिष्वज्याथ वत्सरम् ॥
अधः शयीत नियतो मुच्यते गुरुतल्पगः ।
कृच्छ्रं वाब्दञ्चरेद्विप्रश्चीरवासाः समाहितः ॥
अश्वमेधावभृथके स्नात्वा वा शुद्ध्यते द्विजः‡ ।
कालेऽष्टमे वा भुञ्जानो ब्रह्मचारी सदाव्रती ॥
स्थानाशनाभ्यां विहरंस्त्रिरह्नोऽभ्युपयन्नतः ।
अधःशायी त्रिभिर्वर्षैस्तद्व्यपोहति पातकम् ॥
चान्द्रायणानि वा कुर्य्यात्पञ्च चत्वारि वा पुनः ।
पतितैः सम्प्रयुक्तात्मा§ अथ वक्ष्यामि निष्कृतिम् ॥
पतितेन तु संसर्गं यो येन कुरुते द्विजः¶ ।
स तत्पापापनोदार्थं‖ तस्यैव व्रतमाचरेत्** ॥
तप्तकृच्छ्रञ्चरेद्वाथ संवत्सरमतन्द्रितः ।
षाण्मासिके तु संसर्गे प्रायश्चित्तार्थमाचरेत्†† ॥
एभिर्व्रतैरपोहन्ति महापातकिनो मलम् ।

---

* अवगूहेदिति B and F. † आतिष्ठेद्दक्षिणामाशामिति B. प्रतिष्ठेदिति F. प्रतिष्ठेत इति साधु । ‡ नरः इति B. § संप्रयुक्तानामिति B. सहयुक्तानामिति F. ¶ नरः इति B. ‖ तत्पापापनाशार्थमिति B. ** चरेद्व्रतमनुत्तममिति B. †† प्रायश्चित्तार्द्धमर्हति इति B. प्रायश्चित्तार्द्धमाचरेदिति F.

पुण्यतीर्थाभिगमनात्पृथिव्यां वाथ निष्कृतिः* ॥
ब्रह्महत्या सुरापानं स्तेयं गुर्व्वङ्गनागमम् ।
कृत्वा तैश्चापि संसर्गं ब्राह्मणः कामचारतः ॥
कुर्य्यादनशनं विप्रः पुनस्तीर्थे† समाहितः ।
ज्वलन्तं वा विशेदग्निं ध्यात्वा देवं कपर्द्दिनम् ॥
न ह्यन्या निष्कृतिर्दृष्टा मुनिभिर्ब्रह्मवादिभिः‡ ।
तस्मात्पुण्येषु तीर्थेषु दहन्वापि स्वदेहकम् ॥

इति श्रीकूर्म्मपुराणे उपविभागे द्वात्रिंशोऽध्यायः ।

त्रयस्त्रिंशोऽध्यायः ।

व्यास उवाच ।

गत्वा दुहितरं विप्रः स्वसारमथवापि वा* ।
प्रविशेज्ज्वलनन्दीप्तं मतिपूर्व्वमिति स्थितिः† ॥
मातृष्वसां‡ मातुलानीं तथैव च पितृष्वसाम्§ ।

---

* पुण्यतीर्थाभिगमनं व्रतान्ते पापनाशनमिति B. † पुण्यतीर्थे इति B and F. ‡ ब्रह्मवादिभिरिति B.

---

* स्वसारं वा स्नुषामपीति B and F. † तत्पापप्रशान्तये इति B. मतिपूर्व्व-मिति श्रुतिरिति F. ‡ मातृष्वसारमिति साधु । § पितृष्वसारमिति साधु ।

भागिनेयीं समारुह्य कुर्य्यात्कृच्छ्रातिकृच्छ्रकौ ॥
चान्द्रायणञ्च* कुर्व्वीत तस्य पापस्य शान्तये ।
ध्यायन्देवं जगद्योनिमनादिनिधनं हरिम्† ॥
भ्रातृभार्य्यां समारुह्य कुर्य्यात्तत्पापशान्तये ।
चान्द्रायणानि चत्वारि पञ्च वा सुसमाहितः ॥
पितृष्वस्रेयीं गत्वा तु‡ स्वस्रीयां§ मातुरेव च ।
मातुलस्य सुतां वापि गत्वा चान्द्रायणञ्चरेत् ॥
सखिभार्य्यां समारुह्य गत्वा श्यालीन्तथैव च ।
अहोरात्रोषितो भूत्वा ततः¶ कृच्छ्रं समाचरेत् ॥
उदक्या‖गमने विप्रस्त्रिरात्रेण विशुध्यति ।
चाण्डालीगमने चैव तप्तकृच्छ्रत्रयं विदुः ।
शुद्धिः सान्तपनेन** स्यान्नान्यथा निष्कृतिः स्मृता ॥
मातृगोत्रां समारुह्य समानप्रवरान्तथा ।
चान्द्रायणेन शुध्येत प्रयतात्मा समाहितः ॥
ब्राह्मणो ब्राह्मणीङ्गत्वा कृच्छ्रमेकं समाचरेत् ।
कन्यकान्दूषयित्वा तु चरेच्चान्द्रायणव्रतम्†† ॥
अमानुषीषु पुरुष उदक्यायामयोनिषु ।
रेतः सिक्त्वा जले चैव कृच्छ्रं सान्तपनञ्चरेत् ॥

---

* चान्द्रायणं वेति B. † परमिति B. ‡ संगत्येति B. § स्वस्रीयीमिति B पितृष्वसेयीं चत्वारि पञ्च वा मातुरेव च इति F. ¶ तप्तेति B. सप्तेति F. ‖ उदक्या ऋतुमती। ** महासान्तपनेनेति B. सह सान्तपनेनास्य इति F. †† चान्द्रायणं व्रतमिति B.

बन्धकी*गमने विप्रस्त्रिरात्रेण विशुद्ध्यति ।
गवि मैथुनमासेव्य चरेच्चान्द्रायणव्रतम् ॥
वेश्यायां† मैथुनङ्कृत्वा प्राजापत्यं चरेद्द्विजः ।
पतिताञ्च स्त्रियङ्गत्वा त्रिभिः कृच्छ्रैर्विशुद्ध्यति ॥
पुक्कसी‡गमने चैव कृच्छ्रञ्चान्द्रायणञ्चरेत् ॥
नटीं शैलूषकीञ्चैव रजकीं वेणुजीविनीम्§ ।
गत्वा चान्द्रायणङ्कुर्य्यात्तथा चर्म्मोपजीविनीम् ॥
ब्रह्मचारी स्त्रियङ्गच्छेत्कथञ्चित्काममोहितः ।
सप्तागारञ्चरेद्भैक्षं वसित्वा गर्द्दभाजिनम् ॥
उपस्पृशेत्त्रिषवणं स्वपापम्परिकीर्त्तयन् ।
संवत्सरेण चैकेन तस्मात्पापात्प्रमुच्यते ॥
ब्रह्महत्याव्रतञ्चापि षण्मासान्विचरन्यमी¶ ।
मुच्यते ह्यवकीर्णी तु ब्राह्मणानुमते स्थितः ॥
सप्तरात्रमकृत्वा तु‖ भैक्षचर्य्याग्निपूजनम् ।
रेतसश्च समुत्सर्गे प्रायश्चित्तं समाचरेत् ॥
ओङ्कारपूर्व्विकाभिस्तु महाव्याहृतिभिः सदा ।
संवत्सरन्तु भुञ्जानो नक्तम्भिक्षाशनः शुचिः ॥
सावित्रीञ्च जपेन्नित्यं सत्वरः क्रोधवर्ज्जितः** ।

---

* बन्धकी पुंश्चली । † अजावीति B. आजावीति F. ‡ पुष्कसीति E. पुल्कसीति H. § वेवजीविनीमिति B. ¶ ब्रह्महत्याव्रतं वापि षण्मासानाचरेद्यतीति B. षण्मासानाचरेद्यमीति F. ‖ सप्तरात्रं स कृत्वा तु इति B. ** जपेच्चैव नित्यं क्रोधं विवर्ज्जयेदिति B.

नदीतीरेषु तीर्थेषु तस्मात्पापाद्विमुच्यते* ॥
हत्वा तु क्षत्त्रियं विप्रः कुर्य्याद्ब्रह्महणो व्रतम्।
अकामतो वै† षण्मासान्दद्यात्पञ्चशतङ्गवाम् ॥
अब्दञ्चरेद्वानयुतो‡ वनवासी समाहितः।
प्राजापत्यं सान्तपनं तप्तकृच्छ्रन्तु वा स्वयम्§ ॥
प्रमादात्कामतो वैश्यं कुर्य्यात्संवत्सरत्नयम्।
गोसहस्रन्तु पादन्तु¶ प्रदद्याद्ब्रह्मणो व्रतम्‖ ॥
निहत्य ब्राह्मणीं विप्रस्त्वष्टवर्षं व्रतञ्चरेत्।
राजकन्यां वर्षषट्कं** वैश्यां संवत्सरत्रयम् ॥
वत्सरेण विशुद्ध्येत शूद्रीं हत्वा द्विजोत्तमः।
वैश्यां हत्वा द्विजातिस्तु†† किञ्चिद्दद्याद्द्विजातये ॥
अन्त्यजानां वधे चैव कुर्य्याच्चान्द्रायणं व्रतम्‡‡।
पराकेणाथवा शुद्धिरित्याह भगवान्मनुः§§ ॥

---

* प्रमुच्यते इति B. † अकामतोऽपीति B. ‡ अब्दञ्चरेद्वा नियतः इति B and F. § त्र्यमिति B and F. ¶ गोसहस्रं सपादञ्चेति B. गोसहस्रञ्च पादञ्चेति F. ‖ दद्याद्ब्रह्महणो व्रतीति B. अतः परं B पुस्तके "कृच्छ्रातिकृच्छ्रौ वा कुर्य्याच्चान्द्रायणमथापि वा। संवत्सरं व्रतं कुर्य्याच्छूद्रं हत्वा प्रमादतः। गोसहस्रार्द्धपादञ्च दद्यात्तत्पापशान्तये। अष्टौ वर्षाणि वा त्रीणि कुर्य्याद्ब्रह्महणो व्रतम्। हत्वा तु क्षत्त्रियं वैश्यं शूद्रञ्चैव यथाक्रममिति अधिकः पाठः दृश्यते। F पुस्तकेऽपि उक्तमधिकमस्ति, विशेषस्तु "गोसहस्रार्द्धपादञ्च" इत्यस्य स्थाने "गोसहस्रार्द्धं पादं वा" इति विद्यते, तथा "अष्टौ वर्षाणि वा त्रीणि" इत्यस्य स्थाने अष्टौ वर्षाणि षट् तीर्थादिति च दृश्यते। ** राजन्यां वर्षपर्य्यन्तमिति B. राजन्यां वर्षषट्कन्तु इति F. †† प्रमादेनेति B and F. ‡‡ चान्द्रायणत्रयमिति H. §§ भगवानजः इति B and F.

मण्डूकं नकुलङ्काकं विड़्वराहञ्च* मूषकम्।
श्वानं हत्वा द्विजः कुर्य्यात्षोड़शांशं महाव्रतम्† ॥
पयः पिबेत्त्रिरात्रन्तु श्वानं हत्वा ह्यतन्द्रितः।
मार्ज्जारं वाथ नकुलं योजनञ्चाध्वनो व्रजेत् ॥
कृच्छ्रं द्वादशरात्रन्तु कुर्य्यादश्ववधे द्विजः।
अर्च्चां‡ कार्ष्णायसीं दद्यात्सर्पं हत्वा द्विजोत्तमः ॥
पलालभारकं षण्ढे सीसकञ्चैकमाषकम्।
घृतकुम्भं वराहे§ तु तिलद्रोणन्तु तित्तिरे¶ ॥
शुके‖ द्विहायनं वत्सं क्रौञ्चं हत्वा त्रिहायनम्।
हत्वा हंसं वलाकाञ्च** वकं वर्हिणमेव च ॥
वानरश्येनभासञ्च स्पर्शयेद्ब्राह्मणाय गाम्।
क्रव्यादांस्तु†† मृगान्हत्वा‡‡ धेनुन्दद्यात्पयस्विनीम् ॥
अक्रव्यादान्वत्सतरीमुष्ट्रं हत्वा तु कृष्णलम्।
किञ्चिद्देयन्तु विप्राय दद्यादस्थिमतां वधे ॥
अनस्थ्नाञ्चैव हिंसायां प्राणायामेन शुध्यति।
फलदानान्तु वृक्षाणां छेदने जप्यमृक्शतम् ॥
गुल्मवल्लीलतानान्तु पुष्पितानाञ्च वीरुधाम्।

---

* दन्दशूकञ्चेति B and F. † व्रतं ततः इति B. ‡ अब्भीमिति B, F and G. अब्भी काष्ठकुद्दालः, तत्कृष्टा भूमिर्वा। § वराहमिति B and F. ¶ तित्तिरिमिति B and F. ‖ शुकमिति B and F. ** वलाकञ्चेति B and F. †† क्रव्यादस्तु इति B. ‡‡ मृगं हत्वा इति B.

अन्येषाञ्चैव वृक्षाणां* सारसानाञ्च† सर्व्वशः ॥
फलपुष्पोद्भवानाञ्च घृतप्राशो विशोधनम् ।
हस्तिनाञ्च‡ वधे दृष्टं तप्तकृच्छ्रं विशोधनम् ॥
चान्द्रायणं पराकं वा गां हत्वा तु प्रमादतः ।
मतिपूर्व्ववधे चास्याः प्रायश्चित्तं न विद्यते ॥

इति श्रीकूर्म्मपुराणे उपविभागे त्रयस्त्रिंशोऽध्यायः।

चतुस्त्रिंशोऽध्यायः।

व्यास उवाच।

मनुष्याणान्तु हरणं कृत्वा स्त्रीणां गृहस्य च ।
वापीकूपजलानाञ्च शुद्धेचान्द्रायणेन तु ॥
द्रव्याणामल्पसाराणां स्तेयं कृत्वान्यवेश्मनः* ।
चरेत्सान्तपनं कृच्छ्रं तन्निर्यात्यात्मशुद्धये ॥
धान्यान्नधनचौर्य्यन्तु कृत्वा कामाद्द्विजोत्तमः ।
स्वजातीयगृहादेव कृच्छ्राब्देन† विशुध्यति ॥

---

* अण्डजानाञ्च सत्त्वानामिति B. अन्नजानान्तु सत्त्वानामिति F. † राजसानाञ्चेति B. अण्डजानान्तु सर्व्वश इति F. ‡ हस्तिनश्चेति B.

---

* कृत्वान्यवेश्मतः इति B. † कृच्छ्रार्द्धेन इति B and F.

भक्ष्यभोज्योपहरणे यानशय्यासनेषु च* ।
पुष्पमूलफलानाञ्च पञ्चगव्यं विशोधनम् ॥
तृणकाष्ठद्रुमाणाञ्च शुष्कान्नस्य† गुड़स्य च ।
चैलचर्मामिषाणाञ्च त्रिरात्रं स्यादभोजनम् ॥
मणिमुक्ताप्रवालानां ताम्रस्य रजतस्य च ।
अयस्कान्तोपलानाञ्च‡ द्वादशाहञ्चरेन्निशम्§ ॥
कार्पासस्यैव हरणे¶ द्विशफैकशफस्य च ।
पुष्प‖गन्धौषधीनाञ्च पिवेच्चैव त्र्यहं पयः ॥
नरमांसाशनं कृत्वा चान्द्रायणमथाचरेत् ॥
काकञ्चैव तथा श्वानञ्जग्ध्वा हस्तिनमेव वा ।
वराहं कुक्कुटं वाथ** तप्तकृच्छ्रेण शुध्यति ॥
क्रव्यादानाञ्च†† मांसानि पुरीषं मूत्रमेव वा ।
गोगोमायुकपीनाञ्च तदेव व्रतमाचरेत् ॥
शिशुमारन्तथा चाषं मत्स्यमांसं तथैव च‡‡ ।
उपोष्य द्वादशाहञ्च कुष्माण्डैर्जुहुयात्ततः§§ ॥
नकुलोलूकमार्जाराञ्जग्ध्वा सान्तपनञ्चरेत् ।
श्वापदोष्ट्रखरान् जग्ध्वा तप्तकृच्छ्रेण शुध्यति ।

---

* भक्ष्यभोज्यापहरणे यानशय्यासनस्य चेति B and F. † शुष्कान्नस्येति E and H. ‡ अयःकांस्योपलानाञ्चेति B and F. § द्वादशाहं कणाशनमिति B. ¶ कार्पासकीटजीर्णानामिति B. कार्पासक्षौमवस्त्राणामिति F. ‖ पक्षीति B. पक्षिणामौषधीनाञ्चेति F. ** चाथेति B. †† क्रव्यादाञ्चैव इति B. ‡‡ एतत्पादद्वयं B F पुस्तकयोर्नास्ति। §§ घृतमिति B, E, F and H.

प्रकुर्य्याच्चैव* संस्कारं पूर्व्वेण विधिनैव तु ॥
वकञ्चैव बलाकाञ्च हंसङ्कारण्डवांस्तथा ।
चक्रवाकपलं† जग्ध्वा द्वादशाहमभोजनम् ॥
कपोतटिट्टिभांश्चैव शुकं सारसमेव च ।
उलूकं जालपादञ्च जग्ध्वाप्येतद्व्रतञ्चरेत् ॥
शिशुमारं तथा चाषं मत्स्यमांसं तथैव च ।‡
जग्ध्वा चैव कटाहारमेतदेव व्रतञ्चरेत् ॥
कोकिलञ्चैव मत्स्यादान्§ मण्डूकं भुजगन्तथा ।
गोमूत्रयावकाहारो मासेनैकेन शुद्ध्यति ॥
जलेचरांश्च जलजान् प्रणुदानथ विष्किरान् ।
रक्तपादांस्तथा जग्ध्वा सप्ताहञ्चैतदाचरेत् ॥
शुनो मांसं¶ शुष्कमांसमात्मार्थञ्च तथा कृतम्‖ ।
भुक्त्वा मासञ्चरेदेतत्तत्पापस्यापनुत्तये ॥
वार्त्ताकं मूलकं** शिग्रुं कुटकञ्चटकं तथा†† ।
प्राजापत्यञ्चरेज्जग्ध्वा खट्वां‡‡ कुम्भीकमेव वा ॥
पलाण्डुं लशुनञ्चैव भुक्त्वा चान्द्रायणं चरेत् ।
नालिकान्तण्डुलीयञ्च प्राजापत्येन शुध्यति ॥

---

* व्रतवच्चैवेति B. † चक्रवाकं नवमिति B. चक्रवाकलवमिति F. ‡ अयमधिकः पाठः A, B, E, F, H पुस्तकेषु दृश्यते। § मत्स्यांश्च इति B. मत्स्यादीनिति F. ¶ शुनां मांसमिति B and F. ‖ हतमिति B. ** भूतृणमिति B. भूस्तृणमिति F. †† कुट्टकं कवकं तथेति E, G and H. कुभाण्डं करकं तथेति F. ‡‡ शङ्खमिति B. खड्गमिति F.

अश्मान्तकं तथा पात*न्तप्तकृच्छ्रेण शुध्यति ।
प्राजापत्येन शुद्धिः स्यात्कुसुम्भस्य च भक्षणे ।
अलावुङ्किंशुकञ्चैव भुक्त्वाप्येतद्व्रतञ्चरेत्† ॥
एतेषाञ्च विकाराणि पीत्वा मोहेन वा पुनः‡ ।
उदुम्बरञ्च कालेन§ तप्तकृच्छ्रेण शुध्यति ॥
भुक्त्वा चैव नवश्राद्धे मृतके सूतके तथा¶ ।
चान्द्रायणेन शुद्ध्येत ब्राह्मणः सुसमाहितः ॥
यस्याग्नौ हूयते नित्यमन्नस्याग्रं न दीयते‖ ।
चान्द्रायणञ्चरेत्सम्यक् तस्यान्नप्राशने द्विजः ॥
अभोज्यान्नन्तु सर्व्वेषां भुक्त्वा चान्नमुपस्कृतम् ।
अन्तावसायिनाञ्चैव तप्तकृच्छ्रेण शुद्ध्यति ॥
चण्डालान्नं द्विजो भुक्त्वा सम्यक् चान्द्रायणञ्चरेत् ।**
बुद्धिपूर्व्वन्तु कृच्छ्राब्दं पुनः संस्कारमेव च ॥
असुरामद्यपानेन†† कुर्य्याच्चान्द्रायणव्रतम् ।
अभोज्यान्नन्तु भुक्त्वा तु प्राजापत्येन शुध्यति ॥
विण्मूत्रप्राशनङ्कृत्वा रेतसश्चैतदाचरेत् ।
अनादिष्टे तु चैकाहं सर्व्वत्र तु यथार्थतः ॥
विड्वराहखरोष्ट्राणां गोमायोः कपिकाकयोः ।

---

* पीतमिति B and F. † भुक्त्वा चैतद्व्रतञ्चरेदिति B. ‡ अतः परं B F पुस्तकयोः गोमूत्रयावकाहारः सप्तरात्रेण शुध्यतीति पाठोऽधिकोऽस्ति । § कामेनेति B. ¶ सूतके मृतकेऽपि वेति B. ‖ नित्यं न यस्यान्नं प्रदीयते इति B. ** अतः परं चतुर्द्दश पादाः B पुस्तके न सन्ति । †† असुरामद्यपानेन—सुराभिन्नं मद्यं पीत्वेत्यर्थः ।

प्राश्य मूत्रपुरीषाणि द्विजश्चान्द्रायणञ्चरेत् ॥
अज्ञानात्प्राश्य विण्मूत्रं सुरासंस्पृष्टमेव च।
पुनः संस्कारमर्हन्ति त्रयो वर्णा द्विजातयः ॥
क्रव्यादां पक्षिणाञ्चैव प्राश्य मूत्रपुरीषकम्।
महासान्तपनं मोहात्तथा कुर्य्याद्द्विजोत्तमः।
भासमण्डूककुररे विष्किरे कृच्छ्रमाचरेत् ॥
प्राजापत्येन शुद्ध्येत* ब्राह्मणोच्छिष्टभोजने।
क्षत्रिये तप्तकृच्छ्रं स्याद्वैश्ये चैवातिकृच्छ्रकम्।
शूद्रोच्छिष्टन्द्विजो भुक्त्वा कुर्य्याच्चान्द्रायणव्रतम् ॥
सुराया भाण्डके† वारि पीत्वा चान्द्रायणञ्चरेत्।
समुच्छिष्टं द्विजो भुक्त्वा त्रिरात्रेण विशुद्ध्यति।
गोमूत्रयावकाहारः पीतशेषञ्च वागमम्‡ ॥
अपो मूत्रपुरीषाद्यैर्दूषिताः§ प्राशयेद्यदि।
तदा सान्तपनङ्कृच्छ्रं व्रतम्पापविशोधनम्¶ ॥
चाण्डालकूपे भाण्डेषु यदि ज्ञानात्पिवेज्जलम्‖।
चरेत्सान्तपनङ्कृत्स्नं ब्राह्मणः पापशोधनम् ॥
चाण्डालेन तु संस्पृष्टम्पीत्वा वारि द्विजोत्तमः।
त्रिरात्रव्रतमुख्येन पञ्चगव्येन शुध्यति** ॥

---

* शुध्येत्तु इति B. † सुराभाण्डोदरे इति B. ‡ वा गवामिति B and F. § दूषितैरिति E and H. ¶ पापविनाशनमिति B. ‖ चण्डालकूपभाण्डेषु यद्यज्ञानात्पिबेज्जलमिति B. यदज्ञानादिति E. ** त्रिरात्रेण विशुध्येत पञ्चगव्येन चैव हीति B.

महापातकिसंस्पर्शे भुक्त्वा स्नात्वा द्विजो यदि* ।
बुद्धिपूर्व्वं यदा मोहात्तप्तकृच्छ्रं† समाचरेत् ॥
स्पृष्ट्वा महापातकिनं चण्डालञ्च‡ रजस्वलाम् ।
प्रमादाद्भोजनङ्कृत्वा त्रिरात्रेण विशुध्यति ॥
स्नानार्हो यदि भुञ्जीत ह्यहोरात्रेण शुध्यति ।
बुद्धिपूर्व्वन्तु कृच्छ्रेण भगवानाह पद्मजः ॥
भुक्त्वा पर्य्युषितादीनि गवादिप्रतिदूषिताः§ ।
भुक्त्वोपवासङ्कुर्व्वीत कृच्छ्रपादमथापि वा ॥
संवत्सरान्ते कृच्छ्रन्तु चरेद्विप्रः पुनः पुनः ।
अज्ञानभुक्तशुद्ध्यर्थं ज्ञातस्य तु विशेषतः ॥¶
व्रात्यानां याजनङ्कृत्वा परेषामन्त्यकर्म्म च ।
अभिचारमहीनञ्च त्रिभिः कृच्छ्रैर्विशुध्यति ॥
ब्राह्मणादिहतानान्तु‖ कृत्वा दाहादिकं द्विजः** ।
गोमूत्रयावकाहारः प्राजापत्येन शुध्यति ॥
तैलाभ्यक्तोऽथ वान्तो वा कुर्य्यान्मूत्रपुरीषके†† ।
अहोरात्रेण शुद्ध्येत श्मश्रुकर्म्मणि मैथुने ॥
एकाहेन विहायाग्निं परिहाप्य‡‡ द्विजोत्तमः ।

---

* द्विजोत्तमः इति B and F. † बुद्धिपूर्व्वन्तु मूढ़ात्मा तप्तकृच्छ्रमिति B and F. ‡ चाण्डालीं वा इति B. § प्रदूषितमिति F. ¶ अतः परं A, F, H पुस्तकेषु व्यास उवाच इत्यधिकः पाठो दृश्यते । ‖ हतानाञ्चेति B. ** दाहादिकाः क्रियाः इति B and F. †† तैलाभ्यक्तोऽथवा कुर्य्याद्यदि मूत्रपुरीषके इति B. ‡‡ परिवार्य्य इति B.

त्रिरात्रेण विशुद्धेरत त्रिरात्रात्षड़हः परम्* ॥
दशाहं द्वादशाहं वा परिहाप्य† प्रमादतः ।
कृच्छ्रञ्चान्द्रायणङ्कुर्य्यात्तत्पापस्योपशान्तये‡ ॥
पतिताद्द्रव्यमादाय तदुत्सर्गेण शुध्यति ।
चरेच्च विधिना§ कृच्छ्रमित्याह भगवान्मनुः ॥
अनाशकान्निवृत्तास्तु प्रव्रज्यावसितास्तथा ।
चरेयुस्त्रीणि कृच्छ्राणि त्रीणि चान्द्रायणानि च ॥
पुनश्च जातकर्म्मादिसंस्कारैः संस्कृता द्विजाः ।
शुद्धेयुस्तद्व्रतं सम्यक् चरेयुर्धर्म्मदर्शिनः¶ ॥
अनुपासितसन्ध्यस्तु तदहर्यावकी‖ भवेत् ।
अनश्नन् संयतमना रात्रौ चेद्रात्रिमेव हि ॥
अकृत्वा समिदाधानं शुचिः स्नात्वा समाहितः ।
गायत्र्यष्टसहस्रस्य जप्यं कुर्य्याद्विशुद्धये** ॥
उपवासी†† चरेत्सन्ध्यां गृहस्थो हि‡‡ प्रमादतः ।
स्नात्वा विशुध्यते सद्यः परिश्रान्तश्च संयतः§§ ॥
वेदोदितानि नित्यानि कर्म्माणि च विलोप्य तु ।
स्नातको व्रतलोपन्तु¶¶ कृत्वा चोपवसेद्दिनम् ॥
संवत्सरञ्चरेत्कृच्छ्रमग्न्युत्सादी द्विजोत्तमः ।

---

* षड़हं पुनरिति B. † परिवार्य्य इति B. ‡ पापस्यापनुत्तये इति B. § चरेत्सान्तपनमिति B. ¶ वर्द्धनाः इति B. ‖ तदहर्जापकः इति B. जापको वसेदिति F. ** विशुध्यतीति B. †† जपादीन्न इति B. उपासीनश्चरेदिति F. ‡‡ गृहस्थोऽपीति B. §§ संयमादिति B. ¶¶ स्नातकव्रतलोपन्तु इति B.

चान्द्रायणञ्चरेद्व्रात्यो गोप्रदानेन शुद्ध्यति ॥
नास्तिक्यं यदि कुर्व्वीत प्राजापत्यञ्चरेद्द्विजः ।
देवद्रोहं गुरुद्रोहं तप्तकृच्छ्रेण शुद्ध्यति ॥
उष्ट्रयानं समारुह्य खरयानञ्च कामतः ।
त्रिरात्रेण विशुद्ध्येच्च नग्नो वा प्रविशेज्जलम्* ॥
षष्ठान्नकालता† मासं संहिताजप एव च ।
होमाश्च शाकला‡ नित्यं अपंक्त्यानां विशोधनम् ॥
नीलं रक्तं वसित्वा च ब्राह्मणो वस्त्रमेव हि ।
अहोरात्रोषितः स्नातः§ पञ्चगव्येन शुद्ध्यति ॥
वेद¶धर्म्मपुराणानां चण्डालस्य तु भाषणे ।
चान्द्रायणेन शुद्धिः स्यान्न ह्यन्या तस्य निष्कृतिः‖ ॥
उद्बन्धनादिनिहतं** संस्पृश्य ब्राह्मणं क्वचित् ।
चान्द्रायणेन शुद्धिः स्यात्प्राजापत्येन वा पुनः ॥
उच्छिष्टो यद्यनाचान्तश्चाण्डालादीन् स्पृशेद्द्विजः ।
प्रमादाद्वै†† जपेत्स्नात्वा गायत्र्यष्टसहस्रकम् ॥
द्रुपदानां शतं वापि‡‡ ब्रह्मचारी समाहितः ।
त्रिरात्रोपोषितः सम्यक् पञ्चगव्येन शुद्ध्यति ॥

---

* उष्ट्रयानमित्यादि श्लोकः B पुस्तके श्लोकद्वयात् परं दृश्यते । † षष्ठान्नकालता-षष्टभागविभक्तस्य दिनस्य षष्ठे भागे भोजनशीलता इत्यर्थः । षष्ठान्नकर्षितमिति B. ‡ शाकलाः शाकलप्रोक्तविधिना सम्पादिताः । § स्नात्वेति B. ¶ देवेति B. ‖ न ह्यन्या तस्य निष्कृतिरित्यारभ्य चान्द्रायणेन शुद्धिः स्यादित्यन्तः पाठः G पुस्तके न दृश्यते । ** विहतमिति B. †† प्रमादाद्धि इति B. ‡‡ चापीति B.

चाण्डालपतितादींश्च* कामाद्यः संस्पृशेद्द्विजः।
उच्छिष्टस्तत्र कुर्व्वीत प्राजापत्यं विशुद्धये॥
चाण्डालसूतकिशवन्तथा† नारीं रजस्वलाम्।
स्पृष्ट्वा स्नायाद्विशुद्ध्यर्थं‡ तत्स्पृष्टपतितांस्तथा॥
चाण्डालसूतकिशवैः संस्पृष्टं संस्पृशेद्यदि।
ततः स्नात्वाथ§ आचम्य जपङ्कुर्य्यात्समाहितः॥
तत्स्पृष्टस्पर्शिनं स्पृष्ट्वा बुद्धिपूर्व्वं द्विजोत्तमः।
स्नात्वाचामेद्विशुद्ध्यर्थं प्राह देवः पितामहः॥
भुञ्जानस्य तु विप्रस्य कदाचित्संस्पृशेद्गुदम्¶।
कृत्वा शौचन्ततः स्नायादुपोष्य जुहुयाद्व्रतम्‖॥
चाण्डालन्तु शवं स्पृष्ट्वा कृच्छ्रं कृत्वा विशुद्ध्यति**।
स्पृष्ट्वाऽभ्यक्तस्त्वसंस्पृश्य अहोरात्रेण शुद्ध्यति॥
सुरां स्पृष्ट्वा द्विजः कुर्य्यात्प्राणायामत्रयं शुचिः।
पलाण्डुं लशुनञ्चैव घृतं प्राश्य ततः शुचिः॥
ब्राह्मणस्तु शुना दष्टस्त्र्यहं सायम्पयः पिवेत्।
नाभेरूर्द्ध्वन्तु दष्टस्य तदेव द्विगुणं भवेत्॥
स्यादेतत्त्रिगुणं†† बाह्वोर्मूर्द्ध्नि च स्याच्चतुर्गुणम्।
स्नात्वा जपेद्वा सावित्रीं श्वभिर्दष्टो द्विजोत्तमः॥
अनिर्वर्त्त्य महायज्ञान्यो भुंक्ते तु द्विजोत्तमः।

---

* पतितादींस्तु इति B. † शवांस्तथेति B. ‡ अतः परं पादाष्टकं B पुस्तके न दृश्यते। § प्रमादात्तदा इति F. ¶ संस्रवेद्गुरुमिति B. ‖ जुहुयाद्घृतमिति B, E, F and H ** कुर्य्याद्विशुद्धये इति B and F. †† स्यादेव त्रिगुणमिति B.

अनातुरस्य निधने* कृच्छ्रार्द्धेन स शुद्ध्यति† ॥
आहिताग्निरुपस्थानं न कुर्य्याद्यस्तु पर्व्वणि ।
ऋतौ न गच्छेद्भार्य्यां वा सोऽपि कृच्छ्रार्द्धमाचरेत् ॥
विनाद्भिरप्सु नाप्यार्त्तशरीरं‡ सन्निवेश्य च§ ।
सचेलो जलमाप्लुत्य गामालभ्य विशुध्यति ॥
बुद्धिपूर्व्वन्त्वभ्युदिते¶ जपेदन्तर्जले द्विजः ।
गायत्र्यष्टसहस्रन्तु त्र्यहं चोपवसेद्विजः‖ ॥
अनुगम्येच्छया शूद्रं प्रेतीभूतं द्विजोत्तमः ।
गायत्र्यष्टसहस्रञ्च जपङ्कुर्य्यान्नदीषु च ॥
कृत्वा तु शपथान्** विप्रो विप्रस्यावधिसंयुतम्†† ।
स चैव यावकान्नेन कुर्य्याच्चान्द्रायणं व्रतम् ॥
पङ्क्तौ‡‡ विषमदानन्तु कृत्वा कृच्छ्रेण शुध्यति ।
छायां श्वपाकस्यारुह्य स्नात्वा सम्प्राशयेद्घृतम् ॥
ईचे§§दादित्यमशुचिर्दृष्ट्वाग्निञ्चन्द्रमेव¶¶ वा ।
मानुषञ्चास्थि संस्पृश्य स्नानं कृत्वा विशुद्ध्यति ॥
कृत्वा तु मिथ्याध्ययनञ्चरेद्भैक्षन्तु वत्सरम् ।

---

* अनातुरः सति धने इति B and F. † विनश्यतीति B. ‡ नाप्यर्द्धं शरीरमिति B. नाप्यार्त्तः शरीरमिति F. § सन्निषेव्य तु इति B and F. ¶ अभ्युदितः इति B, E, F and H. ‖ चोपवसेदितीति B and F. ** शपथमिति B and F. †† विप्रस्य वधसंयुतमिति B and F. ‡‡ पङ्क्त्यामिति B. पङ्क्तौ विषमदानम्—एकपङ्क्तिस्थितेभ्यो भोजनङ्कुर्व्वद्भ्यो ब्राह्मणेभ्यो विसदृशदानं परिवेशनमित्यर्थः । §§ ईचेदित्यार्षम्. ईक्षेत इति साधु । ¶¶ म्लेच्छान्नमेवेति B.

कृतघ्नो ब्राह्मणगृहे* पञ्चसंवत्सरव्रती† ॥
हुङ्कारं‡ ब्राह्मणस्योक्त्वा त्वङ्कारञ्च गरीयसः ।
स्नात्वा नाश्नन्नहःशेषं प्रणिपत्य प्रसादयेत् ॥
ताड़यित्वा तृणेनापि कण्ठे बद्ध्वाथ वाससा ।
विवादे चापि निर्जित्य प्रणिपत्य प्रसादयेत् ॥
अवगूर्य§ चरेत्कृच्छ्रमतिकृच्छ्रं निपातने ।
कृच्छ्रातिकृच्छ्रौ कुर्व्वीत विप्रस्योत्पाद्य शोणितम् ॥
गुरोराक्रोशमनृतं कुर्य्यात्कृत्वा¶ विशोधनम् ।
एकरात्रं निराहारः‖ तत्पापस्यापनुत्तये ॥
देवर्षीणामभिमुखं ष्ठीवनाक्रोशने कृते ।
उल्मुकेन दहेज्जिह्वां दातव्यञ्च हिरण्यकम् ॥
देवोद्यानेषु** यः कुर्य्यान्मूत्रोच्चारं सकृद्द्विजः†† ।
छिन्द्याच्छिश्नं विशुध्यर्थञ्चरेच्चान्द्रायणं व्रतम् ॥
देवतायतने मूत्रं कृत्वा मोहाद्द्विजोत्तमः ।
शिश्नस्योत्कर्त्तनं कृत्वा चान्द्रायणमथाचरेत् ॥
देवतानामृषीणाञ्च देवानाञ्चैव‡‡ कुत्सनम् ।
कृत्वा सम्यक् प्रकुर्व्वीत प्राजापत्यं द्विजोत्तमः ॥
तैस्तु सम्भाषणं कृत्वा स्नात्वा देवं समर्च्चयेत् ।
दृष्ट्वा वीक्षेत भास्वन्तं स्मृत्वा विश्वेश्वरं स्मरेत् ॥

---

* ब्राह्मणः शुध्येदिति B. † संवत्सरं प्रतीति B. ‡ ओङ्कारमिति B. § अवगूह्य इति B. अवगृह्य इति F. ¶ कृत्वा कुर्य्यादिति B and F. ‖ एकरात्रं त्रिरात्रं वेति B and F. ** देवोद्याने तु इति B. †† तथेति B. ‡‡ वेदानाञ्चैवेति B.

यः सर्व्वभूताधिपतिं विश्वेशानं विनिन्दति।
न तस्य निष्कृतिः शक्या कर्त्तुं वर्षशतैरपि॥
चान्द्रायणं चरेत्पूर्व्वं कृच्छ्रञ्चैवातिकृच्छ्रकम्।
प्रपन्नः शरणन्देवं तस्मात्पापाद्विमुच्यते॥
सर्व्वस्वदानं कथितं पातकानां विशोधनम्।*
पुण्यक्षेत्राभिगमनं सर्व्वपापविशोधनम्†॥
अमावास्यां तिथिं प्राप्य यः समाराधयेद्भवम्‡।
ब्राह्मणान् पूजयित्वा तु सर्व्वपापैः प्रमुच्यते॥
कृष्णाष्टम्यां महादेवीं§ तथा कृष्णचतुर्द्दशीम्।
सम्पूज्य ब्राह्मणमुखे सर्व्वपापैः प्रमुच्यते॥
त्रयोदश्यां तथा रात्रौ सोपहारं त्रिलोचनम्।
दृष्ट्वेशं प्रथमे यामे मुच्यते सर्व्वपातकैः॥
उपोषितश्चतुर्द्दश्यां कृष्णपक्षे समाहितः।
यमाय धर्म्मराजाय मृत्यवे चान्तकाय च।
वैवस्वताय कालाय सर्व्वप्राणहराय¶ च॥
प्रत्येकं तिलसंयुक्तान्दद्यात्सप्तोदकाञ्जलीन्।
स्नात्वा दद्याच्च‖ पूर्व्वाह्णे मुच्यते सर्व्वपातकैः॥

---

* एतच्छ्लोकार्द्धं B पुस्तके भिन्नरूपमेव दृश्यते, यथा—सर्व्वस्वदानं विधिवत् सर्व्वपाप-विशोधनम्। चान्द्रायणञ्च विधिना कृच्छ्रं चैवातिकृच्छ्रकम्॥ सर्व्वपापप्रशोधनमित्यत्र तत्-पापस्य विशोधनमिति F. † विनाशनमिति B. ‡ शिवमिति B. § महादेवमिति B and F. ¶ सर्व्वभूतरताय इति B. ‖ नद्याञ्चेति B. नद्यान्तु इति F.

ब्रह्मचर्य्यमधःशय्या* उपवासो† द्विजार्च्चनम् ।
तेष्वेतेषु प्रकुर्व्वीत‡ शान्तः संयतमानसः ॥
अमावास्यायां ब्रह्माणं समुद्दिश्य पितामहम् ।
ब्राह्मणांस्त्रीन् समभ्यर्च्य मुच्यते सर्व्वपातकैः ॥
षष्ठ्यामुपोषितो देवं शुक्लपक्षे समाहितः ।
सप्तम्यामर्च्चयेद्भानुं मुच्यते सर्व्वपातकैः ॥
भरण्याञ्च चतुर्थ्याञ्च§ शनैश्चरदिने यमम् ।
पूजयेत्सप्तजन्मोत्थैर्मुच्यते सर्व्वपातकैः¶ ॥
एकादश्यां निराहारः समभ्यर्च्य जनार्द्दनम् ।
द्वादश्यां शुक्लपक्षस्य महापापैः प्रमुच्यते ॥
तपो जपस्तीर्थसेवा देवब्राह्मणपूजनम् ।
ग्रहणादिषु कालेषु महापातकशोधनम् ॥
यः सर्व्वपापयुक्तोऽपि पुण्यतीर्थेषु मानवः ।
नियमेन त्यजेत्प्राणान्मुच्यते सर्व्वपातकैः ॥
ब्रह्मघ्नं वा कृतघ्नं वा महापातकदूषितम्‖ ।
भर्त्तारमुद्धरेन्नारी प्रविष्टा सह पावकम्** ।
एतदेव परं स्त्रीणाम्प्रायश्चित्तं विदुर्बुधाः ॥
पतिव्रता तु या नारी भर्तृशुश्रूषणे रता ।

---

* अधःशय्यामिति B. † उपवासमिति B. ‡ व्रतेष्वेतेषु कुर्व्वीत इति B and F.
§ भरण्यान्तु चतुर्थ्यां यः इति B. ¶ सप्तजन्मोत्थैर्मुच्यते पातकैर्नरः इति B. सप्तजन्माद्यैरिति F. ‖ महापातकिनं नरमिति B. ** पावकैरिति B.

न तस्या विद्यते पापमिहलोके परत्र च* ॥
पतिव्रता धर्म्मरता भद्राण्येव न संशयः ।
नास्याः पराभवङ्कर्त्तुं शक्नोतीह जनः क्वचित् ॥
यथा रामस्य सुभगा सीता त्रैलोक्यविश्रुता ।
पत्नी दाशरथेर्देवी विजिग्ये राक्षसेश्वरम् ॥
रामस्य भार्य्यां सुभगां† रावणो राक्षसेश्वरः ।
सीतां विशालनयनाञ्चकमे कालनोदितः ॥
गृहीत्वा मायया वेषं‡ चरन्तीं विजने वने ।
समाहर्त्तुं मतिञ्चक्रे तापसः किल कामिनीम्§ ॥
विज्ञाय सा च तद्भावं स्मृत्वा दाशरथिम्पतिम् ।
जगाम शरणं वह्निमावसथ्यं शुचिस्मिता ॥
उपतस्थे महायोगं सर्व्वलोकविदाहकम्¶ ।
कृताञ्जली राजपत्नी‖ साक्षात्पतिमिवाच्युतम् ॥
नमस्यामि महायोगङ्कृशानुङ्गह्वरम्परम्** ।
दाहकं सर्व्वभूतानामीशानङ्कालरूपिणम् ॥
प्रपद्ये†† पावकं देवं ब्रह्मण्यं ब्रह्मरूपिणम्‡‡ ।

---

* सर्व्वपापविनिर्म्मुक्ता नास्ति कार्य्या विचारणा इति B. अतः परं B पुस्तके पतिव्रता तु या नारी भर्त्तृशुश्रूषणोत्सुका । न तस्या विद्यते पापमिहलोके परत्र च ॥ इत्यधिकः पाठः दृश्यते । † विमलामिति B. ‡ क्षेमामिति B. § भाविनीमिति B. ¶ सर्व्वदोषविनाशनमिति B. सर्व्वदोषविदाहकमिति E. सर्व्वरोगविनाशनमिति F. ‖ रामपत्नीति B, E and F. ** कृतान्तं गह्वरं परमिति B. कृत्वा नगह्वरं परमिति F. †† नमस्ये इति B. ‡‡ साक्षिणं विश्वतोमुखमिति B.

योगिनङ्कृत्तिवासानं* भूतेशं परमम्पदम्† ॥
तम्प्रपद्ये जगन्मूर्त्तिं प्रभवं सर्व्वतेजसाम्‡।
महायोगेश्वरं वह्निमादित्यम्परमेष्ठिनम् ॥
प्रपद्ये शरणं रुद्रं महाग्रासं त्रिशूलिनम्।
कालाग्निं योगिनामीशं भोगमोक्षफलप्रदम् ॥
प्रपद्ये त्वां विरूपाक्षं भूर्भुवःस्वःस्वरूपिणम्।
हिरण्मये गृहे गुप्तं§ महान्तममितौजसम् ॥
वैश्वानरम्प्रपद्येऽहं सर्व्वभूतेष्ववस्थितम्।
हव्यकव्यवहं देवं प्रपद्ये वह्निमीश्वरम् ॥
प्रपद्ये तत्परं¶ तत्त्वं वरेण्यं सवितुः शिवम्‖।
स्वर्गमग्निं** परं ज्योतिः स्वाक्षयं हव्यवाहनम्†† ॥
इति वह्न्यष्टकं जप्त्वा रामपत्नी यशस्विनी।
ध्यायन्ती मनसा तस्थौ राममुन्मीलितेक्षणा ॥
अथावसथ्याद्भगवान्हव्यवाहो महेश्वरः।
आविरासीत्सुदीप्तात्मा तेजसा निर्द्दहन्निव ॥
सृष्ट्वा मायामयीं सीतां स रावणवधेच्छया‡‡।

---

* कृत्तिवासानं – स्वार्थे णिजन्तादसधातोः शानच्। कृत्तिवसनमिति B and F.
† आत्मानं दीप्तवपुषं सर्व्वभूतहृदि स्थितमिति B. आत्मानं दान्तवपुषं सर्व्वभूतहृदि स्थितमिति F. ‡ प्रपद्ये शरणं वह्निं ब्रह्मण्यं ब्रह्मरूपिणमिति B. § सुप्तमिति B. ¶ परममिति B. ‖ स्वयमिति B. ** भागमग्निमिति B. भार्गवाग्निमिति F. †† रक्ष मां हव्यवाहन इति B and F. ‡‡ रावणवधेप्सया इति B.

सीतामादाय रामेष्टां* पावकोऽन्तरधीयत॥
तां दृष्ट्वा तादृशीं† सीतां रावणो राक्षसेश्वरः।
समादाय ययौ लङ्कां सागरान्तरसंस्थिताम्॥
कृत्वा तु रावणवधं रामो लक्ष्मणसंयुतः।
समादायाभवत्सीतां शङ्काकुलितमानसः॥
सा प्रत्ययाय भूतानां सीता मायामयी पुनः।
विवेश पावकं दीप्तं‡ ददाह ज्वलनोऽपि ताम्॥
दग्ध्वा मायामयीं सीतां भगवानुग्रदीधितिः§।
रामायादर्शयत्सीतां पावकोऽभूत्सुरप्रियः॥
प्रगृह्य भर्त्तुश्चरणौ कराभ्यां सा सुमध्यमा।
चकार प्रणतिम्भूमौ रामाय जनकात्मजा॥
दृष्ट्वा हृष्टमना रामो विस्मयाकुललोचनः।
ननाम वह्निं शिरसा तोषयामास राघवः॥¶
तमाह देवो लोकानां दाहको हव्यवाहनः।
यथा वृत्तं दाशरथिं भूतानामेव सन्निधौ॥
इयं सा परमा साध्वी पार्व्वतीव प्रिया तव‖।
आराध्य लब्ध्वा तपसा देव्याश्चात्यन्तवल्लभा**॥
भर्त्तुः शुश्रूषणोपेता सुशीलेयं पतिव्रता।

* धर्म्मिष्ठामिति B and F. † तामसीमिति B. ‡ क्षिप्रमिति B. § भगवानुग्रदीधितिरिति B. ¶ अतः परं B पुस्तके उवाच वह्निं भगवान् किमेषा वरवर्णिनी। दग्धा भगवता पूर्व्वं दृष्टा मत्पार्श्वमागता॥ इत्यधिकः पाठो दृश्यते। ‖ इत्थं सा मिथिलेशेन पार्व्वतीं रुद्रवल्लभामिति B and F. ** दुर्लभेति B. आराध्य हरिवल्लभामिति F.

भवानीवेश्वरे गुप्ता* माया रावणकामिता ॥
या नीता राक्षसेशेन सीता बलवताहृता† ।
मया मायामयी सृष्टा रावणस्य वधेच्छया‡ ॥
तदर्थं§ भवता दृष्टो रावणो राक्षसेश्वरः ।
मायोपसंहृता चैव हतो लोकविनाशनः ॥
गृहाण चैतां विमलां¶ जानकीं वचनान्मम ।
पश्य नारायणन्देवं स्वात्मानम्प्रभवाव्ययम् ॥
इत्युक्त्वा भगवांश्चण्डो विश्वार्च्चिर्विश्वतोमुखः ।
मानितो राघवेणाग्निर्भूतै‖श्चान्तरधीयत ॥
एतत्पतिव्रतानां वै माहात्म्यङ्कथितं मया ।
स्त्रीणां सर्व्वाघशमनम्प्रायश्चित्तमिदं स्मृतम् ॥
अशेषपापसंयुक्तः** पुरुषोऽपि सुसंयुतः ।
स्वदेहं पुण्यतीर्थेषु त्यक्त्वा मुच्येत किल्विषात् ॥
पृथिव्यां सर्व्वतीर्थेषु†† स्नात्वा पुण्येषु वा द्विजः ।
मुच्यते पातकैः सर्व्वैः सञ्चितैरपि‡‡ पूरुषः ॥§§
इत्येष¶¶ मानवो धर्म्मो युष्माकङ्कथितो मया ।
महेशाराधनार्थाय ज्ञानयोगश्च शाश्वतः ॥

---

* भवानीपार्श्वमानीतेति B. † सीता सा भस्मसङ्गतेति B. सीता भगवती मयेति F. ‡ वधाय सेति B. § यदर्थमिति B and F. ¶ विमलामेनामिति B. ‖ सचैवान्तरधीयतेति F. ** युक्तास्तु इति B. †† देहेष्विति B. ‡‡ समस्तैरपीति B and F. §§ अतः परं व्यास उवाच इति B पुस्तके दृश्यते। ¶¶ इत्येवमिति B and F.

योगेन विधिना युक्तो* ज्ञानयोगं समाचरेत् ।
स पश्यति महादेवं नान्यः कल्पशतैरपि ॥
स्थापयेद्यः परं धर्म्मं ज्ञानं तत्पारमेश्वरम् ।
न तस्मादधिको लोके स योगी परमो मतः ॥
यः संस्थापयितुं शक्तो न कुर्य्यान्मोहितो जनः ।
स योगयुक्तोऽपि मुनिर्नात्यर्थं भगवत्प्रियः ॥
तस्मात्सदैव दातव्यं ब्राह्मणेषु विशेषतः ।
धर्म्मयुक्तेषु शान्तेषु श्रद्धया चान्वितेषु वै ॥
यः पठेद्भवतान्नित्यं संवादं मम चैव हि ।
सर्व्वपापविनिर्मुक्तो गच्छेत† परमाङ्गतिम् ॥
श्राद्धे वा दैविके कार्य्ये ब्राह्मणानाञ्च सन्निधौ ।
पठेत‡ नित्यं सुमनाः श्रोतव्यञ्च द्विजातिभिः ॥
योऽर्थं विचार्य्य युक्तात्मा श्रावयेद्वा द्विजान्§ शुचीन् ।
स दोषकञ्चुकन्त्यक्त्वा याति देवं महेश्वरम् ॥
एतावदुक्त्वा भगवान् व्यासः सत्यवतीसुतः ।
समाश्वास्य मूनीन्सूतं¶ जगाम च यथागतम् ॥

इति श्रीकूर्म्मपुराणे उपविभागे चतुस्त्रिंशोऽध्यायः ।

व्यासगीता च समाप्ता ।||

---

* योऽनेन विधिना युक्तमिति B and F. † गच्छेत इत्यार्षमात्मनेपदम् । गच्छेत्स इति B. स गच्छेदिति F. ‡ पठेत इत्यार्षमात्मनेपदम् । § श्रावयेद्ब्राह्मणानिति B. श्रावयेद्वै इति F. ¶ समीभूतमिति A. मुनीन् सर्व्वानिति F. || एतत्पाठः A पुस्तके नास्ति.।

पञ्चत्रिंशोऽध्यायः ।

ऋषय ऊचुः ।

तीर्थानि यानि लोकेऽस्मिन्विश्रुतानि महान्त्यपि* ।
तानि त्वङ्कथयास्माकं रोमहर्षण साम्प्रतम् ॥

रोमहर्षण उवाच ।

शृणुध्वङ्कथयिष्येऽहं तीर्थानि विविधानि च ।
कथितानि पुराणेषु मुनिभिर्ब्रह्मवादिभिः ॥
यत्र स्नानञ्जपो होमः श्राद्धदानादिकङ्कृतम् ।
एकैकशो मुनिश्रेष्ठाः पुनात्यासप्तमङ्कुलम् ॥
पञ्चयोजनविस्तीर्णं ब्रह्मणः परमेष्ठिनः ।
प्रयागम्प्रथितं तीर्थं यस्य† माहात्म्यमीरितम् ॥
अन्यच्च तीर्थप्रवरं कुरूणां देववन्दितम् ।
ऋषीणामाश्रमैर्जुष्टं सर्व्वपापविशोधनम्‡ ॥
तत्र स्नात्वा विशुद्धात्मा दम्भमात्सर्य्यवर्ज्जितः ।
ददाति यत्किञ्चिदपि पुनात्युभयतः कुलम् ॥
परं गुह्यं गयातीर्थं पितॄणाञ्चातिदुर्ल्लभम् ।
कृत्वा पिण्डप्रदानन्तु न भूयो जायते नरः§ ॥
सकृद्गयाभिगमनङ्कृत्वा पिण्डं ददाति यः ।

---

* महान्ति चेति B. † तस्येति B and F. ‡ प्रणाशनमिति B. § एषः श्लोकः A, E, F, H पुस्तकेषु नास्ति ।

तारिताः पितरस्तेन* यास्यन्ति परमाङ्गतिम् ॥
तत्र लोकहितार्थाय रुद्रेण परमात्मना ।
शिलातले पदं न्यस्तं तत्र पितॄन् प्रसादयेत्† ॥
गयाभिगमनङ्कर्त्तुं यः शक्तो नाधिगच्छति‡ ।
शोचन्ति पितरस्तं वै वृथा तस्य परिश्रमः ॥
गायन्ति पितरो गाथाः कीर्त्तयन्ति महर्षयः ।
गयां यास्यति यः कश्चित्सोऽस्मान्सन्तारयिष्यति ॥
यदि स्यात्पातकोपेतः स्वधर्म्मपरिवर्ज्जितः ।
गयां यास्यति वंशोत्थः§ सोऽस्मान् सन्तारयिष्यति ॥
एष्टव्या बहवः पुत्राः शीलवन्तो¶ गुणान्विताः ।
तेषान्तु समवेतानां यद्येकोऽपि गयां व्रजेत् ॥
तस्मात्सर्व्वप्रयत्नेन ब्राह्मणस्तु विशेषतः ।
प्रदद्याद्विधिवत्पिण्डान् गयाङ्गत्वा समाहितः ॥
धन्यास्तु खलु ते मर्त्त्या गयायां पिण्डदायिनः ।
कुलान्युभयतः सप्त समुद्धृत्याप्नुयुः‖ परम् ॥
अन्यच्च तीर्थप्रवरं सिद्धावासमुदाहृतम् ।
प्रभासमिति विख्यातं यत्रास्ते भगवान्भवः ॥
तत्र स्नानं ततः** श्राद्धं ब्राह्मणानाञ्च पूजनम् ।

---

* पितरस्तारितास्तेनेति B. † एषः श्लोकः A, E, H पुस्तकेषु नास्ति । ‡ नाभिगच्छतीति B and F. § यः कश्चिदिति B. ¶ बलवन्त इति B. ‖ समुद्धृत्याप्नुयुरिति B and F. ** स्नानन्तु यः इति B. तत्र स्नानं तपः श्राद्धमिति F.

ज्ञात्वा योग*मवाप्नोति ब्राह्मणोऽक्षयमुत्तमम्† ॥
तीर्थन्त्रियम्बकं‡ नाम सर्व्वदेवनमस्कृतम् ।
पूजयित्वा तत्र रुद्रं ज्योतिष्टोमफलं लभेत्§ ॥
सुपर्णाक्षं¶ महादेवं समभ्यर्च्य कपर्द्दिनम् ।
ब्राह्मणान् पूजयित्वा च‖ गाणपत्यं लभेद्ध्रुवम् ॥
सोमेश्वरं तीर्थवरं रुद्रस्य परमेष्ठिनः ।
सर्व्वव्याधिहरं पुण्यं रुद्रसालोक्य**कारणम् ॥
तीर्थानां परमं तीर्थं विजयं नाम शोभनम् ।
तत्र लिङ्गं महेशस्य विजयं नाम विश्रुतम् ॥
षण्मासनियताहारी ब्रह्मचारी समाहितः ।
उषित्वा तत्र विप्रेन्द्रा यास्यन्ति परमम्पदम्†† ॥
अन्यच्च तीर्थप्रवरं‡‡ पूर्व्वदेशेषु शोभनम् ।
एकान्तं देवदेवस्य गाणपत्यफलप्रदम् ॥
दत्त्वात्र शिवभक्तानां किञ्चित् शश्वन्महीं शुभाम् ।
सार्व्वभौमो भवेद्राजा मुमुक्षुर्मोक्षमाप्नुयात्§§ ॥
महानदीजलं पुण्यं सर्व्वपापविनाशनम् ।
ग्रहणे तदुपस्पृश्य¶¶ मुच्यते सर्व्वपातकैः ॥
अन्या च विरजा नाम नदी त्रैलोक्यविश्रुता ।

---

* लोकमिति B and F. † ब्राह्मणोऽक्षय्यमुत्तममिति B, E, F and H. ‡ तीर्थन्त्रैयम्बकमिति B and F. § लभेत इति साधु । ¶ सुवर्णाक्षमिति B and F. ‖ तु इति B. ** रुद्रसायुज्येति B. †† प्रयास्यन्ति परम्पदमिति B. ‡‡ तीर्थं परममिति B. §§ एषः श्लोकः A, E, H पुस्तकेषु नास्ति । ¶¶ समुपस्पृश्येति B.

तस्यां स्नात्वा नरो विप्रो ब्रह्मलोके महीयते ॥
तीर्थं नारायणस्यान्यन्नाम्ना तु पुरुषोत्तमम् ।
तत्र नारायणः श्रीमानास्ते परमपूरुषः ॥
पूजयित्वा परं विष्णुं स्नात्वा तत्र द्विजोत्तमः ।
ब्राह्मणान् पूजयित्वा तु विष्णुलोकमवाप्नुयात् ॥
तीर्थानाम्परमं तीर्थङ्गोकर्णं* नाम विश्रुतम् ।
सर्व्वपापहरं शम्भोर्निवासः परमेष्ठिनः ॥
दृष्ट्वा लिङ्गन्तु देवस्य गोकर्णम्परमुत्तमम्† ।
ईप्सिताँल्लभते कामान्रुद्रस्य दयितो भवेत् ॥
उत्तरञ्चापि गोकर्णं लिङ्गं देवस्य शूलिनः ।
महादेवञ्चार्च्चयित्वा शिवसायुज्यमाप्नुयात् ॥
तत्र देवो महादेवः स्थाणुरित्यभिविश्रुतः ।
तं दृष्ट्वा सर्व्वपापेभ्यस्तत्क्षणान्मुच्यते‡ नरः ॥
अन्यत्कुब्जाश्रमम्पुण्यं§ स्थानं विष्णोर्म्महात्मनः ।
सम्पूज्य पुरुषं विष्णुं श्वेतद्वीपे महीयते ॥
यत्र नारायणो देवो रुद्रेण त्रिपुरारिणा ।
कृत्वा यज्ञस्य मथनं दक्षस्य तु विसर्ज्जितः ॥
समन्ताद्योजनङ्क्षेत्रं सिद्धर्षिगणसेवितम् ।
पुण्यमायतनं विष्णोस्तत्रास्ते पुरुषोत्तमः ॥

---

* Situated on the Coromandal Coast. See Raghuvaṃśa, Chapter VIII.

† गोकर्णेश्वरमुत्तममिति B. ‡ मुच्यते तत्क्षणादिति B. § अन्यत् कुब्जाममतुलमिति B. अन्यद्दै परमं स्थानं विष्णोर्यंच्च महात्मन इति F.

अन्यत्कोकामुखे* विष्णोस्तीर्थमद्भुतकर्म्मणः।
मुक्तोऽत्र पातकैर्म्मर्त्त्यो† विष्णुसारूप्यमाप्नुयात् ॥
शालग्रामं‡ महातीर्थं विष्णोः प्रीतिविवर्द्धनम्।
प्राणांस्तत्र नरस्त्यक्त्वा हृषीकेशम्प्रपश्यति§ ॥
अश्वतीर्थमिति ख्यातं सिद्धावासं सुशोभनम्¶।
आस्ते हयशिरो‖ नित्यं तत्र नारायणः स्वयम्।
तीर्थं त्रैलोक्यविख्यातं सिद्धावासं** सुशोभनम् ॥
तत्रास्ति पुण्यदं तीर्थं ब्रह्मणः परमेष्ठिनः।
पुष्करं†† सर्व्वपापघ्नं मृतानां ब्रह्मलोकदम् ॥
मनसा संस्मरेद्यस्तु पुष्करं वै द्विजोत्तमः।
पूयते पातकैः सर्व्वैः शक्रेण सह मोदते ॥
तत्र देवाः सगन्धर्व्वाः सयक्षोरगराक्षसाः।
उपासते सिद्धसङ्घा ब्रह्माणं पद्मसम्भवम् ॥
तत्र स्नात्वा लभेच्छुद्धो‡‡ ब्रह्माणं परमेष्ठिनम्।
पूजयित्वा द्विजवरं ब्रह्माणं सम्प्रपश्यति ॥
तत्राभिगम्य देवेशं पुरुहूतमनिन्दितम्।
तद्रूपो जायते मर्त्यः§§ सर्व्वान् कामानवाप्नुयात्¶¶ ॥

---

* कोकामुखमिति B. कोखामुखमिति F. † मृतोऽत्र पातकैर्मुक्तः इति B. च्युतोऽत्र पातकैर्मर्त्त्यं इति F. ‡ शालिग्राममिति E and H. § प्रपद्यते इति B. ¶ सुपावनमिति B. ‖ हरशिराः इति B and F. ** B पुस्तके सिद्धावासमित्यारभ्य तीर्थमित्यन्तं पादद्वयं नास्ति। †† Near Ajmere in Rájputáná. ‡‡ नरः शुद्धः इति B. तावत् शुद्ध इति E and F. §§ सद्यः इति B. सुरूपी जायते मर्त्त्य- इति E, F and H. ¶¶ कामान् समश्नुते इति B.

सप्तसारस्वतन्तीर्थं* ब्रह्माद्यैः परिषेवितम्† ।
पूजयित्वा तत्र रुद्रमश्वमेधफलं लभेत् ॥
यत्र मङ्कणको रुद्रं प्रपन्नं‡ परमेश्वरम् ।
आराधयामास शिवं§ तपसा गोवृषध्वजम्¶ ॥
प्रजज्वालाथ तपसा मुनिर्मङ्कणकस्तदा‖ ।
ननर्त्त हर्षवेगेन ज्ञात्वा रुद्रं समागतम् ॥
तं प्राह भगवान्रुद्रः किमर्थं नर्त्तितन्त्वया ।
दृष्टापि देवमीशानं नृत्यति स्म पुनः पुनः ।
सोऽन्वीक्ष्य भगवानीशः सगर्व्वं गर्व्वशान्तये ॥
स्वयं देहं विहायास्मै भस्मराशिं प्रदर्शयन् ।
पश्येमं मम शरीरोत्थं भस्मापि त्वं द्विजोत्तम** ॥
माहात्म्यमेतत्तपसस्त्वादृशोऽन्योऽपि विद्यते ।
यः†† सगर्व्वं हि भवता नर्त्तितं मुनिपुङ्गव ॥
न युक्तं‡‡ तापसस्यैतत्त्वत्तोऽप्यभ्यधिको ह्यहम्§§ ।
इत्याभाष्य मुनिश्रेष्ठं स रुद्रः किल विश्वदृक्¶¶ ॥
आस्थाय‖‖ परमं भावं ननर्त्त जगतो हरः ।

---

* सप्तगोदावरन्तीर्थमिति B. † सेवितं परमिति B and F. ‡ प्रपन्नः इति B, E, F and H. § हरमिति B. ¶ पञ्चाक्षरपरायण इति B and F. ‖ तथा इति B. ** स्वकं देहं विदार्थ्यास्मै भस्मराशिमदर्शयत् । पश्येमं मच्छरीरोत्थं भस्मराशिं द्विजोत्तमः ॥ इति B and F. †† यदिति B. ‡‡ युक्तमिति B. स्मयहमिति F. §§ लुप्तोऽप्यत्राधिकोह्ययमिति B. ¶¶ विश्वधृगिति B, E and F. ‖‖ आस्थाय इति E and H. आस्थाय स्वं परमिति F.

सहस्रशीर्षा भूत्वा स सहस्राक्षः सहस्रपात् ॥
दंष्ट्राकरालवदनो ज्वालामाली भयङ्करः ।
सोऽन्वपश्यद्रथेशस्य पार्श्वे तस्य* त्रिशूलिनः ॥
विशाललोचनामेकां देवीञ्चारुविलासिनीम् ।
सूर्य्यायुतसमाकारां† प्रसन्नवदनां शिवाम् ॥
सस्मितं प्रेक्ष्य विश्वेशन्तिष्ठन्तममितद्युतिम् ।
दृष्ट्वा सन्त्रस्तहृदयो वेपमानो मुनीश्वरम्‡ ॥
ननाम शिरसा रुद्रं रुद्राध्यायं जपन्वशी ।
प्रसन्नो भगवानीशस्त्र्यम्बकोभक्तवत्सलः ॥
पूर्व्ववेषं स जगृहे§ देवी चान्तर्हिताभवत् ।
आलिङ्ग्य भक्तम्प्रणतं देवदेवः स्वयं शिवः ॥
न भेतव्यं त्वया वत्स प्राह किन्ते ददाम्यहम् ।
प्रणम्य मूर्द्ना गिरिशं हरं त्रिपुरसूदनम् ॥
विज्ञापयामास तदा हृष्टः प्रष्टुमना¶ मुनिः ।
नमोऽस्तु ते महादेव महेश्वर नमोऽस्तु ते ॥
किमेतद्भगवद्रूपं सुघोरं विश्वतोमुखम् ।
का च सा‖ भगवत्पार्श्वे राजमाना व्यवस्थिता ॥
अन्तर्हिते च सहसा सर्व्वमिच्छामि वेदितुम् ।
इत्युक्ते व्याजहारेशस्तदा मङ्कणकं हरः ॥

---

* शाश्वतस्येति B. † समप्रख्यामिति B, E, F, G and H. ‡ मुनीश्वरः इति B, E, F and H. § जग्राहेति B. ¶ सुस्थमनाः इति B. ‖ का च सेत्यारभ्य दश पादाः B पुस्तके न सन्ति ।

महेशः स्वात्मनो योगं देवीञ्च त्रिपुरानलः।
अहं सहस्रनयनः सर्व्वात्मा सर्व्वतोमुखः॥
दाहकः सर्व्वपाशानां* कालः कालकरो हरः।
मयैव प्रेर्य्यते विश्वं† चेतनाचेतनात्मकम्॥
सोऽन्तर्य्यामी स पुरुषो‡ ह्यहं वै पुरुषोत्तमः।
तस्य सा परमा माया प्रकृतिस्त्रिगुणात्मिका॥
प्रोच्यते मुनिभिः शक्तिर्जगद्योनिः सनातनी।
स एष मायया विश्वं व्यामोहयति विश्वकृत्§॥
नारायणः परोऽव्यक्तो मायारूप इति श्रुतिः।
एवमेतज्जगत्सर्व्वं¶ सर्व्वदा स्थापयाम्यहम्॥
योजयामि प्रकृत्याहं पुरुषं पञ्चविंशकम्।
तथा वै‖ सङ्गतो देवः कूटस्थः सर्व्वगोऽमलः॥
सृजत्यशेषमेवेदं स्वमूर्त्तेः प्रकृतेरजः।
स देवो भगवान् ब्रह्मा विश्वरूपः पितामहः**॥
तवैतत्कथितं सम्यक् स्रष्टृत्वं परमेष्ठिनः††।
एकोऽहं भगवान् कालो ह्यनादिश्चान्तकृद्विभुः॥
समास्थाय परं भावं प्रोक्तो रुद्रो मनीषिभिः।
ममैव सा परा शक्तिः‡‡ देवी विद्येति विश्रुता॥

---

* सर्व्वपापानामिति B. † कृत्स्नमिति B and F. ‡ सोऽन्तर्यामीशपुरुषः इति B. § विश्वधृगिति B. विश्वविदिति F. ¶ कृत्स्नमिति B. ‖ तथा स इति B. तथा वै इति E and F. ** विश्वरूपधरः प्रभुरिति B. †† परमात्मन इति B. ‡‡ शक्ति-रिति B, E and F.

दृष्टो हि भवता नूनं विद्यादेहः स्वयं ततः।
एवमेतानि तत्त्वानि प्रधानपुरुषेश्वरः॥
विष्णुर्ब्रह्मा च भगवान्रुद्रः काल इति श्रुतिः।
त्रयमेतदनाद्यन्तं ब्रह्मण्येव व्यवस्थितम्॥
तदात्मकं तदव्यक्तं तदक्षरमिति श्रुतिः।
आत्मानन्दपरं* तत्त्वं चिन्मात्रं† परमम्पदम्॥
आकाशं निष्कलं ब्रह्म तस्मादन्यन्न विद्यते॥
एवं विज्ञाय भवता भक्तियोगाश्रयेण तु।
सम्पूज्यो वन्दनीयोऽहं ततस्तं पश्यसीश्वरम्‡॥
एतावदुक्त्वा भगवान् जगामादर्शनं हरः।
तत्रैव भक्तियोगेन रुद्रमाराधयन्मुनिः॥
एतत्पवित्रमतुलं तीर्थं ब्रह्मर्षिसेवितम्।
संसेव्य ब्राह्मणो विद्वान्मुच्यते सर्व्वपातकैः॥

इति श्रीकूर्म्मपुराणे उपविभागे पञ्चत्रिंशोऽध्यायः।

---

* आत्मानन्दं परमिति B. आत्मानन्दः इति E, F and H. † चिन्मयमिति B.
‡ पश्य शाश्वतमिति B.

षट्त्रिंशोऽध्यायः।

सूत उवाच।

अन्यत्पवित्रं विपुलं तीर्थं त्रैलोक्यविश्रुतम्।
रुद्रकोटिरिति ख्यातं रुद्रस्य परमेष्ठिनः॥
पुरा पुण्यतमे काले देवदर्शनतत्पराः।
कोटिब्रह्मर्षयो दान्तास्तं देशमगमन् परम्॥
अहं द्रक्ष्यामि गिरिशं पूर्व्वमेव पिनाकिनम्।
अन्योऽन्यं भक्तियुक्तानां विवादोऽभून्महान् किल*॥
तेषां भक्तिं तदा दृष्ट्वा गिरिशो योगिनां गुरुः। †
कोटिरूपोऽभवद्रुद्रो‡ रुद्रकोटिस्ततोऽभवत्§॥
ते स्म सर्व्वे महादेवं हरं गिरिगुहाशयम्।
अपश्यन्¶ पार्व्वतीनाथं हृष्टपुष्टधियोऽभवन्॥
अनाद्यन्तं‖ महादेवं पूर्व्वमेवाहमीश्वरम्।
दृष्टवानिति भक्त्या ते रुद्रन्यस्तधियोऽभवन्॥
अथान्तरिक्षे विमलम्पश्यन्ति स्म महत्तरम्।
ज्योतिस्तत्रैव ते सर्व्वेऽभिलषन्तः परम्पदम्**॥

---

* व्याघाती जायते न हीति B. व्याघाती जायते किलेति F. † एतत्पादद्वयं A पुस्तके नास्ति। ‡ कोटिशः सुषुवे रुद्रानिति F. § ततः स्मृतः इति B. ¶ पश्यन्तः इति B. पश्यन्तीति F. ‖ अपश्यन्तः इति B. अमन्यन्त इति F. ** व्यलीयन्त परस्परमिति B.

यतः स देवोऽध्युषितस्तीर्थं* पुण्यतमं शुभम्।
दृष्ट्वा रुद्रं समभ्यर्च्य रुद्रसामीप्य†माप्नुयात्॥
अन्यच्च तीर्थप्रवरं नाम्ना मधुवनं शुभम्‡।
तत्र गत्वा नियमवानिन्द्रस्यार्द्धासनं लभेत्§॥
अथान्या पद्मनगरी¶ देशः पुण्यतमः शुभः।
तत्र गत्वा‖ पितॄन् पूज्य कुलानान्तारयेच्छतम्॥
कालञ्जरं महातीर्थं रुद्रलोके महेश्वरः।
कालञ्जरं भजन्देवं तत्र भक्तप्रियो हरः॥
श्वेतो नाम शिवे भक्तो राजर्षिप्रवरः पुरा।
तदाशीस्तन्नमस्कारैः पूजयामास शूलिनम्॥
संस्थाप्य विधिना रुद्रं भक्तियोगपुरःसरः।
जजाप रुद्रमनिशं तत्र सन्न्यस्तमानसः॥
सितङ्कार्ष्णाजिनं दीप्तं शूलमादाय भीषणम्।
नेतुमभ्यागतो देशं स राजा यत्र तिष्ठति॥
वीक्ष्य राजा भयाविष्टः शूलहस्तं समागतम्।
कालङ्कालकरं घोरं भीषणं चण्डदीपितम्॥
उभाभ्यामथ हस्ताभ्यां स्पृष्ट्वासौ लिङ्गमुत्तमम्।
ननाम शिरसा रुद्रं जजाप शतरुद्रियम्॥
जपन्तमाह राजानं नमन्तं मनसा भवम्।

---

* एतत् स्वदेशाध्युषितं तीर्थमिति B. एतत्सदेवाध्युषितमिति F. † सारूप्यमिति E. सायुज्यमिति F. ‡ स्मृतमिति B and F. § परस्मैपदमार्षम्। ¶ पुष्पनगरीति B. ‖ अतः परं B पुस्तके सार्द्धद्वादशश्लोकाः न सन्ति।

एह्येहीति पुरः स्थित्वा कृतान्तः प्रहसन्निव॥
तमुवाच भयाविष्टो राजा रुद्रपरायणः।
एकमीशार्च्चनरतं विहायान्यान्निषूदय॥
इत्युक्तवन्तं भगवानब्रवीद्भीतमानसम्।
रुद्रार्च्चनरतो वान्यो मद्दशे को न तिष्ठति॥
एवमुक्त्वा स राजानं कालो लोकप्रकालनः।
बबन्ध पाशै राजापि जजाप शतरुद्रियम्॥

अथान्तरीचे विपुलं दीप्यमानं
तेजोराशिं भूतभर्त्तुः पुराणम्।
ज्वालामालासंवृतं व्याप्य विश्वं
प्रादुर्भूतं संस्थितं सन्ददर्श॥
तन्मध्येऽसौ पुरुषं रुक्मवर्णं
देव्या देवं चन्द्रलेखोज्ज्वलाङ्गम्।
तेजोरूपं पश्यति स्मातिहृष्टो
मेने चात्मानमप्यागच्छतीति*॥
आगच्छन्तं नातिदूरेति† दृष्ट्वा
कालो रुद्रं देवदेव्या महेशम्।
व्यपेतभीरखिलेशैकनाथं‡
राजर्षिस्तन्नेतुमभ्याजगाम॥

---

* मेने तासां नाथ आगच्छतीति इति B. मेने चास्य नाथ आगच्छतीति इति F. मेने चात्मानमथागच्छतीति इति E. † नातिदूरेऽथ इति B and F. ‡ अखिलेनैक-नाथमिति B. अखिलस्यैकनाथमिति F.

आलोक्यासौ भगवानुग्रकर्म्मा
देवो रुद्रो भूतभर्त्ता पुराणः।
एवं भक्तं सत्वरं मां स्मरन्तं
देहीतीमङ्कालरूपं ममेति ॥
स्मृत्वा* वाक्यं गोपते रुद्रभावः
कालात्मासौ मन्यमानः स्वभावम्।
बद्ध्वा भक्तं पुनरेवाथ पाशै-
रुद्रो रौद्रं चाभिदुद्राव वेगात् ॥
प्रेक्ष्यायान्तं शैलपुत्रीमथेशः
सोऽन्वीक्ष्यान्ते विश्वमायाविधिज्ञः।
सावज्ञं वै वामपादेन काल-
ञ्चेतस्येनं† पश्यतो व्याजघान ॥
ममार सोऽतिभीषणो महेशपादघातितः‡।
विराजते सहोमया महेश्वरः§ पिनाकधृक् ॥
निरीक्ष्य देवमीश्वरं प्रहृष्टमानसो हरम्¶।
ननामासौ तमव्ययं स राजपुङ्गवस्तदा ॥
नमो‖ भवाय हेतवे हराय विश्वशम्भवे।
नमः शिवाय धीमते नमोऽपवर्गदायिने ॥
नमो नमो नमो नमो महाविभूतये नमः।

---

* शुत्वा इति B and F. † श्वेतस्य इति E, F and H. ‡ ताड़ित इति B. § रराज देवतापतिः सहोमयेति B. रराज देवता शिवः सहोमया इति F. ¶ हरः इति B. ‖ इतः प्रभृति चतुर्द्दश पादाः B पुस्तके न दृश्यन्ते।

विभागहीनरूपिणे नमो नराधिपतये ॥
नमोऽस्तु ते गणेश्वर प्रपन्नदुःखशासन ।
अनादिनित्यभूतये वराहशृङ्गधारिणे ॥
नमो वृषध्वजाय ते कपालमालिने नमः ।
नमो महानगाय* ते विवाहवे हराय ते† ॥
अथानुगृह्य शङ्करः प्रणामतत्परं नृपम् ।
स्वगाणपत्यमव्ययं स्वरूपतामथो ददौ ॥
सहोमया सपार्षदः सराजपुङ्गवो हरः ।
मुनीशसिद्धवन्दितः क्षणाददृश्यतामगात् ॥
काले महेशनिहते‡ लोकनाथः पितामहः ।
अयाचत वरं रुद्रं सजीवोऽयं भवत्विति ॥
नास्ति कश्चिदपीशान दोषलेशो§ वृषध्वज ।
कृतान्तस्यैव भविता¶ तत्कार्य्ये विनियोजितः ॥
स देवदेववचनाद्देवदेवेश्वरो हरः ।
तथास्त्वित्याह विश्वात्मा सोऽपि तादृग्विधोऽभवत् ॥
इत्येतत्परमं तीर्थं कालञ्जरमिति श्रुतिः‖ ।
गत्वाभ्यर्च्य महादेवं गाणपत्यं च** विन्दति ॥

इति श्रीकूर्म्मपुराणे उपविभागे कालवधे षट्त्रिंशोऽध्यायः ।

---

* नटाय इति B. महानगाय ते इति F. † नमो वृषध्वजाय ते इति B and F. ‡ महेशाभिहते इति B. § दोषरेव: इति A. ¶ कृतान्तस्यैष भवता इति B and F. कृतान्तस्यैव भवता इति F. ‖ श्रुतमिति B, E, F and H. ** गाणपत्यं सः इति B.

सप्तत्रिंशोऽध्यायः ।

सूत उवाच ।

इदमन्यत्परं स्थानं गुह्याद्गुह्यतरं महत् ।
महादेवस्य देवस्य महालय इति श्रुतिः* ॥
तत्र देवाधिदेवेन† रुद्रेण त्रिपुरारिणा ।
शिलातले पदं न्यस्तं नास्तिकानां निदर्शनम् ॥
तत्र पाशुपताः शान्ता भस्मोद्धूलितविग्रहाः ।
उपासते महादेवं वेदाध्ययनतत्पराः ॥
स्नात्वा तत्र पदं शार्व्वं दृष्ट्वा भक्तिपुरःसरम् ।
नमस्कृत्वाथ‡ शिरसा रुद्रसामीप्य§माप्नुयात् ॥
अन्यच्च देवदेवस्य स्थानं शम्भोर्महात्मनः ।
केदारमिति विख्यातं सिद्धानामालयं शुभम् ॥
तत्र स्नात्वा महादेवमभ्यर्च्च वृषकेतनम् ।
पीत्वा चैवोदकं शुद्धं गाणपत्यमवाप्नुयात् ॥
श्राद्ध¶दानादिकङ्कृत्वा ह्यक्षयं लभते फलम् ।
द्विजातिप्रवरैर्जुष्टं योगिभिर्जित‖मानसैः ॥
तीर्थं प्लक्षावतरणं** सर्व्वपापविनाशनम् ।

---

* श्रुतमिति B and F. † देवादिदेवेनेति B and F. ‡ आर्षोऽयं प्रयोगः नमस्कृत्य इति साधु । § सारूप्यमिति B. ¶ श्राद्धमिति B and E. ‖ यतेति B and F.

** A fountain at the foot of a plaksha tree, from which the river Sarswatí takes its rise.

तत्राभ्यर्च्च श्रीनिवासं विष्णुलोके महीयते ॥
अन्यच्च मगधारण्यं सर्व्वलोकगतिप्रदम् ।
अक्षयं विन्दते* स्वर्गं तत्र गत्वा द्विजोत्तमः ॥
तीर्थङ्कनखलं† पुण्यं महापातकनाशनम् ।
यत्र देवेन रुद्रेण यज्ञो दक्षस्य नाशितः ॥
तत्र गङ्गामुपस्पृश्य शुचिर्भावसमन्वितः ।
मुच्यते सर्व्वपापैस्तु ब्रह्मलोके वसेन्नरः‡ ॥
महातीर्थमिति ख्यातं पुण्यं नारायणप्रियम् ।
तत्राभ्यर्च्च हृषीकेशं श्वेतद्वीपं निगच्छति§ ॥
अन्यच्च तीर्थप्रवरं नाम्ना श्रीपर्व्वतं शुभम् ।
अत्र प्राणान्परित्यज्य रुद्रस्य दयितो भवेत् ॥
तत्र सन्निहितो रुद्रो देव्या सह महेश्वरः ।
स्नानपिण्डादिकं तत्र दत्तमक्षय्यमुत्तमम् ॥
गोदावरी नदी पुण्या सर्व्वपापप्रणाशनी‖ ।
तत्र स्नात्वा पितॄन्देवान्तर्पयित्वा यथाविधि ।
सर्व्वपापविशुद्धात्मा गोसहस्रफलं लभेत्** ॥
पवित्रसलिला पुण्या कावेरी विपुला नदी ।
तस्यां स्नात्वोदकङ्कृत्वा†† मुच्यते सर्व्वपातकैः ॥

---

* विन्दतीति B. † A sacred place about two miles south of Hardwár.
‡ ब्रह्मलोकं लभेन्मृतः इति B and E. लोकं व्रजेन्नर इति F. § विगच्छतीति B.
¶ स्नानमिति B. ‖ विनाशिनीति B. ** आर्षोऽयं प्रयोगः लभेत इति साधु ।
†† उदकं कृत्वा—उदककार्य्यं पितृतर्पणं कृत्वा इत्यर्थः ।

त्रिरात्रोपोषितेनाथ एकरात्रोषितेन वा ।*
द्विजातीनान्तु कथितं तीर्थानामिह सेवनम् ॥
यस्य वाङ्मनसी शुद्धे हस्तपादौ च संयतौ† ।
अलोलुपो ब्रह्मचारी तीर्थानां फलमाप्नुयात् ॥
स्वामितीर्थं महातीर्थं त्रिषु लोकेषु विश्रुतम् ।
तत्र सन्निहितो नित्यं स्कन्दोऽमरनमस्कृतः ॥
स्नात्वा कुमारधारायाङ्कृत्वा देवादितर्पणम् ।
आराध्य षण्मुखं देवं स्कन्देन सह मोदते ॥
नदी त्रैलोक्यविख्याता ताम्रपर्णीति‡ नामतः ।
तत्र स्नात्वा पितॄन् भक्त्या तर्पयित्वा यथाविधि ।
पापकर्तॄनपि पितॄंस्तारयेन्नात्र संशयः ॥
चन्द्रतीर्थमिति ख्यातं कावेर्याः प्रभवेऽत्त्वयम्§ ।
तीर्थं तत्र भवेद्दत्तं मृतानां सद्गतिप्रदम्¶ ॥
विन्ध्यपादे प्रपश्यन्ति देवदेवं सदाशिवम् ।
भक्त्या ये ते न पश्यन्ति यमस्य वदनं द्विजाः ॥

---

* अतः परं B पुस्तके विमुक्ताः सर्व्वपापेभ्यो रुद्रसारूप्यमाप्नुयादित्यधिकः पाठोऽस्ति । रुद्रसायुज्यमाप्नुयादिति F. † संस्थितौ इति B. ‡ The name of a river rising in Malaya, celebrated for its pearls. There is a famous lake called Gokarṇa and a mountain called Vaidúrya-parvata, near which a hermitage of the renowned sage Agastya and his disciples is situated. § कावेर्याश्च भवत्त्वयमिति B and F. प्रभव means the source here. ¶ स्वर्गतिर्ध्रुवा इति B.

देविकायां* वृषो नाम तीर्थं सिद्धनिषेवितम् ।
तत्र स्नात्वोदकञ्चत्वा† योगसिद्धिञ्च विन्दति ॥
दशाश्वमेधिकं‡ तीर्थं सर्व्वपापविनाशकम् ।
दशानामश्वमेधानां तत्राप्नोति फलं नरः ॥
पुण्डरीकं तथा§ तीर्थं ब्राह्मणैरुपशोभितम् ।
तत्राभिगम्य युक्तात्मा पुण्डरीकफलं¶ लभेत् ॥
तीर्थेभ्यः परमं तीर्थं ब्रह्मतीर्थमिति‖ स्मृतम्** ।
ब्रह्माणमर्च्चयित्वात्र ब्रह्मलोके महीयते ॥
सरस्वत्या विनशनं प्लक्षप्रस्रवणं शुभम् ।
व्यासतीर्थमिति ख्यातं मैनाकश्च नगोत्तमः ।
यमुनाप्रभवश्चैव सर्व्वपापविनाशनः ।
पितॄणां दुहिता देवी गन्धकालीति विश्रुता ।
तस्यां स्नात्वा दिवं यान्ति मृतो जातिस्मरो भवेत् ॥
कुवेरतुङ्गं पापघ्नं सिद्धचारणसेवितम् ।
प्राणांस्तत्र परित्यज्य कुवेरानुचरो भवेत् ॥
उमातुङ्गमिति†† ख्यातं यत्र सा रुद्रवल्लभा ।
तत्राभ्यर्च्य महादेवीं गोसहस्रफलं लभेत् ॥
भृगुतुङ्गे तपस्तप्तं श्राद्धं दानं तथा कृतम् ।

---

* Name of a river four miles wide and extending forty miles. It is sacred to a class of sages called Devarshis. † दत्त्वेति B and F. ‡ A holy place at Benares. § महेति B and F. ¶ पौण्डरीकं फलमिति B. ‖ Another name for Pushkara. ** श्रुतमिति B and F. †† उत्तमाङ्गमितीति B.

कुलान्युभयतः सप्त पुनातीति मतिर्म्मम ॥
काश्यपस्य महातीर्थं कालसर्पिरिति श्रुतम्।
तत्र श्राद्धानि देयानि नित्यं पापक्षयेच्छया ॥
दशार्णायां* तथा दानं श्राद्धं होमस्तपो जपः।
अक्षयञ्चाव्ययञ्चैव कृतं भवति सर्व्वदा† ॥
तीर्थं द्विजातिभिर्जुष्टं नाम्ना वै कुरुजाङ्गलम्‡।
दत्त्वा तु§ दानं विधिवद्ब्रह्मलोके महीयते ॥
वैतरण्यां महातीर्थे स्वर्णवेद्यां¶ तथैव च।
ब्रह्मपृष्ठे‖ च शिरसि ब्रह्मणः परमे शुभे।
भरतस्याश्रमे पुण्ये पुण्ये गृध्रवने** शुभे।
महाह्रदे च कौशिक्यां दत्तं भवति चाक्षयम् ॥
मुण्डपृष्ठे†† पदं न्यस्तं महादेवेन धीमता।
हिताय सर्व्वभूतानां नास्तिकानां निदर्शनम् ॥
अल्पेनापि तु कालेन नरो धर्म्मपरायणः।
पाप्मानमुत्सृजत्याशु‡‡ जीर्णान्त्वचमिवोरगः ॥

---

* Name of a district lying to the east, and also of another to the west of Indraprastha. Both Bhima, who went forth to the east, and Nakula, who undertook an expedition to the west, are said to have conquered Dasárnas.

† दत्तं भवति नान्यथा इति B. ‡ Another name for Kurukshetra, a district near Karnaul (E. I. Railway Station.) § दत्त्वाच इति B. ¶ स्वर्णवल्यामिति B. स्वर्णनद्यामिति F. ‖ धर्म्मपृष्ठे इति B and F. ** चैत्रे श्राद्धवटे इति B. पुण्ये श्राद्धवटे इति F. †† मुञ्जपृष्ठे इति B. मुण्डापृष्ठे इति E and H. ‡‡ उत्सृजत्यचेति B.

नाम्ना कनकनन्देति तीर्थं त्रैलोक्यविश्रुतम् ।
उदीच्यां ब्रह्मपृष्ठस्य* ब्रह्मर्षिगणसेवितम् ॥
तत्र स्नात्वा दिवं यान्ति सशरीरा द्विजातयः ।
दत्तं वापि† सदा श्राद्धमक्षयं समुदाहृतम् ।
ऋणैस्त्रिभिर्नरः स्नात्वा मुच्यते क्षीणकल्मषः‡ ॥
मानसे सरसि स्नात्वा शक्रस्यार्द्धासनं लभेत् ।
उत्तरं मानसं गत्वा सिद्धिं प्राप्नोत्यनुत्तमाम्§ ॥
तस्मान्निर्वर्त्तयेच्छ्राद्धं यथाशक्ति यथाबलम् ।
स कामान्¶ लभते दिव्यान्मोक्षोपायञ्च विन्दति ॥
पर्व्वतो हिमवान्नाम नानाधातुविभूषितः ।
योजनानां सहस्राणि साशीतिस्त्वायतो गिरिः ।
सिद्धचारणसङ्कीर्णो देवर्षिगणसेवितः ॥
तत्र पुष्करिणी रम्या सुषुम्ना‖ नाम नामतः ।
तत्र गत्वा द्विजो विद्वान् ब्रह्महत्यां विमुञ्चति ॥
श्राद्धं भवति चाक्षय्यं तत्र दत्तं महोदयम्** ।
तारयेच्च पितॄन् सम्यग्दश पूर्व्वान्दशापरान् ॥
सर्व्वत्र हिमवान् पुण्यो गङ्गा पुण्या समं†† ततः ।
नद्यः समुद्रगाः पुण्याः समुद्रश्च विशेषतः‡‡ ॥

---

* मुञ्जपृष्ठस्येति B. मुण्डापृष्ठस्येति F. † चापीति B. ‡ घोरकल्मषः इति B. § अनुत्तमाम्—नास्ति उत्तमा यस्याः सा अनुत्तमा ताम् सर्व्वोत्कृष्टामित्यर्थः । ¶ कामान् स इति B. कामं स इति F. ‖ सुपुष्टा इति B. ** एतत्पादद्वयं A, E, H पुस्तकेषु नास्ति । †† गत्वा पुण्यालयमिति B. ‡‡ समुद्राश्च द्विजोत्तमाः इति B.

वदर्य्याश्रम*मासाद्य मुच्यते सर्व्व†किल्विषात्।
तत्र नारायणो देवो नरेणास्ते‡ सनातनः॥
अक्षयं तत्र दानं स्याच्छ्राद्धदानादिकञ्च यत्§।
महादेवप्रियं तीर्थं पावनं तद्विशेषतः।
तारयेच्च पितॄन् सर्व्वान्दत्त्वा श्राद्धं समाहितः॥
देवदारुवनं पुण्यं सिद्धगन्धर्व्वसेवितम्।
महता देवदेवेन¶ तत्र दत्तं महेश्वरम्‖।
मोहयित्वा मुनीन् सर्व्वान् समस्तैः सम्प्रपूजितः** ॥
प्रसन्नो भगवानीशो मुनीन्द्रान् प्राह भावितान्।
इहाश्रमवरे रम्ये निवसिष्यथ†† सर्व्वदा।
मद्भावनासमायुक्तास्ततः सिद्धिमवाप्स्यथ॥
यत्र‡‡ मामर्च्चयन्तीह लोके धर्म्मपरायणाः।
तेषां ददामि परमङ्गाणपत्यं हि शाश्वतम्§§॥
अत्र नित्यं वसिष्यामि सह नारायणेन तु¶¶।

---

* Badarikáśrama is situated on the Alakanandá, about 25 days journey to the north of Hardwar; it is resorted to, by pilgrims from various parts of the country. But owing to excessive cold, the hermitage is left utterly deserted from September to March. The place is noted for four images of Nara, Náráyaṇa, Chaturbhuja and Kuvera. † कलीति B. कलिकल्मषादिति F. ‡ नरश्चास्ते इति B and F. § जप्ता वापि तथाविधमिति B. ¶ महादेवेन देवेन इति B and F. ‖ महद्वलमिति B. ** पुनस्तैः सम्प्रपूजितः इति E, F and H. †† निवत्स्यथेति साधु। ‡‡ येऽत्र इति B and F. §§ एतत्पादद्वयं B पुस्तके नास्ति। ¶¶ चेति B.

प्राणानिह नरस्त्यक्त्वा न भूयो जन्म चाप्नुयात्* ॥
संस्मरन्ति च ये तीर्थं देशान्तरगता जनाः।
तेषाञ्च सर्व्वपापानि नाशयामि द्विजोत्तमाः ॥
श्राद्धं दानं तपो होमः पिण्डनिर्व्वपणं तथा।
ध्यानं जपश्च नियमः सर्व्वमत्राक्षयङ्कृतम्† ।
तस्मात्सर्व्वप्रयत्नेन द्रष्टव्यं हि द्विजातिभिः ॥
देवदारुवनं पुण्यं महादेवनिषेवितम्।
यत्रेश्वरो महादेवो विष्णुर्वा पुरुषोत्तमः।
तत्र सन्निहिता गङ्गा तीर्थान्यायतनानि च ॥

इति श्रीकूर्म्मपुराणे उपविभागे तीर्थवर्णनं नाम
सप्तत्रिंशोऽध्यायः।

अष्टात्रिंशोऽध्यायः।

ऋषय ऊचुः।
कथं दारुवनम्प्राप्तो* भगवान् गोवृषध्वजः।
मोहयामास विप्रेन्द्रान् सूत तद्वक्तुमर्हसि† ॥

---

* विन्दतीति B and F. † एतत्पादद्वयं B पुस्तके नास्ति।

---

* दारुवने देवः इति B and F. † वक्तुमिहार्हसीति B. नस्तं वक्तुमिहार्हसीति F.

सूत उवाच।

पुरा दारुवने रम्ये देवसिद्धनिषेविते।
सपुत्त्रदारतनयास्तपश्चेरुः सहस्रशः॥
प्रवृत्तं विविधङ्कर्म्म प्रकुर्व्वाणा यथाविधि।
यजन्ति विविधैर्यज्ञैस्तपन्ति च महर्षयः॥
तेषां प्रवृत्त*विन्यस्तचेतसामथ शूलभृत्†।
व्याख्यापयन् सदा दोषं‡ ययौ दारुवनं§ हरः॥
कृत्वा विश्वगुरुं विष्णुं पार्श्वे देवो महेश्वरः।
ययौ निवृत्तविज्ञानस्थापनार्थञ्च शङ्करः॥
आस्थाय विपुलञ्चैष जनं विंशतिवत्सरम्¶।
लीलालसो‖ महाबाहुः पीनाङ्गश्चारुलोचनः॥
चामीकरवपुः श्रीमान् पूर्णचन्द्रनिभाननः।
मत्तमातङ्गगमनो दिग्वासा जगदीश्वरः॥
जातरूपमयीं** मालां सर्व्वरत्नैरलङ्कृताम्।
दधानो भगवानीशः समागच्छति सस्मितः॥
योऽनन्तः पुरुषो योनिर्लोकानामव्ययो हरिः।
स्त्रीवेषं विष्णुरास्थाय सोऽनुगच्छति शूलिनम्††॥
सम्पूर्णचन्द्रवदनं पीनोन्नतपयोधरम्।

---

* प्रवृत्तीति B. † शूलधृगिति B. ‡ व्यापयन् स महादेवः इति B. ख्यातवान् सुमहद्दोषमिति F. महादोषमिति E and H. § दारुवने इति B. ¶ आस्थाय विपुलं वेशमूनविंशतिवत्सरमिति B and E. वेशं गूढमिति F. ‖ सलालसः इति B and F.
** कुशेशयमयीमिति B. †† शोभनमिति B.

शुचिस्मितं सुप्रसन्नं रणन्नूपुरकद्वयम् ॥
सुपीतवसनं दिव्यं श्यामलञ्चारुलोचनम्।
उदारहंसगमनं* विलासि सुमनोहरम् ॥
एवं स भगवानीशो देवदारुवनं† हरः।
चचार हरिणा सार्द्धं मायया मोहयञ्जगत् ॥
दृष्ट्वा चरन्तं विश्वेशं तत्र तत्र पिनाकिनम्।
मायया मोहिता नार्य्यो‡ देवदेवं समन्वयुः ॥
विस्रस्ताभरणाः सर्व्वाः§ त्यक्त्वा लज्जां पतिव्रताः।
सहैव तेन कामार्त्ता विलासिन्यश्चरन्ति हि ॥
ऋषीणां पुत्त्रका ये स्युर्युवानो जितमानसाः¶।
अन्वागमन्हृषीकेशं‖ सर्व्वे कामप्रपीड़िताः ॥
गायन्ति नृत्यन्ति विलासयुक्ता**
नारीगणा नायकमेकमीशम्††।
दृष्ट्वा सपत्नीकमतीवकान्त-
मिष्टन्तथालिङ्गितमाचरन्ति‡‡ ॥
ते सन्निपत्य स्मितमाचरन्ति§§
गायन्ति गीतानि मुनीशपुत्त्राः।

---

* हंसचलनमिति B. दधार हंसचलनमिति F. † देवदारुवने इति B. ‡ मोहितात्मानः इति A, E and H. § विस्रस्तवस्त्राभरणाः इति B, E, F and H. ¶ यतमानसाः इति B. ‖ अन्वगच्छन् हृषीकेशमिति B, E and F. ** यं गोपतिं नित्यविलासवाञ्छा इति B. †† मायिनमेकमीशमिति B, E and F. ‡‡ मिच्छन्त्यथालिङ्गनमाचरन्तीति B. §§ पार्श्वे निपेतुः स्मितमाचरन्तीति B. पदे निपत्य इति F.

आलोक्य पद्मापतिमादिदेवं
भ्रूभङ्गमन्ये* विचरन्ति तेन ॥
आशामथैकामपि† वासुदेवो
मायी मुरारिर्मनसि प्रविष्टः ।
करोति भोगान्मनसि प्रवृत्तिं‡
मायानुभूयन्त इतीव सम्यक्§ ॥
विभाति विश्वामरविश्वनाथः¶
रमाधवस्त्रीगणसन्निविष्टः ।
अशेषशक्त्या समयं निविष्टो‖
यथैकशक्त्या सह देवदेवः ॥
करोति नित्यं परमं प्रधानं**
तदा विरूढः†† पुनरेव भूयः ।
ययौ समारुह्य हरिः स्वभावं
तमीदृशं नाम तमादिदेवम्‡‡ ॥
दृष्ट्वा नारीकुलं रुद्रं पुत्रानपि च केशवम् ।
मोहयन्तं मुनिश्रेष्ठाः कोपं सन्दधिरे भृशम् ॥

---

* शुभाङ्गमन्ये इति B and F. † आशामथैषामपीति B, ‡ मनसानुवृत्तिमिति B. करोति भावं मनसापि वृत्तिमिति F. § मायानुभूतान् स इतीव सम्यक् इति B. मायानुरूपं त इति च सम्यक् इति F. ¶ भूतभर्त्ता इति B. विश्वात्मकभूतभर्त्ता इति F. ‖ अशेषशक्त्यासनसन्निविष्टः इति B. अशेषपंक्त्यासनसन्निविष्ट इति F. ** नृत्यं परमप्रभावमिति B. नक्तं परमं प्रभावमिति F. †† तदाधिरूढः इति B, E and F. ‡‡ तदीशवृत्तात्स्तमादिदेवः इति B.

अतीवपरुषं वाक्यं प्रोचुर्द्देवं कपर्द्दिनम्* ।
शेपुश्च विविधैर्वाक्यै†र्मायया तस्य मोहिताः ॥
तपांसि तेषां सर्व्वेषां प्रत्याहन्यन्त शङ्करे ।
यथादित्यप्रतीकाशे‡ तारका नभसि स्थिताः ॥
तं भर्त्स्य§ तापसा विप्राः समेत्य वृषभध्वजम् ।
को भवानिति देवेशं पृच्छन्ति स्म विमोहिताः ॥
सोऽब्रवीद्भगवानीशस्तपश्चर्तुमिहागतः¶ ।
इदानीं भार्य्यया देशं‖ भवद्भिरिह सुव्रताः ॥
तस्य ते वाक्यमाकर्ण्य भृग्वाद्या मुनिपुङ्गवाः ।
ऊचुर्गृहीत्वा वसनं** त्यक्त्वा भार्य्यां तपश्चर ॥
अथोवाच विहस्येशः पिनाकी नीललोहितः ।
सम्प्रेक्ष्य जगतां योनिं पार्श्वस्थञ्च जनार्द्दनम् ॥
कथं भवद्भिरुदितं†† स्वभार्य्यापोषणोत्सुकैः ।
त्यक्तव्या मम भार्य्येति धर्म्मज्ञैः शान्तमानसैः ॥

मुनयः‡‡ ऊचुः ।

व्यभिचाररता भार्य्याः§§ सन्त्याज्याः पतिनेरिताः¶¶ ।

---

* अतीवासहृशं वाक्यं प्रोचुर्देवकपर्द्दिनमिति B. † पापैर्विविधैरिति B. शापैर्विविधैरिति F. ‡ यथादित्यप्रकाशेन इति B and F. § भर्त्स्येति आर्षः प्रयोगः, भर्त्संयित्वेति साधु। ¶ तपस्तप्तुमिहागतः इति B. ‖ देशे इति B and F. ** वचनमिति A, E and F. †† भवद्भिरुद्दिष्टमिति B. ‡‡ ऋषय इति B. व्यास उवाचेति F. §§ नार्य्य इति B, E, F and H. ¶¶ पतिनेरितमिति E, F and H.

अस्माभिर्भर्त्ता: सुभगा नेदृशास्त्यागमर्हति* ॥

महादेव† उवाच ।

न कदाचिदियं विप्रा मनसाप्यन्यमिच्छति ।
नाहमेनामपि तथा विमुञ्चामि कदाचन ॥

ऋषय ऊचुः ।

दृष्टा व्यभिचरन्तीह ह्यस्माभिः‡ पुरुषाधम ।
उक्तं ह्यसत्यं भवता गम्यताङ्क्षिप्रमेव हि§ ॥
एवमुक्तो महादेवः सत्यमेव मयेरितम् ।
भवतां प्रतिभा¶ ह्येषा व्यक्तासौ विचचार ह‖ ॥
सोऽगच्छद्धरिणा सार्द्धं मुनीन्द्रस्य महात्मनः ।
वसिष्ठस्याश्रमं पुण्यं भिक्षार्थी परमेश्वरः ॥
दृष्ट्वा समागतं देवं भिक्षमाणमरुन्धती ।
वसिष्ठस्य प्रिया भक्त्या प्रत्युद्गम्य ननाम तम् ॥
प्रक्षाल्य पादौ विमलं दत्त्वा चासनमुत्तमम् ।
सम्प्रेक्ष्य शिथिलं गात्रमभिघातहतं द्विजैः ।
सन्धयामास** भैषज्यैर्विषण्णवदना सती ॥
चकार महतीं पूजां प्रार्थयामास भार्य्यया ।
को भवान् कुत आयातः किमाचारो भवानिति ।

---

* नास्माभिरेषा सुभगा तादृशी त्यागमर्हतीति B and F. मूलपाठे तु अर्हन्तीति साधु। † देव इति B. देवदेव इति F. ‡ व्यभिचरन्तीयमस्माभिरिति B and F. § तु इति B. ¶ अतः परं B पुस्तके द्वादश पादाः न दृश्यन्ते । ‖ भवतां प्रतिभाषेणात्युक्तोऽसौ विचचार ह इति F. ** बन्धयामासेति B. सान्त्वयामासेति F.

उच्यतामाह भगवान् सिद्धानाम्प्रवरो ह्यहम्* ॥
यदेतन्मण्डलं शुभ्रं भाति ब्रह्ममयं सदा।
एषैव देवता मह्यं धारयामि सदैव तु† ॥
इत्युक्त्वा प्रययौ श्रीमाननुगृह्य पतिव्रताम्।
ताड़याञ्चक्रिरे दण्डैर्लोष्टिभि‡र्मुष्टिभिर्द्विजैः ॥
दृष्ट्वा चरन्तं गिरिशं नग्नं विकृतिलक्षणम्§।
प्रोचुरेतद्भवल्लिङ्गमुत्पाटय सुदुर्मतिः¶ ॥
तानब्रवीन्महायोगी करिष्यामीति शङ्करः।
युष्माकं मामके लिङ्गे यदि द्वेषोऽभिजायते ॥‖
उक्त्वा तूत्पाटयामास** भगवान् भगनेत्रहा।
नापश्यंस्तत्क्षणाच्चेशं†† केशवं लिङ्गमेव च‡‡ ॥
तदोत्पाता बभूवुर्हि लोकानां भयशंसिनः ॥
न राजते सहस्रांशुश्चचाल पृथिवी पुनः।
निष्प्रभाश्च ग्रहाः सर्व्वे चुक्षुभे च महोदधिः ॥
अपश्यच्चानुसूयात्रेः स्वप्नं भार्य्या पतिव्रता।
कथयामास विप्राणां भयादाकुलितेन्द्रिया§§ ॥

---

* भवत्तामाह देवानां सिद्धानां प्रवरोऽस्म्यहमिति B. सर्व्वेषामेव देवानां सिद्धानां प्रवरोऽस्म्यहमिति F. † सदैवतः इति B. सदेव तदिति F. ‡ लोष्टाभिरिति B. रिपुभिरिति F. § विकृतलक्षणमिति B and F. ¶ प्रोचुरेतद्भवाँल्लिङ्गमुत्पाटयतु दुर्म्मतिरिति B. सुदुर्म्मते इति F. ‖ एतत्पादद्वयं A F पुस्तकयोः नास्ति। ** इत्युक्त्वोत्पाटयामासेति B. †† तत्क्षणे नेहेति B. तत्क्षणेनेशमिति F. ‡‡ तु इति B. §§ आकुलितेक्षणा इति B and F.

तेजसा भासयन् कृत्स्नं नारायणसहायवान्।
भिक्षमाणः शिवो नूनं दृष्टोऽस्माकं गृहेष्विति* ॥
तस्या वचनमाकर्ण्य शङ्कमाना महर्षयः।
सर्व्वे जग्मुर्महायोगं ब्रह्माणं विश्वसम्भवम् ॥
उपास्यमानममलैर्योगिभिर्ब्रह्मवित्तमैः।
चतुर्वेदैर्मूर्त्तिमद्भिः सावित्र्या सहितं प्रभुम् ॥
आसीनमासने रम्ये नानाश्चर्य्यसमन्विते।
प्रभासहस्रकलिले ज्ञानैश्वर्य्यादिसंयुते ॥
विभ्राजमानं वपुषा सस्मितं शुभ्र†लोचनम्।
चतुर्मुखं महाबाहुं छन्दोमयमजं परम् ॥
विलोक्य देववपुषं प्रसन्नवदनं शुचिम्‡।
शिरोभिर्द्धरणीं गत्वा तोषयामासुरीश्वरम् ॥
तान् प्रसन्नो महादेव§श्चतुर्मूर्त्तिश्चतुर्मुखः।
व्याजहार मुनिश्रेष्ठाः किमागमनकारणम् ॥
तत्तस्य वृत्तमखिलं¶ ब्रह्मणः परमात्मनः।
ज्ञापयाञ्चक्रिरे सर्व्वे कृत्वा शिरसि चाञ्जलिम् ॥

ऋषय ऊचुः।

कश्चिद्दारुवनं पुण्यं पुरुषोऽतीवशोभनः।
भार्य्यया चारुसर्व्वाङ्ग्या प्रविष्टो नग्न एव हि ॥

---

* गृहेष्विहेति B. † बभ्रु इति B. ‡ प्रभुमिति B. शुचिरिति E and H. शुभमिति F. § तान् प्रसन्नमना देव इति B and F. ¶ तस्य ते वृत्तमखिलमिति B and F. तस्य प्रवृत्तमखिलमिति E, F and G.

मोहयामास वपुषा नारीणाङ्कुलमीश्वरः* ।
कन्यकानां प्रिया चास्य† दूषयामास पुत्त्रकान् ॥
अस्माभिर्विविधा वाताः प्रदत्तास्ते‡ पराहताः ।
ताड़ितोऽस्माभिरत्यर्थं लिङ्गन्तु विनिपातितम् ॥
अन्तर्हितश्च§ भगवान् सभार्य्यो लिङ्गमेव च ।
उत्पाताश्चाभवन् घोराः सर्व्वभूतभयङ्कराः ॥
क एष पुरुषो देव भीताः स्मः पुरुषोत्तम ।
भवन्तमेव शरणं प्रपन्ना वयमच्युत ॥
त्वं हि वेत्सि¶ जगत्यस्मिन्यत्किञ्चिदिह‖ चेष्टितम् ।
अनुग्रहेण युक्तेन** तदस्मानुपपालय†† ॥
विज्ञापितो मुनिगणैर्विश्वात्मा कमलोद्भवः ।
ध्यात्वा देवं त्रिशूलाङ्कं कृताञ्जलिरभाषत ॥

ब्रह्मा उवाच ।

हा कष्टम्भवतामद्य जातं सर्व्वार्थनाशनम् ।
धिग्बलं धिक् तपश्चर्य्या मिथ्यैव भवतामिह ॥
सम्प्राप्य पुण्यसंस्कारान्निधीनां‡‡ परमं निधिम् ।
उपेक्षितं वृथाभावै§§र्भवद्भिरिह मोहितैः ॥

---

* कुलमाशु चेति B. † प्रियो यस्तु इति B. ‡ शापाः प्रवृत्ताश्चेति B and F.
§ अन्तर्हितस्तु इति B. ¶ वेत्थ इति B and F. ‖ किञ्चिदपि इति B and F.
** विशेषेति B and F. †† तदस्माननुपालयेति B and F. ‡‡ पुण्यसंस्थानां निधीनामिति B. §§ वृथाचारैरिति B and F.

काङ्क्ष्न्ते* योगिनो नित्यं यतन्तो† यतयो निधिम्।
यमेव तं समासाद्य हा भवद्भिरुपेक्षितम्‡ ॥
यजन्ति यज्ञैर्विविधैर्यत्प्राप्तैर्वैदवादिनः।
महानिधिं समासाद्य§ हा भवद्भिरुपेक्षितम् ॥
यमर्च्चयित्वा सततं¶ विश्वेशत्वमिदं मम।
स देवोपेक्षितो‖ दृष्ट्वा निधानभाग्यवर्ज्जिताः** ॥
यस्मिन् समाहितं दिव्यमैश्वर्य्यं यत्तदव्ययम्।
तमासाद्य निधिं ब्रह्म†† हा भवद्भिर्वृथाकृतम्‡‡ ॥
एष देवो महादेवो विज्ञेयस्तु महेश्वरः।
न तस्य परमं किञ्चित्पदं समभिगम्यते§§ ॥
देवतानामृषीणां वा¶¶ पितृणाञ्चापि शाश्वतः‖‖।
सहस्रयुगपर्य्यन्ते प्रलये सर्व्वदेहिनाम्।
संहरत्येष भगवान् कालो भूत्वा महेश्वरः।
एष चैव प्रजाः सर्व्वाः सृजत्येष*** स्वतेजसा ॥
एष चक्री चक्रवर्त्ती श्रीवत्सकृतलक्षणः।
योगी कृतयुगे देवस्त्रेतायां यज्ञ एव च†††।
द्वापरे भगवान्कालो धर्म्मकेतुः कलौ भव‡‡‡ ॥

---

* काङ्क्षन्तीति साधु। † यतमाना इति साधु। ‡ ऐश्वर्य्यमखिलं ध्रुवमिति B. § तमासाद्याच्चयं देवमिति B. ¶ यं समासाद्य जनितमिति B and F. ‖ तद्देवोपेक्षितमिति B. ** भाग्यवर्ज्जितैरिति B. †† ब्राह्ममिति F. ‡‡ यथाकृतमिति B. §§ समधिगम्यते इति B. ¶¶ चेति B. ‖‖ शाश्वतमिति A. *** सृजत्येकः इति B and F. ††† उच्यते इति B. ‡‡‡ युगे इति B. भवेदिति F.

रुद्रस्य मूर्त्तयस्तिस्रो याभिर्विश्वमिदं ततम्* ।
तमो ह्यग्नी रजो ब्रह्मा सत्वं विष्णुरिति स्मृतिः† ॥
मूर्त्तिरन्या स्मृता‡ चास्य दिग्वासा च§ शिवा ध्रुवा ।
यत्र तिष्ठति तद्ब्रह्म योगेन तु समन्वितम् ॥
या चास्य पार्श्वगा भार्य्या भवद्भिरभिभाषिता¶ ।
स हि नारायणो देवः परमात्मा सनातनः ॥
तस्मात्सर्व्वमिदं जातं तत्रैव च लयं व्रजेत् ।
स एष मोचयेत्कृत्स्नं स एष च परा गतिः‖ ॥
सहस्रशीर्षा पुरुषः सहस्राक्षः सहस्रपात् ।
एकशृङ्गो महानात्मा** नारायण इति श्रुतिः†† ॥
रेतोऽस्य‡‡ गर्भो भगवानापो माया तनुः§§ प्रभुः ।
स्तूयते विविधैर्मन्त्रैर्ब्राह्मणैर्मोक्षकाङ्क्षिभिः ॥
संहृत्य सकलं विश्वं कल्पान्ते पुरुषोत्तमः ।
शेते योगामृतं पीत्वा यत्र विष्णोः परम्पदम्¶¶ ॥
न जायते न म्रियते वर्द्धते न च विश्वहृक्‖‖ ।

---

* यानि चार्चन्ति पण्डिताः इति B. † प्रभुरिति B. स्थितिरिति F. ‡ अन्याश्रिता इति B. § वै इति B. ¶ भवद्भिरभिवीक्षिता इति B and F. ‖ स एव परमा गतिरिति B and F. ** अतः परं B F पुस्तकयोः चतुर्व्वेदश्चतुर्मूर्त्तिस्त्रिगुणः परमेश्वरः। एकमूर्त्तिरनन्तात्मा इत्यधिकः पाठो दृश्यते। †† पुराणोऽष्टाक्षरो हरिरिति B and F. ‡‡ स तस्येति B. स तस्य शब्दो भगवानिति F. §§ आपोमयः तनुरिति B and F. ¶¶ तद्विष्णोः परमं पदमिति B and F. ‖‖ विश्वसृगिति B. विश्वधृगिति E and F.

मूलप्रकृतिरव्यक्ता गीयते वैदिकैरजः॥
ततो निशायां वृत्तायां* सिसृक्षुरखिलं जगत्।
अजनाभौ तु† तद्बीजं क्षिपत्येष महेश्वरः॥
तं मां वित्त‡ महात्मानं ब्रह्माणं विश्वतोमुखम्।
महान्तं पुरुषं विश्वमपाङ्गर्भमनुत्तमम्॥
न तं जानीत§ जनकं मोहितास्तस्य मायया।
देवदेवं महादेवं भूतानामीश्वरं हरम्¶॥
एष देवो महादेवो ह्यनादिर्भगवान्हरः।
विष्णुना सह संयुक्तः करोति विकरोति च॥
न तस्य विद्यते कार्य्यं न तस्माद्विद्यते परम्।
स वेदान् प्रददौ पूर्व्वं योगमायातनुर्मम॥
स मायी मायया सर्व्वङ्करोति विकरोति च।
तमेव मुक्तये ज्ञात्वा व्रजध्वं शरणं शिवम्‖॥
इतीरिता भगवता मरीचिप्रमुखा विभुम्।
प्रणम्य देवं ब्रह्माणं पृच्छन्ति स्म समाहिताः**॥

मुनय ऊचुः।

कथं पश्येम तं देवं पुनरेव पिनाकिनम्।
ब्रूहि विश्वामरेशान त्राता त्वं शरणैषिणाम्॥

---

* व्युष्टायामिति B. † अजस्य नाभौ इति B and F. ‡ तमाविष्टमिति A, E and H. § विदाथेति A, E and H. जानीष्व इति F. ¶ हरिमिति A, E and F. ‖ व्रजेत शरणं भवमिति B. ** सुदुःखिताः इति B and F.

ब्रह्मोवाच ।

यद्दृष्टं भवता तस्य लिङ्गं भुवि निपातितम्* ।
तल्लिङ्गानुकृतीशस्य कृत्वा लिङ्गमनुत्तमम् ।
पूजयध्वं सपत्नीकाः सादरं† पुत्त्रसंयुताः ।
वैदिकैरेव नियमैर्व्विविधैर्ब्रह्मचारिणः ॥
संस्थाप्य शाङ्करैर्म्मन्त्रैरृग्यजुःसामसम्भवैः ।
तपः‡ परं समास्थाय गृणन्तः शतरुद्रियम् ।
समाहिताः पूजयध्वं सपुत्त्राः सह बन्धुभिः ।
सर्व्वे प्राञ्जलयो भूत्वा शूलपाणिं प्रपद्यथ ॥
ततो द्रक्ष्यथ देवेशं दुर्द्दर्शमकृतात्मभिः ।
यं दृष्ट्वा सर्व्वमज्ञानमधर्म्मश्च प्रणश्यति ॥
ततः प्रणम्य§ वरदं ब्रह्माणममितौजसम् ।
जग्मुः संहृष्टमनसो¶ देवदारुवनं पुनः ॥
आराधयितुमारब्धा ब्रह्मणा कथितं यथा ।
अजानन्तः परं भावं‖ वीतरागा विमत्सराः ॥
स्थण्डिलेषु विचित्रेषु पर्व्वतानां गुहासु च ।
नदीनाञ्च विविक्तेषु पुलिनेषु शुभेषु च ।
शैवालभोजनाः** केचित्केचिदन्तर्जलेशयाः ।
केचिदभ्रावकाशास्तु†† पादाङ्गुष्ठे ह्यधिष्ठिताः ॥

---

* लिङ्गन्तु विनिपातितमिति B. † सदैवमिति B. ‡ ततः इति A. § प्रसाद्येति B. ¶ सुप्रीतमनसः इति B. ‖ दैवमिति B. ** शैवानां भाजनमिति B. †† केचिद्दर्भावकाशास्तु इति B, E, F and H.

दन्तो*लूखलिनस्त्वन्ये ह्यश्मकुट्टास्तथा परे ।
शाकपर्णाशनाः† केचित्सम्प्रक्षाला मरीचिपाः ॥
वृक्षमूलनिकेताश्च शिलाशय्यास्तथापरे ।
कालं नयन्ति तपसा पूजयन्तो महेश्वरम् ॥
ततस्तेषां प्रसादार्थं‡ प्रपन्नार्त्तिहरो हरः ।
चकार भगवान्बुद्धिं बोधयन् वृषभध्वजः§ ॥
देवः कृतयुगे ह्यस्मिञ्छृङ्गे हिमवतः शुभे¶ ।
देवदारुवनम्प्राप्तः प्रसन्नः परमेश्वरः ॥
भस्मपाण्डुरदिग्धाङ्गो नग्नो विकृतलक्षणः ।
उल्मूकव्यग्रहस्तश्च रक्तपिङ्गललोचनः ॥
क्वचिच्च हसते रौद्रं क्वचिद्गायति विस्मितः ।
क्वचिन्नृत्यति शृङ्गारी क्वचिद्रौति मुहुर्मुहुः ॥
आश्रमे ह्यटति‖ भिक्षु**र्याचते च पुनः पुनः ।
मायाङ्कृत्वात्मनो रूपन्देवस्तद्वनमागतः ॥
कृत्वा गिरिसुतां गौरीं†† पार्श्वे देवः पिनाकधृक् ।
सा च पूर्व्ववद्देवेशी देवदारुवनं गता ॥
दृष्ट्वा समागतं देवं देव्या सह कपर्द्दिनम् ।
प्रणेमुः शिरसा भूमौ तोषयामासुरीश्वरम् ॥

---

* दम्भेति B. † शालपर्णाशिनः इति B. शाकपत्राशिन इति F. ‡ प्रसादार्थमिति B, E, F and H. § प्रबोधाय वृषध्वजः इति B. बोधयंस्तान् वृषध्वज इति F. ¶ भृगोर्हिमवतः सुतेति A, E and H. ‖ स्वागतः इति B. ** भिक्षामिति B. भैक्षमिति F. †† देवीमिति B and F.

वैदिकैर्विविधैर्म्मन्त्रैस्तोत्रैर्*म्माहेश्वरैः शुभैः ।
अथर्व्वशिरसा चान्ये रुद्राद्यैरर्च्चयन् भवम् ॥
नमो देवाधिदेवाय† महादेवाय ते नमः ।
त्र्यम्बकाय नमस्तुभ्यं त्रिशूलवरधारिणे ॥
नमो दिग्वाससे तुभ्यं विकृताय पिनाकिने ।
सर्व्वप्रणतदेवाय‡ स्वयमप्रणतात्मने ॥
अन्तकान्तकृते तुभ्यं सर्व्वसंहरणाय च ।
नमोऽस्तु नृत्यशीलाय नमो भैरवरूपिणे ॥
नरनारीशरीराय योगिने गुरवे§ नमः ।
नमो दान्ताय शान्ताय तापसाय हराय च ॥
विभीषणाय रुद्राय नमस्ते कृत्तिवाससे ।
नमस्ते लेलिहानाय श्रीकण्ठाय च¶ ते नमः ॥
अघोरघोररूपाय वामदेवाय वै नमः ।
नमः कनकमालाय देव्याः प्रियकराय च ॥
गङ्गासलिलधाराय शम्भवे परमेष्ठिने ।
नमो योगाधिपतये भूता‖धिपतये नमः ॥
प्राणाय च नमस्तुभ्यं नमो भस्माङ्गधारिणे** ।
नमस्ते हव्यवाहाय दंष्ट्रिणे हव्यरेतसे ॥
ब्रह्मणश्च शिरोहर्त्रे†† नमस्ते कालरूपिणे ।

---

* सूक्तैरिति B and F. † देवादिदेवाय इति B. ‡ देहायेति B and E. § योगिनां गुरवे इति B and F. ¶ शितिकण्ठायेति B. ‖ ब्रह्माधिपतये इति E and H. ** भागिने इति B. †† हन्त्रे इति B and F.

आगतिं ते न जानीमो गतिं नैव च नैव च ॥
विश्वेश्वराय सौम्याय महाप्रलयकारिणे* ।
नमः प्रमथनाथाय दात्रे च शुभ†सम्पदाम् ॥
कपालपाणये तुभ्यं नमो जुष्टतमाय ते ।
नमः कनकपिङ्गाय वारिलिङ्गाय ते नमः ॥
नमो वह्न्यर्कलिङ्गाय ज्ञानलिङ्गाय ते नमः‡ ॥
नमो भुजङ्गहाराय कर्णिकारप्रियाय च ।
किरीटिने कुण्डलिने कालकालाय ते नमः ॥
महादेव महादेव§ देवदेव त्रिलोचन ।
क्षम्यतां यत्कृतं मोहात्त्वमेव शरणं हि नः ॥
चरितानि विचित्राणि गुह्यानि गहनानि च ।
ब्रह्मादीनाञ्च सर्व्वेषां दुर्विज्ञेयो हि¶ शङ्करः‖ ॥
अज्ञानाद्यदि वाज्ञानात्किञ्चिद्यत्कुरुते नरः ।
तत्सर्व्वं भगवानेव कुरुते योगमायया ॥
एवं स्तुत्वा महादेवं प्रविष्टैरन्तरात्मभिः ।
ऊचुः प्रणम्य गिरिशं पश्यामस्त्वां यथा पुरा ॥
तेषां संस्तवमाकर्ण्य** सोमः सोमविभूषणः ।

---

* विश्वेश्वर महादेव योगिकोऽसि नमोऽस्तु ते इति B. विश्वेश्वर महादेव योऽसि सोऽसि नमोऽस्तु ते इति F. † सुखेति B. सर्व्वेति F. ‡ एतत्पादद्वयं B पुस्तके नास्ति। § वामदेव महेशान इति B. नमो देव महादेव महादेव त्रिलोचन इति F. ¶ दुर्विज्ञेयोऽसि इति B and E. ‖ अतः परं B पुस्तके श्लोकत्रयं न दृश्यते। ** संस्तवं सम्यक् स्तवमित्यर्थः। अत्र संस्तवशब्दः न परिचयार्थकः।

स्वयमेव परं रूपं दर्शयामास शङ्करः॥
तं ते दृष्ट्वाथ गिरिशं देव्या सह पिनाकिनम्।
यथापूर्व्वं स्थिता विप्राः प्रणेमुर्हृष्टमानसाः॥
ततस्ते मुनयः सर्व्वे संस्तूय च महेश्वरम्।
भृग्वङ्गिरा* वसिष्ठस्तु विश्वामित्रस्तथैव च।
गौतमोऽत्रिः सुकेशश्च पुलस्त्यः पुलहः क्रतुः।
मरीचिः कश्यपश्चापि संवर्त्तकमहातपाः।
प्रणम्य देवदेवेशमिदं वचनमब्रुवन्॥
कथं त्वान्देवदेवेश कर्म्मयोगेन वा प्रभो।
ज्ञानेन वाथ योगेन पूजयामः सदैव हि॥
केन वा देव मार्गेण सम्पूज्यो भगवानिह।
किं तत्सेव्यमसेव्यं वा सर्व्वमेतद्ब्रवीहि† नः॥

देवदेव‡ उवाच।

एतद्वः सम्प्रवक्ष्यामि गाढं§ गहनमुत्तमम्।
ब्रह्मणा¶ कथितं पूर्व्वं महादेवे महर्षयः॥
सांख्ययोगाद्द्विधा ज्ञेयं‖ पुरुषाणां हि साधनम्।
योगेन सहितं सांख्यं पुरुषाणां विमुक्तिदम्॥
न केवलं हि** योगेन दृश्यते पुरुषः परः।
ज्ञानन्तु केवलं सम्यगपवर्गफलप्रदम्॥

---

* भृग्वङ्गिराः—भृगुणा सहितः अङ्गिराः। † ब्रूहि। आर्षः प्रयोगोऽयम्। ‡ देव इति B. § गूढमिति B and F. ¶ ब्रह्मणे इति B. ‖ सांख्ययोगौ द्विधा ज्ञेयः इति B and F. ** केवलेनेति B. न केवलं वियोगेनेति E and H.

भवन्तः केवलं योगं समाश्रित्य विमुक्तये।
विहाय सांख्यं विमलमकुर्व्वत* परिश्रमम् ॥
एतस्मात्कारणाद्विप्रा नृणां केवलकर्म्मणाम्† ।
आगतोऽहमिमं देशं ज्ञापयन्मोहसम्भवम् ॥
तस्माद्भवद्भिर्विमलं ज्ञानङ्कैवल्यसाधनम् ।
ज्ञातव्यं हि प्रयत्नेन श्रोतव्यं धर्म्म एव च‡ ॥
एकः सर्व्वत्रगो ह्यात्मा केवलश्चितिमात्रकः ।
आनन्दो निर्म्मलो नित्य एतद्वै§ सांख्यदर्शनम् ॥
एतदेव परं ज्ञानमथ¶ मोक्षोऽनुगीयते ।
एतत्कैवल्यममलं|| ब्रह्मभावश्च वर्णितः** ॥
आश्रित्य चैतत्परमं तन्निष्ठास्तत्परायणाः ।
पश्यन्ति मां महात्मानो यतयो विश्वमीश्वरम् ॥
एतत्तत्परमं†† ज्ञानं केवलं सन्निरञ्जनम् ।
अहं हि वेद्यो भगवान्मम मूर्त्तिरियं शिवा ॥
बहूनि साधनानीह सिद्धये कथितानि तु ।
तेषां‡‡मभ्यधिकं ज्ञानं मामकं द्विजपुङ्गवाः ॥
ज्ञानयोग§§रताः शान्ता मामेव शरणं गताः ।
ये हि मां भस्मनि रता ध्यायन्ति सततं हृदि ॥

---

* अकुर्व्वन्तः इति A, E and H. चिकुर्व्वत इति F. † केवलधर्म्मिणामिति B. ‡ द्रष्टव्यमेव चेति B. श्राव्यमेव च इति F. धर्म्ममेव च इति E and H. § स्यादेतदिति B and F. ¶ ज्ञानमेष इति B and F. || अतुलमिति B. ** ब्रह्मभावस्तुवर्ण्यत इति F. †† परममिति B, E, F and H. ‡‡ येषामिति B. §§ योगे इति B.

मद्भक्तितत्परा* नित्यं यतयः क्षीणकल्मषाः।
नाशयाम्यचिरात्तेषां घोरं संसारगह्वरम्† ॥
निर्म्मितं हि मया पूर्व्वं व्रतं पाशुपतं शुभम्‡।
गुह्याद्गुह्यतमं सूक्ष्मं वेदसारं विमुक्तये ॥
प्रशान्तः संयतमनाः भस्मोद्धूलितविग्रहः।
ब्रह्मचर्य्यरतो नग्नो व्रतं पाशुपतञ्चरेत् ॥
यद्वा कौपीनवसनः स्यादेकवसनो मुनिः§।
वेदाभ्यासरतो विद्वान्ध्यायेत्पशुपतिं शिवम् ॥
एष पाशुपतो योगः सेवनीयो मुमुक्षुभिः।
तस्मिन् स्थितैस्तु पठितं¶ निष्कामैरिति हि श्रुतम्‖ ॥
वीतरागभयक्रोधा मन्मया मामुपाश्रिताः।
बहवोऽनेन योगेन पूता मद्भावमागताः ॥
अन्यानि चैव शास्त्राणि लोकेऽस्मिन्मोहनानि तु।
वेदवादविरुद्धानि मयैव कथितानि तु ॥
वामं पाशुपतं सोमं लाकुरञ्चैव** भैरवम्।
असेव्यमेतत्कथितं वेदबाह्यं तथेतरम् ॥
वेदमूर्त्तिरहं विप्रा नान्यशास्त्रार्थवेदिभिः††।
ज्ञायते मत्स्वरूपन्तु मुक्त्वा देवं सनातनम् ॥

---

* मद्भक्तिपरमा इति B and F. † संसारसागरमिति B, E, F, G and H. ‡ यत्नात्पाशुपतं परमिति B. § स्याद्वा दिग्वाससो मुनिरिति B. ¶ भस्मच्छन्नैर्हि सततमिति B and F. ‖ विश्रुतमिति B. ** लाञ्जनञ्चैवेति B. वकुलमिति F. †† शास्त्रानुसारिभिरिति B. शास्त्रार्थवादिभिरिति F.

स्थापयध्वमिदं मार्गं पूजयध्वं महेश्वरम् ।
ततोऽचिराद्वरं ज्ञान*मुत्पत्स्यति† न संशयः ॥
मयि भक्तिश्च विपुला भवतामस्तु सत्तमाः ।
ध्यानमात्रं‡ हि सान्निध्यं दास्यामि मुनिसत्तमाः ॥
इत्युक्त्वा भगवान् सोमस्तत्रैवान्तर्हितोऽभवत्§ ।
तेऽपि दारुवने स्थित्वा ह्यर्चयन्ति स्म शङ्करम्¶ ॥
ब्रह्मचर्य्यरताः शान्ता ज्ञानयोग‖परायणाः ।
समेत्य ते महात्मानो मुनयो ब्रह्मवादिनः ।
विचक्रिरे बहून्वादान् स्वात्मज्ञानसमाश्रयान् ॥**
किमस्य जगतो मूलमात्मा चास्माकमेव हि ॥
कोऽपि स्यात्सर्व्वभावानां†† हेतुरीश्वर एव च ।
इत्येवं मन्यमानानां ध्यानमार्गावलम्बिनाम् ।
आविरासीन्महादेवी ततो‡‡ गिरिवरात्मजा ॥
कोटिसूर्य्यप्रतीकाशा ज्वालामालासमावृता ।
स्वभाभिर्निर्म्मलाभिः सा§§ पूरयन्ती नभस्तलम् ॥

---

* अचिरादैश्वरं ज्ञानमिति B and F. † उत्पत्स्यते इति साधु। ‡ ध्यातमात्रमिति B. § तत्रैवान्तरधीयत इति B and F. ¶ तेऽपि दारुवने तस्मिन् पूजयन्ति स्म शङ्करमिति B and G. देवदारुवने तस्मिन् पूजयन्ति स्म शङ्करमिति F. ‖ सांख्ययोगेति B and F. ** एतत्पादद्वयं B पुस्तके न दृश्यते। वितौ नरे इति E, F and H. †† भूतानामिति B. ‡‡ देवीति B, E and H. गौरिति F. §§ स्वभाभिर्विमलाभिस्तु इति B.

तामन्वपश्यन्गिरिजाममेयां
ज्वालासहस्रान्तरसन्निविष्टाम् ।
प्रणेमुरेता*मखिलेशपत्नीं
जानन्ति चैतत्परमस्य† वीजम् ॥
अस्माकमेषा परमस्य‡ पत्नी
गतिस्तथात्मा गगनाभिधाना ।
पश्यन्त्यथात्मानमिदञ्च कृत्स्नं
तस्यामथैते मुनयः प्रहृष्टाः§ ॥
निरीक्षितास्ते परमेशपत्न्या
तदन्तरे देवमशेषहेतुम् ।
पश्यन्ति शम्भुं कविमीशितारं
रुद्रं वृहन्तं पुरुषं पुराणम् ॥
आलोक्य देवीमथ देवमीशं
प्रणेमुरानन्दमवापुरग्र्यम् ।
ज्ञानं तदीशं भगवत्प्रसादा-
दाविर्बभौ जन्मविनाशहेतु ॥
इयं या सा जगतो योनिरेका
सर्व्वात्मिका सर्व्वनियामिका च ।
माहेश्वरी शक्तिरनादिसिद्धा
व्योमाभिधाना दिवि राजतीव ॥

---

* प्रणेमुरेकामिति B. प्रणेमुरेनामिति F. † ते तत्परमस्येति B. ‡ परमेशेति B and F. § मुनयश्च विप्राः इति B.

अस्यां महान्* परमेष्ठी परस्तात्
महेश्वरः शिव एकः स† रुद्रः ।
चकार विश्वं परशक्तिनिष्ठं
मायामथारुह्य च‡ देवदेवः ॥
एको देवः सर्व्वभूतेषु गूढ़ो
मायी रुद्रः सकलो निष्कलश्च ।
स एव देवी न च तद्विभिन्न-
मेतज्ज्ञात्वा ह्यमृतत्वं§ व्रजन्ति ॥
अन्तर्हितोऽभूद्भगवान्महेशो¶
देव्या तया‖ सह देवाधिदेवः ।
आराधयन्ति स्म तमादिदेवं**
वनौकसस्ते पुनरेव रुद्रम् ॥

एतद्वः कथितं सर्व्वं देवदेवस्य चेष्टितम्†† ।
देवदारुवने पूर्व्वं पुराणे यन्मया श्रुतम् ॥
यः पठेच्छृणुयान्नित्यं मुच्यते सर्व्वपातकैः ।
श्रावयेद्वा द्विजान् शान्तान् स याति परमां गतिम्‡‡ ॥

इति श्रीकूर्म्मपुराणे उपविभागे देवदारुवनप्रवेशो नाम
अष्टात्रिंशोऽध्यायः ।

---

* अस्यामहमिति B. † एकोऽथेति B and F. ‡ स इति B. समारुह्य च इति F. § ह्यमृतत्वमिति B and F. ¶ भगवानथेशः इति B and F. ‖ देव्याः सर्गः इति B and H. देव्या शक्त्या इति F. ** तमेव देवमिति B and F. †† देवदेवविचेष्टितमिति B and F. ‡‡ श्रावयित्वा द्विजान् भक्तान् प्रयाति परमां गतिमिति B.

ऊनचत्वारिंशोऽध्यायः।

सूत उवाच।

एषा पुण्यतमा देवी देवगन्धर्व्वसेविता।

नर्म्मदा लोकविख्याता तीर्थानामुत्तमा नदी॥

तस्याः शृणुध्वं माहात्म्यं मार्कण्डेयेन भाषितम्।

युधिष्ठिराय तु शुभं सर्व्वपापप्रणाशनम्॥

युधिष्ठिर उवाच।

श्रुतास्ते* विविधा धर्म्मास्त्वत्प्रसादान्महामुने।

माहात्म्यञ्च प्रयागस्य तीर्थानि विविधानि च॥

नर्म्मदा सर्व्वतीर्थानां मुख्या हि भवतेरिता।

तस्यास्त्विदानीं माहात्म्यं वक्तुमर्हसि सत्तम॥

मार्कण्डेय उवाच।

नर्म्मदा सरितां श्रेष्ठा रुद्रदेहाद्विनिःसृता।

तारयेत्सर्व्वभूतानि स्थावराणि चराणि च†॥

नर्म्मदायास्तु माहात्म्यं पुराणे यन्मया श्रुतम्।

इदानीं तत्प्रवक्ष्यामि शृणुष्वैकमनाः‡ शुभम्॥

पुण्या कनखले गङ्गा कुरुक्षेत्रे सरस्वती।

ग्रामे वा यदि वारण्ये पुण्या सर्व्वत्र नर्म्मदा॥

त्रिभिः सारस्वतन्तोयं सप्ताहाद्यामुनं जलम्§।

---

* श्रुतास्तु इति B and F. † स्थापनानि च नर्म्मदेति B. ‡ शृणु इति साधु।

§ सप्ताहेन तु यामुनमिति B and F.

सद्यः पुनाति गाङ्गेयं दर्शनादेव नार्मदम् ॥
कलिङ्गदेशपश्चार्द्धे पर्व्वतेऽमरकण्टके* ।
पुण्या त्रिषु त्रिलोकेषु† रमणीया मनोरमा ॥
सदेवासुरगन्धर्व्वा ऋषयश्च तपोधनाः ।
तपस्तप्त्वा तु राजेन्द्र सिद्धिन्तु परमाङ्गताः ॥
तत्र स्नात्वा नरो राजन्नियमस्थो जितेन्द्रियः ।
उपोष्य रजनीमेकां कुलानां तारयेच्छतम् ॥
योजनानां शतं साग्रं श्रूयते सरिदुत्तमा ।
विस्तारेण तु राजेन्द्र योजनद्वयमायता ॥
षष्टितीर्थसहस्राणि षष्टिकोट्यस्तथैव च ।
पर्व्वतस्य समन्तात्तु तिष्ठन्त्यमरकण्टके ॥
ब्रह्मचारी शुचिर्भूत्वा जितक्रोधो जितेन्द्रियः ।
सर्व्वहिंसानिवृत्तस्तु सर्व्वभूतहिते रतः ॥
एवं शुद्धसमाचारो‡ यस्तु प्राणान्परित्यजेत् ।
तस्य पुण्यफलं राजन् शृणुष्वावहितोऽनघ§ ॥
शतं वर्षसहस्राणि स्वर्गे मोदति¶ पाण्डव ।
अप्सरोगणसङ्कीर्णो दिव्यस्त्रीपरिवारितः ॥
दिव्यगन्धानुलिप्तश्च दिव्यपुष्पोपशोभितः ।
क्रीड़ते दिव्यलोके तु विबुधैः‖ सह मोदते ॥

---

* अमरकङ्कटे इति G and H. † पुण्याश्च त्रिषु लोकेष्विति B. पुण्या च त्रिषु लोकेषु इति F. ‡ सर्व्वसमाचारः इति B and F. § नृपेति B. ¶ मोदते इति साधु। ‖ देवलोके तु दैवतैरिति B and F.

तत: स्वर्गात्परिभ्रष्टो राजा भवति धार्म्मिक:।
गृहन्तु लभतेऽसौ वै* नानारत्नसमन्वितम्॥
स्तम्भैर्मणिमयैर्दिव्यैर्वज्रवैदूर्यभूषितम्।
आलेख्यवाहनै: शुभ्रैर्दासीशतसमन्वितम्† ॥
राजराजेश्वर: श्रीमान् सर्व्वस्त्रीजनवल्लभ:।
जीवेद्दर्षशतं साग्रन्तत्र भोगसमन्वित:॥
अग्निप्रवेशेऽथ जले वाथवानशने कृते।‡
अनिवर्त्तिका§ गतिस्तस्य पवनस्याम्बरे यथा॥
पश्चिमे पर्व्वततटे सर्व्वपापविनाशन:।
ह्रदो¶ जलेश्वरो नाम त्रिषु लोकेषु विश्रुत:॥
तत्र पिण्डप्रदानेन सन्ध्योपासनकर्म्मणा।
दशवर्षसहस्राणि तर्पिता: स्युर्न संशय:॥
दक्षिणे नर्म्मदाकूले कपिलाख्या महानदी।
सरसार्जुन‖सञ्छन्ना नातिदूरे व्यवस्थिता॥
सा तु पुण्या महाभागा त्रिषु लोकेषु विश्रुता।
तत्र कोटिशतं साग्रं तीर्थानान्तु युधिष्ठिर॥
तस्मिंस्तीर्थे तु ये वृक्षा: पतिता: कालपर्य्ययात्।
नर्म्मदातोयसंस्पृष्टास्ते यान्ति** परमाङ्गतिम्॥

---

* शौरेरिति B. † दासीदाससमन्वितमिति B and F. ‡ अथ वह्निप्रवेशे तु-कूले वानाशके कृते इति A, F and H. आशी भोजनमेव आशक:, न आशक: अनाशकस्तस्मिन् प्रायोपवेशने इत्यर्थ:। § अनिवर्त्तिका अपुनरावर्त्तिनीत्यर्थ:। ¶ नद: इति B. ‖ सरलार्ज्जुनेति B and F. ** यान्ति ते इति B.

द्वितीया तु महाभाग विशल्यकरणी शुभा।
तत्र तीर्थे नरः स्नात्वा विशल्यो भवति क्षणात्॥
कपिला च विशल्या च श्रूयेते सरिदुत्तमे*।
ईश्वरेण पुरा प्रोक्ते लोकानां हितकाम्यया॥
अनाशकन्तु यः कुर्य्यात्तस्मिंस्तीर्थे नराधिप।
सर्व्वपापविशुद्धात्मा रुद्रलोके† स गच्छति॥
तत्र स्नात्वा नरो राजन्नश्वमेधफलं लभेत्।
ये वसन्त्युत्तरे कूले रुद्रलोके वसन्ति ते॥
सरस्वत्याञ्च गङ्गायां नर्म्मदायां युधिष्ठिर।
समं स्नानञ्च दानञ्च यथा मे शङ्करोऽब्रवीत्॥
परित्यजति यः प्राणान् पर्व्वतेऽमरकण्टके।
वर्षकोटिशतं साग्रं रुद्रलोके महीयते॥ ‡
नर्म्मदायां जलं पुण्यं फेनोर्म्मिसफलीकृतम्§।
पवित्रं शिरसा वन्द्यं¶ सर्व्वपापैः प्रमुच्यते॥
नर्म्मदा सर्व्वतः‖ पुण्या ब्रह्महत्यापहारिणी।
अहोरात्रोपवासेन मुच्यते ब्रह्महत्यया॥
जालेश्वरं तीर्थवरं सर्व्वपापप्रणाशनम्**।
तत्र गत्वा नियमवान् सर्व्वकामान्†† लभेन्नरः॥

---

* राजसत्तमेति B. † रुद्रलोकमिति B. ‡ एतदन्तं श्लोकद्वयं A, E, H पुस्तकेषु नास्ति। § समलं कृतमिति B. सकलं कृतमिति E. बहुलं कृतमिति F. सफलीकृतमिति H. ¶ धृत्वा इति B. ‖ सर्व्वदेति B. ** विनाशनमिति B. †† सर्व्वान् कामानिति B.

चन्द्रसूर्य्योपरागे तु गत्वा चामरकण्टकम्* ।
अश्वमेधाद्दशगुणं पुण्यमा†प्नोति मानवः ॥
एष पुण्यो गिरिवरो देवगन्धर्व्वसेवितः ।
नानाद्रुमलताकीर्णो नानापुष्पोपशोभितः ॥
तत्र सन्निहितो राजन्देव्या सह महेश्वरः ।
ब्रह्मा विष्णुस्तथा रुद्रो विद्याधरगणैः सह ॥
प्रदक्षिणन्तु यः कुर्य्यात्पर्व्वतेऽमरकण्टके‡ ।
पौण्डरीकस्य यज्ञस्य फलम्प्राप्नोति मानवः ॥
कावेरी नाम विख्याता§ नदी कल्मषनाशिनी ।
तत्र स्नात्वा महादेवमर्च्चयेद्वृषभध्वजम् ॥
सङ्गमे नर्म्मदायास्तु रुद्रलोके महीयते ।

इति श्रीकूर्म्मपुराणे मार्कण्डेययुधिष्ठिरसंवादे नर्म्मदामाहात्म्यं नाम ऊनचत्वारिंशोऽध्यायः ।

---

* काङ्कटमिति E and H. † इतः परं सर्गान्तपर्य्यन्तः परसर्गस्थोनविंशश्लोकपर्य्यन्तश्च पाठः A पुस्तके नास्ति । ‡ नगश्चामरकङ्कटमिति E and H. § विपुलेति E and H.

चत्वारिंशोऽध्यायः।

मार्कण्डेय उवाच।

नर्म्मदा सरितां श्रेष्ठा सर्व्वपापविनाशिनी।
मुनिभिः* कथिता पूर्व्वमीश्वरेण स्वयम्भुना॥
मुनिभिः संस्तुता ह्येषा नर्म्मदा प्रवरा नदी।
रुद्रगात्राद्विनिष्क्रान्ता लोकानां हितकाम्यया॥
सर्व्वपापहरा नित्यं सर्व्वदेवनमस्कृता।
संस्तुता देवगन्धर्व्वैरप्सरोभिस्तथैव च॥
उत्तरे चैव कूले च तीर्थे त्रैलोक्यविश्रुते†।
नाम्ना भद्रेश्वरं पुण्यं सर्व्वपापहरं शुभम्।
तत्र स्नात्वा नरो राजन्देवतैः सह मोदते‡॥
ततो गच्छेत राजेन्द्र तीर्थमाम्रातकेश्वरम्§।
तत्र¶ स्नात्वा नरो राजन् गोसहस्रफलं लभेत्॥
ततोऽङ्गारकेश्वरं गच्छेन्नियतो नियताशनः।
सर्व्वपापविशुद्धात्मा रुद्रलोके महीयते॥
ततो गच्छेत राजेन्द्र केदारं नाम पुण्यदम्।
तत्र स्नात्वोदकं पीत्वा सर्व्वान् कामानवाप्नुयात्॥
निष्पलेशन्ततो गच्छेत्सर्व्वपापविनाशनम्।

---

* मुनिभ्यइति E and H. † त्रैलोक्यविश्रुतमिति E and H. ‡ रुद्रलोके महीयते इति E and H. § विमलेश्वरमुत्तममिति E and H. ¶ अतः परं श्लोकार्द्धषट्कं E H पुस्तकयोर्न दृश्यते।

तत्र स्नात्वा महाराज रुद्रलोके महीयते ॥
ततो गच्छेत राजेन्द्र बाणतीर्थमनुत्तमम् ।
तत्र प्राणान्परित्यज्य रुद्रलोकमवाप्नुयात् ॥
ततः पुष्करिणीं गच्छेत्स्नानं तत्र समाचरेत् ।
तत्र स्नात्वा नरो राजन् सिंहासनपतिर्भवेत् ॥
शक्रतीर्थं ततो गच्छेत्कूले चैव तु दक्षिणे ।
स्नातमात्रो नरस्तत्र इन्द्रस्यार्द्धासनं लभेत् ॥
ततो गच्छेत राजेन्द्र मूलभेद* इति श्रुतिः ।
तत्र† स्नात्वा च पीत्वा च गोसहस्रफलं लभेत् ॥
उपोष्य रजनीमेकां स्नानं कृत्वा यथाविधि ।
आराधयेन्महायोगं देवदेवं‡ नरोऽमलः ॥
गोसहस्रफलम्प्राप्य विष्णुलोकं स गच्छति ॥
ऋषितीर्थं ततो गत्वा सर्व्वपापहरं नृणाम् ।
स्नातमात्रो नरस्तत्र शिवलोके महीयते ॥
नारदस्य तु तत्रैव तीर्थं परमशोभनम् ।
स्नातमात्रो नरस्तत्र गोसहस्रफलं लभेत् ॥
यत्र तप्तन्तपः पूर्व्वं नारदेन सुरर्षिणा ।
प्रीतस्तस्य ददौ योगं देवदेवो महेश्वरः ॥
ब्रह्मणा निर्म्मितं लिङ्गं ब्रह्मेश्वरमिति श्रुतम् ।

---

* मूलभेद इति E, F and H. † तत्र स्नात्वार्च्चयेद्देवं गोसहस्रफलं लभेदिति E and H. ‡ देवं नारायणं हरिमिति E and H.

यत्र स्नात्वा नरो राजन् ब्रह्मलोके महीयते ॥
ऋणतीर्थं ततो गच्छेद्दणान्मुच्येन्नरो ध्रुवम् ।
वटेश्वरं ततो गच्छेत्पर्य्याप्तं* जन्मनः फलम् ॥
भीमे†श्वरं ततो गच्छेत्सर्व्वव्याधिविनाशनम् ।
स्नातमात्रो नरस्तत्र सर्व्वदुःखैः प्रमुच्यते ॥
ततो गच्छेत राजेन्द्र पिङ्गलेश्वरमुत्तमम् ।
अहोरात्रोपवासेन त्रिरात्रफलमाप्नुयात् ॥
तस्मिंस्तीर्थे तु राजेन्द्र कपिलां यः प्रयच्छति ।
यावन्ति तस्या रोमाणि तत्प्रसूतिकुलेषु च ।
तावद्वर्षसहस्राणि रुद्रलोके महीयते ॥
यस्तु प्राणपरित्यागं कुर्य्यात्तत्र नराधिप ।
अक्षयं मोदते कालं यावच्चन्द्रदिवाकरौ ॥
नर्मदातटमाश्रित्य ये च तिष्ठन्ति‡ मानवाः ।
ते मृताः स्वर्गमायान्ति सन्तः सुकृतिनो यथा ॥
ततो दीप्तेश्वरं गच्छेद्व्यासतीर्थं तपोवनम्§ ।
निवर्त्तिता पुरा तत्र व्यासभीता महानदी ।
हुङ्कारिता तु व्यासेन तत्क्षणेन¶ ततो गता ॥
प्रदक्षिणन्तु यः कुर्य्यात्तस्मिंस्तीर्थे युधिष्ठिर ।
प्रीतस्तत्र‖ भवेद्व्यासो वाञ्छितं लभते फलम् ॥

---

* ततो गच्छेत राजेन्द्र संप्राप्तमिति E and H. † एतत्पर्य्यन्तं A पुस्तके नास्ति । ‡ तिष्ठन्ति ये तु इति B. § तपोवनमिति A, F and H. ¶ दक्षिणेनेति B and F. ‖ प्रीतस्त्वेति B.

ततो गच्छेत राजेन्द्र इषुनद्यास्तु* सङ्गमम्।
त्रैलोक्यविश्रुतं पुण्यं तत्र सन्निहितः शिवः।
तत्र स्नात्वा नरो राजन् गाणपत्यमवाप्नुयात्॥
स्कन्दतीर्थं† ततो गच्छेत्सर्व्वपापप्रणाशनम्।
आजन्मनः कृतं पापं स्नातस्तत्र व्यपोहति॥
तत्र देवाः सगन्धर्व्वा भगात्मजमनुत्तमम्।
उपासते महात्मानं‡ स्कन्दं शक्तिधरं प्रभुम्॥
ततो गच्छेदाङ्गिरसं स्नानं तत्र समाचरेत्।
गोसहस्रफलम्प्राप्य§ रुद्रलोकं स गच्छति¶॥
अङ्गिरा यत्र देवेशं ब्रह्मपुत्रो वृषध्वजम्।
तपसाराध्य विश्वेशं लब्धवान्योगमुत्तमम्॥
कुशतीर्थं‖ ततो गच्छेत्सर्व्वपापप्रणाशनम्।
तत्र स्नानं** प्रकुर्व्वीत अश्वमेधफलं लभेत्॥
कोटितीर्थं ततो गच्छेत्सर्व्वपापप्रणाशनम्††।
आजन्मनः कृतं पापं स्नातस्तत्र व्यपोहति‡‡॥
चन्द्रभागां ततो गच्छेत्स्नानं तत्र समाचरेत्।

---

* इक्षुनद्यास्तु इति B and F. † स्वर्गतीर्थमिति B. ‡ महाज्ञानमिति B. महात्मान इति F. § फलं तस्येति B and F. ¶ रुद्रलोके महीयते इति B and F. ‖ कुलतीर्थमिति B. E and F. ** स्नानं तत्रेति B. †† सर्व्वपापहरं परमिति B. एतत्पादद्वयं G पुस्तके न दृश्यते। एतत्पादद्वयं E H पुस्तकयोर्व्युत्क्रमेण पठ्यते। ‡‡ तत्र स्नात्वा नरो राज्यं लभते नात्र संशयः इति B. लभेत पुण्यमुत्तममिति F.

स्नातमात्रो नरस्तत्र सोमलोके महीयते ॥
नर्म्मदादक्षिणे कूले सङ्गमेश्वरमुत्तमम् ।
तत्र स्नात्वा नरो राजन् सर्व्वयज्ञफलं लभेत् ॥
नर्म्मदा चोत्तरे* कूले तीर्थं परमशोभनम् ।
आदित्यायतनं रम्यमीश्वरेण तु भाषितम् ॥
तत्र स्नात्वा तु राजेन्द्र दत्त्वा दानन्तु शक्तितः ।
तस्य तीर्थप्रभावेण लभते चाक्षयम्फलम् ॥
दरिद्रा व्याधिता ये च ये च दुष्कृतकर्म्मिणः† ।
मुच्यन्ते सर्व्वपापेभ्यः सूर्य्यलोकं प्रयान्ति च ॥
मातृतीर्थं‡ ततो गच्छेत्स्नानं तत्र समाचरेत् ।
स्नातमात्रो नरस्तत्र स्वर्गलोकमवाप्नुयात् ॥
ततः पश्चिमतो गच्छेन्मरुतालयमुत्तमम्§ ।
तत्र स्नात्वा तु राजेन्द्र शुचिर्भूत्वा समाहितः¶ ॥
काञ्चनञ्च यतौ‖ दद्याद्यथाविभवविस्तरम् ।
पुष्पकेण विमानेन वायुलोकं स गच्छति ॥
ततो गच्छेत राजेन्द्र अहल्यातीर्थमुत्तमम्** ।
स्नानमात्रादप्सरोभिर्मोदते कालमुत्तमम्†† ॥
चैत्रमासे तु सम्प्राप्ते शुक्लपक्षे त्रयोदशी ।

* नर्म्मदायोत्तरे इति B. † ये तु ये तु दुष्कृतकारिणः इति B and F. ‡ मार्गेश्वरमिति B and F. § मरुदालयमुत्तममिति B. ¶ प्रयतः इति B and F. ‖ द्विजे इति B. द्विजाय काञ्चनं दद्यादिति F. ** अहिल्यातीर्थमुत्तममिति E, G and H. †† कालमक्षयमिति B and F.

कामदेवदिने शुभ्रे* अहल्यां† यस्तु पूजयेत् ॥
यत्र तत्र समुत्पन्नो नरोऽत्यर्थप्रियो भवेत्‡ ।
स्त्रीवल्लभो भवेच्छ्रीमान्§ कामदेव इवापरः ॥
सरिद्वरां¶ समासाद्य तीर्थं शक्रस्य विश्रुतम् ।
स्नातमात्रो नरस्तत्र गोसहस्रफलं लभेत् ॥
सोमतीर्थं ततो गच्छेत्स्नानं तत्र समाचरेत् ।
स्नातमात्रो नरस्तत्र सर्व्वपापैः प्रमुच्यते ॥
सोमग्रहे‖ तु राजेन्द्र पापक्षयकरं भवेत् ।
त्रैलोक्य**विश्रुतं राजन् सोमतीर्थं महाफलम् ॥
यस्तु चान्द्रायणङ्कुर्य्यात्तत्र तीर्थे समाहितः ।
सर्व्वपापविशुद्धात्मा सोमलोकं स गच्छति ॥
अग्निप्रवेशं यः कुर्य्यात्सोमतीर्थे नराधिप†† ।
जले चानशनं‡‡ वापि नासौ मर्त्त्यो हि जायते§§ ॥
स्तम्भतीर्थं¶¶ ततो गच्छेत्स्नानं तत्र समाचरेत् ।
स्नातमात्रो नरस्तत्र सोमलोके महीयते ॥
ततो गच्छेत राजेन्द्र विष्णुतीर्थमनुत्तमम् ।

---

* तस्मिन्निति B and F. † अहिल्यामिति E, G and H. ‡ वरस्तत्र धियी भवेदिति B. वरस्तत्र प्रियी भवेदिति F. § भवेद्धीमानिति B. ¶ अयोध्यान्तु इति B. अयोध्यायामिति F. ‖ सोमग्रहमिति B. ** त्रैलोक्ये इति B. †† समाहितः इति B. ‡‡ वानाशके इति A, E and H. नाशकं वापीति F. §§ मर्त्त्योऽभिजायते इति B, E and F. ¶¶ शुम्भतीर्थमिति B.

योधनीपरमाख्यातं* विष्णोः स्थानमनुत्तमम्।
असुरा योधितास्तत्र वासुदेवेन कोटिशः॥
तत्र तीर्थं समुत्पन्नं विष्णुश्रीकोत्† भवेदिह।
अहोरात्रोपवासेन ब्रह्महत्यां व्यपोहति॥
नर्म्मदादक्षिणे कूले तीर्थं परमशोभनम्।
कामतीर्थमिति ख्यातं यत्र कामोऽर्च्चयद्धरिम्‡॥
तस्मिंस्तीर्थे नरः स्नात्वा उपवासपरायणः।
कुसुमायुधरूपेण रुद्रलोके महीयते॥
ततो गच्छेत राजेन्द्र ब्रह्मतीर्थमनुत्तमम्॥
ऊमाहकमिति§ ख्यातं तत्र सन्तर्पयेत्पितॄन्।
पौर्णमास्याममावास्यां श्राद्धं कुर्य्याद्यथाविधि॥
गजरूपा शिला तत्र तोयमध्ये व्यवस्थिता।
तस्मिंस्तु दापयेत्पिण्डान्वैशाखे तु समाहितः¶॥
स्नात्वा समाहितमना दम्भमात्सर्य्यवर्ज्जितः।
तृप्यन्ति पितरस्तस्य‖ यावत्तिष्ठति मेदिनी॥
सिद्धेश्वरं** ततो गच्छेत्स्नानं तत्र समाचरेत्।
स्नातमात्रो नरस्तत्र गाणपत्यपदं†† लभेत्‡‡॥

---

* योधनीपुरमाख्यातमिति B. योधनापरमाख्यातमिति G. योधनापुरमिति E. योधनापरमिति H. † विष्णुप्रीतः इति B. ‡ कामोऽर्च्चयद्भवमिति B and F. कामोऽर्च्चयद्धरमिति G and H. § अमीघमिति विख्यातमिति B. अमोहकमिति ख्यातमिति F. ¶ वैशाख्यान्तु विशेषतः इति B. ‖ पितरस्तावदिति B. ** विश्वेश्वरमिति F. †† गाणपत्यं पदमिति B. ‡‡ अतः परं श्लोकाद्वैदशकं F पुस्तके नास्ति।

ततो गच्छेत राजेन्द्र लिङ्गो* यत्र जनार्द्दनः।
तत्र स्नात्वा नरो भक्त्या† विष्णुलोके महीयते॥
यत्र नारायणो देवो मुनीनां भावितात्मनाम्।
स्वात्मानं दर्शयामास लिङ्गं तत्परमं पदम्॥
अङ्कोल्लन्तु‡ ततो गच्छेत्सर्व्वपापविनाशनम्।
स्नानं दानञ्च तत्रैव ब्राह्मणानाञ्च भोजनम्।
पिण्डप्रदानञ्च कृतं प्रेत्यानन्तफल§प्रदम्॥
त्रियम्बकेन¶ तोयेन यश्चरुं श्रपयेद्द्विजः‖।
अङ्कुल्लमूले** दद्याच्च पिण्डांश्चैव यथाविधि।
तारिताः†† पितरस्तेन तृप्यन्त्याचन्द्रतारकम्॥
ततो गच्छेत राजेन्द्र तापसेश्वरमुत्तमम्।
तत्र स्नात्वा तु राजेन्द्र प्राप्नुयात्तपसः फलम्॥
शुक्लतीर्थं‡‡ ततो गच्छेत्सर्व्वपापविनाशनम्।
नास्ति तेन समन्तीर्थं नर्म्मदायां युधिष्ठिर॥
दर्शनात्स्पर्शनात्तस्य स्नानाद्दानात्तपोजपात्।
होमाच्चैवोपवासाच्च शुक्लतीर्थे§§ महत्फलम्॥
योजनन्तत्स्मृतं क्षेत्रं देवगन्धर्व्वसेवितम्।

---

* लिङ्गमस्यास्तीति लिङ्गः लिङ्गरूपीत्यर्थः अर्शआदित्वादच्। लिङ्गे इति B. † तत्र स्नात्वा तु राजेन्द्रेति B. ‡ अङ्कोल्लन्तु इति B, E, G and H. § प्रेत्यानन्देति B. ¶ त्रैपञ्चकेनेति B. त्रैयम्बकेन इति E and H. ‖ श्रापयेत्ततः इति B. ** अङ्कोल्लमूले इति B. †† तर्पिताः इति B. ‡‡ शुक्रतीर्थमिति B and F. §§ शुक्रतीर्थे इति B and F.

शुक्लतीर्थ*मिति ख्यातं सर्व्वपापविनाशनम्† ॥
पादपाग्रेण दृष्टेन ब्रह्महत्यां व्यपोहति।
देव्या‡ सह§ सदा भर्गस्तत्र तिष्ठति शङ्करः ॥
कृष्णपक्षे चतुर्द्दश्यां वैशाखे मासि सुव्रत।
लोकात्स्वकाद्विनिष्क्रम्य तत्र सन्निहितो हरः ॥
देवदानवगन्धर्व्वाः सिद्धविद्याधरास्तथा।
गणाश्चाप्सरसो नागास्तत्र तिष्ठन्ति पुङ्गवाः ॥
रञ्जितं हि यथा वस्त्रं शुक्लं भवति वारिणा।
आजन्मजनितं पापं शुक्लतीर्थे¶ व्यपोहति‖ ॥
कार्त्तिकस्य तु मासस्य कृष्णपक्षे चतुर्द्दशी।
घृतेन स्नापयेद्देवमुपोष्य परमेश्वरम् ॥
एकविंशत्कुलोपेतो न च्यवेदीश्वरालयात्** ॥
तपसा ब्रह्मचर्य्येण यज्ञैर्दानेन वा पुनः।
न ताङ्गतिमवाप्नोति शुक्लतीर्थे†† तु यां लभेत् ॥
शुक्लतीर्थं‡‡ महातीर्थमृषिसिद्धनिषेवितम्।
तत्र स्नात्वा नरो राजन् पुनर्ज्जन्म न विन्दति§§ ॥

---

* शुक्लतीर्थमिति B and F. † प्रणाशनमिति B. ‡ श्लोकोऽयं F पुस्तके न दृश्यते। § देव्या सहेत्यारभ्य चतुर्द्दश पादाः B पुस्तके न दृश्यन्ते। ¶ शुक्लतीर्थं इति B. ‖ शुक्लतीर्थं व्यपोहतीति F. स्नानं दानं तपः श्राद्धमनन्तं तत्तु दृश्यते। शुक्लतीर्थात्परं तीर्थं न भविष्यति पावनम् ॥ पूर्व्वे वयसि कर्म्माणि कृत्वा पापानि मानवः। अहोरात्रोपवासेन शुक्लतीर्थे व्यपोहतीति अधिकं F पुस्तके दृश्यते। ** न च्यवेदैश्वरात्पदादिति B. †† शुक्लतीर्थं इति B and F. ‡‡ शुक्लतीर्थमिति B and F. §§ विद्यते इति B and F.

अयने वा चतुर्द्दश्यां संक्रान्तौ विषुवे तथा* ।
स्नात्वा तु सोपवासः सन्विजितात्मा† समाहितः ॥
दानं दद्याद्यथाशक्ति प्रीयेतां हरिशङ्करौ ।
एतत्तीर्थप्रभावेण सर्व्वं भवति चाक्षयम् ॥
अनाथं दुर्गतं विप्रं नाथवन्तमथापि वा ।
उद्वाहयति यस्तीर्थे तस्य पुण्यफलं शृणु ॥
यावत्तद्रोमसंख्या तु तत्प्रसूतिकुलेषु च ।
तावद्वर्षसहस्राणि रुद्रलोके महीयते ॥
ततो गच्छेत राजेन्द्र यमतीर्थमनुत्तमम् ।
कृष्णपक्षे चतुर्द्दश्यां माघमासे युधिष्ठिर ।
स्नानङ्कृत्वा नक्तभोजी न पश्येद्योनिसङ्कटम् ॥
ततो गच्छेत राजेन्द्र एरण्डीतीर्थमुत्तमम् ।
सङ्गमे तु नरः स्नात्वा उपवासपरायणः ।
ब्राह्मणं भोजयेदेकं कोटिर्भवति भोजिताः ॥
एरण्डीसङ्गमे स्नात्वा भक्तिभावात्तु रञ्जितः ।
मृत्तिकां शिरसि स्थाप्य‡ अवगाह्य च तज्जलम् ।
नर्म्मदोदकसंमिश्रं मुच्यते सर्व्वकिल्बिषैः ॥
ततो गच्छेत राजेन्द्र तीर्थङ्कल्लोलकेश्वरम् ।
गङ्गावतरते तत्र दिने§ पुण्ये न संशयः ॥
तत्र स्नात्वा च पीत्वा च दत्त्वा चैव यथाविधि ।

---

* विषुवेऽथवा इति B. † निर्जितात्मा इति B. ‡ स्थापयित्वा इति साधु।
§ स्थाने इति B.

सर्व्वपापविनिर्मुक्तो ब्रह्मलोके* महीयते ॥
नन्दितीर्थं ततो गच्छेत्तत्र स्नानं† समाचरेत् ।
प्रीयते तत्र‡ नन्दीशः सोमलोके महीयते ॥
ततो गच्छेत राजेन्द्र तीर्थं त्वनरकं शुभम् ।
तत्र स्नात्वा नरो राजन्नरकं नैव§ पश्यति ॥
तस्मिंस्तीर्थे तु राजेन्द्र स्वान्यस्थीनि विनिक्षिपेत् ।
रूपवाञ्जायते लोके धनभोगसमन्वितः ॥
ततो गच्छेत राजेन्द्र कपिलातीर्थमुत्तमम् ।
तत्र स्नात्वा नरो राजन् गोसहस्रफलं लभेत् ॥
ज्येष्ठमासे तु सम्प्राप्ते चतुर्द्दश्यां विशेषतः ।
तत्रोपोष्य नरो भक्त्या दत्त्वा दीपं¶ घृतेन तु ।
घृतेन स्नापयेद्रुद्रं ततो वै श्रीफलं लभेत्‖ ॥
घण्टाभरणसंयुक्तां कपिलां वै प्रदापयेत्** ।
सर्व्वाभरणसंयुक्तः†† सर्व्वदेवनमस्कृतः ।
शिवतुल्यबलो भूत्वा शिववत्क्रीड़ते सदा ॥
अङ्गारकदिने प्राप्ते चतुर्थ्यान्तु विशेषतः ।
स्नापयित्वा शिवं दद्याद्ब्राह्मणेभ्यस्तु भोजनम्‡‡ ॥
सर्व्वदेवसमायुक्तो§§ विमाने सर्व्वकामिके ।

---

* रुद्रलोके इति B. † स्नानं तत्रेति B. ‡ तस्येति B, E, G and H. § नरकन्तु नेति B. ¶ दद्याद्दीपमिति B and F. ‖ सघृतं श्रीफलं दहेदिति B. सघृतं गुग्गुलं दहेदिति F. ** प्रदाय तु इति B. †† सर्व्वपापविनिर्मुक्तः इति B. ‡‡ दक्षिणामिति B. §§ सर्व्वभोगसमायुक्तः इति B and F.

गत्वा शक्रस्य भवनं* शक्रेण सह मोदते ।
ततः स्वर्गात्परिभ्रष्टो द्युतिवान्† भोगवान् भवेत् ॥
अङ्गारक‡नवम्यान्तु अमावास्यां तथैव च ।
स्नापयेत्तत्र यत्नेन रूपवान् सुभगो भवेत् ॥
ततो गच्छेत राजेन्द्र गणेश्वरमनुत्तमम् ।
श्रावणे मासि सम्प्राप्ते कृष्णपक्षे चतुर्द्दशी ।
स्नातमात्रो नरस्तत्र ब्रह्मलोके§ महीयते ।
पितॄणां तर्पणङ्कृत्वा मुच्यते स ऋणत्रयात् ॥
गङ्गेश्वरसमीपे तु गङ्गावदनमुत्तमम् ।
अकामो वा सकामो वा तत्र स्नात्वा तु मानवः ।
आजन्मजनितैः पापैर्मुच्यते नात्र संशयः ॥
तस्य वै पश्चिमे भागे¶ समीपे नातिदूरतः ।
दशाश्वमेधिकं तीर्थं त्रिषु लोकेषु विश्रुतम् ॥
उपोष्य रजनीमेकां मासि भाद्रपदे शुभे ।
अमावास्यां हरं स्नाप्य‖ पूजयेद्गोवृषध्वजम्** ॥
काञ्चनेन विमानेन किङ्किणीजालमालिना ।
गत्वा रुद्रपुरं रम्यं रुद्रेण सह मोदते ॥

---

* भुवनमिति E, G and H. † धनवानिति B, E, G and H. ‡ अङ्गारकेत्यादिश्लोकः B पुस्तके नास्ति । § रुद्रलोके इति B and F. ¶ देशे इति B and F. ‖ स्नापयित्वा इति साधु । ** अमावास्यां नरः स्नात्वा पूजयेद्वृषभध्वजमिति B. स्नापयेद्वृषभध्वजमिति F.

सर्व्वत्र सर्व्वदिवसे स्नानं तत्र समाचरेत् ।
पितॄणां तर्पणं कृत्वा चाश्वमेधफलं* लभेत् ॥

इति श्रीकूर्म्मपुराणे उपविभागे नर्म्मदामाहात्म्ये चत्वारिंशोऽध्यायः ।

* अश्वमेधफलमिति B. कुर्य्यादश्वमेधफलं लभेदिति F.

एकचत्वारिंशोऽध्यायः ।

मार्कण्डेय उवाच ।

ततो गच्छेत राजेन्द्र भृगुतीर्थमनुत्तमम् ।
तत्र देवो भृगुः पूर्व्वं* रुद्रमाराधयत्पुरा ।
दर्शनात्तस्य देवस्य सद्यः पापात्प्रमुच्यते ॥
एतत्क्षेत्रं सुविपुलं† सर्व्वपापप्रणाशनम् ।
तत्र स्नात्वा दिवं यान्ति ये मृतास्तेऽपुनर्भवाः ॥
उपानहौ तथा युग्मं देयमन्नञ्च काञ्चनम्‡ ।
भोजनञ्च यथाशक्ति तस्याप्यक्षयमुच्यते§ ॥
क्षरन्ति सर्व्वदानानि यज्ञदानं तपःक्रिया¶ ।
अक्षय्यं तत्तपस्तप्तं‖ भृगुतीर्थे युधिष्ठिर ॥

* यत्र देवभृगुर्भर्गमिति B. यत्र देवं भृगुः पूर्व्वमिति F. † सुविस्तीर्णमिति B. ‡ देयमन्नं सकाञ्चनमिति B. § तदस्याक्षयमुच्यते इति B and F. ¶ यज्ञदानतपःक्रिया इति B and F. ‖ न क्षरेयत्तपस्तप्तमिति B, E and F.

तस्यैव तपसोग्रेण रुद्रेण* त्रिपुरारिणा ।
सान्निध्यं तत्र कथितं भृगुतीर्थे युधिष्ठिर ॥
ततो गच्छेत राजेन्द्र गौतमेश्वरमुत्तमम् ।
यत्राराध्य त्रिशूलाङ्कं गौतमः सिद्धिमाप्नुयात् ॥
तत्र स्नात्वा नरो राजन्नुपवासपरायणः ।
काञ्चनेन विमानेन ब्रह्मलोके महीयते ॥
वृषोत्सर्गं ततो गच्छेच्छाश्वतं पदमाप्नुयात्† ।
न जानन्ति नरा मूढ़ा विष्णोर्मायाविमोहिताः ॥
धौतपापं ततो गच्छेद्धौतं यत्र वृषेण तु‡ ।
नर्म्मदायां स्थितं राजन् सर्व्वपातकनाशनम् ।
तत्र तीर्थे नरः स्नात्वा ब्रह्महत्यां विमुञ्चति ॥
तत्र तीर्थे§ तु राजेन्द्र प्राणत्यागं करोति यः ।
चतुर्भुजस्त्रिनेत्रश्च हरतुल्यबलो भवेत् ॥
वसेत्कल्पायुतं साग्रं शिवतुल्यपराक्रमः ।
कालेन महता जातः पृथिव्यामेकराड्भवेत् ॥
ततो गच्छेत राजेन्द्र हस्ततीर्थमनुत्तमम्¶ ।
तत्र स्नात्वा नरो राजन् ब्रह्मलोके महीयते ॥
ततो गच्छेत राजेन्द्र यत्र सिद्धो जनार्द्दनः‖ ।
वराहतीर्थमाख्यातं विष्णुलोकगतिप्रदम् ॥

---

* तुष्टेनेति B and E. † शाश्वतीं गतिमाप्नुयादिति B. ‡ चेति B. § तत्तत्तीर्थे इति B. ¶ हंसतीर्थमनुत्तममिति B, E, F and H. ‖ सिद्धो यत्र जनार्द्दनः इति B.

ततो गच्छेत राजेन्द्र चन्द्रतीर्थमनुत्तमम्।
पौर्णमास्यां विशेषेण स्नानन्तत्र समाचरेत्।
स्नातमात्रो नरस्तत्र पृथिव्यामेकराट् भवेत्* ॥
देवतीर्थं† ततो गच्छेत्सर्वतीर्थ‡नमस्कृतम्।
तत्र स्नात्वा च राजेन्द्र दैवतैः सह मोदते ॥
ततो गच्छेत राजेन्द्र शङ्खितीर्थ§मनुत्तमम्।
यत्तत्र दीयते दानं सर्व्वं कोटिगुणं भवेत् ॥
ततो गच्छेत राजेन्द्र तीर्थं पैतामहं शुभम्।
यत्तत्र दीयते¶ श्राद्धं सर्व्वं तस्याक्षयं भवेत्‖ ॥
सावित्रीतीर्थमासाद्य यस्तु प्राणान्परित्यजेत्।
विधूय सर्व्वपापानि ब्रह्मलोके महीयते ॥
मनोहरन्तु तत्रैव तीर्थं परमशोभनम्**।
तत्र स्नात्वा नरो राजन्रुद्रलोके महीयते ॥
ततो गच्छेत राजेन्द्र कन्यातीर्थमनुत्तमम्।
स्नात्वा तत्र नरो राजन् सर्व्वपापैः प्रमुच्यते ॥
शुक्लपक्षे तृतीयायां स्नानमात्रं समाचरेत्।
स्नातमात्रो नरस्तत्र पृथिव्यामेकराड्भवेत् ॥††
सर्गविन्दुं‡‡ ततो गच्छेत्तीर्थं देवनमस्कृतम्।

---

* चन्द्रलोके महीयते इति B. † B पुस्तके देवतीर्थवर्णनात्पूर्व्वं कन्यातीर्थवर्णनं दृश्यते। ‡ देवैरिति B and F. § शिखितीर्थमिति B and F. ¶ क्रियते इति B. ‖ तत्तदस्याक्षयं भवेदिति B. ** पैतामहं शुभमिति B. †† एषः श्लोकः A, E, F and H पुस्तकेषु नास्ति। ‡‡ कर्म्मविन्दुमिति F.

तत्र स्नात्वा नरो राजन्दुर्गतिं वै* न पश्यति ॥
अप्सरेशं ततो गच्छेत्स्नानं तत्र समाचरेत् ।
क्रीड़ते नाकलोकस्थो ह्यप्सरोभिः स मोदते ॥
ततो गच्छेत राजेन्द्र भारभूतिमनुत्तमम्† ।
उपोषितो यजेतेशं‡ रुद्रलोके महीयते ।
अस्मिंस्तीर्थे मृतो राजन् गाणपत्यमवाप्नुयात् ॥
कार्त्तिके मासि देवेशमर्च्चयेत्पार्व्वतीपतिम् ।
अश्वमेधाद्दशगुणं प्रवदन्ति मनीषिणः ॥
वृषभं यः प्रयच्छेत§ तत्र कुन्देन्दुसप्रभम्¶ ।
वृषयुक्तेन यानेन रुद्रलोकं स गच्छति ॥
एतत्तीर्थं समासाद्य यस्तु प्राणान् परित्यजेत् ।
सर्व्वपापविनिर्मुक्तो‖ रुद्रलोकं स गच्छति ॥
जलप्रवेशं यः कुर्य्यात्तस्मिंस्तीर्थे नराधिप ।
हंसयुक्तेन यानेन स्वर्गलोकं स गच्छति ॥
एरण्ड्या नर्म्मदायास्तु सङ्गमं लोकविश्रुतम् ।
तच्च तीर्थं महापुण्यं सर्व्वपापप्रणाशनम् ॥
उपवासकृतो** भूत्वा नित्यं व्रतपरायणः ।

---

* ह्रीति B. † भावभूतिमनुत्तममिति B and G. भारभूरिमनुत्तममिति E. भारभूतिजमुत्तममिति F. ‡ उपोषितोऽर्च्चयित्वेशमिति B. उपोषितोऽर्च्चयेद्देनमिति F. § प्रयच्छेत्तु इति B. ¶ सन्निभमिति B. सुप्रभमिति F. ‖ सर्व्वपापविमुक्तात्मेति B. सर्व्वपापविशुद्धात्मा इति F. ** उपवासपरः इति B. उपवासरत इति F. उपवासव्रत इति E and H.

तत्र स्नात्वा तु राजेन्द्र मुच्यते ब्रह्महत्यया॥
ततो गच्छेत राजेन्द्र नर्म्मदोदधिसङ्गमम्।
जमदग्निमिति* ख्यातं सिद्धो यत्र जनार्द्दनः॥
तत्र स्नात्वा नरो राजन्नर्म्मदोदधिसङ्गमे।
त्रिगुणञ्चाश्वमेधस्य फलम्प्राप्नोति मानवः॥
ततो गच्छेत राजेन्द्र पिङ्गलेश्वरमुत्तमम्† ।
तत्र स्नात्वा नरो राजन् ब्रह्मलोके‡ महीयते॥
तत्रोपवासं यः कृत्वा§ पश्येत विमलेश्वरम्।
सप्तजन्मकृतं पापं हित्वा¶ याति शिवालयम्॥
ततो गच्छेत राजेन्द्र अलितीर्थ‖मनुत्तमम्।
उपोष्य रजनीमेकां नियतो नियताशनः।
अस्य तीर्थस्य माहात्म्यान्मुच्यते ब्रह्महत्यया॥
एतानि तव सङ्क्षेपात्प्राधान्यात्कथितानि च**।
न शक्या विस्तराद्वक्तुं संख्या तीर्थेषु पाण्डव॥
एषा पवित्रा विपुला नदी त्रैलोक्यविश्रुता††।
नर्म्मदा सरितां श्रेष्ठा महादेवस्य वल्लभा॥
मनसा संस्मरेद्यस्तु नर्म्मदां वै युधिष्ठिर।

---

* जमदग्निरितीति B and F. † विमलेश्वरमुत्तममिति B. ‡ रुद्रलोके इति B and F. § कुर्य्यादिति B and F. ¶ भित्त्वेति B. ‖ अलिकातीर्थमुत्तममिति E. अलकातीर्थमुत्तममिति F. ** तु इति B, E and H. ब्रह्मणः कथितानि तु इति F. †† एतत्पादद्वयं B पुस्तके न दृश्यते।

चान्द्रायणशतं* साग्रं लभते नात्र संशयः॥
अश्रद्धधानाः पुरुषा नास्तिक्यं घोरमाश्रिताः।
पतन्ति नरके† घोरे इत्याह परमेश्वरः॥
नर्म्मदां सेवते नित्यं स्वयं देवो महेश्वरः।
तेन पुण्या नदी ज्ञेया ब्रह्महत्यापहारिणी॥

इति श्रीकूर्म्मपुराणे उपविभागे नर्म्मदामाहात्म्ये
एकचत्वारिंशोऽध्यायः।

द्विचत्वारिंशोऽध्यायः।

सूत उवाच*।

इदं त्रैलोक्यविख्यातं तीर्थं नैमिषमुत्तमम्।
महादेवप्रियतरं† महापातकनाशनम्॥
महादेवं‡ दिदृक्षूणामृषीणां परमेष्ठिना।
ब्रह्मणा निर्म्मितं स्थानं तपस्तप्तुं द्विजोत्तमाः॥
मरीचयो§ऽत्रयो विप्रा वसिष्ठाः क्रतवस्तथा¶।

---

* जीववर्षशतमिति B. † निरये इति B and F.

---

* एष पाठः A पुस्तके न दृश्यते। † प्रियकरमिति B. ‡ पुरा देवमिति B.
§ मारीचयोऽथ ये विप्रा इति E and H. ¶ वासिष्ठा ध्रुवतस्तथा इति E and H.

भृगवोऽङ्गिरसः पूर्व्वं ब्रह्माणं कमलोद्भवम् ।
समेत्य सर्व्ववरदं चतुर्म्मूर्त्तिं चतुर्म्मुखम् ।
पृच्छन्ति प्रणिपत्यैनं* विश्वकर्म्माणमव्ययम्† ॥

षट्कुलीया ऊचुः ।

भगवन्देवमीशानं तमेवैकं कपर्द्दिनम् ।
केनोपायेन पश्यामो ब्रूहि देव नमस्तव ॥

ब्रह्मोवाच ।

सत्रं सहस्रमासध्वं‡ वाङ्मनोदोषवर्ज्जिताः ।
देशञ्च वः प्रवक्ष्यामि यस्मिन्देशे चरिष्यथ ॥
मुक्त्वा मनोमयं चक्रं संस्पृष्ट्वा§ तानुवाच ह ।
क्षिप्तमेतन्मया चक्रमनुव्रजत मा चिरम् ।
यत्रास्य नेमिः शीर्य्येत स देशस्तपसः शुभः¶ ॥
ततो मुमोच तच्चक्रं ते च तत्समनुव्रजन्‖ ॥
तस्य वै व्रजतः क्षिप्रं यत्र नेमिरशीर्य्यत ।
नैमिषं तत् स्मृतं नाम्ना पुण्यं सर्व्वत्र पूजितम् ॥
सिद्धचारणसम्पूर्णं** यक्षगन्धर्व्वसेवितम् ।
स्थानं भगवतः शम्भोरेतन्नैमिषमुत्तमम् ॥
अत्र देवाः सगन्धर्व्वाः सयक्षोरगराक्षसाः ।

---

* प्रणयाच्चैनमिति A, E and H. † विश्वकर्म्माणमच्युतमिति B. ‡ सत्रं महत्समासध्वमिति B and F. § संस्पृश्य इति साधु । ¶ स देशः पुरुषर्षभाः इति B. ‖ तेन तन्मनसोऽभवन्निति F. समनुव्रजन्नित्यत्र समन्वव्रजन्निति साधु । अड़ागमाभावः आर्षः । ** सङ्कीर्णमिति B and F.

तपस्तप्त्वा पुरा देवा लेभिरे प्रवरान्वरान्* ॥
इमं देशं समाश्रित्य† षट्कुलीयाः समाहिताः ।
सत्रेणाराध्य देवेशं दृष्टवन्तो महेश्वरम् ॥
अत्र दानं‡ तपस्तप्तं श्राद्धयागादिकं§ञ्च यत् ।
एकैकं नाशयेत्पापं¶ सप्तजन्मकृतं तथा ॥
अत्र पूर्व्वं स भगवानृषीणां सत्रमासताम्‖ ।
स वै प्रोवाच ब्रह्माण्डं पुराणं ब्रह्मभावितम् ॥
अत्र देवो महादेवो रुद्राण्या किल विश्वदृक्** ।
रमतेऽद्यापि भगवान् प्रमथैः परिवारितः ॥
अत्र प्राणान् परित्यज्य नियमेन द्विजातयः ।
ब्रह्मलोकं गमिष्यन्ति यत्र गत्वा न जायते ॥
अन्यच्च तीर्थप्रवरं जाप्येश्वरमिति श्रुतम्†† ।
जजाप रुद्रमनिशं यथा‡‡ नन्दी महागणः ॥
प्रीतस्तस्य महादेवो देव्या सह पिनाकधृक् ।
ददावात्म§§समानत्वं मृत्युवञ्चनमेव च¶¶ ॥
अभूदृषिः स धर्म्मात्मा‖‖ शिलादो नाम धर्म्मवित् ।
आराधयन्महादेवं प्रसादार्थं वृषध्वजम्*** ॥

---

* प्रभवान् वरानिति F. † समागम्य इति B. ‡ अन्नदानमिति B. § श्राद्धं जप्यादिकमिति E, F and H. ¶ पावयेत्पापमिति B. ‖ नित्यमासतामिति F. ** विश्वधृगिति B. and E. विश्वकृदिति F. †† जप्येश्वरमनुत्तममिति B. जप्येश्वरमिति श्रुतमिति F. ‡‡ यत्रेति B and F. §§ दत्त्वा चात्मेति B. ¶¶ तु इति B. ‖‖ सर्व्वभूतात्मा इति B. सुधर्म्मात्मा इति E and F. *** पुत्रार्थं वृषभध्वजमिति B and F.

तस्य वर्षसहस्रान्ते तप्यमानस्य विश्वधृक्* ।
शर्व्वः सोमो गणवृतो वरदोऽस्मीत्यभाषत ॥
स वव्रे वरमीशानं वरेण्यं गिरिजापतिम् ।
अयोनिजं मृत्युहीनं याचे† पुत्त्रं त्वया समम् ॥
तथास्त्वित्याह भगवान्देव्या सह महेश्वरः ।
पश्यतस्तस्य विप्रर्षेरन्तर्द्धानं गतो हरः ॥
ततो युयोज‡ तां§ भूमिं शिलादो धर्म्मवित्तमः ।
चकर्ष लाङ्गलेनोर्व्वीं भित्वाहृश्यत शोभनः ॥
संवर्त्तकोऽनलप्रख्यः कुमारः प्रहसन्निव ।
रूपलावण्यसम्पन्नस्तेजसा भासयन्दिशः ॥
कुमारतुल्योऽप्रतिमो मेघगम्भीरया गिरा ।
शिलाद तात तातेति प्राह नन्दी पुनः पुनः ॥
तं दृष्ट्वा नन्दनं¶ जातं शिलादः परिषस्वजे ।
मुनीनां‖ दर्शयामास तत्राश्रमनिवासिनाम्** ॥
जातकर्म्मादिकाः सर्व्वाः क्रियास्तस्य चकार ह ।
उपनीय यथाशास्त्रं वेदमध्यापयत् स्वयम्†† ॥
अधीतवेदो भगवान्नन्दी मतिमनुत्तमाम् ।
चक्रे महेश्वरं दृष्ट्वा जेष्ये मृत्युमिव‡‡ प्रभुम् ॥

---

* विश्वकृदिति B and F. † देहीति B. ‡ ययिचुरिति B and F. § स्वामिति B and F. ¶ दृष्टानन्दितमिति B. नन्दिनमिति F. ‖ मुनिभ्यः इति B and F. ** ये तदाश्रयवासिनः इति B and F. †† सुतमिति B. ‡‡ मृत्युमितीति B. जन्ने मृत्युमिति F.

स गत्वा सागरं पुण्य*मेकाग्रः श्रद्धयान्वितः ।
जजाप रुद्रमनिशं महेशासक्तमानसः ॥
तस्य कोट्याञ्च पूर्णायां शङ्करो भक्तवत्सलः† ।
आगतः सर्व्वसगणो‡ वरदोऽस्मीत्यभाषत§ ॥
स वव्रे पुनरेवेशं¶ जपेयं कोटिमीश्वरम् ।
भवदाहं‖ महादेवं देहीति परमेश्वरम्** ॥
एवमस्त्विति सम्प्रोच्य देवोऽप्यन्तरधीयत ।
जजाप कोटिं भगवान् भूयस्तद्गतमानसः ॥
द्वितीयायाञ्च कोट्यां वै पूर्णायाञ्च†† वृषध्वजः ।
आगत्य वरदोऽस्मीति प्राह भूतगणैर्वृतः ॥
तृतीयाञ्जप्तुमिच्छामि कोटिं भूयोऽपि शङ्कर ।
तथास्त्वित्याह विश्वात्मा देव्या चान्तरधीयत ॥
कोटित्रयेऽथ सम्पूर्णे देवः प्रीतमना भृशम् ।
आगत्य वरदोऽस्मीति प्राह भूतगणैर्वृतः ॥
जपेयं कोटिमन्यां वै भूयोऽपि तव तेजसा ।
इत्युक्ते भगवानाह न जप्तव्यं त्वया पुनः ॥
अमरो जरया त्यक्तो मम पार्श्वे गतः‡‡ सदा ।
महागणपतिर्द्देव्याः पुत्त्रो भव महेश्वरः ॥

---

* सरितं पुण्यामिति B and F. † एतत्पादद्वयं B पुस्तके नास्ति । ‡ आगत्य स्वात्मनगणः इति B. आगत्य शम्भुः सगण इति F. § वरदोऽस्मीत्युवाच हेति B. ¶ पुनरेवाहमिति B. ‖ तावदायुरिति B and F. ** वरमीश्वरेति B वरमुत्तममिति F. †† सम्पूर्णायामिति B and F. ‡‡ पार्श्वगतः इति B, F and H.

योगेश्वरो* महायोगी† गणानामीश्वरेश्वरः।
सर्व्वलोकाधिपः श्रीमान् सर्व्वयज्ञमयो हितः‡॥
ज्ञानन्तन्नामकं दिव्यं हस्तामलकसंज्ञिकम्§।
आभूतसंप्लवस्थायी ततो यास्यसि तत्पदम्॥
एतदुक्त्वा¶ महादेवो गणानाहूय शङ्करः।
अभिषेकेण युक्तेन नन्दीश्वरमयोजयत्॥
उद्वाहयामास च तं स्वयमेव पिनाकधृक्।
मरुताञ्च शुभाङ्गन्यां स्वयमेति च विश्रुताम्‖॥
एतज्जप्येश्वरं स्थानं देवदेवस्य शूलिनः।
यत्र तत्र मृतो मर्त्त्यो रुद्रलोके महीयते॥

इति श्रीकूर्म्मपुराणे उपविभागे जप्येश्वरमाहात्म्ये
द्विचत्वारिंशोऽध्यायः।

---

* योगीश्वरः इति B † योगनेत्रः इति B. योगत इति F. ‡ सर्व्वज्ञो मद्दरान्वितः इति B. सर्व्वज्ञो मद्गबलान्वित इति F. § ज्ञानन्तु मामकं दिव्यं हस्तामलकवत्तक इति B and F. ¶ एवमुक्त्वा इति B. ‖ विश्रुतामिति B, F and H.

त्रिचत्वारिंशोऽध्यायः ।

सूत उवाच ।*

अन्यच्च तीर्थप्रवरं जप्येश्वरसमीपतः† ।
नाम्ना पञ्चनदं पुण्यं सर्व्वपापप्रणाशनम् ॥
त्रिरात्रमुषितस्तत्र‡ पूजयित्वा महेश्वरम् ।
सर्व्वपापविशुद्धात्मा रुद्रलोके महीयते ॥§
अन्यच्च तीर्थप्रवरं शक्रस्यामिततेजसः¶ ।
महाभैरवमित्युक्तं|| महापातकनाशनम् ॥
तीर्थानाञ्च परं तीर्थं वितस्ता परमा नदी ।
सर्व्वपापहरा पुण्या स्वयमेव गिरीन्द्रजा ॥
तीर्थं पञ्चतपो नाम शम्भोरमिततेजसः ।**
यत्र देवाधिदेवेन शक्रार्थे†† पूजितो भवः ॥
पिण्डदानादिकं तत्र प्रेत्यानन्दसुखप्रदम्‡‡ ।
मृतस्तत्राथ नियमाद्ब्रह्मलोके§§ महीयते ॥
कायावरोहणं नाम¶¶ महादेवालयं शुभम् ।
यत्र माहेश्वरा धर्म्मा मुनिभिः सम्प्रवर्त्तिताः|||| ॥

---

* एष पाठः A H पुस्तकयोर्नास्ति । † जप्येश्वरमनुत्तममिति B. ‡ त्रिरात्रो-पोषितस्तत्रेति B. § श्लोकद्वयं F पुस्तके नास्ति । ¶ शङ्करस्यामितौजसः इति B. || महाभैरवमित्युक्तमित्यादि श्लोकद्वयं A पुस्तके नास्ति । महाभारतमित्युक्तमिति F. ** श्लोकार्द्धचतुष्टयं E H पुस्तकयोर्नास्ति । †† चक्रार्थमिति B. पूजितोहर इति F. ‡‡ प्रेत्यानन्तफलप्रदमिति B, E and F. §§ मृतस्तत्रापि नियम्य ब्रह्मलोके इति B. ¶¶ कामेति B. |||| सम्प्रकीर्त्तिताः इति B.

श्राद्धं दानं तपो होम उपवासस्तथाक्षयः* ।
परित्यजति यः प्राणान् रुद्रलोकं स गच्छति ॥
अन्यच्च तीर्थप्रवरं कन्यातीर्थमनुत्तमम्† ।
तत्र गत्वा त्यजेत्प्राणाँल्लोकान् प्राप्नोति‡ शाश्वतान् ॥
जामदग्न्यस्य च शुभं रामस्याक्लिष्टकर्म्मणः ।
तत्र स्नात्वा तीर्थवरे गोसहस्रफलं लभेत् ॥
महाकालमिति ख्यातं तीर्थं लोकेषु विश्रुतम्§ ।
गत्वा प्राणान् परित्यज्य गाणपत्यमवाप्नुयात् ॥
गुह्याद्गुह्यतमं तीर्थं नकुलीश्वरमुत्तमम् ।
तत्र सन्निहितः श्रीमान् भगवान्नकुलीश्वरः ॥
हिमवच्छिखरे रम्ये गङ्गाद्वारे सुशोभने¶ ।
देव्या सह महादेवो नित्यं शिष्यैश्च संवृतः‖ ॥
तत्र स्नात्वा महादेवं पूजयित्वा वृषध्वजम् ।
सर्व्वपापैर्विशुद्धेत्र** मृतस्तज्ज्ञान††माप्नुयात् ॥
अन्यच्च देवदेवस्य स्थानं पुण्यतमं शुभम् ।
भीमेश्वरमिति ख्यातं गत्वा मुञ्चति पातकम् ॥
तथान्यच्चण्डवेगायाः सम्भेदः पापनाशनः ।
तत्र स्नात्वा च पीत्वा च मुच्यते ब्रह्महत्यया ॥

---

* तथाक्षयमिति A. † कन्यातीर्थमिति श्रुतमिति B. ‡ लोकानाप्नोति इति E. § त्रैलोक्यविश्रुतमिति B. ¶ गङ्गाद्वारं सुशोभनमिति A, E and H. ‖ मानवः इति A, E and H. संवृत इति F. ** विमुच्येतेति B and F. †† मृतस्तु ज्ञानमिति B and F.

सर्व्वेषामपि चैतेषां तीर्थानां परमा पुरी।
नाम्ना वाराणसी दिव्या कोटिकोट्ययुताधिका॥
तस्याः पुरस्तान्माहात्म्यं भाषितं वो मया त्विह।
नान्यत्र लभते मुक्तिं योगेनाप्येकजन्मना॥
एते प्राधान्यतः प्रोक्ता देशाः पापहरा नृणाम्।
गत्वा सङ्क्षालयेत्पापं जन्मान्तरशतैरपि* ॥
यः स्वधर्म्मान् परित्यज्य तीर्थसेवां करोति हि।
न तस्य फलते† तीर्थमिह लोके परत्र च॥
प्रायश्चित्ती च विधुर‡स्तथा यायावरो§ गृही।
प्रकुर्य्यात्तीर्थसंसेवां यश्चान्यस्तादृशो जनः¶॥
सहाग्निर्वा सपत्नीको गच्छेत्तीर्थानि यत्नतः।
सर्व्वपापविनिर्मुक्तो यथोक्तां गतिमाप्नुयात्॥
ऋणानि त्रीण्यपाकुर्य्यात्कुर्व्वन्वा तीर्थसेवनम्‖।
विधाय वृत्तिं पुत्त्राणां भार्य्यां तेषु निधाय च॥
प्रायश्चित्तप्रसङ्गेन तीर्थमाहात्म्यमीरितम्।
यः पठेच्छृणुयाद्वापि सर्व्वपापैः प्रमुच्यते**॥

इति श्रीकूर्म्मपुराणे उपविभागे तीर्थमाहात्म्यं नाम त्रिचत्वारिंशोऽध्यायः।

---

* जन्मान्तरशतैः कृतमिति B. एतत्पादद्वयं F पुस्तके नास्ति। † फलदमिति B and F. ‡ विबुध इति B. § पापचरः इति B. जायावर इति F. ¶ ये चान्ये तादृशा जनाः इति B, E, F and H. ‖ ऋणानि त्रीण्यपाकृत्य कुर्य्यादिति B. ऋणानि त्रीण्यपाहृत्य कुर्य्याद्वा इति F. ** मुच्यते सर्व्वपातकैरिति B and F.

चतुश्चत्वारिंशोऽध्यायः ।

सूत उवाच ।

एतदाकर्ण्य विज्ञानं नारायणमुखेरितम् ।
कूर्म्मरूपधरं देवं पप्रच्छुर्मुनयः प्रभुम् ॥

मुनय ऊचुः ।

कथितो भवता धर्म्मो* मोक्षज्ञानं सविस्तरम् ।
लोकानां सर्गविस्तारो वंशो मन्वन्तराणि च ॥
इदानीं देवदेवेश प्रलयं वक्तुमर्हसि† ।
भूतानां भूतभव्येश यथापूर्व्वं त्वयोदितम् ॥

सूत उवाच ।

श्रुत्वा तेषां तदा वाक्यं भगवान् कूर्म्मरूपधृक् ।
व्याजहार महायोगी भूतानां प्रतिसञ्चरम्‡ ॥

कूर्म्म उवाच ।

नित्यो नैमित्तिकश्चैव प्राकृतोऽत्यन्तिकस्तथा§ ।
चतुर्द्धायं पुराणेऽस्मिन् प्रोच्यते प्रतिसञ्चरः ॥
योऽयं सन्दृश्यते नित्यं लोके भूतक्षयस्त्विह ।
नित्यः सङ्कीर्त्यते नाम्ना मुनिभिः प्रतिसञ्चरः ॥
ब्राह्मनैमित्तिको नाम कल्पान्ते यो भविष्यति ।

---

* कथिता भवता धर्म्माः इति B and F. † प्रतिसर्गमिदानीं नो वक्तुमर्हसि माधव इति B. इदानीं प्रतिसर्गान्वा वक्तुमर्हसि माधवेति F. ‡ प्रतिसञ्चरम्—आत्मनि पुनःसंग्रहम् प्रतिसंहारमित्यर्थः। § प्राकृतात्यन्तिको मतः इति B.

त्रैलोक्यस्यास्य कथितः प्रतिसर्गो मनीषिभिः ॥
महदाद्यं विशेषान्तं यदा संयाति सङ्क्षयम् ।
प्राकृतः प्रतिसर्गोऽयं प्रोच्यते कालचिन्तकैः ॥
ज्ञानादात्यन्तिकः प्रोक्तो योगिनः परमात्मनि ।
प्रलयः प्रतिसर्गोऽयं कालचिन्तापरैर्द्विजैः ॥
आत्यन्तिकस्तु* कथितः प्रलयो ज्ञानसाधनः† ।
नैमित्तिकमिदानीं वः कथयिष्ये‡ समासतः ॥
चतुर्व्यूहसहस्रान्ते§ सम्प्राप्ते प्रतिसञ्चरे ।
स्वात्मसंस्थाः प्रजाः कर्त्तुम्प्रतिपेदे प्रजापतिः ॥
ततोऽभवत्त्वनावृष्टिस्तीव्रा सा शतवार्षिकी ।
भूतक्षयकरी घोरा सर्व्वभूतक्षयङ्करी ॥
ततो यान्यल्पसाराणि सत्त्वानि पृथिवीपते ।
तानि चाग्रे प्रलीयन्ते भूमित्वमुपयान्ति च ॥
सप्तरश्मिरथो भूत्वा समुत्तिष्ठन्दिवाकरः ।
असह्यरश्मिर्भवति पिबन्नम्भो गभस्तिभिः ॥
तस्य ते रश्मयः सप्त पिबन्त्यम्बु महार्णवे ।
तेनाहारेण ता दीप्ता सप्तसूर्य्या भवन्त्युत¶ ॥
ततस्ते रश्मयः सप्त शोषयित्वा चतुर्द्दिशम्‖ ।
चतुर्लोकमिमं** सर्व्वं दहन्ति शिखिनो यथा ॥

---

* आत्यन्तिकश्चेति B. † लयसाधनः इति B. ‡ कीर्त्तयिष्ये इति B. § चतुर्युगसहस्रान्ते इति B and F. ¶ भवन्ति हि इति B and F. ‖ सूर्य्या भूत्वा चतुर्द्दिशेति B. ** चातुर्ल्लोकमिममिति A and F.

व्याप्नुवन्तश्च ते दीप्ता* ऊर्द्ध्वञ्चाधः स्वरश्मिभिः† ।
दीप्यन्ते भास्कराः सप्त युगान्ताग्निप्रदीपिताः‡ ॥
ते सूर्य्या वारिणा दीप्ता बहुसाहस्ररश्मयः ।
खं समावृत्य तिष्ठन्ति प्रदहन्तो§ वसुन्धराम् ॥
ततस्तेषां प्रतापेन दह्यमाना वसुन्धरा ।
साद्रि¶नद्यर्णवद्वीपा निःस्नेहा सम्प्रपद्यते‖ ॥
दीप्ताभिः सन्तताभिश्च रश्मिभिर्वै** समन्ततः ।
अधश्चोर्द्ध्वञ्च लग्नाभिस्तिर्य्यक् चैव समावृतम्†† ॥
सूर्य्याग्निना प्रसृष्टानां‡‡ संसृष्टानां परस्परम् ।
एकत्वमुपयातानां§§मेकज्वालं भवत्युत ॥
सर्व्वलोकप्रणाशश्च सोऽग्निर्भूत्वा तु मण्डली ।
चतुर्लोकमिमं सर्व्वं निर्द्दहत्याशु तेजसा¶¶ ॥
ततः प्रलीने सर्व्वस्मिञ्जङ्गमे स्थावरे तथा ।
निर्वृक्षा निस्तृणा भूमिः कूर्म्मपृष्ठा प्रकाशते ॥
अम्बरीष इवाभाति‖‖ सर्व्वमापूरितं जगत् ।
सर्व्वमेव तदर्च्चिर्भि*** पूर्णं जाज्वल्यते पुनः ॥

---

* तीव्रा इति B and F. † च रश्मिभिरिति B and F. ‡ प्रतापिन इति B. प्रतापिता इति E, G and H. § निर्दहन्त इति B and F. प्रलापिता इति F. ¶ यातीति A. ‖ समपद्यतेति B and F. ** मरीचिभिः प्रदीप्ताभिः सन्तताभिरिति B and F. †† एतत्पादद्वयं B पुस्तके न दृश्यते। ‡‡ प्रतप्तानामिति B. सूर्य्याग्नीनां प्रवृत्तानामिति F. §§ एकत्वमुपजातानामिति B and F. ¶¶ निर्दहत्यात्मतेजसेति B. निहन्त्याशु स्वतेजसा इति F. ‖‖ अम्बरीषमिवाभातीति B and F. *** सर्व्वमेतत्तदर्च्चिर्भिरिति B and F.

पाताले यानि सत्त्वानि* महोदधिगतानि च।
ततस्तानि† प्रलीयन्ते भूमित्वमुपयान्ति च‡॥
द्वीपांश्च पर्व्वतांश्चैव वर्षाण्यथ महोदधीन्।
तान् सर्व्वान् भस्मसाच्चक्रे सप्तात्मा पावकः प्रभुः॥
समुद्रेभ्यो नदीभ्यश्च आपः शुष्काश्च सर्व्वशः।
पिवन्नपः समिद्धोऽग्निः पृथिवीमाश्रितो ज्वलन्॥
ततः संवर्त्तकः शैलानतिक्रम्य महांस्तथा।
लोकान्दहति§ दीप्तात्मा मारुतेयो विजृम्भितः¶॥
स दग्ध्वा पृथिवीं देवो रसातलमशोभयत्‖।
अधस्तात्पृथिवीं दग्ध्वा दिवमूर्द्ध्वं दहिष्यति**॥
योजनानां शतानीह सहस्राण्ययुतानि च।
उत्तिष्ठन्ति शिखास्तस्य वह्नेः संवर्त्तकस्य तु††॥
गन्धर्व्वांश्च पिशाचांश्च सयक्षोरगराक्षसान्।
तदा दहत्यसौ दीप्तः कालरुद्रप्रणोदितः‡‡॥
भूर्लोकञ्च भुवर्लोकं महर्ल्लोकं तथैव च§§।
दहेदशेषङ्कालाग्निः कालाविष्टतनुः¶¶ स्वयम्॥
व्याप्तेष्वेतेषु‖‖ लोकेषु तिर्य्यगूर्द्ध्वमथाग्निना।

---

* तीर्थानीति B. † तत्र तानीति B. ‡ वै इति B. अतः परं श्लोकद्वयं B पुस्तके नास्ति। § नाकान्दहतीति B. ¶ रुद्रतेजोविजृम्भित इति B and F. ‖ अशोषयदिति F and H. ** धक्ष्यति। इडागम आर्षः। †† हीति B. तु इति F and H. ‡‡ प्रचोदित इति B and F. §§ स्वर्लोकञ्च तथा परमिति B. स्वर्लोकञ्च तथा मह इति F. ¶¶ कालो विश्वतनुरिति B. ‖‖ व्याप्तेषु तेषु इति B and F.

तत्तेजः समनुप्राप्य कृत्स्नं जगदिदं शनैः।
अतो गूढ़मिदं* सर्व्वं तदेवैकम्प्रकाशते† ॥
ततो गजकुलाकारास्तड़िद्भिः‡ समलङ्कृताः।
उत्तिष्ठन्ति तदा व्योम्नि घोराः संवर्त्तका घनाः ॥
केचिन्नीलोत्पलश्यामाः केचित्कुमुदसन्निभाः।
धूम्रवर्णा§स्तथा केचित्केचित्पीताः पयोधराः ॥
केचिद्रासभवर्णास्तु लाक्षारसनिभाः परे¶।
शङ्खकुन्दनिभाश्चान्ये जात्यञ्जननिभास्तथा‖ ॥
मनःशिलाभाश्च परे** कपोतसदृशाः परे।
इन्द्रगोपनिभाः केचिद्धरितालनिभास्तथा††।
इन्द्रचापनिभाः‡‡ केचिदुत्तिष्ठन्ति घना दिवि ॥
केचित्पर्व्वतसङ्काशाः केचिद्गजकुलोपमाः।
कूटाङ्गार§§निभाश्चान्ये केचिन्मीनकुलोद्वहाः ॥
बहुरूपा घोररूपा घोरस्वरनिनादिनः।
तदा जलधराः सर्व्वं पूरयन्ति नभस्तलम् ॥
ततस्ते जलदा घोरा राविणो भास्करात्मजाः।

---

* अथोगूढ़मिति B. अम्बरीकनिभमिति F. † तदा चैकम्प्रकाशयेदिति B. ‡ गजकुलोन्नादाः स्तनितैः इति B. गजकुलोन्मादास्तड़िद्भिरिति F. § धूमवर्णा इति E, F and H. ¶ तथा इति B. ‖ जात्याञ्जननिभाः परे इति B. ** मनःशिलाभास्त्वन्ये चेति B. मनःशिलाभास्त्वपरे इति F. †† इदं पादद्वयं F पुस्तके नास्ति। इतः पूर्व्वमिदमधिकं F पुस्तके दृश्यते—केचिद्दुद्रावणवर्णाभास्तथान्ये चौरसन्निभाः। तथा कर्पूरवर्णाश्च भिन्नाञ्जननिभास्तथा ॥ ‡‡ काकाण्डकनिभाः इति B. §§ कूटागारेति B and F.

सप्तधा संहतात्मानं तमग्निं शमयेत्पुनः* ॥
ततस्ते जलदा वर्षं मुञ्चन्तीह महौघवत् ।
सुघोरमशिवं वर्षं नाशयन्ति च† पावकम् ॥
अतिवृद्ध‡स्तदात्यर्थमम्भसा पूर्य्यते जगत् ।
अद्भिस्तेऽम्भोऽभिभूतत्वात्तदग्निः§ प्रविशत्यपः ॥
नष्टे चाग्नौ वर्षशतैः पयोदाः क्षयसम्भवाः¶ ।
प्लावयन्तो जगत्सर्व्वं‖ महाजलपरिस्रवैः ॥
धाराभिः पूरयन्तीदं नोद्यमानाः** स्वयम्भुवा ।
अत्यन्तसलिलौघास्तु वेला इव महोदधेः†† ॥
साद्रिद्वीपा‡‡ ततः पृथ्वी जलैः सञ्छाद्यते शनैः ।
आदित्यरश्मिभिः पीतं जलमभ्रेषु तिष्ठति ।
पुनः पतति तद्भूमौ पूर्य्यन्ते तेन चार्णवाः ॥
ततः समुद्राः स्वां वेलामतिक्रान्तास्तु§§ कृत्स्नशः ।
पर्व्वताश्च विलीयन्ते मही चाप्सु निमज्जति ॥
तस्मिन्नेकार्णवे घोरे नष्टे स्थावरजङ्गमे ।
योगनिद्रां समास्थाय शेते देवः प्रजापतिः¶¶ ॥
चतुर्युगसहस्रान्तं कल्पमाहुर्म्मनीषिणः‖‖ ।

---

* ततः इति B. एकवचनमार्षम् । शमयन्त्युत इति F. † नेति A and F. ‡ प्रवृद्धैस्तैरिति B. प्रवृत्तैस्तैरिति F. § तेजोऽभिभूतात्मा तदाग्निरिति B. अग्नितेजोऽभिभूतत्वात्तदाग्निः प्रविशत्यपः इति F. ¶ पक्षसम्भवा इति B. ‖ प्लावयन्तोऽथ भुवनमिति B. ** मेघमाला इति B. †† अत्यन्तसलिलौघैश्च परिप्लाव्य दिशो दश इति B. ‡‡ साब्धिद्वीपा इति B. §§ क्रम्याशु इति E and H. ¶¶ जगत्पतिरिति B. ‖‖ महर्षय इति B.

वाराहो वर्त्तते कल्पो यस्य विस्तर ईरितः ॥
असंख्यातास्तथा* कल्पा ब्रह्मविष्णुशिवात्मकाः।
कथिता हि पुराणेषु मुनिभिः कालचिन्तकैः ॥
सात्विकेष्वथ कल्पेषु माहात्म्यमधिकं हरेः।
तामसेषु हरस्योक्तं† राजसेषु प्रजापतेः ॥
योऽयं प्रवर्त्तते कल्पो वाराहः सात्विको मतः‡।
अन्ये च सात्विकाः कल्पा मम तेषु परिग्रहः ॥
ध्यानं तपस्तथा ज्ञानं लब्ध्वा ते योगिनः परम्§।
आराध्य तञ्च गिरिशं यान्ति तत्परमम्पदम् ॥
सोऽहन्तत्त्वं¶ समास्थाय मायी मायामयां‖ स्वयम्।
एकार्णवे जगत्यस्मिन्योगनिद्रां व्रजामि तु ॥
मां पश्यन्ति महात्मानः सुप्तकाले** महर्षयः।
जनलोके वर्त्तमानास्तापसा†† योगचक्षुषा ॥
अहं पुराणः पुरुषो भूर्भुवःप्रभवो विभुः।
सहस्रचरणः श्रीमान् सहस्राक्षः‡‡ सहस्रपात् ॥
मन्त्रोऽहं ब्राह्मणाः§§ गावः कुशोऽथ समिधो ह्यहम्।

---

* तदेति B. † शिवस्योक्तमिति B. ‡ एतत्पादद्वयं B पुस्तके नास्ति। § तेष्वेव योगिनः इति B. तेषु च योगिन इति F. ¶ सत्त्वमिति B, F and G. ‖ मायामयीमिति H. मायामयमिति F. ** सुप्तकालमिति G. मां पश्यन्ति महात्मानः सुप्तं कालविपर्य्यये इति F. †† तपसेति B and F. ‡‡ सहस्रांशुरिति B. सहस्रांशुः सहस्रदृगिति F. §§ मन्त्रोऽग्निर्ब्राह्मणः इति B. मैत्राग्निब्राह्मणा इति F.

प्रोक्षणीयं स्रुवश्चैव सोमो व्रत*मथास्म्यहम् ॥
संवर्त्तको महानात्मा† पवित्रं परमं यशः ।
मेधाप्यहं‡ प्रभुर्गोप्ता गोपतिर्ब्राह्मणो मुखम् ॥
अनन्तस्तारको योगी गतिर्गतिमतां वरः ।
हंसः प्राणोऽथ कपिलो विश्वमूर्त्तिः सनातनः ॥
क्षेत्रज्ञः प्रकृतिः कालो जगद्बीजमथामृतम् ।
माता पिता महादेवो§ मत्तो ह्यन्यो न विद्यते ॥
आदित्यवर्णो भुवनस्य गोप्ता
नारायणः पुरुषो योगमूर्त्तिः ।
तं पश्यन्ते¶ यतयो योगनिष्ठा
ज्ञात्वात्मानं मम तत्त्वं व्रजन्ति|| ॥

इति श्रीकूर्म्मपुराणे उपविभागे व्यासगीतासु
चतुश्चत्वारिंशोऽध्यायः ।

---

* प्रोक्षणी च स्रुवश्चैव सोमो घृतमिति B and F. † महात्माहमिति F and G. ‡ वेदवेद्यमिति B and F. § महादेव्यः इति F. ¶ पश्यन्ते इति आर्षमात्मनेपदम् । मां पश्यन्तीति B and F. || ज्ञात्वात्मानममृतत्वं व्रजन्तीति B. अमृतं त्वां व्रजन्ति इति F.

पञ्चचत्वारिंशोऽध्यायः ।

कूर्म्म उवाच ।

अतः परं प्रवक्ष्यामि प्रतिसर्गमनुत्तमम् ।
प्राकृतं तत्समासेन* शृणुध्वङ्गदतो मम ॥
गते परार्द्धद्वितये काले लोकप्रकालनः ।
कालाग्निर्भस्मसात्कर्त्तुं चरते चाखिलं जगत्† ॥
स्वात्मन्यात्मानमावेश्य‡ भूत्वा देवो महेश्वरः ।
दहेदशेषं ब्रह्माण्डं सदेवासुरमानुषम् ॥
तमाविश्य महादेवो भगवान्नीललोहितः ।
करोति लोकसंहारं भीषणं रूपमाश्रितः ॥
प्रविश्य मण्डलं सौरङ्कृत्वाऽसौ बहुधा पुनः ।
निर्द्दहत्यखिलं लोकं सप्तसप्तिस्वरूपधृक् ॥
स दग्ध्वा सकलं विश्वमस्त्रं§ ब्रह्मशिरो महत् ।
देवतानां शरीरेषु क्षिपत्यखिलदाहकम्¶ ॥
दग्धेष्वशेषदेवेषु देवी गिरिवरात्मजा ।
एषा‖ सा साक्षिणी शम्भोस्तिष्ठते वैदिकी श्रुतिः ॥
शिरःकपालैर्देवानाङ्कृतस्रग्वरभूषणः ।
आदित्यचन्द्रादिगणैः पूरयन्व्योममण्डलम् ॥

---

* प्राकृतं हि समासेनेति B. प्राकृतं वः इति F. † करोति निखिलां मतिमिति B and F. ‡ स्वात्मनात्मानमावेश्येति G and H. § सत्त्वमस्त्रमिति B. लोकमस्त्रमिति F. ¶ अखिलदाहकः इति B and F. ‖ एका इति B and F.

सहस्रनयनो देवः सहस्राच इतीश्वरः* ।
सहस्रहस्तचरणः सहस्रार्च्चिर्म्महाभुजः ॥
दंष्ट्राकरालवदनः प्रदीप्तानललोचनः ।
त्रिशूलकृत्तिवसनो योगमैश्वरमास्थितः ॥
पीत्वा तत्परमानन्दं† प्रभूतममृतं स्वयम्‡ ।
करोति ताण्डवं देवीमालोक्य परमेश्वरः ॥
पीत्वा नृत्यामृतं देवी भर्त्तुः परममङ्गलम्§ ।
योगमास्थाय देवस्य देहमायाति शूलिनः ॥
स भुक्त्वा¶ ताण्डवरसं स्वेच्छयैव पिनाकधृक् ।
ज्योतिः‖स्वभावं भगवान्दग्ध्वा ब्रह्माण्डमण्डलम् ॥
संस्थितेष्वथ देवेषु ब्रह्मा विष्णुः पिनाकधृक्** ।
गुणैरशेषैः पृथिवी विलयं याति वारिषु ॥
स वारि तत्त्वं सगुणङ्ग्रसते हव्यवाहनः ।
तेजः स्वगुणसंयुक्तं†† वायौ संयाति सङ्क्षयम् ॥
आकाशे सगुणो वायुः प्रलयं याति विश्वभृत् ।
भूतादौ च तथाकाशे‡‡ लीयते गुणसंयुतः§§ ।
इन्द्रियाणि च सर्व्वाणि तैजसे¶¶ यान्ति सङ्क्षयम् ॥

---

* सहस्राकृतिरीश्वर इति B and F. † परमानन्दः इति B. ‡ स्वकमिति B. शिवमिति F. § परममङ्गलेति B and F. ¶ संत्यक्त्वा इति B. आर्षः प्रयोगः। ‖ जातीति B. यातीति E, F and H. ** ब्रह्मविष्णुपिनाकिषु इति B and F. †† तैजसं गुणसंयुक्तमिति B. तेजस्तु गुणसंयुक्तमिति F. ‡‡ तथाकाशमिति B. §§ गुणसंयुतमिति B. ¶¶ तेजांसीति B.

वैकारिको देवगणैः* प्रलयं याति† सत्तमाः ।‡
त्रिविधोऽयमहङ्कारो महति प्रलये व्रजेत् ॥
महान्तमेभिः सहितं ब्रह्माणममितौजसम्§ ।
अव्यक्तञ्जगतो योनिः संहरेदेकमव्ययम् ॥
एवं संहृत्य भूतानि¶ तत्त्वानि च महेश्वरः ।
वियोजयति चान्योऽन्य‖म्प्रधानं पुरुषम्परम् ॥
प्रधानपुंसोरजयोरेष संहार ईरितः ।
महेश्वरेच्छाजनितो न स्वयं विद्यते लयः ॥
गुणसाम्यं तदव्यक्तं प्रकृतिः परिगीयते ।
प्रधानं जगतो योनिर्मायातत्त्वमचेतनम् ॥
कूटस्थश्चिन्मयो** ह्यात्मा केवलं†† पञ्चविंशकः ।
गीयते मुनिभिः साक्षी महानेष‡‡ पितामहः ।
एवं संहारशक्तिश्च§§ शक्तिर्माहेश्वरी ध्रुवा¶¶ ॥
प्रधानाद्यं विशेषान्तं देहे रुद्र‖‖ इति श्रुतिः ।
योगिनामथ सर्व्वेषां ज्ञानविन्यस्तचेतसाम् ॥
आत्यन्तिकञ्चैव लयं विदधातीह शङ्करः ।
इत्येष भगवान्रुद्रः संहारं कुरुते वशी ।

---

* वैकारिकि देवगणा इति B. † यान्तीति B. ‡ अतः परं B पुस्तके--वैकारिकस्तैजसश्च भूतादिश्चेति सत्तमाः—इत्यधिकं दृश्यते । § अतितेजसमिति B and F. ¶ भूतादिरिति B. ‖ वियोजयत्यथोऽन्योन्यमिति B. ** कूटस्थ चिन्मय इति A, E and H. †† केवलः इति B. ‡‡ महानेकः इति B and F. §§ संसारकरणीति B and F. ¶¶ शुभेति B. ‖‖ दहेद्रुद्र इति B and F.

स्थापिका* मोहिनी शक्तिर्नारायण इति श्रुतिः ॥
हिरण्यगर्भो भगवाञ्जगत्सदसदात्मकम् ।
सृजेदशेषं प्रकृतेस्तन्मयः पञ्चविंशकः ॥
दुर्ब्बलाः† सर्व्वगाः‡ शान्ताः स्वात्मन्येव व्यवस्थिताः ।
शक्तयो ब्रह्मविष्ण्वीशा भुक्तिमुक्तिफलप्रदाः ॥
सर्व्वेश्वराः सर्व्ववन्द्याः§ शाश्वतानन्तभोगिनः ।
एकमेवाक्षरं तत्त्वं पुम्प्रधानेश्वरात्मकम् ॥
अन्याश्च शक्तयो दिव्यास्तत्र सन्ति¶ सहस्रशः ।
इत्येते‖ विविधैर्यज्ञैः शक्त्यादित्यादयो**ऽमराः ॥
एकैकस्याः†† सहस्राणि देहानां वै शतानि च ।
कथ्यन्ते चैव‡‡ माहात्म्याच्छक्तिरेकैव निर्गुणा ॥
तां शक्तिं स्वयमास्थाय§§ स्वयं देवो महेश्वरः ।
करोति विविधान्देहान्दृश्यते¶¶ चैव लीलया ॥
इज्यते सर्व्वयज्ञेषु ब्राह्मणैर्वेदवादिभिः ।
सर्व्वकामप्रदो रुद्र इत्येषा वैदिकी श्रुतिः ॥
सर्व्वासामेव शक्तीनां ब्रह्मविष्णुमहेश्वराः ।

---

* स्थायिकेति B. स्थापिता इति F. † सर्व्वतः सर्व्वगः शान्तः स्वात्मन्येव व्यवस्थित इति F. ‡ सर्व्वज्ञाः सर्व्वगाः इति G. § वन्द्या इति E, F and H. ¶ दिव्याः सन्ति तत्र इति B. ‖ युज्यन्ते इति B. इज्यन्ते इति E, G and H. इत्थं ते इति F. ** शक्रादित्यादयः इति B, E and F. †† एकैकस्य इति B and F. ‡‡ देवेति B. §§ तां तां शक्तिं समाधायेति B. तां स्वशक्तिं समास्थायेति G. इमां शक्तिं समास्थाय इति F. ¶¶ ग्रसते इति B and F.

प्राधान्येन स्मृता देवाः शक्तयः परमात्मनः॥
आभ्यः परस्ताद्भगवान् परमात्मा सनातनः।
गीयते सर्व्वमायात्मा* शूलपाणिर्महेश्वरः॥
एकमेके† वदन्त्यग्निं नारायणमथापरे।
इन्द्रमेके परे प्राणं‡ ब्रह्माणमपरे जगुः॥
ब्रह्मविष्ण्वग्निवरुणाः सर्व्वे देवास्तथर्षयः।
एकस्यैवाथ रुद्रस्य भेदास्ते परिकीर्त्तिताः॥
यं यं भेदं§ समाश्रित्य यजन्ति परमेश्वरम्।
तत्तद्रूपं¶ समास्थाय प्रददाति फलं शिवः॥
तस्मादेकतरं भेदं समाश्रित्यापि शाश्वतम्।
आराधयन्महादेवं याति तत्परमं पदम्॥
किन्तु देवं महादेवं सर्व्वशक्तिं सनातनम्।
आराधयेद्‖ गिरिशं सगुणं वाथ निर्गुणम्॥
मया प्रोक्तो हि भवतां योगः प्रागेव निर्गुणः।
आरुरुक्षुस्तु सगुणं पूजयेत्परमेश्वरम्॥
पिनाकिनं त्रिनयनं जटिलङ्कृत्तिवाससम्।
रुक्माभं वा सहस्रार्काञ्चिन्तयेद्वैदिकी** श्रुतिः॥
एष योगः समुद्दिष्टः सबीजो मुनिपुङ्गवाः††।

---

* सर्व्वशक्त्यात्मा इति B and F. † एवमेकमिति E. एनमेकमिति F. एकमेव-मिति H. ‡ विप्राः इति B. § देवमिति B. ¶ तत्तद्रूपमित्यारभ्य चतुर्द्दश पादाः A, E, H पुस्तकेषु न दृश्यन्ते। ‖ आराधयेद्वै इति F. ** पद्मासनस्थं रुक्माभं चिन्तयेद्वैदिकीति B and F. †† मुनिसत्तमा इति B.

अत्राप्यशक्तोऽथ हरं विश्वं* ब्रह्माणमर्च्चयेत् ॥
अथ चेदसमर्थः स्यात्तत्रापि मुनिपुङ्गवाः ।
ततो वाय्वग्निशक्रादीन् पूजयेद्भक्तिसंयुतः ॥
तस्मात्सर्व्वान् परित्यज्य देवान् ब्रह्मपुरोगमान् ।
आराधयेद्विरूपाक्षमादिमध्यान्तसंस्थितम् ॥
भक्तियोगसमायुक्तः स्वकर्म्मनिरतः† शुचिः ।
तादृशं रूपमास्थाय आसाद्यात्यन्तिकं शिवम् ॥
एष योगः समुद्दिष्टः सवीजोऽत्यन्तभावनः ।
यथाविधि प्रकुर्व्वाणः प्राप्नुयादैश्वरम्पदम् ॥
द्वे‡ चान्ये भावने शुद्धे प्रागुक्ते भवतामिह ।
अथापि§ कथितो योगो निर्व्वीजश्च सवीजकः ॥
ज्ञानं तदुक्तं निर्व्वीजं पूर्व्वं हि भवतां मया ।
विष्णुं रुद्रं विरञ्चिञ्च¶ सवीजे साधयेद्बुधः ॥
अथ वाय्वादिकान्देवान्तत्परो नियतात्मवान्‖ ।
पूजयेत्पुरुषं विष्णुं चतुर्मूर्त्तिधरं हरिम्** ॥
अनादिनिधनं देवं वासुदेवं सनातनम् ।
नारायणं जगद्योनिमाकाशं परमम्पदम् ॥
तल्लिङ्गधारी नियतं यद्युक्तस्तदुपाश्रयः†† ।

---

* विष्णुमिति B and C. † स्वधर्म्मनिरत इति B and C. ‡ ये इति B. विधाने भावने शुद्धे इति C. § अत्रापीति B and C. ¶ विरिञ्चिं वा इति B. ‖ संयतेन्द्रियः इति B. ** हरमिति A, E and H. इतः पूर्व्वं पादषट्कं C पुस्तके नास्ति । †† तद्भक्तस्तदपाश्रय इति B. नियतस्तद्भक्तस्तदुपाश्रय इति C.

एष एव विधिर्वा स्वभावने चान्तिमे मतः* ॥
इत्येतत्कथितं ज्ञानं भावनासंश्रयम्परम्।
इन्द्रद्युम्नाय मुनये कथितं यन्मया पुरा† ॥
अव्यक्तात्मकमेवेदं चेतनाचेतनं जगत्।
तदीश्वरं परं ब्रह्म तस्माद्ब्रह्ममयं जगत् ॥

सूत उवाच।

एतावदुक्त्वा भगवान्विरराम जनार्द्दनः।
तुष्टुवुर्मुनयो विष्णुं शक्रेण‡ सह माधवम् ॥

मुनयः§ ऊचुः।

नमस्ते कूर्म्मरूपाय विष्णवे परमात्मने।
नारायणाय विश्वाय वासुदेवाय ते नमः ॥
नमो नमस्ते कृष्णाय गोविन्दाय च ते नमः¶।
माधवाय च ते नित्यं‖ नमो यज्ञेश्वराय च ॥
सहस्रशिरसे तुभ्यं सहस्राक्षाय ते नमः।
नमः सहस्रहस्ताय सहस्रचरणाय च ॥
ओं नमो ज्ञानरूपाय विष्णवे परमात्मने**।
आनन्दाय नमस्तुभ्यं मायातीताय ते नमः ॥
नमो गूढ़शरीराय निर्गुणाय नमोऽस्तु ते।

---

* विधिर्ब्राह्मे भावने चान्तिके मतः इति B and C. विधिर्वाह्यभावने इति G.

† प्रद्युम्नाय कथितं मुनये यन्मया पुरेति B. ‡ शक्रेणेति B, C, E and G.

§ ऋषय इति B. ¶ गोविन्दाय नमो नम इति B. ‖ माधवाय नमस्तुभ्यमिति B.

** परमात्मस्वरूपिणे इति B. परमार्थस्वरूपिणे इति C.

पुरुषाय पुराणाय सत्तामात्नस्वरूपिणे ॥
नमः सांख्याय योगाय केवलाय* नमोऽस्तु ते ।
धर्म्मज्ञानाभिगम्याय निष्कलाय नमोऽस्तु ते† ॥
नमस्ते योगतत्त्वाय‡ महायोगेश्वराय च ।
परावराणां प्रभवे वेदवेद्याय ते नमः ॥
नमो बुद्धाय शुद्धाय नमो युक्ताय हेतवे ।
नमो नमो नमस्तुभ्यं मायिने वेधसे नमः§ ॥
नमोऽस्तु ते वराहाय नारसिंहाय ते नमः ।
वामनाय नमस्तुभ्यं हृषीकेशाय ते नमः ॥
स्वर्गापवर्गदानाय नमोऽप्रतिहतात्मने¶ ।
नमो योगाधिगम्याय योगिने योगदायिने ॥
देवानां पतये तुभ्यं देवार्त्तिशमनाय ते‖ ।
भगवंस्त्वत्प्रसादेन सर्व्वसंसारनाशनम् ॥
अस्माभिर्व्विदितं ज्ञानं यज्ज्ञात्वाम्टतमश्नुते ।
श्रुताश्च विविधा धर्म्मा वंशा मन्वन्तराणि च ॥
सर्गश्च प्रतिसर्गश्च ब्रह्माण्डस्यास्य विस्तरः ।
त्वं हि सर्व्वजगत्साक्षी विश्वो नारायणः परः ।

---

* कैवल्याय इति B. एतत्पादचतुष्टयं B पुस्तके श्लोकद्वयात्परं दृश्यते । C पुस्तके तु एतत्पादचतुष्टयं नास्ति । † धर्म्मज्ञानाधिगम्याय निष्कलाय नमो नम इति B. ‡ व्योमरूपाय इति B and C. § नमो मायाविने तुभ्यं वेधसे च नमो नमः इति B and C. ¶ स्वर्गापवर्गदात्रे च नमोऽप्रतिहताय चेति B. ‖ चेति B.

त्रातुमर्हस्यनन्तात्मा* त्वामेव शरणङ्गताः† ॥

सूत उवाच ।

एतद्वः कथितं विप्रा भोगमोक्षप्रदायकम् ।
कौर्म्मं पुराणमखिलं यज्जगाद गदाधरः ॥
अस्मिन् पुराणे लक्ष्म्यास्तु सम्भवः कथितः पुरा ।
मोहायाशेषभूतानां‡ वासुदेवेन योजितः§ ॥
प्रजापतीनां सर्गास्तु¶ वर्णधर्म्माश्च वृत्तयः ।
धर्म्मार्थकाममोक्षाणां यथावल्लक्षणं शुभम् ॥
पितामहस्य विष्णोश्च महेशस्य च धीमतः ।
एकत्वञ्च पृथक्त्वञ्च विशेषश्चोपवर्णितः ॥
भक्तानां लक्षणम्प्रोक्तं समाचारश्च भोजनम्‖ ।
वर्णाश्रमाणाङ्कथितं यथावदिह लक्षणम् ॥
आदिसर्गस्ततः** पश्चादण्डावरणसप्तकम् ।
हिरण्यगर्भः सर्गश्च कीर्त्तितो मुनिपुङ्गवाः ॥
कालसंख्याप्रकथनं माहात्म्यञ्चेश्वरस्य च†† ।
ब्रह्मणः‡‡ शयनञ्चाप्सु नामनिर्व्वचनं तथा ।
वराहवपुषो भूयो भूमेरुद्धरणं पुनः ॥

---

* अनन्तात्मन्निति B. त्रातुमर्हसि नः सर्व्वानिति C. † त्वमेव शरणं गतिरिति B. ‡ मोहाय सर्व्वभूतानामिति B. माहात्म्यं शेषभूतानामिति C. § योजनमिति B and C. ¶ सर्गश्च इति B. सर्गस्तु इति C. ‖ शोभनः इति B and C. ** आदित्यसर्गतः इति B. †† तु इति B. ‡‡ ब्रह्मण इत्यारभ्य दश पादाः A, C, E, H पुस्तकेषु न सन्ति ।

मुख्यादिसर्गकथनं मुनिसर्गस्तथापरः।
व्याख्यातौ रुद्रसर्गश्च ऋषिसर्गश्च तापसः॥
धर्म्मस्य च प्रजासर्गस्तामसात्पूर्व्वमेव तु।
ब्रह्मविष्णोर्विवादः स्यादन्तर्देहप्रवेशनम्॥
पद्मोद्भवत्वं देवस्य मोहस्तस्य च धीमतः।*
दर्शनञ्च महेशस्य माहात्म्यं विष्णुनेरितम्॥
दिव्यदृष्टिप्रदानञ्च ब्रह्मणः परमेष्ठिनः।
संस्तवो देवदेवस्य ब्रह्मणा परमेष्ठिना॥
प्रसादो गिरिशस्याथ वरदानं तथैव च†।
संवादो‡ विष्णुना सार्द्धं शङ्करस्य महात्मनः॥
वरदानं तथा पूर्व्वमन्तर्द्धानं पिनाकिनः।
वधश्च कथितो विप्रा मधुकैटभयोः पुरा§॥
अवतारोऽथ¶ देवस्य ब्रह्मणो नाभिपङ्कजात्।
एकीभावश्च देवेन ब्रह्मणा कथितः पुरा‖॥
विमोहो** ब्रह्मणश्चाथ संज्ञानात्तु†† हरेस्ततः।
तपश्चरणमाख्यातं देवदेवस्य धीमतः॥
प्रादुर्भावो महेशस्य ललाटात्कथितस्ततः‡‡।
रुद्राणाङ्कथिता सृष्टिर्ब्रह्मणः प्रतिषेधनम्।

---

* एतत्पादद्वयं B पुस्तके नास्ति। † वरदस्य ततः परमिति B. ‡ विवाद इति B. § परमिति B. तथा इति C. ¶ अवतारोऽस्य इति B. ‖ देवस्य कथितस्तवेति B. देवस्य विष्णुना सह तत्त्वत इति G. ** विनीह इत्यारभ्य पादषट्कं A, E, H पुस्तकेषु नास्ति। †† शिवालाभ इति C. ‡‡ इतः पूर्व्वं पादचतुष्टयं C पुस्तके नास्ति।

भूतिश्च* देवदेवस्य वरदानोपदेशकौ† ॥
अन्तर्द्धानञ्च देवस्य‡ तपश्चर्य्याम्बुजस्य च§ ।
दर्शनं देवदेवस्य नरनारीशरीरता ॥
देव्या विभागकथनं देवदेवात्पिनाकिनः ।
देव्याश्च¶ पश्चात्कथितं दक्षपुत्रीत्वमेव च ॥
हिमवद्दुहितृत्वञ्च देव्या याथात्म्यमेव‖ च ।
दर्शनं दिव्यरूपस्य विश्वरूपाक्षदर्शनम्** ॥
नाम्नां सहस्रङ्कथितं पित्रा हिमवता स्वयम् ।
उपदेशो महादेव्या वरदानं तथैव च ॥
भृग्वादीनां प्रजासर्गो राज्ञां वंशस्य विस्तरः ।
प्राचेतसत्वं दक्षस्य दक्षयज्ञविमर्द्दनम्†† ॥
दधीचस्य च यज्ञस्य विवादः कथितस्तदा‡‡ ।
ततश्च शापः कथितो मुनीनां मुनिपुङ्गवाः ॥
रुद्रागतिः प्रसादश्च अन्तर्द्धानं पिनाकिनः ।
पितामहोपदेशः स्यात्§§ कीर्त्यते वै रणाय¶¶ तु ॥
दक्षस्य च‖‖ प्रजासर्गः कश्यपस्य महात्मनः ।
हिरण्यकशिपोर्नाशो हिरण्याक्षवधस्तथा ॥

---

* ततश्चेति B. श्रुतिश्च इति C. † वरदानोपदेशनमिति B. ‡ रुद्रस्य इति B and C. § तु इति B. ¶ देव्यास्तु इति B. ‖ माहात्म्यमेव च इति B and C. ** वैश्वरूपस्य दर्शनमिति B. विश्वरूपस्य दर्शनमिति C. †† विमर्द्दकमिति B. ‡‡ कथितस्तथेति B and C. §§ पितामहस्योपदेश इति B and C. ¶¶ रक्षणाय इति B. कीर्त्तितं रक्षणाय चेति C. ‖‖ तु इति B.

ततश्च शापः कथितो देवदारुवनौकसाम् ।
निग्रहश्चान्धकस्याथ गाणपत्यमनुत्तमम् ॥
प्रह्लादनिग्रहश्चाथ बलेः संयमनन्त्वथ* ।
वाणस्य निग्रहश्चाथ प्रसादस्तस्य शूलिनः† ॥
ऋषीणां वंशविस्तारो राज्ञां वंशाः प्रकीर्त्तिताः ।
वसुदेवात्ततो विष्णोरुत्पत्तिः स्वेच्छया हरेः ॥
दर्शनञ्चोपमन्योर्वै तपश्चरणमेव च ।
वरलाभो महादेवं दृष्ट्वा साम्बं त्रिलोचनम्‡ ।
कैलासगमनञ्चाथ निवासस्तस्य§ शार्ङ्गिणः ॥
ततश्च कथ्यते भीतिर्द्वारवत्यां निवासिनाम् ।
रक्षणङ्गरुडेनाथ जित्वा शत्रून्महाबलान्¶ ॥
नारदागमनञ्चैव यात्रा चैव गरुत्मतः ।
ततश्च कृष्णागमनं मुनीनामाश्रमस्ततः‖ ॥
नैत्यकं** वासुदेवस्य शिवलिङ्गार्च्चनं तथा ।
मार्कण्डेयस्य च मुनेः प्रश्नः प्रोक्तस्ततः परम् ॥
लिङ्गार्च्चननिमित्तञ्च लिङ्गस्यापि सलिङ्गिनः†† ।
याथात्म्यकथनञ्चाथ लिङ्गाद्वै भीतिरेव च‡‡ ॥

---

* संयमनन्तथा इति B. † एतत्पादद्वयं B पुस्तके नास्ति । ‡ सार्द्धत्रिशूलिनमिति C. § तत्रेति B, C, G and H. ¶ त्रिधा शक्तिर्महात्मना इति B. जित्वा शत्रून् महात्मनेति C. ‖ मुनीनामागतिस्ततः इति B and C. मुनीनामागम इति E. ** नैष्ठिकमिति B. नैत्तिकमिति C and E. †† च लिङ्गिनः इति B and C. ‡‡ यथार्थं कथितञ्चाथ लिङ्गाविर्भावएव चेति B. सर्व्वात्मकथनञ्चाथ लिङ्गाविर्भाव एव च इति C.

ब्रह्मविष्णोस्तथा मध्ये कीर्त्तिता मुनिपुङ्गवाः।
मोहस्तयोर्वै* कथितो गमनञ्चोर्द्धतो ह्यधः† ॥
संस्तवो देवदेवस्य प्रसादः परमेष्ठिनः।
अन्तर्द्धानञ्च लिङ्गस्य साम्बोत्पत्तिस्ततः परम्।
कीर्त्तिता चानिरुद्धस्य समुत्पत्तिर्द्विजोत्तमाः ॥
कृष्णस्य गमने बुद्धिर्ऋषीणामागतिस्तथा।
अनुशासनञ्च‡ कृष्णेन वरदानं महात्मनः§ ॥
गमनञ्चैव कृष्णस्य पार्थस्याप्यथ¶ दर्शनम्।
कृष्णद्वैपायनस्योक्तं युगधर्म्माः सनातनाः ॥
अनुग्रहोऽथ पार्थस्य वाराणस्याङ्गतिस्ततः।
पाराशर्य्यस्य च मुनेर्व्यासस्याद्भुतकर्म्मणः।
वाराणस्याश्च‖ माहात्म्यं तीर्थानाञ्चैव वर्णनम्** ॥
व्यासस्य तीर्थयात्रा च†† देव्याश्चैवाथ दर्शनम्।
उद्वासनञ्च कथितं वरदानं तथैव च ॥
प्रयागस्य च माहात्म्यङ्क्षेत्राणामथ कीर्त्तनम्‡‡।
फलञ्च विपुलं§§ विप्रा मार्कण्डेयस्य निर्गमः¶¶ ॥
भुवनानां स्वरूपञ्च ज्योतिषाञ्च निवेशनम्।

---

* मोहस्तयोस्तु इति B and C. † ऽप्यधः इति B and C. ‡ अनुशासितञ्च इति B. § महात्मनामिति B and C. ¶ पार्थस्यापि च इति B. ‖ वाराणस्यास्तु इति B. ** एष पादः B पुस्तके नास्ति। †† तीर्थयात्रा तु व्यासस्य इति B. ‡‡ क्षत्राणां मुनिपुङ्गवाः इति B. §§ फलं सुविपुलमिति B. ¶¶ एष पादः B पुस्तके नास्ति।

कीर्त्तितश्चापि वर्षाणां* नदीनाञ्चैव निर्णयः ॥
पर्व्वतानाञ्च कथनं स्थानानि च दिवौकसाम्।
द्वीपानां प्रविभागश्च श्वेतद्वीपोपवर्णनम्† ॥
शयनं केशवस्याथ माहात्म्यञ्च महात्मनः।
मन्वन्तराणाङ्कथनं विष्णोर्माहात्म्यमेव च ॥
वेदशाखाप्रणयनं व्यासानाङ्कथनं ततः‡।
अवेदस्य च वेदस्य कथितं मुनिपुङ्गवाः ॥
योगेश्वराणाञ्च कथा शिष्याणाञ्चाथ कीर्त्तनम्§।
गीताश्च विविधा गुह्या ईश्वरस्याथ कीर्त्तिताः¶ ॥
वर्णाश्रमाणामाचाराः‖ प्रायश्चित्तविधिस्ततः।
कपालित्वञ्च रुद्रस्य भिक्षाचरणमेव च ॥
पतिव्रतानामाख्यानं** तीर्थानाञ्च विनिर्णयः।
तथा मङ्कणकस्याथ निग्रहः कीर्त्तितो द्विजाः ॥
वधश्च कथितो विप्राः कालस्य च समासतः।
देवदारुवने शम्भोः प्रवेशो माधवस्य च।
दर्शनं षट्कुलीयानां देवदेवस्य धीमतः।
वरदानञ्च देवस्य नन्दने तु प्रकीर्त्तितम् ॥
नैमित्तिकश्च कथितः प्रतिसर्गस्ततः परम्।

---

* कीर्त्यन्ते चैव वर्षाणीति B and C. † श्वेतद्वीपस्य वर्णनमिति B. ‡ तथा इति B. एतत्पादद्वयं B पुस्तके परवर्त्तिपादद्वयस्य पश्चात्पठ्यते। § तथा शिष्याणाञ्चानुकीर्त्तनमिति B. ¶ पुण्या ईश्वरस्यानुकीर्त्तिताः इति B. ‖ आचार इति B and C. ** पतिव्रतायाश्चाख्यानमिति B and C.

प्राकृतः प्रलयश्चोर्द्ध्वं सवीजो योग एव च* ॥
एवं ज्ञात्वा पुराणस्य सङ्क्षेपङ्कीर्त्तयेत्तु यः ।
सर्व्वपापविनिर्मुक्तो ब्रह्मलोके† महीयते ॥
एवमुक्त्वा श्रियं देवीमादाय पुरुषोत्तमः ।
सन्त्यज्य कूर्म्मसंस्थानं प्रजगाम हरस्तदा§ ॥
देवाश्च सर्व्वे मुनयः स्वानि स्थानानि भेजिरे ।
प्रणम्य पुरुषं विष्णुं गृहीत्वा ह्यमृतं द्विजाः ॥
एतत्पुराणं सकलं¶ भाषितङ्कूर्म्मरूपिणा ।
साक्षाद्देवाधिदेवेन‖ विष्णुना विश्वयोनिना ॥
यः पठेत्सततं विप्रा नियमेन समासतः** ।
सर्व्वपापविनिर्मुक्तो ब्रह्मलोके महीयते ॥
लिखित्वा चैव यो दद्याद्वैशाखे कार्त्तिकेऽपि वा†† ।
विप्राय वेदविदुषे तस्य पुण्यं निबोधत ॥
सर्व्वपापविनिर्मुक्तः सर्व्वैश्वर्य्यसमन्वितः ।
भुक्त्वा तु विपुलान्मर्त्त्यो भोगान्दिव्यान् सुशोभनान् ॥
ततः स्वर्गात्परिभ्रष्टो विप्राणां जायते कुले ।
पूर्व्वसंस्कारमाहात्म्याद्ब्रह्मविद्यामवाप्नुयात् ॥

---

* मरीच्याद्याश्च एव चेति B. † रुद्रलोके इति B. विष्णुलोके इति C. § स्वस्थानञ्च जगाम हेति B. स जगाम हरिः प्रभुरिति C. ¶ एतत्पुराणममलमिति B. परममिति C. ‖ देवादिदेवेनेति B and C. ** मर्त्त्यो नियमेन समाहितः इति B and C. †† वैशाखे मासि सुव्रतः इति B and C.

पठित्वाध्यायमेवैकं* सर्व्वपापैः प्रमुच्यते।
योऽर्थं विचारयेत्सम्यक् प्राप्नोति परमम्पदम्† ॥
अध्येतव्यमिदं पुण्यं विप्रैः पर्व्वणि पर्व्वणि।
श्रोतव्यञ्च द्विजश्रेष्ठा महापातकनाशनम् ॥
एकतस्तु पुराणानि सेतिहासानि कृत्स्नशः।
एकत्र परमं वेद‡मेतदेवातिरिच्यते ॥
इदं पुराणं मुक्त्यैकं नान्यत्साधनकं§ परम्।
यथावदत्र भगवान्देवो नारायणो हरिः।
कीर्त्यते¶ हि यथा विष्णुर्न तथाऽन्येषु सुव्रताः ॥
ब्राह्मी पौराणिकी चेयं संहिता पापनाशनी।
अत्र तत्परमं ब्रह्म कीर्त्यते हि यथार्थतः ॥
तीर्थानां परमं तीर्थं तपसाञ्च परं तपः।
ज्ञानानां परमं ज्ञानं व्रतानां परमं व्रतम् ॥
नाध्येतव्यमिदं शास्त्रं वृषलस्य च सन्निधौ।
योऽधीते चैव मोहात्मा स याति‖ नरकान् बहून् ॥
श्राद्धे वा दैविके** कार्य्ये श्रावणीयं द्विजातिभिः।
यज्ञान्ते तु विशेषेण सर्व्वदोषविशोधनम् ॥

---

* पठित्वाध्यायने चैवेति B. पठित्वाध्यायमेकैकमिति C. † स प्राप्नोति परं पदमिति B and G. प्राप्नोति परमाङ्गतिमिति C. ‡ वेदपरममिति B. § नास्त्यन्यत्साधनमिति B. धर्म्मनैपुण्यकामानां ज्ञानिनां पुण्यकामिनाम्। इदं पुराणं त्यक्त्वैकं नास्त्यन्यत्साधनं परमिति C. ¶ कथ्यते इति B. ‖ योऽधीते सत्तमो ज्ञात्मा प्रयातीति B. योऽधीते चैव माहात्म्यं स याति इति C. ** वैदिके इति B.

मुमुक्षूणामिदं* शास्त्रमध्येतव्यं विशेषतः।
श्रोतव्यञ्चाथ मन्तव्यं वेदार्थपरिवृंहणम्॥
ज्ञात्वा यथावद्विप्रेन्द्रान् श्रावयेद्भक्तिसंयुतान्।
सर्व्वपापविनिर्मुक्तो ब्रह्मसायुज्यमाप्नुयात्॥
योऽश्रद्दधाने पुरुषे दद्याच्चाधार्म्मिके तथा।
सम्प्रेत्य गत्वा निरयान् शुनां योनिं व्रजत्यधः॥
नमस्कृत्य हरिं विष्णुं जगद्योनिं सनातनम्।
अध्येतव्यमिदं शास्त्रङ्कृष्णद्वैपायनं तथा†॥
इत्याज्ञा देवदेवस्य विष्णोरमिततेजसः।
पाराशर्य्यस्य विप्रर्षेर्व्यासस्य च महात्मनः‡॥
श्रुत्वा नारायणाद्देवान्नारदो भगवानृषिः।
गौतमाय ददौ पूर्व्वं तस्माच्चैव पराशरः॥
पराशरोऽपि भगवान् गङ्गाद्वारे मुनीश्वराः§।
मुनिभ्यः कथयामास धर्म्मकामार्थमोक्षदम्॥
ब्रह्मणा कथितं पूर्व्वं सनकाय च धीमते।
सनत्कुमाराय तथा सर्व्वपापप्रणाशनम्॥
सनकाद्भगवान् साक्षाद्देवलो योगवित्तमः।
अवाप्तवान्पञ्चशिखो देवलादिदमुत्तमम्॥
सनत्कुमाराद्भगवान्मुनिः सत्यवतीसुतः।

---

* मुमुक्षुभिरिदमिति B. † कृष्णद्वैपायनोऽब्रवीदिति B. ‡ परमात्मनः इति A, C, E and H. § गङ्गाद्वारे मुनीश्वरा इत्यारभ्य द्वादश पादाः B पुस्तके न सन्ति।

एतत्पुराणं परमं* व्यासः सर्व्वार्थसञ्चयम् ॥
तस्माद्व्यासादहं श्रुत्वा भवतां पापनाशनम्† ।
उचिवान्वै भवद्भिश्च दातव्यं धार्म्मिके जने‡ ॥
तस्मै व्यासाय मुनये§ सर्व्वज्ञाय महर्षये ।
पाराशर्य्याय शान्ताय नमो नारायणात्मने ॥
यस्माल्सञ्जायते कृत्स्नं यत्र चैव प्रलीयते ।
नमस्तस्मै परेशाय¶ विष्णवे कूर्म्मरूपिणे ॥

इति श्रीकूर्म्मपुराणे षट्साहस्र्यां संहितायामुपविभागे
व्यासगीतासु पञ्चचत्वारिंशोऽध्यायः ।

समाप्तञ्चेदं‖ कूर्म्मपुराणम् ।

---

* लेभे पुराणममलमिति B and C. † भवत्पापप्रणाशनमिति B. ‡ एतत्पादद्वयं B पुस्तके नास्ति । § गुरवे इति B and C. ¶ सुरेशाय इति B, C, E, G and H. ‖ समाप्तमिदमिति B.